BUILDING COMMUNITY RESILIENCE POST-DISASTER

A Guide For Affordable Housing and Community Economic Development Practitioners

DORCAS R. GILMORE AND DIANE M. STANDAERT
EDITORS

AMERICAN BAR ASSOCIATION

Forum on Affordable Housing and Community Development Law

Cover by Tamara Kowalski/ABA Publishing.

Credit for the photo in the bottom right corner of the cover goes to FEMA/Barry Bahler. It shows the lower 9th Ward/St. Bernard Parish in New Orleans, La. in 2008, three years following Hurricane Katrina.

Printed in the United States of America

17 16 15 14 13 5 4 3 2 1

Library of Congress Cataloging-in-Publication Data

Building community resilience post-disaster : a guide for affordable housing and community economic development practitioners / edited by Dorcas R. Gilmore and Diane M. Standaert, ABA Forum on Affordable Housing and Community Development Law. — First edition.

pages cm

Includes bibliographical references and index.

ISBN 978-1-62722-178-8 (print : alk. paper)

1. Disaster relief—Law and legislation—United States. 2. Housing—Law and legislation—United States. 3. Federal aid to housing—United States. I. Gilmore, Dorcas R., editor of compilation. II. Standaert, Diane M., editor of compilation. III. American Bar Association. Forum on Affordable Housing and Community Development Law.

KF3750.B85 2013

363.34'80973—dc23

2013022595

Brief Contents

Part 1
Framework for Recovery 1

Chapter 1
Federal Funding and Financing Programs Post-Disaster 3

Chapter 2
The Role of the U.S. Department of Housing and Urban Development in Post-Disaster Community Recovery 29

Chapter 3
Beyond the Stafford Act: A Human Rights Approach to Disaster Policy 53

Chapter 4
Equity in Disasters: Civil and Human Rights Challenges in the Context of Emergency Events 91

Chapter 5
Local Government and Interjurisdictional Coordination in Disaster Response and Recovery 109

Chapter 6
The Role of Nonprofits and Religious Organizations in Emergency Response 133

Part 2
Economic Recovery 165

Chapter 7
The 9/11 Attack on America and Lessons on How to Rebuild a Mixed-Use Business District 167

Chapter 8
Small Business Disaster Assistance 187

Chapter 9
Restoring Small Business: A State Agency Response to the 2008 Iowa Disasters 205

Part 3
Housing Recovery 215

Chapter 10
The 2008 Texas Hurricanes: Working for Equitable
and Transparent Redevelopment. 217

Chapter 11
Public Housing Post-Disaster: To Rehabilitate or Replace? 249

Chapter 12
Locked Out and Torn Down: Public Housing
Post–Hurricane Katrina 275

Part 4
Community Resilience: Challenges and Opportunities. 301

Chapter 13
Wolf at the Door: Protecting Homeowners from
Predatory Housing Activities in the Wake of Disaster 303

Chapter 14
Housing Choice in Crisis: Short-Term Post–Hurricane
Katrina Relief 319

Chapter 15
Disasters' Long-Term Impact on Fair Housing: Rebuilding as
an Engine to Perpetuate or Challenge Entrenched Segregation 345

Chapter 16
Innovative Post-Disaster Community-Based
Housing Strategies 371

Chapter 17
Disaster as a Catalyst for Collaboration and Innovation: Workforce
Development in Mississippi Following Hurricane Katrina 391

Resources 405

Index. 433

Contents

Acknowledgments . . . . **xvii**
About the Contributors . . . . **xix**
About the Editors . . . . **xxv**
Editors' Introduction . . . . **xxvii**
Reports from the Frontlines of Disaster Recovery & Community Resilience . . . . **xxxiii**
Ingrid Norton

Part 1
Framework for Recovery **1**

Chapter 1
Federal Funding and Financing Programs Post-Disaster **3**
Antoinette M. Jackson
I. Introduction 3
II. Creation of Funding Sources 4
A. National Response to Disasters 4
B. State and Local Responses to Disasters 5
C. Process for Presidential Declaration 6
III. Identification of Resources 7
A. Robert T. Stafford Disaster Relief and Emergency Assistance Act 7
B. Community Development Block Grants Disaster Recovery Funds 10
C. HOME Funds 11
D. Section 108 Loan Guarantee Program 12
E. Capital Fund Emergency/Natural Disaster Funds/Disaster Housing Assistance Program 12
F. Small Business and USDA Loans 13
G. U.S. Department of Commerce Disaster Relief Opportunity Funds 13

H. U.S. Department of Labor National Emergency Grants 14
I. Agricultural Disaster Assistance Act 15
Recent Developments in Federal Government Support of Tribal Governments' Disaster Recovery Efforts (by Dorcas R. Gilmore and Diane M. Standaert) 15
IV. Funding Incentives and Public Support 19
A. GO Zone Credits 19
B. GO Zone Bonds 19
C. Bonus Depreciation 20
D. Other Incentives 20
E. Public Support—Charitable Contributions and Volunteerism 20
V. The Good and the Bad: What Makes a Successful Program 21
A. Implementing Lessons Learned 21
B. Effective Distribution of Funding 22
C. Use Funding to Address Long-Range Goals 22
D. Leverage Government Funds by Stimulating Private Investment 22
E. Eliminate Regulatory Barriers 23
F. One-Stop Resource Centers 23
G. Provide Pre-Disaster Information 23
H. Eliminate the Political Response 23
VI. Conclusion 23
Notes 24

Chapter 2
The Role of the U.S. Department of Housing and Urban Development in Post-Disaster Community Recovery 29
Helen R. Kanovsky and Carey Catherine Whitehead
I. Introduction 29
A. HUD's Historical Involvement in Federal Disaster Response 30
B. Evolution of HUD's Disaster Recovery Role. 31
II. Discussion and Case Studies 32
A. HUD's Toolbox for Recovery 32
B. Using the Toolbox to Meet Housing Needs 33
C. CDBG-DR: Using the Toolbox to Meet Economic and Other Development Needs 42
D. HUD's Role in the Overall Federal Response 43
III. Best Practices and Lessons Learned. 45
IV. Conclusion 46
Notes 47

Chapter 3
Beyond the Stafford Act: A Human Rights Approach to Disaster Policy 53
Eric Tars and Catherine Galitzine
I. Introduction 54
II. International Human Rights Law in the United States 55
A. Domestic Legal Effect of International Human Rights Law 55
B. Using International Human Rights Law in Domestic Courts 57
C. Using International Human Rights Law in Policy Advocacy 57
III. Using International Human Rights Law to Defend the Housing Rights of Internally Displaced Persons 58
A. Introduction to Human Rights of Internally Displaced Persons 58
B. General Principles 60
C. Rights in Planning for Displacement 67
D. Rights during Displacement 68
E. Rights after Displacement 73
IV. Case Study: Using Human Rights Standards and Processes to Advance Housing Rights of Internally Displaced People in Post–Katrina New Orleans 75
A. Engaging with the Human Rights System: Advocacy with the Human Rights Committee, 2005–2006 75
B. Building Momentum and Empowering Victims on an International Stage: Working with the Committee on Elimination of Racial Discrimination, 2007–2008 77
C. Visits from Human Rights Monitors: Specific Recommendations and Increased Visibility, 2008–2009 79
D. Putting Housing Rights in Context: 2010 Universal Periodic Review 81
V. Conclusion 83
Notes 85

Chapter 4
Equity in Disasters: Civil and Human Rights Challenges in the Context of Emergency Events 91
Jacqueline Patterson
I. Introduction 91
II. A Post-Disaster Equity Framework 92
III. Preexisting Community Vulnerabilities 93
IV. Socio-cultural Impacts of Disaster Cripple Families and Cause Irreversible Community Changes 94
V. Housing 96
VI. Employment 98

VII. Community Infrastructure 99
VIII. Transportation. 100
IX. Business 101
X. Redevelopment Following the Disaster 101
XI. Recommendations 102
XII. Conclusion 103
Notes 104

Chapter 5
Local Government and Interjurisdictional Coordination in Disaster Response and Recovery. 109
Dina Schlossberg
I. Introduction 109
II. All Disasters Are Local: Roles of Local Government Post-Disaster 110
III. Local Government Considerations in Disaster Planning, Response, and Recovery 111
A. State of Existing Infrastructure 112
B. Size of the Local Jurisdiction. 112
C. The Beleaguered State of Local Economies 113
D. Vulnerable and At-Risk Populations 113
IV. Planning and Cooperation among Local Governments 116
A. Continuity of Operations / Continuity of Government Plans. 116
B. Mutual Aid Compacts 116
C. Council of Governments as Facilitating Disaster Recovery. 117
V. State and Local Government Interaction 118
VI. Federal Support for Local Government Response 120
A. Public Assistance Program. 120
B. Community Development Block Grant—Disaster Recovery 121
VII. Local Government Framework for Long-Term Recovery 122
VIII. Challenges: Inclusive, Long-term Planning in the Midst of Disaster. . . . 123
IX. Opportunity: Building Stronger Communities Post-Disaster. 124
A. East Grand Forks, Minnesota. 125
B. Greensburg, Kansas 126
X. Conclusion 127
Notes 128

Chapter 6
The Role of Nonprofits and Religious Organizations in Emergency Response 133
Brenda Bratton Blom (with contribution by Woody Widrow)
I. Introduction 133
II. Turbulence on the Rise and Community Resilience. 134

A. Community 135
B. Resilience 136
III. Emergency Housing Post-Disaster 137
A. The Paradigm and Critical Orientations 137
B. International Lessons 137
IV. The Role of Nonprofit Organizations 139
A. National and International Nonprofits 139
B. Local Nonprofit Initiatives 143
V. The Role of Religious Organizations 146
A. National Religious Organizational Response 146
B. Local Religious Organizations Respond 147
VI. Innovations Post-Disaster 149
Portable Individual Development Accounts: Supporting Individual and Community Assets after Major Disasters 150
VII. Best Practices and How Attorneys Can Make a Difference 156
A. Emergency Preparedness and Coordination 156
B. Common Platforms 158
C. Communication 158
D. Reflection 159
VIII. Conclusion 159
Notes 160

Part 2

Economic Recovery 165

Chapter 7

The 9/11 Attack on America and Lessons on How to Rebuild a Mixed-Use Business District 167

Richard M. Froehlich

I. Introduction 167
II. Downtown: The History and Base Case 168
III. Building the World Trade Center Towers and Battery Park City 169
IV. Impact of 9/11 on Housing and Community Economic Development . . 170
V. Creation of Lower Manhattan Development Corporation 171
VI. Case Example: Federal Recovery Funds 172
VII. Specific Aid for Transit, Small Businesses, and Economic Development 174
VIII. Voluntary Charitable Giving 175
IX. Liberty Zone Tax Benefits and Liberty Bonds 176
X. Rebuilding at Ground Zero: Commercial Space, Arts, the Memorial, and Museum 177

A. Commercial Space 177
B. The Memorial 179
C. The Arts 179
XI. From Liberty Zone to GO Zone: Lessons Learned 180
XII. Conclusion: Taking Stock of What Worked and What Did Not 180
XIII. Epilogue 181
Notes 182

Chapter 8
Small Business Disaster Assistance 187
Peggy Maisel and Natalie Roman
I. Introduction 187
II. Federal Assistance 188
A. Small Business Administration 188
B. Internal Revenue Service 192
C. Community Development Block Grants Disaster Recovery 193
III. State Assistance 195
IV. Conclusion 197
Notes 198

Chapter 9
Restoring Small Business: A State Agency Response to the 2008 Iowa Disasters 205
Meridith Marshall
I. Introduction 205
II. Disaster Recovery Funding and State Assistance 206
III. Personal Property Assistance 208
IV. Commercial and Residential Rental Assistance 209
V. Case Management 209
VI. Lessons Learned 210
VII. Conclusion 213
Notes 213

Part 3
Housing Recovery 215

Chapter 10
The 2008 Texas Hurricanes: Working for Equitable and Transparent Redevelopment 217
Heather K. Way and Maddie Sloan
I. Introduction 217
II. Background: The 2008 Texas Hurricanes Dolly and Ike 218

III. The Federal Response 219
IV. Texas's Initial Response: Inequities and Long Delays 221
V. Legal and Community-Based Strategies 225
A. State-Level Advocacy 225
B. Local Advocacy 230
VI. Nuts and Bolts of Section 3 Law 237
VII. Lessons Learned 240
VIII. Conclusion 242
Notes 243

Chapter 11
Public Housing Post-Disaster: To Rehabilitate or Replace? 249
Michael H. Reardon and Nathaniel S. Cushman
I. Introduction 249
II. An Introduction to the "Big Four": The Housing Authority of New Orleans Confronts Hurricane Katrina 250
III. Rehabilitating Public Housing 251
A. Disaster under the Stafford Act: The Public Assistance Program . . . 252
B. Non–Stafford Act Disaster: HUD Funds for Emergency Capital Needs 254
IV. Demolition and Disposition of Public Housing 255
A. Section 18 General Requirements for Demolition or Disposition . . . 256
B. Section 18 Requirements Specific to Dispositions 257
C. Section 18 Requirements Specific to Demolitions 258
D. Special Guidance for Exigent Cases, Including Disasters 259
V. Programmatic Options for Redevelopment of Public Housing 259
A. Disposition in Support of Mixed-Finance Development 260
B. The HOPE VI Program and the Choice Neighborhoods Initiative . . 262
C. The Rental Assistance Demonstration Program 263
VI. Issues in Public Housing Rehabilitation and Replacement 265
A. One-for-One Replacement Requirement 265
B. Fair Housing, Deconcentration, and Site and Neighborhood Standards 267
VII. Conclusion 268
Notes 268

Chapter 12
Locked Out and Torn Down: Public Housing Post–Hurricane Katrina 275
Bill Quigley and Sara H. Godchaux
I. Introduction 275
II. Low-Income Housing in New Orleans Pre–Hurricane Katrina 277
III. Public Housing in New Orleans Pre–Hurricane Katrina 278

IV. Hurricane Katrina Damage to Public Housing. 280
V. Political Response to Damaged Public Housing 281
VI. What Happened to Public Housing Residents during and after Hurricane Katrina: An Unequal Opportunity to Return. 282
VII. Response of HUD. 285
A. Demolition or Rehabilitation? 286
B. Consultation and Offer to Residents 286
C. The Failures of the Federal Demolition Procedure 287
VIII. Litigation to Reopen Public Housing. 288
IX. Low-Income Housing in New Orleans 2012 289
X. Conclusion 293
Notes 294

Part 4
Community Resilience: Challenges and Opportunities. 301

Chapter 13
Wolf at the Door: Protecting Homeowners from Predatory Housing Activities in the Wake of Disaster 303
Kate Titford and Rutledge Simmons
I. Introduction 303
II. Challenges of the Post-Disaster Environment 304
III. Predatory Housing Transactions in the Wake of Disaster 306
A. Contractor Fraud 307
B. Insurance Fraud 308
C. Government Relief Scams 308
D. Mortgage Fraud 310
E. Affiliation with Government Entities. 310
IV. After the Storm: Ways to Protect Homeowners from Financial Predators after Disasters. 310
A. Consumer Education and Outreach 311
B. Presence of High-Capacity Service Providers in the Post-Disaster Vacuum. 311
C. Design Programs That Avert Scammers' Access to Potential Victims 312
D. Develop Technology That Is Responsive to New Scams 313
E. State and Federal Enforcement Actions. 313
V. Conclusion 315
Notes 316

Chapter 14
Housing Choice in Crisis: Short-Term Post–Hurricane Katrina Relief . . . 319
James H. Perry and Monika Gerhart-Hambrick
I. Introduction . . . 319
II. Shelter as Dwelling . . . 320
III. Vouchers as Disaster Housing . . . 321
A. Katrina Disaster Housing Assistance Program . . . 322
IV. "I'm Not Racist, but Whites Only" . . . 324
V. Compounding Burdens: People with Disabilities . . . 327
VI. Sex Discrimination . . . 330
VII. No Se Puede . . . 333
VIII. Recommendations . . . 336
Notes . . . 339

Chapter 15
Disasters' Long-Term Impact on Fair Housing: Rebuilding as an Engine to Perpetuate or Challenge Entrenched Segregation . . . 345
Morgan Williams and Nisha Arekapudi
I. Introduction . . . 345
II. Recent Post-Disaster Redevelopment Programs on the Gulf Coast and the Perpetuation of Entrenched Patterns of Segregation . . . 347
A. Road Home Program . . . 347
B. Gulf Opportunity Zone Tax Credit Program . . . 350
C. Redevelopment of Public Housing . . . 353
D. Disaster Housing Assistance Program . . . 356
III. Fair Housing Law Mandates That Post-Disaster Redevelopment Programs Employ Federal Housing Funds to Promote Integration . . . 357
A. Practices Needed to Ensure Post-Disaster Redevelopment Occurs in a Manner That Furthers Fair Housing Choice . . . 360
B. Policies Needed to Counteract Identified Barriers to Fair Housing Choice . . . 362
C. Enforcement Techniques Available to Challenge Post-Disaster Redevelopment Plans That Do Not Further Fair Housing Choice . . . 364
IV. Conclusion . . . 366
Notes . . . 366

Chapter 16
Innovative Post-Disaster Community-Based Housing Strategies..........371
Diane Glauber and David Zisser
I. Introduction 371
II. Barriers to Rebuilding 372
A. Exclusionary Zoning 372
B. Government Programs 373
C. Private-Sector Barriers 374
D. Planning Problems 375
III. Community-Based Strategies 375
A. Community Land Trusts 376
B. Developing Vacant and Blighted Properties 379
C. Volunteer Construction Model 380
D. Title Clearing 383
IV. Lessons Learned 385
Notes 386

Chapter 17
Disaster as a Catalyst for Collaboration and Innovation: Workforce Development in Mississippi Following Hurricane Katrina..........391
Ed Sivak
I. Introduction 391
II. Case Examples 392
A. Hurricane Katrina Damage Estimates 392
B. Workforce Development before Hurricane Katrina 394
C. After Katrina: The First Weeks of Recovery 395
D. National Emergency Grant Program 396
E. Temporary Jobs 397
F. Workforce Training: Mississippi Gulf Coast 398
G. Workforce Training in Rural Areas 399
H. Women in Construction Program 400
III. Lessons Learned 401
A. Do Not Waste a Crisis 401
B. Hierarchy of Needs Matters 401
C. Supportive Services Matter—Particularly for Low-Income Families 402
D. Nonprofits Have a Role to Play—Yet Scale Remains a Challenge... 402
IV. Conclusion 402
Notes 403

Resources 405
Federal Government Resources 405
Tools You Can Use 405

Consumer Financial Protection Bureau 406
Federal Emergency Management Agency (FEMA) 406
Internal Revenue Service 407
Small Business Administration (SBA) 408
U.S. Department of Agriculture 408
U.S. Department of Commerce Economic Development Administration 409
U.S. Department of Housing and Urban Development (HUD) 409
Community Development Block Grants-Disaster Recovery (CDBG-DR) 409
Federal Housing Administration (FHA) 410
HOME 410
Office of Public and Indian Housing 410
Office of Fair Housing and Equal Opportunity 411
Section 3 of the HUD Act of 1968 411
U.S. Department of Justice 411
U.S. Department of Labor 412
Tribal Governments 412
Evaluations of Federal Support Post-Disaster 413
International Human Rights Law 415
Tools You Can Use 415
For Further Reading 415
Equitable Recovery 416
Tools You Can Use 416
For Further Reading 417
State Government Resources 418
Local Government Resources 418
Nonprofit and Religious Organizations 419
Emergency Housing 420
Fair Housing 420
Public Housing 421
Predatory Financial Transactions 423
Small Businesses 423
Workforce Development 423
Centers and Think Tanks 424
Select Disaster-Specific Recovery Resources 425
New York City Post–9/11 425
2005 Hurricane Katrina 425
2008 Texas Hurricanes 426
2008 Iowa Storms 428
2010 BP Oil Spill 429
2012 Hurricane Sandy 430

Index 433

Acknowledgments

This book would not have been possible without the support, ideas, and guidance of our colleagues on the ABA Forum on Affordable Housing and Community Development Law's Governing Committee. The Forum's first foray into post-disaster concerns for affordable housing and community economic development was its 2008 conference "Lessons Learned from Katrina and Rita" held in New Orleans, just as seismic shifts began occurring in the Low Income Housing Tax Credit market and the broader economy due to turbulence in the mortgage market that would eventually lead to an unprecedented wave of millions of foreclosures across the country. *Building Community Resilience Post-Disaster* furthers the Forum's commitment to creating strong communities, particularly after natural and human-made disasters.

We thank Rochelle Lento for her guidance, comments, and mentorship throughout the publication process. The editing advice of Roger Clay and Susan Jones was important as we embarked on this book project.

ABA Forum Manager Dawn Holiday, as always, encouraged our initiative and work throughout. As chair of the Forum when we proposed this book project, Toni Jackson supported our vision from the beginning. The ABA publishing team under the leadership of Rick Paszkiet patiently and thoughtfully guided us through the publication process.

From the start to the end of the editing process, there were several people who graciously assisted with securing authors, reviewed chapter drafts, offered suggestions, and provided editing support: Sherrod Banks, Joanne Boy, Roger Clay, Amy Curry, Chad Harris, Susan Jones, Julie McGovern, Kim Pate, Chaundi Randolph, and Carey Whitehead.

The chapter authors have generously shared their time, insights, and experiences, which have made this book a useful resource for the field. Your work is the inspiration for this publication, and your contributions to advancing affordable housing and community economic development are invaluable. It has been an honor to work with you.

Finally, and most importantly, thank you to the community leaders, elected officials, advocates, government personnel, volunteers, and the countless others whose stories and lives are woven into the fabric of this book as they work day in and day out to ensure community resilience.

We are especially thankful for our families, friends, and colleagues who have nurtured our dreams and supported us in life and throughout the process of developing this book.

To my parents, Ray and Ella J. Gilmore; my husband, Chad E. Harris; my sister and her family, Tabitha, Kwame, and Kaelynn Curtis; my second parents, Jack and Carolyn Harris; my extended family; my friends; and my mentors, I am eternally grateful for your insight, encouragement, unwavering support, friendship, and love.

Dorcas R. Gilmore

To my parents, Joseph and Dr. Mary Standaert; my sister, Patricia Ravenhorst, and her family Wil, Maria Sebastian, Harm, and Jake; my colleagues at Self-Help; my mentors; and my friends, thank you so much for your support, wisdom, inspiration, laughter, and patience.

Diane M. Standaert

About the Contributors

Nisha Arekapudi is a JD candidate at American University Washington College of Law and was a National Fair Housing Alliance 2012 summer law clerk.

Brenda Bratton Blom, JD, PhD, is a law school professor, recently retired from the University of Maryland Francis King Carey School of Law. Her interests revolve around the legal and social policies that support or hinder the development of communities, particularly low-income communities. She taught clinically and has written in the areas of community economic development, community justice, and professionalism, culminating in the publication of *Community Economic Development Law: A Text for Engaged Learning* with coauthors Susan Bennett (American University), Louise Howells (University of the District of Columbia), and Deborah Kenn (Syracuse University) in August of 2012.

Nathaniel S. Cushman is an associate at Nixon Peabody, LLP. He received his JD from the Georgetown University Law Center, where he participated in the Harrison Institute for Housing and Community Development starting in 2008. He has practiced at Nixon Peabody, LLP, since 2010, focusing on affordable housing regulatory and transactional matters, including representation of both developers and public housing authorities in connection with HUD mixed-finance transactions.

Richard M. Froehlich is the chief operating officer, executive vice president, and general counsel of the New York City Housing Development Corporation. Prior to joining the Housing Development Corporation, Mr. Froehlich was of counsel at O'Melveny & Meyers, LLP, where he was involved in numerous multifamily housing transactions representing equity investors, lenders, credit enhancers, and issuers in bond-financed transactions. He is an adjunct assistant professor at Columbia University

Graduate School of Architecture, Planning, and Preservation. He is a 1988 graduate of Columbia Law School and a 1985 graduate of Columbia University's Columbia College.

Catherine (Katusha) Galitzine served as the Program on Human Rights and the Global Economy Fellow with the National Law Center for Homelessness and Poverty. She is a graduate of Northeastern University School of Law and currently serves as a graduate fellow with the Legal Skills in Social Context program.

Monika Gerhart is a senior policy analyst for the Greater New Orleans Fair Housing Action Center, leading local, state, and federal policy efforts. She contributed to or led disaster-housing work in the aftermath of Hurricane Katrina with Amnesty International USA and the Louisiana Disaster Recovery Foundation.

Diane Glauber is the director of the Community Development Project at the Lawyers' Committee for Civil Rights Under Law and she has over two decades of experience in the area of community development in the public, private, and nonprofit sectors. She has served as director of Human Services for the city of Baltimore, syndication counsel at Enterprise Community Investment, director of Supportive Housing at the Enterprise Foundation, and program officer at the Baltimore Community Foundation. She graduated from the University of Maryland Francis King Carey School of Law and holds a master's in public administration from New York University and a bachelor of arts from Emory University.

Sara Helene Godchaux is a Social Justice Fellow in New Orleans. She is a 2012 graduate of Loyola University New Orleans College of Law, where she was an editor of the law review and named Outstanding Ignatian Law Student for distinction in scholarship and service.

Antoinette M. "Toni" Jackson is a partner at Coats Rose in Houston, Texas, and graduate of Thurgood Marshall School of Law. She has served as chair of the ABA Forum on Affordable Housing and Community Development Law, president of the Texas Affiliation of Affordable Housing Providers, and chair of the National Bar Association Real Estate Section.

Helen R. Kanovsky is the general counsel of the U.S. Department of Housing and Urban Development (HUD). She was sworn in by Secretary Shaun Donovan on May 4, 2009. She received her JD cum laude from the Harvard Law School in 1976. She previously worked at HUD from 1979 to 1981, when she served as a special assistant to Secretary of Housing and Urban Development Patricia Roberts Harris.

Margaret (Peggy) Maisel is the founding and current director of the Clinical Legal Education Program and professor of law at Florida International University College of Law. She also founded and taught Florida International University's Community Development Clinic and now teaches an interdisciplinary Health Law and Policy Clinic.

Meridith Marshall is a senior project manager for the Community Development Division of the Iowa Economic Development Authority. She has worked with the Iowa Economic Development Authority for more than three years, managing $98 million of disaster recovery economic development funding and overseeing the duplication of benefits assessment for Iowa's Community Development Block Grants Disaster Recovery allocation. In 2009, she graduated from Drake University with a bachelor of science in business administration with a major in economics and a master of business administration.

Ingrid Norton is a freelance writer with a special interest in urban history, community resilience, and poverty. Her essays and reportage span subjects from the effects of long-standing housing discrimination in Detroit, Michigan, to hurricanes in the Gulf of Mexico. Her work has appeared in publications such as *Dissent*, *The Guardian*, *The Los Angeles Review of Books*, *Next City*, *Open Letters Monthly*, and *Religion and Politics*.

Jacqui Patterson, MSW, MPH, is the director of Environmental and Climate Justice at the NAACP. Over the years she has served as a trainer, organizer, researcher, program manager, and policy analyst on international and domestic issues, including women's rights, HIV and AIDS, violence against women, racial justice, economic justice, and environmental and climate justice, with organizations including the U.S. Peace Corps, Center on Budget and Policy Priorities, Baltimore City Healthy Start, IMA World Health, Federal Emergency Management Agency, United for a Fair Economy, ActionAid, Health GAP, and the organization she cofounded, Women of Color United.

James Perry is the executive director of the Greater New Orleans Fair Housing Action Center. Under his leadership, the organization has tripled in size and helped thousands of residents to challenge unfair practices based on race, sex, sexual orientation, income, and disability. He is a member of the National Fair Housing Alliance and Louisiana Housing Alliance Board of Directors.

Bill Quigley is a human rights lawyer and law professor at Loyola University New Orleans College of Law. He was part of the legal team representing thousands of displaced public housing residents in New Orleans who challenged the demolition of their apartments.

Michael H. Reardon is a partner at Nixon Peabody, LLP, and was previously assistant general counsel for assisted housing at the U.S. Department of Housing and

Urban Development. For over 30 years, he has concentrated his practice on affordable housing and real estate matters, in particular the public housing and Section 8 housing assistance programs.

Natalie Roman is currently a research fellow at Florida International University College of Law. She received her JD summa cum laude from Florida International University College of Law. For the last 15 years, she has operated a small business providing tutoring services.

Dina Schlossberg is deputy director/senior attorney for Multifamily Housing at Regional Housing Legal Services. She was of counsel at two law firms and an associate practice professor of law at University of Pennsylvania Law School. She has more than 20 years of experience in the area of real estate and nonprofit law, concentrating primarily on community development and economic development initiatives.

Rutledge Simmons is deputy general counsel of NeighborWorks America, a Washington, D.C.–based national nonprofit that provides technical and financial assistance to a network of community economic-development organizations. He handles all legal matters and leads significant corporate initiatives on foreclosure and rescue scam prevention, acquisitions, new program designs, and fund investments. He is the chair of the African American Experience Fund of the National Park Foundation, former chair of the ABA Business Law Section's Community Economic Development Committee, and a member of the American Bar Association's Commission on Homelessness and Poverty. He practiced corporate law at the law firms of Hale and Dorr, LLP, and Holland and Knight, LLP, and he is a graduate of Harvard College and Columbia Law School.

Ed Sivak is the director of the Mississippi Economic Policy Center and the senior vice president for Policy and Evaluation at the Hope Enterprise Corporation. As director, Sivak manages the strategic direction, sustainability, research, training, and advocacy agenda for the center. The Mississippi Economic Policy Center uses its analysis to ensure that the needs of low- and moderate-income Mississippians in particular are considered in the development and implementation of public policy with the ultimate goal of improving access to economic opportunity.

Madison Sloan manages Texas Appleseed's disaster relief and fair housing projects. She first joined Texas Appleseed as an Equal Justice Works Legal Fellow working on systemic issues related to Hurricane Katrina. She received a JD from the University of Michigan Law School and a master of public affairs from the University of Texas, and she previously worked for Legal Services of South Central Michigan.

Eric S. Tars is the director of Human Rights and Children's Rights Programs at the National Law Center on Homelessness and Poverty. In his human rights capacity, he works with homelessness and housing advocacy organizations to train and strategically utilize human rights as a component of their work. In his youth rights capacity, he works to protect homeless students' right to education and advocates for homeless youth and families through trainings, litigation, and policy advocacy at the national and local levels.

Kate Titford is an attorney in the Office of General Counsel at NeighborWorks America. In this capacity, she manages the legal assistance component of the National Foreclosure Mitigation Counseling Program. She has represented NeighborWorks America at numerous foreclosure mediation working groups. Before coming to NeighborWorks in 2009, she served as managing director of Baltimore City's nonprofit vacant building receiver and managing editor of a quarterly housing law digest published by the Housing and Development Law Institute. She holds a JD from the University of Maryland Francis King Carey School of Law and a bachelor of science from Spring Hill College in Mobile, Alabama.

Heather K. Way is a professor at the University of Texas School of Law, where she serves as director of the Community Development Clinic. She is also the cofounder and a leader of the UT Opportunity Forum, an interdisciplinary collaborative of University of Texas faculty working to foster the expansion of equitable opportunities for low-income Texans. Her work as an attorney and policy advocate focuses on equitable communities, affordable housing, problem properties, and land-title issues in low-income neighborhoods—and also family-friendly communities, which she blogs about at www.whichwayaustin.blogspot.com.

Carey Catherine Whitehead is an attorney advisor in HUD's Office of General Counsel, Community Development Division. Since joining HUD in 2009, she has served as a program counsel working on disasters and other issues with HUD's Office of Community Planning and Development and Office of Disaster Management and National Security. She received her JD cum laude from Lewis and Clark Law School in 2009.

Woody Widrow is the executive director of RAISE Texas, the first incorporated, nonprofit, statewide asset-building coalition in the country. He has over 40 years of experience in housing, community development, and asset building. Before moving to Texas in 1999, he served as the vice president of the National Community Reinvestment Coalition, the deputy director of the National Association for Affordable Housing Lenders, and the executive director of the National Housing Institute and editor of *SHELTERFORCE*.

Morgan Williams is the Director of Enforcement and Investigations at the National Fair Housing Alliance, where he provides technical support to fair housing offices across the country and manages a docket of systemic fair housing cases. Previously, he was General Counsel of the Greater New Orleans Fair Housing Action Center, managing fair housing enforcement in post–Katrina New Orleans and throughout Louisiana and southern Mississippi. He graduated with a B.A. in environmental studies at Oberlin College, and with a J.D., magna cum laude, from Tulane Law School. He has served on the adjunct faculty at American Law School and Loyola Law School of New Orleans.

David Zisser is counsel in the Community Development Project at the Lawyers' Committee for Civil Rights Under Law. The Community Development Project represents more than 15 community-based organizations in the Gulf Coast that are engaged in community revitalization, fair housing, affordable housing, environmental justice, and food access. He obtained his law degree from University of California Hastings College of Law and his master's in city planning from UC Berkeley.

About the Editors

Dorcas R. Gilmore and Diane M. Standaert

Dorcas R. Gilmore is assistant general counsel in the NAACP legal department, where she represents the NAACP national office and assists its more than 1,000 branches and units nationwide. In this role, she advances the NAACP's racial justice advocacy mission on issues of economic justice and provides corporate counsel. Prior to her current position, Gilmore was a Skadden Fellow and staff attorney at the Community Law Center. She created the Youth Entrepreneurship Initiative, providing a range of business and nonprofit legal services to youth-led organizations. She also directed the Small Business Legal Services Program & Youth Entrepreneurship Initiative and the Equitable Development Project. Gilmore has represented businesses, community organizations, social ventures, and coalitions seeking to promote racial and economic equity in their communities. Gilmore has written several articles and book chapters on youth entrepreneurship legal services, community economic development, community lawyering, and law and leadership.

Gilmore earned her law degree from the University of Maryland Francis King Carey School of Law, where she was the 2004 Gilbert & Jaylee Mead Public Interest Scholar. Prior to law school, she provided workforce development training in the Dominican Republic as a part of the national government's Presidential Plan Against Poverty. Gilmore graduated magna cum laude from Rollins College with an honors bachelor of arts.

Gilmore is a member of the Governing Committee of the ABA Forum on Affordable Housing and Community Development Law and a founding member of its Young Lawyers Network. She also serves on the board of directors of the Women's Law Center of Maryland and the Racial Justice Advisory Committee for the Sargent Shriver National Center on Poverty Law.

Diane M. Standaert is a senior legislative counsel at the Center for Responsible Lending, working with stakeholders and policymakers to curb predatory lending. The Center for Responsible Lending is the policy and research arm to Self-Help, the nation's largest community-development financial institution. Standaert's articles on consumer finance, mortgage lending, and foreclosures have appeared in national publications for lawyers and community development practitioners.

Standaert graduated summa cum laude from Florida State University, where she was recognized as Humanitarian of the Year for her leadership with the campus chapter of Habitat for Humanity. Following college, Standaert was selected to serve as Jane Addams–Andrew Carnegie Fellow at the Indiana University-Purdue University School of Philanthropy, where she focused on the role of the nonprofit sector in affordable housing production and worked with the Indianapolis Neighborhood Housing Partnership to support the city's community development corporations.

She received her law degree from the University of North Carolina at Chapel Hill in 2006 as a Chancellor's Scholar, during which time she directed the law school's pro bono program. In the months following Hurricane Katrina, the UNC School of Law Pro Bono Program spearheaded post-disaster pro bono opportunities in New Orleans, primarily helping the New Orleans Pro Bono Project address title issues for low-income homeowners seeking access to disaster-relief funds. Following law school, Standaert served as a staff attorney at the University of North Carolina Center for Civil Rights, working with communities in the rural South to gain access to clean water, build wealth through preservation of family-owned land, and combat discriminatory housing practices.

Standaert currently serves on the Governing Committee for the ABA Forum on Affordable Housing and Community Development Law. Previous ABA involvement includes serving as the Forum's Law Student Liaison; Young Lawyer Liaison; co-chair for the Forum's 2008 Regional Conference in New Orleans, "Lessons Learned from Hurricanes Katrina and Rita;" and cochair for the Forum's 2010 national annual conference, "Restoration, Revitalization, and Resiliency."

Building Community Resilience Post-Disaster: A Guide for Affordable Housing & Community Economic Development Practitioners

Editors' Introduction

Dorcas R. Gilmore and Diane M. Standaert

In the late fall of 2012 Superstorm Sandy devastated communities from the Caribbean to Canada. It followed Hurricane Isaac's landfall on the Gulf Coast less than three months earlier. In the wake of these storms, many news reports raised the question of whether disasters are "the new normal," especially as such events are increasing in frequency and intensity. With more than 655 major disaster declarations in the last decade[1] and 71 percent of the United States facing disaster drought conditions in 2012,[2] examination and public discussion of the post-disaster roles of government and nongovernmental entities are warranted. Human-created disasters are an equally important part of the analysis. The 9/11 terrorist attacks redefined governmental responses and preparedness for human-created disasters. Subsequent events like the 2010 BP oil drilling disaster, one of the largest environmental disasters in U.S. history, reignited the national debate on the impacts of these disasters and respective roles of public and private actors in post-disaster recovery.

Whether rising floodwaters, ravages of a financial crisis, oil-polluted seafood, or fatalities from terrorist attacks, the toll disasters exact on communities is immediate, profound, and long-lasting. Disasters spotlight many long-standing affordable housing and community economic-development questions: How and where to create housing and economic opportunities? How will these opportunities be financed? Who will benefit from them? Who will bear the environmental and economic costs of development? And who will be included in these important decisions? Lawyers and other practitioners in the field of affordable housing and community economic development confront these issues head-on, from the immediate aftermath through the long-term recovery. In facing these post-disaster realities, *Building Community Resilience Post-Disaster* calls upon practitioners to advance communities' abilities to rebound and create stronger and healthier places to live, work, worship, and play—to be more resilient.

With enhancing community resilience as a primary goal in the post-disaster landscape, practitioners must evaluate the way disasters reshape the possibilities and challenges for affordable housing and community economic development generally. For example, disaster-recovery funding is far outpacing traditional community development resources. The U.S. Department of Housing and Urban Development funding request for Community Development Block Grants in fiscal year 2013 was $2.948 billion[3] compared with the $16 billion allocation of Community Development Block Grant Disaster Recovery funding for areas affected by Superstorm Sandy.[4] This financing reality presents important challenges and opportunities for communities and practitioners. The number of communities affected by disasters; the amount of federal, state, and local resources devoted to disaster preparation and response; and the extent of increased vulnerability, discrimination, and exclusion in post-disaster contexts require ongoing research, analysis, and focus by the affordable housing and community economic development field.

Building Community Resilience Post-Disaster aims to contribute to this growing body of work by detailing disasters' various impacts on the affordable housing and community economic development landscapes at local, state, regional, and national levels. Examining disasters that span every region of the United States, the book raises and answers many pivotal affordable housing and community economic-development questions with similar and some conflicting viewpoints. Programs that are developed in one disaster are modified and often incorporated into the disaster response toolkit for a future disaster. An example is the creation of the Liberty Zone in the post–9/11 economic recovery and its evolution four years later to the Gulf Opportunity Zone following Hurricanes Katrina and Rita. The chapters present past failures, best practices, and a range of opportunities to improve local, regional, and national disaster response frameworks and processes.

Critical to the post-disaster framework is equity and a decided emphasis on the civil and human rights of those impacted by the disaster. Because "[d]isasters occur at the intersections of hazards and vulnerabilities,"[5] structural inequalities often create the conditions that lead to disasters' disparate effects in communities. The colonias in Texas along the Mexican border serve as an example of the lack of infrastructure investment in water and sewer lines as a pre-disaster vulnerability in many low-income communities. This vulnerability regularly results in flooding and sewage backups. Disasters then compound the inadequate infrastructure, creating very hazardous conditions following a storm or hurricane: flooding communities with water and sewage.

Post-disaster responses also have long-term effects on how communities rebound from the disaster; whether the recovery includes all members of impacted communities, particularly those most vulnerable; and to what extent the communities are healthier post-disaster than they were before. As such, in the process of building community resilience post-disaster, advocates and government actors must create mechanisms that promote inclusion in disaster response as well as combat new and existing forms of economic exclusion and housing segregation through both policy and practice.

Building Community Resilience Post-Disaster begins with a post-disaster snapshot, through a journalist's eye, that highlights uneven recovery, multiple vulnerable communities, and numerous parallels between disasters separated by time and geography. Part 1 examines the components of the disaster recovery framework that exists in the United States. With specific attention to housing and economic development, it focuses on the multiple roles of federal, tribal, state, and local governments, nonprofit organizations, and religious organizations in first response, financing recovery efforts, and ensuring a more holistic and equitable recovery. The first two chapters highlight the current federal and tribal government framework for disaster relief and the significant funding devoted to disaster recovery, discussing the specific role of the U.S. Department of Housing and Urban Development as a key federal agency in the housing and community economic development recovery. Using a civil and human rights framework, the next two chapters offer an expanded view of the role of the federal government in disaster response and underscore the importance of equity as central to greater community resilience. Part 1 ends with the roles of first responders—local government and nonprofit and religious organizations—in filling the gaps in the recovery systems and reaching those most vulnerable.

Part 2 emphasizes the federal, state, and local economic development incentives that fueled business and economic recovery following the 9/11 terrorist attacks in New York, Hurricane Andrew in 1992, the Los Angeles Riots in 1992, Hurricanes Katrina and Rita in 2005, the Iowa disasters in 2008, and the BP oil drilling disaster in 2010. Whether the disaster is human-created or natural, these chapters stress the need to restore local and regional economies and the important roles of multiple government entities in sustainable economic recovery. The recovery of local economies is dependent not only on jobs and business development but also on ensuring communities have accessible, affordable housing as the bedrock for strong and resilient communities.

Part 3 focuses on the recovery of affordable housing for those most economically insecure, very low-income residents of public housing. With case examples of 2008 Hurricanes Ike and Dolly and 2005 Hurricane Katrina, these chapters highlight the importance of housing recovery for all residents and bring into clear view many of the challenges, stakeholders' roles, and questions in ensuring meaningful housing access.

Part 4 accentuates the challenges and opportunities disasters pose for community resilience. The challenges include new predatory housing practices and discriminatory practices with short-term and long-term fair housing consequences, which undermine community resilience and can lead to greater inequities than existed before the disaster. Disasters simultaneously can be opportunities, as discussed in the final two chapters. These chapters identify innovations in new housing models that meet the needs of local communities and investigate expanded workforce development options for vulnerable populations to become full participants in and benefit from the local and regional economy.

Finally, the book concludes with a resources section, which mirrors the book's chapter topics and provides practitioners with additional tools and disaster-specific information.

As practitioners in multiple roles and phases of post-disaster response and recovery, the nearly two dozen authors reveal many valuable recommendations for all those engaged in disaster response, recovery, mitigation, and preparation:

- Begin with an equity framework in which the goal is to expand the economic and housing opportunities and safety net for more members of the community.
- Pay attention to the existing disaster recovery frameworks at the community, local, regional, state, tribal, and national levels, along with their shortcomings.
- Involve communities most affected by disasters in the needs assessment, funds allocation, and evaluation phases of planning and recovery. This is central to effective, equitable, and sustainable recovery.
- Allocate and disburse funds through mechanisms that are transparent and traceable, ensuring accountability, assessments of equitable distribution, and long-term evaluation of effectiveness.
- Plan to assess the preexisting vulnerabilities in communities that lead to long-term, and sometimes fatal, effects post-disaster.
- Enforce civil and human rights laws and standards to promote equity in immediate response, recovery, and redevelopment, and educate the public about these laws and standards.
- Ensure nonprofits at the local, regional, and national levels are fully engaged, communicating with one another, government entities, and communities.
- Leverage the philanthropic resources of individuals, corporations, and foundations to develop a strategic and coordinated approach using the experience, community-based knowledge, and relative strengths of local, regional, and national nonprofit and religious organizations.

- Create a means of communication that ensures affected communities remain an integral part of the decision-making processes, despite post-disaster challenges such as displacement and disrupted traditional communication mechanisms.
- Be prepared to combat the multiple ways disasters can create opportunities for predatory housing and consumer practices, and broadly communicate this, in multiple languages, to disaster survivors.
- Develop systems to document and replicate housing and community economic-development innovations that emerge in the post-disaster response.

Affordable housing and community economic development practitioners continue to play vital roles in post-disaster recovery as advocates, regulators, planners, developers, and financing agents. Building community resilience requires a commitment to ensuring interconnected systems, effective communication, strong community engagement, public and private collaboration, and equity that lifts up those most vulnerable and advances all members of communities in the process.

Although acute natural and human-created disasters are the focus of this book, the lessons and warnings are important for addressing the long-term disasters of disinvestment, predatory financial practices, and discrimination that have led to decline in too many cities and towns throughout the country. These long-term disasters and those detailed in *Building Community Resilience Post-Disaster* remind us that a community's ability to thrive in the aftermath of disaster depends on a collective commitment to a broad and shared vision of every community as a healthy and resilient community.

Notes

1. *Disaster Declarations by Year*, FED. EMERGENCY MGMT. AGENCY, http://www.fema.gov/disasters/grid/year (last visited Mar. 19, 2013).

2. Press Release, U.S. Dep't of Agriculture, USDA Designates 597 Counties in 2013 as Disaster Areas Due to Drought (Jan. 9, 2013), *available at* http://www.usda.gov/wps/portal/usda/usdahome?contentid=2013/01/0002.xml&contentidonly=true (last visited Mar. 19, 2013).

3. *Community Development Allocations and Appropriations*, U.S. DEP'T OF HOUS. AND URBAN DEV., http://portal.hud.gov/hudportal/HUD?src=/program_offices/comm_planning/communitydevelopment/budget (last visited Mar. 19, 2013).

4. Press Release, U.S. Dep't of Hous. and Urban Dev., HUD Announces First Round of Allocations of Hurricane Sandy Recovery Funds (Feb. 6, 2013), *available at* http://portal.hud.gov/hudportal/HUD?src=/press/press_releases_media_advisories/2013/HUDNo.13-014.

5. Bonnie Allen et al., *Community Recovery Lawyering: Hard-Learned Lesson from Post-Katrina Mississippi*, 4 DEPAUL J. SOC. JUST. 97, 121 (2010).

Reports from the Frontlines of Disaster Recovery & Community Resilience

Ingrid Norton

Communities face existential questions in the wake of civil unrest, natural disasters, and terrorist attacks. In the aftermath of such events, questions of change, civic collaboration, and fairness often haunt residents and local leaders for years. The sudden displacement of people and economic disruption can reveal the presence of long-standing inequality and make individuals newly vulnerable. This book directly concerns itself with the difficult trade-offs recovery involves, both in the immediate aftermath of disasters and in subsequent months and years. By shattering the status quo, these events provide opportunities for new collaborations between those directly affected and concerned leaders, empowering communities to weather future catastrophes.

The chapters in *Building Community Resilience Post-Disaster* illuminate the common struggles as well as the institutional and legal ambiguities involved in efforts to rebuild following human-made and natural disasters. One chapter delves into the urban rebuilding following the 9/11 terrorist attacks in New York City that destroyed the World Trade Center. The city faced difficult practical and symbolic choices about how to honor the dead and reconstitute a shaken economy, severed public transit networks, and incinerated buildings in the city's financial district. Another author describes neighborhood economic development in southeast Los Angeles following the 1992 Los Angeles riots, and in Cedar Rapids, Iowa, following the severe 2008 Upper Mississippi River floods: in both instances, small businesses proved integral to bulwarking local economies and repairing sundered civic fabric.

Economic collapse, political instability, and natural disasters destabilize legal norms meant to guide development and fair housing during ordinary circumstances. Just as the devastation of Hurricane Katrina galvanized national debate about corruption and long-standing inequality in New Orleans, in the realm of international law, disasters such as the 2006 Typhoon Durian in the Philippines and the civil unrest in the South

Ossetia region in the country of Georgia demonstrated the integral role of emerging international human rights standards in improving the housing situations of those displaced by disaster within their own country.

Every case study in this book depicts a prolonged and ongoing, multiyear recovery process. By bringing together a wide range of examples, from post–9/11 New York City to workforce development on the Mississippi coast post–Hurricane Katrina, *Building Community Resilience Post-Disaster* illuminates how much community leaders, lawyers, government officials, and nonprofit workers responding to major destruction and privation have to learn from each other, and how high the stakes are.

New Orleans after the Brink

Post–Hurricane Katrina New Orleans remains a central example in the field of disaster recovery because of the confusion and devastating pain caused by the complete lack of coordination and cooperation that marked every step of response to the hurricane. In the days after Hurricane Katrina, residents of low-lying neighborhoods, particularly those who lacked cars, were trapped as the floodwaters rose.[1] More than 50 levees in the city's notoriously outdated system failed or were overtopped: most famously, in the Lower Ninth Ward a barge had exploded through the Army Corps of Engineers levee meant to protect the Lower Ninth Ward from the Industrial Canal. The accompanying wave crushed some houses, warped others, and engulfed those on low ground and set back from the levee, sometimes to a height of 13 feet. As the waters subsided and the winds died down across the city, Council on Foreign Relations representatives made recommendations to the Department of Homeland Security that led to FEMA ordering the police and National Guard to go house to house to seize the guns of jittery residents waiting to be rescued.[2]

Visiting the city in late February 2006 to cover "the first Mardi Gras after the storm" for *The Daily Texan*, my colleagues and I, photographers Joey Castillo and Peter Franklin, drove through a landscape of boarded-up storefronts, darkened streets, and rubble. In the Mid-City neighborhood, driving down one of the long avenues that were completely blacked out, we saw Mayor Ray Nagin's face smiling down from a fresh billboard at twisted telephone poles and rubble—"Reunite Our City"—part of his reelection campaign. Signs for building and roofing work seemed to have been staked into the middle of every avenue. Predominantly Mexican migrant workers were arriving from other parts of the country to do poorly paid and uninsured rebuilding work,[3] often on behalf of opportunist contractors, a fact that caused tension—first with the city's long-standing and largely African-American unions of builders and craftsmen, and ultimately for city building inspectors as residents finally rebuilt their homes in subsequent years, a process still ongoing under a FEMA program called Road Home.

Six months after the storm, the Lower Ninth Ward remained so damaged that overnight stays were prohibited: the entire neighborhood was on a policy called Look and Leave. Residents were allowed to visit their homes during daylight hours—or allowed to visit the shards of tile, wood from furniture, and tears of cloth embedded in the mud that remained. It was during this time that I met Al Andrews, who had spent his entire life in that neighborhood, on a desolate stretch of St. Claude Avenue, near a parking lot where workers were delivering hot food from a Red Cross truck. He and I stood near his battered, boarded-up former school and former church, but what was left of his house was at the other end of the neighborhood, so he just showed me a picture from his first visit back after evacuating to friends in Jackson, Mississippi. Less than two months after the storm, he stood in front of a pile of rubble, arms spread, looking exhausted and defiant. He still hadn't heard from some of his cousins. His friends and extended family had all lived in neighborhoods now uninhabitable and were scattered to Mississippi, Missouri, Tennessee, and Virginia.

Andrews explained that a lot of people weren't interested in the annual pre-Lenten festival itself, "so much as in using it as a meeting place" to find lost loved ones at the season's gathering spots. Andrews, however, brightened when asked about the Mardi Gras Indians, crews of traditionally working-class African-American men who meet in secret to create elaborate suits and headdresses of beads and feathers, a practice that dates back to the 1880s. Andrews described the plans of one tribe to dance across the rubble in the Lower Ninth Ward, and then over the bridge next to the burst levee. On Mardi Gras day itself, Indians ended up on the front page of *The Times-Picayune*, a sign of change and new attention to the city's vibrant working-class culture from the traditionally mainstream newspaper.

But in addition to highlighting the city's communal and cultural resilience, focusing on the survival of unique Louisiana traditions may just have been camouflage for a more uncomfortable truth: tens of thousands of people had been displaced, and a major American city and international tourist destination felt like a war zone. Almost three-quarters of homes in New Orleans were damaged by winds or floodwaters, according to most estimates. The city government's attempts to attract private sponsorship for the $2.7 million that Mardi Gras cost had failed, attracting only donated trash bags from Glad.

On that trip, Mark Ruffino, a U.S. postal carrier, was driving his old route in the Bywater, where mail wasn't deliverable. He told me from his van that "[t]he city brought this on itself as far as not everybody coming back. . . . Over the past 10 years, it's been so focused on tourism . . . the people have been forgotten about." The suburbs hadn't saved him: his home in working-class St. Bernard Parish, where he was born, had been wiped out by the same levee failures that devastated the Lower Ninth Ward.

Katrina's seventh anniversary in August 2012 was supposed to be better than that six-month pulse-check: the election of Mayor Mitch Landrieu (the former lieutenant governor and the first white mayor since the 1970s) by a demographically shrunken but majority-black voter base was seen as a sign of burgeoning trust and public will for cooperation and innovation. The Hurricane Katrina anniversary coincided with the midway point of Mayor Landrieu's term and was supposed to be a good time to applaud the tremendous progress the mayor had made: reopened schools, returned residents, and economic recovery supported by federal recovery investment, including a 350-mile ring of updated levees, built at a cost of $14.5 billion.

But when Hurricane Isaac hooked west toward Haiti from its original course seven years to the week from when Hurricane Katrina had also shifted west from Puerto Rico, the anniversary became an occasion for a renewed sense of vulnerability among many residents. Reporting for *The Guardian* in the Iberville public housing development two days before Hurricane Isaac hit, I met Darren Williams, a 16-year-old who had come of age in the fraught post–Hurricane Katrina education system, where thousands of African-American educators were displaced in a sweeping reform that dismantled the existing public school system, created a new school district, and incentivized the opening of new charter schools. In coming years, the Iberville will be converted into mixed-income units as part of President Obama's Choice Neighborhoods Initiative. Williams told me he remembered evacuating to Mississippi when he was nine years old and coming back just two months after the storm. "I'm wondering if it's going to flood like it did from Katrina," he said.

A woman named Faynell Thomas, 37, was carrying water out to her friends. She had taken three years to return, and told me, "I wish I never came back!" Her 19-year-old son was in the hospital with a gunshot wound to the head, causing her to stay. Thomas's anxiety harkened back to the nightmarish week after Hurricane Katrina, when power failures threatened the lives of patients on life support at nearby hospitals, and inmates at Orleans Parish Prison were left in rising floodwaters.

The uncertainty felt by residents like Williams and Thomas provided a reminder of how deep-seated the post–Hurricane Katrina sense of mistrust and vulnerability still is for the many residents still in the process of reestablishing a sense of normalcy. However, Hurricane Isaac, which lowered to a Category 1 storm of pounding rain, proved an opportunity to reflect on the extent to which, at an institutional level, local officials had internalized the mistakes of Hurricane Katrina and taken steps to avoid repeating them. The weekend that the storm threatened New Orleans, the Landrieu administration began voluntarily evacuating patients to hospitals in Baton Rouge, and his representatives went door to door in the Iberville and other housing projects with pamphlets about buses for evacuations—a protective measure directly informed by the city's failure to take care of needy citizens after Hurricane Katrina.

"Cooperation is now the norm. . . . Hurricanes are nonpartisan events in Louisiana," Michael Hecht told me. He is president and CEO of GNO, Inc., an economic development nonprofit responsible for the metro region. I reached him by phone the night after Hurricane Isaac made landfall at his darkened house in uptown New Orleans, as rains continued to pound southeast Louisiana. Before becoming president of GNO, Inc., Hecht had joined Louisiana Economic Development during the difficult year after Hurricane Katrina when more than half, and then a third, of residents remained displaced, and many of those who had returned were crammed into FEMA trailers with poor electric connections which later proved to be leaking formaldehyde.

"If you go back and do an analysis, it was not only lack of coordination but of trust that resulted in a delay in assistance [during Hurricane Katrina]," he said.

He said that the moment he realized the extent of the protocol in place for Hurricane Isaac was Monday morning before the storm. President Obama convened a phone call with representatives from FEMA, Louisiana Gov. Bobby Jindal, and Mayor Landrieu so that representatives from each level of government could coordinate preparations, like the FEMA trucks near the Lower Ninth Ward loaded with crates of bottled water, and the city emergency warnings that were translated in Spanish and Vietnamese for local immigrant populations.

A New Normal?

Yet New Orleans' local success in preparing for Hurricane Isaac was quickly overshadowed when the infrastructure of eastern seaboard cities was overwhelmed by Superstorm Sandy two months later. "We Are All from New Orleans Now," ran the headline of a *Nation* op-ed penned by Mike Tidwell, who has authored a book about how rising sea levels threaten major coastal cities. A month before Superstorm Sandy hit the East Coast, a *New York Times* article explored the extent to which parts of the city, such as the low-lying financial district where the World Trade Center was located, were unprepared for a storm surge. Since the 1993 World Trade Center bombing, and in the wake of 9/11, many of New York's disaster response resources had been focused on potential terrorist attacks. Following the massive hurricane, officials, residents, and advocates worked to repair damage to transportation systems, deal with emergency housing needs as freezing temperatures began to set in, and solve a long-term housing shortage. "We don't have a lot of empty housing in this city," Mayor Michael Bloomberg stated at an early November press conference about the estimated 20,000 people living without electricity in dank, damaged apartments, particularly in Brooklyn and Queens' coastal high-rise apartments.[4]

On November 8—almost two weeks after Superstorm Sandy dissipated—Matthew Power wrote a story for *Outside Online* about Doctors Without Borders' first deployment in the United States, with an emergency medical clinic at a public housing development in shattered, coastal Far Rockaway, Queens, meant to fill the potential gaps in government response. Sophie Delaunay, the group's executive director, explained to Power, "When these things happen in developed countries, we assume the government knows how to deal with it. That isn't necessarily the case. We assumed with Hurricane Katrina that authorities would cope with medical needs. By the time we realized we were wrong, it was too late, and the moment when we could have most helped had passed. It was a bitter experience."

Nor were the problems confined to public housing. In December 2012, Sheri Fink published a long *New York Times Magazine* report about Superstorm Sandy and a 200-unit private high-rise, also in Far Rockaway Queens, where Thomas Anderson, an 89-year-old African-American WWII veteran, died on his back next to his bed, likely of heart problems induced by stress. In the 1970s the complex was built for retired unionized auto workers but was acquired by an investor group called Sarasota Gold, LLC, in the mid-2000s. Because of New York's excellent tenant laws, when the new owner hiked the rents, the state government paid the difference for residents like Anderson.

A short video of panicked residents at the condo, taken by a young reporter a week after Superstorm Sandy, drew international attention and inspired other Internet videos where people pleaded for the city of New York to help residents of the darkened building. Yet no one involved was aware of or accountable for the building's sole casualty of the storm. Thomas Anderson's body was found two weeks later when electricity came back on and a building superintendent checked on the elderly veteran. Anderson's problem, the article implies, may have been a World War II–era one: expecting a well-organized command chain with a clear mission in a city that hasn't experienced a major hurricane for decades, and where the mismatch between unleveraged, in-depth community knowledge and Internet-based panic and public sympathy may have compounded murky communication between volunteers, first responders, and officials.

Are events like this the new normal? The litany of problems that attended Superstorm Sandy in the New York area recall the failures and controversies that followed Hurricane Katrina, and on a much larger scale: elderly and disabled residents left in cold apartments; city buses mobilized as triage after crucial subway tunnels flooded; hospitals and nursing homes unprepared for electricity shortages; massive damage to housing, particularly in middle-class areas of coastal New Jersey and Staten Island and in areas of concentrated poverty such as Far Rockaway; a rise in medical cases of cold-exposure and carbon monoxide poisoning. Much coverage of and commentary on Hurricane Katrina in 2005 depicted the city as a troubled third-world hold-out of violence and corruption, exoticizing conditions of poverty that had pervaded the city for decades and that are common in major urban areas nationwide—and ignoring the Mississippi Gulf Coast, where towns such as Biloxi and Gulfport collectively form a major regional economic hub, which was devastated by Hurricane Katrina's direct hit to the area. Coverage of the aftermath of Superstorm Sandy, on the other hand, seems characterized by a kind of fatigued, detached resilience. The unfolding assessment of the damage and resources that will be involved in post–Superstorm Sandy recovery is a reminder of the extent to which the case studies of recovery and coordination in this book will continue to be relevant in coming years.

The subsequent chapters describe in detail how resiliency can be built—how advocates have worked hard to improve fair housing for residents following hurricanes and to recoup and empower a scattered middle class in the Gulf Coast; how state government officials created incentives to bring small businesses back to Cedar Rapids, Iowa, following devastating floods; how Greensburg, Kansas, used rebuilding from tornadoes as an opportunity to rebuild its future on green and sustainable principles; how Downtown New York reconstituted itself following 9/11 a decade ago. Despite all of the post-disaster challenges, leaders and residents are working hard to rebuild within the context of past hardship and the exigencies that follow catastrophe. The long, uncertain process of rebuilding can be as fraught and harrowing as disaster itself—yet again and again, despite being damaged, stakeholders in the communities profiled in this book were undaunted, and through tenacity and collaboration are emerging stronger than ever before. Their lessons provide a lamp for continuing recovery, and for whatever disasters come next.

—Ingrid Norton

San Antonio, Texas
Winter 2013

Notes

1. Reporting at the Iberville public housing development in central Treme six months later, I heard from residents a lot of angry, conspiratorial-sounding stories about the days after the storm—for instance, about inmates trapped at Orleans Parish Prison in rising water. What they said was entirely true and ultimately led to landmark ACLU and Department of Justice reports regarding the constitutional rights of inmates, which in turn led to a Southern Poverty Law Center lawsuit, pending as of this writing. This is still unfolding and a lot of resources are helpful here; they are listed in the Resources section of the book.

2. Doug Babwin, The Associated Press, "Corpses, Guns Found in New Orleans Homes," (SARASOTA) HERALD-TRIBUNE (Sept. 6, 2005), http://www.heraldtribune.com/article/20050909/BREAKING/50909004.

3. The Latino population spiked by 57 percent from 2000 to 2010, largely credited to the influx of migrant workers and anchored by preexisting Central American communities. Press Release, Greater New Orleans Cmty. Data Ctr., Facts for Features: Hurricane Katrina Recovery, http://www.gnocdc.org/Factsforfeatures/HurricaneKatrinaRecovery/index.html.

4. Mireya Navarro, *New York Is Lagging as Seas and Risks Rise, Critics Warn*, N.Y. TIMES, Sept. 10, 2012, http://www.nytimes.com/2012/09/11/nyregion/new-york-faces-rising-seas-and-slow-city-action.html?pagewanted=all; Michael Schwirtz, *Housing Nightmare Looms in Wake of Storm*, N.Y. TIMES, Nov. 4, 2012, http://www.nytimes.com/2012/11/05/nyregion/freezing-temperatures-complicate-storm-recovery.html?pagewanted=all&_r=0.

PART 1

Framework for Recovery

CHAPTER 1

Federal Funding and Financing Programs Post-Disaster

Antoinette M. Jackson

I. Introduction

In recent years, the United States has seen an increase of natural and human-made disasters that have required the need for governmental funding. These disasters and emergencies have ranged from hurricanes, fires, floods, and drought to terrorism, oil spills, and hazards associated with nuclear power plants.[1] There are many sources that work to predict the top disaster threats to the United States by providing safety warnings, and because of these prediction systems, the number of lives lost has begun to decrease. However, Matthew Kohn, a professor at the University of California–Los Angeles, has gathered statistics showing that although the loss of life has decreased, the number of people left homeless and displaced due to these disasters has increased.[2] As a result, this has increased the need for state and, more specifically, federal post-disaster funding.

This chapter will provide an overview of the history of how the federal government became involved in disaster response. It will also explain how disasters are declared and thus become eligible for federal funding. The chapter will conclude by providing an overview of the various disaster funding programs and incentives, as well as provide a short discussion about public support.

Although there are many funding programs designated for disasters, most legislation is passed in response to the disaster after the needs for appropriate response have been identified. The issue raised in this chapter is not entirely when the funds are designated or appropriated by Congress but rather how the funds are distributed post-disaster and the responsiveness of the agencies handling the distribution.

II. Creation of Funding Sources

A. National Response to Disasters

The coordination of the federal government's response to domestic disasters can be traced to as early as the Congressional Act of 1803. This act was created to provide assistance to a town in New Hampshire after an extensive fire. After this act, legislation was passed more than 100 times to respond to natural disasters such as floods, fires, hurricanes, and earthquakes. In the early 1930s, the Reconstruction Finance Corporation, which was created to provide assistance to railroads, financial institutions, and corporations, offered loans for repair after earthquakes and, subsequently, following other disasters.[3] These duties were expanded to include aid to agriculture and financing for state and local public needs as a result of the Emergency Relief Act of 1932. These loans have been recognized as the earliest disaster loans provided by the federal government. The Reconstruction Finance Corporation was abolished under the Eisenhower administration in the 1950s and its powers were transferred to several agencies, including the Housing and Home Finance Agency.[4]

Other early authority allowed the Bureau of Public Roads to provide funding for highways and bridges damaged by natural disasters, and the Flood Control Act provided authority to implement flood control projects. However, it was soon recognized that the government did not have a comprehensive plan and that the scattered approach was not as effective. The result was the creation of the Disaster Relief Act of 1950. This legislation would provide better oversight and cooperation between federal agencies while authorizing the president, rather than Congress, to manage the disaster activities. The act also allowed that assistance could be distributed through the American Red Cross.[5] The Federal Disaster Assistance Administration was the entity created as a result of the Disaster Relief Act, and it operated within the U.S. Department of Housing and Urban Development (HUD) to provide response and recovery to the growing disasters that were being experienced in the United States.

As a wave of severe and massive natural disasters struck the U.S. in the 1960s and 1970s, it became more and more necessary for the federal government to respond to them and provide recovery operations. In 1974, the Disaster Relief Act was further expanded to set out regulation for presidential declarations of natural disasters.[6] Even with these steps, there were more than 100 federal agencies involved in responding to natural disasters. Additionally, in 1979 following the nuclear power plant accident at Three Mile Island, hazards associated with nuclear power plants were added to the lists of emergencies that required federal attention and funding.[7] Many agreed that the approach to handling these emergencies was haphazard and sought to decrease the number of agencies and centralize the federal emergency functions.

Under Executive Order 12127, President Jimmy Carter centralized the federal emergency functions by merging many of the disaster-related responsibilities into one agency. The agency created was called the Federal Emergency Management Agency (FEMA). It was created to coordinate "the federal government's role in preparing for, preventing, mitigating the effects of, responding to, and recovering from all domestic disasters, whether natural or human-made, including acts of terror."[8] Since its inception, FEMA has struggled with creating a cohesive and responsive agency. It has received harsh criticism as a result of its handling of several disasters, including Hurricanes Hugo, Andrew, and Katrina, the terrorist attacks of 9/11, and most recently Superstorm Sandy.[9]

In March 2003, along with 22 other federal agencies, programs, and departments, the Department of Homeland Security was created as a stand-alone, cabinet-level department. FEMA was among the agencies included in the new department. Homeland Security now has the directive of creating a comprehensive and coordinated approach and response to national security, which includes both natural and human-made disasters and emergencies. The Post-Katrina Emergency Management Reform Act, which was signed into law in 2006, reorganized FEMA and includes a more comprehensive and stronger preparedness mission for the agency.[10]

B. State and Local Responses to Disasters

Prior to the assistance that was provided by the federal government, each state was required to provide response to natural disasters within its borders. However, as the size of the disasters grew, states and local jurisdictions began to look more often to the federal government for assistance and intervention. When a disaster occurs, state and local governments are the first to respond to determine the level of the emergency and the needs of those affected. They are also responsible for mobilizing state and local agencies and determining the level of resources it has to offer on the state level. The emergency services for each state are directed through the state's homeland security or emergency management office.[11] Most states have one entity, but there are a number of states that have several agencies handling these responsibilities.[12] However, the Congressional Budget Office (CBO) has determined that although many states appropriate some funds for disasters, the funding for most states is very limited. Most states appropriate small amounts to a disaster account legislatively but supplement these accounts after a disaster occurs through unobligated state funds.[13] Testimony provided to the CBO has indicated that there does not appear to be a set standard or formula used by states to determine funding level for emergencies, but most states are prepared to mobilize funding quickly as needed through the use of general funds, rainy-day funds, and other funding as determined by each individual state.

In 1993, Florida created a Disaster Trust Fund, which is funded from insurance policy surcharges. These funds are then equally distributed to each county for local emergency management.[14] The Governors Contingency and Emergency Fund for Arizona allocates a small amount from its general funds for emergencies. There were few examples found of other states that similarly fund their emergency management in advance.[15]

If the state determines that it does not have the resources necessary to address the disaster, its state agency along with FEMA assesses the damages to determine if the damages are too costly for the state. If this is determined, the governor may request a federal disaster declaration, but it is still expected to significantly contribute to the recovery. As disasters increase, states are becoming more and more dependent upon the resources that are provided by the federal government.

C. Process for Presidential Declaration

The presidential process for declaring a disaster allows the president to authorize a declaration for a major disaster or emergency that cannot be handled by state and local resources.[16] There are essentially two types of declarations that can be made by the president. The first is an emergency declaration that is issued to protect public health and safety or to avert a major catastrophe. Emergency declarations are usually more limited in scope and require the assistance of the federal government for recovery or prevention of the emergency. The second is a major disaster declaration, which is issued to help a state or local community after a disaster or catastrophic event. The assistance can be given in the form of individual assistance that is directed to individuals and families or it can be public assistance to address infrastructure repairs. Major disaster declarations are often a result of natural disasters that require long-term funding from the federal government to assist with recovery and rebuilding.[17] FEMA also tracks Fire Management Assistance Declarations. Fire Management Assistance Declarations are declarations used to provide assistance for management, control, and mitigation of fires on public and private land.[18]

A requirement of a presidential declaration is that the governor of the affected state must first request the declaration. The gubernatorial request must provide information regarding state and local resources and certify to the compliance of cost sharing. The governor makes this determination based upon knowledge of state resources and the level of the damage. The president then has the discretion whether to grant the request and may then declare a disaster based upon this request.[19]

As a part of FEMA's assessment of the level of state and local assistance for a disaster, it conducts a Preliminary Damage Assessment (PDA). The PDA process "is a mechanism used to determine the impact and magnitude of damage and the resulting unmet needs of individuals, businesses, the public sector, and the community as a whole."[20] The PDA, which is used to support a governor's request for disaster funding, looks at six factors: (1) estimated costs of the assistance, (2) localized impacts, (3) insurance coverage, (4) hazard mitigation, (5) recent multiple disasters, and (6) programs of other federal assistance. The team conducting the PDA is made up of at least one state and one federal official.[21] However, the requirement of a joint

PDA may be waived in those cases of "unusual severity and magnitude."[22] As FEMA assesses estimated costs, it considers as a threshold of $1 million of public assistance damage and an estimated threshold of $1.30 per capita in estimated disaster costs dependent on the size of the state.[23] These factors also consider the local impact of infrastructure damage at approximately $3.27 per capita, amount of insurance coverage, and whether there were mitigation efforts made that could have lessened the disaster's impact.[24] Additionally, the state may request a reduction of its state share in those cases of extreme economic impact.[25]

Although all gubernatorial requests are reviewed by FEMA, the agency considers whether other federal programs are available to respond to the emergency or disaster. Because of the differences in locations and factors impacting each state, the disaster requests have varied in type and scope. However, since 1953, when the presidential declaration process was put into place, a disaster request has been made and granted to every state and the numbers of presidential declarations have continued to rise.[26] In fact, almost half of all presidential disaster declarations have come from the last three presidents: President Barack Obama, President George W. Bush, and President Bill Clinton.[27] As a result, the amount of money spent on disasters has also increased as the disaster declarations increase.

III. Identification of Resources

A. Robert T. Stafford Disaster Relief and Emergency Assistance Act

The Robert T. Stafford Disaster Relief and Emergency Assistance Act, known as the Stafford Act, "finds and declares that—

(1) Because disasters often cause loss of life, human suffering, loss of income and property loss and damage; and

(2) Because disasters often disrupt the normal function of governments and communities"

—the president can enable federal agencies to provide assistance in response to these disasters through the presidential disaster declaration process.[28] Congress created this act to "alleviate the suffering and damage which result from such disasters."[29]

The Stafford Act specifically establishes programs for preparedness and mitigation assistance, coordination of agencies, and procedures for presidential declarations, and identifies assistance programs. Eligible applicants under the Stafford Act can be states, local governments, individuals, families, and owners of certain nonprofit facilities such as hospitals. Not everyone affected by a disaster is eligible for aid under the Stafford Act. If an individual, family, or business is determined to have sufficient insurance coverage or financial capacity, they may not be eligible for assistance under the Act. The act provides for aid to those people in need of assistance as determined by FEMA officials. The Stafford Act provides for a number of different assistance programs available in response to a disaster or emergency. The major funding programs under the Stafford Act include (1) General Federal Assistance, (2) Essential Assistance and (3) Hazard Mitigation.[30]

General Federal Funding provides support to state and local response and recovery efforts. This assistance may or may not reimburse the federal agency providing the assistance. It also provides for the coordination of relief assistance such as evacuations and recovery. Most important, the funding from General Federal Assistance provides for an accelerated federal response as needed "to save lives, prevent human suffering or mitigate severe damage"—which may not be prevented if the assistance is not provided.[31]

Essential Assistance offers assistance to address immediate threats to life and property. Assistance under this portion of the act includes the distribution of medicine, medical equipment, food, and other consumable supplies and services. The work done under Essential Assistance also includes search and rescue, medical care, clearance of roads, construction of temporary bridges, demolition of unsafe structures, and provision of temporary facilities. The federal share under this section of the act cannot be less than 75 percent of eligible cost of the assistance. The work under this section of the act is often performed by the Department of Defense.[32]

Hazard Mitigation allows the president to determine that the contribution of funding for hazard mitigation measures is cost-effective and will reduce the risk of future damages and loss. This may include land acquisition to erect a new structure for relocation out of a hazardous area to prevent or mitigate additional suffering as a result of the disaster.[33]

The Public Assistance Grant Program provides grants to state, tribal, and local governments so that they are able to quickly and effectively respond to a disaster. (For examples of the use of Public Assistance Programs, see chapters 5, 11, and 17.) This program is also available to certain private nonprofit corporations. The repair, restoration, and replacement of governmental facilities are often covered by these funds in addition to other immediate response activities such as debris and wreckage removal and other emergency matters.[34]

Other funding programs under the act include:

Funding Programs	Authorization[35]
Federal facilities	repair, restoration, and replacement of federal facilities
Repair, Restoration, and Replacement of Damaged Facilities	repair, restoration, or replacement of a public facility or private nonprofit facility
Debris removal	clear debris and wreckage from lands and waters publicly and privately owned

Funding Programs	Authorization
Federal Assistance to Individuals and Households	assistance to individuals and households unable to meet certain needs through other means, including temporary housing, provisions for repairs, replacement housing, or permanent construction of housing
Unemployment assistance	provides unemployment assistance to those not eligible for unemployment benefits
Food coupons and distributions	provides food coupons from the Department of Agriculture to those low-income households unable to purchase nutritious food as long as it is determined necessary
Food Commodities	authorizes emergency mass feeding
Relocation Assistance	authorizes that no person will be denied assistance because they are unable to meet occupancy requirements
Legal Services	coordinates federal agencies with state and local bar associations to provide legal services to low-income individuals who need legal assistance
Crisis Counseling and Training	provides counseling services and financial assistance for those whose mental health problems have been caused or aggravated as a result of a disaster
Community Disaster Loans	offers loans to local governments who have sustained substantial loss of tax and revenues and need the funding in order to continue their governmental functions
Emergency Communications	establishes temporary communication systems in anticipation and during a disaster and makes the systems available to state and local officials
Emergency Public Transportation	establishes temporary transportation to places necessary to resume normal life such as governmental offices, supply centers, stores, post offices, schools, and major employment centers
Fire Management Assistance	provides assistance for the management, mitigation, and control of fires whose destruction of public or private forest land or grassland would be determined a major disaster

In December 2011, Congress passed the Disaster Relief Appropriations Act, which provided an additional $6.4 billion in the Disaster Relief Fund to remain available until expended.[36] The Disaster Relief Fund is funded through FEMA's budget in its annual appropriations for major disasters declared pursuant to the Stafford Act. Until recently, funds have remained in the FEMA budget for disasters and emergencies without fully depleting the budget. However, due to the rising number of natural disasters as determined by the National Oceanic and Atmospheric Administration (NOAA) National Weather Service, the budget has become vulnerable to the rising costs and the increased requests for state assistance through presidential disaster declarations.

B. Community Development Block Grants Disaster Recovery Funds

Community Development Block Grants Disaster Recovery (CDBG-DR) funds may be appropriated by Congress to provide additional funding in the event of a disaster. These CDBG-DR funds are provided in addition to those funds administered by FEMA, the Small Business Administration and the U.S. Army Corps of Engineers. The CDBG-DR funds are administered by HUD as grants to state and local governments to supplement other disaster programs. Congress has appropriated CDBG-DR funds since 1993 as needed for disaster recovery assistance. To date, Congress has appropriated the following CDBG-DR funding:

- **FY 2013**—$16 billion to assist recovery from Superstorm Sandy ($15.18 billion after sequester)[37]
- **FY 2012**—$400 million to assist recovery from multiple disasters occurring in 2011
- **FY 2010**—$100 million to assist recovery in areas affected by severe storms and flooding from March 2010 through May 2010
- **FY 2008**—$6.1 billion to assist recovery from all 2008 disasters, including Hurricanes Ike, Gustav, and Dolly
- **FY 2008**—$300 million to assist recovery from the Midwest floods
- **FY 2008**—$3.0 billion to supplement the LA homeowner assistance program
- **FY 2006**—$16.7 billion to assist the victims of Hurricanes Katrina, Rita, and Wilma
- **FY 2005**—$150 million to assist recovery from multiple disasters
- **FY 2002**—$2.783 billion to assist post–9/11 New York City's recovery efforts
- **FY 2001**—$700 million to assist post–9/11 New York City's recovery efforts
- **FY 1999**—$20 million to assist recovery from multiple disasters
- **FY 1998**—$130 million to assist recovery from multiple disasters
- **FY 1997**—$500 million to assist recovery from upper Midwest floods
- **FY 1996**—$50 million to assist recovery from multiple disasters
- **FY 1995**—$39 million to assist with recovery from the Oklahoma City bombing
- **FY 1994**—$180 million to assist with recovery from Tropical Storm Alberto
- **FY 1994**—$225 million for the Northridge earthquake
- **FY 1994**—$425 million for the recovery from the earthquake in Southern California and Midwest floods
- **FY 1993**—$85 million to assist with recovery from Hurricanes Andrew and Iniki and Typhoon Omar[38]

Because CDBG-DR funds are often a more flexible funding source and not always paid on a reimbursement basis, CDBG-DR funds have even been considered to be the best-suited federal funds for addressing post-disaster needs.[39] Additionally, CDBG funds have the ability for local jurisdictions to target the use of the funds with private investment and stimulate redevelopment. The CDBG-DR funds are provided as a grant to communities to assist with the needs of its low-income residents impacted by a disaster. As long as the funds do not duplicate funding from other disaster sources and benefit at least 51 percent of the low- and moderate-income population, they can be used for housing, infrastructure, economic development, and the prevention of additional damage.[40] Eligible activities range from acquisition and infrastructure costs for housing, technical assistance, building of public facilities, planning and administration costs, job training, and financial support to small business, just to name a few.[41]

The national objective set out for regular CDBG funding must also be met for the CDBG-DR funds. These three objectives are to (1) benefit low- and moderate-income people, (2) aid in the prevention or elimination of slums or blight, and (3) meet other urgent community development needs because the conditions pose a serious and immediate threat to the community.[42] Although populations often shift as a result of people relocated after a disaster, the funding is based upon pre-disaster data to determine a jurisdiction's funding eligibility.

Since fiscal year 1993, HUD has had approximately $40 billion appropriated to assist with the recovery of multiple and specific disaster and recovery efforts, including $16.7 billion that was appropriated to assist the victims of Hurricanes Katrina, Rita, and Wilma. When the funds are made available, eligible governments must develop and submit an action plan before receipt of the grants. The action plan must describe the needs and uses of the CDBG-DR funds. Although federal funding requirements must be met in the disbursement of these funds, the Stafford Act authorizes the secretary of HUD to suspend certain requirements of funding except those related to public notice, nondiscrimination, fair housing, labor standards, environmental standards, and activities that benefit low- and moderate-income people.[43] The suspension of certain requirements eliminates some of the impediments to utilizing the funds and allows jurisdictions to more promptly disburse the funds.

C. HOME Funds

HOME funds are authorized under the HOME Investment Partnerships Act, as amended.[44] These funds provide for a participating jurisdiction to receive an annual allocation based upon a formula grant for the purpose of creating low-income housing. As with CDBG-DR funds, HOME statutory and regulatory requirements may be suspended for disaster activities. HUD may reduce the match requirement for those disaster areas in order to address the damage and may determine that competitive bidding is not required.[45] Grantees will be required to designate the disaster activities in its consolidated plan so that the activities are distinguishable. Any HOME funds used must also meet the "duplication of benefits" test to ensure that the same activities are not being paid for by multiple governmental agencies or private insurance.

D. Section 108 Loan Guarantee Program

The Section 108 Loan Guarantee Program, which is the loan guarantee provision of the CDBG-DR program, may also be utilized for the redevelopment of disaster areas. Those communities entitled to CDBG-DR funds may receive loan guarantees equal to five times their entitled amount, and those not in entitled areas may receive a guarantee against the state's grant program for a period of 20 years. These funds can be utilized for property acquisition, rehabilitation of publicly owned property, infrastructure, housing rehabilitation, public facilities, and economic development. The funds must be administered pursuant to CDBG-DR statutory requirements, and unlike the CDBG-DR and HOME funds, authority has not been provided to waive these requirements.[46]

E. Capital Fund Emergency/Natural Disaster Funds/Disaster Housing Assistance Program

Congress has appropriated funds for housing authorities from capital funds to be used for unforeseen emergencies and natural disasters in the amount of $20 million. Unlike some of the other disaster funds available, those emergencies and disasters that have been identified by presidential declaration are excluded.[47] These funds also are available to a public housing authority to be used for safety and security reasons. The safety and security grants are for a maximum of $250,000. However, HUD has the discretion to determine the amount that will be granted for natural disasters. The funds are available to a public housing authority (PHA) who sets out the reason for the funding, the number of units that will be served by the funding, and the severity of the emergency or disaster through a preliminary request to the HUD local field office. The emergency or disaster must pose a threat to public housing tenants and will be funded for capital expenditures on a one-time basis. Often, the identified needs for disasters exceed the amounts reimbursed by insurance and other sources.[48] PHAs that require immediate funding for temporary repairs to ensure habitability or the structural integrity of units and buildings may request preliminary disaster grant funding from HUD. These preliminary grant applications for funding are usually reviewed and funded by HUD within 30 days. Unlike as required by other PHA funding, the authority is not required to hold public meetings or consult its residents before applying for these funds. However, resident and public consultation is recommended when possible and the PHA must inform the residents of any funding received by the PHA.

The Bush administration set up the Disaster Housing Assistance Program (DHAP) as a solution to provide long-term rental housing assistance to those families affected by Hurricanes Katrina and Rita. Families receiving rental assistance from FEMA were transferred to the DHAP where local public housing authorities administered the program. Through the DHAP, HUD oversaw the administration of rental vouchers for approximately 45,000 families.[49] Although no additional funding has been put into the DHAP, the program set up the model for the transition of long-term rental assistance to be transitioned from FEMA to HUD should future disasters require this type of long-term administration. (For further discussion on the use of vouchers post-disaster, see chapter 14.)

F. Small Business and USDA Loans

Business owners may receive low-interest loans from the Small Business Administration (SBA) and U.S. Department of Agriculture (USDA) after a disaster. These loans may be used to replace real estate, business property, machinery and equipment, and other inventory damaged or destroyed as a result of a disaster. SBA loans can be used for both economic injury to meet financial obligations and physical damage assistance to replace property and inventory. The loans can be in amounts up to $2 million. These loans can also be made available to nonprofit organizations impacted by a disaster.[50] (For further discussion of small business redevelopment post-disaster, see chapters 8 and 9.)

The USDA offers assistance for agriculture related disasters, such as drought and emergencies affecting crop production. The USDA provides assistance to farmers and other businesses affected by these disaster conditions. This assistance can be through emergency loans, moving water to livestock, emergency haying, and other measures that provide assistance and response to these conditions. The USDA, through the Farm Service Agency, also administers programs that address crop loss, livestock loss, and damaged farm loss.[51]

G. U.S. Department of Commerce Disaster Relief Opportunity Funds

The U.S. Department of Commerce, through the Economic Development Administration (EDA), provides long-term disaster recovery grants to communities via a competitive application process. In fiscal year 2012, Congress appropriated $200 million in Disaster Relief Opportunity Funds for the EDA to allocate to local communities across three categories: strategic planning and technical assistance; infrastructure design and development; and capital to leverage additional funds.[52] In its request for applications, the EDA notes that applicants must make a direct connection between the funds and community resiliency, describing resiliency as follows within the context of economic development:

> Disaster resiliency is broadly defined as a community's or region's ability to reduce the probability of system failure and other negative consequences resulting from a disaster or incident. Disaster resiliency also focuses on reducing the time a community needs to recover from a disaster. Within the context of economic development, disaster resiliency should include

> methods and measures to mitigate the potential for future economic injury, promote a faster "up-time" for economic anchors (e.g. key businesses and/or industries), and enable a stronger capacity to troubleshoot vulnerabilities within the regional economy.
>
> There exists a need to deepen the capacity of communities to be disaster resilient and absorb the "shock" of disasters and incidents. Enhancing community resiliency becomes a multi-dimensional effort emphasizing engagement and support from all aspects of the community, including from economic development practitioners. Some examples include efforts to broaden the industrial base with diversification initiatives, enhance business retention and expansion programs to further strengthen existing high-growth businesses, and comprehensive planning efforts that involve extensive engagement from the community to define and implement a collective vision for recovery in response to disasters and incidents.[53]

To be eligible, applicants have to be located in an area that received a major presidential disaster designation during the time specified in the notice of funding availability.[54] Eligible recipients include states or political subdivisions of states; public or private nonprofit organizations or associations; district organizations (e.g., economic development districts, regional planning commissions); institutions of higher education; and Indian tribes or consortium of tribes.[55]

Examples of post-disaster economic recovery projects funded in part through these EDA funds range from direct small business assistance to infrastructure improvements. For example, following the 2007 tornadoes, Greensburg, Kansas, decided to rebuild as a model of green and sustainable development, and the city sought and received EDA funding. (For a case study of Greensburg's redevelopment, see chapter 5.) The $2.35 million grant was used specifically to finance "the construction of basic infrastructure in their central business district to serve a USDA Rural Development-supported business incubator project. This incubator provides much needed space at affordable rent for businesses wishing to re-locate downtown."[56] Other examples of EDA's Disaster Relief Opportunity grants include upgrading railroads following floods, supporting a university to help vulnerable businesses recover from natural and human-made disasters, creating a revolving loan fund to provide low-cost capital to businesses rebuilding in a disaster-damaged area, and many other types of local economic resiliency projects.[57]

H. U.S. Department of Labor National Emergency Grants

Another critical federal funding source designated to support communities' economic recovery post-disaster is the U.S. Department of Labor's National Emergency Grant (NEG) program, which was authorized as part of the Workforce Investment Act of 1998.[58] The grants provide supplemental funding to quickly reemploy or train individuals following unexpected events that lead to significant job loss. (For a discussion on the use of the National Emergency Grants to support workforce redevelopment in Mississippi following Hurricanes Katrina and Rita, see chapter 17.) NEG funds can be sought when a community's needs exceed the funding already available through the Workforce Investment Act.[59]

Eligible applicants are generally state workforce agencies, local workforce investment boards, or Indian and Native American tribes.[60] Following a disaster, the NEG program can be used to "provide temporary employment, humanitarian services, and retraining for workers affected by natural disasters and other catastrophic events."[61] In its most recent assessment of the NEG program (in 2006), the U.S. Government Accountability Office noted that while post-disaster grants were on average awarded significantly faster than other NEG funds, state and local government recipients reported that consistent guidance across local Department of Labor regional offices and information about best practices would aid in the efficient deployment of the funds.[62]

I. Agricultural Disaster Assistance Act

The Agricultural Disaster Assistance Act was passed in early August 2012 to provide funding to farmers who have experienced higher than normal deaths of livestock due to extreme weather. These funds also cover losses to farm-raised fish, honeybees, and tree production due to adverse weather.[63] According to the summaries provided to Congress, this bill was introduced to address the extreme drought being experienced by more than 65 percent of the country. This act, which will cost approximately $383 million, reauthorized previous livestock disaster legislation that had expired in 2011.[64]

Recent Developments in Federal Government Support of Tribal Governments' Disaster Recovery Efforts

Dorcas R. Gilmore and Diane M. Standaert

Tribal governments are sovereign nations and, as such, govern and manage the safety and security of their land, resources, and citizens. Tribal government borders often cross multiple local jurisdictions within any given state and, in some circumstances, cross state boundaries, which can create unique challenges in planning for and responding to disasters. Examples of disasters on tribal lands were highlighted by the Associated Press:

> At Santa Clara Pueblo [in northern New Mexico], two-thirds of the tribe's forests have been charred by wildfires that have started outside the reservation's boundaries over the last 14 years. The most recent one has left the tribe with the threat of flooding for the past two summers.
>
> In Montana, floodwaters from the Little Bighorn River and other waterways devastated parts of the Crow Indian Nation in 2011, swamping homes, businesses and churches.

continued

Recent Developments in Federal Government Support of Tribal Governments' Disaster Recovery Efforts *(continued)*

> A Havasupai village at the bottom of the Grand Canyon—accessible only by foot, mule or helicopter—was flooded in 2010, forcing the evacuation of tourists and causing more than $1.6 million in damages. That marked the first disaster declaration in Arizona for which a sovereign tribal nation was the sole applicant.[65]

Although tribal governments are recognized as sovereign nations, until recently, tribal governments were more akin to local governments than sovereign states within the construct of federal disaster relief and recovery. Prior to the passage of legislation following Superstorm Sandy, federally recognized tribal governments were not permitted to make a direct request for a major disaster or emergency declaration from the president under the Stafford Act. Instead, they were resigned to making a request through the state or states in which the tribal communities were located. The previous law was considered not only in contradiction to tribes' sovereignty, but also failed to account for whether the tribes—not just the states—had adequate resources to respond to and recover from the unique and disproportionate impact that disasters had on their communities.[66]

Tribal governments had been pushing for a change in these rules for more than a decade, seeking the ability to directly access federal relief.[67] By 2012, FEMA, the American Red Cross, and the Obama administration all publicly declared their support for a legislative change to the Stafford Act that would authorize a tribal government to make a request directly to the president for a federal emergency or disaster declaration.[68]

On January 29, 2013, Congress made this important change as part of the federal Sandy Recovery Improvement Act of 2013 to provide more than $50 billion in supplemental aid.[69] The legislation also included a provision amending the Stafford Act granting federally recognized tribal governments a direct route to request federal relief aid.[70] Specifically, it provides tribal governments the option of either applying directly to the president for post-disaster aid or through the governor of the state in which they are located. Applauding the amendment, FEMA Administrator Craig Fugate noted, "This amendment to the Stafford Act follows on the President's commitments to Indian Country, strengthens the government to government relationship between FEMA and federally recognized Tribes, and will enhance the way FEMA supports Tribal communities before, during, and after disasters."[71]

Tribal government leaders heralded the long-sought change.[72] Former governor of the Santa Clara Pueblo Walter Dasheno stated, "We should not be treated as third world countries. . . . We should be there at the table, sitting across from the president, addressing our needs and concerns. I think we've been on the back burner for a number of years."[73] The Santa Clara Pueblo bore the brunt of the destruction caused by the 2011 Las Conchas wildfires in New Mexico, which, as noted, destroyed the majority of the community's woodlands and increased the susceptibility to floods. Robert Holden, deputy director of the National Congress of American Indians, highlighted the importance of the amendment in eliminating delays in emergency response. He stated further, "It was the frustration over the years in terms of the interaction and the process and how tribal lands and citizens have been shortchanged and left stranded by natural and technical disasters. . . . It's just unfair

Recent Developments in Federal Government Support of Tribal Governments' Disaster Recovery Efforts *(continued)*

and inequitable, and we're just trying to right what should be righted."[74] Finally, Navajo Nation President Ben Shelly reaffirmed these sentiments:

> The Navajo Nation has had a distinct government since before the United States gained its independence from a colonial power. The United States is committed by law and treaty to the self-governance of the Navajo Nation, and working with us on a government-to-government basis. The passage of this bill is a welcoming sign of the blossoming recognition nationally of the sovereignty of the Navajo Nation as a co-equal government within the United States.[75]

The need for allowing federally recognized tribal governments to directly access federal aid, rather than depend upon state governors, is exemplified by the following incidents:

1. *Cheyenne River Indian Reservation*

The 2009 and 2010 ice storms in South Dakota had a devastating impact on the Cheyenne River Indian Reservations and other native communities. Then-governor Mike Rounds sought on February 24, 2010 and received on March 10, 2010 a presidential declaration of a major disaster for impacted counties, including portions of the reservations located in those counties.[76] This declaration provided $23 million in "Public Assistance requested by the Governor available to State and eligible local governments and certain private non-profit organizations on a cost-sharing basis for emergency work and the repair or replacement of facilities damaged by the severe winter storm" in 29 enumerated counties "and those portions of the Cheyenne River Indian Reservation, Sisseton-Wahpeton Indian Reservation, and Standing Rock Indian Reservation that lie within these counties. This declaration also made Hazard Mitigation Grant Program assistance requested by the Governor available for hazard mitigation measures in all counties and Tribal Reservations within the State of South Dakota."[77]

When the governor's office issued its press release announcing the presidential declaration of disaster, it failed to state that the reservations were included in this declaration coverage, creating confusion, criticism, and delay.[78] This omission compounded already existing criticisms that the governor acted too slowly in seeking the presidential declaration.[79]

2. *Quinault Nation*

The experience of the Quinault Nation following a severe storm in 2007 in Washington state underscores the importance of the 2013 amendment to the Stafford Act. According to Fawn Sharp, president of the Quinault Nation, "The Quinault Reservation experienced an eight-day power and water outage. Because we didn't have authority to declare a natural disaster, services on our reservation were offered inconsistently. Citizens in Queets, which is in Jefferson County, were treated differently than our citizens in Taholah and Amanda Park, in Grays Harbor County. One was declared a disaster, but not the other."[80] The new law will permit tribes to bypass such obstacles entirely by providing a direct application process.

The streamlined process, which seeks to address the complications described above, is now moving into implementation stage. As of February 2013, rulemaking and guidance for

continued

Recent Developments in Federal Government Support of Tribal Governments' Disaster Recovery Efforts *(continued)*

implementing these changes are under way, as FEMA notes: "Fully implementing this historic provision will require consultation with Tribes and other stakeholders, particularly as FEMA develops the administrative and programmatic requirements and procedures necessary to execute the law. FEMA will provide interim guidance in the coming weeks explaining how and when Tribal governments may seek declarations, while more comprehensive consultations and administrative procedures are undertaken."[81]

While this change is a monumental step in providing a more equitable disaster response system, other challenges to tribal and federal government coordination persist. For example, in January 2013, the same month in which Congress recognized tribal sovereignty for federal disaster aid purposes, a report by the U.S. Government Accountability Office revealed the disparate service received by tribes as part of FEMA's National Flood Insurance Program (NFIP).[82] NFIP, created by Congress in 1968 and managed by FEMA, provides federally backed flood insurance protection for property owners. As noted in *Indian Country Today*, "Flooding, the most common, destructive natural hazard in the U.S., causes catastrophic harm to tribal lands too, some of which flood repeatedly."[83]

Summarizing its findings, the GAO reports:

> First, the Federal Emergency Management Agency (FEMA) has not placed a high priority on mapping rural areas, including many Indian lands, for flood risk, and most tribal lands remain unmapped. Without flood hazard maps, tribal communities may be unaware of their flood risk, even in high-risk areas. Partly for this reason, the risk of flooding is perceived as relatively low on many tribal lands. Further, tribes may lack the resources and administrative capacity needed to administer NFIP requirements, and NFIP premiums are often too high for low-income tribal members. Finally, unique tribal issues can make participation difficult. For example, some Indian tribes do not have reservations over which they can enact and enforce the land use ordinances that are required for NFIP participation. Instead, many have lands that were allotted to individuals rather than to a tribal entity, limiting the tribes' jurisdiction.[84]

The report concludes with recommendations concurred with by both FEMA and Tribal representatives, such as the FEMA Administrator examining ways to make mapping of tribal lands in flood-prone areas a higher priority.

Holden, of the National Congress of American Indians, underscores the importance of continued vigilance in improving tribal government and federal government coordination post-disaster: "There are just numerous instances where not only property but lives have been lost and there has been economic disruption. . . . It's throughout Indian Country. Disasters aren't restricted to certain areas."[85] Improved coordination among governmental jurisdictions is important for any community, and these developments related to Native American tribes' access to resources and direct access are a promising next step, but more remains to be done.

IV. Funding Incentives and Public Support

In addition to the funding programs created by the federal government to respond to disaster relief, the government has sought to create responses that provide opportunity for rebuilding businesses. These responses have come in the form of tax incentives that are intended to provide immediate relief and create opportunities for jobs. These tax incentives also assist with the rebuilding and expansion of the businesses in the impacted areas and thus provide economic opportunities. These incentives include tax relief, deductions, bonds, and even the opportunity for receiving a refund of taxes paid in earlier years. Unfortunately, because the incentives are benefits that a business owner may or may not choose to utilize, there is no way of tracking the number of businesses that have taken advantage of these incentives.

A. GO Zone Credits

The Gulf Opportunity Zone Act of 2005 was signed into law on December 21, 2005, by President George Bush.[86] The Gulf Opportunity Zone, or GO Zone, was specifically designated in the act by those areas impacted by Hurricane Katrina and provided certain tax incentives for people and businesses in the GO Zone.[87] The incentives set forth in the GO Zone Act have been some of the most substantial incentives set out by Congress. This was a result of Hurricane Katrina's devastating destruction in the Gulf Coast region and the amount of money needed for recovery and rebuilding of the area. The areas affected by Hurricanes Wilma and Rita were also addressed in the act and designated as the Wilma GO Zone and Rita GO Zone.[88] The act also set out the incentives specific to those other areas. Overall, the incentives included an extra allocation of low-income housing tax credits to the GO Zone states of Louisiana, Mississippi, and Alabama, an extra allocation of New Market Tax Credits, [89] a basis boost for credits, and certain bonus depreciation extensions.[90]

The act initially provided extra allocations of low-income housing tax credits to those GO Zone states for a period of three years. This extra allocation of $18 per capita was intended to be utilized only in the GO Zone region and required the states to allocate the GO Zone credits before its annual allocation of credits. Any credits that states were unable to award were lost without an extension of carryover.[91] Initially, developments utilizing the credits had to be placed in service by the end of 2008, but later legislation extended this date to the end of 2011 for GO Zone counties and parishes located in Louisiana and Mississippi due to the extensive damage sustained in these states.[92] (For further discussion on the fair housing implications of the GO Zone, see chapter 15.)

B. GO Zone Bonds

The GO Zone Bonds provided for the issuance of tax-exempt, private activity bonds for the acquisition, construction and rehabilitation of residential and commercial real estate, and public utility property located in the GO Zone. These bonds were not subject to the state's private activity bond cap, which allowed the states to issue bonds as needed for the rebuilding of communities and businesses. The GO Zone Bonds, which were tailored after the Liberty Bonds, were intended to encourage business development by providing low-interest capital to businesses and stimulate investment in the affected areas. Unlike the Liberty Bonds, which were targeted for specific areas and authorized between state and local entities, the criteria for issuance of the GO Zone Bonds was more broad.[93] (For further discussion on the Liberty Bonds and tax incentives, see chapter 7.)

C. Bonus Depreciation

The act also provided for a bonus depreciation deduction, which is a tax incentive that allows an additional depreciation for qualified property.[94] This depreciation bonus accelerated the normal depreciation by allowing a bonus depreciation of 50 percent of the cost in the first year the property is placed in service. This type of tax incentive is beneficial to small businesses because it allows them to write off most or all of the property or equipment needed to reestablish the business after the disaster or emergency. By taking advantage of these tax incentives, small businesses can enjoy this write-off more quickly rather than having to wait over a several-year period. A property was only allowed to take advantage of either the tax-exempt bonds or the bonus depreciation, but not both.

D. Other Incentives

The GO Zone Act also provided for incentives directed toward business owners, commercial activity, and reinvestment. The act authorized an additional $1 billion of New Market Tax Credits for the years 2005–07. The New Market Tax Credits were intended for substantial commercial investments to community development entities serving in the areas affected by the hurricanes. The employee-retention credit provided that an employer could receive a credit of 40 percent of an eligible employee's wages. The amount of qualified wages could not exceed $6,000 per employee. Employers were eligible for this credit if they owned a business prior to the hurricanes and the business was rendered inoperable as a result of the hurricanes. Employers were also eligible for a work tax credit if they hired an eligible employee who was displaced during the storm. Business owners were also provided a tax credit for debris cleanup and demolition by allowing employers to expense up to 50 percent of the costs.[95]

E. Public Support—Charitable Contributions and Volunteerism

The American Red Cross, which was founded in 1881, is a nonprofit humanitarian organization whose purpose is "to carry out a system of national and international relief in time of peace, and to apply that system in mitigating the suffering caused by pestilence, famine, fire, floods, and other great national calamities, and to devise and carry out measures for preventing those calamities."[96] It was chartered by Congress under Title 36 to recognize an official relationship, but it is not a governmental entity.[97] Attending to people affected by disasters and emergencies is a critical area addressed by the Red Cross, as well as responding to the needs of military families. Because it is an entity that people are familiar with, people give in great amounts to the Red Cross to respond to disasters and emergencies both in the United States and abroad.

After the 9/11 attacks, there was an outpouring of public support to numerous existing and newly created charitable organizations to respond to the emergency. The funds were raised by approximately 111 organizations with 40 of those organizations raising and distributing more than $2.2 billion.[98] These funds were raised to address certain needs and fill gaps of needs that were unmet through governmental and other funding sources. Superstorm Sandy has experienced a similar outpouring of public support that is helping to fill the needs that have gone unmet from governmental support. The Red Cross reported that it has deployed more than 9,000 volunteers to the affected areas and spent more than $110 million for emergency relief.[99]

People affected by disasters and emergencies in the United States and around the world have received incredible public support. This support comes in the form of charitable donations, volunteerism, and other methods of responding to disasters and emergencies. In the United States, we have seen generous examples of widespread public response to disasters and emergencies following 9/11, Hurricane Katrina, the Joplin tornadoes, and Superstorm Sandy. People unwilling to wait for governmental response and feeling the need to provide more personal assistance have flocked to these areas to provide personal assistance with response, recovery, and rebuilding efforts. (See generally chapter 6.)

V. The Good and the Bad: What Makes a Successful Program

As the number of declared disasters escalates, the amount of money appropriated by the federal government will continue to also increase unless different criteria for assistance is set. Although many of the disaster programs are already set out by federal and state legislation, an increasing number of programs and legislative appropriations are created in response to particular disasters. This increase of appropriated funds and agency resources requires more efficiency in responding, processing, and distributing the funding and resources necessary to effectively respond to the disasters. It requires us to take a closer look at what makes a successful program.

A. Implementing Lessons Learned

Many of the programs have been criticized because of slow response and delays of funding. After each disaster Congress and the responding agencies have continued to assess the effectiveness of the response and promptness of distributing the funding. This is done through Congressional hearings, agency reviews, and public assessments. Over the years, these assessments have identified the need for less complex regulatory requirements and more coordinated approaches to the disasters and emergencies. Federal and state agencies must continue to learn from these lessons and revamp programs in an effort to become more coordinated, streamlined, and responsive. The lessons learned are of no use if the lessons are not implemented and programs revamped in preparation for the next disaster or emergency. However, as the numbers of declared disasters increases, it is imperative for the government to assess best practices in order to more effectively identify and distribute disaster funding.

B. Effective Distribution of Funding

Federal and state governments must consider distributing funding in a way that allows families, individuals, and businesses to more effectively address immediate needs. This may require less restrictive criteria for distribution of funding, as well as providing the funding on an audit basis rather than a reimbursement basis. Persons impacted by disasters and emergencies are often displaced and don't have the resources to replace and repair and then request the funds, especially low-income individuals and small-business owners who have even more limited resources.[100] Post-disaster funding must be distributed in a manner that is more sensible of the circumstances of the recipient.

C. Use Funding to Address Long-Range Goals

Funding must be used to rebuild communities with long-range goals. If the funding only allows families and individuals to rebuild to pre-disaster requirements rather than building better, the funding has not been utilized to its full capacity or to address more long-range goals.[101]

D. Leverage Government Funds by Stimulating Private Investment

Funding must be utilized in a manner that stimulates additional private investment in communities. This can be done through leveraging funding in a way that serves as a catalyst for private companies, foundations, and others to also invest along with governmental funding. Examples of this type of private investment were seen in New York after 9/11 and New Orleans after Hurricane Katrina and should continue to be encouraged in other communities.

E. Eliminate Regulatory Barriers

Individuals, families, and businesses that are impacted and displaced continue to seek and even expect more efficiency when working with governmental agencies. They seek the ability to access funding more expediently and without many of the traditional governmental requirements such as a requiring a permanent address or public notice prior to applying for funding. Legislation must be created that addresses these issues and eliminates barriers created to prevent those affected individuals, families, and businesses from receiving prompt assistance.

F. One-Stop Resource Centers

Other permanent changes are needed to address effective distribution of post-disaster funds. The creation of one-stop resource centers provides more efficiency and prevents recipients from having to go to different agencies to have all of their disaster needs met or even having to try to identify which agencies can assist them in meeting their needs.

G. Provide Pre-Disaster Information

In addition to efficient and coordinated distribution of funding, federal and state agencies will also have to find ways to more effectively respond to the needs of those who have been affected by creating pre-disaster steps and information that will assist with post-disaster response and distribution of funds.[102]

H. Eliminate the Political Response

More and more, the response to disasters and the subsequent funding has become a part of political maneuvering that has slowed responses and funding distribution in impacted communities. Congress must find a way to objectively respond to disasters without politicizing the process to the point of delay. This may require that Congress create a formula based upon the initial declaration process to determine how much funding will be allocated for any presidentially declared disaster.

VI. Conclusion

Newspapers across the country continue to be filled with human-interest stories relaying both the positive and negative reactions to federal and state responses following disasters and emergencies. It is through these stories that we learn of the real lives that are touched through the applied use of disaster funds. And it will be through these lenses that we are able to more effectively determine the success of post-disaster funding programs.

Appendix
Chart of Eligible Activities and Funding Source

	1	2	3	4	5	6	7	8	9	10	11	12
Acquisition					X	X	X	X				X
Rehabilitation		X	X	X	X	X	X	X	X			
Road Repair		X			X		X			X		
Housing					X	X		X				
Demolition		X	X		X	X			X			
Debris Removal			X	X	X							
Public Facilities		X	X	X	X	X	X			X		
Individual Assistance				X	X							
Business Assistance				X			X		X	X	X	X
Evacuation	X							X				
Recovery	X	X						X	X			X
Food/Medicine		X		X					X			X
Employment/ Training				X	X						X	
Infrastructure					X		X	X		X		
Relocation				X								

1. General Federal Funding
2. Essential Assistance
3. Hazard Mitigation
4. Public Assistance
5. CDBG
6. HOME
7. 108
8. Capital Funding-PHA Only
9. Small Business USDA
10. Commerce Disaster Relief Opportunity Funds
11. National Emergency Grants
12. Agricultural Disaster Assistance

Notes

1. As used in this chapter, "disaster" and "emergency" have the meanings set forth in 42 U.S.C. § 5122(1) (2012) and 42 U.S.C. § 5122(2) (2012).
2. Matthew Bandyk, *Why Natural Disasters Are More Expensive—But Less Deadly*, US News and World Rep., Mar. 24, 2010.
3. *About*, FEMA, http://www.fema.gov/about/history.shtm (last updated Oct. 15, 2012).
4. 15 U.S.C. § 14.
5. 42 U.S.C. § 5143(b)(3).
6. 42 U.S.C. § 5190.

7. *About*, *supra* note 3.
8. 44 Fed. Reg. 19,367, 3 C.F.R., 1979 Comp., p. 376.
9. According to the FEMA disaster database, a major disaster was declared in 11 states (New York, New Jersey, Connecticut, Rhode Island, Delaware, Maryland, Virginia, West Virginia, New Hampshire, Massachusetts, Ohio) and the District of Columbia for Superstorm Sandy.
10. Title VI of Pub. L. No. 109-295 (H.R. 5441) (2006).
11. Although every state has an office of emergency management or homeland security, these offices primarily handle disaster and emergency preparedness, disaster information, and coordination with federal resources.
12. *State Homeland Security and Emergency Services*, U.S. DEP'T OF HOMELAND SEC., http://www.dhs.gov/files/resources/editorial_0306.shtm (last visited Mar. 27, 2013).
13. VERONICA ROSE, OLR RESEARCH REPORT, 2007-R-0643, STATE DISASTER FUNDING (2007).
14. FLA. STAT. § 215.555 (1993).
15. *How States Budget and Plan for Emergencies: Hearing Before the Task Force on Budget Process*, 105th Cong. (1998).
16. FRANCIS X. MCCARTHY, CONG. RESEARCH SERV., RL34146, FEMA'S DISASTER DECLARATION PROCESS: A PRIMER.
17. *Disaster Declaration Fact Sheet*, FEMA (May 2011), http://www.fema.gov/pdf/media/factsheets/dad_disaster_declaration.pdf.
18. *Program Details*, FEMA, http://www.fema.gov/fire-management-assistance-grants-program-details (last updated June 15, 2012).
19. 42 U.S.C. § 5170.
20. 44 C.F.R. § 206.33.
21. Department of Homeland Security, Office of Inspector General, *Opportunities to Improve FEMA's Public Assistance Preliminary Damage Assessment Process* (May 2012), http://www.oig.dhs.gov/assets/Mgmt/2012/OIG_12-79_May12.pdf.
22. 44 C.F.R. § 206.33(d).
23. FRANCIS MCCARTHY, CONG. RESEARCH SERV., RL34146, FEMA'S DISASTER DECLARATION PROCESS: A PRIMER 12, *available at* http://assets.opencrs.com/rpts/RL34146_20100318.pdf.
24. *Id.*
25. 42 U.S.C. § 5193.
26. FRANCIS X. MCCARTHY, CONG. RESEARCH SERV., RL34146, FEMA'S DISASTER DECLARATION PROCESS: A PRIMER.
27. *Disaster Declarations by Year*, FEMA, http://www.fema.gov/disasters/grid/year (last visited Mar. 27, 2013).
28. 42 U.S.C. § 5121.
29. *Id.*
30. Pub. L. No. 93-288, as amended, 42 U.S.C. §§ 5121–5207.
31. 42 U.S.C. § 5170a.
32. 42 U.S.C. § 5170b.
33. 42 U.S.C. § 5170c.
34. *Public Assistance: Local, State, Tribal and Non-Profit*, FEMA, http://www.fema.gov/public-assistance-local-state-tribal-and-non-profit (last updated Jan. 7, 2013).
35. 42 U.S.C. §§ 5170–87.
36. Disaster Relief Appropriations Act of 2012, Pub. L. No. 112-77.
37. At the time of publication, legislation providing additional funding in an amount projected to total $60 billion had been introduced but had not yet been passed by Congress.
38. *CDBG Disaster Recovery Assistance*, U.S. DEP'T OF HOUS. & URBAN DEV., http://portal.hud.gov/hudportal/HUD?src=/program_offices/comm_planning/communitydevelopment/programs/drsi (last visited Mar. 27, 2013).
39. ROBERT OLSHANSKY & LAURIE JOHNSON, IMPROVING POST-DISASTER RECOVERY: INITIAL THOUGHTS FOR A NEW ADMINISTRATION, (Nov. 17, 2008), http://www.disasterrecoveryresources.net/OlshanskyJohnson_RecoveryPolicyPaper_111708.pdf.
40. 24 C.F.R. pt. 570.
41. HUD CPD, ECONOMIC DEVELOPMENT TOOLKIT 18–23 (April 2010), *available at* http://www.hud.gov/offices/cpd/economicdevelopment/toolkit/edt_manual.pdf.
42. 24 C.F.R. § 570.208
43. 42 U.S.C. § 5321.

44. 42 U.S.C. § 12750.
45. *Id.*
46. 24 C.F.R. pt. 570.
47. FY 2011 Act, Pub. L. No. 111-117.
48. Comprehensive Grant Handbook (7485.3G).
49. *Disaster Housing Assistance Program*, U.S. Dep't of Hous. & Dev., http://www.hud.gov/news/dhap.cfm.
50. 13 C.F.R. pt. 123.
51. 7 C.F.R. § 1945.
52. U.S. Economic Development Administration, *Disaster Recovery Overview*, http://www.eda.gov/disasterrecovery.htm.
53. U.S. Economic Development Administration, *Announcement of Federal Funding Opportunity: FY 2012 Disaster Relief Opportunity*, http://www.eda.gov/pdf/FY2012_Disaster_Relief_Opportunity_FFO_FINAL.pdf.
54. *Id.*
55. U.S. Economic Development Administration, *Disaster Recovery Overview*, http://www.eda.gov/disasterrecovery.htm.
56. U.S. Economic Development Administration, *EDA Disaster Recovery Webinar, in Partnership with the National Association of Regional Councils*, at slide 9 (Aug. 2, 2012), http://narc.org/wp-content/uploads/EDA-Disaster-FFO-NARC-briefing_FINAL.pdf.
57. *Id.* at slide 10.
58. 29 U.S.C. § 2918, *et seq.*
59. 29 U.S.C. § 2918(a)(3).
60. Eligible applicants are defined in 29 U.S.C § 2918(c)(1)(a) and 29 U.S.C § 2911(c).
61. *U.S. Gov't Accountability Office, National Emergency Grants: Labor Has Improved Its Grant Award Timeliness and Data Collection, but Further Steps Can Improve Process*, at 12 (Sept. 2006), http://www.gao.gov/assets/260/251274.pdf.
62. *Id.*
63. Agricultural Disaster Assistance Act of 2012, H.R. 6233, 112th Cong. (2012).
64. *Id.*
65. Susan Montoya Bryan, *New Law Allows American Indian Tribes to Seek Direct Federal Aid After Natural Disasters*, Star Tribune, Jan. 31, 2013, *available at* http://www.startribune.com/nation/189269351.html?refer=y.
66. Rob Capriccioso, *President Obama Signs Law Putting Tribes on Equal Footing as States for Federal Emergency Aid*, Indian Country Today, Jan. 31, 2013, http://indiancountrytodaymedianetwork.com/2013/01/31/president-obama-signs-law-putting-tribes-equal-footing-states-federal-emergency-aid.
67. Bryan, *supra* note 65.
68. *Id.*; *see also* Rob Capriccioso, *FEMA Supporting Specific Legislation on Making Tribes Equal to States*, Indian Country Today, June 15, 2012, http://indiancountrytodaymedianetwork.com/article/fema-supporting-specific-legislation-on-making-tribes-equal-to-states-118481.
69. H.R. 219 113th Cong. (P.L. 113-2) (2013). The language included in the Sandy relief package bill came from legislation that had been pending at least since 2011, H.R. 2903, sponsored by Rep. Nick Rahall, D-West Virginia, and S. 2283, sponsored by Sen. Jon Tester, D-Montana.
70. H.R. 219, 113th Cong., § 1110 (amending the Robert T. Stafford Disaster Relief and Emergency Assistance Act (42 U.S.C. §§ 5121–5207)).
71. Press Release, FEMA, Statement by FEMA Administrator Craig Fugate on Sandy Recovery Improvement Act of 2013 (Jan. 30, 2013), http://www.fema.gov/news-release/2013/01/30/statement-fema-administrator-craig-fugate-sandy-recovery-improvement-act.
72. *See generally Tribes Applaud Sandy Recovery Improvement Act*, Indian Country Today, Feb. 4, 2013, http://indiancountrytodaymedianetwork.com/2013/02/04/tribes-applaud-sandy-recovery-improvement-act-147453.
73. Bryan, *supra* note 65.
74. Bryan, *supra* note 65.
75. *Tribes Applaud Sandy Recovery Improvement Act, supra* note 72.
76. FEMA, South Dakota Severe Winter Storm—FEMA-1887-DR, Declared March 10, 2010, http://www.fema.gov/pdf/news/pda/1887.pdf.
77. *Id.*

78. *Governor Rounds Office Announces Presidential Disaster Declaration Approved for South Dakota Reservations*, NORTH DAKOTA NATIVE NEWS (Mar. 10, 2010), http://ndnnews.com/2010/03/governor-rounds-office-annouces-presidential-disaster-declaration-approved-for-south-dakota-reservations/.

79. *Id.*

80. *Tribes Applaud Sandy Recovery Improvement Act, supra* note 72.

81. Press Release, *supra* note 71.

82. U.S. GOV'T ACCOUNTABILITY OFFICE, FLOOD INSURANCE: PARTICIPATION OF INDIAN TRIBES IN FEDERAL AND PRIVATE PROGRAMS (2013), *available at* http://www.gao.gov/assets/660/651160.pdf.

83. Terri Hansen, *Limited FEMA Mapping on Indian Reservations Increases Flood Risk, Lessens Federal Flood Insurance*, INDIAN COUNTRY TODAY, Jan. 22, 2013, http://indiancountrytodaymedianetwork.com/2013/01/22/limited-fema-mapping-indian-reservations-increases-flood-risk-lessens-federal-flood.

84. U.S. GOV'T ACCOUNTABILITY OFFICE, *supra* note 45.

85. Bryan, *supra* note 65.

86. Gulf Opportunity Zone Act of 2005, H.R. 4440, 109th Cong. (Dec. 22, 2005).

87. Hurricane Katrina, which hit landfall on August 29, 2005, was a Category 3 hurricane that primarily affected the Gulf states of Louisiana, Mississippi, and Alabama.

88. Hurricane Wilma was a hurricane that primarily affected southern Florida, and Hurricane Rita primarily affected southeast Texas. Like Hurricane Katrina, both hurricanes hit landfall during the 2005 hurricane season.

89. Gulf Opportunity Zone Act of 2005, Pub. L. No. 109-135, § 1400N, 119 Stat. 2577 (2005).

90. *Id.* at § 105.

91. The IRS allows a carryover allocation for any project not placed in service during the year of the credit reservation. The GO Zone did not provide for an extension of carryover beyond the date that was set forth in the legislation.

92. Tax Relief, Unemployment Insurance Reauthorization and Job Creation Act of 2010 (H.R. 4853), 111th Cong. (Dec. 17, 2010).

93. U.S. GOV'T ACCOUNTABILITY OFFICE, GAP-08-913, GULF OPPORTUNITY ZONE TAX INCENTIVES (2008).

94. Gulf Opportunity Zone Act of 2005 (H.R. 4440), 109th Cong. (Dec. 22, 2005).

95. *Id.*

96. 36 U.S.C. § 300102(4) (2006).

97. *Id.*

98. FOUND. CTR., 9/11 RELIEF AND REGRANTING FUNDS: A SUMMARY REPORT ON FUNDS RAISED AND ASSISTANCE PROVIDED (2004).

99. AM. RED CROSS, *SUPERSTORM SANDY: ONE MONTH UPDATE* (Dec. 3, 2012).

100. ROBERT OLSHANSKY & LAURIE JOHNSON, IMPROVING POST-DISASTER RECOVERY: INITIAL THOUGHTS FOR A NEW ADMINISTRATION, (Nov. 17, 2008), *available at* http://www.disasterrecoveryresources.net/OlshanskyJohnson_RecoveryPolicyPaper_111708.pdf.

101. AMY LIU, FEDERAL POST-DISASTER RECOVERY: A REVIEW OF FEDERAL PROGRAMS (May 2010).

102. *Id.*

CHAPTER 2

The Role of the U.S. Department of Housing and Urban Development in Post-Disaster Community Recovery

Helen R. Kanovsky and Carey Catherine Whitehead*

I. Introduction

Using the programs and resources of the U.S. Department of Housing and Urban Development (HUD) to address economic, housing, and community development issues following a disaster is critical to fulfilling HUD's mission to create strong, sustainable, and inclusive communities and quality affordable homes for all. HUD was created, in part, to further coordination of "Federal activities which have a major effect upon urban community, suburban, or metropolitan development . . . to encourage the solution of problems of housing [and] urban development" at the national level.[1] The department's support for rebuilding from disasters fits soundly within this purpose.

HUD has used many avenues to assist communities following a disaster. This chapter discusses those mechanisms, from the department's historical response to disasters to current federally coordinated procedures when disaster strikes. Our goal is to demonstrate the flexibility within HUD's programs to assist communities and support recovery

*The authors would like to thank Althea Forrester, Associate General Counsel for Assisted Housing and Community Development, and Richard J. Washington III, attorney advisor in OGC's Assisted Housing Division, for their significant contributions to this chapter.

after a disaster.[2] We hope examples and discussion in this chapter will help readers understand HUD's role in a coordinated response to devastating events that affect our nation.

A. HUD's Historical Involvement in Federal Disaster Response

The Federal government's current role in responding to major disasters is rooted in the structure Congress established through the Federal Disaster Act of 1950[3] (the 1950 Act). This law authorized the president to declare a major disaster at the request of a governor and provide federal disaster assistance to "supplement the efforts and available resources of the State and local governments."[4] The 1950 Act identifies the major underpinning of federal disaster assistance—the federal role is limited and not a substitute for relief afforded by state, local, or private resources. This posture has remained intact through significant changes to the scope of federal disaster response.

HUD has contributed to the federal government's supplementary role in disaster recovery and flood protection since Congress established the department in 1965.[5] In 1968, HUD began to administer the new National Flood Insurance Program,[6] which was delegated within HUD to the Federal Insurance Administration. HUD's significant involvement in its early years following devastating disasters such as Hurricanes Camille (1969) and Agnes (1972) led to a major role in recovery assistance and coordination.

In 1973, through a series of executive orders,[7] President Richard Nixon consolidated administration of certain disaster relief functions within the department and delegated to HUD's secretary the authority vested in the president by the Disaster Relief Act of 1970 (the 1970 Act)[8] and other related authorities. Under the 1970 Act, the president had broad authority to designate a major disaster area, to direct federal agencies to provide emergency services or supplies, and to direct or authorize various types of disaster preparation and relief assistance to states, localities, and individuals. The 1970 Act also directed the president to appoint a federal coordinating officer who would make an initial appraisal of needed relief and coordinate work of federal agencies and relief organizations such as the American Red Cross and the Mennonite Disaster Service. Also in 1973, Congress authorized HUD to establish a special disaster assistance fund and use HUD's resources to finance disaster recovery.[9] Additionally, the secretary of HUD created the Federal Disaster Assistance Administration (FDAA) to lead the department's new role.[10]

Although President Nixon's plan consolidated many disaster response functions within HUD and the FDAA, some emergency, mitigation and response activities still resided within other departments. On April 1, 1979, President Jimmy Carter implemented a plan to merge disaster recovery agencies from within the Departments of Defense and Commerce, HUD, and the General Services Administration to create the Federal Emergency Management Agency (FEMA).[11] This coordinating role has remained with FEMA through its consolidation into the U.S. Department of Homeland Security (DHS)[12] and subsequent reorganization.[13]

As part of its role, FEMA administers the Robert T. Stafford Disaster Relief and Emergency Assistance Act (Stafford Act). The Stafford Act replaced or amended other federal disaster legislation and sets forth the current federal response and recovery role. Response under the Stafford Act is triggered by a presidential declaration of a major disaster or emergency based on a finding that the disaster or situation is of "such severity and magnitude that effective response is beyond the capabilities of the State and the affected local governments and that Federal assistance is necessary."[14]

B. Evolution of HUD's Disaster Recovery Role

Although HUD no longer retains the responsibility for coordinating federal disaster response, the department has continued to play a significant part in disaster recovery. While HUD's primary disaster recovery roles have developed in its program offices, HUD has established an operational structure designed to layer with current programs to further a coordinated HUD response to disasters. In 2010, HUD established an Office of Disaster Management and National Security (ODMNS) that advises departmental leadership on disaster management and national security. While ODMNS serves as one focal point to improve coordination, HUD works through its program offices to maximize use of existing programs, tools, staff, and financial resources to address community disaster recovery needs.[15]

Using the framework of existing programs to respond to disasters provides advantages. First, affected existing grantees are familiar with basic program requirements and have the advantage of additional flexibility. Second, communities can respond to recovery needs while advancing the objectives of HUD programs.

In large part, the use of HUD programs for disasters has evolved through the department's response to, and consideration of, requests by program participants. The post–Hurricane Agnes recovery marked an early example of program-centric policy development in response to requests for guidance. In 1972, Hurricane Agnes caused $3.1 billion in damage, approximately $2.1 billion of which was in Pennsylvania. There, the storm reportedly caused 48 deaths, destroyed 68,000 homes, and left 220,000 homeless.[16]

HUD responded to Hurricane Agnes principally through its urban renewal program, a predecessor to the Community Development Block Grant (CDBG) program, to assist recovery from storm-related flooding and damage.[17] Along the Susquehanna River, communities that experienced devastating floods sought HUD approval to pay pre-flood values for acquisition of affected properties (this flood "buyout" practice is still a common use of CDBG disaster recovery (CDBG-DR) grant funds). HUD considered the question, finding that compensation for property should be determined under principles of state law. Pennsylvania law permitted use of pre-flood values in connection with flood control projects. When the Government Accountability Office (GAO) questioned whether some projects qualified under state law, HUD contended that the nature and intent of the projects called for a liberal and humanitarian interpretation and application of the law. Ultimately, the GAO ended the inquiry after a change in state law more clearly permitted the use of pre-flood values. But HUD's policy to permit use of pre-flood values when permissible under state law remains in place for CDBG-funded flood buyout programs, so long as grantees use one method of valuation for all acquisitions. Over time, program-based responses have resulted in a set of recovery tools that offer flexibility, and that states, local governments, and other grantees can mold to fill gaps not addressed by other resources.

II. Discussion and Case Studies

The department's programs and authorities that support disaster recovery and response have undergone minimal changes in recent decades. Even so, HUD's ability to contribute to sound recovery has developed through efforts to use existing authorities to address needs, and from questions presented by program participants as they integrate HUD funds into successful program designs.

A. HUD's Toolbox for Recovery

HUD's avenues for providing assistance following a disaster can be generally categorized into three sources of authorities: (1) permanent statutory authorities, (2) waiver authorities, and (3) supplemental appropriations. Permanent avenues to provide special considerations or assistance in the event of a disaster are limited. For example, section 310 of the Stafford Act[18] directs HUD to prioritize processing applications from major disaster areas under certain programs. Within the CDBG program, the secretary may use funds available as a result of adjustments or noncompliance findings under title I, sections 104(e) and 111 of the of the Housing and Community Development Act of 1974 (HCD Act)[19] to meet disaster-related community development needs. Recently, HUD provided assistance from this CDBG sanctions fund following the spring 2011 tornadoes, granting $350,000 each to Birmingham and Tuscaloosa, Alabama, and Joplin, Missouri. HUD makes use of available permanent authorities when feasible, but as these examples suggest, their availability is restricted.

Most HUD programs are not designed primarily as disaster recovery tools. To adapt existing programs for this purpose, HUD has relied heavily on its waiver authorities. Pursuant to section 106 of the Department of Housing and Urban Development Reform Act of 1989 (HUD Reform Act),[20] HUD may waive regulatory provisions not required by statute for good cause. Congress also provided disaster-specific waiver and suspension authority for certain programs. For example, title I, section 122 of the HCD Act[21] permits suspension of CDBG requirements in major disaster areas, except for those related to public notice of funding availability, nondiscrimination, fair housing, labor standards, environmental standards, and requirements that activities benefit persons of low and moderate income.[22]

Finally, Congress has provided supplemental appropriations that increase HUD's role in providing recovery resources. Historically, supplemental appropriations have built on existing programs by providing authority to tailor program requirements to address recovery needs. For example, beginning with CDBG-DR assistance for Hurricane Andrew and other major disasters provided by the Emergency Supplemental Appropriations Act of 1993, Congress has approved no less than 24 appropriations supplementing funding for the CDBG program.[23] Supplemental disaster recovery appropriations for CDBG and other HUD programs have served as avenues to respond to immediate housing and other disaster recovery needs, to rebuild affected areas, and to provide crucial seed money to stimulate the recovery process.

B. Using the Toolbox to Meet Housing Needs

HUD's efforts to address various post-disaster housing needs provide examples of how HUD employs the tools Congress has authorized and how past experience has influenced HUD's current disaster responses. In the days and weeks following a disaster when community-specific needs may be unknown, HUD can draw from its understanding of basic housing needs common across many disasters. For example, HUD has used its authority under section 290 of the Cranston-Gonzalez National Affordable Housing Act, as amended,[24] and its HUD Reform Act authority to suspend, waive, or provide alternative requirements for immediate use with HOME Investment Partnerships Program funds. HUD focuses on requirements that might hinder disaster response, such as limits on the use of HOME Funds for administrative costs, requirements for source documentation for HOME income determinations, and match contributions. HUD generally requires participating jurisdictions to request a waiver or suspension of HOME requirements through the local Community Planning and Development director after consulting with the local HUD office.

While HUD's initial responses are designed to address the most common needs, HUD's overall response to post-disaster housing needs is largely dependent on the types of housing affected and the extent to which buildings are insured. HUD has collaborated with federal agencies, states, local governments, public housing authorities, and others to assess damage and short-term and long-term recovery needs. The department's consideration of the best response within existing authorities has resulted in significant developments in disaster housing policies and programs.

1. *Multifamily Needs: The Development of HUD's Response*

HUD's policies and procedures that apply to all HUD-insured and assisted multifamily properties in disaster areas and in other situations in which the local Hub[25] director determines that an emergency exists are now captured in chapter 38 of HUD handbook 4350.1.[26] This guidance applies to HUD staff, owners of HUD-insured and assisted multifamily properties, and communities. It covers multiple aspects of servicing damaged multifamily properties.

Much of chapter 38 is informed by the response to Hurricane Charley, which devastated the Gulf Coast of Florida in 2004. In communities hardest hit by Charley, damage was severe and resulted in widespread power outages, debilitation of emergency services, loss of life, and economic losses.[27]

Within five days after Charley struck Florida, HUD's Jacksonville Hub and Florida field offices completed preliminary damage assessments of all properties in HUD's Florida inventory and sent staff to conduct property inspections in the most affected areas. Other staff continued damage assessments by phone and in person in other areas of the state. These initial assessments indicated more than 200 projects were seriously affected and more than 700 residents were relocated. The Jacksonville Hub and field offices began working with HUD headquarters to explore every means to help with the disaster response.

The nature and volume of damage sustained during Hurricane Charley spurred HUD to answer questions not previously considered and to develop new comprehensive guidance for multifamily assets. HUD's Office of General Counsel was asked within days of the storm to address critical questions. These included whether HUD could direct owners of HUD-insured and HUD-assisted properties not to evict, for a period of time, disaster-affected individuals who had returned to their units, and whether HUD could direct mortgagees not to file a claim or foreclose on delinquent loans for some period. HUD quickly proposed potential regulatory relief, such as approval of liberal use of residual receipts to address damage.

The scope of HUD's initial impact assessment was far-reaching and indicated that the damage would affect all HUD housing programs (including Section 202 Supportive Housing for the Elderly, Section 8, capital grants, insured housing, HUD-held and HUD-owned properties). HUD inventoried the number of vacant units in assisted and insured properties in Florida and Georgia, provided a list of the vacant units to FEMA, and explored the department's ability to waive temporary income and occupancy restrictions. In an effort to use vacant risk-sharing units financed by low-income housing tax credits (LIHTC) as a resource for displaced residents, the Department immediately began conversations with the Florida Housing Finance Corporation (FHFC), which had oversight responsibility for this portfolio. FHFC successfully sought a temporary suspension of LIHTC income restrictions from the IRS, subject to FHFC approval, when vacant units were rented to individuals displaced by Hurricanes Charley and Frances.[28]

After its initial assessment, HUD began to develop additional guidance to ease short-term recovery from Hurricane Charley. Within roughly 90 days, HUD issued a notice, *Disaster Recovery Guidance by Multifamily Housing After a Presidentially-Declared Disaster*.[29] The notice addressed reliance on FEMA eligibility determinations for temporary rental housing; included a policy to permit, with owner approval, multiple occupants in a residence to accommodate displaced residents; described the department's practice to postpone all Real Estate Assessment Center (REAC) physical assessments for a minimum of 30 days following the disaster; and encouraged owners to take action to support recovery, such as allowing community space to be used for shelter and holding vacant units off the market in anticipation of providing temporary housing.

On September 9, 2005, immediately following Hurricane Katrina, the department updated post–Hurricane Charley guidance through a memorandum, *Multifamily Disaster Clarification of Notice H 04-22 and Additional Guidance*. A superseding memorandum dated October 28, 2005, provided more thorough guidance.[30] It recognized that given the extent of immediate housing needs, it was impractical to rely on FEMA certification of eligibility. Instead, HUD directed owners to require only documentary identification that the applicant lived in the disaster-declared county at the time of the disaster. The department clarified which programs had a statutory requirement to give priority to disaster-displaced residents (Sections 221(d)(3), 221(d)(4), and 236 properties), and when disaster-displaced residents *may* be given priority in other HUD-assisted or HUD-insured properties. The memorandum distinguished policies applicable to temporary housing for disaster-displaced residents from those applicable to permanent housing, and added guidance related to the right of disaster-displaced residents to return to their units. It also addressed development issues related to Federal Housing Administration (FHA) mortgage insurance for all project mortgages with insured advances under applicable sections of the National Housing Act[31] (except Section 242 hospital insurance) with the goal of hastening 100 percent project completion and occupancy.

When HUD assembled all of the disaster-related multifamily housing guidance previously issued through the notice and memorandum into a comprehensive update to chapter 38, it incorporated lessons learned during the response to Hurricane Katrina. Chapter 38 addresses a critical element of HUD's mission, "that the residents of HUD's multifamily housing properties live in decent, safe, and sanitary housing without discrimination," in three ways. First, it describes options available to address quickly the needs of owners and occupants. Second, it provides guidance to housing staff charged with relaying information to owners and residents and sets protocol for field offices to service and protect HUD assets. And third, it emphasizes planning, both before a disaster strikes and during recovery.

2. Single-Family Rehabilitation, Replacement, Foreclosure Prevention

To support rehousing and rehabilitation of damaged single-family housing stock, HUD's Office of Housing has promulgated regulations and used other tools that meld discretion with permanent disaster-related authorities to create a comprehensive disaster approach. These tools have been swiftly and widely employed following major disasters. First, HUD has the authority to sell and lease its properties in order to assist disaster survivors under the provisions of the National Housing Act (NHA) and related regulations.[32] Under section 203(k) of the NHA, HUD can also insure mortgages covering the purchase or refinancing and rehabilitation of a home in a disaster area. Section 203(h) of the NHA expressly permits HUD to provide financing to disaster survivors. HUD is authorized to provide financing up to 100 percent of the property's appraised value to individuals with homes in presidentially declared disaster areas if their homes were destroyed or damaged to such an extent that reconstruction or replacement is necessary. HUD clarified the availability of section 203(h) in its "Hurricane Sandy Frequently Asked Questions" document, explaining that disaster survivors are not required to buy a home in a disaster area and that section 203(h) is available to both renters and owners of affected properties.[33]

HUD has previously by mortgagee letter and handbook taken measures to assist individuals affected by disasters. Specifically, HUD has extended the appraisal validity period and the period in which lenders can submit closed loans for insurance endorsement, allowed the homeownership centers to endorse delinquent mortgages on a case-by-case basis if the delinquency was due to disaster-related circumstances, automatically imposed a 90-day moratorium on foreclosures for disaster survivors, and allowed disaster survivors to have total fixed payment to gross income ratios of 45 percent.[34] HUD has also encouraged mortgagees to make loss mitigation options available to disaster survivors and to consider alternatives to foreclosure on disaster survivors such as the pre-foreclosure sales program or deed in lieu of foreclosure, to make assistance available to mortgagors related to hazard and flood insurance proceeds, and to consider using the construction/permanent mortgage program in the affected areas.[35] By handbook waiver, HUD also has extended the maximum age of mortgage loan documentation.[36]

3. *Iowa Buyouts: Gap Funding, Resilience, and Housing Recovery Needs*

The faster a community can work with FEMA to assess damage, the earlier it can design recovery programs and identify HUD funds that may be available to fill gaps in assistance to meet those needs. Recovery from the 2008 storms, tornadoes, and record-breaking floods that ravaged the state of Iowa offers a prime example of how HUD funds can be used to fill gaps and address resilience while meeting housing needs. Iowa experienced extreme flooding that submerged whole portions of communities. Across the state, more than 21,000 housing units were damaged and more than 4,000 of those units suffered severe structural damage or were destroyed.[37] The state estimated that after all insurance and government assistance, the remaining unmet housing needs (measured in the cost to repair or replace the damage to housing) would amount to $946 million, of which $856 million was for single-family dwellings.

Iowa received allocations for recovery needs from two supplemental CDBG-DR appropriations: $156,690,815 under the Supplemental Appropriation Act of 2008[38] (First Appropriation), and a total of $734,178,651, including a distribution under the Disaster Recovery Enhancement Fund (DREF), under the Consolidated Security, Disaster Assistance, and Continuing Appropriations Act of 2009[39] (Second Appropriation). The DREF provided an incentive match for activities that promoted resiliency while responding to the disasters of 2008, such as buyout programs under an optional relocation plan.

At the time it submitted its first action plan describing the planned use of the First Appropriation, Iowa had already set aside $5 million for local governments to provide a 15 percent local match from state CDBG funds for the FEMA Hazard Mitigation Grant Program (HMGP) for housing buyouts (an additional 10 percent match was available from state funds). The state described property acquisition as "the state's number one priority under this program, with the intent of removing houses from flood hazard areas."[40] When planning its use of funds from the Second Appropriation, Iowa had a better understanding of the resources FEMA would make available and which units would meet the program requirements. The state set aside additional funds from the Second Appropriation, bringing the total available for FEMA local match to $21.3 million. To buy homes that did not meet FEMA buyout requirements, Iowa's action plan for the Second Appropriation identified $240,406,941 for buyouts in flood-prone areas for which FEMA funds were not available, but for which CDBG-DR funds could cover all or a portion of the cost.

Local governments implemented Iowa's buyout programs. The city of Cedar Rapids used voluntary buyouts to address the roughly 1,300 blocks of the city's center where flooding was so severe that rehabilitation would have been difficult to impossible. The city's program was designed to respond to damage and reduce future loss of life and property along the Cedar River.[41] It was open to an estimated 1,300 commercial and residential properties identified in a strategy for voluntary acquisitions in three flood-impacted areas. The city developed the strategy in conjunction with the U.S. Army Corps of Engineers, Iowa State Homeland Security and Emergency Management, FEMA, and other experts.

Generally, the Cedar Rapids strategy identified three eligibility areas based on location, land purpose, and availability of funding beyond the local match.[42] The first covered 192 properties eligible for FEMA's HMGP in an unprotected area between the river and a proposed flood management system. Properties there must remain open space. A reported 1,154 properties in the other two areas were eligible for voluntary property acquisition with CDBG-DR assistance. In the first, the plan permitted construction of compatible infrastructure, utilities, and flood management structures. In the second, the plan contemplated redevelopment, but used buyouts to address the many units damaged beyond reasonable repair. As of June 2011, the city had combined the three funding sources to acquire a total of 1,015 properties at a cost of more than $60 million. Across Iowa, as of September 2012, CDBG disaster funds had contributed to buyouts on a total of 1,769 properties. Iowa was diligent when combining funding sources to prevent the duplication of benefits (DOB) under section 312 of the Stafford Act. HUD's technical assistance in Iowa and on related issues in other states prompted the 2011 consolidation of CDBG-DR DOB guidance into a Federal Register notice applicable to future grantees and new programs funded by CDBG-DR.[43] Iowa's buyout program dovetailed with the state's other rehousing programs (including new construction) to ensure that permanent housing recovery needs incorporated resilience to future flooding events.

4. *Immediate Housing Needs: Post–Katrina*

On August 29, 2005, Hurricane Katrina struck the Gulf Coast of the United States causing significant loss of life and catastrophic damage to property. At the time, it was the most destructive natural disaster in the nation's history.[44] Approximately 300,000 homes were either destroyed or made uninhabitable and more than one million people were displaced.[45] The storm devastated the economy, power infrastructure, and communications of Louisiana, Mississippi, and Alabama and caused environmental and health hazards across the affected region. This was the first domestic hurricane to cause nearly $100 billion in damage, with $67 billion attributable to damaged housing.[46]

a. *HUD's Immediate Response*

HUD's response to Katrina began before the storm. Upon learning the storm's size and potential destructive force, HUD began preparations to devolve operations from its office in New Orleans to other field offices within the region and created program disaster teams.[47] When disasters strike, they are not discriminating; the local office and many HUD staff suffered significant effects from Katrina.[48] Responding quickly requires communication within the department, and externally with partners in crisis (program participants and federal, state, and local governments). A coordinated effort had already begun among program offices (field and headquarters) to determine the extent to which the department had statutory and regulatory authority to undertake proposed recovery activities. Immediately, HUD field staff began to put in place the process to carry out damage assessments and determine ways to assist relief efforts for tenants, owners, and others affected.

Katrina tested the limits of HUD's public housing and Section 8 programs in the face of significant displacement of assisted housing residents and tremendous loss of housing property. Losses to rental housing and the public housing stock were particularly significant. Within days HUD was faced with multiple policy issues regarding use of funds and assisted housing property to aid response. Finding immediate housing for displaced assisted housing residents was critical. HUD's Office of Public and Indian Housing (PIH)[49] knew from prior disasters that housing providers (including public housing agencies (PHAs))[50] needed to process applications, determine eligibility, and admit applicants at a rapid pace.

By August 31, 2005, two days after landfall, the PIH disaster team was in communication with its public housing staff and local PHAs in HUD Regions IV and VI. By then, the team had decided that the REAC would assist field staff in identifying all available units within a 600-mile radius of New Orleans. Once this vacant unit list was completed, field staff would be responsible for assisting with the placement of HUD-assisted families. The city of Houston identified 1,000 units available for families, and the Houston Housing Authority agreed to set up a booth at the Astrodome to begin processing those displaced from New Orleans. PIH staff was working on legislative language and a budget for the purpose of obtaining additional funds and statutory waivers to facilitate recovery, and the team had outlined a method to streamline its regulatory waiver process. HUD established an 800 number for the public, and PIH began to select and educate a contractor to respond to questions and concerns.

This was an unprecedented effort within days of the storm. Among the notable recommendations: HUD instructed field offices to advise PHAs to amend their Admission and Continued Occupancy Plan to add a preference for those displaced. This advice subsequently was formalized as a PIH notice to staff and housing providers addressing the immediate needs of displaced HUD-assisted residents. The notice, Hurricane Katrina Disaster Policy for PIH, made clear that the first priority of the department and PHAs was "to assist existing public housing and voucher program participants who [had] been affected by Hurricane Katrina." The notice encouraged PHAs to use vacant or turnover units to house displaced residents. Assuming a PHA did not have an existing selection preference for disaster-affected individuals, it could adopt a preference to include displaced public housing and Section 8 residents who qualified for public housing and add these individuals to its waiting list. In accordance with this guidance, the PHA could admit affected individuals ahead of other applicants. Accompanying the notice was a certification form for use by PHAs to verify quickly that a displaced resident had been assisted by HUD.

The initial PIH notice was soon followed by PIH's Guidance for Public Housing Agencies in Assisting Families Displaced by Hurricane Katrina.[51] The guidance was a set of questions and answers related to the Housing Choice Voucher (HCV) and public housing programs that had been raised by PHAs, HUD field staff, and disaster-affected individuals, many in connection with prior disasters.[52] On October 3, 2005, PIH published in the Federal Register another notice setting out the regulatory and administrative waivers granted by PIH.[53]

The PIH notice dated October 3, 2005, was part of the larger departmental effort to identify regulatory obstacles that HUD could waive to assist the recovery. Days after landfall, HUD's program offices issued notices and memoranda informing housing providers and communities of actions that could be taken immediately. The Office of Community Planning and Development (CPD) issued a memorandum within seven days[54] of the hurricane notifying field directors of a statutory waiver under the CDBG program to allow entitlement grantees to use CDBG funds for food, temporary shelter, and related services for affected families and individuals.[55] The department published all of its waivers and guidance on a central website for the public: Program Guidance, Waivers, and Notices in Response to Hurricane Katrina.[56]

Weeks after Katrina, FEMA began to transition families out of temporary shelters and into intermediate and permanent housing. Many families who registered with FEMA were able to receive assistance under section 408 of the Stafford Act.[57] However, more was needed to respond to intermediate housing needs. As discussed below, FEMA tasked HUD with a major role in this effort.

b. *Katrina Disaster Housing Assistance Program and Disaster Voucher Program*

The Katrina Disaster Housing Assistance Program (KDHAP) was a HUD-FEMA initiative to provide temporary housing through local PHAs. HUD and FEMA recognized that PHAs with experience administering the HCV program were uniquely positioned to help displaced families. The HCV program is a PHA-administered program that provides assistance on behalf of low-income families, allowing them to obtain private-market housing. FEMA issued a mission assignment[58] tasking HUD to implement a similarly designed program (with reimbursement from FEMA) that provided rent subsidy assistance and assistance for a housing search, transportation, security deposit, and utilities. KDHAP included a special-needs component that allowed for enhanced services to pre-disaster homeless families and those who received special-needs housing program assistance prior to Katrina.

Under KDHAP, PHAs that had administered an HCV program pre-Katrina provided a temporary monthly rent subsidy for housing in the private rental market for no more than 18 months. Eligible families were displaced by Katrina, registered with FEMA, and either qualified as pre-disaster homeless families or were assisted pre-Katrina under certain HUD assisted housing programs.[59]

In 2006, the Disaster Voucher Program (DVP) replaced KDHAP. The Department of Defense Appropriations Act of 2006[60] (DVP Supplemental) appropriated $390 million to HUD for temporary rental voucher assistance for certain families displaced by Hurricanes Katrina and Rita.[61] Both KDHAP and DVP were modeled on the HCV program; however, DVP was funded by the DVP Supplemental and authorized under section 8(o) of the Housing Act of 1937, the authorizing provision for the HCV program.[62]

DVP provided temporary rental assistance for HUD-assisted, special-needs, and homeless families displaced as a result of Hurricanes Katrina and Rita. DVP funds were also made available to assist pre-disaster HCV families who had returned to heavily affected areas of Louisiana and Mississippi and who were subject to the federal disaster declarations in connection with Hurricanes Katrina or Rita. To expedite the delivery of assistance to DVP eligible families not yet receiving KDHAP assistance and simplify the transition from KDHAP to DVP for assisted families, HUD retained the KDHAP model for DVP. Under the authority of the DVP Supplemental, HUD waived income eligibility and tenant contribution requirements for families participating under the DVP for the statutory maximum term of 18 months.[63]

5. *Intermediate Housing Needs: Post–Katrina Disaster Housing Assistance Program*

One year after Katrina, HUD had done much to address the immediate housing needs of the Katrina survivors using statutory and administrative flexibility:

- On June 30, 2006, FHA extended the foreclosure moratorium to August 31, 2006, to allow mortgagors to rebuild homes or preserve good credit standing by paying off their mortgage debt. At the one-year mark, more than 13,000 borrowers had been assisted through HUD-initiated mortgage foreclosure relief programs.
- Ginnie Mae expanded its Targeted Lending Initiative (TLI), which provides incentives for lenders to increase loan volumes in traditionally underserved areas, to Katrina-damaged areas. Between October 2005 and June 2006, Ginnie Mae securities receiving this TLI discount included 3,069 loans from the Katrina census tracts with original principal balances of more than $368 million.
- HUD staff conducted housing counseling sessions to assist families in the purchase of homes in their new communities. Beyond the fundamentals of the home-buying process, evacuees were also advised of their eligibility under HUD's 203(h) and other mortgage insurance programs.[64]

Still, housing needs continued to exist two years after Katrina and Rita. By early 2007, FEMA had begun talks with HUD to extend coverage. On July 26, 2007, HUD and FEMA signed an Interagency Agreement (IAA), which governed the formation and implementation of the Disaster Housing Assistance Program (DHAP), a temporary housing assistance program, to assist an estimated 45,000 individuals still in need of housing or housing assistance, with an anticipated cost of $565 million.[65]

HUD and FEMA initially discussed the possibility of new legislation to transfer FEMA's administrative responsibility to HUD for the FEMA-assisted families who were at the time receiving rental assistance as a result of Hurricanes Katrina and Rita. As envisioned, the legislation would have provided appropriations to HUD to administer tenant-based assistance for these families through PHAs. As an alternative to a legislative approach, HUD and FEMA negotiated the terms of the IAA. Based on HUD's HCV program expertise and successful implementation of KDHAP and DVP, FEMA asked HUD to design DHAP in the model of those three programs. HUD, on FEMA's behalf, continued its administrative role of providing rental assistance through its network of housing providers (i.e., PHAs) to a broader demographic of families under the provisions of the Stafford Act.

FEMA funded the program, including rental assistance and case management services, from its Disaster Relief Fund. PHAs that administered the HCV program were designated by HUD to administer DHAP in their jurisdictions. Grants were provided to local PHAs to administer DHAP on behalf of FEMA. Subject to FEMA's approval, HUD operated the program in accordance with HUD's DHAP operating requirements and developed the grant agreement used by PHAs to govern the use of the funds.[66]

To be eligible for DHAP, families had to have been displaced by Hurricanes Katrina or Rita and consequently were either receiving or were eligible to receive rental assistance administered by FEMA. FEMA determined the eligibility of families, and PHAs verified eligibility through a HUD-managed system. PHAs had a number of responsibilities, including calculating rent subsidies, making payments on behalf of participants, performing housing quality standards inspections when necessary, and terminating participation for noncompliance. Unlike previous non-disaster-related rental assistance programs, DHAP included elements designed to transition participating households from the temporary program. These included declining rental assistance payments that encouraged greater responsibility for housing costs over time and the provision of case management services to help move households to more stable, permanent housing options.

Administering the suite of DHAP-model programs to meet short- and intermediate-term housing needs was a new post-disaster role for the department. With the understanding that HUD and FEMA may deploy a similar program in response to future disasters, HUD's Office of Policy Development and Research (PD&R) commissioned a study of participating households' transitions out of the DHAP program. The study explores program outcomes seven years after Hurricanes Katrina and Rita. These outcomes may inform future post-disaster housing responses. PD&R published a report in March 2013 to present the results of the study.[67]

Over the course of its response to Hurricanes Katrina and Rita, the department refined its available statutory and administrative tools in response to the needs of the families and communities it served and in recognition of the need to maximize use of resources related to the department's programs. In sum, the Hurricane Katrina experience provided many valuable lessons and strengthened HUD's capacity to assess and respond to other disasters.[68]

C. CDBG-DR: Using the Toolbox to Meet Economic and Other Development Needs

In response to disasters and other emergencies, Congress may appropriate additional funding for the CDBG program to award CDBG-DR grants for long-term activities authorized under title I of the HCD Act. Because these recovery funds may assist a broader range of recovery activities than many other federal programs, CDBG-DR grants provide a flexible funding source that can facilitate a comprehensive response and help achieve objectives that might otherwise be unattainable due to limits on other resources. Congress has frequently provided the secretary of HUD with additional waiver authority (subject to limitations) to facilitate the use of funds for recovery. HUD publishes applicable requirements in the Federal Register.

Although Congress had been providing supplemental disaster recovery funds to communities through the CDBG program since 1993, the use of CDBG-DR in the overall recovery from the 9/11 terrorist attacks marked the first time that Congress used CDBG-DR as a multibillion-dollar vehicle for recovery. A total of $3.483 billion in CDBG-DR funds were available to help New York City, and America as a whole, rebound. These funds supported crucial, large-scale recovery initiatives, including planning and property acquisition related to the World Trade Center site and cultural projects such as the National September 11 Memorial & Museum.[69]

Many CDBG-DR supplemental appropriations have provided that, among other activities, funds are available for economic revitalization. CDBG-DR funds provided critical support for this purpose following the World Trade Center attacks, which resulted in staggering physical destruction that damaged or eliminated approximately 30 million square feet of commercial space and displaced more than 100,000 jobs.[70] Given the scope of investment necessary to jump-start economic recovery, HUD waived the public benefit standards for economic development activities, which typically limit for each activity "the amount of CDBG assistance per job retained or created," or the "amount of CDBG assistance per low- and moderate-income person to which goods or services are provided."[71]

HUD's funds were invested in a number of economic development programs[72] in close consultation and coordination with New York's Empire State Development Corporation (ESDC), the New York City Economic Development Corporation, and the Lower Manhattan Development Corporation (a subsidiary of ESDC formed in October 2001). These included the Business Recovery Grant program, the Small Firm Attraction and Retention Grant program, the Small Business Technical Assistance program, the Small Business Recovery Loan Fund, and the Job Creation and Retention Program. The breadth of CDBG-funded programs resulted in a full-scale economic recovery. In 2006, the Louis Berger Group found that nearly $1.1 billion in HUD resources were invested in more than 16,000 firms that directly employed more than 250,000 people.[73] This assistance helped retain businesses and indirectly generated an additional 10,000 jobs. A recent *Crain's New York Business* article noted that the recovery in Lower Manhattan has resulted in a model of a sustainable, vibrant, livable, modern urban center in only 10 years.[74]

D. HUD's Role in the Overall Federal Response

In 2008, as required by the National Strategy for Homeland Security, DHS and FEMA published the National Response Framework (NRF or the Framework) to guide the interagency response coordination structure for major disasters and other incidents (DHS updated this framework in May 2013). When an incident triggers the NRF, a Joint Field Office (JFO) serves as the point for coordinating federal, state and other responders. Under the NRF, FEMA maintains lead coordinating responsibility. The Framework describes the support roles of other federal agencies and describes Emergency Support Functions (ESFs) used to coordinate response support. HUD supports FEMA's work as the coordinating agency for sheltering and interim housing.

Long-term recovery is outside the scope of the NRF. In September 2009, President Barack Obama charged DHS and HUD with establishing a Long-Term Disaster Recovery Working Group.[75] This effort resulted in the National Disaster Recovery Framework (NDRF). It defines six new Recovery Support Functions (RSFs) and identifies the federal agencies responsible for RSF coordination and support. The NDRF operates from the interim period following a disaster through long-term recovery. HUD is the coordinating agency for disaster-related housing under the Housing RSF. HUD also serves as a support organization under the Community Planning and Capacity Building RSF.

Housing support coordinated under the NRF and the NDRF is informed by the National Disaster Housing Strategy (the Strategy), which was published by FEMA in 2009. Under the Strategy, FEMA and HUD will "partner to provide Federal interim housing assistance, each bringing its expertise and experience to bear. When Federal permanent housing assistance is needed, HUD will have the lead responsibility under this Strategy and will coordinate with its partners to provide housing and community development resources."[76] HUD supports this effort by assessing damage to HUD-assisted and insured properties, and through resources such as the National Housing Locator System (NHLS).[77] The Strategy acknowledges that HUD may need new authorities and resources to implement the Strategy, such as permanent authorizing legislation for DHAP or a successor program. Absent changes, FEMA can use its Stafford Act authority to request that HUD provide housing services through a mission assignment.

HUD drew from the Strategy and the NRF to inform its response and to provide support to FEMA after hundreds of tornadoes ripped through the South and Midwest in April and May of 2011, causing massive damage and loss of life. HUD worked in the first days to assess the damage to HUD-assisted housing assets, such as the Rosedale Courts public housing project in Tuscaloosa, Alabama, where 11 people lost their lives and 100 of 188 units were destroyed. To support rehousing efforts through FEMA's JFOs, HUD worked to identify available units for rehousing, calling on property owners to list available units in the NHLS. FEMA and state and local recovery workers have access to the system and can refer displaced families to a suitable place to live. HUD's Office of Fair Housing and Equal Opportunity (FHEO) added fair housing tips to the NHLS and helped ensure that landlords who list properties know they must comply with the Fair Housing Act's[78] prohibition against housing discrimination based on race, color, national origin, religion, sex, familial status, or disability.[79]

The multiple-vortex EF5 tornado that struck Joplin, Missouri, also provided an opportunity to improve regional and field coordination in support of the NRF and NDRF. HUD established a strong internal coordination effort to assist other federal partners. HUD established the Joplin tornado field working group and began assessing the damage to HUD properties and clients. They met with the local PHA director, checked on homeless grantees and their clients, and looked firsthand at storm-decimated multifamily properties. The Joplin tornado field working group made several visits to the city and forged a strong partnership between HUD, the city, and other federal agencies to help rebuild. The field working group helped to get public and multifamily housing units back online and to secure disaster funding for Joplin. The group met with city management to offer edits on Joplin's proposed use of the funding and helped celebrate the reopening of a multifamily property for seniors that was heavily damaged.

In other recent work under the national frameworks, HUD collaborated with various agencies in 2010 and 2011 to address short-term and long-term flood damage and response needs suffered by the North Dakota Spirit Lake Tribe and other northern plains tribes. Working under FEMA's lead through the NRF's ESF No. 14 (the long-term recovery predecessor to the NRSF) HUD collaborated with the Department of Transportation, Indian Health Service, the Department of Agriculture, and other state and federal agencies to develop the Spirit Lake Long-Term Flood Recovery Plan, which addresses ongoing flooding affecting the Spirit Lake Tribe Nation in North Dakota. In March 2011, HUD's Northern Plains Office of Native American Programs established a Tribal Special Assistance Team to provide focused technical assistance in coordination with other federal agency partners.

HUD's cross-program and cross-agency collaborations in Joplin and in the northern plains mark a change in the way HUD's regional offices approach recovery after similarly scaled disasters.

III. Best Practices and Lessons Learned

Over time, HUD has developed tools to protect its existing investments, to assist participants and grantees and to build back better. These tools are now employed in a series of common responses following a major disaster. Included below are lessons that may benefit disaster recovery practitioners.

Pre-disaster planning is irreplaceable. Although most communities have disaster plans in place, plans should be revisited in the context of the NRF and NDRF. Planning supports basic functions such as communications and initial damage assessments, and also aids long-term recovery. For example, adopting a programmatic agreement to assist cultural and historic resource review after a disaster may allow communities to shorten review periods for compliance with the National Environmental Policy Act[80] and related laws.

Practitioners can review HUD research on past disasters and integrate data-driven results into disaster planning and programs. PD&R's Disaster Recovery Tool Kit provides guidance to aid recovery and resilience (home rehabilitation, design and construction practices that promote moisture resistance, disaster preparedness, and other relevant content). PD&R's reports are available online.[81]

HUD's waiver and suspension authorities are based on a finding of good cause and meeting other required standards. With any request, data or other support are necessary. Waiver requests are not guaranteed, and will be considered on a case-by-case basis under applicable standards of review.

HUD recommends communicating with the department early and often. For disaster recovery, regional administrators have delegated authority for collecting local information, measuring community impact, initiating cross-program communication and coordination, and facilitating resolution of potential program differences. HUD's field offices are the initial point of contact for inquiries. Variances in practices between HUD regions may be based on applicable facts. When flexibility is an option, HUD's previous responses to those similarly situated in other regions may be considered.

Finally, plans should address the issues that may arise with respect to duplication of benefits (DOB). The essence of this prohibition under section 312 of the Stafford Act is that a beneficiary of federal disaster assistance may not receive more than the cost of the need for which assistance is provided (including funds from insurance, another disaster program, or any other source). HUD grantees administering disaster programs must ensure DOB compliance. It is much easier to avoid duplication through good planning than to require repayment.

IV. Conclusion

As a matter of course, HUD has a particular post-disaster role in protecting the department's assets and those supported by its resources. HUD's primary responses to disasters remain consistent with HUD's mission to create safer, more affordable and sustainable communities. From time to time HUD may be called upon to participate in an enhanced role by the president, Congress, or FEMA (in its lead disaster recovery coordination role), as it has in response to Superstorm Sandy.

In December 2012, President Obama signed Executive Order 13632[82] to establish the Hurricane Sandy Rebuilding Task Force and appoint Secretary Shaun Donovan as chair. "The task force is charged with creating a comprehensive regional plan, based on local vision for redevelopment, to guide long-term disaster recovery efforts."[83] On January 2, 2013, Secretary Donovan announced that his chief of staff, Laurel Blatchford, will serve as executive director. He also summarized the five major responsibilities of the task force. It will (1) coordinate with stakeholders to deliver rebuilding strategies in a comprehensive regional plan within six months; (2) reduce regulatory burdens and cut red tape; (3) manage the flow of federal recovery funds and make sure that federal resources are aligned with local priorities; (4) monitor progress and strengthen accountability measures; and (5) offer technical assistance, track clear metrics to monitor progress, and capture best practices and set standards for long-term disaster recovery. It is too soon to predict how the task force will implement these responsibilities, but Secretary Donovan has made clear that the task force will support local visions and encourage resiliency in carrying out its functions.

Already, HUD's response to Superstorm Sandy has demonstrated better interdepartmental coordination and a unified HUD response. Whereas information for previous disasters was provided by various program offices or as a Q&A with partners and grantees, HUD quickly published a frequently asked questions guidance document specific to Superstorm Sandy following the disaster.[84] On February 6, 2013, HUD allocated the first third of the $16 billion in CDBG-DR funds made available by the Disaster Relief Appropriations Act of 2013.[85] This is the fastest HUD has ever allocated CDBG-DR funding to grantees.

In the wake of a major disaster, HUD's partners can expect that HUD's overall response will be specific to the disaster at hand, but draw from past experience. Although HUD has an arsenal of examples and models for recovery programs that can be easily deployed, communities are best positioned to mold these options for localized use after assessing needs and identifying priorities for recovery and resilience.

Notes

1. Department of Housing and Urban Development Act § 2, 42 U.S.C. § 3531 (2011).
2. Disclaimer: HUD's OGC appreciates this opportunity to communicate with practitioners about HUD's mission and programs. Inclusion of this chapter does not represent an endorsement of the American Bar Association, its Forum on Affordable Housing and Community Development Law, the Forum's Community Development Committee, or the other contributors to this book.
3. Federal Disaster Act of 1950, Pub. L. No. 81-875, 64 Stat. 1109, *repealed by* Disaster Relief Act of 1970, Pub. L. No. 91-606, 84 Stat. 1744.
4. *Id.* at § 2(a) 64 Stat. 1109.
5. Department of Housing and Urban Development Act, Pub. L. No. 89-174, 79 Stat. 667 (codified as amended at 42 U.S.C. §§ 3531–3537 (2011)) (transferring to HUD the functions of agencies such as the Housing and Home Finance Agency, which had disaster-related and flood protection roles).
6. National Flood Insurance Act of 1968, Pub. L. No. 90-448, 82 Stat. 476 (codified as amended at 42 U.S.C. §§ 4001–4129 (2011)).
7. Exec. Order No. 11,725, 3 C.F.R. 779 (1973), *reprinted in* 38 Fed. Reg. 17,175 (June 29, 1973) (for the transfer of certain functions of the Office of Emergency Preparedness); Exec. Order No. 11,749, 3 C.F.R. 324 (1973), *reprinted in* 38 Fed. Reg. 34,177 (Dec. 12, 1973) (consolidating disaster relief functions assigned to the Secretary of HUD).
8. Disaster Relief Act of 1970, Pub. L. No. 91-606, 84 Stat. 1744, *repealed by* Disaster Relief Act of 1974, Pub. L. No. 93-288, 88 Stat. 143 (codified as amended at 42 U.S.C. §§ 5121–5207 (2011)).
9. Department of Housing and Urban Development; Space, Science, Veterans, and Certain Other Independent Agencies Appropriations Act of 1973, Pub. L. No. 92-383, § 406, 86 Stat. 553.
10. Cong. Research Serv., Comm. on Gov't Operations, 93d Cong., After Disaster Strikes: Federal Programs and Organizations III (Comm. Print 1974), *available at* https://bulk.resource.org/gao.gov/93-288/0000FB71.pdf.
11. Reorganization Plan No. 3 of 1978, 3 C.F.R. 389 (1978 Comp.2), *reprinted in* 5 U.S.C. app. 229, *and in* 92 Stat. 3788 (implemented through Exec. Order No. 12,127, 3 C.F.R. 376 (1979) and Exec. Order No. 12,148, 3 C.F.R. 412 (1979)). This plan was an effort to unify, for the first time, key emergency management and assistance functions into one agency directly accountable to the president.
12. Homeland Security Act of 2002, Pub. L. No. 107-296, 116 Stat. 2135 (codified in scattered titles of U.S.C.). The secretary of Homeland Security implements overall coordination of federal response activities. The FEMA administrator helps the secretary in meeting these responsibilities. U.S. Dep't. of Homeland Sec., National Response Framework 12, 24, 25 (2008).
13. The Post Katrina Emergency Management Reform Act of 2006 (PKEMRA), Pub. L. No. 109-295, 120 Stat. 1355 (codified at 6 U.S.C. §§ 313–321e, 311 note, 313 note 701, 701 note) (amending title V of the Homeland Security Act of 2002). PKEMRA provided that FEMA's primary mission is "to reduce the loss of life and property and protect the Nation from all hazards, including natural disasters, acts of terrorism, and other man-made disasters" by leading the nation in preparedness, protection, response, and recovery. 6 U.S.C. § 313 (2011).
14. Robert T. Stafford Disaster Relief and Emergency Assistance Act, as amended (Stafford Act), §§ 401, 501, 42 U.S.C. §§ 5170, 5191 (2011).
15. Delegation of Authority to the Office of Disaster Management and National Security, 76 Fed. Reg. 62,433 (Oct. 7, 2011); *What HUD Services and Resources Are Available for Disaster Relief and*

Recovery in FY 2012?: Statement to the S. Comm. on Appropriations, Subcomm. on Homeland Sec., 111th Cong. 3 (2010) (written testimony of Frederick Tombar, Senior Advisor for Disaster Programs, Office of the Secretary, HUD), *available at* http://www.appropriations.senate.gov/ht-homeland-security.cfm ?method=hearings.download&id=e1e7eb23-26c7-4cf9-bf0a-e0116f05ed62.

16. *Hurricane Agnes Still Ranks as Pa.'s Worst Disaster*, USA TODAY (June 20, 2002), http://usatoday30 .usatoday.com/weather/hurricane/2002/6-20-agnes-revisited.htm#more.

17. Authorized under title I of the Housing Act of 1949 (1949 Act) (ch. 338, § 100, 42 U.S.C. § 1450) (omitted pursuant to 42 U.S.C. § 5316), the urban renewal program authorized assistance to local public agencies for eliminating slums and blight in urban areas through planning and eligible renewal activities. Section 111 of the 1949 Act authorized HUD to permit grantees to disregard certain program requirements in areas declared a major disaster to complete "Disaster Urban Renewal Projects." *Id.* § 1462.

18. Stafford Act, 42 U.S.C. § 5153.

19. 42 U.S.C. §§ 5304(e), 5311 (2011).

20. 42 U.S.C. § 3535(q)(4) (2011).

21. 42 U.S.C. § 5321 (2011).

22. *Id.*

23. A list of supplemental CDBG-DR appropriations is included within the chapter on CDBG-DR grants in HUD's online publication, *Programs of HUD*. This publication is regularly updated to include new supplemental appropriations. *Programs of HUD*, DEP'T OF HOUS. AND URBAN DEV., http://portal .hud.gov/hudportal/HUD?src=/hudprograms/disaster-recovery (last visited Feb. 16, 2013).

24. 42 U.S.C. § 12840 (2011).

25. Processing of HUD housing programs is done within the department's Multifamily Hubs and Program centers.

26. U.S. DEP'T OF HOUS. & URBAN DEV., HANDBOOK 4350.1 MULTIFAMILY ASSET MGMT. AND PROJECT SERVICING HANDBOOK, EMERGENCY/DISASTER ASSISTANCE GUIDANCE, CH. 38 (2010), *available at* http://portal.hud.gov/hudportal/HUD?src=/program_offices/housing/mfh/disasterguide.

27. THE INSTITUTE FOR BUILDING TECHNOLOGY & SAFETY, AN ASSESSMENT OF DAMAGE TO MANUFACTURED HOMES CAUSED BY HURRICANE CHARLEY 1 (2005), *available at* http://www.huduser.org /Publications/pdf/HurricaneCharley04.pdf.

28. I.R.S. Notice 2004-66 I.R.B. (Oct. 18, 2004), *available at* http://www.irs.gov/irb/2004-42_IRB /ar12.html.

29. Housing Notice 04-22, Disaster Recovery Guidance by Multifamily Housing After a Presidentially-Declared Disaster (Nov. 10, 2004), *available at* http://www.hud.gov/offices/adm/ hudclips/notices/hsg/04hsgnotices.cfm.

30. Multifamily Disaster Clarification of Notice H 04-22 and Additional Guidance (Oct. 28, 2005), *available at* http://www.hud.gov/offices/hsg/mfh/hto/clarifyh04-22.pdf.

31. *Id.*

32. National Housing Act (NHA), § 204(g), 12 U.S.C. § 1710(g) (2011). The NHA provides that the "Secretary shall have power to deal with . . . or sell for cash or credit, in his discretion, any properties conveyed to him . . ." and authorizes the secretary to sell real and personal property upon such terms and conditions as he/she may prescribe. The implementing regulations regarding the disposition of HUD-acquired single-family property provide that HUD will lease property "to comply with other designated HUD programs, or when the Secretary determines that it is in the interest of HUD" and that HUD may conduct direct sales of properties to displaced persons. *See* 24 C.F.R. §§ 291.10, 291.90(c)(2), 291.210(b) (2012).

33. DEP'T OF HOUS. & URBAN DEV., FREQUENTLY ASKED QUESTIONS (FAQS) SPECIFIC TO SANDY 4 (2012), *available at* http://portal.hud.gov/hudportal/documents/huddoc?id=SandyQAs.pdf.

34. *See* U.S. DEP'T OF HOUS. & URBAN DEV., HANDBOOK 4330.1, ADMINISTRATION OF INSURED HOME MORTGAGES (1994), *available at* http://portal.hud.gov/hudportal/HUD?src=/program_offices/ administration/hudclips/handbooks/hsgh/4330.1; U.S. DEP'T OF HOUS. & URBAN DEV., HANDBOOK 4155.1, MORTGAGE CREDIT ANALYSIS FOR MORTGAGE INSURANCE ON ONE- TO FOUR-UNIT MORTGAGE LOANS (2011) [hereinafter HANDBOOK 4155.1], *available at* http://portal.hud.gov/hudportal/HUD?src=/ program_offices/administration/hudclips/handbooks/hsgh/4155.1; U.S. DEP'T OF HOUS. & URBAN DEV., MORTGAGEE LETTER 2005-33, UNDERWRITING AND SERVICING POLICIES TO ASSIST VICTIMS OF PRESIDENTIALLY-DECLARED MAJOR DISASTER AREAS (2005) [hereinafter ML 2005-33], *available at* portal.hud.gov/hudportal/documents/huddoc?id=DOC_16752.doc; U.S. DEP'T OF HOUS. & URBAN DEV., MORTGAGEE LETTER 2012-23, GUIDANCE FOR FHA-APPROVED MORTGAGEES ORIGINATING AND SERVICING MORTGAGES IN PRESIDENTIALLY-DECLARED MAJOR DISASTER AREAS (2012) [hereinafter ML 2012-23], *available at* http://portal.hud.gov/hudportal/documents/huddoc?id=12-23ml.pdf.

35. *See* ML 2005-33, *supra* note 35; ML 2012-23, *supra* note 35; HANDBOOK 4155.1, *supra* note 35; U.S. DEP'T OF HOUS. & URBAN DEV., MORTGAGEE LETTER 2012-19, HAZARD AND FLOOD INSURANCE REQUIREMENT REMINDER (2012).

36. HANDBOOK 4155.1, *supra* note 35, at 1.B.1.h.

37. IOWA DEP'T OF ECON. DEV., STATE OF IOWA ACTION PLAN FOR DISASTER RECOVERY #2 1, 2 (2013) [hereinafter IOWA ACTION PLAN], *available at* http://www.iowaeconomicdevelopment.com/userdocs/documents/ieda/actionplan2.pdf.

38. Supplemental Appropriation Act of 2008, Pub. L. No. 110-252, 122 Stat. 2323.

39. Consolidated Security, Disaster Assistance, and Continuing Appropriations Act of 2009, Pub. L. No. 110-329, 122 Stat. 3574.

40. IOWA ACTION PLAN, *supra* note 38, at 9.

41. *Voluntary Property Acquisition (Buyout) Program*, CITY OF CEDAR RAPIDS, http://www.cedar-rapids.org/city-news/flood-recovery-progress/floodrecoveryresources/buyoutprogram/Pages/default.aspx (last visited Feb. 16, 2013).

42. The city's interactive map of flood areas and acquisitions are available online. *CR Progress Map*, CITY OF CEDAR RAPIDS, http://crgis.cedar-rapids.org/CR-Progress/FlexViewer/index.html (last visited Feb. 16, 2013).

43. Clarification of Duplication of Benefits Requirements Under the Stafford Act for Community Development Block Grant (CDBG) Disaster Recovery Grantees, 76 Fed. Reg. 71,060 (Nov. 16, 2011), *available at* http://www.gpo.gov/fdsys/pkg/FR-2011-11-16/pdf/2011-29634.pdf.

44. Hurricane Katrina destroyed more residential property than Hurricane Andrew, which destroyed or damaged approximately 80,000 homes in 1992, or the combined damage of the four major 2004 hurricanes—Charley, Frances, Ivan, and Jeanne—which, together, destroyed or damaged approximately 85,000 homes. EXEC. OFFICE OF THE PRESIDENT, THE FEDERAL RESPONSE TO HURRICANE KATRINA: LESSONS LEARNED 7 (2006) [hereinafter LESSONS LEARNED].

45. *Id.* at 7. Hurricane Rita closely followed Hurricane Katrina, making landfall on September 24, 2005, once again hitting the Gulf Coast area of the United States and causing further displacement of individuals and families and property damage. *Id.* at 8.

46. *Id.* at 7.

47. HUD is organized in 10 regions. Each region is managed by a Regional Administrator, who also oversees the regional office. Each field office within a region is managed by a Field Office Director, who reports to the Regional Administrator. Regions IV and VI include the states most heavily affected by Hurricane Katrina and the displacement of residents: Louisiana, Mississippi, Alabama, and Texas.

48. Other federal agencies and resources were also affected. The National Finance Center (NFC), which is headquartered in New Orleans, is a federal government agency that provides human resources, financial, and administrative services for other federal agencies—including processing payroll for HUD. Because of the hurricane, the NFC shut down all operations in Louisiana and resumed operations at its Philadelphia and Texas sites.

49. HUD's Office of Public and Indian Housing administers the programs authorized under the Housing Act of 1937, Pub. L. No. 75-412, 50 Stat. 888 (codified as amended at 42 U.S.C §§ 1437–1437bbb-9 (2011)), which includes HUD's public housing programs and the Section 8 Housing Choice Voucher Program, as well as related assisted housing programs.

50. Public housing agencies own and/or operate public housing projects and are the entities primarily authorized to administer the department's Section 8 programs. *See* 42 U.S.C. § 1437a(b)(6) (2011).

51. DEP'T OF HOUS. & URBAN DEV., GUIDANCE FOR PUBLIC HOUSING AGENCIES IN ASSISTING FAMILIES DISPLACED BY HURRICANE KATRINA (2005), *available at* http://www.afhh.org/aboutus/pubs/HUD_Katrina_facts.pdf. This guidance was dated September 13, 2005.

52. As noted earlier, the department's primary programs and authorities that support disaster recovery and response have undergone only minimal changes in recent decades, and prior experience was key to HUD's immediate response.

53. Regulatory and Administrative Waivers Granted for Public and Indian Housing Programs to Assist with Recovery and Relief in Hurricane Katrina Disaster Areas, 70 Fed. Reg. 57,716 (Oct. 3, 2005).

54. Memorandum from Pamela H. Patenaude, Assistant Sec'y for Cmty. Planning and Dev. to CPD Field Office Directors (Sept. 5, 2005), *available at* http://www.hud.gov/offices/cpd/library/katrina/revkatpswaive.pdf.

55. As early as September 28, 2005, HUD began to request confirmation that FEMA would reimburse state and local governments for eligible emergency services that were temporarily funded with CDBG and other HUD assistance. HUD's OGC worked diligently to confirm and interpret FEMA's

response. By November 2005, OGC had confirmation that FEMA would reimburse these costs to the extent they were paid by CDBG. OGC continued to push for clarification as to reimbursement of HOME funding. On March 28, 2006, FEMA's chief counsel confirmed by letter to HUD's general counsel that FEMA's authority to provide emergency shelter under section 403 of the Stafford Act is more specific than HOME's program authority, and therefore communities that used HOME funds for emergency sheltering might also be eligible for reimbursement through FEMA's public assistance program. Letter from David A. Trissell, FEMA Chief Counsel, to Keith E. Gottfried, HUD General Counsel (Mar. 28, 2006), *available at* http://www.hud.gov/offices/cpd/library/katrina/051206_femaletter.pdf.

56. *Program Guidance, Waivers, and Notices in Response to Hurricane Katrina*, DEP'T OF HOUS. & URBAN DEV., http://www.hud.gov/katrina/proguidance.cfm (last visited Feb. 16, 2013).

57. 42 U.S.C. § 5174.

58. The Mission Assignment, issued in accordance with section 402 of the Stafford Act, was dated September 29, 2005.

59. On December 1, 2005, HUD issued notices describing KDHAP operating requirements. PIH Notice 2005-36 (HA), (Dec. 1, 2005), *available at* http://portal.hud.gov/hudportal/documents/huddoc?id=DOC_10916.pdf; DEP'T OF HOUS. & URBAN DEV., OFFICE OF PUB. & INDIAN HOUS., KDHAP SPECIAL NEEDS FACT SHEET (2005), *available at* http://lhpd.law.uiowa.edu/dpn_hi/98.pdf.

60. Pub. L. No. 109-148, 119 Stat. 2680, 2779 (2005).

61. Hurricane Rita caused additional displacement of individuals and families and damage to property affected by Hurricane Katrina. *See* LESSONS LEARNED, *supra* note 45, at 7.

62. 42 U.S.C. § 1437f(o) (2006).

63. HUD issued a notice providing more detail on DVP. *See* PIH Notice 2006-12 (Feb. 3, 2006), *available at* http://portal.hud.gov/hudportal/documents/huddoc?id=DOC_9052.pdf.

64. U.S. DEP'T HOMELAND SEC., HURRICANE KATRINA: WHAT GOVERNMENT IS DOING 2–3 (2006).

65. DHAP was authorized under the Department of Homeland Security's general grant authority under section 102(b)(2) of the Homeland Security Act (6 U.S.C. § 112 (2011)); sections 408(b)(1), 426, and 306(a) of the Stafford Act (42 U.S.C. §§ 5174(b)(a), 5189d, 5149 (a) (2011)); and the Economy Act (31 U.S.C. § 1535 (2011)).

66. Notice PIH-2007-26 (Aug. 16, 2007), *available at* http://portal.hud.gov/hudportal/documents/huddoc?id=DOC_9040.pdf.

67. DEP'T OF HOUS. & URBAN DEV., OFFICE OF POLICY DEV. & RESEARCH, STUDY OF HOUSEHOLD TRANSITION FROM THE DISASTER HOUSING ASSISTANCE PROGRAM (DHAP-KATRINA) FINAL REPORT (2013), http://www.huduser.org/Publications/pdf/HUD-495-DHAP-Katrina.pdf.

68. On September 23, 2008, HUD and FEMA entered a similar interagency agreement to establish the DHAP-Ike program for families affected by Hurricane Ike. DHAP-Ike was based on the Katrina DHAP model, but modified the program so that payments were made directly to a landlord on behalf of a family. As of September 2009, 24,649 of the 51,624 families referred by FEMA were participating in DHAP-Ike across 104 PHAs. *See A Year Later: Lessons Learned, Progress Made, and Challenges That Remain from Hurricane Ike: Hearing Before the S. Comm. on Small Bus. and Entrepreneurship, the Comm. on Homeland Sec. and Governmental Affairs Ad Hoc Subcomm. on Disaster and Recovery*, 111th Cong. 67 (2009) (statement of Frederick Tombar, Senior Advisor, Office of the Secretary, HUD), *available at* http://www.gpo.gov/fdsys/pkg/CHRG-111shrg66459/pdf/CHRG-111shrg66459.pdf.

69. Activities funded by CDBG-DR and carried out by the Lower Manhattan Development Corporation (LMDC) are described in detail in partial action plans. Each partial action plan describes planned use of a portion of CDBG-DR funds, and undergoes a multistage approval process that includes community input. These partial action plans are available on LMDC's website. *Partial Action Plans*, LOWER MANHATTAN DEV. CORP., http://www.renewnyc.com/FundingInitiatives/PartialActionPlans.aspx (last visited Feb. 16, 2013). All CDBG-DR supplemental appropriations and Federal Register notices of funding allocations, waivers, and alternative requirements are available on HUD's website at http://portal.hud.gov/hudportal/HUD?src=/program_offices/comm_planning/communitydevelopment/programs/drsi/afwa.

70. *Recovery Snapshot: 9/11 Business Recovery Grant Program*, DEP'T OF HOUS. & URBAN DEV., http://portal.hud.gov/hudportal/documents/huddoc?id=DOC_22573.pdf (last visited Feb. 16, 2013).

71. Statutory and Regulatory Waivers Granted to New York State for Recovery from the September 11, 2001, Terrorist Attacks: Technical Correction, 67 Fed. Reg. 5845 (Feb. 7, 2002).

72. Department of Defense and Emergency Supplemental Appropriations for Recovery from and Response to Terrorist Attacks on the United States, 2002, Pub. L. No. 107-117, 115 Stat. 2230, one of three CDBG-DR supplemental acts for New York City recovery, stipulated the use of $500 million for economic losses suffered by individuals, nonprofits, or small businesses located in an area south of 14th

Street in Lower Manhattan. HUD issued a waiver and alternative requirement to implement this provision, permitting "payment of compensation to an individual, nonprofit or small business for economic losses" resulting from the attacks as a distinct eligible activity for purposes of that appropriation. Statutory Waiver Granted to New York State for Recovery from the September 11, 2011, Terrorist Attacks, 67 Fed. Reg. 12,042 (Mar. 18, 2002). Although the economic loss program was developed to respond to specific legislative direction, CDBG-DR funds from other supplemental appropriations have supported economic revitalization through other activities eligible under the CDBG program.

73. *HUD's Role in the Recovery and Rebirth of Lower Manhattan after 9/11*, DEP'T OF HOUS. AND URBAN DEV., http://portal.hud.gov/hudportal/HUD?src=/press/HUD's_role_in_the_recovery_and_rebirth_of_lower%20manhattan_after_9.11 (last visited Feb. 16, 2013).

74. Theresa Agovino, *Lower Manhattan Is Surprising Urban Model*, CRAIN'S N.Y. BUS., July 17, 2011, *available at* http://www.crainsnewyork.com/article/20110717/REAL_ESTATE/307179979.

75. FEMA, NATIONAL DISASTER RECOVERY FRAMEWORK: STRENGTHENING DISASTER RECOVERY FOR THE NATION 3 (2011), *available at* http://www.fema.gov/pdf/recoveryframework/ndrf.pdf.

76. FEMA, NAT'L DISASTER HOUS. STRATEGY 17, 55 (2009), *available at* http://www.fema.gov/pdf/emergency/disasterhousing/NDHS-core.pdf.

77. HUD has activated the National Housing Locator System following past disasters. The system is not available to the public.

78. Pub. L. No. 90-284, tit. VIII, 82 Stat. 73, 81–89 (codified as amended at 42 U.S.C. §§ 3601–31 (2006)).

79. FHEO plays an important role in HUD's overall disaster response, most importantly in educating emergency housing providers on Fair Housing Act compliance. HUD's disaster resources include information about its Housing Discrimination Hotline and how victims of housing discrimination may file a complaint with HUD. FHEO collaborates with partners to provide multilingual information on fair housing rights, responsibilities, and resources, and has assisted a network of foreign consulates to reach otherwise hard-to-contact local residents. During the long-term recovery phase, FHEO has worked with communities to ensure future plans to affirmatively further fair housing.

80. National Environmental Policy Act of 1969, 42 U.S.C. §§ 4321–47 (2006).

81. *PD&R Disaster Recovery Tool Kit*, DEP'T OF HOUS. & URBAN DEV., http://www.huduser.org/portal/sandy.html (last visited Feb. 16, 2013).

82. Exec. Order No. 13,632, 77 Fed. Reg. 74,341 (Dec. 14, 2012) (establishing the Hurricane Sandy Rebuilding Task Force).

83. *Secretary Shaun Donovan,* U.S. DEP'T HOUS. AND URBAN DEV., http://portal.hud.gov/hudportal/HUD?src=/about/principal_staff/secretary_donovan (last visited April 9, 2013).

84. *Frequently Asked Questions (FAQs) Specific to Sandy*, DEP'T OF HOUS. & URBAN DEV., http://portal.hud.gov/hudportal/documents/huddoc?id=SandyQAs.pdf.

85. Pub. L. No. 113-2, approved Jan. 29, 2013.

86. *HUD's Local Office Directory*, DEP'T OF HOUS. & URBAN DEV., http://portal.hud.gov/hudportal/HUD?src=/localoffices (last visited Feb. 16, 2013).

CHAPTER 3

Beyond the Stafford Act: A Human Rights Approach to Disaster Policy

Eric Tars and Catherine Galitzine

Hurricane Katrina was one of the worst human rights and humanitarian disasters the United States has ever faced, and its immediate and lingering effects showed the inadequacy of our laws, policies, and practices to protect the rights of the most vulnerable in times of disaster. The international human rights system contains a wealth of standards, both general and specific to the rights of internally displaced victims of disasters. Standard-setting documents such as the United Nations' Guiding Principles on Internal Displacement, the Basic Principles and Guidelines on Development-Based Evictions and Displacement, and the Principles on Housing and Property Restitution for Refugees and Displaced Persons, as well as human rights treaties such as the International Covenant on Civil and Political Rights and the International Covenant on Economic, Social and Cultural Rights,[1] protect people's right to housing and other related rights in preparation for, during, and after displacement due to disaster. These rights include the right to adequate housing during displacement, the right to return and restitituion, and the right to participate in decisions about prevention and reconstruction policies. Beyond these documents, at the request of U.S. advocates, U.N. human rights monitors have visited the United States and assessed the government's response to Hurricane

Katrina according to human rights standards numerous times in recent years, making concrete and specific recommendations for policy improvements. Advocates and policymakers at the local and national levels are using these standards and recommendations successfully in addressing policy for housing and other services for victims of natural and human-made disasters.

I. Introduction

Following Hurricane Katrina, more than one million people were displaced from their homes in New Orleans and the Gulf Coast. Many said they felt like refugees in their own land. The media struggled with what to call them, eventually settling on the term "evacuees."[2] But under international law, these victims were a clearly defined group, internally displaced persons (IDPs), with clearly defined rights. The U.S. government in fact recognizes the United Nations Guiding Principles on Internal Displacement (the Guiding Principles) as the gold standard for addressing the rights of displaced victims of disasters abroad.[3] However, the government refused to adopt this terminology or apply the Guiding Principles domestically, although (or perhaps because) it would create far better assurances of basic rights of IDPs than those granted under the Robert T. Stafford Disaster Relief and Emergency Assistance Act (the Stafford Act), the primary federal law addressing disasters.[4] Whereas Hurricane Katrina victims were given one-way tickets out of hurricane-affected areas, the Guiding Principles guarantee the right of return. Whereas victims here were given inadequate accommodations in camps far from jobs and services, sometimes in formaldehyde-laced trailers, the Guiding Principles guarantee a right to adequate housing. And whereas victims here were denied the right to vote in New Orleans elections from their displaced locations,[5] the Guiding Principles guarantee victims the right to participate in the decisions affecting their recovery.

All these rights, and many more, should have been protected by the U.S. government as their obligations under the Guiding Principles and the treaties and other international law upon which the Guiding Principles are based. However, while an ever-growing number of advocates in the United States campaigned vigorously for application of the Guiding Principles and other basic human rights standards, many advocates, policymakers, and practitioners were, and are, unaware of these standards of international law that could be used to protect displaced people in future disasters.

This chapter is a step in changing that reality. It begins by explaining the general framework of international human rights law and its applicability in the United States. It continues with a discussion of international human rights of IDPs, in particular related to the right to housing, but also addressing other intersecting rights. It then takes an in-depth look at the post–Hurricane Katrina Gulf Coast and how advocates there worked with the tools and mechanisms of human rights law as part of their domestic advocacy on behalf of Hurricane Katrina's victims. It concludes with thoughts for further steps in deepening U.S. use of and adherence to human rights principles and law following (and in preparation for) natural and human-made disasters.

II. International Human Rights Law in the United States

International human rights law is useful to those dealing with disasters as an additional framework from which to think about the effects of disasters on housing. Recent polling indicates that three-quarters of Americans believe that adequate housing is a human right, and two-thirds believe that government programs need to be expanded to ensure this right.[6] International human rights law is a system of legal instruments that developed in response to the atrocities of World War II, which taught the international community that in addition to a system that mediated the interests of governments against one another, individuals must have a way of holding their own governments responsible for the protection of individuals' rights.[7]

The legal system that developed to protect human rights has a hierarchy of legal instruments, with treaties as the most important sources of binding law. It is often criticized for lacking an enforcement mechanism beyond international condemnation (often called "shame and blame"). However, proponents of the legal system argue that international enforcement is beside the point, and that treaty standards are best implemented by the domestic democratic legislative, regulatory, and judicial processes within each country.

While significant challenges exist to the use of international human rights law as a binding legal system, ever-growing numbers of advocates and policymakers in the United States have been turning to human rights in recent years. Courts and legislators have constructed a number of roadblocks for litigants attempting to sue for rights guaranteed by international treaties. Advocates have had success, however, in human rights standards as interpretive guidance in areas where domestic standards are vague, in order to shape a court's interpretation of domestic legislation to reflect the collective international wisdom about how to protect people in a particular situation. Recognizing the difficulty of arguing for binding human rights standards in domestic settings, some may choose to advocate for human rights standards using constitutional, statutory, and policy arguments that utilize the language of human rights standards without citing the international instrument or guidance from which the language comes. However executed, advocates and policymakers can use human rights standards and mechanisms to frame public debate, propose legislative solutions, and supplement litigation both in disaster preparedness and in the response to natural or human-made disasters.

A. Domestic Legal Effect of International Human Rights Law

The United States has signed and ratified three of the nine major international human rights treaties: the International Covenant on Civil and Political Rights (ICCPR), the Convention on the Elimination of All Forms of Racial Discrimination (CERD) and the Convention against Torture and Other Forms of Cruel, Inhuman, or Degrading Treatment or Punishment (CAT).[8] Once signed and ratified by the Senate, human rights treaties are the "supreme Law of the Land," binding on both state and federal courts.[9] However, the United States takes advantage of treaty law that allows a ratifying nation to attach reservations, understandings, or declarations (RUDs) to the treaty as it is ratified.[10] Because the United States attaches declarations to international human rights treaties that state that the treaties are not "self-executing," those treaties do not create an independent cause of action for enforcing the rights granted by the treaties in domestic courts, absent specific implementing legislation. This view of the obligations of human rights treaties makes it difficult for individual citizens to bring cases in state and federal court to defend their human rights, unless those rights are codified elsewhere in domestic law.

Other international human rights treaties have been signed by the president, but not ratified by the Senate. Treaties at this point have no binding domestic effect, though international law requires that a state that has signed a treaty not take any affirmative steps that contravene the object and purpose of the treaty.[11]

Some of these treaties, including the International Covenant on Economic, Social and Cultural Rights, codify human rights norms that are considered customary international law. Principles of customary international law require that some degree of human rights protections are required of all governments, regardless of ratification status.[12]

On the international stage, ratification of a treaty by the Senate means the United States is bound to adhere to the obligations in the treaty, and report periodically on its progress to the treaty bodies that oversee compliance. During the reporting cycle, the United States reports on the progress of compliance with treaty provisions, and nongovernmental organizations (NGOs) can submit "shadow reports" on issues related to the treaty that they believe should be part of the conversation.[13] The treaty-monitoring bodies issue "concluding observations" that can provide specific, authoritative guidance on how countries should be implementing the treaty's provisions, though the U.S. government takes the position that these observations are not binding.

In addition, the U.N. Human Rights Council, under a process called the Universal Periodic Review (UPR), reviews every country in the world every four years for its compliance with all relevant treaties and the Universal Declaration of Human Rights. Just as in the individual treaty reporting process, advocates can highlight issues of concern and press the council for specific language useful to their advocacy through the shadow report process, and can use the council's recommendations as a sort of jurisprudence on human rights.[14]

The Human Rights Council also appoints special rapporteurs who are individuals empowered to track the progress of human rights work, either in a thematic area, or in a geographic area. Special rapporteurs are experts in their area, and their visits can generate precise criticism and recommendations on a specific issue or geographic area. Advocates can draw attention to a particular situation covered by a special rapporteur's mandate, asking for the rapporteur's evaluation and recommendations. A special rapporteur's report can clarify what compliance with human rights instruments means in a unique situation. Though, again, the U.S. government does not consider the recommendations binding, both advocates and policymakers at the local, state, and national levels can look to them in addresing concerns. The specific use of all these processes as applied to the rights of disaster victims in the United States will be discussed in section IV.

B. Using International Human Rights Law in Domestic Courts

Though the U.S. Senate through its reservations has made it difficult to bring claims in domestic courts to defend human rights protections, the definitions and principles that make up human rights law can be informative and persuasive in litigation. Judges in both federal and state courts are turning more often to international standards and comparative practice of other countries to inform their decisions. Judges have relied on international law standards in their decisions, in some cases including statements about the importance of international law.[15]

In 1804, the Supreme Court found that "an act of Congress ought never to be construed to violate the law of nations if any other possible construction remains."[16] This includes those principles of customary international law to which the United States has not affirmatively signed on. This generally includes the protections of the Universal Declaration of Human Rights (UDHR), the first human rights document, signed by the United States in 1948, and the protections of the ICCPR and International Covenant on Economic, Social and Cultural Rights (ICESCR), the two earliest and broadest human rights instruments.[17]

This interpretive use of international law avoids the common criticism that using international law requires ceding sovereignty to the United Nations. Using treaties as interpretive guidance brings their standards into the judicial discourse without stepping outside the domestic statutory framework. As the Supreme Court said in *Roper v. Simmons*, "The opinion of the world community, while not controlling our outcome, does provide respected and significant confirmation for our own conclusions."[18] This principle allows advocates to argue that a state or federal housing law, for example, should be interpreted to give effect to the human right to housing as that right has been defined by the international instruments. Additionally, litigators can look to international standards to inform the crafting of remedies after winning a case or during settlement discussions.

C. Using International Human Rights Law in Policy Advocacy

The use of human rights language to shape policy in the United States is limited only by the imagination of those seeking to employ it. Numerous examples of changes to housing policy using human rights standards have been documented in the United States, even outside of the disaster context.[19] The substantive language regarding the protections of disaster victims specifically has also been developing quickly in recent years, driven by the Guiding Principles on Internal Displacement.[20] This and other documents articulate the substantive protections to which disaster victims are entitled, and can be used domestically at the federal, state, and local levels.

The next section covers the language of the human rights protections, and guidance from experts on how to ensure that displaced people can access housing, participation, health care, and other rights.

III. Using International Human Rights Law to Defend the Housing Rights of Internally Displaced Persons

The growing presence of internally displaced persons all over the world as the result of civil war, other conflicts, or disasters has meant a rapid development of the international human rights law that protects these people. In the United States, disaster victims must rely on the protections of the Stafford Act as the basis for disaster relief.[21] As shown in Section B, while serving as the primary legal infrastructure for disaster response by the federal government, the Stafford Act does not provide for a human rights–based approach to the major issues facing those displaced by disaster. The U.S. government and domestic advocates are in constant conversation with the international structures of human rights law, working to incorporate human rights standards into domestic policy at the national, state, and local levels. Standards for compliance, both general and specific to countries and situations are being constantly refined. The growing international jurisprudence on these human rights standards lays the foundation for specific guidance to domestic courts, agencies, and legislatures about how to amend or interpret domestic law to include the protections experience has taught us disaster victims need.

A. Introduction to Human Rights of Internally Displaced Persons

As stated by the U.N. Special Rapporteur on Adequate Housing (Housing Rapporteur) as a component of the right to an adequate standard of living:

> [n]atural disasters result in displacement, loss of housing and livelihood thereby impacting peoples' rights to adequate housing and its congruent rights. Recent natural disasters and their aftermath, have demonstrated the need to integrate human rights standards into prevention, relief and rehabilitation efforts. In many of these situations, concerns raised include discrimination, gender insensitivity, lack of participation, and corruption and delay in distribution of aid, compensation and reconstruction work.[22]

Treaties in force articulate numerous rights that are particularly important to, and at risk for, populations affected by disaster. These include the rights to adequate housing; freedom from discrimination; life; family; and civic participation; among others. Based on the rights present in the treaties, the U.N. Special Rapporteur on the Rights of Internally Displaced Persons has articulated specific principles for the treatment of people forced to flee their homes because of disasters or strife, but who do not cross international borders. Recognizing the vulnerability of these populations, many nations, including the United States, have agreed on a set of principles drawn from treaty law that speak to their particular needs.

1. History

In the early 1990s, following a rash of humanitarian emergency situations in Somalia, Sudan, and Iraq, among others, the international community recognized the need to expressly defend the human rights of a growing vulnerable population of people displaced from their homes but who had not crossed national borders.[23] The Commission on Human Rights and the General Assembly asked the U.N. Special Rapporteur on the Rights of Internally Displaced Persons to study the issues specific to this population and determine a framework for ensuring their rights. The resulting Guiding Principles, completed in 1998 by Dr. Francis Deng, provide a rights-based framework for disaster recovery.[24]

The Guiding Principles have been used to develop a number of responses to internal displacement worldwide, including *Addressing Internal Displacement: A Framework for National Responsibility,* a publication of the Brookings Institution that has been used by a number of national and international bodies as well as NGOs to develop policies that protect the rights of IDPs.[25]

The rights articulated in the Guiding Principles include the rights of people before, during, and after disaster-related displacement. They speak to a government's responsibility to prepare for disaster so as to minimize evacuation, (the right to be free from arbitrary displacement), the care of IDPs during the course of their displacement (rights to housing, life, liberty, and participation for those currently displaced), and ensuring the right and ability of those IDPs who choose to return to do so as soon as possible (the right of return and restitution). The Guiding Principles do not create new human rights specific to IDPs. They explain how responsible governments can ensure that the human rights of this population are realized despite the challenges of their displacement. The Guiding Principles rest on, and are consistent with, existing human rights norms embodied in the core human rights treaties and their supporting documents.

2. Definition

International law defines "internally displaced persons" as:

> [P]ersons or groups of persons who have been forced or obliged to flee or to leave their homes or places of habitual residence, in particular as a result of or in order to avoid the effects of armed conflict, situations of generalized violence, violations of human rights or natural or human-made disasters, and who have not crossed an internationally recognized [national] State border.[26]

This definition clearly encompasses those displaced due to natural and human-made disasters in the United States, from Hurricane Katrina to wildfires, tornadoes, earthquakes, or other smaller-scale disasters. Regardless of the cause of displacement, this population is particularly vulnerable to the loss of a number of human rights. When homes are destroyed, people's access to medical care, food, water, and sanitation may be disrupted. People may be forced to relocate away from their families and local communities. This relocation can make it difficult for people to exercise their civil and political rights to participation in local government and decision making. Under international human rights standards, governments have a duty to mitigate these difficulties and restore an affected population's access to realization of their human rights to the best of its ability, and, importantly, in a nondiscriminatory manner. Unlike the legal status of a refugee, an internally displaced person does not possess specific rights not granted to other people. It simply presents challenges to governments in guaranteeing those rights that are universal.

3. *Status in the United States*

The Guiding Principles are recognized by and incorporated into the work of the U.S. Agency for International Development (USAID) outside the United States.[27] USAID states that it "supports the goals of these principles, and will encourage its partners and host governments to use them as a practical reference."[28] However, it also notes that "[a]lthough the United States does not accept the U.N. Guiding Principles as an expression of governing international law, it recognizes the valuable practical role the principles can play in the protection of IDPs."[29] Though the United States has repeatedly affirmed the usefulness of the Guiding Principles in situations of strife and disasters abroad, the federal government has not applied the Guiding Principles to its policies or practices in addressing domestic disasters.

B. General Principles

There are some general principles that apply to human rights law that sets it apart from a domestic legal system. Human rights are considered universal, inalienable, interdependent, and indivisible. Many of the rights articulated by the international community are enabling rights, meaning they facilitate the achievement of other rights. The most important general principles in distinguishing a human rights approach to the rights of disaster victims are the concepts of national responsibility and nondiscrimination. International human rights law places the responsibility to respect (codify the right), protect (against third parties), and fulfill or make manifest an individual's right with the national government. This concept runs counter to a libertarian view of the role of the federal government but is necessary for the protection of people who have been cut off from their local structures of protection by disaster.

1. *National Responsibility*

Under the Guiding Principles, "[n]ational authorities have the primary duty and repsonsibility to provide protection and humanitarian assistance."[30] This is an important distinction for their applicability in the United States, as many domestic IDPs may cross state lines in the course of their displacement. The Stafford Act leaves primary responsibility for disaster prevention and the care of displaced people to the states. Following Hurricane Katrina, this policy left IDPs in widely varying situations of displacement depending on where they found themselves displaced.

In a federal system, this language has been interpreted to require that the government take proactive measures that are necessary to prepare for displacement and care for the victims, identifying the responsible parties and ensuring they are fit to the task.[31] Even if their responsibility extends only to expressly delegating responsibility, the national government must be ultimately accountable for the care of those within its borders. Hurricane Katrina demonstrated the inadequacy of our current system, in which many obligations fell through the cracks as federal, state, and local agencies argued about which of them should be responsible for specific assistance and, in some cases, even worked at counter purposes. For example, even as FEMA recertified occupants for extensions of subsidized trailers placed on their own land, local governments passed zoning ordinances prohibiting the siting of trailers anywhere in the community, leading to the eviction of the residents; neither government assumed responsibility for providing housing following the evictions, leading victims into homelessness.[32]

As Hurricane Katrina has taught us, internal displacement may last much longer than the immediate effects of a disaster. The responsibility for IDPs, therefore, needs an independent institutional focal point within the government to address both long-term planning and emergency coordination needs. Some countries have established a ministry-level position dedicated to this population (Colombia, Georgia, Iraq, Yemen) while other countries have established a position within their disaster agency (Afghanistan, Pakistan, Turkey).[33]

The Guiding Principles specify that the national government has, at minimum, the following responsibilities:

- "The primary duty and responsibility to provide protection and humanitarian assistance to internally displaced persons within their jurisdiction."[34]
- Ensure displacement lasts no longer than necessary.[35]
- Prioritize IDP participation in planning and management of resettlement and reintegration plans.[36]
- Help IDPs recover their property or provide restitution for damaged property.[37]
- Ensure protections in a nondiscriminatory manner, in accordance with international standards recognizing disparate impact, as well as intentional discrimination.[38]

As will be discussed in further depth in section IV, the contrast of the requirements of the Guiding Principles with the experience of the victims of Hurricane Katrina shows just how valuable institutionalizing the Guiding Principles as the framework for disaster relief in the United States would be. The chart on the next page, prepared by the

Advocates for Environmental Human Rights, compares the Guiding Principles with the existing federal law addressing disaster relief, the Robert T. Stafford Act.

Issue	Robert T. Stafford Disaster Relief and Emergency Assistance Act	United Nations' Guiding Principles on Internal Displacement
Should the federal government have primary responsibility for disaster recovery?	**No.** States have primary responsibility for disaster recovery (42 U.S.C. § 5191). The federal government's responsibility is limited to matters under exclusive federal control as established by the U.S. Constitution or federal law (42 U.S.C. § 5191(b)). All other federal responses to a disaster are discretionary acts that are completely immune from lawsuits (42 U.S.C. § 5148).	**Yes.** National governments have the primary duty to provide relief to displaced people and establish the conditions that allow the safe return and reintegration of displaced people (Principle 3, 28).
Should the federal government be required to take precautions that can prevent displacement?	**No.** The federal government has the discretion to assist in the development of state mitigation plans and emergency preparedness programs (42 U.S.C. § 5165). The federal government also has the discretion to warn the public of hazards and reduce immediate threats to life, property, public safety, and health (42 U.S.C. § 5170b).	**Yes.** It is the obligation of national governments to prevent the conditions that can cause displacement (Principle 5).

Issue	Robert T. Stafford Disaster Relief and Emergency Assistance Act	United Nations' Guiding Principles on Internal Displacement
Should people who have been displaced by a disaster have a right to humanitarian assistance and assistance to either return to their residences or resettle?	**No.** Individuals do not have a legal right to assistance, and the federal government is immune from lawsuit for its actions or inactions under the act. The federal government is not even required to provide essential assistance, which includes emergency medical care, shelter, clearing roads and bridges, demolition of unsafe buildings, dissemination of health and safety information, and reduction of immediate life-threatening risks (42 U.S.C. § 5170b).	**Yes.** People displaced by a disaster are entitled to relief under the principles (Principle 2). All displaced people have the right to request and receive protection and humanitarian assistance from governmental authorities (Principle 3). National governments have the primary duty and responsibility to provide humanitarian assistance, as well as the means for displaced people to return, resettle, and/or reintegrate (Principles 24–30).
Should the federal government be required to ensure that displaced people can meaningfully participate in governmental decisions affecting recovery?	**No.** The act does not require or address voting or civic participation; nor does the act require or address participation of displaced people in recovery planning and management.	**Yes.** Displaced people have the right to vote and participate in governmental and public affairs (Principle 22). National governments have the obligation to make special efforts to ensure the full participation of displaced people in planning and management of return, resettlement, and reintegration (Principle 28). ***continued***

Issue	Robert T. Stafford Disaster Relief and Emergency Assistance Act	United Nations' Guiding Principles on Internal Displacement
Should displaced people be protected from governmental actions that result in discriminatory impacts?	**No.** Although the federal government is prohibited from discriminating on the basis of race, color, nationality (42 U.S.C. § 5151), disability, or English-language proficiency (Katrina Reform Act § 689(a)), courts have limited this obligation to only prohibit an intentional act of discrimination, not an act that results in a discriminatory impact.	**Yes.** Displaced people have a right to governmental assistance and protection that does not intentionally discriminate or result in a discriminatory impact based on race, color, nationality, sex, age, economic status, disability, political opinion, ethnic or social origin, disability, property, or birth status (Principles 4, 18, 24).
Should displaced people have the right to housing, education, and healthcare?	**No.** Any housing assistance is provided at the discretion of the federal government (42 U.S.C. § 5174(b)). Temporary housing assistance cannot exceed a period of 18 months (42 U.S.C. § 5174I). Temporary educational facilities can be provided at the discretion of the federal government (42 U.S.C. § 5170b.a.3.D.). Emergency medical care and reduction of immediate threats to life and health can be provided at the discretion of the federal government (42 U.S.C. § 5170b.a.3.D). The rebuilding of medical facilities is also discretionary (42 U.S.C. § 5172).	**Yes.** Displaced people have the right to: • housing that requires governments to provide temporary housing for the duration of the displacement and support for the rebuilding of permanent homes (Principle 17); • education that requires governments to make education and training facilities available as soon as conditions permit (Principle 23); and • medical services, including psychological and social services (Principles 7, 18, 19).

Chart care of Advocates for Environmental Human Rights, available at http://www.ehumanrights.org/ourwork_residents_USDRLvHRS.html.

In order to implement the Guiding Principles, the agencies and actors responsible for preparedness and recovery plans may need to be trained on the Guiding Principles and successful implementation of them in other countries. Many countries with IDP populations, including Central African Republic, Colombia, the Democratic Republic of the Congo, Georgia, Iraq, Kenya, Nepal, Sudan, Turkey, Uganda, and Yemen, have conducted trainings with government personnel, led by U.N. experts and international NGOs on the needs of IDPs, giving officials a broad understanding of the special vulnerabilities of this population.[39]

2. Nondiscrimination

Following a disaster, it may be more difficult for poor citizens to access their rights than those with more resources. Because economic factors are closely tied to gender and racial disparities in the United States, evacuation and reconstruction plans may have a disparate impact on communities of color and on women and families. A human rights framework is particularly important in this context, because international treaties recognize the de facto discrimination of plans that favor the economically advantaged, including those that own their own forms of transportation and their own homes. Because domestic equal protection jurisprudence often requires proof of a specific discriminatory intent beyond disparate impact, and because economic factors are so closely tied to racial and gender disparities, international anti-discrimination language is vital to address facially neutral discriminatory policies.

In the Guiding Principles, IDPs are protected from discrimination based on their displacement, as well as discrimination among IDPs based on other arbitrary characteristics. The Guiding Principles specify that they be applied to internally displaced people "without discrimination of any kind, such as race, color, sex, language, religion or belief, political or other opinion, national, ethnic or social origin, legal or social status, age, disability, property, birth or any other similar criteria," a comprehensive list, and broader than our own federally recognized protected classes.[40] This requirement tracks the definitions in other international human rights instruments, including the ICCPR, UDHR, ICERD, Convention on the Elimination of All Forms of Descrimination against Women (CEDAW), ICESCR, and Convention on the Rights of the Child (CRC). Human rights law does not consider equitable treatment to be the same as equal treatment, therefore requiring that special protections be granted to populations that need them.

a. Racial Discrimination

The Guiding Principles' prohibition on discrimination references the requirements of the International Covenant on the Elimination of All Forms of Racial Discrimination (ICERD), which requires that "[e]ach State Party shall take effective measures to review governmental, national and local policies, and to amend, rescind or nullify any laws and regulations which have the effect of creating or perpetuating racial discrimination wherever it exists."[41]

The ICERD definition references discriminatory effect, focusing on the practical consequences of even facially neutral policies. This means that U.S. disaster and recovery policies that have a discriminatory effect should be reevaluated. For example, the evacuation plan in New Orleans relied in large part on people evacuating in personal cars, leaving mostly low-income people of color without a means of evacuation. Under international human rights law, this policy would be considered discriminatory on the basis of race and the basis of property.

b. *Gender Discrimination*

The Guiding Principles make special mention of the role of women in multiple contexts:

> "Certain internally displaced persons, such as children . . . expectant mothers, mothers with young children, female heads of household, . . . shall be entitled to protection and assistance required by their condition and to treatment which takes into account their special needs."[42]
>
> "Special efforts should be made to ensure the full participation of women in the planning and distribution of [food, potable water, basic shelter, clothing, medical services, and sanitation]."[43]
>
> "Women and men shall have equal rights to obtain such necessary documents [for the exercise of their legal rights] and shall have the right to have such documentation issued in their own names."[44]
>
> "Special efforts should be made to ensure the full and equal participation of women and girls in educational programmes."[45]

These principles track the requirements of the CEDAW, which requires state parties to take affirmative steps to increase the role of women in public discourse and decision making, and to undertake measures that equalize the historic power imbalance between women and men.

In disaster planning and relief, this requires that plans take into account the situation of woman-headed households during displacement and women's role in the planning and distribution of aid.

c. *Disability Discrimination*

Because the Guiding Principles require assistance to displaced people that is commensurate with their special needs, a government is required to create disaster-preparedness plans and recovery missions that take into account the needs of people with all forms of disability.

The Convention on the Rights of Persons with Disabilities reqiures that "States Parties shall take . . . all necessary measures to ensure the protection and safety of persons with disabilities in situations of risk, including . . . the occurrence of natural disaster."[46] Protection of IDPs with a disability requires that evacuation, as well as housing during displacement, be appropriate to the specific challenges of a disability.

3. *Indivisibility of Human Rights*

The principle of the indivisibility of human rights means that a government cannot choose which human rights it chooses to fulfill. Human rights instruments are meant to be implemented with an understanding that rights depend on each other for full realization. The human right to participation in government, for example, is dependent on a person's right to life, health, and education. As a result, all the content of the underlying rights that people maintain after a disaster are a part of the rights of internally displaced people.

C. Rights in Planning for Displacement

Prevention is the most important step a state can take in protecting (potentially) internally displaced people, but requires a preliminary dedication of resources that is difficult in the absence of a recent or pending disaster. Turkey, Myanmar, Sri Lanka, and Pakistan, among others, have adopted legislation to prepare for natural disasters and provide services to the inevitable displaced populations.[47] International guidance suggests these measures should be focused on keeping people in or near their homes, leaving only in conditions that endanger health or safety, because displacement has far-reaching consequences and a tendency to prolong itself.

Though scholars agree that emergency preparedness is the most effective way to prevent displacement, national governments have been slow to adopt the preventive framework. Development organizations, on the other hand, have prioritized prevention of displacement in areas made vulnerable by climate change.[48] Because preparedness is harder to implement and harder to document than the humanitarian assistance that follows a disaster, the effectiveness of the Guiding Principles on the lives of displaced people has only been studied in the context of a post-displacement response. As explained in Section IV, NGOs have started to incorporate the Guiding Principles into their relief efforts with promising results.

The Guiding Principles prioritize the prevention of displacement and the quick and voluntary return of displaced people to their homes.

> All authorities and international actors shall respect and ensure respect for their obligations under international law, including human rights and humanitarian law, in all circumstances, so as to prevent and avoid conditions that might lead to displacement of persons. . . . (1.) Every human being shall have the right to be protected against being arbitrarily displaced from his or her home or place of habitual residence. (2.) The prohibition of arbitrary displacement includes displacement . . . [i]n cases of disasters, unless the safety and health of those affected requires their evacuation (3.) Displacement shall last no longer than required by the circumstances.[49]

In the case of natural or human-made disasters, displacement is considered arbitrary if it is undertaken for any reason other than the safety or health of the residents.[50]

Compliance with the Guiding Principles require that a government consider the prevention of displacement in disaster planning and prepare for disasters in order to shorten the length of time people are displaced from their homes in the event of a disaster. This principle is a specific application of the right contained in article 12 of the ICCPR, the right to choose one's residence, and the implicit right to remain there barring necessary displacement. The Housing Rapporteur has pointed out that the right to "habitable" housing implies requirements of habitability that takes into account the likelihood of natural disasters, such as earthquakes.[51]

The Guiding Principles also state that the government has a particular responsibility to prevent displacement of indigenous people and other groups with a special dependency on and attachment to their lands.[52] International Labor Organization Convention No. 169 also specifies that "[indigenous] peoples shall have the right to return to their traditional lands, as soon as the ground for relocation cease to exist" or, when this is not possible, to be provided "with lands of quality and legal status at least equal" to their pre-displacement lands.[53] The U.N. Declaration on the Rights of Indigenous Peoples, recently endorsed by the United States, similarly maintains that "States shall provide effective mechanisms for the prevention of, and redress for, . . . any action which has the aim or effect of dispossessing them of their lands, territories or resources . . ." and "[i]ndigenous peoples shall not be forcibly removed from their lands or territories. No relocation shall take place without the free, prior and informed consent of the indigenous peoples concerned and after agreement on just and fair compensation and, where possible, with the option of return."[54]

D. Rights during Displacement

As the U.N. General Assembly stated in 1993, "[a]ll human rights are universal, indivisible and interdependent and interrelated."[55] The failure of a government to protect any human right for IDPs may infringe on a number of other human rights. Lack of housing may prevent people in the United States from participating in civic and political life, and is closely linked to poor health outcomes. The Guiding Principles remind us that life, health, family, and shelter are all essential during displacement.

When Typhoon Durian in the Philippines caused massive landslides and volcanic ash that covered the provincial capital of Legazpi, the government relocated approximately 55,000 people into transitional sites when their homes and communities were destroyed.[56] The original relocation plan housed the displaced in substandard housing where concerns about hunger and disease were rampant. International NGOs led by Oxfam GB determined that the substandard conditions were due to a lack of coordination and resources rather than ill will or corruption, and sought to test the effectiveness of the Guiding Principles as a tool for organization and advocacy. The NGOs trained private-sector, government, and community leaders and IDPs themselves on their rights and strategies. These trainings focused the assistance on tangible goals (a toilet per 20 people for example) and gave IDPs, their government, and the organizations providing assistance a set of priorities they could all agree on. As the plans moved forward, government officials recognized that distributing the Guiding Principles and formulating a plan based on them prevented unrest among the IDPs, who could measure improvement by a concrete set of human rights standards everyone agreed on.[57]

In areas where prolonged conflict has led to a continuing IDP crisis, the Guiding Principles and a human rights approach have been used successfully to assess and improve the housing rights of long-term displaced people.

In Georgia, widespread displacement that began during the outbreak of conflict in South Ossetia (also known as Tskhinvali) and Abkhazia in the early 1990s, and exacerbated by further conflict in the same regions in 2008, has forced the country to develop formalized national procedures for ensuring the human rights of internally displaced people.[58] This displacement crisis developed contemporaneously with the development of international standards for internally displaced people.

Though financial assistance and housing accommodations were provided by the national government (and supplemented by the Abkhaz government in exile) from the start of displacement in the early 1990s, the application of the Guiding Principles as they were developed in the following years crystallized a national plan and shifted the government's focus in dealing with the issues unique to IDPs. Following a mission to Georgia by the U.N. representative for IDPs in 1996, the government adopted a formal comprehensive national strategy for addressing internal displacement, as recommended by the visiting representative.[59] A government commission was established, and government ministers sat in working groups with NGO leaders to address a variety of issues faced by IDPs. Recommendations of working groups led to the adoption of the State Strategy for Internally Displaced Persons—Persecuted. The strategy was brought in line with the Guiding Principles, and was adopted into law in February 2007. Once adopted, the strategy led to concrete gains in Georgian legislation and the court system, including the right to vote in local and parliamentary elections and the right to purchase property without losing IDP status.[60]

1. Housing

Internally displaced people retain their human right to housing during the period of their displacement. The Guiding Principles require the following:

> Regardless of the circumstances, and without discrimination, competent authorities shall provide internally displaced persons with and ensure safe access to . . . basic shelter and housing.[61]
>
> Every internally displaced person has the right to liberty of movement and freedom to choose his or her residence.[62]

The Guiding Principles require that IDPs be able to choose their location during their displacement and that human rights protections during displacement cannot be dependent on their willingness to live in camps or settlements.

When the Guiding Principles refer to the right to housing, it is reflective of a body of human rights law that began with the Universal Declaration of Human Rights and is defined in several key documents.

The UDHR is the first major international agreement on human rights. Although it is not a treaty, it is considered to have been the inspiration to all subsequent human rights treaties. Many scholars consider it binding customary international law. Adopted and proclaimed by the General Assembly on December 10, 1948, article 25(1) of the UDHR provides the first human rights standard to recognize housing rights, enshrining a specific right for everyone to adequate housing:

> Everyone has the right to a standard living adequate for the health and well-being of himself [or herself] and of his [or her] family, including food, clothing, housing and medical care and necessary social services, and the right to security in the event of unemployment, sickness, disability, widowhood, old age or other lack of livelihood in circumstances beyond his [or her] control.[63]

The ICESCR recognizes "the right of everyone to an adequate standard of living for himself and his family, including adequate food, clothing, and housing, and to the continuous improvement of living conditions."[64] As a binding treaty, the ICESCR is the most legally significant universal codification provision recognizing this right. Of all international legal sources of housing rights, it has been subject to the greatest analysis, application, and interpretation. The ICESCR recognizes the right to housing within the larger right to an adequate standard of living; however, international human rights law generally has developed the right to adequate housing as an independent or freestanding right, while also recognizing its interdependence with other rights.

Treaty bodies that oversee implementation of the treaties routinely issue guidance, known as "General Comments" as to definitions of key terms in the treaties, and guidance for implementation. The General Comments of treaty bodies are similar to domestic regulations, in that they provide more specific guidance and procedures for compliance with the legal standards set out in the treaty.

The Committee on Economic, Social and Cultural Rights, which oversees the ICESCR, defines the right to adequate housing in its General Comment 4 as consisting of seven core components: (1) legal security of tenure, (2) availability of services and infrastructure, (3) affordability, (4) habitability, (5) accessibility, (6) location, and (7) cultural adequacy.[65] Implementation of these rights may require the expenditure of resources and, under the human rights framework, the obligation on states (or countries) is to realize the implementation of the right progressively.[66]

The Guiding Principles require that during displacement the government work to ensure all seven aspects of the right to adequate housing for internally displaced people, despite the possibly temporary nature of the displacement. This means that the government should ensure that even temporary housing for IDPs be safe, affordable, habitable, and located to facilitate other human rights, such as civic participation, employment, and education.

The ICCPR, ratified by the United States, while focused on civil and political rights, guarantees several rights relevant to ensuring the right to adequate housing. The following are some guarantees of the ICCPR:

- nondiscrimination based on a wide range of characteristics including race, color, sex, language, religion, political or other opinion, national or social origin, property, birth, or other status[67]
- equal access to rights for men and women[68]
- the inherent right to life[69]
- protection from torture and cruel, inhuman or degrading treatment[70]
- equality before the law and protection against discrimination on any ground such as race, color, sex, language, religion, political or other opinion, national or social origin, property, birth, or other status[71]

Read together, these interrelated articles of the treaty mean that all rights must be ensured on an equal basis, prohibiting discrimination in more forms than are recognized by domestic jurisprudence.

Various U.N. bodies have established advisory groups on areas of particular interest. UN-HABITAT, the United Nations Human Settlements Program, for example, created the Advisory Group on Forced Evictions (AGFE) in 2004. AGFE reports on forced evictions around the world with the goal of advancing security of tenure as a part of the human right to housing. As discussed in Section IV below, the AGFE conducted a visit to New Orleans in 2009 to assess the housing situation in New Orleans and determine how to avoid future forcible evictions in cases of disaster. AGFE issued recommendations focused on ending forced evictions in policy or practice.[72] The findings of the group have been used by a number of housing advocates to draw attention to the failures of housing policy in New Orleans.[73]

2. *Life and Health*

The Guiding Principles specify, "Every human being has the inherent right to life, which shall be protected by law."[74] This right is closely related to the right to an adequate standard of living, cited above, that includes food and water, shelter or housing, clothing, and medical services.[75] Including all these in the right to an adequate standard of living reflects the understanding in human rights law that these four elements are basic necessities for the realization of all human rights including the right to life. These rights reflect similar articulations in the UDHR and ICCPR, as well as the Geneva Conventions in humanitarian law.[76]

3. *Family*

According to the Guiding Principles:

> Every human being has the right to respect of his or her family life . . . family members who wish to remain together should be allowed to do so. Families which are separated by displacement should be reunited as quickly as possible. All appropriate steps shall be taken to expedite the reunion of such families, particularly when children are involved. The responsible authorities shall facilitate inquiries made by family members and encourage and

> cooperate with the work of humanitarian organizations engaged in the task of family reunification.[77]
>
> All internally displaced persons have the right to know the fate and whereabouts of missing relatives.[78]

These requirements in the Guiding Principles reflect Geneva Convention laws regarding wartime responsibilities of a government, as well as Council of Europe recommendations that protection of family life includes a government's obligation to facilitate the reunification of families separated by internal displacement.[79]

"Family" as used in human rights law has no universal definition and, according to the Human Rights Committee, should "be given a broad interpretation to include all those comprising the family as understood in the society of the state party concerned."[80] The right to government assistance in family reunification is drawn from humanitarian law and the requirement that governments attempt to reunite families following armed conflicts.[81]

4. Participation

During displacement, IDPs maintain the right to participate in government. The Guiding Principles state:

> Every human being has the right to recognition everywhere as a person before the law. To give effect to this right for internally displaced persons, the authorities concerned shall issue to them all documents necessary for the enjoyment and exercise of their legal rights, such as passports, personal identification documents, birth certificates and marriage certificates. In particular, the authorities shall facilitate the issuance of new documents or the replacement of documents lost in the course of displacement, without unreasonable conditions.[82]

> Internally displaced persons, whether or not they are living in camps shall not be discriminated against as a result of their displacement in the enjoyment of the following rights. . . . (c) the right to associate freely and participate equally in community affairs; (d) the right to vote and to participate in governmental and public affairs, including the right to have access to the means necessary to exercise this right.[83]

In order to effect this right, some countries with protracted displacement have systems of data collection or registration that allows governments and NGOs to facilitate access to participation. This kind of data collection can be essential to ensuring even short-term displaced persons have access. In Iraq, displaced persons can sign up to vote in their home district from anywhere in the country they find themselves displaced.[84] This kind of protection would require domestic legislation, but may be a significant protection for the interests of internally displaced people.

The right to participation in community and government tracks the requirements of the ICCPR that "[e]very citizen shall have the right and the opportunity, without unreasonable restrictions: (a) To take part in the conduct of public affairs, directly or through freely chosen representatives; (b) To vote and to be elected at genuine periodic elections which shall be by universal and equal suffrage."[85] In cases of displacement, IDPs have the right to participate in the civic life of the community in which they are displaced, as well as the right to have a voice in the development of the community from which they are temporarily displaced.

The Inter-Agency Standing Committee is a body that coordinates humanitarian relief in situations of disaster and conflict. Recognizing that implementing human rights norms facilitates the delivery of humanitarian relief, they created operational guidelines to protect victims of disaster. Because the effective delivery of humanitarian aid is dependent on the participation of those in need, the guidelines stress the importance of participation:

> Affected persons should be informed and consulted on measures taken on their behalf and given the opportunity to take charge of their own affairs to the maximum extent and as early as possible. They should be able to participate in the planning and implementation of the various stages of the disaster response. Targeted measures should be taken to include those who are traditionally marginalized from participating in decision-making.[86]

E. Rights after Displacement

The human rights protections guaranteed by the Guiding Principles do not end with the period of displacement.

> Competent authorities have the primary duty and responsibility to establish conditions, as well as provide the means, which allow internally displaced persons to return voluntarily in safety and with dignity, to their homes or places of habitual residence, or to resettle voluntarily in another part of the country. Such authorities shall endeavour to facilitate the reintegration of returned or resettled internally displaced persons. . . . Special efforts should be made to ensure the full participation of internally displaced persons in the planning and management of their return or resettlement and reintegration.[87]

This principle was distilled into a separate international human rights document by Special Rapporteur on Housing and Property Restitution Paulo Sergio Pinheiro in 2002.[88] Sergio Pinheiro's recommendations have been accepted by the CERD, and are generally refered to as the Pinheiro Principles.

The Pinheiro Principles state that internally displaced people have a right to government assistance in getting back property and possessions lost in displacement or to restitution for lost property and possessions. The Pinheiro Principles clarify the rights available to IDPs returning home. These, like all human rights obligations, must be fulfilled in a nondiscriminatory manner and include the following:

- The right to have restored to them any housing, land or property of which they were arbitrarily or unlawfully deprived, or to be compensated for any housing, land or property that is factually impossible to restore as determined by an independent, impartial tribunal.[89]
- The right to return voluntarily to their former homes, lands, or places of habitual residence, in safety and dignity. Voluntary return in safety and dignity must be based on a free, informed, individual choice. Refugees and displaced persons should be provided with complete, objective, up-to-date, and accurate information, including on physical, material, and legal safety issues in countries or places of origin.[90]
- States should adopt positive measures aimed at alleviating the situation of refugees and displaced persons living in inadequate housing.[91]

Another complementary set of standards that apply in both disaster and non-disaster contexts are the Basic Principles and Guidelines on Development-Based Evictions and Displacement (Basic Guidelines), developed by the Housing Rapporteur in 2007. These can be used as a human rights response to intervening development in areas affected by disasters or strife that prevents IDPs from returning to their homes or places of habitual residence.[92] In the United States, many advocates worried that decision makers in New Orleans prioritized development over the human rights to return and restitution, destroying low-income housing in favor of new development projects that would price the IDPs out of returning to New Orleans. The Basic Guidelines take a human rights perspective and require recognition of the residents of an area even when those residents are temporarily displaced.

- The guidelines reiterate the human right to housing, including the security of tenure articulated in General Comment 4.[93]
- States must recognize that the prohibition of forced evictions includes arbitrary displacement that results in altering the ethnic, religious, or racial composition of the affected population.[94]
- States should take preventive measures to avoid underlying causes of forced evictions, review housing and tenancy markets, and intervene to ensure that market forces do not increase the vulnurability of low-income and other marginalized groups.[95]
- Priority in housing and land should be ensured to disadvantaged groups such as the elderly, children, and persons with disabilities.[96]
- During planning processes, opportunity for dialogue and consultation must be extended to vulnurable and marginalized groups.[97]
- Special efforts should be made to ensure equal participation of women in all planning processes.[98]
- The state must ensure fair and just compensation for any losses, and return and restitution should be prioritized.[99]

The next section discusses some ways in which those fighting for the rights of the IDPs displaced by Hurricane Katrina sought to use these standards as tools in their advocacy.

IV. Case Study: Using Human Rights Standards and Processes to Advance Housing Rights of Internally Displaced People in Post–Katrina New Orleans

After Hurricane Katrina, many Gulf Coast residents were evicted, relocated, and excluded from the decision-making processes in contravention of their human rights. In response, local and national advocates used international instruments to reframe domestic policy failures as human rights violations and utilized human rights reporting processes and visits of human rights monitors to advance specific standards applicable to the concerns of displaced people in the Gulf Coast and promote a rights-based approach to recovery. This section will discuss both those standards and the advocacy used to create them, as both contain potential utility for advocates dealing with future disasters.

This advocacy began immediately after the hurricane, as advocates tapped into the coordinated work around the upcoming 2006 review of the United States' compliance with the ICCPR to raise the human rights violations of IDPs and work for the recognition of the Guiding Principles as the framework for recovery. This advocacy was repeated during the ICERD review process in 2008, and then enhanced by bringing human rights fact-finding monitors to the Gulf Coast through visits by the Special Rapporteurs on Racism and the Right to Adequate Housing and the AGFE. Each of these visits produced detailed reports condemning specific violations and making specific recommendations for reform reflective of advocates' demands. Advocates then, in 2010, used the opportunities for domestic and international advocacy during the Universal Periodic Review (UPR), the most comprehensive nation-specific human rights review to revisit these previous recommendations and continue pressing for recognition of the violations and the human rights standards applicable to their continuing recovery.

Each time U.S. policies regarding IDPs in the Gulf Coast were presented to the international community, experts found them inadequate to preserve human rights. Domestic advocates can and are using the reports, recommendations, and observations of these experts in shifting the conversation about housing into a rights-based framework and publicizing the gulf that exists between current policies and what is possible when the government prioritizes human rights.

A. Engaging with the Human Rights System: Advocacy with the Human Rights Committee, 2005–2006

As noted above, under each treaty the United States has ratified, it is obligated to make periodic reports to the treaty oversight body on its implementation of the rights in the treaty. Three months after Hurricane Katrina, the United States filed its report on compliance with the ICCPR with the Human Rights Committee (HRC). Despite coming on the heels of arguably one of the biggest human rights and humanitarian disasters in our country's history, the report stunningly made no reference to the human rights situation in the Gulf Coast.[100] National and Gulf Coast activists used this interaction with the international human rights system to begin a concerted effort to develop a body of law and commentary with international human rights bodies for domestic use in response to the housing situation in the United States, including the plight of IDPs displaced by Hurricane Katrina.

Following the government's submission of its report to the HRC, the U.S. Human Rights Network, in conjunction with Advocates for Environmental Human Rights (AEHR), based in New Orleans, hosted a training on human rights for advocates in the Gulf Coast. Local groups then worked with national ones to coordinate a "shadow report" in response to the U.S. government's inadequate report.[101] In their shadow report, advocates presented their concerns about pre– and post–Hurricane Katrina violations and suggested language for the HRC to use in condemning and recommending remedies for those violations.

After the submission of shadow reports, advocates met with the members of the HRC during sessions in New York City in March 2006 and Geneva, Switzerland, in July 2006. The testimony of directly affected victims of Hurricane Katrina made an impact on the committee, and created a sense of empowerment in the victims. As a result, the committee questioned the U.S. government extensively on Hurricane Katrina violations. Although the ICCPR does not address housing rights specifically, it does guarantee the right to life,[102] the right to family,[103] the right to education,[104] the right to vote,[105] and the right to be free from discrimination based on property status, gender, and race.[106] The concluding observations of the committee reflected the concerns of the community:

> The Committee . . .remains concerned about information that the poor, and in particular African-Americans, were disadvantaged by the rescue and evacuation plans implemented when Hurricane Katrina hit the United States, and continue to be disadvantaged under the reconstruction plans.
>
> The State party should review its practices and policies to ensure the full implementation of its obligation to protect life and of the prohibition of discrimination, whether direct or indirect, as well as of the United Nations Guiding Principles on Internal Displacement, in matters related to disaster prevention and preparedness, emergency assistance and relief measures. In the aftermath of Hurricane Katrina, the State party should increase its efforts to ensure that the rights of the poor, and in particular African-Americans, are fully taken into consideration in the reconstruction plans with regard to access to housing, education and healthcare.[107]

To bring public attention to the concluding observations, AEHR organized a press conference in the Gert Town neighborhood of New Orleans, in front of a home that had collapsed and remained in the street 10 months after the hurricane. The U.S. Army Corps of Engineers heard of the press conference plans and directed a work crew stationed in the Lower Ninth Ward to travel across the city and remove the collapsed home before the conference. However, the news reporters and cameras were set up just before the work crew arrived. When a Gert Town resident was asked by a news reporter if the HRC's concluding observations would make any difference, the resident pointed to the work crew hovering as proof that the committee's report has been able to achieve what letters and phone calls to FEMA, the Army Corps of Engineers, and the mayor could not.[108]

Thus, although the observations are not binding judicial decrees, they are designed to be disseminated to the appropriate government branches to be incorporated into domestic democratic processes. While the U.S. government did not widely publicize the committee's observations, advocates were able to attract signficant local and national media attention to the observations and the deficiencies in the reconstruction plans, with some very concrete effects. AEHR and other advocates also held follow-up meetings with FEMA representatives, as well as state and local government officials to work to realize the recommendations. Additionally, by obtaining specific reference to the Guiding Principles in the treaty body's observations, advocates were able to elevate these nonbinding principles within the context of a legally binding treaty, an important point for the potential use of the Guiding Principles in future legal advocacy.

B. Building Momentum and Empowering Victims on an International Stage: Working with the Committee on Elimination of Racial Discrimination, 2007–2008

Two years after its ICCPR report to the Human Rights Committee, the United States presented a similar report to the Committee on the Elimination of Racial Discrimination in compliance with its obligation as a signatory to the ICERD. This report made brief reference to, and simultaneously dismissed the concerns of, advocates that responses to Hurricanes Katrina and Rita reflected and reinforced a disparate racial impact in housing. The sole reference in the official U.S. report begins:

> Concern has been expressed about the disparate effects of Hurricane Katrina on housing for minority residents of New Orleans. Recognizing the overlap between race and poverty in the United States, many commentators conclude nonetheless that the post-Katrina issues were the result of poverty (i.e. the inability of many of the poor to evacuate) rather than racial discrimination *per se*.[109]

This paragraph ignores the definition of discrimination used in the treaty, which includes both intentional discrimination and facially neutral policies that allow the kind of de facto discrimination referred to in the report.

By this point, local communities and advocates in the Gulf Coast were facing new problems in the longer-term aftermath of Hurricane Katrina. These included the threatened demolition of 70 percent of public housing, most of which was not seriously damaged by the storm, as part of a larger effort to "clean up" the city; the discovery that IDPs were being exposed to formaldehyde in FEMA trailers; and broader violations of the right to housing, political participation, and other rights due to extended displacement in inadequate camps or in cities far from their homes.[110] Advocates again included analysis of these issues in their shadow report to the CERD.

Housing advocates again participated in the several days of meetings and hearings that preceded the U.S. delegation review in Geneva. During these days, the CERD heard from legal and policy experts, as well as those directly affected by the policies following Hurricane Katrina. For those victims and local activists who attended the hearings, the opportunity to tell their stories and influence the conversation, and to watch the government delegation put on the spot before the committee, was a vital boost to people who had been fighting an uphill battle at home.

Again, the advocacy resulted in questioning of the government by the committee in its oral review and concluding observations directly reflecting the advocates' concerns:

> The Committee . . . remains concerned about the disparate impact that this natural disaster continues to have on low-income African American residents, many of whom continue to be displaced after more than two years after the hurricane (art. 5 (e) (iii)).
>
> The Committee recommends that the State party increase its efforts in order to facilitate the return of persons displaced by Hurricane Katrina to their homes, if feasible, or to guarantee access to adequate and affordable housing, where possible in their place of habitual residence. In particular, the Committee calls upon the State party to ensure that every effort is made to ensure genuine consultation and participation of persons displaced by Hurricane Katrina in the design and implementation of all decisions affecting them.[111]

While the U.S. and local governments did not take a proactive approach to incorporating the committee's observations into local policy, advocates added this language to the language from the ICCPR review, building momentum for a human rights–based approach to housing rights in New Orleans and beyond. Advocates again were able to gain national and local media coverage, including a joint op-ed in the *Miami Herald* with Congressman Alcee Hastings of Florida.[112]

In addition to working with the CERD, while in Geneva the National Law Center on Homelessness and Poverty (Law Center) coordinated a meeting with the Housing Rapporteur, Miloon Kothari, and the staff of the U.N. Independent Expert on minority issues for groups dealing with housing issues specifically in the aftermath of Hurricane Katrina. As noted in the Law Center's report following the meeting, "[t]he demolition of four public housing projects were at that point imminent, and advocates urged the Rapporteur to call for a halt to the demolitions. Following this meeting, in which the Rapporteur was visibly moved by stories from the Gulf Coast, Kothari invited groups to send him information and talking points on the situation, and a week later the Rapporteur and the Independent Expert issued a joint statement calling for a moratorium on demolitions of public housing."[113] Though the housing projects were eventually demolished as planned, housing advocates succeeded in reframing the issue as a human rights violation, and the move generated a wealth of bad press for the New Orleans reconstruction plan that ignored the needs of the poor residents and discriminated against African-American evacuees.[114]

Later that year, the city council proposed an anti-camping ordinance in response to the increased visibility of a homeless population that had doubled since the storms. With local activists, the Law Center drafted a letter to the city counsel, citing the recent observations of the treaty committees alongside constitutional arguments. The letter made clear that future human rights violations would garner the same kind of negative press attention that had accompanied the demolition of the housing projects. Housing advocates had proven that they could use human rights law to influence public opinion, and the anti-camping ordinance was defeated.[115]

C. Visits from Human Rights Monitors: Specific Recommendations and Increased Visibility, 2008–2009

With the ICCPR and ICERD reporting processes concluded, advocates looked for other ways to keep the international human rights spotlight on the Gulf Coast by arranging visits from United Nations human rights monitors, the Special Rapporteurs on Racism and the Right to Adequate Housing, and the UN-HABITAT Advisory Group on Forced Evictions to the Gulf Coast.

The Special Rapporteur on Racism visited eight cities across the United States, including New Orleans, on his first official mission to the country in 2008. He held town hall meetings and met directly with advocates and victims, as well as government officials. His visit generated more media coverage for human rights advocates, and his final report again reflected language drawn from local advocates, specifically highlighting standards from the Guiding Principles:

> The Federal Government and the States of Louisiana, Alabama and Mississippi should increase its assistance to the persons displaced by Hurricane Katrina, particularly in the realm of housing. The principle that "competent authorities have the primary duty and responsibility to establish conditions, as well as provide the means, which allow internally displaced persons to return voluntarily, in safety and with dignity, to their homes or places of habitual residence" should be respected.[116]

In 2009, the Housing Rapporteur, Raquel Rolnik, at the request of advocates, included New Orleans in her eight-city visit to the United States. She visited the sites of demolished public housing units and again talked directly with advocates and victims. Her visit similarly generated further media attention and continued to frame the post–Hurricane Katrina violations through a human rights lens. The Rapporteur's report gave a detailed assessment of many housing policies in the United States, and specifically condemned the closure of public housing units in New Orleans:

> The Special Rapporteur deeply regrets the demolition of thousands of public housing units in New Orleans. Many residents and victims of Hurricane Katrina were prevented from returning to their homes (many of which according to residents sustained little storm damage) and had their homes demolished.
>
> The current housing crisis in New Orleans reflects the disastrous impact of the demolition policy. In particular, the demolition of the "Big Four" housing complexes (B.W. Cooper, C.J. Peete, Lafitte and St. Bernard) has displaced approximately 20,000 individuals. Only one public housing complex still remains, Iberville, which is in need of better maintenance. Residents of Iberville fear demolition of their homes. In addition, former public housing residents of New Orleans are facing grave housing challenges in other cities. One New Orleans resident told the Special Rapporteur that he had met Katrina survivors who are homeless or close to homeless in other cities, "the legacy of the demolition policy."[117]

These missions, like the treaty reporting process, generated language that advocates could lean on in making the argument that the way the United States was dealing with Katrina victims constituted a human rights violation.

In addition to the Special Rapporteurs, housing advocates reached out to the UN-HABITAT Advisory Group on Forced Evictions to direct specific attention to the ongoing housing crisis in New Orleans. In contrast to the individual Rapporteurs appointed by the Human Rights Council, AGFE is composed of members of a pool of housing experts from around the globe who advise the executive director of UN-HABITAT, the United Nation's housing and development agency, on urgent issues. Groups in the United States interested in bringing AGFE's attention to New Orleans, including the National Economic & Social Rights Initiative, May Day New Orleans, and the Law Center, joined the expert pool, and together with two international members, conducted a mission to New Orleans. The mission received additional support through a preparatory report by the Center for Constitutional Rights and Loyola University New Orleans College of Law.[118] This enabled local advocates to closely craft the agenda and outcome report, measuring the experience of the IDPs and those who had returned to New Orleans against the Guiding Principles, Pinheiro Principles, and General Comment 4 to the ICESCR.[119]

While in New Orleans, the AGFE members met with local advocates and government officials, held town hall meetings to hear victims' concerns, and conducted site visits, all of which again generated extensive media attention, including front-page coverage in the local paper and innovative social media coverage.[120] The mission explicitly categorized the Hurricane Katrina evacuees as IDPs,[121] and the situations that separated them from their former homes as forced evictions. Framing in these existing international definitions allowed them to evaluate the situation in New Orleans under the same standards used to judge mass evictions and displacement due to disaster or armed conflict abroad.[122] The mission found that the plans in place for survivors of Katrina fell short of the government's obligation to IDPs and violated the human rights of New Orleans residents.[123] The findings are too extensive to fully cite, but make reference to many of the standards discussed in Section III, and advocates can use the report as a model for addressing future violations.

As discussed throughout this section, advocates for domestic human rights have incorporated the findings of international human rights monitors into their ongoing work for the victims of Hurricane Katrina. The 2010 Universal Periodic Review of the United States gave housing rights groups the opportunity to incorporate the growing body of statements by international experts into a larger conversation about the domestic role of human rights in the United States.

D. Putting Housing Rights in Context: 2010 Universal Periodic Review

In 2010, the United States prepared for its inaugural review by the U.N. Human Rights Council under the Universal Periodic Review (UPR) mechanism, and as part of the process hundreds of advocates from across the country testified before representatives from HUD and other government agencies.[124] While not focused exclusively on the problems of disaster victims, this unprecedented process was a vital step in bringing the human rights conversation out of the exclusive State Department domain and into the domestic policy agencies and the public sphere across the board, in ways that may indicate broader hope for future advocacy.[125]

The UPR process, as the first international human rights review undertaken by the Obama administration, marked an opportunity to set a new standard for integration of human rights domestically. The UPR calls for government consultation with civil society in advance of the government preparing its report, and advocates worked with government officials to ensure this consultation process would not be mere window dressing. This meant a series of a dozen regional consultations, not just meetings in Washington, D.C., and involvement not just of the State Department but with representatives of domestic agency officials responsible for actually implementing policies which affect human rights.

The first consultation organized by the State Department as part of the UPR process took place in New Orleans. Officials from the State Department, the Department of Justice, the Department of Housing and Urban Development, the Department of Homeland Security, and the Department of Health and Human Services attended and heard testimony from hundreds of advocates and victims. Given the extensive preparation through the treaty reviews and monitor visits, housing advocates were well prepared to take advantage of this opportunity. According to one State Department official, housing was the "number one human rights issue" brought to the attention of federal officials through the consultation process, both in New Orleans and in other regional consultations.[126]

Despite the compelling testimony of advocates and citizens and the fact that we are in the midst of an unprecedented housing crisis, the right to adequate housing received short shrift in the U.S. official report to the Human Rights Council. The report carefully sidesteps naming housing and other economic and social rights as rights, stating, "On subjects such as 'freedom from want,' the United States has focused on democratic solutions and civil society initiatives while the U.S. courts have defined our federal constitutional obligations narrowly and primarily by focusing on procedural rights to due process and equal protection of the law."[127]

After all the work done to bring international attention to housing issues, the international audience did not dismiss housing concerns as readily as the United States. Advocates again traveled to Geneva in November 2010, presenting their concerns at side panels to the Human Rights Council on housing and homelessness broadly as well as post–Katrina violations specifically. At the official review, the Human Rights Council made dozens of specific housing, homelessness, and poverty-related recommendations.[128] HUD issued an unprecedented press statement affirming that "[t]he U.N.'s Universal Periodic Review process helps to inform and influence our nation's effort to dramatically increase the amount of affordable housing, especially for those struggling to find a place to call home."[129] The Law Center led follow-up meetings with HUD, the Departments of Justice and State, and the U.S. Interagency Council on Homelessness (USICH). In March 2011, the government officially responded to the recommendations, supporting a large number of recommendations regarding housing rights and homelessness.[130] This support was then cited by the USICH as part of the federal government's progress in implementing the Federal Strategic Plan to Prevent and End Homelessness.[131]

Immediately following the UPR process, U.S. Assistant Secretary of State for Democracy, Human Rights, and Labor Michael Posner announced a new U.S. policy officially embracing economic and social rights, including the right to housing, on an equal footing with civil and political rights.[132] Equally as important, Posner made clear that human rights have both international and domestic implications, explicitly citing increased funding for homelessness as a relevant representation of our work to promote these rights.[133]

In March 2012, the U.S. government unveiled its plan for implementing the recommendations of the council, including ongoing working group meetings led by domestic agency representatives. These working groups provide an excellent opportunity to deepen domestic agency understanding of international standards and their relevance and importance to human rights here at home, including the human rights of those facing displacement due to disasters.

These recent steps are the product of advocates working in close concert with international human rights bodies and capitalizing on the reports of those bodies on the national and local level. As the AGFE pointed out in its report, the relatively privileged position of the United States in terms of availability of housing stock, and comparatively wealthy populations, prior to Hurricane Katrina, had sheltered the government from having to think critically about its domestic compliance with the Guiding Principles regarding IDPs and the human right to housing more broadly. Beyond infrastructure and emergency plans, part of the job of preparing for disasters domestically will be the incorporation of human rights standards in preparation and response. Many of the lessons learned from the response to Hurricane Katrina, as reflected in the various international reports, show that prioritizing the human rights of the affected populations and involving them directly in recovery efforts is necessary to develop a plan that is responsive and not discriminatory. Contrasting the goals of the various levels of government with the goals of a human rights–based recovery plan, the AGFE said:

> [T]he government approach appears to have focused on how New Orleans could become a "better" or more affluent, prettier, cleaner city. It appears to have been based in stereotypes about public housing tenants, and in an assumption that Black residents are not likely to struggle to maintain residency in the city—create a few barriers and they will decide not to return. The human rights approach, based in principles of dignity, the right to adequate housing, and the indivisibility of all human rights, is fairly straight-forward and markedly different: no one—regardless of their source or level of income or their racial or ethnic identity—shall be rendered homeless as a result of Katrina and the resettlement policies implemented to address Katrina.[134]

Following any disaster, the poor and minority people in a community are going to be the most at risk. Adopting a human rights–based model that prioritizes human need in the recovery process ensures that the most vulnerable are not displaced or overlooked.

V. Conclusion

The content of international human rights law prioritizes the needs of rights holders (individuals) and the associated responsibilities of governments. Advocates and policymakers can and should use this model in preparing for and responding to disasters to help centralize or clearly allocate responsibility, and keep the needs of directly affected victims, particularly those traditionally marginalized, at the core of disaster planning and recovery.

There is a broad and growing movement for the human right to housing, as well as for the broader integration of human rights standards into domestic policy at all levels of government. The organizing and advocacy conducted by local and national organizations following Hurricane Katrina laid important groundwork for gains in the domestic use of international human rights standards, which open doors for similar integration both within and beyond the disaster context. At the federal level, following consistent advocacy, the USICH and Department of Justice issued a report stating that the criminalization of homelessness may violate the ICCPR and CAT, the first time a federal policy report has ever acknowledged domestic practices may violate human rights standards.[135] At the state level, advocates in Vermont passed a universal health-care bill on a campaign for the human right to health.[136] Locally, advocates in Madison, Wisconsin, passed an ordinance recognizing the human right to housing and authorizing hiring a planner to develop loal implementation strategies.[137] Advocates are taking the principles of human rights off the paper, beyond the halls of the United Nations in Geneva, and putting them to work making a difference in the lives of people every day.

The human rights frameworks presented in this chapter present a clear and cogent alternative to existing models that either neglect the needs of traditionally marginalized communities or prioritize economic development over basic human rights and human needs. According to human rights standards, a government's responsibility to its residents affected by disaster begins with planning, and continues through resettlement and integration of affected populations. Whether working at the federal, state, or local level, lawyers working to help communities affected by disaster, or working to craft disaster-prevention policy, can utilize the tools of international human rights law described in this chapter to ensure the human rights of their clients and their communities are upheld. Some steps advocates and policymakers could take include the following:

- Working with FEMA, the Department of Homeland Security, and Congress to explicitly adopt the Guiding Principles as a framework for legislation and regulation in addressing disasters.
- Advocating for specific aspects of the Guiding Principles to be integrated into federal, state, or local policy, with or without reference to their international origin, such as:
    - Primary duty for the federal government to provide or clearly allocate responsibility (and be ultimately accountable for) for protection and humanitarian assistance during disaster;
    - Appointment of an institutional focal point within FEMA (or other federal agency) and state and local governments for the rights and needs of IDPs;
    - Integrating the needs of traditionally marginalized communities into disaster planning and recovery, including active consideration of

how facially-neutral policies could disparately affect different racial, gender, ability and economic populations;
  - Providing a clear right to adequate housing (including access to necessary healthcare services, employment, education, etc.) for those displaced due to disaster for the full duration of displacement;
  - Providing clear rights to either return to disaster-affected areas and receive assistance in recovering property or receive resitution and resettlement assistance;
  - Providing for the right to participation and voting for those displaced by disasters.
- Educating their communities about relevant human rights standards and working with them to develop plans to claim their rights.

For advocates and policymakers who believe that existing policies under the Stafford Act or other domestic law are inadequate, the time has come to join the movement for the implementation of human rights into domestic policy and practice. While not replacing existing laws and advocacy strategies, human rights law presents a helpful additional tool for implementing and enforcing existing domestic laws, promoting a rights-based approach to creating new policies, and maximizing recovery efforts.

Notes

1. *See infra* notes 64 and 67.
2. *See, e.g.*, Mike Pesca, *Are Katrina's Victims Refugees or Evacuees?*, NPR, Sept. 5, 2005, http://www.npr.org/templates/story/story.php?storyId=4833613; *Calling Katrina Survivors Refugees Stirs Debate*, Associated Press, Sept. 7, 2005, *available at* http://www.msnbc.msn.com/id/9232071/ns/us_news-katrina_the_long_road_back/t/calling-katrina-survivors-refugees-stirs-debate/.
3. U.S. Agency for Int'l Dev., USAID Assistance to Internally Displaced Persons Policy, PD-ACA-558 (2004), *available at* http://www.usaid.gov/policy/ads/200/200mbc.pdf.
4. Robert T. Stafford Disaster Relief and Emergency Assistance Act, Pub. L. No. 93-288, as amended, 42 U.S.C. §§ 5121–5207 (1992) [hereinafter Stafford Act].
5. Advisory Grp. on Forced Evictions, Mission Report to New Orleans, U.S. 43 (2010), *available* at www.unhabitat.org/downloads/docs/10009_1_593996.pdf, [hereinafter AGFE].
6. Nat'l Law Ctr. on Homelessness & Poverty, "Simply Unacceptable": Homelessness and the Human Right to Housing in the United States 2011 (2011) (citing Opportunity Agenda, Human Rights in the U.S.: Opinion Research with Advocates, Journalists, and the General Public 19, 22 (2007)).
7. *See e.g.*, Dinah L. Shelton, An Introduction to the History of International Human Rights Law, GWU Legal Studies Research Paper No. 346 (2007), *available at* http://ssrn.com/abstract=1010489.
8. The United Nations considers the following treaties the core international human rights instruments: International Convention on the Elimination of All Forms of Racial Discrimination (CERD), International Covenant on Civil and Political Rights (ICCPR), International Covenant on Economic, Social and Cultural Rights (ICESCR), Convention on the Elimination of All Forms of Discrimination Against Women (CEDAW), Convention Against Torture and Other Cruel, Inhuman, or Degrading Treatment or Punishment (CAT), Convention on the Rights of the Child (CRC), International Convention on the Protection of the Rights of All Migrant Workers and Members of Their Families (ICRMW), International Convention for the Protection of All Persons from Enforced Disappearance (CPED), Convention on the Rights of Persons with Disabilities (CRPD). *Core International Human Rights Instruments and Their Monitoring Bodies*, http://www.ohchr.org/EN/ProfessionalInterest/Pages/CoreInstruments.aspx.

9. "[A]ll Treaties made, or which shall be made, under the Authority of the United States, shall be the supreme Law of the Land; and the Judges in every State shall be bound thereby, any Thing in the Constitution or Laws of any State to the Contrary notwithstanding." U.S. CONST. art. VI, § 2.

10. Vienna Convention on the Law of Treaties art. 2(d), 19–23, 1155 U.N.T.S. 331. Some explain this process as analogous to signing a contract and then attaching a statement explaining what you believe the contract means. Reservations limit the effect of the treaty. For example, the United States has attached a reservation to the ICERD limiting the requirements of the treaty so as not to conflict with current understandings of the requirements of the First Amendment. Understandings are meant to clarify terms and provisions of international treaties in accordance with domestic law. For example, the United States attached an understanding to the ICCPR stating that in our system of federalism, the state and local governments will be responsible for implementing those aspects of the treaty over which they have jurisdiction, despite the treaty language that gives the national government sole responsibility for implementing the treaty.

11. Treaties the United States has signed but not ratified include the ICESCR, CEDAW, CRC, and CRPD.

12. Customary International Law is composed of those concepts so central to international law that no treaty is required to bind states to compliance with them. *See e.g.*, TULIO TREVES, *Customary International Law*, MAX PLANCK ENCYCLOPEDIA OF PUB. INT'L LAW, http://www.mpepil.com/sample_article?id=/epil/entries/law-9780199231690-e1393&recno=34& (last updated Nov. 2006).

13. For a full discussion on how to use shadow reporting in advocacy see Eric Tars, *Who Knows What Lurks in the Hearts of Human Rights Violators? The Shadow (Reporter) Knows—Human Rights Shadow Reporting: A Strategic Tool for Domestic Justice*, 42 CLEARINGHOUSE REV. 475 (2009), *available at* http://www.nlchp.org/content/pubs/ShadowReportArticleCR.pdf.

14. For a full discussion on using the UPR process for advocacy, see Eric Tars & Deodonne Bhattarai, *Opening the Door to the Human Right to Housing: The Universal Periodic Review and Strategic Federal Advocacy for a Rights-Based Approach to Housing*, 45 CLEARINGHOUSE REV. 197 (2011).

15. *See, e.g.*, Roper v. Simmons, 543 U.S. 551, 575–78 (2005); Grutter v. Bollinger, 539 U.S. 306 (2003) (Breyer, J. and Ginsberg, J. concurring); *see also* OPPORTUNITY AGENDA, HUMAN RIGHTS IN STATE COURTS (2011), *available at* http://opportunityagenda.org/legal_and_policy_analysis_human_rights_state_courts_2011 (surveying state courts' use of international law).

16. Murray v. Schooner Charming Betsy, 6 U.S. (2 Cranch) 64, 118 (1804).

17. Though the case speaks only to laws written after the ratification of the international instrument, the United States includes statements when it ratifies a treaty stating that existing U.S. law is in compliance with the requirements of the treaty, making the principle equally effective retrospectively.

18. Roper v. Simmons, 125 S. Ct. 1183, 1200 (2005).

19. Public housing residents in Chicago used the international human right to housing to secure temporary housing when they were forcibly evicted from their homes. Advocates campaigned succesfully to have the human right to housing included as a guiding principle of Los Angeles's homelessness initiative. *See* Maria Foscarinis & Eric Tars, *Housing Rights and Wrongs: The U.S. and the Right to Housing*, *in* HUMAN RIGHTS AT HOME (Cynthia Soohoo, Catherine Albisa & Martha Davis eds., Praeger Publishers 2007).

20. Representative of the Secretary-General, *Report on the Guiding Principles on Internal Displacement*, (Feb. 11, 1998), *delivered to the Commission on Human Rights*, U.N. Doc. E/CN.4/1998/53/Add.2 [hereinafter *Guiding Principles*].

21. Stafford Act, *supra* note 4.

22. Special Rapporteur on Adequate Housing, *Promotion and Protection of All Human Rights, Civil, Political, Economic Social and Cultural Rights, Including the Right to Development*, Human Rights Council, ¶ 81, U.N. Doc. A/HRC/7/16, (Feb. 13, 2008), *available at* www.hic-net.org/content/srh_eng.pdf.

23. A person who flees disaster or strife into another country may be protected under the international agreements governing the treatment of refugees.

24. *Guiding Principles*, *supra* note 20.

25. *See* ELIZABETH FERRIS, ERIN MOONEY, AND CHAREEN STARK, FROM RESPONSIBILITY TO RESPONSE: ASSESSING NATIONAL APPROACHES TO INTERNAL DISPLACEMENT vii, Brookings Institution-LSE Project on Internal Displacement, (2011) [hereinafter NATIONAL APPROACHES].

26. *Guiding Principles*, *supra* note 20, at Introduction:2.

27. U.S. AGENCY FOR INT'L DEV., USAID ASSISTANCE TO INTERNALLY DISPLACED PERSONS POLICY, PD-ACA-558 (2004), *available at* http://www.usaid.gov/policy/ads/200/200mbc.pdf.

28. *Id.* at 6.

29. *Id.*

30. *Guiding Principles*, *supra* note 20, at Principle 3:1.

31. Walter Kälin, Annotation, *Guiding Principles of Internal Displacement*, 38 Stud. in Transnat'l Pol'y, 20 (American Society of International Law and Brookings Institution 2008) [hereinafter *Principles Annotation*], *available at* http://www.asil.org/pdfs/stlp.pdf.

32. *See* Ctr. for Constitutional Rights and Loyola Univ. of New Orleans Coll. of Law, International Human Rights Obligations and Post-Katrina Housing Policies 20 (2009) [hereinafter Ctr. for Constitutional Rights and Loyola University of New Orleans College of Law].

33. *See* National Approaches, *supra* note 25.

34. *Guiding Principles*, *supra* note 20, § I:3:1.

35. *Id.* § II:6:3.

36. *Id.* § V:28.

37. *Id.* § V:29.

38. *Id.* § I:4.

39. National Approaches, *supra* note 25.

40. *Guiding Principles*, *supra* note 20, § I:4:1.

41. International Covenant on the Elimination of All Forms of Racial Discrimination art. 2, 660 U.N.T.S. 195; G.A. Res. 2106 (XX), Annex, 20 U.N. GAOR, Supp. No. 14, U.N. Doc. A/6014, at 47 (1966).

42. *Guiding Principles*, *supra* note 20, § I:4.

43. *Id.* § III:18.

44. *Id.* § III:20.

45. *Id.* § 23:3.

46. Convention on the Rights of Persons with Disabilities G.A. Res. 61/106, art. 11, U.N. Doc. A /RES/61/106 (Jan. 24 2007), *available at* http://www.unhcr.org/refworld/docid/45f973632.html.

47. National Approaches, *supra* note 25, at 28.

48. *See generally* Khalid Koser, *Gaps in IDP Protection*, 31 Forced Migration Rev. 17 , *available at* http://www.fmreview.org/sites/fmr/files/FMRdownloads/en/FMRpdfs/FMR31/17.pdf; Megan Bradley & Jane McAdam, Rethinking Durable Solutions to Displacement in the Context of Climate Change (Brookings–LSE Project on Internal Displacement 2012).

49. *Guiding Principles*, *supra* note 20, § II:5, 6.

50. *Principles Annotation*, *supra* note 31, at 34.

51. Office of the U.N. High Comm'r for Human Rights, Protection of Internally Displaced Persons in Situations of Natural Disaster: A Working Visit to Asia by the Representative of the United Nations Secretary-General on the Human Rights of Internally Displaced Persons Walter Kalin 12 (2005), *available at* http://www.ohchr.org/Documents/Issues/IDPersons/Tsunami.pdf.

52. *Guiding Principles*, *supra* note 20, § II:9.

53. Convention Concerning Indigenous and Tribal Peoples in Independent Countries (ILO Conv. No. 169), 72 ILO Official Bull. No. 59, art. 16(3) (entered into force Sept. 5, 1991); *see also Principles Annotation*, *supra* note 31, at 23.

54. Declaration on the Rights of Indigenous Peoples, G.A. Res. 61/295, art. 8(2), 10, U.N. Doc. A/RES/47/1 (2007); *see also Announcement of U.S. Support for the United Nations Declaration on the Rights of Indigenous Peoples* (Dec. 10, 2010), http://www.state.gov/documents/organization/184099.pdf.

55. World Conference on Human Rights, June 14–15, 1993, *Vienna Declaration and Programme of Action*, U.N. Doc. A/CONF.157/23 (July 12, 1993).

56. Sara McHattie, *Guiding Principle 27 and the Philippine Typhoon Response*, Forced Migration Rev., Special Issue on 10 Years of the Guiding Principles on Internal Displacement, December 2008, at 30.

57. *Id.* at 31.

58. Erin Mooney, *From Solidarity to Solutions: The Government Response to Internal Displacement in Georgia*, *in* From Responsibility to Response: Assessing National Approaches to Internal Displacement 179 (Brookings-LSE Project on Internal Displacement 2011).

59. *Id.* at 185. The position of Representative for IDPs later became the Special Rapporteur for IDPs.

60. Iulia Kharashvili, Ilya Kharashvili & Koba Subeliani, *Experience of the Guiding Principles in Georgia*, *in* Forced Migration Rev., Special Issue on 10 Years of the Guiding Principles on Internal Displacement, December 2008, at 16–17.

61. *Guiding Principles*, *supra* note 20, § III:18.

62. *Id.* § III:14.

63. Universal Declaration of Human Rights, G.A. Res. 217 (III) A, U.N. Doc. A/810 (1948), at 71, art. 25(1) [hereinafter UDHR].

64. International Covenant on Economic, Social and Cultural Rights, G.A. res. 2200A (XXI), 21 U.N. GAOR Supp. (No. 16) at 49, U.N. Doc. A/6316 (1966), 993 U.N.T.S. 3, *entered into force* Jan. 3, 1976 [hereinafter ICESCR].

65. General Comment 4, The Right to Adequate Housing, 6th session, (III) Annex, U.N. Doc. E/1992/23/, at 114 (1991), *reprinted in* Compilation of General Coments and General Recommendations Adopted by Human Rights Treaty Bodies, U.N. Doc. HRI/GEN/1/Rev.6 at 18 (2003).

66. *Id.* ¶ 8. The term "progressive realization" recognizes that full realization of economic, social, and cultural rights are generally not achievable in a short period of time, but "should not be misinterpreted as depriving the obligation of all meaningful content. It is on the one hand a necessary flexibility device, reflecting the realities of the real world and the difficulties involved for any country in ensuring full realization of economic, social and cultural rights. On the other hand, the phrase must be read in the light of the overall objective, indeed the *raison d'être*, of the Covenant which is to establish clear obligations for States parties in respect of the full realization of the rights in question. It thus imposes an obligation to move as expeditiously and effectively as possible towards that goal. Moreover, any deliberately retrogressive measures in that regard would require the most careful consideration and would need to be fully justified by reference to the totality of the rights provided for in the Covenant and in the context of the full use of the maximum available resources." General Comment 3, The Nature of States Parties' Obligations, 5th session, (III) Annex, U.N. Doc. E/1991/23, at 86 (1990), *reprinted in* Compilation of General Comments and General Recommendations Adopted by Human Rights Treaty Bodies, U.N. Doc. HRI/GEN/1/Rev.6 at 14 (2003) ¶ 9.

67. International Covenant on Civil and Political Rights, G.A. Res. 2200 (XXI) A, U.N. GAOR, 21st Sess., Supp. No. 16, U.N. Doc. A/6316 (1966), at 52, 999 U.N.T.S. 171 (entered into force Mar. 23, 1976), [hereinafter ICCPR].

68. *Id.* art. 3.

69. *Id.* art. 6.

70. *Id.* art. 7.

71. *Id.* art. 26.

72. AGFE, *supra* note 5.

73. *See, e.g.*, National Law Center on Homelessness & Poverty et al., *United States of America, Submission to the United Nations Universal Periodic Review, Right to Adequate Housing* (2010), http://www.ushrnetwork.org/sites/default/files/housing_joint_report.pdf.

74. *Guiding Principles*, *supra* note 20, § 3:10.

75. *Id.* § 3:18.

76. UDHR, *supra* note 63, art. 3; ICCPR, *supra* note 67, art. 6; Geneva Convention Relative to the Protection of Civilian Persons in Time of War art. 3, Aug. 12, 1949, 6 U.S.T. 3516, 75 U.N.T.S. 287 [hereinafter Geneva Convention].

77. *Guiding Principles*, *supra* note 20, § III:17.

78. *Guiding Principles*, *supra* note 20, § III:16.

79. *Principles Annotation*, *supra* note 31, at 74 (citing Council of Europe, Rec(2006)6 of the Committee of Ministers to member states on internally displaced persons of 5 April 2006, ¶ 6 (2006)).

80. *Principles Annotation*, *supra* note 31, at 77 (citing Human Rights Committee, General Comment 19, Article 23 (Thirty-ninth session, 1990), Compilation of General Comments and General Recommendations Adopted by Human Rights Treaty Bodies, U.N. Doc. HRI/GEN/1/Rev.1 at 28 (1994), para. 39).

81. *See* Geneva Convention, *supra* note 76.

82. *Guiding Principles*, *supra* note 20, § III:20.

83. *Id.* § III:22.

84. National Approaches, *supra* note 25, at 122.

85. ICCPR, *supra* note 67, art. 25.

86. Inter-Agency Standing Comm., IASC Operational Guidelines on the Protection of Persons in Situations of Natural Disaster 11 (Brookings-Bern Project on Internal Displacement 2011), *available at* http://ochanet.unocha.org/p/Documents/Operational%20Guidelines.pdf.

87. *Guiding Principles*, *supra* note 20, § V:28.

88. This Special Rapporteur was a separate mandate than the Special Rapporteur on IDPs, created by the now-defunct U.N. Subcommission on the Promotion and Protection of Human Rights. *See Pinhiero Principles Initiative*, Displacement Solutions, http://displacementsolutions.org/ds-initiatives/201-2/ (last visited Apr. 2, 2013).

89. CTR. ON HOUS. RIGHTS AND EVICTIONS, THE PINHEIRO PRINCIPLES: UNITED NATIONS PRINCIPLES ON HOUSING AND PROPERTY RESTITUTION FOR REFUGEES AND DISPLACED PERSONS, princ. 2.1 (2005).

90. *Id.* at princ. 10.1.

91. *Id.* at princ. 8.1.

92. Special Rapporteur on Adequate Housing as a Component of the Right to an Adequate Standard of Living (Feb. 5, 2007), *Basic Principles and Guidelines on Development-Based Evictions and Displacement*, U.N. Doc. A/HRC/4/18.

93. *Id.* ¶ 19.

94. *Id.*

95. *Id.* ¶ 30.

96. *Id.* ¶ 31.

97. *Id.* ¶ 39.

98. *Id.* ¶ 53.

99. *Id.* ¶ 59–68.

100. *See* United States, Second and Third periodic reports of States parties due in 2003 UNITED STATES OF AMERICA, CCPR/C/USA/3 (Nov. 28, 2005).

101. U.S. HUMAN RIGHTS NETWORK, HURRICANE KATRINA AND VIOLATIONS OF ICCPR ARTICLES 6 AND 26: A RESPONSE TO THE THIRD PERIODIC REPORT OF THE UNITED STATES OF AMERICA (2006), *available at* http://www2.ohchr.org/english/bodies/hrc/docs/ngos/USHRN.pdf.

102. ICCPR, *supra* note 67.

103. *Id.* art. 23.

104. *Id.* art. 24.

105. *Id.* art. 25.

106. *Id.* art. 26.

107. Human Rights Committee, *Consideration of Reports Submitted by States Parties Under Article 40 of the Covenant, Concluding Observations of the Human Rights Committee United States of America*, ¶ 26 CCPR/C/USA/CO/3/Rev.1 (Dec. 18, 2006).

108. *See* ADVOCATES FOR ENVTL. HUMAN RIGHTS, GRANT REPORT ON THE PROTECTING THE HUMAN RIGHTS OF DISPLACED GULF COAST RESIDENTS PROJECT (2007) (on file with author).

109. UNITED STATES, PERIODIC REPORT OF THE UNITED STATES OF AMERICA TO THE U.N. COMMITTEE ON THE ELIMINATION OF RACIAL DISCRIMINATION CONCERNING THE INTERNATIONAL CONVENTION ON THE ELIMINATION OF ALL FORMS OF RACIAL DISCRIMINATION (2007) ¶ 255.

110. *See generally* AGFE, *supra* note 5.

111. *See* Concluding Observations of the Committee on the Elimination of Racial Discrimination: United States of America, U.N. Doc. CERD/C/USA/CO/6, ¶ 31 (2008).

112. Alcee Hastings & Maria Foscarinis, *End Racial Disparities in Housing*, MIAMI HERALD, Mar. 14, 2008, at A21.

113. *See* Press Release, United Nations, U.N. Experts Call on U.S. Government to Halt Ongoing Evictions and to Take Immediate Steps to Protect the Human Rights of African-Americans Affected by Hurricane Katrina and the Demolition of Public Housing in New Orleans, Louisiana (Feb. 28, 2008), *available at* http://www.unhchr.ch/huricane/huricane.nsf/view01/907604B6DAF5E2F1C12573FD007AD7DC?opendocument.

114. Martha Carr, *U.N. experts, HUD disagree on housing*, TIMES-PICAYUNE, Feb. 28, 2008, http://www.nola.com/news/index.ssf/2008/02/un_experts_hud_disagree_on_hou.html.

115. *See* Eric Tars, *Who Knows What Lurks in the Hearts of Human Rights Violators? The Shadow (Reporter) Knows—Human Rights Shadow Reporting: A Strategic Tool for Domestic Justice*, 42 CLEARINGHOUSE REV. 475 (2009).

116. U.N. Human Rights Council, Report of the Special Rapporteur on Contemporary Forms of Racism, Racial Discrimination, Xenophobia and Related Intolerance, ¶ 110, U.N. Doc. A/HRC/11/36/Add.3 (Apr. 28, 2009) (by Doudou Diéne) (citing U.N. Guiding Principles on Internal Displacement, E/CN.4/1998/53/Add. 2 at 14. (2001)).

117. Human Rights Council, Report of the Special Rapporteur on adequate housing as a component of the right to an adequate standard of living, and on the right to nondiscrimination in this context, Addendum, mission to the United States of America, ¶ 30, U.N. Doc. A/HRC/13/20/Add.4 (Feb. 12, 2010) (by Raquel Rolnik).

118. *See* CTR. FOR CONSTITUTIONAL RIGHTS AND LOYOLA UNIVERSITY OF NEW ORLEANS COLLEGE OF LAW, *supra* note 32.

119. AGFE, *supra* note 5.

120. *See id.*, at app. 6; *see also Advocacy Manual, New Orleans & Gulf Coast*, NAT'L LAW CTR. ON HOMELESSNESS & POVERTY (2009), http://wiki.nlchp.org/display/Manual/New+Orleans+and+Gulf+Coast.

121. *Id.* § 4.4.

122. *Id.* § 5.

123. *Id.* § 4.

124. National Law Center on Homelessness & Poverty, *"Simply Unacceptable": Homelessness and the Human Right to Housing in the United States 2011* (June 2011), http://www.nlchp.org/content/pubs/SimplyUnacceptableReport.pdf, *citing* Opportunity Agenda, *Human Rights in the U.S.: Opinion Research with Advocates, Journalists, and the General Public*, 19, 22 (2007).

125. For an in-depth discussion of the 2010 UPR process and housing advocacy, see Eric S. Tars & Déodnné Bhattarai, Opening the Door to the Human Right to Housing: The Universal Periodic Review and Strategic Federal Advocacy for a Rights-Based Approach to Housing, 45 CLEARINGHOUSE REV. 197 (2011).

126. David Sullivan, Office of Legal Adviser, State Department, Human Rights on the Hill, May 25, 2010 (oral remark in response to a question (unscripted). Notes on file with author).

127. National report submitted in accordance with paragraph 15 (a) of the annex to Human Rights Council resolution 5/1, Working Group on the Universal Periodic Review, United States of America, U.N. Doc. A/HRC/WG.6/9/USA/1 (2010) [hereinafter U.S. UPR Report].

128. Human Rights Council, Report of the Working Group on the Universal Periodic Review United States of America § 2, U.N. Doc. A/HRC/16/11.

129. U.S. Dept. of Housing and Urban Development Statement on the U.S. Participation in the United Nations' Universal Periodic Review, Nov. 5, 2011, http://portal.hud.gov/hudportal/HUD?src=/press/speeches_remarks_statements/2010/statement-110510.

130. Report of the Working Group on the Universal Periodic Review, United States of America, Addendum, A/HRC/16/11/Add.1 (2011), *at* paras. 6, 19.

131. U.S. INTERAGENCY COUNCIL ON HOMELESSNESS, OPENING DOORS: FEDERAL STRATEGIC PLAN TO PREVENT AND END HOMELESSNESS, UPDATE 2011 (2011).

132. Asst. Sec. of State for Democracy, Human Rights & Labor, Michael Posner, "The Four Freedoms Turns 70," (Mar. 24, 2011) (speech given to the American Society of International Law), http://www.state.gov/j/drl/rls/rm/2011/159195.htm.

133. *Id.* ("Our government's commitment to provide for the basic social and economic needs of our people is clear and it reflects the will of the American people. They ask us to provide shelter for the destitute . . . and we do. . . . In the wake of the housing crisis, last year the federal government committed almost $4 billion to target homelessness.").

134. AGFE, *supra* note 5, ch. V.7.

135. U.S. INTERAGENCY COUNCIL ON HOMELESSNESS & DEP'T OF JUSTICE, SEARCHING OUT SOLUTIONS: CONSTRUCTIVE ALTERNATIVES TO THE CRIMINALIZATION OF HOMELESSNESS 8 (2012), *available at* http://www.usich.gov/resources/uploads/asset_library/RPT_SoS_March2012.pdf.

136. Mariah McGill, *Human Rights from the Grassroots Up: Vermont's Campaign for Universal Health Care*, 14 HEALTH & HUM. RTS. J. 1 (2012), *available at* http://hhrjournal.org/index.php/hhr/article/view/456/722.

137. Pat Schneider, *Grassroots: Madison Recognizes Housing as a Human Right*, CAPITAL TIMES (Dec. 2, 2011), http://host.madison.com/ct/news/local/grassroots/grass-roots-madison-recognizes-housing-as-a-human-right/article_30d9d280-1c7b-11e1-858a-001871e3ce6c.html.

CHAPTER 4

Equity in Disasters: Civil and Human Rights Challenges in the Context of Emergency Events

Jacqueline Patterson

> *"Disasters, however 'natural,' are profoundly discriminatory. Preexisting structures and social conditions determine how a community will be affected and who will pay the highest price."*[1]
>
> — Oxfam Report, *"Exposed: Social Vulnerability and Climate Change in the US Southeast"*

I. Introduction

Given the progression of climate change and the resulting increase in the frequency and severity of extreme weather events, there is a critical need to protect civil and human rights before, during, and after disasters. The occurrence of an emergency event may be random and not targeting a specific population, but the experience of and recovery from disasters varies widely based on a person's placement in society.

Recent history shows the disproportionate and disparate impact that disasters have had on certain populations:

- During ***Hurricane Katrina***, women in New Orleans and Mississippi experienced spikes in partner and familial violence, which often occurs in times of disaster.[2,3] People living with HIV and AIDS did not have access to life-preserving medicines in the aftermath of the storm. People who were deaf or hard of hearing were at a disadvantage in getting access to recovery information.[4,5] In addition to African-Americans, there were thousands of Native Americans living in southeast Louisiana who were displaced and faced great challenges in getting post-disaster assistance.[6] Undocumented immigrants also risked deportation if they obtained disaster-relief support.[7]

- The ***BP Oil Drilling Disaster*** spilled approximately 660,000 barrels of oil into the Gulf of Mexico,[8] directly affecting communities from the Florida Panhandle to the eastern tip of Texas and indirectly affecting countless more. The most affected groups were indigenous communities, immigrant communities, communities of color, low-income communities, and women, because of social, political, economic, and cultural differences that fostered preexisting vulnerabilities and differential access to recovery resources.
- In the wake of ***Superstorm Sandy***, low-income communities of color in Far Rockaway, New York, returned to live in their homes that were inundated with toxic mold.[9] Even months after the disaster, thousands remained without power, while more affluent neighborhoods' power was quickly restored.[10]

Although the research continues, there is an abundance of evidence showing that race, poverty, age, ability, gender, and immigration status can influence risk in times of disasters. According to Daniel A. Farber, Sho Sato professor of law and chair of the Energy and Resources Group at the University of California, Berkeley, "Those who already suffer from societal disadvantage are more likely to be in harm's way, and they are less likely to be able to take defensive action or to reconstruct their lives after a disaster."[11] Systematic, inclusive, and equitable preparation and response to disasters are necessary to ensure that the entire community can rebound from a disaster. This is critical to building community resilience post-disaster.

II. A Post-Disaster Equity Framework

A working definition of equity is the "fair access to livelihood, education and resources; full participation in the political and cultural life of the community; and self-determination in meeting fundamental needs."[12] "Defining Equity: A Framework for Evaluating Equity in the Context of Ecosystem Services," authored by a team of researchers from Rutgers University, Australian National University, and University of Southampton, provides an equity framework that is useful for developing a post-disaster recovery plan. The equity framework has three dimensions:

1. **Procedural equity** encompasses fairness in political processes and participation in decision making.
2. **Distributive equity** highlights the need to consider not just the allocation of benefits, but also the costs and risks with a focus on the outcomes of allocation decisions.

3. **Contextual equity** recognizes the fact that the playing field is never level but that people's capabilities and their access to resources and power determine the extent to which they are able to utilize procedural equity to determine the best distributive outcome for themselves.[13]

These three dimensions of equity address the process by which communities are able to engage in decisions that affect them, the social and economic implications of those decisions, and the extent to which existing vulnerabilities and disparate access to resources facilitate or impede the recovery of all communities. An equity framework throughout all phases of the disaster preparedness and response continuum is critical to fostering the resilience of all members of communities impacted by disaster.

This chapter will provide an overview and analysis of how preexisting vulnerabilities and biases in systemic responses combine to result in economic, social, political, and cultural impacts on certain populations. It will have a specific focus on housing, employment, and community infrastructure. The situations that arise during disasters shine a spotlight on the civil and human rights issues faced by racial and ethnic minorities, low-income communities, immigrant communities, people with different levels of ability, people with special health needs, and women. These issues require vigilance and deliberate action from all agencies, organizations, and individuals involved in community development, as well as the emergency management continuum.

III. Preexisting Community Vulnerabilities

Communities' preexisting vulnerabilities serve as an important foundation for an equity analysis. Due to preexisting vulnerabilities including economic, political, cultural, and social marginalization, an array of populations are predisposed to greater impact from the ravages of disasters. Economic inequalities often result in low-income communities being the least able to weather a disaster and rebound in the aftermath.[14] For example, people who were poor, elderly, or sick had the highest mortality rates and composed the largest proportion of people who died in Hurricane Katrina, largely because they were unable to evacuate.[15] In addition, communities of color disproportionately face daunting challenges during and after a disaster. In 1995, out of the more than 700 people who died during a weeklong heat wave in Chicago, African-Americans were 1.5 times more likely to die than whites. Racial segregation, poverty, and lack of political capital were principal reasons for this disparity.[16] At the Orleans Parish Prison, in the aftermath of Hurricane Katrina, prisoners were abandoned and left locked in sewage-tainted floodwaters of their cells without food or drink or even proper ventilation, and others were bused to an open field where they spent days in the elements.[17]

In some communities, patterns and policies of spatial segregation cause greater vulnerability to disasters. The topography of New Orleans puts economically disadvantaged communities at greater risk in times of hurricanes and flooding because the lowest-lying and poorest areas are in the Ninth Ward, yet the most affluent neighborhoods are on higher ground, away from where floodwaters drain. This specific example is true throughout the country with low-income communities and communities of color occupying the least desirable land that is also the most prone to natural and human-created disasters.[18]

Systemic inequities that are manifested through infrastructure, policies, and practices result in compounded victimization of vulnerable populations when disasters occur. The continuum of emergency management has multiple points where certain populations are at a differential disadvantage, from the preparedness through to the redevelopment phase. In the recent 2012 Hurricane Isaac, which largely impacted coastal areas in Florida, Mississippi, and Louisiana, it came to light in the hurricane's aftermath that the U.S. Army Corps of Engineers based its formula for where to reinforce levees on prioritizing areas of greatest economic impact.[19,20] This formula led to communities with higher property values being prioritized over communities with lower property values. It also meant that regardless of how many people lived in an area, value was only placed on material assets.

In addition to diminished economic value assigned to certain communities before a disaster, nuclear facilities, sewage treatment facilities, coal-fired power plants, and refineries are more likely to be in communities of color.[21,22,23] In times of disaster, these facilities pose extreme danger to the surrounding communities, as witnessed by the impact of the earthquake and tsunami on Fukushima.[24] The nearly breached Grand Gulf Nuclear station in the flooding of Port Gibson, Mississippi, in 2011 could have spelled disaster in this low-income African-American community for which its inadequate evacuation routes have long been acknowledged, though no efforts by local government authorities have been made to improve them.[25] Recently, the spillage of tons of sewage in the Little Patuxent River in Maryland during Superstorm Sandy exposed those in nearby communities to noxious odors, which are especially risky for those with heightened sensitivity to respiratory contamination.[26]

IV. Socio-cultural Impacts of Disaster Cripple Families and Cause Irreversible Community Changes

Given the pervasive nature of disasters, extensive social and cultural impacts on individuals, families, and communities are inevitable. Disaster can cause displacement, illness, mortality, or criminalization. The sociocultural issues can also include the separation of families, dispersion of communities, and erosion of place-based cultures.

The 2011 Deepwater Horizon Oil Spill's deluge of oil overlaid another travesty upon a region still recovering from the 2005 Hurricanes Rita and Katrina. The oil spill—the largest environmental disaster in U.S. history—was visited upon communities who already suffered from compromised economic status, displacement and substandard housing, fragile mental and physical health status, and sociocultural disruption due to one of the most costly hurricanes in U.S. history. Alabama's Senator Richard Shelby noted at a 2011 senate hearing that during the period after the oil spill, Alabama had a 50 percent drop in tourism, with a loss of $850 million to $1 billion.[27] Shrimpers, bait and tackle shops, processors, and others experienced extreme loss of jobs.[28]

In the aftermath of the oil spill, the United Houma Nation, already struggling with issues of sovereignty, was impacted by the contamination of the land, which holds a deeply cultural connection for the Houma people.[29] At the same time, Vietnamese fishermen and fisherwomen who came to the United States seeking a land of democracy and opportunity found themselves separated from their only means of earning a livelihood for their families. Complicated by language and cultural differences, they also were challenged by navigating the systems in place to provide assistance to those impacted by the crisis.

During the 2011 string of tornadoes in Alabama, some entire communities were completely leveled. Multiple low-income African-American communities were obliterated with little chance of recovery due to issues of underinsurance or noninsurance.[30,31] Where there had been families that played and socialized together and local place-based cultures, there was rubble.

For example, there is a gas station in Pratt City, Alabama, where one can look out over an expanse that used to be a densely populated housing development. Now, there is nothing but piles of brick, plywood, furniture, and other debris. With so many questions surrounding the ability to rebound and return, one can definitively say many of the communities will not be even close to the same again. Whether temporary or long-term, families were split from each other as alternative housing measures often did not suit the needs of all, and often families and individuals were separated from communities that formed their cultural and social fabric. One gentleman in Pratt City, who stood marveling and lamenting the destruction, stated, "There's nothing left." The question remains, what will become of that community?

Pratt City, Alabama, after the 2011 tornadoes. (Photo credit: Jacqueline Patterson)

V. Housing

When crisis is at its peak and shelter is at a premium, it is the most vulnerable in society who are further marginalized with inadequate attention to their needs. A range of preexisting conditions render low-income communities, communities of color, women, and incarcerated people extremely vulnerable to the impact of disasters. Women, who compose 70 percent of people living in poverty, are often renting or own homes of poor housing stock.[32,33] Communities of color, which are also disproportionately low income and low wealth, face similar circumstances.[34] Incarcerated people have no control over their environments, and the infrastructure of their dwellings is compromised due to underinvestment in safe prison housing.[35]

Women are differentially affected by disaster in multiple ways, The BP Oil Drilling Disaster illustrated these impacts that were seen in other disasters like Hurricane Katrina where similar patterns of impact emerged. One example of differential impact that is linked to housing is the increase in violence against women because women have few options for alternative sheltering when they are threatened by or subjected to violence. Mayor Stan Wright of Bayou La Batre, Alabama, said that domestic violence had risen by 320 percent since the Gulf oil spill began.[36] This trend is consistent with previous reports finding that marital and partner discord and divorce rise in the wake of disaster.[37] Divided families have left many women and children struggling, especially in situations where the husband was the only skilled laborer and principal breadwinner.

Homelessness increased dramatically in some areas of the gulf after the BP Oil Drilling Disaster. Abigail Folkes, who runs a housing program in Fort Walton Beach, Florida, described one case that shows the intersecting and layered needs that hit communities in the Gulf Coast.

> A single mom, with an 18 month old child, came to us after she became pregnant again. She left her boyfriend because when she got pregnant the second time, her partner became increasingly frustrated because he had lost his job due to the oil spill. He was stressed out because he feared that they couldn't manage to feed another person. His anger reached the point where he began to beat her because he was so worried that he couldn't take on the extra responsibility. So she had no health insurance and a baby on the way. Plus she was not in an employable situation. She had been working as a waitress lifting heavy trays, but she couldn't continue [sic] keep up. So they asked her to leave.[38]

The prison population is also a notable example of people with limited options seeking to cope in post-disaster contexts. Whether in jail or in long-term prison, the process of relocating prisoners in past disasters, such as Hurricane Katrina, showed that the respect and care in the transfer process varies widely, leaving prisoners vulnerable to abuse.[39] Also, given the limited number of facilities, there is a risk that prisoners would be transferred from one level of security to another, which is a violation of the terms of their incarceration.

Where there is home ownership, communities of color and low-income communities are more likely to own homes with poor housing stock, which means that when disaster strikes, these houses are far more likely to be damaged or destroyed. Communities of color and low-income communities are also more likely to own or rent homes located in floodplains, which leaves them inundated in extreme water events.[40] Also, in community after community, families of color and families with low income are less likely to have homeowners insurance and more likely to be underinsured when they do have insurance. In the South, many low-income families have ancestral homes. Therefore there is no mortgage or any obligation to maintain homeowners insurance. In these circumstances, when there is a choice between feeding the family, keeping electricity flowing, and paying insurance "just in case" something happens, they choose to deal with the dilemma facing them instead of protecting against a catastrophe that may occur. Thus, when disaster strikes, even as homeowners, they are likely to find themselves with no safety net to cover the loss of home and property. This lack of insurance then serves as a barrier for post-disaster recovery funds. For those with insurance, the disproportionately lower home values in communities of color and low-income communities further inhibit rebuilding possibilities, due to inadequate funds to cover the full rebuilding costs.

One family in Crenshaw, Mississippi, following the flooding of 2011, experienced some of these dynamics combined with unfortunate results, which included total loss of home and property. Their home was built in a floodplain, and the political marginalization in this community was such that requests for improvement in the inadequate drainage system were long ignored.[41] After the disaster struck, this family discovered they did not have a flood clause in their homeowners insurance and they emerged from consultation with their insurance agent empty handed. Without the cushioning savings to compensate for the insurance gap, their outlook was bleak. They were not alone, as their neighbors were in similar circumstances.

One representative example of land loss due to low wealth and underinsurance is the story of Lewis, of Linden, Alabama. She and her husband had moved from the city, built their dream home, and enjoyed several years there with their grandson. Then, the tornados of 2011 took it all away. "The insurance is giving us money, but it is not enough to rebuild. We can't come back from this. We'll have to go back to the city and start over."[42] Her entire community was leveled by the storms and it is unclear who, if any, will be able to return.

Exacerbated by the underinsurance issue, low-income and low-wealth communities are preyed upon by predatory contractors promising a better deal. (See chapter 13.) Therefore, many end up spending their meager resources on subpar work out of desperation borne of a perceived lack of options. In the aftermath of the 2011 tornadoes, in Limestone County, Alabama, one resident stated, "They all came around here afterwards and they were giving such wildly different prices, I didn't know whom to trust!" Also in Limestone County, another resident said, "I paid hundreds of dollars to them guys and they took my money and left me with the same pile of rubble I started with! I haven't seen them since and I wasn't the only one."[43]

VI. Employment

Low-income people on the entry or low-wage rungs of the employment ladder have the least employment security when disasters strike because they often have no benefits and are considered to be the most expendable when operations cease. Plus, they tend to have the least contractually guaranteed income.

In Greenville and Tunica, Mississippi, in the wake of the flooding of 2011, casino workers found their livelihoods underwater after the river overtook the banks and completely submerged their place of work.[44] Whether it is lost wages from the temporary closure of the facility or long-term unemployment, as the casino reduced its ranks in the economic downturn in the aftermath of the disaster, it is always those with the least income and ability to withstand lost wages who are least secure and most affected.

Similarly with the BP Oil Drilling Disaster, the crab pickers and deckhands were no longer able to work after the disaster. Because they were paid in cash, they were not able to prove their wages. This made them ineligible for income through the Gulf Coast Claims Facility compensation system. This left them in dire straits with no recourse.

Opportunities for work as part of the cleanup or remediation efforts in the wake of disasters can be discriminatory in terms of who is hired for the jobs. And for those who do obtain the positions, the hazardous working conditions and lack of proper protective training and gear can detract from the benefit of being employed. As an example of those who simply do not have access to employment, during the BP Oil Drilling Disaster, women were trained and promised work but were denied jobs when placements were subsequently made. The employers exhibited gender bias against women, who were deemed less able to carry out manual labor efforts.[45,46] Therefore, women were not afforded the same level of opportunity for economic recovery as men in the wake of the disaster.

In recent disasters, when labor is required for cleanup or otherwise, the most vulnerable workers—incarcerated persons and day laborers—are enlisted. During the recent Mississippi and Louisiana floods, instances have been reported in which the prisoners were used to pile up sandbags as the floodwaters were rising. Given the disproportionate representation of African-Americans among the incarcerated population and among low-wage workers, there is a greater likelihood of impact of infractions on prisoners' rights and workers' rights for African-Americans. In addition, day laborers, who are predominantly migrant workers, are often engaged in such work, some of which can involve handling hazardous materials or toxic waste. Finally, all of these workers face significant health and safety violations. In the BP Oil Drilling Disaster, there were reports of insufficient protective covering to protect the health and well-being of workers.[47]

Post-disaster remediation jobs are the most dangerous, dirtiest jobs, and this work is being done by the most vulnerable populations with the least amount of choice (prison labor and undocumented immigrants). With little regard to laws in place to protect workers, this post-disaster environment is ripe for labor violations and exploitation. In many cases in a non-disaster context, dangerous jobs are rewarded with high pay, but in these cases, the opposite tends to be true.

VII. Community Infrastructure

A community's infrastructure includes its systems of education, transportation, and economic growth. In each of these systems, the destruction of the physical buildings, rail lines and roads, or commercial real estate is only one aspect of recovering the community's infrastructure. The quest for good schools, reliable transportation, and shared, sustainable economic opportunity are at the heart of recovery. These systems have the potential to hold communities together, foster existing tensions, or create new dividing lines. Each of these interdependent systems determines whether communities will fully recover or will be further marginalized based on how, when, and where they are rebuilt.

Schools are often institutions that bind communities. Displacement of educational facilities and student housing, and resulting setbacks in educational progress occurred in many facilities from elementary schools to universities. With school quality often tied to property values, communities of color and low-income communities already suffer disproportionately from compromised school systems. Therefore, days or even weeks missed from school due to disaster can spell major setbacks and affect the likelihood of achievement for students. In the aftermath of major displacement, the impact of this is widespread, but there are several ways African-American students were differentially impacted. Students facing closed schools due to damaged facilities and dormitories or appropriation of schools for relief purposes found themselves having to study from home without the benefit of a structured environment, or not at all because the family was consumed with recovery from the disasters.

In Mississippi and Alabama, multiple elementary and high schools were used as makeshift disaster recovery centers, resulting in the cessation of the classes in the public schools, most of which were in communities of color where the schools were the only facilities that could accommodate disaster-relief operations. Ongoing absenteeism from class has shown to negatively impact students' achievement rates in school.[48] Therefore, days and even weeks of missed school due to disaster can spell major setbacks and affect the likelihood of achievement for students. Also, most of today's public schools are still segregated by race and class and those "students in high-poverty racially segregated schools are not exposed to high-quality curricula, highly qualified teachers, or important social networks as often as students in wealthier, predominantly White schools."[49] Given those circumstances, African-American and Latino students or students from low-income families cannot afford interruptions in class attendance.

The impacts are even felt at the undergraduate level. At Alabama A&M University, students had to return home because their storm-damaged dormitories were uninhabitable. Due to financial constraints, many of those students were not able to return to finish their studies in a classroom and were instead relegated to distance education. Professors feared the impact of this on their outcomes for the semester. This issue disproportionately impacted both African-American and low-income students. According to Dr. Tonya Perry, professor at the School of Social Work, "They can't come back. They can't afford to come back. So they just have to finish the year from home, which is a shame."[50]

Often forgotten when considering disaster displacement are the teachers. Hurricane Katrina–ravaged New Orleans underwent a radical reform of the school system. Before the storm, there was a system to attract teachers to schools that combined government pensions, control over work assignment, small classes, and limits on working hours. After the storm, in the "reformed" system, teachers were selected and rewarded based on high performance on test scores. Because testing is inherently racially biased, this effectively stewarded a system of structural racism that changed the complexion and culture of New Orleans schools.[51] The damaged system is then further weakened when post-disaster decision making dealing with redistricting of school districts inevitably works out in favor of the vocal majority that is least affected by the storm. So the cycle of disenfranchisement and lack of access to quality public services continues.

VIII. Transportation

Transportation access was a key contributor to the economic, ability, and racial disparities in mortality. Hurricane Katrina made it clear that access to a car can actually be a matter of life or death: The evacuation of New Orleans worked very well for people with cars, but hundreds died because they didn't have the ability to drive away.[52] And others were shipped off as far away as Salt Lake City, Utah, in a rush by well-intended first responders to "save" them, but the evacuees had no way to return home, particularly for those without income or savings to reestablish their lives in their former homes.

Mobility has also proved to be a significant barrier in survival rates for persons with physical impairments in times of disaster as evacuation becomes a much more complex endeavor when accessible facilities are needed to accommodate movement. A 2005 Harris Interactive survey found that 53 percent of people with disabilities have not made plans to evacuate or escape their homes quickly in case of an emergency.[53]

According to analysis of the 2000 U.S. Census, African-Americans are five times more likely than white Americans to rely on public transportation to get to work.[54] This signifies a lack of a personal vehicle and means that when the time comes for the need for urgent movement, they are almost completely reliant on external systems for their survival. Therefore, in situations like Hurricane Sandy where the subway system was completely inundated, people who are dependent on public transportation have no means of escape. Even where there is private vehicle ownership, highways that are not meant to accommodate simultaneous movement of massive numbers of personal vehicles can become death traps when floodwaters overtake traffic that has become paralyzed by sheer volume and insufficient space.

IX. Business

Finally, disasters have disparate impacts on businesses, and the pre-disaster economic condition of businesses greatly determines their ability to rebound after the disaster. Financial security in women- and minority-owned businesses is already shallow compared with other businesses,[55] which renders them vulnerable to any destabilizing event. The U.S. Department of Labor estimates over 40 percent of businesses never reopen following a disaster. According to the Association of Records Managers and Administrators, over 60 percent of businesses close within two years of being confronted with a major disaster.[56] Small businesses are hardest hit by disaster because they have fewer resources to fall back on in terms of non-affected revenue streams, insurance, and other cushioning forces that allow them to be more resilient. Given the preexisting vulnerabilities of women- and minority-owned businesses—less cash reserves—they are the first and most likely to go under due to the impact of disasters.[57] Two women's stories in the wake of disasters in the Gulf Coast were illustrative of the vulnerability of women-owned businesses, which resulted in differential impact.

One African-American woman had been scraping and saving for years as a single mother with a high-school diploma and no college education. She was able to earn a living wage but not much more. However, she had finally realized her dream of starting her own business, a hair salon, when Hurricane Katrina came and swept it all away. She had not been "employed" at the time of the disaster, and so could demonstrate no lost wages. Compounding this problem, she did not have any revenue because her business had not become operational, and she was a renter on top of all of that. As such, she could not qualify for the assistance or the loans that were available through the emergency response system to small-business owners or to the unemployed. She fell through the cracks of the disaster response infrastructure, from being on the brink of realizing her dreams, to utter destitution.[58]

A Vietnamese woman and her daughter ran a laundry service. In the aftermath of the BP Oil Drilling Disaster, they no longer had any business. Their biggest contract was with a ship that docked weekly in Biloxi, Mississippi, but they only had a handshake agreement with the shipping company, which suited them fine until the disaster. However, to qualify for compensation post-disaster, they needed paperwork to prove lost income, which they could not produce. They felt like they had to be a bit lax with business practices to survive in a competitive environment, but it ended up being their downfall when disaster struck.[59]

X. Redevelopment Following the Disaster

If previous disasters and early observations of Superstorm Sandy are predictors, the continued trajectory toward increased disasters means both the incidents and the post-disaster efforts will result in disparities in redevelopment and civic disengagement through voter disenfranchisement and redistricting. This combination results in hemorrhaging of political power of low-income communities and communities of color, thus marginalizing their ability to help shape the rebuilding of their own communities.

Equitable decision making regarding the determination of adequately safe infrastructure, zoning, and siting of hazardous facilities; allocation of recovery funding; and more is dependent on having representative and responsive elected officials. In 2005, voting was disrupted for thousands due to the ongoing displacement of Hurricane Katrina survivors, and the level of dispersion resulted in redistricting decisions that significantly changed the political landscape of New Orleans.[60] In 2012, about one week before the presidential election, Superstorm Sandy ravaged the northeast United States and lowered the level of civic engagement by displacing residents and forcing the closure of early voting sites in many states.

When one layers the disproportionate displacement of certain communities and the documented disparities in mobility, disasters deepen already-existing differential impact of voter disenfranchisement, regressive voting rights policies, and redistricting on communities of color and low-income communities. This political disenfranchisement then ingrains the cycle of lack of engagement in decision making of the most vulnerable communities. The political cycle then perpetuates the cycle of preexisting vulnerability, disproportionate disaster impacts, and less resilience of the entire community. At any point in this cycle, communities are less able to rebound and build stronger communities.

XI. Recommendations

- A civil rights and equity analysis must be used when developing emergency preparation and response policies. Civil rights violations in the areas of housing, education, transportation, employment, and contracting are pervasive in the aftermath of a disaster. Strong monitoring and enforcement of civil rights protections is important to equitable recovery. The equity analysis must include an assessment of the various pre-disaster vulnerabilities, a strategy for the distribution of recovery resources to address the disaster's compounding impacts on communities, and a fair and transparent process that involves all communities.
- Enact policies that support community-resilience building initiatives. Community resilience is defined as "the sustained ability of a community to withstand and recover from adversity."[61] Tools necessary to help ensure a resilient community must feature a model of community-designed planning that encompasses vulnerability assessment; physical and structural protection; early warning systems; transportation systems; preparedness and contingency planning; public knowledge, awareness, and skills; and other measures.[62]

- Research initiatives must be supported and implemented to identify and evaluate equity issues in the context of disasters. Given the influx of federal and state dollars post-disaster, as well as private foundations to community-based organizations, to research the effectiveness of disaster-recovery efforts, these assessments must be undertaken with an equity lens. This includes moving beyond the simply quantifiable outcomes of the number of dollars deployed and utilized, but also examining who benefited or were excluded from these resources.
- For example, in assessing transportation redevelopment dollars, look beyond just the number of roads rebuilt to the larger picture of whether those roads were rebuilt in communities of color and low-income communities. Or, as another example, in assessing emergency housing responses, look beyond simply the number of people served to whether special populations such as women, people with disabilities, and survivors of domestic violence were appropriately included in those response and recovery efforts.
- Infrastructure development, such as decision making on levee reinforcement, must be based on impact on people. A justice-based framework must be the determining lens through which considerations are made regarding infrastructure development projects.
- Improve and reform siting and zoning and development processes and regulations.

    a. Future construction should avoid building homes in floodplains. Where there are existing homes in floodplains, provisions should be made to relocate the homes to safer ground.

    b. Homes must not be located in proximity to hazardous facilities. Where there are existing homes located near hazardous facilities, provisions should be made to relocate facilities and shut them down.

- Ensure that every community that has a hazardous facility has a comprehensive disaster and evacuation plan, as well as the proper infrastructure to support the highest level of safety if disasters occur.
- First responders must provide consistent guidance to all returning residents regarding safe reentry into homes contaminated with toxic mold or other hazards. This guidance should also be translated into the languages of the displaced communities.

XII. Conclusion

Disasters underscore the point that place really does matter. Without a civil and human rights approach to disaster recovery, one disaster compounds another and leads to additional and persistent inequities.

Identifying and understanding the existing vulnerabilities in communities is essential to advancing equitable recovery.

Existing vulnerabilities include the location of low-income communities and communities of color more often along floodplains; the siting of hazardous facilities in these communities; the poor condition of vital infrastructure like sewer and transportation systems; the quality and type of housing; the lack of economic options for work and business development; and socioeconomic vulnerabilities of women, people with disabilities, incarcerated people, immigrant communities, and others. These circumstances are then exacerbated by lack of political power and influence of those most vulnerable, which means decision making around rebuilding and future disaster mitigation also fails to encompass the needs of those most at risk.

Further compounding these dynamics is the rise of what some refer to as "disaster capitalism," taking advantage of a major disaster to adopt free-market policies that the population would be less likely to accept under normal circumstances. For example, Superstorm Sandy has resulted in the allocation of $60 billion in disaster relief funding, which means there is a lot of money to be gained from being engaged in post-disaster recovery. There are those who view a disaster as an opportunity to make money without regard to the civil and human rights violation in their practices. From price gouging to developers who advance projects that result in land loss for vulnerable property owners, these predatory practices are all done in a context of post-disaster chaos and lack of protective measures for consumers, landowners, small-business owners, and more.

Therefore, a thorough analysis of the myriad pre-disaster vulnerabilities is necessary to design policies, programs, processes, and infrastructure that encompass the needs of all. Measures to assess circumstances that arise in disasters that deepen vulnerabilities or create new risks and hazards for some more than others must also be included. Past post-disaster policies and practices that have resulted in inequitable school reforms, marginalizing redistricting processes, and redevelopment that resulted in disparate property and small-business losses must be examined in order to create mechanisms to ensure equitable recovery in all sectors. Decision-making processes must be inclusive of a representative population, with a special emphasis on those who are most vulnerable.

Notes

1. OXFAM AMERICA, RECOVERING STATES? THE GULF COAST SIX MONTHS AFTER THE STORM (2006), *available at* http://reliefweb.int/sites/reliefweb.int/files/resources/1C601FC87F7D5AB249257122000D3FFA-oxfam-usa-23feb.pdf.

2. Pamela Jenkins & Brenda Philips, *Chapter VIII, Domestic Violence and Hurricane Katrina*, KATRINA AND THE WOMEN OF NEW ORLEANS, http://tulane.edu/nccrow/upload/NCCROWreport08-chapter8.pdf (last visited on April 9, 2013).

3. *See, e.g.*, OXFAM, *The Tsunami's Impact on Women* (March 2005), http://www.preventionweb.net/files/1502_bn050326tsunamiwomen.pdf.

4. B. Phillips & B. Morrow, *Social Science Research Needs: Focus on Vulnerable Populations, Forecasting, and Warnings*, 8(3) NAT. HAZARDS REV. 61–8 (2007).

5. Nick A. Gilbert et al., *Emergency Preparedness for Vulnerable Populations: People with Special Health-care Needs*, PUB. HEALTH REP., Mar.–Apr. 2009, 124(2), at 338–43, http://www.ncbi.nlm.nih.gov/pmc/articles/PMC2646456/.

6. Gregory Berger, *Isolated Native American Communities Struggle in the Aftermath of Hurricanes Katrina and Rita*, DEMOCRACY NOW (Nov. 24, 2005), http://m.democracynow.org/stories/6422.

7. CHESTER HARTMAN & GREGORY D. SQUIRES, THERE IS NO SUCH THING AS A NATURAL DISASTER: RACE, CLASS AND HURRICANE KATRINA (2006).

8. Campbell Robertson and Clifford Krauss, *Gulf Spill is the Largest of Its Kind, Scientists Say*, N.Y. TIMES, Aug. 2, 2010, http://www.nytimes.com/2010/08/03/us/03spill.html?_r=0.

9. Anemona Hartocollis & Julie Turkewitz, *Storm Victims, in Cleanup, Face Rise in Injuries and Illness*, N. Y. TIMES, Nov. 19, 2012, http://www.nytimes.com/2012/11/20/nyregion/improvised-emergency-rooms-rise-amid-hurricane-sandys-debris.html?pagewanted=all.

10. Stephen Nessen, "Thousands Still Cold and Struggling Months After Superstorm Standy, National Public Radio, at http://www.npr.org/2013/01/24/170198110/thousands-still-cold-and-struggling-months-after-superstorm-sandy (January 24, 2013) (last visited on April 8, 2013).

11. Daniel A. Farber, *Disaster Law and Inequality*, 25 LAW & INEQUALITY 297, Summer 2007.

12. *Reliable Prosperity: Social Equity*, ECOTRUST, http://www.reliableprosperity.net/social_equity.html (last visited Apr. 2, 2013).

13. Melanie McDermott et al., *Defining Equity: A Framework for Evaluating Equity in the Context of Ecosystem Services* (2011), http://redd-net.org/files/ESPA%20Equity%20Paper%20for%20website%20final1.pdf.

14. DEANNA BURNEY, KEITH SIMMONDS & GILBERT QUEELEY, FORUM ON PUB. POLICY, THE RELATIONSHIP BETWEEN SOCIO-ECONOMIC CONDITIONS AND THE IMPACT OF NATURAL DISASTERS ON RURAL AND URBANIZED REGIONS LEVEL OF PREPAREDNESS AND RECOVERY (2007), *available at* http://forumonpublicpolicy.com/archivesum07/burney.pdf.

15. David Hall, *Katrina: Spiritual Medicine for Political Complacency and for Social Activists Who Are Sleepwalking*, 23 HARV. BLACKLETTER L.J. 1, 2 n.4 (2007).

16. Dennis P. Andrulis et al., *Preparing Racially and Ethnically Diverse Communities for Public Health Emergencies*, 26 HEALTH AFF. 1269, 1269 (2007).

17. *Abandoned and Abused*, AM. CIVIL LIBERTIES UNION (Aug. 9, 2006), http://www.aclu.org/prisoners-rights/abandoned-and-abused.

18. Amy Vanderwarker, *Water and Environmental Justice*, *in* A TWENTY-FIRST CENTURY U.S. WATER POLICY (2012).

19. Bob Marshall, *Hurricane Isaac Lays Bare the Painful Economics of Flood Protection*, TIMES-PICAYUNE (Sept. 12, 2012), http://www.nola.com/hurricane/index.ssf/2012/09/hurricane_isaac_lays_bare_the.html.

20. Mark Schleifstein, *Corps Puts Breaks on Donaldsonville to the Gulf Levee Project*, TIMES-PICAYUNE, June 27, 2012.

21. Adrian Wilson, *Coal Blooded: Putting Profits before People* 4–5, NAACP (2012), http://naacp.3cdn.net/ab160002359dc4e863_mlbleopn9.pdf.

22. UNITED CHURCH OF CHRIST, TOXIC WASTES AND RACE AT TWENTY 1987–2007 (2007), *available at* http://www.ucc.org/justice/pdfs/toxic20.pdf.

23. CERD WORKING GRP. ON HEALTH AND ENVTL. HEALTH, UNEQUAL HEALTH OUTCOMES IN THE UNITED STATES (2008), 27–28.

24. Evan Osnos, *Sandy, Fukushima, and the Nuclear Industry*, NEW YORKER (Nov. 2, 2012), http://www.newyorker.com/online/blogs/evanosnos/2012/11/sandy-fukushima-and-the-nuclear-industry.html.

25. SW MISS. PLANNING & DEV. DISTRICT, SOUTHWEST MISSISSIPPI MULTI-JURISDICTIONAL HAZARD MITIGATION PLAN (2010), *available at* http://www.swmpdd.com/services/SWMPDD_Hazard_Mitigation_Plan.pdf.

26. Agency for Toxic Substances and Disease Registry. Public Health Statement for Hydrogen Sulfide (July 2006) #CAS-m http://www.aecf.org/upload/publicationfiles/fact_sheet3.pdf.

27. *Gulf Coast Recovery: An Examination of Claims and Social Services in the Aftermath of the Deepwater Horizon Oil before the U.S. Comm. on Homeland Sec. and Governmental Affairs Subcomm. for Disaster Recovery and Intergovernmental Relations*, 112th Cong. (Jan. 27, 2011) (testimony by Sen. Richard Shelby), beginning at 34:08, video at http://www.hsgac.senate.gov/subcommittees/disaster-recovery-and-intergovernmental-affairs/hearings/gulf-coast-recovery-an-examination-of-claims-and-social-services-in-the-aftermath-of-the-deepwater-horizon-oil-spill.

28. *Id.*; *see also* Richard Andrew Robinson Jr., The Gulf of Mexico Oil Disaster: A Case Study on the Projected Economic Impact on Tourism Among the Gulf States of Louisiana, Mississippi, Alabama,

and Florida (Aug. 1, 2010) (unpublished A.B. thesis, University of Nevada, Las Vegas), *available at* http://digitalscholarship.unlv.edu/cgi/viewcontent.cgi?article=1567&context=thesesdissertations.

29. Daniel A. Farber, *The BP Blowout and the Social and Environmental Erosion of the Louisiana Coast*, 13 MINN. J.L. SCI. & TECH. 37 (2012), *available at* http://scholarship.law.berkeley.edu/facpubs/144/.

30. *See, e.g.*, Tonya Ott, *In Alabama, Tornadoes Wiped Out Uninsured Homes*, NPR, http://www.npr.org/2011/05/05/136028754/in-alabama-tornadoes-wiped-out-uninsured-homes.

31. Associated Press, *Tornado Victims Are Often Uninsured* (May 26, 2011), http://www.nola.com/business/index.ssf/2011/05/tornado_victims_are_often_unin.html.

32. *Poverty & Economics*, UNIFEM WOMEN, http://www.unifem.org/gender_issues/women_poverty_economics/.

33. ERIC S. BELSKY & RACHEL BOGARDUS DREW, JOINT CTR. FOR HOUS. STUDIES, HARVARD UNIV., TAKING STOCK OF THE NATION'S RENTAL HOUSING CHALLENGES AND A HALF CENTURY OF PUBLIC POLICY RESPONSES (2007), *available at* http://jchs.harvard.edu/sites/jchs.harvard.edu/files/rr07-1_belsky_drew.pdf.

34. *See generally* RAKESH KOCHHAR, RICHARD FRY & PAUL TAYLOR, PEW RESEARCH CTR., TWENTY-TO-ONE: WEALTH GAPS RISE TO RECORD HIGHS BETWEEN WHITES, BLACKS AND HISPANICS (July 27, 2011), *available at* http://www.pewsocialtrends.org/files/2011/07/SDT-Wealth-Report_7-26-11_FINAL.pdf (finding that "[t]he median wealth of white households is 20 times that of black households and 18 times that of Hispanic households"); *see also* THOMAS M.SHAPIRO, TATJANA MESCHEDE & LAURA SULLIVAN, BRANDEIS UNIV. INST. ON ASSETS AND SOC. POLICY, THE RACIAL WEALTH GAP INCREASES FOURFOLD (May 2010), http://www.insightcced.org/uploads/CRWG/IASP-Racial-Wealth-Gap-Brief-May2010.pdf.

35. *See, e.g.*, Craig Haney, *The Wages of Prison Overcrowding: Harmful Psychological Consequences and Dysfunctional Correctional Reactions*, 22 WASH. U.J.L. & POL'Y 265–93 (2006), *available at* http://law.wustl.edu/Journal/22/p265Haney.pdf.

36. Yvonne Yen Liu, *Some Gulf Coast Oil Spill Toxins Are Harder to See*, COLORLINES (Apr. 20, 2011), http://colorlines.com/archives/2011/04/the_fallout_of_the_gulf_coast_oil_spill_on_communities_of_color.html.

37. Catherine L. Cohan & Steve W. Cole, *Life Course Transitions and Natural Disaster: Marriage, Birth, and Divorce Following Hurricane Hugo*, 16(1) J. FAM. PSYCHOL., March 2002, at 14–25.

38. JACQUELINE PATTERSON, NAACP, "MY NAME IS 6508799": STATE OF THE GULF, ONE YEAR AFTER THE OIL DRILLING DISASTER (2011), *available at* http://naacp.3cdn.net/201f13fed7009f7191_z8m6bkkhv.pdf.

39. Elaine Rundle, *When Disaster Strikes, Inmates Can Move to the Frontlines of Community Response*, *in* EMERGENCY MANAGEMENT, *available at* http://www.emergencymgmt.com/disaster/Inmates-Community-Response.html.

40. Amy Vanderwarker, *Water and Environmental Justice*, *in* A TWENTY-FIRST CENTURY U.S. WATER POLICY (2012).

41. Interview by Jacqueline Patterson (May 10, 2011).

42. Interview by Jacqueline Patterson (May 10, 2011).

43. Interview by Jacqueline Patterson (May 9, 2011).

44. Howard Stutz, *Tunica Casinos to Reopen after Flooding*, LAS VEGAS REVIEW-JOURNAL, May 17, 2011, http://www.reviewjournal.com/business/casinos-gaming/tunica-casinos-reopen-after-flooding?mobile=y.

45. Jacqueline Patterson, *Gulf Oil Drilling Disaster: Gendered Layers of Impact*, ON THE ISSUES MAG., http://www.ontheissuesmagazine.com/2011spring/2011spring_Patterson.php (last visited Apr. 2, 2013).

46. Mark Schleifstein, *BP Agrees to $5.4 Million Settlement of Complaints of Gender Bias in Oil Spill Cleanup Hiring*, TIMES-PICAYUNE (June 28, 2012), http://www.nola.com/news/gulf-oil-spill/index.ssf/2012/06/bp_agrees_to_54_million_settle.html.

47. Nicole Santa Cruz & Julie Cart, *Oil Cleanup Workers Report Illness*, L.A. TIMES, May 26, 2010, http://articles.latimes.com/2010/may/26/nation/la-na-oil-workers-sick-20100526.

48. R. BALFANZ & V. BYRNES, JOHNS HOPKINS UNIV. CTR. FOR SOC. ORG. OF SCH. BALTIMORE, THE IMPORTANCE OF BEING IN SCHOOL: A REPORT ON ABSENTEEISM IN THE NATION'S PUBLIC SCHOOLS (2012), *available at* http://new.every1graduates.org/wp-content/uploads/2012/05/FINALChronicAbsenteeismReport_May16.pdf.

49. THE ANNIE E. CASEY FOUNDATION, *Race Matters: Unequal Opportunities in EDUCATION Fact Sheet* (2006), *available at* http://www.aecf.org/upload/publicationfiles/fact_sheet3.pdf.

50. Interview by Jacqueline Patterson (May 13, 2011).

51. DANIELLE ANN COOK, VOICES CRYING OUT FROM THE WILDERNESS: THE STORIES OF BLACK EDUCATORS ON SCHOOL REFORM IN POST KATRINA NEW ORLEANS (2008), *available at* http://dc.lib.unc.edu/cgi-bin/showfile.exe?CISOROOT=/etd&CISOPTR=1518&filename=1509.pdf.

52. JULIE CIDELL, SUSTAINABLE TRANSPORTATION: ACCESSIBILITY, MOBILITY, AND DERIVED DEMAND, *available at* http://cnx.org/content/m42717/latest/.

53. DISASTERSRUS.ORG, http://www.disastersrus.org/MyDisasters/disability/disability_preparedness.htm.

54. U.S. CENSUS BUREAU, THE AMERICAN COMMUNITY—BLACKS: 2004 22, fig.18 (American Community Survey Reports 2007), http://www.census.gov/prod/2007pubs/acs-04.pdf.

55. U.S. DEPARTMENT OF COMMERCE, MINORITY BUSINESS DEVELOPMENT AGENCY, DISPARITIES IN CAPITAL ACCESS BETWEEN MINORITY AND NON-MINORITY OWNED BUSINESSES: THE TROUBLING REALITY OF CAPITAL LIMITATIONS FACED BY MBEs (Jan. 2010), http://www.mbda.gov/sites/default/files/DisparitiesinCapitalAccessReport.pdf; NATIONAL WOMEN'S BUSINESS COUNCIL, 2012 ANNUAL REPORT, http://www.nwbc.gov/sites/default/files/NWBC_2012AnnualReport_FINAL.pdf.

56. Darrell Zahorsky, *Disaster Recovery Decision Making for Small Businesses*, ABOUT.COM, http://sbinformation.about.com/od/disastermanagement/a/disasterrecover.htm (last visited Apr. 2, 2013).

57. Brenda Berkman, *How to Support Women and Girls in Disaster Recovery*, FEMINISTING (Nov. 21, 2012) http://feministing.com/2012/11/21/how-to-support-women-and-girls-in-disaster-recovery/.

58. JACQUELINE PATTERSON, NAACP, "MY NAME IS 6508799": STATE OF THE GULF, ONE YEAR AFTER THE OIL DRILLING DISASTER (2011), *available at* http://naacp.3cdn.net/201f13fed7009f7191_z8m6bkkhv.pdf.

59. *Id.*

60. Campbell Robertson, *Smaller New Orleans after Katrina, Census Shows*, N. Y. TIMES, Feb. 12, 2011, http://www.nytimes.com/2011/02/04/us/04census.html?pagewanted=all&_r=0.

61. BUILDING COMMUNITY RESILIENCE TO DISASTER: A WAY FORWARD TO ENHANCE NATIONAL HEALTH SECURITY (2012).

62. JOHN TWIGG, DFID, CHARACTERISTICS OF A DISASTER-RESILIENT COMMUNITY: A GUIDANCE NOTE (2007), *available at* https://practicalaction.org/docs/ia1/community-characteristics-en-lowres.pdf.

CHAPTER 5

Local Government and Interjurisdictional Coordination in Disaster Response and Recovery

Dina Schlossberg

I. Introduction

In December 2006, a severe windstorm ravaged the western part of the state of Washington, leaving millions of residents in 17 counties without electrical power. Dubbed the Hanukkah Eve Wind Storm of 2006, the storm caused the deaths of 15 people, including nine from the effects of carbon monoxide poisoning.[1] The effects of this storm were most keenly felt in King County, Washington, where the severity of the windstorm caused unprecedented damage to the electrical grid, knocking out electrical power to more than one million people. At least 100,000 people remained without electricity for more than 10 days.[2] The immediate strain of the storm on the King County government was immense. More than 17,000 calls for emergency assistance were placed to the county's 9-1-1 service within the first 18 hours after the storm emerged, four times the number of calls normally received by the county.[3] In King County, as well as some of the neighboring counties, high winds and loss of power resulted in closure of some county offices and an additional burden on functioning governmental resources.[4] It is the chaos following the storm, such as in King County, in which local governments begin their response to disaster and build the road to recovery.

This chapter will explain the roles and responsibilities of local governments in the context of disaster preparedness, response, and recovery. This chapter also will provide a framework for the opportunities of local government to receive funding and provide much-needed relief services within the context of the federal disaster relief system. Beyond meeting basic needs, local governments may also address disaster relief and the longer-term process of recovery utilizing a holistic and community-based approach. As such, this chapter concludes with examples of local jurisdictional responses to disaster that are creative, community driven, and forward looking.

II. All Disasters Are Local: Roles of Local Government Post-Disaster

Whether the result of human or natural causes, disasters most profoundly affect the individuals, families, neighborhoods, and communities in which the disaster occurs. It is images of a mother and her children who have lost their home as the result of a tornado, or the picture of a senior citizen pulled to safety in a flood that conveys to the outside world the immediacy of the suffering that strikes a particular community. "All disasters are local" is a recurrent theme in all aspects of disaster planning, response, recovery, and mitigation. This was also the central theme of Federal Emergency Management Agency (FEMA) Deputy Administrator Richard Serino's keynote speech in November 2011, at the International Association of Emergency Managers' Annual Conference.[5] Serino's speech occurred in a year in which more than 1,000 deaths occurred in the United States in local disasters, and 10 major disasters resulted in more than $1 billion in damages.[6] "FEMA started in 1979," he remarked. "Did we have disasters before 1979? It was locals taking care of each other, the states helping, and eventually the federal government."[7]

In many respects the organizational construct described by Serino continues to guide disaster response and recovery despite the creation of FEMA. The system of distribution of responsibility that puts the primary burden of emergency response on the local government with support from the state government has been in existence since the time of World War I and is consistent with the American federalism system of government.[8] With disasters of any magnitude, it is the local government that is most familiar with the needs of the community, the impact of the incident, and the governmental body responsible for taking the initial lead in the incident response and recovery. This response and recovery includes maintaining public order and safety, providing access to temporary safe and secure shelter, protecting the lives of those unable to assist themselves, and assessing the costs and resources needed for recovery.

Regardless of the geographic size and scope of the local community, it is local government leaders who are primarily and ultimately responsible for overseeing all four phases of emergency and disaster management: preparedness, response, recovery, and mitigation against future disasters.[9] It is the locally elected or appointed governmental official (mayor, town manager, borough manager, etc.) who is responsible for the health, safety, and welfare of a community, and it is this same official's responsibility to lead in the response and recovery of a disaster. The local government has the primary obligation to plan, undertake, and manage all aspects of the community's recovery.

III. Local Government Considerations in Disaster Planning, Response, and Recovery

At its most basic, disaster response is generally recognized as those activities necessary to address the immediate and short-term effects of an emergency or disaster. Response involves the immediate actions to save lives, protect property, and meet basic human needs.[10] Given their immediate proximity to those affected and intimate knowledge of the community landscape and networks, a fundamental obligation of local government bodies is to aid and protect the community in the aftermath of a disaster by addressing the most immediate needs of public safety, security, and shelter. Yet, local governments are often also burdened with the same post-disaster obstacles as their constituents and the needs for recovery may far exceed local resources. As a result, local governments must plan and prepare for this role with the support of the state and federal governments, as well as the support of the nonprofit and private business sectors. Local response to disaster includes undertaking the following: (1) acting as the primary "first provider" of emergency response services; (2) coordinating a response with public agencies, area nonprofit organizations, and private agencies; (3) proclaiming a local state of emergency to authorize using local resources or the expenditure of funds, such as for snow removal, and waiving the usual bidding process for goods and services; and (4) activating area mutual aid compacts with other local governments and area organizations.

Once disaster response is under way, and the incident stabilized, disaster recovery begins. In an article published in *Public Management Magazine* in 2009, Frances L. Edwards, then associate director of the Collaboration for Disaster Mitigation in San Jose, California, aptly described the commencement of disaster *recovery* as that point "when the situation is no longer getting worse, all the living have been rescued, and the community has found the floor."[11] Examples of activities taken during the response period include restoring electricity and other power to the area, securing shelter for area residents, clearing roads and highways for travel, and removal of debris.

Some experts believe the recovery process begins well in advance of the completion of the response period. Brett Kriger, director of the Institute for Building Technology and Safety's Disaster Management Group, notes that the recovery process begins even prior to completing the response stage because decisions made while responding affect the recovery process. He states, "There's usually a 30 percent overlap in the middle where the community is still responding while gearing up for recovery."[12] Many professionals involved with disaster planning and response believe that the key to a healthy community response to a disaster is the ability to begin the recovery phase while still in the disaster response mode.[13]

Just as no two communities are precisely alike, so may the same be said for a local community's ability to prepare, respond, and recover from a disaster. Each local government is tasked with the obligation to prepare for and respond to a disaster in a manner that best protects the health, welfare, and public safety of that particular community. Local government leaders and their emergency response teams must address the particular dangers and concerns of a specific crisis and must provide attention to both the protection and security of the people and the property within the jurisdiction. Despite these differences and particularities, there are also a number of external factors that can influence a local government's ability to effectively meet this basic obligation, including the state of existing infrastructure, size of the jurisdiction, state of local economies, and the needs of the local community's vulnerable and at-risk populations.

A. State of Existing Infrastructure

As evident in the Hanukkah Eve Wind Storm, the loss of a major utility—public or private—can cripple a region, causing havoc and even loss of life. According to the King County Department of Natural Resources and Parks, the cost of damage to public property in King County and its cities (including public roads, sewage pipes, and buildings) due to the Hanukkah Eve Storm was roughly estimated to be $28.5 million.[14] In many parts of the country, the existing infrastructure—be it utility lines, bridges, roads, or breached levees—is crumbling or decaying, thereby compromising the safety of the community's residents. The American Society of Civil Engineers (ASCE) ranks the quality of the country's infrastructure as a D, due to the overall state of neglect and decay.[15] According to the ASCE, for example, the average bridge in the United States is 43 years old, and one in four of the 60,000 bridges in this country are structurally deficient.[16] Similarly, an analysis by the *New York Times* found that across the United States, a water line bursts roughly every two minutes, or 720 times a day.[17] Compromised, old, and decaying infrastructure challenges the ability of local governments to effectively plan for a disaster and increases the likelihood of an unknown and unplanned event, such as a bridge collapse or a dam break, to occur. In addition, the cost to repair the infrastructure makes the cost of recovery ever more challenging.

Nowhere is this made more compelling than in the aftermath of the Category 1 Superstorm Sandy in the densely packed regions of New York and New Jersey. Rebuilding costs may exceed exceed $70 billion, which would cover just replacement of existing, aging public works without additional improvements. [18]

B. Size of the Local Jurisdiction

The size of the jurisdiction and its composition of government are factors in disaster recovery and response and in the ability of a local government to act swiftly and effectively. In New York City, for example, it is estimated that due to the magnitude of damage inflicted by Superstorm Sandy, the need for housing is overwhelming, with an estimated 30,000 to 40,000 people seeking replacement housing as a result of the storm.[19] In contrast, in Greensburg, Kansas, the entire community was affected by a violent tornado in 2007, and the loss was significant; however, rebuilding efforts involved a community of 1,500 households.[20]

Likewise, while major cities will likely have professional emergency management systems and chains of command, in some smaller towns, boroughs, and rural communities, the responsibility for being the first to aid the public in a local emergency may be assigned to volunteer participants rather than paid government employees. For example, the Commonwealth of Pennsylvania is home to 12 percent of the nation's 20,000 all-volunteer fire companies, more than any other state.[21] Increasingly, these volunteer fire departments are being called upon to meet not only the challenges of local fire needs but to also be first responders in all level of emergencies, regardless of magnitude or cause of event.[22]

C. The Beleaguered State of Local Economies

The capacity of many local jurisdictions has been impaired by the larger economic downturn. Doing more with less is a familiar theme as local governments have to cut back budgets due to rising expenditures, reduced local tax revenue, and less revenue sharing from the state and federal governments.[23] In some jurisdictions, the twin effects of reduced tax revenue and loss of needed federal and state funds have resulted in a significant reduction in direct services and investment in infrastructure, even without the additional hardships of a disaster. Some jurisdictions, such as Pontiac, Michigan, due to their dire financial conditions, are now under emergency management control pursuant to state law that strips local government of authority in favor of a lone emergency manager. In Pontiac, as a cost-saving measure, the emergency manager eliminated both the local police and fire departments.[24] Throughout the United States, a number of cities and local utilities have filed for bankruptcy—for example, San Bernardino in California—shredding the police department and decimating common everyday services.[25] For certain municipalities, it would seem likely that the ability to respond in the event of a natural or human-made disaster would be strained by the overall economic condition of the local government.

D. Vulnerable and At-Risk Populations

In all cycles of an emergency, special consideration needs to be given to address the needs of vulnerable or special-needs populations. This may be defined differently for each community, but vulnerable populations may be defined as people who cannot comfortably or safely access and use the standard resources offered in disaster preparedness, relief, and recovery. Such person might include (but need not be limited to) community members who have physical, mental, or developmental disabilities;

have limited English skills or are non-English speaking; or are geographically or culturally isolated, medically or chemically dependent, homeless, elderly, or children.[26] Communities that are economically less secure tend to also bear the brunt of certain natural disasters. An example of this is the effect of tornadoes on people who live in less permanent housing structures such as mobile or manufactured homes. Nationwide, statistics from 2001 to 2010 indicate that people who live in mobile homes die in tornadoes at a rate 15 times higher than residents of permanent homes.[27]

Standard protocol for emergency preparedness is to advise the public that in the event of emergency each household prepare to be self-reliant for up to three days and to have on hand at least three days' worth of food and water and other emergency supplies.[28] Putting aside that in many recent disasters large numbers of people have gone without power or aid for a week or more,[29] for many vulnerable residents and at-risk members, health, age, or physical ability may limit their capacity to safely and securely reside without basic systems of water, power, and access to medical care for even these first few days. For low-income residents, the ability to stockpile food, water, and other emergency supplies is not within financial reach. In certain disasters where there is a call to evacuate, the lack of a car or lack of funds to evacuate by means of public transportation may render an order to evacuate meaningless.[30]

Where language is a barrier to instructions in English, the ability to comprehend the warnings or to follow emergency orders is equally rendered without effect. For instance, in King County, Washington, a major problem revealed one week into the storm and power outage was that safety messages needed to be translated into more languages than other types of messages, and these messages needed to reach targeted and smaller audiences, with the Somali population being one example. The county officials found that some non-English-speaking populations may not have received the intended messages due to lack of literacy in their native tongue.[31]

Planning for disaster recovery by local government or first-responder agencies such as the Red Cross is especially critical when addressing the needs of vulnerable and disadvantaged communities. No disaster made this more evident than Hurricane Katrina, in which the vulnerability indices of the communities affected were not adequately addressed in the planning for or the recovery aftermath of the storm.[32] One study conducted by the nonprofit Fritz Institute found that 28 percent of the people who did not evacuate in Hurricane Katrina did not leave because they had limited resources. Of these who could not evacuate because of limited resources, 71 percent said they had nowhere else to go, 37 percent did not own a car, and 32 percent had a physical disability or were responsible as caretaker for someone with a disability.[33]

To effectively meet the needs of vulnerable populations, local governments must plan before disasters strike local areas. Below are two case studies of local governments' engagement in pre-disaster planning efforts to better serve vulnerable populations post-disaster. The first case study highlights a local government-initiated program, and the second case study describes collaboration between local government and a nonprofit organization.

1. City of Philadelphia, Pennsylvania

As described in the publication *Emergency Management*, Philadelphia's Department of Public Health decided to partner in advance of an upcoming disaster with organizations that serve vulnerable populations.[34] The Health Department reached out to human services agencies and community- and faith-based organizations to leverage the existing information and communication network within the city's culturally and economically vulnerable communities. The department sought to build and understand these relationships before disasters occurred. A plan was developed to reach out to these various organizations and discuss how the city could best serve its respective constituent populations in the event of an emergency or disaster. Dr. Esther Chernak, director of Philadelphia's Department of Public Health's Emergency Preparedness Program from 1999 to 2008, and now director of Drexel University's Center for Public Health Readiness and Communication, suggested the following principles be followed when developing an emergency preparedness and recovery program to serve culturally and ethnically vulnerable communities:

- Work with large organizations like the American Red Cross, United Way, and volunteer organizations active in disaster, because they should have a roster of which organizations and agencies are doing what in which communities.
- Conduct a needs assessment of who in the community has what functional needs; this will help to prioritize where to initiate the community-based work.
- Make clear that communication is to be bidirectional. Reinforce the importance of learning from and providing information to the community and its leaders, but also be sure to listen to and be open to the discussion on community needs and the community's understanding of the priority needs during and immediately after a disaster or other emergency.
- Have patience—understand that planning and relationship building will take a long time.[35]

2. "Ready Neighborhoods" in Northern and Central California

In Northern California in 2011, the Red Cross commenced a massive multiyear program to improve the disaster readiness in more than 50 local neighborhoods throughout Northern and Central California. Working in collaboration with local governments, business leaders, and community organizations, the Red Cross initiated a program called Ready Neighborhoods, which uses a partnership and community-based approach to train California residents, particularly those in underserved and vulnerable communities, on how to prepare for and respond in the event of an emergency.[36] Under Ready Neighborhoods, each target community is building partnerships and setting goals to meet its specific needs. The Red Cross then facilitates the collaboration of community leaders, local businesses, government departments and agencies, and nonprofit organizations to set community-specific goals.[37] Assessing the needs of vulnerable populations, creating goals to meet those needs, and developing disaster strategies before a disaster occurs is a part of local government's role.

IV. Planning and Cooperation among Local Governments

Local government officials are tasked with leading local disaster preparedness activities and systems and, in furtherance thereof, coordinating emergency preparation activities across and among all departments and agencies of a local jurisdiction, with the state and federal governments, and with the nonprofit and private sector. Various tools discussed in this section help ensure that local governments are prepared for this task by having the proper planning and networks with other local governments or regional networks in place when disaster strikes.

A. Continuity of Operations / Continuity of Government Plans

An important disaster planning tool used by local and state governments includes the adoption of a Continuity of Operations Plan (COOP), which details how essential functions of an agency or unit of local government will be handled during any emergency or situation that may disrupt normal operations,[38] and a Continuity of Government Plan (COGP).[39] A COGP helps to ensure that, in all instances, the functions of the local government are maintained, and typically consists of several key components, including order of succession, how to meet essential functions, storage and maintenance of vital records, alternate facilities, and ongoing communications.[40] Taken together, these two plans focus on the local jurisdiction's ability to perform essential government functions during any unplanned or exigent situation. These two plans are also intended to address how vital parts of the community's overall critical health, welfare, and economic needs will be maintained during any given disaster.

B. Mutual Aid Compacts

Local jurisdictions may not have the ability or the resources to effectively manage disaster relief efforts without assistance. In some jurisdictions, the emergency manager and governing official may coordinate recovery activities with neighboring jurisdictions through the use of Intrastate Mutual Aid Compacts.[41] Fashioned on the concepts of the Emergency Management Assistance Compact (EMAC), a national interstate mutual aid agreement that allows states to share resources across state lines during disasters and emergencies, an Intrastate Mutual Aid Compact is an agreement by and between neighboring local jurisdictions to provide mutual aid in the event of a disaster or time of other crucial need. Terms of each Intrastate Mutual Aid Compact are determined by state-enabling law and will typically cover such issues as who may declare an emergency, who may authorize deployment of assistance, and allocation of liability and costs in connection with the deployment of resources.[42] In addition, a compact may address protections for emergency responders in the areas of workers' compensation, tort liability, reciprocity of licensure, and reimbursement.[43] In most states, authorizing legislation deems participation automatic for each town, city, and other local municipality, but provides a mechanism to opt out through a referendum or other local vote. Participation in a local Mutual Aid Compact does not mean a local jurisdiction is obligated to provide support when called upon by a neighboring jurisdiction. The compact simply provides the framework for the allocation of expenses, risk, and liability, and provides immunity to the parties providing assistance. In 2011, the Washington legislature passed enabling legislation, which established an Intrastate Mutual Aid Compact.[44] Washington is the 35th state to pass such legislation.[45]

Businesses and local utilities may also enter into volunteer compacts to address emergency needs arising from extreme circumstances such as a disaster. For instance, during the Hanukkah Eve Wind Storm of 2006, the area utility companies invoked the use of a voluntary Mutual Aid Compact to address the severe power outages affecting the western counties of the state.[46]

C. Council of Governments as Facilitating Disaster Recovery

Another means of collaboration between neighboring jurisdictions is to utilize a Council of Governments (COG). According to the National Association of Regional Councils, "A COG is a multiservice entity with state and locally defined boundaries that delivers a variety of federal, state, and local programs while continuing its function as a planning organization, technical assistance provider, and 'visionary' to its member local governments. As such, they are accountable to local units of government and effective partners for state and federal governments."[47] A COG is a form of volunteer association among local governments of a specific geographic region that come together with the intent to bolster the economic opportunities of the region or to address other issues of mutual concern.[48] This structure provides the opportunity to bring together multiple local government entities to coordinate any number of issues, such as land use, infrastructure development, tourism, transportation, and emergency disaster preparedness and recovery. A COG may set regional priorities for a variety of federal and state funding programs, oversee regional programs for member municipalities, and provide technical assistance to municipalities, local organizations, and the general public.

In the aftermath of a disaster, recovery needs often transcend beyond geographic boundaries. When a presidential declaration of disaster is made, it is often for a large geographic area comprising multiple jurisdictions and counties. As federal and state disaster relief funds are made available, a COG can operate to facilitate the receipt and disbursement of these funds. A COG can also be used to leverage other sources of funds, such as low-interest business loans or foundation and grant funds. The National Association of Development Organizations (NADO) Research Foundation, with support from the U.S. Economic Development Administration, along with support from other partners, focuses its research on exploring methods that hasten post-disaster economic recovery and reduce the long-term financial burden of disasters on impacted communities, businesses, and individuals.[49] In its December 2012 report, NADO focused on the experiences of the East Central Iowa Council of Governments (ECICOG) after the 2008 Iowa floods (for further discussion of the 2008 Iowa floods, see chapter 9) and the Houston-Galveston Area Council (HGAC) in the wake of Hurricane Ike. (For further discussion of COGs following Hurricane Ike, see chapter 10.) The report concluded that to maximize opportunities for success, COGs or other regional development organizations should make sure to incorporate the following:

- Develop a Pre-Disaster Plan.
- Collaborate early and often in the recovery process.
- Set expectations appropriately, however this can best be defined. Recognize that recovery may take months, if not years.
- Clarify with public officials at federal, state, and local levels the core competencies of regional development organizations and the efficacy of delivery of services through this model.
- Expect roles and funding guidelines to change during the recovery process.
- Develop a rainy day fund. These funds can be used for immediate post-disaster grants and loans to keep afloat local businesses and to address other emergency community needs.[50]

A COG is also positioned to serve an important role in the opportunity for community input in the design of post-disaster recovery funding. For example, in 2011, the South East Texas Regional Planning Commission (SETRPC), located in the Beaumont, Texas, region, wished to engage the public to participate in a discussion on community development and housing needs resulting from a disaster. Through a number of different forms of communication in English, Spanish, and Vietnamese, the SETRPC encouraged residents of the region, particularly those of low income or living in heavily impacted communities, to submit their views regarding housing and community development needs post-disaster.[51]

V. State and Local Government Interaction

In addition to the assistance of other local jurisdictions, the state government plays a key role in the allocation of additional resources and provides leadership within the federal disaster response framework. The governor of a state may, in accordance with state law, make, amend, or suspend certain orders or regulations in response to or in anticipation of a disaster or declaration of an emergency. In addition, each state governor commands the state military forces and gives the orders for deployment for disaster planning and response. Additionally, all states (and U.S. territories) have laws mandating the establishment of a state emergency management agency and the emergency plans coordinated by that agency. The director of each state's emergency management agency is responsible for coordinating the state's response to an incident, including working and coordinating with impacted local and tribal governments within that particular state.[52]

If the governor of a state believes that its own resources may be exceeded as a result of the scope of the crisis, the governor can request assistance from the federal government through a Stafford Act presidential declaration of an emergency or major disaster,[53] or from other states through mutual aid and assistance arrangements, such as the EMAC.[54] A recent example of the implementation of the EMAC is in the aftermath of Superstorm Sandy. Because of the magnitude of the storm, the need for immediate support from other states was tremendous. Under the authority granted by EMAC, 27 states deployed more than 2,000 personnel and lent equipment to the impacted areas of New York and New Jersey.[55]

A state's understanding of what and how many resources are needed in a disaster's immediate aftermath is largely driven by assessments made by local governments. Local officials will undertake a needs assessment to determine the scope and magnitude of the disaster, including determining how many people are affected and whether there is a risk to life, security, and health.[56] If the need is sufficient, the chief local official will make a request for state and, in some instances, federal aid to the state emergency management agency.[57] The state emergency management agency will coordinate with local officials and its authorized representatives to develop a preliminary damage assessment as supporting documentation for the governor's request for a presidential disaster declaration.[58]

In accordance with the Stafford Act, when the president determines federal assistance is necessary, the president will request that the governor of the affected state designate a state coordinating officer for the purpose of coordinating state and local disaster-assistance efforts with those of the federal government.[59] The state coordinating official, along with the state emergency management agency, is tasked to work with the local jurisdictions on defining the need, assessing the damage, and determining the cost of recovery.[60] A state's determination of how to engage and involve local jurisdictions, which local jurisdictions to engage, and how much federal funding will be dispersed to particular jurisdictions has very direct and important consequences for local recovery. Also, the manner in which state governments utilize regional and/or local jurisdictions and organizations to prioritize and allocate disaster funds shapes the recovery landscape. For example, in the aftermath of Hurricanes Ike and Dolly in 2008, the state of Texas delegated approximately $1.1 billion to 11 COGs serving 250 local government entities with little guidance and oversight for allocation of the funds. (See generally chapter 10.)

As communities move from response to recovery, the state and local governments' coordination becomes equally important in resource allocation and accountability. The state and local coordination in disbursing funds, particularly those that come from federal programs and agencies, becomes an important, continual balancing act of leveraging the local government's intimate knowledge of needs, while ensuring the expended funds can be tracked in a centralized manner and are not used for discriminatory purposes.

VI. Federal Support for Local Government Response

When the combined efforts of the local and state governments are not sufficient to effectively and efficiently address the direct results of the devastating effects of the disaster, the local government may apply for federal assistance, either directly or through its state government and depending on whether the area is granted a presidential disaster declaration. (For a discussion on the role of federal government assistance post-disaster, see chapter 1.) As described above, the Stafford Act authorizes the president to provide federal assistance to supplement the disaster recovery efforts of local, state, and tribal governments. This federal assistance is primarily provided through FEMA's Public Assistance Program.[61] (For a discussion on the use of Public Assistance Grants in the contexts of public housing and workforce development post-disaster, see chapters 11 and 17 respectively.)

A. Public Assistance Program

According to James A. Walke, director of FEMA's Public Assistance Division, Disaster Assistance Directorate, the Public Assistance Program provides more than $2.5 billion a year to cost-sharing grants for local communities and nonprofit organizations.[62] The mission of the Public Assistance Program is to assist communities in rebounding from the overwhelming effects of disasters and natural emergencies by providing technical assistance and financial grants in an efficient, effective, and consistent manner.[63] Public Assistance Grants are most often awarded for recovery costs associated with debris removal, emergency protective measures, and the repair, replacement, or restoration of disaster-damaged, publicly owned facilities, and facilities of certain private nonprofit institutions.[64]

Under the Public Assistance Program, an applicant (as defined below) must register a request for assistance within 60 days of the date of the disaster. Four categories of applicants are eligible to apply for public assistance funds: (1) state government agencies; (2) local governments; (3) private nonprofit organizations that own or operate facilities open to the general public and that provide certain services otherwise performed by a government agency, such as colleges and universities, medical centers and other institutions, custodial care for the elderly or homeless, and other essential governmental services; and (4) federally recognized tribal governments and Alaska Native village organizations.[65]

Eligibility for the Public Assistance Program requires that an applicant meet four preliminary criteria:

1. Applicant must be eligible for assistance as listed above.[66]
2. The damaged area must be eligible for funding for replacement or rehabilitation.[67]
3. The work to be done to repair the facility or institution must be eligible for disaster-related relief (i.e., the work must be located in the disaster area, and the work must not be eligible for funding from another program).[68]
4. The costs of the emergency or repair work must be eligible. This is interpreted by FEMA as "reasonable and necessary to accomplish the eligible work;" the work must be conducted in accordance with federal, state, and local laws and regulations, and all costs to be paid by FEMA must take into consideration the deduction of any eligible insurance proceeds and salvage value.[69]

Public Assistance funds are awarded to the state, which passes them on to the local government. The federal share of assistance is no less than 75 percent of the eligible cost for emergency measures and the permanent restoration, rebuilding, and repair of the public facilities. The state, as the program grantee, determines how the non-federal share (up to 25 percent) is split with the eligible applicants (the affected local governments or nonprofit organizations).[70]

B. Community Development Block Grant—Disaster Recovery

An additional source of disaster recovery funds for local governments is federal Community Development Block Grants Disaster Recovery (CDBG-DR) funds.[71] Unlike FEMA funds, once an appropriation has been made, local jurisdictions, as well as states and federal Indian tribes, may apply directly to the Department of Housing and Urban Development (HUD) for assistance.[72] HUD notifies eligible governments of the appropriation, who must then develop and submit an action plan for disaster recovery before receiving CDBG-DR grants.[73] The action plan must describe the needs, strategies, and projected uses of the disaster recovery funds.[74] CDBG-DR funds are subject to the same regulatory requirement of the CDBG program unless waivers are otherwise provided. This means that, in general, grantees must use at least half of disaster recovery funds for activities that principally benefit low- and moderate-income people.[75] CDBG-DR funds may only be used to fund necessary expenses related to disaster relief, long-term recovery, and restoration of infrastructure, housing, and economic revitalization. CDBG-DR funds will not be provided to a grantee for disaster recovery if the need is otherwise funded by FEMA or other federal disaster relief programs.[76]

For instance, East Grand Forks, Minnesota (discussed later in this chapter), received $10.8 million in CDBG-DR funds after devastating floods in 1997.[77] These funds were used between 1997 and 2002 for economic development to assist 22 businesses and construction of several buildings for the purposes of creating and retaining jobs.[78] The use of CDBG-DR funds in rebuilding the Riverwalk Center, a commercial and recreation area located in downtown East Grand Forks, is noted as an example of the need to be flexible in using such funds from the local government's perspective:

> The Riverwalk Center is an example of how disaster grantees must be flexible to meet constantly shifting financial situations. The Riverwalk Center project was removed from the CDBG Disaster Recovery grant in 2000 and moved to a State CDBG grant for commercial rehabilitation. The $550,000 that had been budgeted for Riverwalk Center was re-budgeted to pay for flood damage repair costs to public facilities that were not covered by FEMA Public Assistance grants.[79]

By 2002, in reporting the use of the disaster relief funds, the city noted, "The business community is active once again and most jobs in the new downtown are occupied by or available to low- and moderate-income people. Job creation data has been carefully maintained by the city."[80]

This federal-state-local flow of money enables increased capacity but also lends itself to the tensions of local governments being on the ground faced with the immediate day-to-day needs as they wait for the wheels of these additional layers of government to move into action. Yet, on the other hand, such layering plays an important role in ensuring such funds are not used for discriminatory or non-disaster relief purposes.

VII. Local Government Framework for Long-Term Recovery

The local government is primarily responsible for the establishment of the long-term plan for recovery of a community. The ideal disaster recovery process recognizes the potential of the circumstance and manages the necessary activities to generate solutions rather than additional problems. In *Holistic Disaster Recovery, a Guide for Building Local Sustainability after a Natural Disaster*, the ideal disaster recovery process is described as one in which the community proactively manages:

- recovery and redevelopment decisions to balance competing interests so constituents are treated equitably and long-term community benefits are not sacrificed for short-term individual gains;
- multiple financial resources to achieve broad-based community support for holistic recovery activities;
- reconstruction and redevelopment opportunities to enhance economic and community vitality;
- environmental and natural resource opportunities to enhance natural functions and maximize community benefits; and
- exposure to risk to a level that is less than what it was before the disaster.[81]

FEMA, in its *Long Term Community Recovery Planning Process: A Self-Help Guide*,[82] echoes the above as the ideal recovery process and sets forth suggested procedures and processes for achieving a holistic recovery. FEMA describes the long-term recovery of a community as "the need to re-establish a healthy, functioning community that will sustain itself over time."[83] In this same guide, FEMA outlines a disaster recovery approach that places emphasis on a community-driven process with significant opportunities for community and citizen involvement and local control.[84]

VIII. Challenges: Inclusive, Long-term Planning in the Midst of Disaster

While the above frameworks are helpful guides, they do not alleviate the inevitable challenges faced on the ground as local governments make long-lasting decisions about the future amid the rubble of the disaster. Perhaps there is no better representation of the role of local government's decision making than zoning and land use. Ideally, all local land-use plans would be designed to incorporate the potential for disaster most likely to occur in that community (tornadoes in the plains, flooding in the coastal areas, etc.) and would be designed to mitigate the risks of loss to life or property should such a disaster occur. However, zoning and land-use laws are most often developed over time and in a piecemeal fashion, and more often than not with the overarching desire to drive economic opportunity, rather than to mitigate for disaster. Even in circumstances where local land use laws are developed to mitigate for one kind of natural disaster, it is possible to have the community negatively impacted by another wholly unexpected human-made or natural disaster.

When a disaster occurs, the local government must identify and then establish the policy objectives that will guide post-disaster zoning and land-use planning. This is especially true when a disaster envelops an entire community such as in Joplin, Missouri, in its 2011 tornado, and more recently Superstorm Sandy as it affected the barrier islands of New Jersey, or the entire community of Breezy Point in Staten Island, New York. Tensions often occur between the emotional needs of the residents, businesses, and organizations of the community that have been personally devastated—and who clamor to be able to rebuild what was lost—and the government's need to engage in a thoughtful, organized, and participatory decision-making process.

While governed by local decision-making processes, state and federal government agencies, through the requirements established by post-disaster funding and existing laws against discrimination, provide input into land-use and construction codes that impact how and when and where rebuilding will occur. Such oversight is an important mechanism by which to prevent local governments from enacting exclusionary and discriminatory land-use and zoning policies post-disaster. Galveston, Texas (see also chapter 10), and St. Bernard Parish, Louisiana (see also chapter 15), are two examples of local governments attempting to use disaster recovery as an opportunity to keep affordable rental housing and public housing out of their communities.

Rebuilding efforts in any given community are often driven by two overarching factors: the need to design in such a way to ensure the public safety of the people and property of the area and the need for economic recovery.[85] One of the biggest post-disaster challenges for a local government is to properly walk the fine line between emergency relief activities and thoughtful planning for a long-term economically productive and safe recovery. Public decisions made in the heat of the emergency period immediately following a disaster often compromise other opportunities for a thoughtful rebuilding process.[86] The understandable pressure imposed by residents and other property owners to allow for immediate rebuilding is a powerful influence on how local, state, and even federal decision makers address post-disaster recovery. At present, this debate is particularly acute post–Superstorm Sandy in New Jersey, which is estimated to have suffered loss or damage to an estimated 30,000 homes and businesses across the state and where repairs to the local infrastructure, schools, and other publicly owned property is estimated to be over $16 billion.[87] Here, significant damage occurred along the coastline, while long-standing local and state land-use laws emphasize a strong right to rebuild for all residents.[88]

Navigating the need for thoughtful rebuilding while also meeting the exigent needs and expectations of the community is a careful mix of managing expectations and engaging the wider community in a thoughtful replanning process. Some short-term decisions may have long-lasting and often unintended consequences and should therefore be carefully considered, including but not limited to:

- the location of temporary housing, which often becomes more permanent than was originally intended;
- the siting of temporary business locations, which begins with the aim of allowing local businesses to continue to operate, but may become de facto, long-term relocations;
- the selection of sites for dumping disaster debris; and
- road and bridge closures and reopenings.[89]

The basic decisions a community must make when choosing how they want to rebuild after a disaster are fundamentally centered on place and geography—how to use it and who owns it and whether to build back the same or to make use of the opportunity to build back differently. When given the opportunity, a comprehensive community-driven process to answer these questions is ideal and the best way to build resilience to withstand the next disaster.

IX. Opportunity: Building Stronger Communities Post-Disaster

Disaster recovery can provide the opportunity for local communities to engage in a thoughtful and engaged process that can result in an economically and environmentally sustainable community-development plan. Below are two case studies of communities that used their disaster recovery processes as opportunities to build their futures anew.

A. East Grand Forks, Minnesota

On April 18, 1997, the Red River flooded the city of East Grand Forks in Minnesota and the city of Grand Forks in North Dakota. More than 58,000 people from the two cities fled with their children, pets, and whatever they could carry. In Minnesota, all 98,000 residents of East Grand Forks had to be evacuated for a minimum of three weeks, with many residents unable to return home for weeks on end, and only seven of the town's 5,500 houses were spared flood damage.[90] On the Grand Forks side, a fire that followed the flood destroyed much of the downtown area. Within weeks of the flood, residents began returning home housed in FEMA trailers, and the local officials of East Grand Forks quickly welcomed a comprehensive community design recovery approach. The town residents and officials decided to embrace the river, not fight its existence and to build a recovery design that would provide assurance against future flood disasters.[91] With access to the river as the guiding principle, the consensus for the new vision of the city was that East Grand Forks should become a destination city, a "place where families would come for shopping, camping, dining and exploring the river," expressed Val Gravseth, the mayor's assistant.[92]

The city of East Grand Forks worked with the University of Minnesota's Center for Rural Design, which brings design as a problem-solving process to rural land issues, to redesign the area.[93] The Center for Rural Design worked with the city. Some of the significant design decisions included establishing new neighborhood developments created further from the river to ensure they would be spared future flooding, establishing sites for new schools, moving downtown business, and focusing on a vision of a grand Roaring Twenties city with emphasis on fine dining, shopping, and recreational activities.

After rebuilding, to protect the downtown area closest to the river, East Grand Forks built a new dike and flood wall, using innovative technology of the United States' installation of the "Invisible Flood Control Wall."[94] The city erects the "Invisible Flood Control Wall" only in times of an impending flood; otherwise, the wall is down and the river visible from downtown.[95]

The redesign of the city also includes what became a new recreation area known as the Red River State Recreation Area, utilizing the lots that used to house the flooded homes.[96] Resources to develop the newly created area came from FEMA Hazard Mitigation Grant Program, Department of Natural Resources, CDBG-DR, and state CDBG funds.[97] After the U.S. Army Corp of Engineers redrew the floodplain, FEMA purchased approximately 500 homes and other buildings situated in the area along the river. The buildings were removed and the land became a 1,200-acre greenway, and a dedicated state recreation area, which includes walking and biking trails, areas for picnicking, boating, fishing, and camping.[98]

B. Greensburg, Kansas

On May 4, 2007, a 1.7-mile-wide F5 tornado destroyed 95 percent of Greensburg, Kansas, a two-mile-long town that was home to 1,500 inhabitants. Greensburg, about 100 miles from Wichita, is located in Kansas's "tornado alley." The Greensburg tornado was the strongest to hit the United States since 1999. The tornado lasted for about an hour and destroyed almost 1,000 homes and businesses, and about 800,000 cubic yards of debris was hauled away after the storm. Eleven residents died during the storm, primarily from being hit by flying debris.[99]

All of the town's residents were evacuated as a result of the tornado. Within a few weeks, more than one-third of the town's residents had returned, most to live in FEMA-provided temporary mobile homes. Within a few months, more than 800 residents had returned. Prior to the storm, the town, as so many others across the country, was diminishing in population and growth. For example, in the 10 years prior to the storm, there had not been one new building permit issued to construct a new home.[100] Because so much of the town was destroyed—over 95 percent of the physical area—the town leadership along with the returning residents participated in an intensive design and community visioning process. This process was facilitated by FEMA and BNIM Architects of Kansas City. The questions asked by the residents and the community leaders included: How are we going to distinguish ourselves? How are we going to make our name known? How can we make our buildings sustainable, as our grandparents did?[101]

The leadership of Greensburg knew they had to slow down the process of rebuilding so that it was done correctly. As Mayor Bob Dixson, elected in 2008, remarked, "The whole town was gone; the only thing we had was each other."[102]

As detailed in its long-term disaster recovery plan, the town of Greensburg decided to embrace sustainable development and green building as its overarching principles, and to rebuild Greensburg, Kansas, as a model green community.[103] The city of Greensburg created a nonprofit organization, Greensburg Greentown, to build and develop its model green city. This initiative has made Greensburg a leader in rural city rejuvenation and disaster recovery. Among the key factors in Greensburg's revitalization efforts are the following:

- The city's goal is to run on 100 percent renewable energy 100 percent of the time. The city is now home to 10 wind turbines, and 100 percent of the town's consumption is met through wind-generated energy.[104] The city is partnering in its efforts with the U.S. Department of Energy and has plans to reduce energy consumption by 30–50 percent. Toward this end, the city replaced all 303 streetlights with LED bulbs, becoming the first city in the country to accomplish this goal. Private companies have also participated in this new green initiative. The local John Deere dealership rebuilt since the tornado and constructed a LEED-platinum-certified building, which became the national distributor of John Deere windmills.

- Greensburg's City Council passed a resolution that all building projects initiated or supported by the city must meet LEED platinum criteria. Homes are encouraged to be built to meet LEED certification but are not required.
- Construction of a new arts center, the 5.4.7 Arts Center, named after the date of the storm, was completed in May 2008. This is the community's first-ever arts center. The building has a white roof that reflects heat with blocks of green roofing that reduce storm water runoff. The arts center is powered by its own wind turbine and geothermal heating and cooling system and also recently installed solar panels.[105]
- The Greensburg schools were destroyed by the tornado, so the city committed to building a new school that would serve its community's school-age children. In 2010, the city opened its new K–12 school in Greensburg. This new building is built to be 60 percent more energy efficient than a similar building constructed to standard code. The school uses numerous renewable-energy technologies, including a 50-kilowatt on-site wind generator and ground-source heat pump system. School leaders and the design/construction team worked closely together to design an environmentally responsible, student-focused academic environment that reinforces Greensburg's community-wide commitment to sustainability. The 120,000-square-foot, two-story facility has the capacity to hold more than 300 students ranging from preschoolers to high-school seniors and is designed to meet LEED platinum certification as per the city's resolution.[106]
- GreenTown launched its Chain of Eco-Homes in the winter of 2009. It is a series of demonstration eco-homes designed to be "living laboratories" featuring a variety of building techniques, prices, sizes, energy-efficiency features, and green living products and services. The Chain of Eco-Homes will consist of unique homes in which visitors can stay to experience green living and will also serve as a key informational source about how different technology performs; it is intended to be a key driver in supporting tourism post-disaster.[107]

X. Conclusion

Disasters affect communities at a base, fundamental level. Everyday basic needs of shelter, food, and safety can become threatened by the effects of a catastrophic event. The challenge of addressing these needs during and immediately after an event occurs is one of the principal obligations of any local government. As this chapter has described, it is the local government that takes responsibility for meeting the needs of its citizens. When a disaster occurs, local governments act first and, if needed, will access support from partners such as nonprofit organizations or seek assistance from the state or neighboring local jurisdictions.

Disasters also affect communities at a collective level. How a community and its government choose to respond to a devastating crisis can have long-lasting effects on the morale and the emotional health of its citizenry, as well as the fiscal health and other indices of quality of life of the community at large. Developing and implementing a plan for long-term recovery is also primarily the obligation of local government. This chapter provided a number of examples of local governments that, when faced with overwhelming devastation, chose to use this unfortunate crisis as a welcome opportunity to engage in a community-wide, community-driven planning process for redevelopment and recovery.

Notes

1. Wash. State Military Dep't., Windstorm Response After Action Report December 2006: A Statewide Report to the Governor [hereinafter Statewide Report], *available at* http://www.emd.wa.gov/publications/documents/FINAL_AAR_040407.pdf (last visited Jan. 22, 2013).
2. *Hanukkah Eve Wind Storm Ravages Washington*, HistoryLink.org, http://www.historylink.org/index.cfm?DisplayPage=output.cfm&file_id=8042.
3. Statewide Report, *supra* note 1, at 18.
4. Statewide Report, *supra* note 1, at 15.
5. Elaine Pittman, *Remember: All Disasters Are Local, Says FEMA Deputy Administrator*, Emergency Mgmt., Nov. 14, 2011, http://www.emergencymgmt.com/disaster/Remember-All-Disasters-Are-Local-Says-FEMA-Deputy-Administrator.html.
6. *Id.*
7. *Id.*
8. For more on the history of the American emergency response system, see Andrew S. Mener, *Disaster Response in the United States of America: An Analysis of the Bureaucratic and Political History of the Failing System*, C. Undergraduate Res. Electronic J., Univ. of Pa. (2007), at 17–19.
9. Christine Becker, *Disaster Recovery: A Local Government Responsibility*, Pub. Mgmt., vol. 91:2, March 2009 [hereinafter *Disaster Recovery*].
10. TRADE Training Resource and Data Exchange, "Emergency Management Issues: Glossary and Acronyms of Emergency Management Terms Third Edition," May 1999, at 40.
11. *Disaster Recovery*, *supra* note 9, at 7.
12. *Id.*
13. *Id.*
14. *See $28.5 million price tag from storm*, Seattle Times, Feb. 6, 2007.
15. Adam Stone, *Falling Apart*, Emergency Mgmt. Jan.–Feb. 2012, 16–22, at 18 [hereinafter *Falling Apart*]; *see also 2009 Report Card for America's Infrastructure*, ASCE, https://apps.asce.org/reportcard/2009/grades.cfm (last visited Feb. 17, 2013).
16. *Falling Apart*, *supra* note 15. Sadly, decayed infrastructure was found to be the cause of the bridge collapse in Minneapolis that resulted in injuries to more than 100 people and the death of 13.
17. *Falling Apart*, *supra* note 15; *see also* Charles Duhigg, *Saving U.S. Water and Sewer Systems Would be Costly*, N.Y. Times, Mar. 14 2012, www.nytimes.com/2012/03/15/us/15water.html.
18. Editorial, *Crumbling Infrastructure Hampers Recovery*, Tampa Bay Times, Nov. 16, 2012, www.tampabay.com/opinion/editorials/crumbling-infrastructure-hampers-recovery/1261975.
19. *Hurricane Sandy: New York's 'massive, massive housing problem*,' Week, Nov. 5, 2012, http://theweek.com/article/index/235850/hurricane-sandy-new-yorks-massive-massive-housing-problem (last visited Jan. 24, 2013).
20. U.S. Environmental Protection Agency, *Region 7 Clean Up: Greensburg, Kansas, Tornado Response*, http://www.epa.gov/region7/cleanup/greensburg/index.htm.
21. Berks Cnty., Pa., *Background Information on the State of the Volunteer Fire Service*, http://www.co.berks.pa.us/Dept/DES/Pages/PAFire Service.aspx.
22. *Id.*
23. *See* City Fiscal Conditions in 2012, Nat'l League of Cities, Sept. 2012, www.nlc.org.

24. Ryan Holeywell, *Emergency Financial Managers: Michigan's Unwelcome Savior*, GOVERNING, May 2012, http://www.governing.com/topics/mgmt/gov-emergency-financial-managers-michigan-municipalities-unwelcome-savior.html.

25. Ian Lovett, *A Poorer San Bernardino, and a More Dangerous One, Too*, N.Y. TIMES, Jan. 14, 2013, http://www.nytimes.com/2013/01/15/us/crime-rises-in-san-bernardino-after-bankruptcy.html?_r=0.

26. *Id.*

27. Bill Estep, *As Tornado Approaches, Flee Mobile Homes in Favor of Vehicles or Ditches, Experts Say*, LEXINGTON HERALD LEADER, Mar. 10, 2013, http://www.kentucky.com/2012/03/10/2104476/as-tornado-approaches-flee-mobile.html (quoting Harold Brooks, research meteorologist with the NOAA/National Severe Storms Laboratory).

28. STATEWIDE REPORT, *supra* note 1, at 10; *see also Build a Kit* FEMA, www.ready.gov/build-a-kit (last visited Feb. 17, 2013) (advising each household to assemble a disaster supply kit of food, water, and other supplies in sufficient quantity for a period of at least 72 hours).

29. In the Hanukkah Eve Wind Storm, more than 100,000 people were without power for more than 10 days. *See A Region at Risk: Improving our Readiness to Respond to Disaster*, UNITED WAY OF KING CNTY., Mar. 20, 2007, www.uwkc.org/assets/files/research-and-reports/region-at-risk.pdf. After Superstorm Sandy, some communities went almost two weeks without power, including parts of Long Island, New York. *See, e.g.*, Frank Eltman & Michael Virtanen, *LIPA Hurricane Sandy Response Angers Residents as Many Remain Without Power*, HUFFINGTON POST, Nov. 13, 2012, http://www.huffingtonpost.com/2012/11/13/lipa-hurricane-sandy-response-angers-residents-without-power_n_2121191.html.

30. Dr. David P. Eisenman & Dr. Kristina M. Cordasco et al, *Disaster Planning and Risk Communication with Vulnerable Communities: Lessons from Hurricane Katrina***,** 97 AM. J. OF PUBLIC HEALTH, Supplement 1, 5109–15, *available at* http://ajph.aphapublications.org/doi/abs/10.2105/AJPH.2005.084335.

31. STATEWIDE REPORT, *supra* note 1, at 31.

32. For example, even pre–Hurricane Katrina, Louisiana and Mississippi, states most affected by the storm, were widely considered as the states with the highest child poverty rates in the in the United States. Additionally 20–25 percent of people in New Orleans either had significant disabilities or were primary caretakers for persons with such challenges. Irwin Redlener, *Population Vulnerabilities, Preconditions, and the Consequence of Disasters*, 75 SOC. RESEARCH, No 3, Fall 2008, at 789–90.

33. Elaine Pittman, *How to Include Diverse, Vulnerable Populations in Emergency Preparedness*, EMERGENCY MGMT., Apr. 11, 2011, http://www.emergencymgmt.com/disaster/Diverse-Vulnerable-Populations-Preparedness-041111.html [hereinafter Pittman].

34. *Id.*

35. *Id.*

36. For more information on Ready Neighborhoods visit http://www.redcross.org/ca/san-francisco/local-programs-services/ready-neighborhoods (last visited Jan. 22, 2013).

37. Justine Brown, *Community Based Program Prepares California for a Disaster*, EMERGENCY MGMT., July-Aug. 2012, 42–46, at 44.

38. Lessons Learned Info. Sharing (LLIS.gov), *State and Local Government Continuity of Operations Planning: Elements of a Continuity of Operations Plan*, http://higheredbcs.wiley.com/legacy/college/perry/0471920770/chap_resource/ch08/coop_elements.pdf.

39. Robin J. Clark and Adrian Wilairat, *Bringing It All Back Home: Continuity of Government Planning for Local Government*, J. OF EMERGENCY MGMT., Sept./Oct. 2009, at 19, *available at* http://www.mdchhs.com/sites/default/files/pdf_articles/JEM-7-5-03-bringing_it_home.pdf.

40. *Id.* at 23.

41. For examples of legislation authorizing the use of Mutual Aid Compacts, see Ohio Intrastate Mutual Aid Compact, found at Ohio Revised Code section 5502.41, as enacted into law in 2002, and Iowa's Mutual Aid Compact, which began as a volunteer program and was recently revised to mandate the participation of local jurisdictions enabling legislation, found at Iowa Code § 29.C.22s. *See also* Nat'l Emergency Mgmt. Assoc. (NEMA), Model Intrastate Mutual Aid Legislation, (2004), *available at* http://www.iafc.org/files/downloads/MASTF/mtlAid_NMEAmodelIntrastateMAlegislation.pdf.

42. MICH. OFFICE OF PUB. HEALTH PREPAREDNESS, MUTUAL AID: UNITY OF PURPOSE, INFORMATION AND RESOURCES (2004), *available at* http://www.michigan.gov/documents/mdch/Mutual_Aid_174881_7.pdf.

43. *Id.*

44. Legislation found at WASH. REV. CODE § 38.56.020 l.

45. TERRENCE EGAN ED.D & CHRIS UTZINGER, WASH. EMERGENCY MGMT. DIV., THE STATE OF MUTUAL AID (2011), *available at* www.emd.wa.gov/plans/documents/WSEMA_2011_Egan_Utzinger.pptx.

46. STATEWIDE REPORT, *supra* note 1, at 20.

47. *See What is a Regional Council?*, NAT'L ASSOC. OF REG'L COUNCILS, http://narc.org/resource-center/cogs-mpos/what-is-a-council-of-government/ (last visited Feb. 17, 2013).

48. A COG is a multiservice entity with state and locally defined boundaries that delivers a variety of federal, state, and local programs while continuing its function as a planning organization, technical assistance provider and "visionary" to its member local governments. As such, they are accountable to local units of government and effective partners for state and federal governments.

49. NAT'L ASSOC. OF DISASTER OFFICIALS (NADO) RESEARCH FOUND., RESTORING ECONOMIES IN THE WAKE OF DISASTER (2010), *available at* http://www.nado.org/disaster-recovery-2/.

50. *Id.*

51. SOUTH EAST TEX. REG'L PLANNING COMM'N, COUNCIL OF GOVERNMENTS METHOD OF DISTRIBUTION CITIZEN PARTICIPATION PLAN FOR ROUND 2.2 DISASTER RECOVERY SUPPLEMENTAL ALLOCATION *available at* http://www.glo.texas.gov/GLO/_documents/disaster-recovery/mod/setrpc-citizen-participation-plan.pdf.

52. NEIGHBORWORKS AM., DISASTER PREPAREDNESS AND RECOVERY FOR COMMUNITY DEVELOPMENT ORGANIZATIONS (2009) [hereinafter NEIGHBORWORKS].

53. Robert T. Stafford Disaster Relief and Emergency Assistance Act, as amended, and related authorities 42 U.S.C. §§ 5121–5207, § 5170 (2007) [hereinafter Stafford Act].

54. EMAC was signed into law by Congress in 1996 with Public Law 104-321. All 50 states, the District of Columbia, Puerto Rico, Guam, and the U.S. Virgin Islands have all enacted legislation to become members of EMAC. *See* www.emacweb.org.

55. *See* EMERGENCY MANAGEMENT ASSISTANCE COMPACT, *EMAC Support Surges for Hurricane Sandy Response and Recovery*, www.emacweb.org.

56. *See, e.g.*, Wyo. Office of Homeland Sec., *Damage Assessment*, app. D, *in* WYOMING RESPONSE PLAN, 231-61, http://wyohomelandsecurity.state.wy.us/Library/Wyoming%20Response%20Plan_07.pdf Oct. 2008, [hereinafter WYOMING RESPONSE PLAN] (providing sample templates, checklists, and resolutions for assessing damage and declaring disaster for local governments).

57. *Id.*

58. *Id.*

59. Stafford Act, 42 U.S.C. § 5143(c).

60. WYOMING RESPONSE PLAN, *supra* note 56.

61. Regulations for the Public Assistance Program are found at 44 C.F.R. § 206.

62. James A. Walke, *The Federal Emergency Management Agency: Partners in Infrastructure Recovery*, *in* UNDERSTANDING THE STAFFORD ACT: ITS EFFECT ON PUBLIC ENTITIES, *available at* http://www.primacentral.org/resources/Public%20Assistance%20Program%20Article.pdf [hereinafter Walke].

63. *Id.*

64. *Public Assistance: Local, State, Tribal and Non-Profit*, FEMA, http://www.fema.gov/public-assistance-local-state-tribal-and-non-profit (last updated Jan. 7, 2013).

65. 44 C.F.R. § 206.222 (2011).

66. *Id.*

67. 44 C.F.R. § 206.223.

68. 44 C.F.R. § 206.223.

69. *See generally Public Assistance: Eligibility*, FEMA, http://www.fema.gov/public-assistance-eligibility (last updated June 21, 2012).

70. 44 CFR § 206.47.

71. *CDBG Disaster Recovery Assistance*, HUD, http://portal.hud.gov/hudportal/HUD?src=/program_offices/comm_planning/communitydevelopment/programs/drsi#summaryCite CDBG regs [hereinafter *CDBG Disaster Recovery*].

72. *Id.*

73. *Id.*

74. *Id.*

75. 24 C.F.R. § 570.208 (2012).

76. *CDBG Disaster Recovery*, *supra* note 71.

77. *See Recovery Snapshot: East Grand Forks Downtown Revitalization*, HUD, available at http://portal.hud.gov/hudportal/documents/huddoc?id=DOC_22571.pdf.

78. *Id.*

79. *Id.*

80. *Id.*

81. Clancy Philipsborn, *The Disaster Recovery Process*, *in* HOLISTIC DISASTER RECOVERY: IDEAS FOR BUILDING LOCAL SUSTAINABILITY AFTER A NATURAL DISASTER 1, 2 (2001) (Natural Hazards Ctr. rev. 2005), *available at* http://csc.uoregon.edu/opdr/sites/csc.uoregon.edu.opdr/files/HDR.pdf.

82. *See Disaster Recovery*, *supra* note 9.

83. FEMA, LONG TERM COMMUNITY RECOVERY PLANNING PROCESS: A SELF HELP GUIDE (2005) [hereinafter SELF HELP GUIDE].

84. *Id.* at 5.

85. FEMA, FEMA 421, PLANNING FOR POST-DISASTER RECOVERY AND RECONSTRUCTION 48 (1998), *available at* http://www.fema.gov/library/viewRecord.do?id=1558 [hereinafter PLANNING FOR POST-DISASTER RECOVERY].

86. *Id.*

87. Chris Kirkham & John Rudolph, *Jersey Shore Development Failures Exposed by Hurricane Sandy*, HUFFINGTON POST, Dec. 11, 2012, http://www.huffingtonpost.com/2012/12/11/jersey-shore-development_n_2267557.html.

88. *Id.*

89. PLANNING FOR POST-DISASTER RECOVERY, *supra* note 85, at 48.

90. Linda Tischler, *Grand Forks and East Grand Forks: After the Flood (Literally)*, FAST CO. (July 30, 2002) http://www.fastcompany.com/node/45153/print.

91. *Id.*

92. *Id.*

93. For more information on the Center for Rural Design, visit http://ruraldesign.cfans.umn.edu/.

94. George Fryklund & Jennifer Reeder, *"Invisible" Wall Protects Red River Valley*, LAND & WATER, http://www.landandwater.com/features/vol47no6/vol47no6_2.html.

95. *Flood Protection in East Grand Forks*, http://www.draves.com/gf/egf_dike.htm.

96. NEIGHBORWORKS, *supra* note 52, at 53.

97. *Id.*; *see also Recovery Snapshot*, *supra* note 77.

98. *See Red River Recreation Area*, MINN. DEP'T OF NATURAL RES., www.dnr.state.mn.us/state_parks/red_river/index.html.

99. *Greensburg, Kansas: Rebuilding After the May 4, 2007 Tornado*, EARTHGAUGE, http://www.earthgauge.net/wp-content/uploads/2009/03/eg_greensburg.pdf (last visited Apr. 3, 2013).

100. *Id.*

101. American Planning Association, *Four Years Later—Rebuilding Greensburg* (podcast of then Greensburg Mayor Bob Dixson, and Stephen Hardy, senior planner with BNIM Architects in Kansas City, who facilitated the preparation of the Greensburg Sustainable Comprehensive Plan following the May 2007 tornado), July 6, 2012, http://podbay.fm/show/194167978/e/1325870437 (last visited May 17, 2013).

102. *Id.*

103. Kansas Office of the Governor and FEMA, *Long-Term Community Recovery Plan: Greensburg and Kiowa County, Kansas*, August 15, 2007, http://www.epa.gov/region7/cleanup/greensburg/pdf/GB_LTCR_PLAN_Final_HiRes070815.pdf.

104. *Id.*

105. *See* http://www.547artscenter.org/.

106. For more information on the green initiatives of Greensburg, visit www.greensburggreentown.org.

107. *Id.*

CHAPTER 6

The Role of Nonprofits and Religious Organizations in Emergency Response

Brenda Bratton Blom
(with contribution by Woody Widrow)

I. Introduction

Nonprofit and religious organizations that deliver guidance, service, and services at the local level bring extreme value to a critical place in disaster response and recovery. Whether they are operating as first responders in rescue of the poor, elderly, and disabled or identifying and filling gaps in services as the response and recovery efforts unfold, organizations driven by mission to service of the poor and forgotten become critical anchors, strengthening resilience in the communities in which they are located and in which they work.

Those who work in communities through nonprofit and religious organizations that are themselves complex systems of interdependence introduce a capacity to embrace loss. They bring the calming order of their own systems to people overwhelmed by the chaos of the crisis. These connections are critical at the ground level. Despite the important role of nonprofit and religious organizations in disaster response, neither they nor the for-profit sector can replace the need for government action and involvement.

This chapter will examine several case studies, highlight best practices, and draw some lessons learned focusing on the role of nonprofits post-disaster, specifically in the areas of emergency housing and individual asset building. It will also examine the call for lawyers to work with these organizations in ways that strengthen the resilience of the people and communities affected by disaster.

II. Turbulence on the Rise and Community Resilience

> *Between 1985 and 1994, Oxfam found that 174 million people were affected by disasters each year. In the following decade, this figure increased by 70 percent to 254 million people per year. The increasing disaster rate has disproportionately affected the poor. . . .*[1]

It should be of no surprise that the data show that the number of disasters annually is increasing. The U.N. Environment Program's collaboration with the GRID-Arendal Center has produced data that has tracked the occurrence of disasters since 1900. Disaster, by their definition, includes "drought, earthquake, extreme temperatures, famine, flood, insect infestations, slides, volcanic eruption, wave and surge, wildfires, and windstorms." Excluding earthquakes, the number of disasters worldwide has increased dramatically.[2] This published graph relies on data from the Center for Research on the Epidemiology of Disasters (CRED), part of the World Health Organization (WHO).

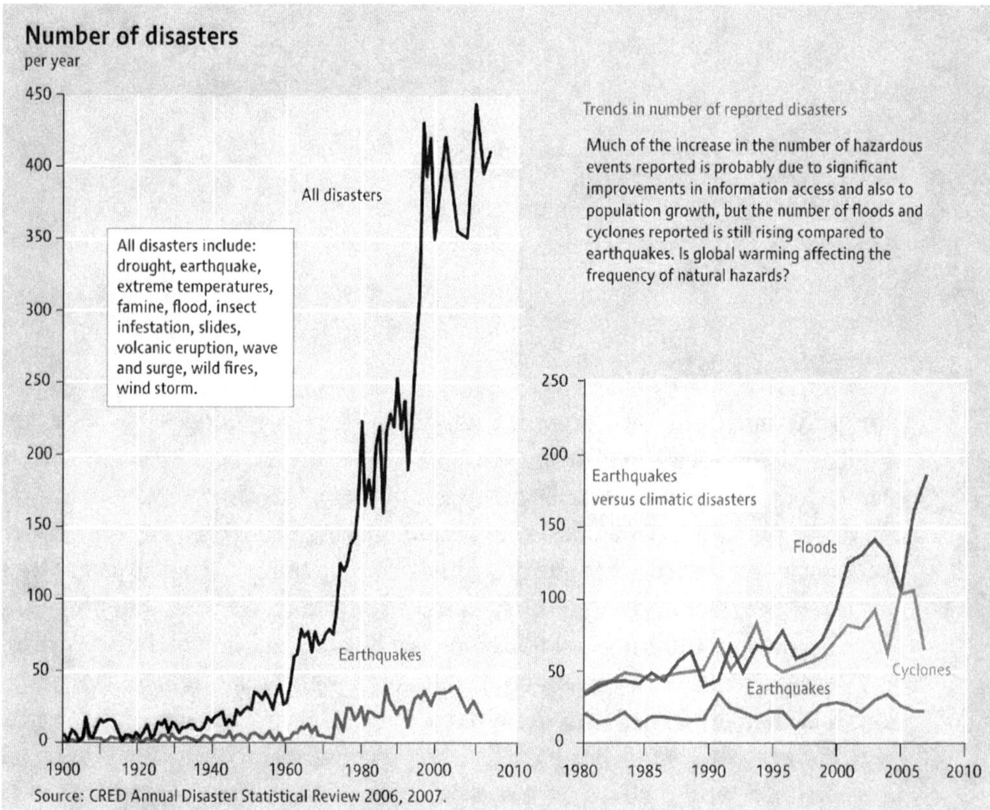

Not only has the frequency of disaster increased, but the severity of weather-related disasters has also increased as the planet continues to warm. Lawyers and community economic-development practitioners are much more likely now to experience the immediacy of a disaster and the life-altering reality of rebuilding lives and communities than two decades ago.

Housing and community development practitioners bring a special lens to the task of transforming capacity to respond to and survive catastrophe and disaster. There are two concepts to explore that are key to effective lawyering in this context. The first is the concept of *community*. The second is the concept of *resilience*.

A. Community

There are multiple ways in which the term "community" is used. One use is simply another word for neighborhood—a geographical, boundaried place that captures the statistical aggregate of individuals who reside within its borders. There might also be a shared governance and cultural and historical heritage, but not necessarily.[3]

Perhaps at the other end of the spectrum might be what Jane Winstone and Francis J. Pakes refer to as "a nostalgic indulgence."[4] "It refers to the spurious memory of a community that never was and typically represents an idealized version of our parents' or grandparents' time."[5]

But there are other descriptions and definitions, as well—and those are the ones that may be helpful in the discussions that will be developed here.

A community of interest: This community may or may not be virtual, but it tends to be decentralized and collected around a set of interests that have been identified or self-identified. These may include very localized interests (e.g., urban farmers in Baltimore) or be part of a much larger network (e.g., a local Rotary Club or Lion's Club). These communities of interest are becoming more powerful engines of disaster response as social media and connections explode. They hold tremendous opportunity, both for good and for exploitation.

Some smaller churches fulfill the definitional requirements that Robert Redfield described for a religious community because (1) it is distinctive, (2) it is small—all members know each other and are often in each other's sight—and (3) it is self-sufficient.[6] Local congregations of some larger denominations might also meet these criteria.

Neighborhoods organized under a Community Development Organization or plan: Groups of people who live in contiguous surroundings or who have a local democratic or structured problem-solving process for issues that are commonly experienced. This, by definition, would include tenants' organizations and housing councils.

Nonprofit organizations are often linked to networks of local residents through some form of service provision or organizing mission. These communities can include nonprofit soup kitchens, homeless services, housing assistance, and job-training groups. While some of these services might be provided by government agencies, the nonprofit providers can see themselves as integrally connected and linked to the mission and those with whom they work.

Whether tightly defined or loosely associated, all of these communities have in common "a complex system of interdependence which recognizes the pursuit of individual goals, provided they are legitimate and socially sanctioned."[7] These relationships and networks—this system of interdependence—is a critical piece of the disaster response and recovery experience. Disasters can destroy the networks within which we live and work. The trauma associated with this wrenching of the individual and family from these networks is significant. But they can also reclaim those relationships and provide critical avenues to restoration of both personal and social lives.

B. Resilience

The core concept of "resilience" is the ability to rebound and recover. Like community, resilience has been used in many ways and in many contexts:

- Psychological resilience refers to an individual's ability to cope with stress and adversity.[8]
- Network resilience refers to the performance of computer networks in use.[9]
- Ecological resilience is used to refer to ecological systems that are damaged and/or under threat.[10]
- Organizational resilience refers to the ability of an organization or group to rebound from catastrophe.

Internationally, there are now organizations that are fully committed to the development of literature and information about system resilience across a broad sweep. The Torrens Resilience Institute in South Australia is studying resilience "to improve the capacity of organizations and societies to respond to disruptive challenges which have the potential to overwhelm local disaster management capabilities and plans."[11] The Resilience Alliance was formed in 1999, and is using scientific research about resilience as a frame for creating sustainable solutions for problems in ecology and society.[12] "As the limiting factor in disaster response is often the coping capacity of those affected, improving their resilience when responding to disasters is a key approach to lessening the consequence of a disaster."[13]

While these definitions do not directly refer to communities, there is little doubt that nonprofit and religious organizations are vital to effective and inclusive disaster response and recovery.

This chapter does not address the role of government in disaster response and recovery. It is important to note, however, the absence of such discussion does not suggest that nonprofit and religious organizations can meet the challenges of disasters without the full support and commitment of resources by local, state, and federal governments.[14] Other chapters in this book discuss the role and resources provided by the government. (For discussion of the federal, state, and local governments' roles in post-disaster recovery, see chapters 1 and 5.)

This book focuses on acute disasters, which "rip the veneer off the ordered lives of storm-ravaged towns and cities and their people."[15] It is important to also note that the lessons learned might also be applied to the "sub-acute" disasters in America—the "decades-long decline of investment and economic exclusion that similarly consign so many Americans to conditions . . . that also cry out for recovery."[16]

III. Emergency Housing Post-Disaster

"[S]helter must be considered as a process, not as an object."[17]

A. The Paradigm and Critical Orientations

Shelter is fundamental. "The need for shelter can be summarized as the need for: Protection from the elements, Preservation of Dignity, and Orientation and Identity."[18] Whether dealing with the subacute issues of homelessness or the explosive issues of shelter in the wake of a disaster, understanding shelter as a process rather than an object captures the wide range of experiences people encounter. People may be staying in their homes that have been flooded—dealing with issues of mold and trash and debris and lack of heat and water services—or they may be evacuees (either temporary or more permanent) or they may have truly lost their capacity to return and must be relocated with or without family and friends. The process of sheltering becomes a significant need that is often addressed by a series of nonprofit and religious organizations. Those most acutely affected are usually the poor.

"Katrina destroyed or rendered uninhabitable over 50% of the low-income housing stock on the Mississippi Gulf Coast. In the apartments that remained livable, rent costs rose by as much as 30%. Seventy-five percent of the federal recovery funds designated for lower-income survivors were redirected to other purposes. . . . [T]housands of low-income individuals and people of color remain displaced."[19] While it is early in the recovery process for the communities affected by Superstorm Sandy, Mayor Michael R. Bloomberg estimated that there would be up to 40,000 new homeless residents of New York, many of them low income.[20] Given the timing of the storm and the cold months, the urgency of the situation, shelter, and housing became a central focus for the region.[21]

"Other than the loss of a loved one, loss of the home is generally the greatest loss individuals and households sustain."[22]

Matching the need for emergency shelter with the appropriate response is a task that we are still grappling to understand.

B. International Lessons

International agencies have been engaged in the struggle to shelter those in large crisis situations for years. There is a recognized language to describe those in crisis. Summarizing Jensen's 1986 work on Typology and Causes of Emergency Settlement, Elizabeth Babister and Ilan Kelman remind us that internally displaced persons (IDPs) are those who "have been forced to flee their homes but remain within the territory of their own country."[23] Externally displaced persons (EDPs) are those who "'have crossed an international border but are not legally recognized as refugees . . . [and] are not included within the mandates of the UN."[24] "Refugees are those who 'owing to a well-founded fear of being persecuted for reasons of race, religion, nationality, membership of a particular social group or political opinion, are outside the country of [their] nationality and [are] unwilling to return to it.' . . . Asylum seekers are those who have crossed an international border and are in the process of applying for refugee status."[25] While those who become evacuees in the United States generally remain IDPs, it may be helpful to understand the international framework and some of the lessons that have been learned as we rise to the task of increasing large and frequent massive disaster situations that require sheltering large numbers of people.

When people are displaced, there is a continuum of possible responses[26]:

- Repair and rehabilitation of houses: essentially staying in place through the rehabilitation of the homes.
- Self-settlement: people who find temporary shelter without assistance. People might stay with friends or family, or they might have the resources to stay in a hotel or find a temporary rental option.
- Conversion of buildings: Mass shelters can be organized, which can be effective ways of distributing aid to large numbers of people, but the effectiveness is complicated by all of the difficulties of having many people sharing one space.[27]
- Assisted self-settlement: often using the mass shelters as transit centers to help people find a more suitable location.[28]
- Temporary settlements: In the international context, these become refugee camps, which are generally considered only a last resort. "A solution that maintains and fosters the self-reliance of the refugees is always preferable."[29]

In the international context, the provision of emergency shelter has not been pleasantly solved. There are many competing interests, including state interests. Funders have multiple ideological and theological frameworks, and resources are more or less difficult to deliver due to both geography and political realities. In fact, "half of [refugee camps] last longer than five years, with under one quarter lasting under two years."[30]

In addition, there are other lessons that have been learned through the study of emergency housing response, highlighting obstacles to reaching the needs of survivors of disaster. First, there should be continued assessment, evaluation, and planning as implementation of emergency shelter unfolds. Second, there should be involvement of the beneficiaries. Third, if possible, there should be an aim to use local resources, because that will work to revitalize the local economy and build capacity for the long term. And fourth, nonprofit responders and NGOs should work to minimize environmental and social impacts. These principles can be applicable to recovery in the United States, as well.[31]

It is also true that one disaster response might lead to a more protracted review and new decisions. After the March 23, 2012, flood due to an ice jam in Perth-Andover, New Brunswick, Canada, the government approved disaster-relief funds immediately for people to repair their homes in a flood-ravaged area of the village. This expense averaged about $25,000 per homeowner. The funds were used to renovate and flood-proof basements. After a mitigation study,[32] the provincial government then decided to give residents the option to move their homes, sell, or stay, with an additional cost of $8 million. About 190 structures were flooded in this small community. There was some discussion about the changing goals of the program, but, in fact, this might be a prime example of the shelter process in recovery and restoration.[33] Best practices learned from the international and national experiences lead to an understanding that immediate responses may be necessary investments, even though the long-term decisions may require investment in different strategies for recovery. As in this case, what may begin as a repair and rehabilitation strategy may end in assisted relocation.

IV. The Role of Nonprofit Organizations

Nonprofit organizations are driven by the mission to serve, educate, and reform, not the mission to accrue profit. The nonprofit sector has continued to expand in the United States and internationally. Internationally, nongovernmental organizations (NGOs) often take the lead in disaster recovery. Many find their funding and base of operations out of the United Nations and its network of government-supported organizations. But none is more widely recognized than the Red Cross.

A. National and International Nonprofits

> *Who is affected more when it's cold? Poor people. Who is affected more when it's hot? Poor people. Who is affected more when it's wet? Poor people. Who is more affected when the economy is bad? Poor people. Poor people are the most fragile.*[34]

1. The Red Cross and Red Crescent Movement

Clara Barton,[35] replicating the work of the International Red Cross, founded the American Red Cross in 1881. It was chartered by Congress in 1900 and 1905 to "carry out a system of national and international relief in time of peace and carry out the same in mitigating the suffering caused by pestilence, famine, fire, floods and other great national calamities, and to devise and carry out measures to prevent those calamities."[36] It is a single national organization with chapters around the country, and it shares fundamental principles with the International Red Cross and Red Crescent movement. Those principles are "humanity, impartiality, neutrality, independence, voluntary service, unity and universality."[37]

While the Red Cross works alongside the Federal Emergency Management Agency (FEMA), it is supported completely by private and corporate donations.[38] The organization is also primarily staffed by volunteers. After the 9/11 terrorist attacks, volunteers literally lined up around the block from Red Cross centers to volunteer their time and effort.[39]

During the 2011 fiscal year, the Red Cross responded to hurricanes affecting Massachusetts, New York, North Carolina, Texas, and the U.S. Virgin Islands; tornadoes affecting communities across 18 states; floods in Minnesota, North Dakota, Montana, Arizona, Oklahoma, and Tennessee; and large-scale wildfires (up to a half million acres in Arizona alone) in Arizona, Colorado, New Mexico, Texas, and Washington State. This does not include the "everyday disasters" when tragedy strikes through house fires, explosions, chemical releases, or environmental emergencies.[40]

The Red Cross delivered those services through a network of volunteers. With 32,000 paid staff, they mobilized 487,000 volunteers. Working with a centralized record base, they are able to follow the training and certification of individual volunteers and locally based partner organizations that prepare to respond long before disaster strikes. The National Association for the Advancement of Colored People (NAACP) is one such partner organization, which is national but with local and regional chapters. The Red Cross has a national memorandum of agreement, does training of NAACP volunteers at regional conferences, and has learned to listen to the deep lessons of cultural competence learned during major disasters such as Hurricanes Katrina and Rita.[41]

The standing army of volunteers is networked locally, and those local networks of trained volunteers are connected to the resources that can be readily mobilized by the national Red Cross to respond. The Red Cross prides itself on its low administrative costs—running about 12 percent of its budget.[42] Its funds are spent on the goods and services needed at the front lines in any disaster.

Because it is standing in readiness and always improving its systems, it is also a key partner for governmental agencies like FEMA and the National Guard. While those entities can mobilize resources, they are, generally, not connected to local networks of volunteers.

While not just working on housing, the Red Cross works across the immediate housing continuum. They coordinate with organizations to provide mass shelters, support self-settlement and assisted self-settlement, and, when possible and necessary, work with partners to provide temporary settlements.

2. National Voluntary Organizations Active in Disaster

Founded more than 40 years ago in response to the havoc created by Hurricane Camille in 1969, the National Voluntary Organizations Active in Disaster (VOAD) that provided disaster relief created an organization that now includes 108 members serving in 50 states, 4 territories and the District of Columbia. The organization is guided by what they call "the 4 Cs: Cooperation, Communication, Coordination and Collaboration."[43]

The National VOAD system serves as a centralized mechanism for engaging volunteer disaster response and recovery organizations across the United States. FEMA's Ready[44] website provides broad information about disaster response issues and resources. National VOAD is given prominence alongside the Red Cross.[45] This level of recognition and integration into the disaster response and recovery framework is an important indicator of the status of this long-standing network.

3. Habitat for Humanity International

One of the foremost providers of housing in America is Habitat for Humanity International. While Habitat's story and achievements could be found in several places in this chapter, its importance as a national housing organization that has developed a more complete disaster response model leads to placement in this bundle of ideas and work. A "nonprofit, ecumenical, Christian ministry founded on the conviction that every man, woman and child should have a decent, safe and affordable place to live,"[46] this organization works internationally, but has a substantial commitment to housing on the national level. Founded in 1976 by Millard and Linda Fuller, it has become one of the most influential housing efforts in the world. The model developed by the Fullers was designed as a model in which simple, decent, and affordable housing was built and provided with sweat equity and no interest loans to low-income purchasers, using donated volunteer labor for the basic housing construction, under the supervision of building specialists.[47]

Dating back to 1998, Habitat has been involved in disaster response. In 1999, when Hurricane Floyd wreaked havoc in North Carolina, Habitat responded. Building more than 60 recovery homes by 2002, "families who lost their homes . . . were back on their feet with the help of volunteers and other partners." And in 2000, 16 homes were built "during a blitz build for families who lost their homes to tornadoes in Camilla, Georgia."[48]

By 2005, Habitat was training and building their "Disaster Corps," providing "skilled and experienced professionals throughout the United States who are trained to work in disaster settings."[49] Matching trained volunteers with centers of need, the Disaster Corps assists with a range of projects that can both build capacity of local areas before disaster strikes or work to provide broad support for redevelopment efforts post-disaster. And, as with all Habitat projects, there is a deep commitment to facilitate "community involvement and support."[50]

Through its deep involvement in disaster response and support of self-sufficiency in its core model of development, Habitat has also begun to take seriously the task of disaster risk reduction. Heeding the lessons outlined in the Hyogo Framework for Action,[51] which emerged from the World Conference on Disaster Reduction that was held in Kobe, Hyogo, Japan, in 2005, Habitat has worked to include risk reduction in everything it does through basic elements of a programmatic approach: "(1) introducing disaster mitigation and climate change adaptations by 'design' in shelter and settlement projects, (2) mainstreaming of disaster-preparedness training within the family selection process, and (3) developing community-based disaster risk-management projects."[52]

Habitat works primarily in the repair and rehabilitation strategy on the housing continuum. While the group may work short term supporting the self-settlement or assisted self-settlement, its primary focus in on creating or re-creating communities. (See also chapter 16.)

Habitat's commitment to housing as a fundamental stabilizing anchor for the poor continues to develop as it responds to disasters around the world. Participating as a full partner in efforts to stabilize housing in an increasingly unstable environment will be an important part of the ongoing work.

4. Other Nonprofits

Other national nonprofits have been developing creative and powerful ways to respond to disasters. Examples of those include the Network for Good[53] that established its Support Hurricane Sandy Relief page almost immediately after the storm. By November 6, 2012, it had raised $2.5 million in relief aid for several different nonprofit organizations. The model is to channel fundraising through to nonprofit organizations ranging from the American Red Cross to World Vision in such a way that donations could be made for the response and recovery through this one website.

National nonprofit organizations also have the capacity to work across interest areas to concentrate resources. Guidestar is a national organization that provides support and information for nonprofit organizations—those with 501(c)(3) status, and those who serve such organizations. A query on its website for "disaster response" revealed nearly 1,000 results across the country.[54] Guidestar plays an important role in providing information to those thinking about providing donations to the relief effort, because it allows potential donors to locate, validate, and research charities. The National Law Center on Homelessness & Poverty developed a "Know Your Rights" information packet for the 1.5 million people who were left homeless post Hurricanes Katrina and Rita. It included information on children and education, disability benefits, housing, and identification issues.[55] At this larger level, organizations can make connections and step back to find resources, both financial and material, but also by identifying organizations that have similar experiences and connections for problem solving on the ground. These types of supports and connections can make a difference in the resilience of the organizations on the ground.

The Neighborhood Investment Corporation (NeighborWorks) was created by an act of Congress in 1978[56] to increase the capacity of local community-based organizations to revitalize their communities. This national organization has created and is supporting a network of local organizations. NeighborWorks has taken disaster response seriously. In January 2009, it released the paper *Disaster Preparedness and Recovery for Community Development Organizations*, written for NeighborWorks by Susan Ude.[57] This thorough and complete manual on preparedness answers the question of "Why Prepare?" "Being prepared can lessen the fear, anxiety and losses associated with disasters."[58]

This manual is a step-by-step guide for Community Development Organizations (CDOs) to prepare for a disaster. Why? Communities count on CDOs to be capable of responding to their needs.

> CDOs have aided their communities' recovery from disaster with counseling services such as foreclosure prevention, help with the FEMA/SBA process, disaster recovery case management, rehabilitation services, recovery fundraising volunteer management, new construction management, assistance in development of economic recovery, temporary housing to disaster victims, funding for day care, providing meeting spaces for recovery planning, communication with clientele, mental health services and so on. CDOs have responded to the needs of the existing clientele as well as disaster victims who were not in need of the CDOs' services previously.[59]

National organizations such as Enterprise Community Partners and Local Initiatives Support Corporation (the intermediary organizations that fund and provide technical support for affordable housing development and community development initiatives across the country) commit resources and raise funds to provide support in the immediate response and in the recovery. By the beginning of November 2012, both organizations had created emergency relief funds for the victims of Superstorm Sandy, and both had committed to support the rebuilding of affordable housing in the affected region. They have established web-based links to resources from the federal government, from state government, and through their national networks.[60]

B. Local Nonprofit Initiatives

Housing and shelter are the greatest challenges in times of disaster. "Typically after disaster, the vast majority (80%) of the affected population is able to manage its own recovery. The remaining 20% will need special assistance that CDOs and nonprofit organizations are uniquely positioned to provide."[61] But the needs presented by the 20 percent, many of whom are already marginally sheltered, can quickly become a problem much beyond local capacities.

> The elevators had been out for four days at the Jacob Riis Houses, a public housing complex in Lower Manhattan, and there was only one way down for Adonis Brice. The stairwell: 11 flights turned pitch black since Hurricane Sandy tore through the city and cut off electricity, water and heat. These 154 steps were his only path to the bread, candles and water he needed to care for his two small children . . . on the Lower East Side, in a housing complex of 19 brick high-rises where about 4,000 poor and working-class New Yorkers reside, life remained darkened and difficult.[62]

While neighbors were looking after neighbors, it is beyond individual or small group capacity to respond in these circumstances. As we saw after Katrina, government organizations can be assisted by local nonprofit and religious organizations in situations where there are high concentrations of people who need emergency shelter or, if sheltering in place, broader provisioning supports (i.e., food, batteries, heat, etc.). But volunteers and nonprofit groups cannot replace the massive assistance that only collective action with government resources can provide. The sheer numbers of people who were stranded in the Lower East Side high-rises outstripped small-group capacity to assist.

Local response can include the work of those providing emergency shelter in churches and mass shelters set up to receive people who have been displaced and who will probably return. This outpouring of care and comfort is important, as has been discussed before. But this work is only the first step.

The recovery process is a place where CDOs and Community Based Organizations (CBOs) have played a more creative role. The challenge is to provide longer-term replacement housing, whether that is in the location where people had evacuated or somewhere else entirely. As the United Way summed up the experiences of IDPs who relocated to Los Angeles following Hurricane Katrina, "[t]he cost and availability of housing in Los Angeles County is the number one problem affecting the ability of Katrina evacuees to stabilize their lives."[63] While recognizing that the primary problems with homelessness, generally, in Los Angeles are systemic—inadequate coordination of the "safety net" and "inadequate longer term planning and linkage of support systems"—the United Way summed up that these systemic problems locally were exacerbated for the people who had come from Louisiana and did not understand the city itself. "Many of the evacuees who came here will wind up being part of the 88,000 homeless. What we need are long term solutions."[64] CBOs and Community Development Organizations are perfectly placed for the rebuilding project, if they themselves have been able to survive the disaster.

"Local" might get even more local in some cases. Neighbors helping neighbors has always been the norm, but the ability to use social media to recruit and organize a local response may change the way disaster response happens. Post–Superstorm Sandy, within two days, there were postings on Facebook for support and opportunities to volunteer. Times and volunteers were listed, along with multiple locations.[65] Further, within 24 hours, an Occupy Sandy site had been set up on the Internet with ways to donate, volunteer, locate a shelter, and track the news.[66] New York Cares was founded in the late 1980s to address the problems in New York "from the ground up." The group immediately had a place on its site where people could post opportunities for volunteering and coordination of the volunteers themselves. But this very decentralized response network, while growing, is still in its infancy.

Nonprofits on the front lines have been organizing responses to disasters, and been a sustained part of the recovery for a very long time. Two case studies shed some light on the choices that nonprofit organizations might need to make in the midst of a disaster as it unfolds.

1. Mississippi Center for Justice

The Mississippi Center for Justice (MCJ) was founded in 2003 as a nonprofit law firm pursuing racial and economic justice in the poorest state in America.[67] Currently, it has three offices across the state, but when Hurricanes Katrina and Rita devastated the coastal region in 2005, MCJ found itself on the front lines of response and recovery, "opening a Katrina Recovery Office in Biloxi to respond to the legal needs of individual survivors, as well as to influence recovery-related policy decisions."[68] In short order, staff attorneys and volunteer attorneys became experts in FEMA regulations and appeals, insurance disputes, title clearance, contractor fraud, and landlord tenant law, to name a few of the areas that were critical. But there were two other areas of work that became the core of the work in Mississippi.

The first area was to become a link to pro bono legal resources across the country. "Martha [Bergmark, MCJ executive director], decided early on that she wanted to be able to use the offers of support and assistance. Within an organization or collaboration, you have to determine that you want to allocate some resources to figure out ways to take advantage of offers."[69] Working with the Lawyers' Committee for Civil Rights Under Law, some of the nation's largest law firms, and Equal Justice Works Fellows, MCJ was able to channel 60,000 pro bono hours into the state between 2006 and 2009.[70] Pro bono attorneys were able to provide "policy advocacy and impact litigation support" for MCJ's efforts. These legal links were to law schools, as well. Even today, each year MCJ hosts 1,000 law students who come to Mississippi to provide service to the ongoing and subacute recovery effort. These links have been important to the students and to the community. "Every few decades, the outside world breaks into Mississippi . . . it happened during Reconstruction, the Civil Rights era, and now, in the aftermath of Katrina."[71]

In addition, through this work, MCJ met and developed relationships with a broad array of grassroots nonprofit and religious organizations advocating for an "equitable recovery" regarding the interests of low-income survivors and communities of color.[72] "Starting with the Community Development Block Grant (CDBG) money, there was very little—actually there was *no* regard—given to community based groups focused on lower income people. They were left out. These local groups who focused on lower income people fought that at every step . . . and it will be fascinating if that is the same or different in the recovery from Sandy. You have to fight your way to the table!"[73]

Legal services on the ground are critical to the recovery of the most vulnerable. The use of volunteers "is energizing for students and staff," according to Bonnie Allen, an MCJ attorney. But "using outside resources must be done strategically."[74]

2. Hope Community Development Agency

Established in 2005 as the East Biloxi Coordination, Relief and Redevelopment Agency, Hope Community Development Agency's mission is "[t]o support the individuals, families, small business, and neighborhoods of Mississippi."[75] William "Bill" Stallworth, the founder, was born in Alabama, but moved to Mississippi when he was in high school. Starting his career in public service, working for the city of Biloxi in many capacities, then as city councilman in Biloxi, he moved into the private sector in 1985. While in the private sector, he served on multiple nonprofit boards, including the Red Cross. His deep ties to the community made the Hurricane Katrina response a logical next step.

The organization has a wide array of services that reflect the wraparound response to a disaster. These services include individual case management, community outreach, the development and support of a block captain system of community engagement, and the design and development of a product to respond to the greatest need: affordable housing.

"Bill Stallworth founded the Hope Community Development Agency which has done wonderful work. It is very much community based, and he partnered with the School of Architecture to create a design studio to develop a house that was affordable and could respond to need. Then, they worked block by block with local community based leadership. Community based solutions happening at the same time the government is driving resources."[76]

Hope Community Development Agency is focused on the repair and rebuilding strategy. It grew out of the disaster of Hurricanes Katrina and Rita. Because of strong local ties, and by connecting this strategy with deep commitments to communication and collaboration, the community and individuals have the chance to emerge in a stronger and more stable condition than before the disaster.

V. The Role of Religious Organizations

"The religious groups with Katrina played an absolutely critical role—they were here because the government was not here. Their response was churches at their best. There was every single kind of group and they just showed up and did what needed to be done. They would drive in a mobile kitchen and cook for people. The Episcopal Church out of Mississippi became the central headquarters for supplies and medical care. But the little scrappy churches were coming from all over. You need the structured large church resource programs and then the scrappy volunteers as well."[77]

A. National Religious Organizational Response

"After the experience of Katrina in 2005, many church agencies and religious groups are now seasoned veterans when it comes to disaster response. They have learned from their own mistakes and built networks to empower their efforts."[78]

Efforts by the Southern Baptists, the Mennonite, Amish, United Methodist, and more across the Gulf Coast were noted again and again. More than one-third of the organizations that are listed as disaster relief agencies on the Disaster Center's website[79] are explicitly based in religious outreach. Some might suggest that this is a perfect match—not only do religious organizations have the capacity to marshal physical and capital resources through their members, they also are able to bring emotional and spiritual resources to the project of response and recovery. After the 9/11 terrorist attacks, not only did religious groups mobilize to respond to the events of the day, but they also opened their doors to those who were stunned and needed a place of quiet reflection or prayer.

For some religious organizations, these response networks are key to their understanding of their mission. According to Ray Nothstine, "Christianity proclaims the future regeneration of a disordered world. The Church is an earthly reminder of that day of restoration."[80] But whether Christian, Jewish, Muslim, Buddhist, Hindu, or Sikh, these organizations are staffed and trained at the local, regional, and national level and are prepared to be able to respond and call on parishioners and members in local areas for support. That response is primarily boots-on-the-ground support of physical and spiritual needs. But they might also interact with local congregations and organizations that might have a different response to the disaster.

More than any other group, religious organizations not in the heart of the disaster convert their buildings for mass shelter in the time period immediately after a disaster. Even the insurance services provided to religious organizations are helping with policies and preparations so that religious communities are prepared for this function. And while some organizations will be available for longer-term repair and rehabilitation efforts in housing, much of the continuing support will be about the personal needs of individuals who have been displaced.

B. Local Religious Organizations Respond

Local congregations in the heart of the disaster might have very different responses to the same disaster. Some who are not destroyed or damaged might open their doors as shelters or a place for volunteers to sleep and eat. For others, the commitment might be more long term. "An interfaith coalition on the coast has played an on-going role in the redevelopment of Mississippi."[81]

And there are some very interesting stories that emerged out of the catastrophe of Hurricane Katrina in New Orleans. Two religious congregations responded in quite different manners.

1. Smoking for Jesus

The Smoking for Jesus Ministry is a nondenominational Christian ministry established in 1996 by Pastor Willie Monnet Sr. and his wife, Claudette. The church was initially located in the Ninth Ward of New Orleans, the ward hit hardest by the floods following the levees' break. They served the congregants who were poor, and were "ex-everything." Pastor Monnet led a ministry through church services, prison ministry, and outreach. The ministry operated a number of small businesses to employ members, including a lawn-care service, a restaurant, a barber and beauty service, and a car wash.[82] It also operated a prekindergarten through eighth-grade school.

The church had previously provided evacuation services for its members, and with Hurricane Katrina looming, the church took a caravan of about 40 cars and nearly 200 people to a church shelter near Beaumont, Texas. Over 85 percent of the members lost their homes and the church was damaged. They made the decision to stay in Texas.

Initially, they traveled between church shelters and hotels throughout Texas. They found a newly constructed apartment complex built in anticipation of a "school district workforce that hadn't materialized."[83] As families were approved, they moved into the Vistas Apartments located in Marble Falls, Texas—a small town with African-Americans making up 1 percent of the population.[84]

The church has since purchased the former Buckner Baptist Boy's Ranch, where they hold church services and allow church members to purchase land to build homes. They operate three New Orleans–style restaurants in the region of the Texas Hill Country and continue to re-create their community. The church now has a membership of 400 people, including white and Hispanic members.

"We brought our community with us; it makes it easier to adjust," said June Roth, the church's events planner, in the *Austin Chronicle*'s article "Finding God in the Gumbo." "But what do you do when life gives you Hurricane Katrina, decimating your entire community and way of life? The answer for one New Orleans East church group was: Stay together, trust the Lord, move to Texas, make gumbo. And create a new life in the Hill Country."[85]

Smoking for Jesus is a good example of a community focused on self-settlement or assisted self-settlement. They were able to clearly analyze the needs and assets of their members and make plans, as a community, for a future together.

2. *Mary Queen of Vietnam Catholic Community*

Emily Chamlee-Wright and Virgil Henry Storr have written an extraordinary account of the journey of the community of the Mary Queen of Vietnam Catholic Church in New Orleans.[86] The data and story of this community's journey is taken almost exclusively from this rich and textured accounting. The journey stands on the opposite end of the spectrum from the Smoking for Jesus community, in some regards, in that the community returned in full to New Orleans. But it shares a similar story, in that the community acted as a unit and acted under the dynamic leadership and loving care of their religious leaders.

Mary Queen of Vietnam (MQVN) Catholic Church was and is located in the Ninth Ward of New Orleans. The community surrounding the church was made up almost exclusively of Vietnamese refugees and their families who fled Vietnam with the help of Catholic Charities at the fall of Saigon. The first wave of the nearly 1,000 residents who had first fled North Vietnam in 1954 were settled in New Orleans East. Another 2,000 Vietnamese arrived in 1976 alone, with migration continuing through the 1980s. By 1985, the MQVN church was built, and in 2003 Father Vien Nguyen became the pastor of the parish.

"The MQVN church was (and remains) the hub around which spiritual, social and commercial life evolved. Father Vien estimates that of the 4,000 people within a one-mile radius of the church pre-Katrina, at least 3,800 of them are Catholic. . . . Further, the MQVN neighborhood has a much higher concentration of ethnic

Vietnamese people than any other residential area in New Orleans."[87] Before Hurricane Katrina, the church served as "host to Vietnamese cultural events, weekly farmers markets, and a periodic arts and crafts market." Homeownership rates were rising among parishioners, and the community was working toward a Vietnamese cultural and commercial center, an urban gardening project and housing for the elderly. Lay leadership was well organized and robust.

When Hurricane Katrina was bearing down on New Orleans, the church leaders, religious and lay, organized the evacuation of members of the community who could, and shelter in the church for those who could not. Over the next year, they tracked the location of all members of their community, and spearheaded efforts for return and redevelopment of their community—against great odds.

"By April 2006, . . . 1,200 of the 4,000 residents who lived within a one-mile radius of the church had returned. Within a year of the storm, more than 3,000 residents had returned. By the summer of 2007, approximately 90 percent of the MQVN residents went back, while the rate of return in New Orleans overall remained at only 45 percent."[88]

Their businesses returned, the school returned, the church began celebrating Mass immediately, and, as a result of the needs of the community, the church took on an overtly political presence in the city to demand that resources be returned to support the residents who had returned.

The church was able to anchor the complex social organization needed to facilitate such a dramatic return to their community, and the "bundle of club goods provided by MQVN are critical to their being able to live spiritually full, socially connected, and independent lives."[89]

This community represents a fine example of the implementation of a "repair and rehabilitation" strategy in the post-disaster of Hurricane Katrina. Using networking and circles of coordination and sophisticated communication, they were able to effectively regroup in the place where their community had been.

VI. Innovations Post-Disaster

> *Social entrepreneurs try to cure what ails society, and they judge their activities by their success in bringing about desired transformations. Because of their close ties to the community, they are often alert to neighborhoods' needs in a way that government agencies are not. Social entrepreneurs don't just fill the gaps in needed services—they also work to galvanize the support that is essential for community resilience.*[90]

When people are on the ground in the heart of a disaster, they face problems for which there might not be an existing answer. And given the boundless creative human spirit, this may become an opportunity to find the answer that solves the problem. Some might suggest that is the nature of capitalism itself. But the emergence of the social entrepreneur blends the creative problem solving of the traditional entrepreneur with the social mission of the nonprofit or environmental organization. Examples of this kind of problem solving can be seen in the area of housing, in particular:

- *Katrina Cottages*: The need for shelter after Hurricane Katrina was extreme. FEMA provided trailers and shelters, but entrepreneurs developed the Katrina Cottage that eventually housed many in the coastal region.

  The Saturday after Hurricane Katrina, Andres Duany and Steve Mouzon spent the day working out the beginnings of the New Urbanist response to the staggering housing problem. . . . "We must have a solution that delivers houses that are manufactured, houses that are modular, houses that are built from kits, houses that are panelized, and houses that are site-built."[91]

  These small cottages were designed by young urban designers, who provided those designs to FEMA and to the world. They were a turning point in providing some affordable-housing relief across the Gulf Coast.[92] The Katrina Cottage movement in small, sustainable and affordable housing continues.[93] Katrina Cottages are being tapped for use in the Superstorm Sandy rebuilding process, and received a much better reception, given the general state of the economy and housing market.[94]
- *ShelterBox:* ShelterBox was founded in 2000 by Tom Henderson, a Rotarian and former Royal Navy search-and-rescue diver. ShelterBox is a nonprofit registered in England and Wales. The organization has a stated goal of assisting 50,000 people a year. The ShelterBox response to disaster is simple. They provide the essentials for a family to survive in a disaster's immediate aftermath. "Each large, green ShelterBox is tailored to a disaster but typically contains a disaster relief tent for an extended family, blankets, water storage and purification equipment, cooking utensils, a stove, a basic tool kit, a children's activity pack, and other vital items."[95] Partnering with international, national, and local organizations with trained volunteers who can effectively allocate the boxes, these containers of resources needed in a disaster-stricken area can create and support communities.

But there have been important entrepreneurial developments in other areas of need, as well, including asset building to help support long-term individual and community economic recovery.

Portable Individual Development Accounts: Supporting Individual and Community Assets after Major Disasters

Woody Widrow

Starting in the late fall of 2005 following the devastating Hurricanes Katrina and Rita, the nonprofit and public sectors came together to discuss what happened in the aftermath of the destruction from these two hurricanes and the life-changing results, including the

Portable Individual Development Accounts: Supporting Individual and Community Assets after Major Disasters *(continued)*

displacement of hundreds of thousands of families and the lessons learned for future disasters. The gatherings provided an initial look at the opportunities and challenges presented to mitigate the crisis and help move people from recovery to the rebuilding of their lives, assets, and community. One particular focus and place for innovation to support asset building among disaster-stricken families and communities was the Individual Development Accounts (IDA) program.

While there has not been a disaster in the United States affecting as many families and for as long a duration as Hurricane Katrina, many families and communities since then have had their lives disrupted through new man-made and natural occurrences, such as the tornados in Mississippi and Joplin, Missouri; the wildfires in Texas; and more recently, Superstorm Sandy. Hopefully, the lessons learned in the recovery of the 2005 Gulf Coast hurricanes about expanding IDAs in a post-disaster context will benefit those communities and families recovering from these and other disasters.

Individual Development Accounts as a Tool for Disaster Recovery

At its core, the IDA program is a matched savings program that allows individuals to save for a long-term asset such as homeownership, small-business creation or expansion, or postsecondary education. Traditionally, IDAs are place-based and move people along a path toward financial success through the purchase of an appreciating asset in a specific target market. In addition to this financial support, many practitioners and advocates cite the longer-term benefits of IDAs in wealth creation. Beyond these tangible benefits tied to the asset purchase, additional wealth building outcomes occur for the IDA participant through completing personal finance education, opening up a bank account with a financial institution, reaching a goal, and the changing behavior reflected in successfully completing the program.

As evacuee families slowly move from crisis to recovery, they will be ready to rebuild their lives and move from transitional living situations to a more permanent lifestyle. To facilitate this transition, there must be a strategy to serve the longer-term asset-building activities required to restore and enhance the lives of these low-income people impacted by the devastation. Not only must we rebuild peoples' homes and lives, we must also rebuild their community and social networks. The loss of community and the local social networks that were destroyed or disrupted must be restored or re-created to fulfill a comprehensive asset-building approach.

Given the extraordinary circumstances that had taken place over the first seven months after Hurricanes Katrina and Rita, it was essential to move beyond the traditional, place-based IDA concept and focus on an updated asset-building strategy. This strategy relates to individuals, families, and communities that were displaced by the devastation in the Gulf Coast and to the areas of the country where large numbers of evacuees have relocated. The traditional place-based IDA program needs to be retooled in serving these families and future families and communities faced with these catastrophic circumstances.

continued

Portable Individual Development Accounts: Supporting Individual and Community Assets after Major Disasters *(continued)*

A New Model: The Portable IDA Product

Through a grant from the Foundation for the Mid South, a meeting was held in Jackson, Mississippi, on June 20 and 21, 2006, for the idea of a portable IDA. The gathering brought together IDA and asset-building leaders from the Gulf Coast, including from Louisiana, Mississippi, and Texas.

Following the meeting, Covenant Community Capital, headquartered in Houston, along with the Texas Asset Building Coalition proposed to act as a lead partner to retool the traditional asset-building IDA product. The goal was to create an expanded product that provides a new program, serving hurricane evacuees through the establishment of portable IDAs. These portable IDAs would serve as the initial product to help the evacuees in rebuilding their lives in their new community or in facilitating their return to their previous community.

As envisioned, the portable IDA program would have the same basic elements of the traditional IDA, but would include additional features to help the evacuees move forward wherever they decided to build roots. In addition to the standard financial education curriculum and asset-specific classes, we proposed to include new educational features to help evacuees understand and adjust in their new community and assist them as they decided where to live in the future. Classes on civic engagement and community building would also be included to strengthen participants' confidence as they rebuilt their lives and developed relocation skills. Additional classes as necessary would be offered to support the evacuee families to enable them to decide on their asset-building strategy.

To enable the participant to have the knowledge, tools, and resources necessary to decide how best to rebuild their family life, it was envisioned that this program must work on potential asset-building skills and activities where the evacuee is currently living, any transitional location that may occur, and a more permanent location over the next six to 24 months. See Table 1 below.

Table 1
Portable IDAs versus Place-based or AFI IDAs

In designing a portable IDA product, there are a number of categorical differences from the traditional place-based IDA program. Below are several components that begin to separate the two products.

Key Categories	AFI or Place-based IDA	Portable IDAs
Income limits	usually 200% of poverty level	200% of poverty level; can also serve up to 80% AMI depending on program funding
Asset limits	$10,000	no asset limits for target population

continued

Table 1
Portable IDAs versus Place-based or AFI IDAs

Key Categories	AFI or Place-based IDA	Portable IDAs
Earned income requirement	yes	yes, but exceptions (e.g., SSI)
Lump sum deposits not from earned income	no	possibly (e.g., insurance)
First-time homebuyer	yes	yes, but exceptions; see former HOME definition*
Educational requirements	financial and asset	financial, asset, and others
Additional educational	usually peer groups	civic engagement and disaster preparedness
Target market	defined areas	defined areas and beyond
Matched funds to participant	defined areas	any market (need at least 10% flexible funds)
Administrative funds for organization	AFI and local funders	local funders and beyond
Matched funds to organization	mostly local	local and targeted funds (at least 10% outside target market)
Financial institution partners	usually one partner	multiple partners needed
Key partners	local partners for marketing, education, asset	local and beyond for marketing, education, asset
Policies and procedures	one set	may be one set or standardized policies
Application	one set	one set or standardized
Application process	in person and online	in person and online
Minimum time in program	six months	possibly less
Transfer of IDA	must find another program	have MOU work out transfer policy including, time, match, and admin funds
Database management	usually AFI2 or MISIDA	may need other system
Outcome and evaluation	local group and funder	common outcomes developed for specific evaluation measures
Maximum time in program	up to 5 years or less	probably three years
Allowable uses	home, education, business	home, education, business, and others as necessary

continued

Table 1 (*continued*)
Portable IDAs versus Place-based or AFI IDAs

Key Categories	AFI or Place-based IDA	Portable IDAs
Homeownership	defined areas	defined areas, partners, national
Homeownership	down payment, closing costs, mortgage buydown	potential additional uses such as build on land
Education	usually local but sometimes national	national
Small business	usually local	national
Home repair	not allowed	possible asset
Car purchase	not allowed	possible asset

* "First-time homebuyer" means an individual or individuals or an individual and his or her spouse who have not owned a home during the three-year period before the purchase of a home with HOME assistance, except that the following individual or individuals may not be excluded from consideration as a first-time homebuyer under this definition:

The state of Texas HOME program previously used this exception. "An individual, or individuals who owns or owned, as a principal residence during the three-year period, a dwelling unit whose structure is:

(i) not permanently affixed to a permanent foundation in accordance with local or state regulations; or

(ii) not in compliance with state, local, or model building codes and cannot be brought into compliance with such codes for less than the cost of constructing a permanent structure."

Portable IDAs: Moving beyond Placed-Based Asset Building Programs

Beyond portable IDAs for the post–Hurricanes Katrina and Rita population and for future large disasters, the creation of a portable IDA product was proposed to address several weaknesses in the placed-based, fixed-geography aspects of current IDA programs. They include the following:

- The declining nature of long-term employment stability that has evolved since 1990 in the U.S. labor market means the typical employee will have 5–7 jobs over a career.
- It appears that the effects of global warming may increase household mobility.
- A static geographic product works against student savers and young savers, who have greater mobility in their early working years.
- The dislocation or evacuation of residents from their local areas, as occurred with Hurricane Katrina.

Portable Individual Development Accounts: Supporting Individual and Community Assets after Major Disasters *(continued)*

To move the portable IDA forward, an initial step would be the creation of the Southern Asset Building Network, a regional association of organizations working to help strengthen the economic resiliency of families through asset-building strategies. If successful, it could be a model for other regional associations. The network would strengthen the asset-building cause by:

1. fostering the use of model enrollment forms and policies and procedures that share certain baseline qualities that can facilitate savings and education mobility;
2. promoting memoranda of understanding between network members to facilitate family mobility;
3. providing a reserve of match funds to bridge temporary shortfalls in local match availability;
4. enabling disaster evacuees to begin or continue an asset strategy while uncertainty remains about their final place of residence;
5. enabling students to enroll with some certitude of flexibility in pursuing the best job opportunities in the region;
6. creating an access point to link new clients with local asset-building resources through a ZIP code–driven network database;
7. promoting portability with funders and policymakers;
8. developing increased civic participation training and educational modules;
9. developing disaster preparedness training and educational modules; and
10. adding additional asset-building products to support family economic resiliency.

While the network never took off, a byproduct of the discussion on creating a portable IDA was that Covenant Community Capital designated 20 percent of its IDA-matched funds to serve markets outside of its direct service area. This allowed participants and areas in Texas and potentially outside the state to participate in an IDA without having to live in Houston.

The portable IDA was initially designed as an alternative asset-building, permanent-housing strategy after the devastation from Hurricanes Katrina and Rita. Though the product was not officially established in the Gulf Coast, it highlighted the limitations of using the placed-based traditional IDA to help families purchase a home. As we look to newer examples of similar situations like Superstorm Sandy, where the rebuilding process is longer term and the disruption of peoples' lives encompasses many months and potentially greater than one year, adding the portable IDA to the asset-building toolbox could make a major difference to individuals and communities moving forward.

Starting over is never easy, but having in place a number of unique asset-building products when a major disaster occurs is one critical step in moving quickly back to financial, housing, and community stability.

Asset building that addresses the needs of low-income communities post-disaster is a critical component of the disaster recovery.

Some innovations that arise during a disaster, particularly economic innovations, also bring risks to communities reeling from disaster. There is a new "disaster economics" that is emerging, both around the tools of economic projections and tabulations about the effects of climate change, challenging the standard assumptions about what we can expect in the future and how we will pay for it.[96] For example, some argue that the reason for the problems in the Superstorm Sandy disaster response was because communities had not allowed the rezoning for a Walmart big-box store to move in to the region.[97] This suggests that not only will local organizations and citizen groups need to be prepared to respond to the small human drama but also to pay attention to the larger trends and economic forces that will attempt to use the disaster for their own economic gain.

VII. Best Practices and How Attorneys Can Make a Difference

Lawyers have a special role in supporting, developing, and implementing the best practices that have been summed up by responders and community organizations in the past decade. Community development and housing lawyers are often called upon to be engaged in community lawyering—lawyering that is "based on a collaborative strategic vision of building community by developing client communities' ability to advocate for themselves."[98] Lawyers bring important skills to the table, but they are only part of the larger team that must respond.

> In the immediate response, lawyers' roles will be changing with mercurial speed to meet the needs that immediately present themselves. And some of those needs will be feet-on-the-ground provision of food, blankets, flashlights, and comfort. But, as Bonnie Allen has reflected, "There is this notion of two recoveries: The first recovery is how people that are middle class and wealthy recover, and then the second recovery is how the poor recover."[99] As those who carry a special responsibility for the quality of justice in America,[100] lawyers must find ways to be present for both recoveries.

A. Emergency Preparedness and Coordination

While some would say that planning for preparedness is a waste of time, there is plenty of evidence to the contrary. It may be true that there is no way to prepare for all emergencies. It may seem hard to justify spending time and resources planning for a response that might not be necessary. There is already so much work to do every day. It is also true that the Boy Scouts were on to something! Being prepared makes a big difference in the ability of persons, organizations, and communities to bounce back in a disaster.

Preparedness: There is a new momentum surrounding the conversations of preparedness. This momentum is driven by the confluence of local, national, and international organizations and governments that are responding to the ever more frequent disasters. Whether it is the Red Cross ramping up its training and certification activities, Habitat's development of the Disaster Corps, or the work that Mississippi Center for Justice has done to systematically train volunteer lawyers in disaster response and recovery short-term and long-term strategies, there is growing acknowledgement that preparation for disaster is a key element of a successful and resilient community response. Lawyers' capacity to identify best practices in advance, help train nonprofit and religious organizations, and put into place systems with backup systems gives the legal community a planning and implementation niche to work with clients in communities in *advance* of disaster.

Coordination: Coordination between nonprofit and religious organizations on the ground during a disaster can bring about stronger long-term networks for response. But key to that longer-term capacity building is the conscious summing up of the response work while it is still fresh in the minds of the participants. One model effort was conducted by the United Way of Greater Los Angeles following Hurricanes Katrina and Rita. In a report released in October 2006, the United Way took the time to conduct a coordinated review of the initiatives of nonprofit, government, and religious efforts to meet the needs of evacuees from Louisiana who came to Los Angeles after the storm.[101] More than 5,500 evacuees arrived in Los Angeles County and "had to be sheltered, fed, clothed, treated for injuries and ailments, registered for FEMA assistance, transported safely and assessed for mental stability."[102]

There were many findings in the report, but perhaps two are critical to the recommendations for Los Angeles and for areas beyond this report:

> Leadership capacity needs to be strengthened, particularly with regard to the role and contributions of the nonprofit community. . . . [T]he nonprofit community should be recognized and supported by the public and private sectors as key responders during an emergency/disaster requirement and "all hands on deck" response.

Coordination came too late and was disorganized.[103]

The group that was convened included 29 representatives from networks of nonprofit and religious organizations and governmental agencies. Their findings and recommendations should strengthen the nonprofit presence in any further disaster response. These recommendations include lessons for local nonprofits and for their relationships. The first recommendation is that there be an emergency network to coordinate the information flow between government agencies (both national and local) and local nonprofit and religious organizations. This should be a two-way information stream about the availability and locality of local resources and local needs, and national resources and national needs. This network should be completely integrated into the planning and design of the emergency response system and the emergency operations center.

The second recommendation is that local organizations should strengthen their leadership and preparedness for response and recovery. This should include the development of dedicated emergency reserves. There should be a line of fundraising so that resources needed during emergencies do not conflict with ongoing local responses.

While the Mary Queen of Vietnam Catholic community is a small example of local coordination, it is a fine example on which to build. This group was able to coordinate resources within the Catholic Church more broadly in the region, within New Orleans, and more locally within the Ninth Ward. Hope Community Development Agency was able to use coordinated resources within the state, using the expertise of the local universities linked with the organizing relationships within the community.

It may be a challenge for religious and nonprofit organizations to include an articulated strategy of coordination and preparedness in their vision of service. Lawyers may well be able to help clients foresee the need to be prepared in this way, and to understand the coordinating role as service in times of great disruption.

B. Common Platforms

A third lesson that was summarized in the Los Angeles reflection was that there should be a universal client tracking system, and forms that allow agencies the right to coordinate information between agencies when serving disaster victims. This reduces the drama for the survivor, having to travel between agencies, and maximizes all resources. It also requires sustained planning and coordination before disaster presents itself, so that the systems are in place, and coordination is seamless.

Issues of integration of computer and information systems is work that must draw in both experts in the systems themselves, but must also include those who pay close attention to the dangers of integrated systems—both the dangers for misuse by the nonprofit sectors, but also the misuse by government actors. In addition, there is a hearty debate about the constitutional protections that need to be in place for the protection of individual rights day to day in our country. Those attorneys and experts who are developing clear policies and procedures need to be actively engaged as the nonprofit sector, in particular, works to streamline and simplify the delivery of post-disaster services.

As the Mississippi Center for Justice quickly found out, it was necessary for all community-based service delivery organizations to collaborate on how to effectively deliver the broadest possible set of services to those in need in Gulf Coast region. Preparing to allocate at least some of the resources of an organization before the disaster will reduce the number of hours spent on this work after the disaster.

C. Communication

Having the ability to communicate within your own organization and with those served, either in your community or the community where you provide services, is a critical component to the ability to provide the kind of support that builds on the resiliency needed for a speedy recovery. "Evidence shows that community participation *before, during, and after* a disaster can greatly reduce the overall mortality as well as improve the use of resources. . . . [T]he greatest number of lives can be saved during the first few hours . . . before help from the outside arrives. . . . The local community must, therefore, be ready to assist since they may only have themselves to rely on."[104] The capacity to prepare community members and develop communication plans inside organizations and with community leaders can make the difference between having an effective response in which lives are saved, and an ineffective response with much more massive loss of life and property.

This is obviously more easily said than done. CBOs should think about their block captain equivalents, or partner organizations that have developed such structures, whether Citizens on Patrol or youth development organizations or even the local school parent teacher organization's phone tree. The "each one reach one" idea is important to think about in advance, building on 200 years of the "each one teach one" model.

The Hope Community Development Agency was able to use local block captains in their redevelopment efforts. People on the ground already knew and trusted these neighbors and leaders. It made work in the field more efficient and more effective.

D. Reflection

While the work in Los Angeles produced an exemplary moment of clarity about the challenges and opportunities of coordination and response, they are not alone in learning lessons and providing best practices.

Church Mutual Insurance Company, in its Spring 2009 "risk reporter," provided resources and suggestions for churches that wish to provide shelter in emergency situations.[105] Insurers of those who provide emergency response and recovery services are helping in the development of policies and procedures that can make the work needed in these moments of disaster productive and satisfying for those who are served, those who volunteer and those who contribute to these efforts. Without preparation and training, the work to be done is more difficult and costly.

"Disaster management conveys the important idea that protecting populations and property also involved the estimation of risk, preparation activities which will mitigate the consequences of predictable hazards and post disaster reconstruction in a way that will decrease vulnerabilities."[106]

VIII. Conclusion

This chapter was written as the disaster that was Superstorm Sandy unfolded across the eastern part of the United States, then moving up into the central provinces of Canada. Having been immersed in the literature of the lessons of Hurricane Katrina and Rita, I was reminded of the wisdom of those who survived and responded to that Gulf Coast nightmare:

As lawyers we took personally the observation that, every day, policy makers, institutions and private citizens alike made decisions *through the structures of law* that determine the effects of disasters. Lawyers are key designers and defenders of the rules, policies, and institutions that failed the people of the Gulf Coast. Disasters occur at the intersections of hazards and vulnerabilities.[107]

Today's culture is one of immediacy. But the lessons for lawyers and practitioners from disaster response might also be about creating an eye for the future. This includes the policies adopted by federal and state governments that engage the reality of our warming planet and the increasing demands of ever more frequent devastation in the lives of our citizens. It also includes adding the task of emergency planning to the compliance work that needs to be done for and with our clients, and raising with those clients the possibility of disaster whenever a policy or practice is recommended and adopted.

Supporting communities and strengthening the resilience of those communities, and the people and the organizations within them, is hard and tricky work. And it cannot be done by mandate or by law, though both laws and mandates can support or make that work more difficult. It is the people themselves, heart to heart, home to home, block to block, who are able to reach out and hold the dreams and hopes of each other. Lawyers can make the moments of disaster response easier: by hoping for the best, but helping clients prepare for the worst.

Notes

1. David Gutierrez, *Natural Disasters Up More than 400 Percent in Two Decades*, NaturalNews, June 5, 2008, http://www.naturalnews.com/z023362_natural_disasters_floods.html.

2. Blue Carbon: The Role of Healthy Oceans in Binding Carbon 31 (Christian Nellemann et al. eds., 2009), *available at* http://www.grida.no/files/publications/blue-carbon/BlueCarbon_screen.pdf.

3. After a lifetime as a community activist and organizer, and 20 years as a lawyer representing community-based organizations, this is the author's working definition of a community.

4. Community Justice: Issues for Probation and Criminal Justice 4 (Jane Winstone & Francis J. Pakes eds., 2005).

5. *Id.* at 4.

6. Robert Redfield, The Little Community and Peasant Society and Culture (Univ. of Chicago Press 1973) (1960).

7. *Id.* at 4.

8. *See Resilience: Build Skills to Endure Hardship*, Mayo Clinic (July 19, 2011), http://www.mayoclinic.com/health/resilience/MH00078.

9. Elie Bursztein & Jean Goubault-Larrecq, *A Logical Framework for Evaluating Network Resilience Against Faults and Attacks*, 4846 Lecture Notes in Computer Sci. 212 (2007); Louise McKeag, *How to . . . Build Network Resilience: Improving Your Network's Availability Without Paying Too Much*, Techworld, Oct. 7, 2004, http://howto.techworld.com/networking/888/how-to—build-network-resilience/; Paul Smith et al., *Network Resilience: A Systematic Approach*, 49 IEEE Comm. Mag. 88 (2011).

10. Lance H. Gunderson, *Ecological Resilience in Theory and Application*, 31 Ann. Rev. Ecology & Systematics 425 (2000); *Key Concepts*, Resilience Alliance (Oct. 16, 2002, 2:53 PM), http://www.resalliance.org/index.php/key_concepts.

11. *Overview*, Torrens Resilience Institute, http://www.torrensresilience.org/ (last visited Jan. 28, 2013).

12. *About RA*, RESILIENCE ALLIANCE (Jan. 8, 2004, 12:11 PM), http://www.resalliance.org/index.php/about_ra.

13. JOHNS HOPKINS BLOOMBERG SCH. OF PUB. HEALTH & INT'L FED'N OF THE RED CROSS AND RED CRESCENT SOCIETIES, PUBLIC HEALTH GUIDE IN EMERGENCIES 26 (2d ed. 2008), *available at* http://www.jhsph.edu/research/centers-and-institutes/center-for-refugee-and-disaster-response/publications_tools/publications/_CRDR_ICRC_Public_Health_Guide_Book/Forward.pdf [hereinafter HOPKINS, PUBLIC HEALTH GUIDE].

14. There has been some debate in the political arena about whether it is necessary to have federal agencies respond to naturally occurring and human-made disasters. Competing social and political interests lay claim to federal dollars. There are few interests, however, that seem more clear than the strong capacity of government to respond to and support response to such devastation when it falls upon our people.

15. Bonnie Allen et al., *Community Recovery Lawyering: Hard-Learned Lesson from Post-Katrina Mississippi*, 4 DEPAUL J. SOC. JUST. 97, 121 (2010).

16. *Id.*

17. Elizabeth Babister & Ilan Kelman, *The Emergency Shelter Process with Application to Case Studies in Macedonia and Afghanistan*, J. HUMANITARIAN ASSISTANCE 1, 2 (2002) (quoting IAN DAVIS, SHELTER AFTER DISASTER (1978)).

18. *Id.* at 4–5.

19. Allen et al., *supra* note 15, at 102–03.

20. *NYC Mayor Bloomberg Says up to 40,000 May Need Relocation*, CBSNEWS, Nov. 4, 2012, http://www.cbsnews.com/8301-201_162-57544884/nyc-mayor-bloomberg-says-up-to-40000-may-need-relocation/.

21. *NYC Housing Recovery to Help Victims Displaced by Hurricane Sandy*, MIKEBLOOMBERG.COM, Dec. 7, 2012, http://www.mikebloomberg.com/index.cfm?objectid=7612AE38-C29C-7CA2-F1A555A5A2E85324.

22. SUSAN UDE, DISASTER PREPAREDNESS AND RECOVERY FOR COMMUNITY DEVELOPMENT ORGANIZATIONS 49 (2009), *available at* www.nw.org/network/documents/DisasterPreparednessManual.pdf.

23. Babister & Kelman, *supra* note 17, at 8 (quoting E. Jensen, *Introduction and Overview: Typology and Causes of Emergency Settlement*, THE FIRST INTERNATIONAL EMERGENCY SETTLEMENT CONFERENCE PAPERS, NEW 'APPROACHES TO NEW REALITIES' (Univ. of Wis.—Disaster Mgmt. Ctr., 1986)).

24. *Id.*

25. *Id.* at 9.

26. *Id.* at 10–11.

27. *Id.* at 10–12.

28. The centers that were established in Texas after Katrina were, essentially, these temporary transit or relocation centers. Some people returned to New Orleans, and some used resources to resettle.

29. Babister & Kelman, *supra* note 17, at 12 (citing U.N. HIGH COMMISSIONER FOR REFUGEES, HANDBOOK FOR EMERGENCIES: FIELD OPERATIONS (1999)).

30. *Id.* at 13.

31. *Id.* at 44.

32. FLOOD MITIGATION CORE GROUP COMMITTEE, PERTH-ANDOVER & TOBIQUE FIRST NATION MITIGATION STUDY FINAL REPORT SUBMITTED TO THE GOVERNMENT OF NEW BRUNSWICK (2012), *available at* http://www2.gnb.ca/content/dam/gnb/Departments/env/pdf/Publications/MitigationStudyFinalReportPerthAndover.pdf.

33. Adam Huras, *Minister Says Quick Response to Victims' Well-being Was Paramount After Flood*, NEW BRUNSWICK TELEGRAPH-JOURNAL, Nov. 9, 2012, at A1.

34. Russel Honoré, a retired Lieutenant General who served as the Commander of the Joint Task Force Katrina for the Department of Defense and the Federal Emergency Management Agency (FEMA), made this statement during the government's response to Hurricane Katrina. Michael H. Cottman, *Honoré Advises New Orleans Residents to Leave, but Refuses to Use Force*, MICHAELH.COTTMAN.COM, Sep. 9, 2005, http://www.michaelhcottman.com/~micha270/publications/mcColumns.php; *Press Room*, GENERAL HONORÉ LLC at Home, http://www.generalhonore.com/PressRoom.html (last visited May 14, 2013).

35. *Founder Clara Barton*, AM. RED CROSS, http://www.redcross.org/about-us/history/clara-barton (last visited Jan. 25, 2013).

36. *Our Federal Charter*, AM. RED CROSS, http://www.redcross.org/about-us/history/federal-charter (last visited Jan. 25, 2013).

37. *The Global Red Cross Network*, AM. RED CROSS, http://www.redcross.org/about-us/history/global-red-cross-network (last visited Apr. 6, 2013).

38. Interview with Lenora Henry, former fundraiser, American Red Cross (Nov. 5, 2012) (on file with the author).

39. *Id.*

40. AM. RED CROSS, DISASTER SERVICES PROGRAM REVIEW: FISCAL YEAR 2011 (2012).

41. *Id.*

42. *Id.*

43. NATIONAL VOLUNTARY ORGANIZATIONS ACTIVE IN DISASTER, http://www.nvoad.org (last visited Jan. 25, 2013).

44. FEDERAL EMERGENCY MANAGEMENT AGENCY, http://www.ready.gov (last visited Jan. 25, 2013).

45. *Volunteer: Volunteer with Community Organizations*, FED. EMERGENCY MGMT. AGENCY (Sept. 13, 2012, 3:17 PM), www.ready.gov/volunteer.

46. *About Habitat for Humanity*, HABITAT FOR HUMANITY, http://www.habitat.org/how (last visited Jan. 25, 2013).

47. *What are Habitat Houses Like?*, HABITAT FOR HUMANITY, https://www.habitat.org/how/whatlike.aspx (last visited Jan. 25, 2013).

48. *Disaster Response: Completed Response Projects*, HABITAT FOR HUMANITY, http://www.habitat.org/disaster/completed_responses.aspx (last visited Jan. 25, 2013).

49. *Disaster Corps*, HABITAT FOR HUMANITY, http://www.habitat.org/disaster/disaster_corps (last visited Jan. 25, 2013).

50. *Disaster Response Programs*, HABITAT FOR HUMANITY, http://www.habitat.org/disaster/programs (last visited Jan. 25, 2013).

51. U.N. INT'L STRATEGY FOR DISASTER REDUCTION, HYOGO FRAMEWORK FOR ACTION 2005-2015: BUILDING THE RESILIENCE OF NATIONS AND COMMUNITIES TO DISASTERS (2005), *available at* www.unisdr.org/2005/wcdr/intergover/official-doc/L-docs/Hyogo-framework-for-action-english.pdf.

52. *Disaster Risk Reduction*, HABITAT FOR HUMANITY, http://www.habitat.org/disaster/mitigation_preparedness (last visited Jan. 25, 2013).

53. NETWORK FOR GOOD, http://www1.networkforgood.org (last visited Jan. 25, 2013).

54. *Search Results*, GUIDESTAR, http://www.guidestar.org (search "disaster response").

55. NAT'L LAW CTR. ON HOMELESSNESS & POVERTY, www.nlchp.org (last visited Jan. 25, 2013).

56. Housing and Community Development Amendments of 1978, Pub. L. No. 95-557, 92 Stat. 2080 (1978).

57. *See* UDE, *supra* note 22.

58. *Id.* at 6.

59. *Id.* at 7.

60. *Search Results*, ENTERPRISE, http://www.enterprisecommunity.com/where-we-work/new-york/priorities-andimpact/hurricane-sandy-rebuilding; *see also* LOCAL INITIATIVES SUPPORT CORP., http://www.lisc.org (search "disaster").

61. *See* UDE, *supra* note 22, at 5.

62. Paul Schwartzman, *Life After Sandy Still Difficult for New York's Poor*, WASH. POST, Nov. 1, 2012, http://articles.washingtonpost.com/2012-11-01/national/35507247_1_hurricane-sandy-lower-manhattan-new-yorkers.

63. UNITED WAY OF GREATER L.A., AFTER THE STORM: A PRELIMINARY ASSESSMENT OF THE NONPROFIT RESPONSE TO HURRICANE KATRINA IN LOS ANGELES COUNTY 22 (2006), *available at* http://uwglacdn.s3.amazonaws.com/wp-content/uploads/2011/11/AftertheStorm_Oct2006.pdf [hereinafter UNITED WAY, AFTER THE STORM].

64. *Id.* (quoting Steve Neal of AFL-CIO Labor Community Services).

65. The author's own network of Facebook friends posted at least three opportunities to volunteer. Neighbor-to-Neighbor Disaster Relief and SandyBaggers are examples of volunteer opportunities with devoted Facebook pages.

66. *Occupy Sandy Recovery*, INTEROCCUPY, http://interoccupy.net/occupysandy/ (last visited Jan. 25, 2013).

67. MISSISSIPPI CENTER FOR JUSTICE, http://www.mscenterforjustice.org (last visited Jan. 25, 2013).

68. Allen et al., *supra* note 15, at 107.

69. Interview with Bonnie Allen, Director of Training and Foundation Development, Mississippi Center for Justice (Nov. 7, 2012) (on file with the author).

70. *See* Allen et al., *supra* note 15, at 108–110.

71. *Id.* at 104 (quoting Derrick Evans, leader of the Turkey Creek Community Initiatives, in the Turkey Creek community of North Gulfport Mississippi).

72. *Id.*

73. Interview with Bonnie Allen, Director of Training and Foundation Development, Mississippi Center for Justice (on file with the author).

74. *Id.*

75. *Hope Community Development Agency*, GULF COAST COMMUNITY FOUND., www.hopecda.org (last visited Jan. 25, 2013).

76. Interview with Bonnie Allen, Director of Training and Foundation Development, Mississippi Center for Justice (Nov. 7, 2012) (on file with the author).

77. *Id.*

78. Ray Nothstine, *The Church and Disaster Relief: Shelter from the Stormy Blast*, 21 ACTON INST. RELIGION AND LIBERTY 4 (2011), *available at* http://www.acton.org/sites/v4.acton.org/files/pdf/rl-21-2.pdf.

79. THE DISASTER CTR., www.disastercenter.com (last visited Jan. 25, 2013). The Disaster Center is a website developed in the aftermath of Hurricane Katrina that updates a list of government, nonprofit and private sector resources available for disaster relief. By providing this information, it is itself another resource in the response network.

80. *See* Nothstine, *supra* note 78, at 4.

81. Interview with Bonnie Allen, Director of Training and Foundation Development, Mississippi Center for Justice (Nov. 7, 2012) (on file with the author).

82. *About Our Pastor*, SMOKING FOR JESUS MINISTRY, http://www.smokingforjesusministry.org/our-pastor—elect-lady.html (last visited Jan. 25, 2013).

83. MM Pack, *Finding God in the Gumbo*, AUSTIN CHRON., May 4, 2007, http://www.austinchronicle.com/food/2007-05-04/471756.

84. Andrea Ball, *After Katrina, New Orleans Church Started Over in Burnet,* STATESMAN.COM, Aug. 28, 2010, http://www.statesman.com/news/news/local/after-katrina-new-orleans-church-started-over-in-1/nRxM6/.

85. Pack, *supra* note 83.

86. Emily Chamlee-Wright & Virgil Henry Storr, *Club Goods and Post-Disaster Community Return*, 21 RATIONALITY & SOC'Y 429 (2009).

87. *Id.* at 433–34.

88. *Id.* at 430.

89. *Id.* at 444.

90. Emily Chamlee-Wright & Virgil Henry Storr, *Post-Disaster Recovery and Social Entrepreneurship*, GEORGE MASON UNIVERSITY, Nov. 11, 2012, http://localknowledge.mercatus.org/articles/post-disaster-recovery-and-social-entrepreneurship/.

91. KATRINA COTTAGES, http://www.katrinacottages.com/delivery/index.html (domain name has expired).

92. KATRINA COTTAGES, http://www.katrinacottages.com (domain name has expired).

93. Tom Gogola, *Katrina Cottages: Years late and $1 Million Over Budget in the 9th Ward*, THE LENS, May 3, 2012, http://thelensnola.org/2012/05/03/katrina-cottages-for-sale/. The last of the New Orleans Katrina Cottages came on line in the Ninth Ward, bringing Louisiana's total to 461 cottages and Mississippi's 500. This article is critical of the Louisiana political maneuvering that caused significant delays and cost overruns.

94. Ben Brown, *Finally Thinkin' Small: But Can We Build on What We've Learned?*, PLACE MAKERS, Nov. 5, 2012, www.placemakers.com/2012/11/05/finally-thinkin-small.

95. SHELTERBOX, http://www.shelterbox.org (last visited Jan. 25, 2013).

96. Michael Reksulak, *Free enterprise: Disaster Economics*, SAVANNAH MORNING NEWS, Nov. 2, 2012, http://savannahnow.com/exchange/2012-11-03/free-enterprise-disaster-economics#.UQL67lEoorU; *see also* Andrew Martin, *The Mad Max Economy*, N.Y. TIMES, Nov. 10, 2012, at BU1.

97. Naomi Shaefer Riley, *Walmart's Answer to NYC's Slaps*, N.Y. POST, Nov. 15, 2012, http://www.nypost.com/p/news/opinion/opedcolumnists/walmart_answer_to_nyc_slaps_wd5d3QXGdlfsZlL7wcwbBI.

98. Allen et al., *supra* note 15, at 99.

99. Interview with Bonnie Allen, Director of Training and Foundation Development, Mississippi Center for Justice (Nov. 7, 2012) (on file with the author).

100. AM. BAR ASS'N, COMPENDIUM OF PROFESSIONAL RESPONSIBILITY: RULES & STANDARDS 19 (2012).

101. *See* United Way, After the Storm, *supra* note 63.
102. *Id.* at 4.
103. *Id.* at 6, 7.
104. Hopkins, Public Health Guide, *supra* note 13, at 39.
105. *Hurricane Readiness*, Church Mutual Insurance Co., http://www.churchmutual.com/hurricane/ (last visited Jan. 25, 2013). For the general hurricane season updates and for the report, see *Church Mutual Risk Reporter*, Church Mutual Insurance Co., http://www.churchmutual.com/index.php/choice/risk/page/rm_Newsletters07/id/38 (last visited Jan. 25, 2013).
106. Hopkins, Public Health Guide, *supra* note 13, at 34.
107. Allen et al., *supra* note 15, at 121.

PART 2

Economic Recovery

CHAPTER 7

The 9/11 Attack on America and Lessons on How to Rebuild a Mixed-Use Business District

Richard M. Froehlich*

The morning of September 11, 2001, started with clear blue skies and a bright sun in New York City, when at 8:46 a.m. and 9:03 a.m., two planes crashed into the two World Trade Center (WTC) towers, leading to the deaths of approximately 2,700 people; destruction of the WTC complex; and damage or destruction of over 30 million square feet of office space, mass transportation facilities, and the communication infrastructure.[1] Although not a natural disaster, the scope of the 9/11 terrorist attack on New York created damage akin to one and required a response commensurate to the incredible losses experienced by the city.

I. Introduction

Usually we think of natural disasters such as an earthquake, hurricane, tornado, or fire as requiring a coordinated federal-state-local response because the affected community cannot respond on its own without shared assistance. What happened on 9/11 was similar: an actual attack

*Mr. Froehlich would like to acknowledge the assistance of Thomas G. James, a legal intern at HDC and a 2014 J.D. candidate from Boston College Law School, who assisted in preparing portions of this chapter.

on American soil that instantaneously triggered a patriotic response but also required a multidimensional approach to address the needs of residents, workers, companies (both large and small), and the region as a whole. Due to the complexities of the physical environment at the WTC site, the cleanup and subsequent redevelopment plans for this area were extremely challenging. President George W. Bush responded to the raw emotions and fears of further terrorism by decisively declaring that the federal government would provide $20 billion to help rebuild New York City.[2]

This chapter provides a review of the needs and responses to the destruction and a case review of the affected area prior to the attack. It also reviews the specific effects of the attack at the site of the WTC complex (Ground Zero), the surrounding neighborhoods, and the region. Finally, this chapter examines the public and private response to the destruction and offers an opportunity to look back over the experience of more than a decade to determine the effectiveness of these efforts. The response to 9/11 established a framework for some of the programs that were created in response to later disasters, including Hurricanes Katrina and Rita and Superstorm Sandy.

II. Downtown: The History and Base Case

Understanding why the World Trade Center was a target is an appropriate place to start. For purposes of this article, Downtown—the original heart of New York City and clearly its historic core—refers to the area south of Canal Street in Manhattan. New York City's first European settlers were the Dutch. Between its modest inception as the trading outpost known as New Amsterdam on the southern tip of Manhattan to the British takeover in 1664, the settlement grew from a few hundred colonists to a city of between 7,000 and 8,000 inhabitants.[3] The influence of the Dutch traders survives in the original street plan of Lower Manhattan as distinguished from the rigid grid system established for the island of Manhattan in the 1811 Commissioner's Plan.[4]

Lower Manhattan's reputation as a commercial hub began to grow with the establishment of its financial foundations as banking and insurance businesses began congregating along Wall Street, one of the original Dutch streets built to protect the early city.[5] The establishment of the nation's second stock exchange (the iconic New York Stock Exchange) as well as construction of banking headquarters signaled the leading role of New York City as a financial center that continues to this day.[6] The destruction of the WTC was an attempt to undermine New York City's role as a world financial center and an overt attack on the perceived wealth and prosperity that was created in its financial headquarters.[7]

The city's first skyscrapers, such as the Equitable Life Assurance Building (built in 1870) and the towers built for its leading newspapers in the 1870s, all reflected the continuing importance of Lower Manhattan. Even as its importance diminished with the expansion of the mass transit system that led to the rapid development of New York's midtown region, Downtown was still extremely relevant when the Woolworth Building was developed as the world's tallest building in 1911 and then 40

Wall Street, which surpassed that achievement in April 1930, only to be outdone by the Chrysler Building a month later.[8] Building the tallest buildings was a consistent theme throughout Downtown's history.

In response to a short economic depression in the late 1950s and a significant migration of large corporations to the east Midtown district, the construction of One Chase Manhattan Plaza and the establishment of the Downtown-Lower Manhattan Association by David Rockefeller was an effort to revitalize the financial district and provided the original impetus to create the WTC. Nelson Rockefeller, David's brother, was governor of New York and not surprisingly followed his brother's recommendations that Downtown needed further investment on the large scale that led to the subsequent creation of the WTC.[9]

III. Building the World Trade Center Towers and Battery Park City

The legendary Twin Towers were the product of negotiations between New York and New Jersey. They were part of a continuing effort to maintain New York City and the surrounding region as the predominant financial center in the country, as well as to redevelop a low-density section of Downtown. Construction of the WTC began in 1966 by the Port Authority of New York and New Jersey, a joint agency of the two states (Port Authority). Consisting of seven buildings, the WTC was noted for the Twin Towers, each rising above 1,350 feet and occupying a one-acre footprint of the 16-acre total site. Each tower contained more than two million square feet of office space. Although the WTC failed to immediately attract its desired clientele, nearly 500 companies, including leading banks and financial institutions, opened offices in the towers by the 1990s.[10] An estimated 50,000 people arrived to work each morning at the Twin Towers[11] while another 200,000 traveled through the site on a daily basis or visited as tourists in the late 1990s.[12]

Construction of the WTC created both the economic and physical base for the establishment of Battery Park City, a new mixed-use community in Downtown. Using landfill material from the excavation and construction of the WTC, the state of New York, acting through a public benefit corporation, the Battery Park City Authority, created a 92-acre foundation on land reclaimed from the Hudson River. Battery Park City was the last major piece of land added to Manhattan, and the construction of this planned neighborhood began in 1976.[13] It currently consists of 9.3 million square feet of commercial space, 7.2 million square feet of residential space, and almost 36 acres of green space. The Urban Land Institute recently declared that it is "a model for successful large-scale planning efforts and marking a positive shift away from the urban renewal mindset of the time."[14]

Battery Park City's housing stock is a mix of high-end home ownership in condominiums and mostly market-rate rental housing. Throughout its history, debates have continued about whether to increase affordable housing in the area, but municipal and state political leaders have consistently decided to use income from Battery Park City to support affordable housing in other parts of New York City.[15]

While new construction sought to revitalize Lower Manhattan's commercial legacy, changes to New York City zoning regulations and tax incentives encouraged developers to breathe new life into existing structures and begin the process of creating a lively mixed-use district. Recognizing the underutilization of Downtown's commercial stock, New York City created initiatives such as the 421-g tax incentive program to facilitate the conversion of commercial buildings or sections of buildings that were located south of Murray Street, City Hall, and the Brooklyn Bridge into multiple dwellings.[16]

One example of such a conversion is the Crystal Building at 47 West Street, directly across from Battery Park City. Its owner lost four commercial tenants in the early 1990s and had 26,000 square feet of nonresidential loft space left vacant for two years.[17] The tax benefits provided an incentive to convert several floors into live-in workspace to attract residents. The program was effective in greatly changing the nature of Downtown; more than 5,000 units of housing were added in the 1990s.[18]

The development of Battery Park City and the shifting nature of Downtown New York as a 24-hour, mixed-use community led to a more vibrant neighborhood than traditional central business districts. The changing area was starting to attract different businesses suitable for residents, as well as corporate clients. But the impact of the 9/11 attacks was particularly challenging to these nascent changes and made the recovery of services for area businesses and residents significantly more complicated for the city and state of New York.

IV. Impact of 9/11 on Housing and Community Economic Development

The destruction created by the attack on the WTC was monumental in scale. Debris from the collapsing Twin Towers, as well as fires that started after the planes hit the towers and spewed jet fuel over the area, destroyed the ancillary WTC buildings and claimed both 7 World Trade Center and St. Nicholas Church. In addition, the underground tunnels for the related mass transit subway stations and the PATH (Port Authority Trans-Hudson) station connecting Downtown New York with New Jersey were destroyed. Significant parts of the World Financial Center, across the highway from the WTC in Battery Park City, were severely damaged. Other nearby damaged buildings included the Deutsche Bank Tower at 130 Liberty Street, which was eventually demolished; 90 West Street, which was substantially rehabilitated with Liberty Bonds, as described below; Fiterman Hall, an extension facility for the Borough of Manhattan Community College that was subsequently rebuilt; Gateway Plaza in Battery Park City; the Millennium Hilton; and other structures.[19]

Job losses, fires from the crash, and debris from collapsing buildings also led to the precipitous drop in residential occupancy in Lower Manhattan. According to the Lower Manhattan Development Corporation, the population in Downtown New York in November 2001 was approximately 40 percent of the number of residents before 9/11. The destroyed buildings and supporting enterprises also meant that nearly 18,000 businesses and 536,000 employees were forced to relocate.[20]

The U.S. economy was already slowing down and entering a recession prior to the attacks. New York's downturn had started in January 2001 and had been continuing when the World Trade Center was destroyed.[21] Although it is difficult to determine the exact economic impact caused by an event like the 9/11 attacks, several efforts have been made to measure the losses. New York City's economic output was estimated to have dropped approximately $27.3 billion during the 15-month period after 9/11. The city was projected to lose over $2 billion in tax revenue in fiscal year 2002 and another $1 billion the following fiscal year due to reduced economic activity. Revenue losses, combined with relief and recovery expenses, further strained New York City's already stretched budget.[22]

The city's comptroller reported in 2002 that the total economic loss might be as high as $90 billion in terms of the combination of lost wealth (both physical and personal) and lost gross domestic product over a three-year period.[23] Other estimates are significantly lower and suggest that the attack exacerbated the effects of the recession, which had been under way for nearly a year.[24]

Regardless of the precise accuracy of these estimates of the attack's economic cost, it was clear that unemployment grew very quickly after the attacks, particularly in the Downtown area near Ground Zero where the economy essentially stopped for several months. The source of Downtown's economic strengths magnified the impact of 9/11 compared with what occurred in other parts of New York City. Manhattan as a whole and Downtown in particular were focused on finance, real estate, the arts, and the high-end professionals who service such industries. The nature of the attack greatly damaged the ability of businesses to function in the Downtown area. Although affected, other parts of the city had more local factors, including resilient businesses such as health care, retail, and government, which limited the lasting impact of the attack.[25] New York City and especially Manhattan, as one of the major tourist attractions in the United States, also experienced significant cuts in its hotel and restaurant industries as a result of the worsening recession and in response to the attacks. Tourists were wary to visit a place perceived to be unsafe or considered a likely future target, and travel to New York plummeted in the aftermath of 9/11.[26]

V. Creation of Lower Manhattan Development Corporation

The Lower Manhattan Development Corporation (LMDC), a subsidiary of the Empire State Development Corporation (ESDC),[27] was formed in 2002 as part of a city-state partnership to lead recovery efforts and revitalize the Downtown area. Among LMDC's stated goals, as the lead agency for determining the scope and plan for the rebuilding at Ground Zero, was the creation of a permanent memorial to commemorate the 9/11 attacks. The future of the actual WTC site was far from clear at the time; debate soon arose about how to remember the tragedy while affirming the resiliency of New York and the United States.[28] In comparison to the future of the ground at the WTC site, it was far easier to determine a pathway for Downtown as a whole.

LMDC was also charged with facilitating the revival of Lower Manhattan to ensure its long-term viability. LMDC was the creator of the plan and the agency meant to coordinate work by departments at both city and state levels to ensure success. It also played the lead role under environmental rules, and all public participation in the decisions on what would be done with the site were through LMDC hearings and meetings.

The controversial decision to build commercial space at WTC, albeit not within the footprints of the original Twin Towers, was in response to a significant debate that continues to this day about whether the site should be considered hallowed ground, whether any buildings built at the site would be perpetual targets, or whether we should rebuild on a very valuable piece of land as a message about resiliency. In the end, after a long and public review period, LMDC developed a general project plan that includes the memorial and museum, five commercial buildings, the transit hub, and the performing arts center.

VI. Case Example: Federal Recovery Funds

President Bush quickly pledged $20 billion in assistance following the 9/11 attacks. It took months, and in some cases years, to bring stability back to Downtown New York. The assistance from the federal government played an important role in making such normalcy possible. (For further discussion on the role of the federal government assistance post-disaster in general, see chapter 1.) The assistance can be characterized in three categories: (1) emergency response and cleanup, (2) rebuilding and development, and (3) budgetary relief for New York State and New York City.[29]

Congress also acted with alacrity in coordination with President Bush's pledge to assist families and regions most affected by the attacks and approved several important pieces of legislation, including the Emergency Supplemental Appropriations Act for Recovery from and Response to Terrorist Attacks on the United States[30] (approved within weeks of the attack); the Department of Defense and Emergency Supplemental Appropriations for Recovery from and Response to Terrorist Attacks on the United States Act[31] (approved in early 2002); the 2002 Supplemental Appropriations Act for Further Recovery from and Response to Terrorist Attacks on the United States;[32] and the Job Creation and Worker Assistance Act of 2002 (JCWAA).[33] These bills collectively defined the federal assistance for the recovery of New York City and included a mix of grants, budgetary relief for New York State and New York City, tax breaks and incentives for businesses and individuals, and funds for both state and local governments.[34]

In a separate action, Congress created the 9/11 Victim Compensation Fund pursuant to the Air Transportation Safety and System Stabilization Act and set aside $7 billion for families of those who perished on 9/11.[35] In 2011, President Obama signed the James Zadroga 9/11 Health and Compensation Act of 2010, which provides for compensation to first responders who subsequently filed claims for medical treatment and compensation related to their work at the WTC site.[36] Although both funds are significant to the direct beneficiaries (i.e., families and first responders), such activities are not going to be explored in this discussion on the rebuilding of WTC and Downtown New York. The money for both funds was not considered to be part of the pool used to revitalize New York City after 9/11.

Of the $20 billion allocated by President Bush and Congress, approximately $6 billion in public-assistance-related funding—including grants for removing debris, replacing destroyed vehicles, and repairing damaged buildings, among other initiatives—came from the Federal Emergency Management Agency (FEMA).[37] The Federal Transit Administration provided $4.55 billion in transportation aid. Almost $3.5 billion in Community Development Block Grants (CDBG) came from the Department of Housing and Urban Development (HUD). At an estimated $5 billion in total cost to the federal government, provisions of the JCWAA created tax incentives for New York State; New York City; and the New York Liberty Zone, a section of Lower Manhattan in proximity to the attacks. Other sources of almost $1.5 billion brought the aid package to the amount promised by President Bush.[38]

Although most of the FEMA funds went for the actual cleanup of the site, nearly $1 billion was used to set up an insurance fund related to claims from the debris cleanup and removal.[39] In addition to the funding allocated toward cleanup and economic revitalization, FEMA and HUD committed nearly $4.81 billion to compensate organizations, businesses, and individuals for losses attributable to the attacks.

LMDC received $2.783 billion in CDBG funding that was used to address a wide variety of projects. Unlike regular CDBG funds, the funds provided by HUD were not subject to the standard use and public participation requirements.[40] LMDC disbursed $807 million to individuals and families. This aid was given in recognition of concerns that occupancy rates in neighborhoods surrounding Ground Zero had fallen by 60 percent after the attacks and that significant efforts would be needed to stabilize these neighborhoods.

LMDC established the $281 million Residential Grant Program, which provided financial incentives to attract and keep residents in Lower Manhattan.[41] Funds for this purpose included the Two-Year Commitment-Based Grant, which offered 30 percent toward monthly rent or housing costs conditioned upon a two-year lease, and the September 11, 2001, Residents Grant and Family Grant, which provided $1,000 per household for individuals who continued to live in the area.[42] FEMA contributed an additional $200 million toward mortgage and rental assistance grants; applicants who had lost 25 percent of their income after the attacks could receive up to 18 months of assistance.[43]

To restore residential life Downtown after 9/11, the first goal was to clean up debris and dust and encourage displaced residents to return. The grants discussed above were very effective in stabilizing the population, and the combination of grants and rent concessions filled any vacancies. Other than displacement, which lasted up to 45 days, no housing was lost as a result of the attack, so many of the emergency housing needs were limited in cost.

VII. Specific Aid for Transit, Small Businesses, and Economic Development

FEMA and the Department of Transportation (DOT) spent a total of $5.7 billion on transit repair and expansion. Such funds were used to repair subway stations, ferry terminals, and streets, as well as to create the signature World Trade Center transportation hub.[44] Without significant investment to rebuild the transit system, many Downtown workers would have been inconvenienced for a much longer period than the two years that PATH trains connecting Downtown New York City and Jersey City were unavailable, or the one year it took to allow subway trains through the WTC site to the southern tip of Manhattan.[45]

Santiago Calatrava, an internationally renowned architect, has designed the transit hub with its distinctive winged features. It will serve approximately 60,000 daily commuters from New Jersey plus additional visitors (expected to be more than 200,000 visits daily). It will have over 500,000 square feet of retail space, making it one of the largest shopping areas in Downtown New York. With a price tag in excess of $3.5 billion and numerous delays, the project is not scheduled to be delivered until early 2015. Critics have suggested that a simpler approach would have been better and clearly cheaper than the design of a celebrated architect. Despite such concerns and delays, the project has moved forward and will be a distinctive addition to Downtown.[46]

The 9/11 attacks physically devastated the financial sector in Lower Manhattan and destroyed 18,000 small businesses in the surrounding area.[47] Because of small or nonexistent cash reserves and an inability to raise capital, small businesses were particularly vulnerable to collapse following destruction or dislocation.[48] Both the federal and New York State governments moved swiftly to help rebuild small business and ward off future economic stagnation Downtown. The funds described below were essential in convincing many firms that were displaced or otherwise affected to continue operations Downtown after the 9/11 attack.

The Small Business Administration (SBA) began meeting with small-business owners two days after the attacks and, by September 30, 2002, issued 5,254 loans (totaling $435 million with average loans of $82,900).[49] Further aid for small businesses came in the form of CDBG funds disbursed by HUD for use by the LMDC.[50] SBA altered its Disaster Loan Program to increase the maximum available loan amounts, approving an estimated $1 billion in loans for victims of the attacks by the end of the fiscal year 2002.[51] (For further discussion of small-business redevelopment post-disaster, see chapter 8.)

By 2007, LMDC awarded 33 grants exceeding $37 million in Community Enhancement Funds to address a variety of projects such as health care, education, community services, recreation, and cultural projects.[52] In response to such a dramatic economic calamity, HUD allocated $578 million to compensate businesses for economic losses and recovery efforts through the ESDC. This program, called the Business Recovery Grant Program (BRG), was used mostly to fund small businesses. More than 15,000 businesses were assisted under BRG, which was an unusual use of HUD funds for nonhousing purposes.[53] Other federal funding geared toward economic revitalization included the Small Firm Attraction and Retention Grant Program (SFARG), which was administered by ESDC. Nearly $457 million in aid was awarded to displaced or otherwise affected small businesses.[54] Although most funds were allocated in the two years following 9/11, some funds have yet to be disbursed, and ESDC has had to modify its action plan several times. The most recent modification, which extends the grant period until December 31, 2013, was submitted in 2011, and other changes to the plan were submitted in 2012.[55]

VIII. Voluntary Charitable Giving

Charitable giving was a significant source of funds for families of victims of the attack, as well as for resident and business relief after 9/11. The leading 30 charities responding to 9/11 raised approximately $2.4 billion. The Red Cross raised more funds (approximately $1 billion) than any other organization. Much of its assistance went to providing funds to the families of the victims, help for displaced residents of Downtown New York, and aid for approximately 50,000 people who lost their jobs because of 9/11 and needed funds to pay living costs. The Red Cross prepared and distributed 14 million meals for disaster workers, those who cleared the debris, and others affected in the months following the attack.[56]

The September 11th Fund raised more than $500 million and spent most of its funds on many of the same activities as the Red Cross. However, it also provided funds for job training, and nearly 1,000 small businesses and nonprofits received grants or loans to help rebuild Downtown.[57] One of its major initiatives was the funding (along with ESDC) of Seedco, a national community-development opportunity intermediary, for the Lower Manhattan Small Business & Workforce Retention Project (LMSB&WRP). LMSB&WRP had two phases. Phase I was disaster relief to help retail and service businesses below Canal Street pay costs related to the attack and provide working capital for businesses. Phase II was assistance to stabilize, expand, or start new operations. As of July 29, 2004, Seedco had provided financial and technical assistance to 1,541 businesses in Lower Manhattan, providing more than $40 million in assistance to small businesses and nonprofits under LMSB&WRP.[58]

IX. Liberty Zone Tax Benefits and Liberty Bonds

Congress created tax incentives for the New York Liberty Zone through the Job Creation and Worker Assistance Act of 2002. The Liberty Zone is defined as the area below Canal Street between the Hudson and East Rivers, and businesses located within the zone or directly affected by the 9/11 attacks were eligible for federal tax benefits. Tax credits, accelerated depreciation tax benefits, additional bond refunding authority for New York City and New York State, and Liberty Zone Bonds were all part of the tool kit of economic development programs created in response to the 9/11 attacks.

Firms were entitled to claim a credit for 40 percent of the first $6,000 of qualified wages for all employees under JCWAA. Furthermore, JCWAA authorized firms to claim a first-year depreciation deduction equal to 30 percent of adjusted basis for tangible personal property.[59] Although the New York City comptroller expressed serious doubts about the use of some depreciation and tax credits and sought to have these benefits converted to direct grants for transit projects,[60] Congress never enacted such changes. Because tax credits are useful only if a business has profits, it is difficult to gauge whether they were used by or helpful to the intended beneficiaries without access to actual tax returns.[61]

Congress allocated an aggregate of $8 billion in exempt facility bonds for the purpose of financing the construction and rehabilitation of both commercial property and residential rental property in the Liberty Zone.[62] Developments eligible for financing with these bonds included buildings and their structural components; fixed tenant improvements; and public utility property (e.g., gas, water, electric, and telecommunication lines). Issuance of Liberty Zone Bonds was limited to projects approved by the mayor of New York City or the governor of New York State, each of whom was authorized to designate up to $4 billion of the aggregate bond authority. Of the $8 billion, a maximum of $1.6 billion was allocated for residential rental property. The residential developments financed with Liberty Zone Bonds were not subject to the normal tax-exempt bond affordability requirements for multifamily housing. The allocated bonds for commercial activity were highly unusual in that commercial office buildings generally are not eligible for financing under existing rules for private activity bonds.

Residential conversions in Downtown New York had begun before 9/11 but accelerated afterward in direct response to federal aid for housing and the assistance described above. At 20 Exchange Place, which was a former bank headquarters around the corner from the New York Stock Exchange, developers in 2004 converted 800,000 square feet to residential space, while retaining limited commercial space on the lower floors.[63] Similar efforts were undertaken on Wall Street with the conversions at 63 and 67 Wall Street receiving award-winning acclaim. Other buildings, such as 90 West Street, which was severely damaged during the attacks, were refurbished and converted.[64] Most office buildings were financed in part through the Liberty Zone Bond program.

Liberty Zone Bonds were used to create thousands of units of housing Downtown and helped create jobs and a sense of renewal in an area severely damaged by the terrorist attack. Between the New York State Housing Finance Agency (HFA) and the New York City Housing Development Corporation (HDC), the entire allocation of $1.6 billion was utilized for the development of housing in the Liberty Zone. Approximately 5,700 units, including conversion of existing office buildings to residential space, as well as new construction, were created south of Canal Street.[65] The units financed by HDC did not have any affordability requirements, but approximately $30 million in fees were charged on its Liberty Zone financings and used as subsidy loans on approximately 600 units of affordable housing in other parts of New York City, mostly in the Bronx and Brooklyn.[66] HFA required its developers to set aside 5 percent of the financed units (approximately 120 units overall) for families at 150 percent of the city's area median income. Several of the HFA-financed projects were part of the residential plan for Battery Park City, and the financing from Liberty Zone Bonds was instrumental in completion of Battery Park's plan.[67]

As noted above, the residential portion of Liberty Zone Bonds led to the growth of people living Downtown. Critics complained that the program subsidized market-rate housing for upper-income individuals and families. Government officials and program supporters responded that Liberty Zone Bonds were not intended as an affordable-housing program but instead were meant to stabilize the region and ensure the vitality of the mixed-use neighborhood. More importantly, at the time the program was created, the future success of such efforts was uncertain at best.[68] Partly in response to concerns about affordable housing, LMDC allocated over $50 million in CDBG funds for the creation and preservation of affordable housing in Downtown New York, including subordinate repair loans for several large, aging developments for moderate-income residents.[69]

X. Rebuilding at Ground Zero: Commercial Space, Arts, the Memorial, and Museum

A. Commercial Space

Redevelopment of office space in both Downtown and Midtown New York City was an important vote of confidence in response to concerns that New York was still vulnerable to terrorist attacks.[70] Of the $6.4 billion in bond authority, all have now been used, but the first $800 million was allocated for projects outside of the Liberty Zone to fund a new headquarters for Bank of America in Midtown New York City, a building for Bank of New York in downtown Brooklyn, and for the headquarters of tech company Interactive Corporation in Chelsea, a few miles north of WTC.[71] Critics lambasted New York City and the state of New York for use of the subsidy outside the Liberty Zone, but the mayor and the governor and their respective administrations rationalized their decision as a vote of confidence in the future of New

York City as a whole. The investment bank Goldman Sachs received $1.65 billion in bonds for the construction of its headquarters in Battery Park City. Not surprisingly, due to the backlash against many financial institutions as a result of the 2007–2008 financial crisis, New York City has been roundly criticized for this subsidy, as well as the other inducements to keep Goldman Sachs Downtown.[72]

Most of the Liberty Zone Bonds were set aside to finance the development of commercial space at Ground Zero. The rebuilding of 7 World Trade Center was funded also from insurance proceeds. It was the first building rebuilt (and now fully leased) and received $475 million in bond financing. Another $3.3 billion is funding a portion of the construction costs of 1 and 4 World Trade Center.

Critics have questioned the need for so much additional office space Downtown. Interestingly, after Bank of America purchased Merrill Lynch, it decided to move many employees from the World Financial Center in Battery Park City to its new Midtown tower, which had been funded with Liberty Zone Bonds. Concern has been expressed that the vacant space will reduce demand for office space that is expected to be delivered at the WTC.[73] When fully built out, the five towers will have approximately 10 million square feet of space with another 600,000 square feet of retail space in WTC and the transit hub. Added to other plans and available space Downtown, developers are looking to populate a business district that has more office space than the entire New Orleans Central Business District. However, the economic challenges after the financial crisis of 2007–2008 dampened demand for large projects, such as the WTC, as well as commercial space throughout Manhattan. In addition, progress on the rebuilding at the WTC was initially delayed by design and security challenges and negotiations with insurance companies.

One World Trade Center, originally labeled the Freedom Tower, has made the most progress and is expected to welcome tenants in 2014. Expected to reach 1,776 feet, including its spire, it will be the tallest building in the Western Hemisphere at a cost of approximately $3.5 billion and with more than 2.6 million square feet of office space.[74] Condé Nast has agreed to be the lead tenant.[75]

Four World Trade Center is also proceeding apace and is projected to be a 61-story, 950-foot tower with 1.8 million square feet. The Port Authority has already agreed to be its major tenant. Work has also begun on 3 World Trade Center, which is planned to be 71 stories and have 2.8 million square feet. However, work on 3 World Trade Center may be suspended at only seven stories if its developer is unable to find a tenant willing to take at least 400,000 square feet.[76] The combination of a weak economy and the glut of office space means that WTC may not be finished until almost 20 years after the attack.[77]

Expecting a large infusion of workers in WTC, retail development has also picked up and will continue to expand business and employment opportunities for both entrepreneurs and job seekers alike. When combined with the already burgeoning tourist trade and residential expansion, the completion of the commercial towers will spur an expansion of shopping opportunities. As noted, the WTC plan has retail components that will play an important role in adding even more vibrancy to Downtown.[78]

B. The Memorial

In 2003, LMDC sponsored an international competition to choose a design for the 9/11 Memorial, fielding 5,201 applications from 63 countries.[79] A 13-member jury selected *Reflecting Absence*, submitted by architects Michael Arad and Peter Walker. The memorial features cascading waterfalls within the original footprints of the Twin Towers, designed as tribute to both physical and emotional voids left by the 9/11 attacks. The names of the 2,983 victims of the attacks in New York City, the Pentagon, and Pennsylvania, as well as the 1993 bombing of the original WTC, surround the memorial pools. Their arrangement reflects "meaningful adjacencies," based on the relationships of individuals, their location during the attacks, and requests by family members and and loved ones.[80]

Construction started on March 13, 2006, and the memorial opened on September 12, 2011, commemorating the 10th anniversary of the attacks. The memorial also will feature an underground museum containing artifacts recovered from the collapsed buildings, although its construction was delayed by prolonged negotiations among the mayor of New York City and the governors of New York and New Jersey. The parties were finally able to reach an agreement to ensure the museum's construction shortly before the 11th anniversary of 9/11. It should be completed within two years.[81]

By the end of 2011, more than one million visitors had seen the 9/11 Memorial, which has attracted more tourists than the original Twin Towers.[82] Open seven days a week, the memorial is accessible to visitors who have reserved a free pass through the memorial's website. Lower Manhattan hosted 9.8 million tourists in 2011, exceeding the previous year by 800,000 visitors.[83]

C. The Arts

In addition to the creation of the 9/11 Memorial as a cultural destination, LMDC has authorized plans for the creation of a 1,000-seat performing arts center.[84] Expected to be occupied by the Joyce Theater Foundation, the performing arts center would be the city's only venue dedicated exclusively to dance. The space will provide performance groups that cannot afford to take the financial risk of renting larger venues with a viable space.[85] LMDC has set aside $155 million from its CDBG allocation for the project. However, with a price tag expected to exceed $450 million, significant fundraising will be needed before the project moves forward. Critics have raised multiple questions about whether the concept of the arts center, which was an original part of the overall plan for the rebuilt WTC, should be built on the WTC campus or if the funds should be used for arts purposes in multiple Downtown locations. Renowned architect Frank Gehry, designer of the Beekman Tower (also funded with Liberty Zone Bonds) in the Financial District, has been commissioned to design the space.[86]

XI. From Liberty Zone to GO Zone: Lessons Learned

On some level, the federal government's response to Hurricanes Katrina, Rita, and Wilma was influenced by its response to 9/11. This is clearest when looking at the Liberty Zone tax benefits created after 9/11 and the Gulf Opportunity Zone (GO Zone) benefits created after the hurricanes. (For further discussion on the GO Zone tax benefits, see chapter 1.) The package of tax credits, accelerated depreciation tax benefits, additional tax-exempt bond authority, and authority to advance refund certain governmental bonds in order to create savings were highly similar. The differences in the tax package mostly related to the need to rebuild an enormous amount of damaged housing stock. In addition, the Liberty Zone was narrowly defined while the GO Zone, reflecting the wide swath of damage in the Gulf area, was considerably larger.[87]

The scale of the devastation caused by the hurricanes was very broad. Of the approximately $120 billion in direct federal assistance, the vast majority relates to temporary and long-term housing ($52 billion), emergency response ($29 billion), and the rebuilding of infrastructure ($19 billion). In comparison to New York, the value of the proposed tax benefits was only $8 billion.[88] But, unlike New York City, the inclusion of a large infusion of additional housing tax credit allocations for the affected states in the Gulf area did have the effect of encouraging the development of affordable housing.[89] Congress's long-term goal of encouraging private ownership of affordable housing led to the creation of the GO Zone tax credit, which was regarded as a natural solution for replacing some of the lost affordable-housing stock.

XII. Conclusion: Taking Stock of What Worked and What Did Not

New York City's enduring prominence as a preeminent financial center in the world can be viewed as the primary success of the rebuilding efforts Downtown. The actual dynamism created in Downtown New York City after 9/11 must also be regarded as a significant accomplishment. The residential population has doubled, Battery Park City has been fully built out, and the World Trade Center area has been re-created "as a vibrant, 24-hour place."[90] On a warm summer weekend afternoon, anyone would be impressed by the energy and sheer number of people flooding through the 9/11 Memorial, Battery Park City, the South Street Seaport, and all the areas in between these sites. Many are visitors to New York, which has become the nation's largest tourist destination since 9/11, but quite a few are the approximately 56,000 Downtown residents (almost double the number of residents in 2001).[91]

Certain aspects of the success relate to the general sustained good health of New York City, even after the deep recession of 2008–2009. Tourism has become an ever-growing engine of activity. The city heavily markets itself, both inside and outside the United States, and has focused great energy on increasing tourism and its beneficial impact on New York's economy.[92] Overall economic activity has grown at a greater pace in New York City than in either New Jersey or New York State as a whole.[93]

Small-business owners and federal audits have been critical of the adequacy of certain relief efforts that were targeted to smaller businesses, although they recognize the government's quick efforts to respond to the disaster.[94] Assessments have generally shown that federal financial assistance was insufficient, and specific complaints highlight the SBA's inability to tailor its programs to New York City business owners. For example, the SBA typically requires some sort of collateral, usually a home, while most New York City residents rent.[95]

Even though the federal government appropriated large sums for disaster relief, internal auditing has revealed doubts as to the aid's efficacy. Specifically, the House Subcommittee of Management, Integration, and Oversight issued a report to the 109th Congress questioning the impact of the $13.7 billion disbursed by federal agencies in Lower Manhattan. No governmental entity catalogued the full extent of the aid provided to New York City until August 2006, despite concern of potential fraud, waste, and abuse of federal funds. The report identified several systematic problems that are typical of disaster response efforts and were evident in the disbursement of the 9/11 funds, including lack of information sharing and agency coordination, inadequate verification prior to disbursing funds, duplicative payments, relaxed controls, and ineffective central oversight.[96]

The subcommittee's report also provided recommendations for disbursement of federal emergency funding in future disasters, including the creation of a full-time independent coordination agency to prevent fraud and duplicative spending, as well as mandatory regularly scheduled audits and stricter screening processes for both contractors and aid applicants. [97] While certain exigencies appear specific to New York City, such as the influence of organized crime on trucking and debris-removal services,[98] these recommendations are applicable to a host of disaster scenarios in urban settings.

As noted throughout this chapter, certain aspects of the efforts were clearly successful. The agencies involved have received complaints, criticism, and praise, and some important projects are still in progress at the actual WTC site. The rebuilding will continue to take shape over the next five to seven years. The critiques are not unusual considering the scope of the endeavor undertaken by so many different parties. For some, the slow pace of the actual redevelopment of the WTC site has been disappointing, but others are now recognizing that, with all of the challenges involved, the entities responsible for planning the revitalization of Downtown Manhattan did an admirable job.

XIII. Epilogue

Downtown New York City was hit particularly hard by the nontropical cyclone named Sandy that passed through the New York metropolitan region October 29–30,

2012. Although more residential losses and loss of life occurred elsewhere in the region, Downtown was badly flooded as the result of its low elevation and proximity to the Hudson and East Rivers and the New York Harbor. On a cost basis, the business losses in Downtown will be staggering compared with the rest of the region. The surging tide damaged many buildings, as well as the infrastructure (mass transit, electrical systems) that allow the area to operate. The irony of a natural disaster causing major disaster in an area devastated by human-made events was not lost on observers. The subway stops rebuilt after 9/11 have been severely damaged as well as the PATH subways connecting New Jersey with Downtown.

The 9/11 Memorial reopened to the public a little more than a week after floodwaters, as high as 10 feet in places, were drained from the 16-acre site. One of the more graphic images of flooding Downtown showed storm-surge water cascading into the memorial. Five huge pumps were used to suck tens of millions of gallons of water out of the entire construction site.[99] The museum was also flooded up to seven feet, potentially impacting some of the artifacts already stored there.[100] Generally, because most of the building systems were not yet installed, work at the WTC site was able to resume without too much permanent damage. It is expected that designs may be modified to ensure operations when future flooding occurs.

Broader questions about the future of Downtown linger after Superstorm Sandy. Numerous buildings operating close to the shoreline have been shuttered for an extended period that probably will last three to six months. Small businesses, such as restaurants, delis, coffee shops, and other service providers, may have limited insurance coverage, and their willingness to locate in an area that is now considered a flood zone will need to be answered in ways similar to the response to 9/11. Unlike 9/11, which engendered a patriotic response, the effects of Superstorm Sandy may be more profound and longer lasting as occupants of Downtown ponder their next steps.[101]

Of course, questions will need to be asked throughout the region on where to rebuild, how to address the vulnerabilities of the infrastructure, and how to survive the next natural disaster. Post-Sandy, all the lessons that can be learned from prior disasters will need to be deployed in the New York metropolitan region as it rebuilds again from this devastating disaster.

Notes

1. LOWER MANHATTAN DEV. CORP., Final Generic Environmental Impact Statement for World Trade Center Memorial and Development Plan (2004), *available at* http://www.renewnyc.com/content/pdfs/eis/04-12-2004/vol1/01%20Project%20Description.pdf.

2. Dave Gatton & Nate Roman, *New York Mayor, Lawmakers Pleased with Bush Aid Package*, U.S. MAYOR NEWSPAPER, Mar. 18, 2002, http://www.usmayors.org/usmayornewspaper/documents/03_18_02/nyc_bush_aid.asp.

3. EXPLORING HISTORIC DUTCH NEW YORK 26 (Gajus Scheltema & Heleen Westerhuijs eds., 2011).

4. *Id.* at 29.

5. CHARLES R. GEISST, WALL STREET: A HISTORY FROM ITS BEGINNINGS TO THE FALL OF ENRON 10 (2004).

6. Charles R. Geisst, Deals of the Century: Wall Street, Mergers, and the Making of Modern America xx (2004).

7. *FAQ About 9/11*, 9/11 Memorial, http://www.911memorial.org/faq-about-911.

8. Andrew S. Dolkart, Guide to New York City Landmarks 25 (Matthew A. Postal ed., 2009).

9. David Rockefeller, Memoirs 310 (2002).

10. *A Look at Former World Trade Center Tenants*, Wall St. J., Jan. 15, 2002, http://interactive.wsj.com/public/resources/documents/Tenant-List.htm.

11. Eric Darton, Divided We Stand: A Biography of New York's World Trade Center 146 (1999).

12. *Id.* at 8.

13. Jane Kolleeny, *Battery Park City Library*, Architectural Rec., Mar. 2011, http://archrecord.construction.com/projects/Building_types_study/libraries/2011/battery-park-city-library.asp.

14. Leigh Franke, *Battery Park City — 2010 Global Award for Excellence Winner*, Urban Land Inst., http://www.uli.org/global-awards-for-excellence/battery-park-city-2010-global-award-for-excellence-winner/.

15. David L.A. Gordon, Battery Park City: Politics and Planning on the New York City Waterfront 91 (1997).

16. N.Y. [Real Prop. Tax] Law § 421-g (Consol. <year>). Under section 421-g, the city was permitted to provide a developer a 14-year abatement of about 80 percent of the real estate taxes paid on the property prior to the conversion of commercial space to residential uses.

17. Alan S. Oser, *Perspectives: New Residential Space Arrives in Lower Manhattan*, N.Y. Times, Feb. 4, 1996, http://www.nytimes.com/1996/02/04/realestate/perspectives-new-residential-space-arrives-in-lower-manhattan.html?pagewanted=all&src=pm.

18. Joseph J. Salvo, Arun Peter Lobo & Joel Alvarez, N.Y. City Dep't. City Planning, A Pre- and Post-9/11 (2000–2005) Look at Lower Manhattan (2007), *available at* http://www.nyc.gov/html/dcp/pdf/census/pre_post_911.pdf., p.3.

19. Lower Manhattan Dev. Corp, *supra* note 1.

20. U.S. Gov't Accounting Office, September 11: Overview of Federal Disaster Assistance to the New York City Area 36 (2003), *available at* http://www.gao.gov/new.items/d0472.pdf.

21. Jason Bram, *New York City's Economy Before and After September 11*, Current Issues in Econ. & Fin. 1 (2003).

22. Gail Makinen, Cong. Research Serv., RL31617, The Economic Effects of 9/11: A Retrospective Assessment 5 (2002), *available at* http://www.fas.org/irp/crs/RL31617.pdf.

23. N. Y. City Office of the Comptroller, One Year Later: The Fiscal Impact of 9/11 on New York City 1 (2002).

24. Bram, *supra* note 21, at 4.

25. Michael L. Dolman & Solidelle F. Wasser, *9/11 and the New York City Economy: A Borough-by-Borough Analysis*, 127 Monthly Lab. Rev. (2004), 3–9.

26. Leslie Eaton, *Attack Gave a Devastating Shove to the City's Teetering Economy*, N.Y. Times, Sept. 8, 2002.

27. The Empire State Development Corporation is a state public-benefit corporation.

28. Michael D. Lemonick, *Should They Be Rebuilt?*, Time, Sept. 24, 2001.

29. N.Y. City Budget Office, The Aftermath: Federal Aid 10 Years After the World Trade Center Attack (2011), *available at* http://www.ibo.nyc.ny.us/iboreports/wtc2011.pdf [hereinafter Federal Aid].

30. Pub. L. No. 107-38, 115 Stat. 220 (2001).

31. Pub. L. No. 107-117, 115 Stat. 220 (2002).

32. Pub. L. No. 107-206 (2002), 43 U.S.C. 2211.

33. Pub. L. No. 116 Stat. 21 (2002).

34. Federal Aid, *supra* note 29, at 2.

35. Air Transportation Safety and System Stabilization Act, Pub. L. No. 107-42, 49 U.S.C. § 40101 (2001).

36. Pub. L. No. 111-347, 124 Stat. 3623 (2011).

37. U.S. Gov't Accountability Office, GAO-03-926, Disaster Assistance: Information on FEMA's POST 9/11 Public Assistance to New York City (2003), http://www.gao.gov/new.items/d03926.pdf [hereinafter FEMA's Disaster Assistance].

38. Federal Aid, *supra* note 29, at 2.

39. *Id.* at 9.

40. *Federal Aid to New York City in the Aftermath of September 11th: How Much, and for What? Before the J. Hearing of the City Council Fin., Lower Manhattan Redevelopment, and State and Fed. Legislation Comms.* 4 (2002) (statement of Ronnie Lowenstein, Dir. N.Y.C. Indep. Budget Office), *available at* http://www.ibo.nyc.ny.us/iboreports/Counciltestimony.pdf.

41. Press Release, Lower Manhattan Dev. Council, Lower Manhattan Development Council Approves First Round of Residential Grant Program Applications (Oct. 7, 2002), *available at* http://www.renewnyc.com/displaynews.aspx?newsid=3142e1fa-27ef-4826-bd28-403d07095f56.

42. FEMA's Disaster Assistance, *supra* note 37, at 43–44.

43. *Id.*

44. Federal Aid, *supra* note 29, at 5.

45. Randy Kennedy, *Tunnel Vision: With Station's Reopening, Even Commuters Smile*, N.Y. Times, Sept. 17, 2002, http://www.nytimes.com/2002/09/17/nyregion/tunnel-vision-with-station-s-reopening-even-commuters-smile.html.

46. Shawn Boburg, *World Trade Center Transportation Hub Costs Increasing*, The Rec., Apr. 25, 2011, http://www.northjersey.com/news/120586299_World_Trade_Center_transportation_hub_costs_increasing.html.

47. Gail Makinen, Cong. Research Serv., RL31617, The Economic Effects of 9/11: A Retrospective Assessment 5 (2002), *available at* http://www.fas.org/irp/crs/RL31617.pdf.

48. *Id.* at 39.

49. *Id.* at 40.

50. *Id.* at 5, 40.

51. U.S. Gov't Accountability Office, Small Business Administration: Response to September 11 Victims and Performance Measures for Disaster Lending (2003) http://www.gao.gov/new.items/d03385.pdf.

52. Press Release, Lower Manhattan Dev. Council, LMDC Announces More Than $37 Million in Grants (Nov. 8, 2007), *available at* http://www.renewnyc.com/displaynews.aspx?newsid=3a002039-985b-4b5c-bb57-3b275521615c.

53. Gail Makinen, Cong. Research Serv., RL31617, The Economic Effects of 9/11: A Retrospective Assessment 40 n.58 (2002), *available at* http://www.fas.org/irp/crs/RL31617.pdf.

54. Federal Aid, *supra* note 29, at 5.

55. New York State Action Plan Amendment (May 30, 2012), *available at* http://www.esd.ny.gov/Resources/05302012_WTCJCRPActionPlanAmendment.pdf.

56. U.S. Gov't Accountability Office, GAO-02-1037, September 11: Interim Report on the Response of Charities 20 (2002), http://www.gao.gov/new.items/d021037.pdf.

57. *Id.*

58. Adina Abramowitz, Beth Lipson & Jon Schwartz, Nat'l Cmty. Capital Ass'n, Assessing Seedco's Lower Manhattan Small Business and Workforce Retention Program (2005), *available at* http://www.seedcofinancial.org/_seedcofinancial.org/dynamic/user_publications-file-14.pdf.

59. *Id.* at 6.

60. N.Y.C. Office of the Comptroller, 9/11 Three Years Later: Securing the Federal Pledge 5 (2004).

61. *Id.* at 13.

62. 26 U.S.C. § 1400L(d) (2012) (the Liberty Zone consists of addresses located on or south of Canal Street, East Broadway (east of its intersection with Canal Street), or Grand Street (east of its intersection with East Broadway) in the Borough of Manhattan).

63. *20 Exchange Place*, Lower Manhattan Constr. Ctr., http://lowermanhattan.info/construction/project_updates/20_exchange_place_95253.aspx (last visited July 18, 2012).

64. Glenn Collins, *Faces at Least a City Can Love*, N.Y. Times, Feb. 28, 2005, http://www.nytimes.com/2005/02/28/nyregion/28west.html.

65. Federal Aid, *supra* note 29, at 8.

66. HDC established a policy of charging a larger fee that it could use to provide subsidies to affordable low-income developments in other parts of the city. The author is an officer of HDC and worked on most of its Liberty Bond transactions. HDC's policy on this matter was established prior to his employment in November 2003.

67. Terry Pristin, *A Pot of Tax-Free Bonds for Post-9/11 Projects Is Empty*, N.Y. Times, July 12, 2006, http://www.nytimes.com/2006/07/12/realestate/12liberty.html?ex=1310356800&en=cf5291a4979664b2&ei=5090&partner=rssuserland&emc=rss.

68. Martin Z. Braun, *New York's Post-9/11 Liberty Bond Program Gets Mixed Grades*, BLOOMBERG, Sept. 11, 2006, http://www.bloomberg.com/apps/news?pid=email_en&refer=munibonds&sid=a.3Ce4rZER9M.

69. FEDERAL AID, *supra* note 29, at 8.

70. David Dunlap, *Liberty Bonds' Yield: A New Downtown*, N.Y. TIMES, May 30, 2004, http://www%.nytimes.com/2004/05/30/realestate/liberty-bonds-yield-a-new-downtown.html?pagewanted=all&src=pm.

71. FEDERAL AID, *supra* note 29, at 7.

72. Nicole Gelinas, *Liberty Misspent*, N.Y. POST, Sept. 6, 2011, http://www.nypost.com/p/news/opinion/opedcolumnists/liberty_misspent_WnVFbDPCBHHmhcgq77JSaL.

73. Terry Pristin, *New York Financial Towers Looking to Diversify*, N.Y. TIMES, July 31, 2012, http://www.nytimes.com/2012/08/01/realestate/commercial/world-financial-center-undergoes-makeover.html?ref=terrypristin.

74. Clare Suddath, *What Took So Long? Why the World Trade Center Still Isn't Finished*, TIME, Sept. 10, 2011, http://www.time.com/time/nation/article/0,8599,2092503,00.html.

75. Gabriel Sherman, *One World Trade Center*, N.Y. MAG., Aug. 27, 2011, http://nymag.com/news/9-11/10th-anniversary/one-world-trade-center/?mid=twitter_nymag.

76. Theresa Agovino, *Silverstein to Call a Halt at 3 WTC*, CRAIN'S N.Y., Jan. 23, 2012, http://www.crainsnewyork.com/article/20120122/REAL_ESTATE/301229973.

77. *Id.*

78. Allison Gregor, *Rise of World Trade Center Spurs a Retail Revival*, N.Y. TIMES, July 5, 2011, http://www.nytimes.com/2011/07/06/realestate/commercial/1-world-trade-center-progress-spurs-retail-revival.html.

79. *Design Competition*, 9/11 MEMORIAL, http://www.911memorial.org/design-competition (last visited Aug. 8, 2012).

80. David W. Dunlap, *Constructing a Story with 2,982 Names*, N.Y. TIMES, May 4, 2011, http://www.nytimes.com/2011/05/05/nyregion/on-911-memorial-constructing-a-story-name-by-name.html?_r=1.

81. Charles Bagli, *Agreement Will Restart Work on Sept. 11 Museum*, N.Y. TIMES, Sept. 10, 2012, http://www.nytimes.com/2012/09/11/nyregion/ground-zero-museum-to-resume-construction-as-cuomo-and-bloomberg-end-dispute.html.

82. Michael Arad, *Visitors to New York's 9/11 Memorial Top 1 million*, CNN (Dec. 29, 2011), http://articles.cnn.com/2011-12-29/us/us_new-york-911-memorial_1_memorial-plaza-michael-arad-memorial-features-two?_s=PM:US.

83. ALLIANCE FOR DOWNTOWN N.Y., LOWER MANHATTAN REAL ESTATE YEAR IN REVIEW (2011), *available at* http://www.downtownny.com/sites/default/files/LM%20Real%20Estate%20Market%20Q4_Final.pdf.

84. *Performing Arts Center*, WORLD TRADE CTR., http://www.wtc.com/about/performing-arts-center (last visited Aug. 8, 2012).

85. Jennifer Maloney, *WTC Arts Center Advances*, WALL ST. J., Mar. 12, 2012, http://online.wsj.com/article/SB10001424052970204603004577269741211268960.html.

86. *Id.*

87. Lynn Lofton, *What's Working—and What's Not—with GO Zone Provisions?*, MISS. BUS. J., Mar. 26, 2007, http://msbusiness.com/2007/03/what8217s-working-8212-and-what8217s-not-8212-with-go-zone-provisions/.

88. MATT FELLOWES & AMY LIU, BROOKINGS INST., FEDERAL ALLOCATIONS IN RESPONSE TO KATRINA, RITA AND WILMA: AN UPDATE (2006), *available at* http://www.brookings.edu/~/media/research/files/reports/2006/8/metropolitanpolicy%20fellowes/20060712_katrinafactsheet.

89. Donna Kimura, *Rebuilding the Gulf Coast*, APARTMENT FIN. TODAY, July 2007, http://www.housingfinance.com/aft/articles/2007/jul/GULF0707.htm.

90. Charles V. Bagli, *Downtown's Rebirth, 10 Years and $24 Billion Later*, N.Y. TIMES, Sept. 11, 2011, http://travel.nytimes.com/2011/09/11/nyregion/10-years-after-911-downtown-area-is-thriving.html?_r=0.

91. ALLIANCE FOR DOWNTOWN N.Y., THE STATE OF LOWER MANHATTAN (2011), *available at* http://www.downtownny.com/sites/default/files/SOLM_2011_9.20.11.pdf.

92. Michael Idov, *And Another Fifty Million People Just Got Off of the Plane*, N.Y. MAG., Nov. 27, 2011, http://nymag.com/news/features/tourism/tourist-increase-2011-12/.

93. JASON BRAM & JAMES ORR, FED. RESERVE BANK OF N.Y., AUGUST INDEXES OF COINCIDENT ECONOMIC INDICATORS SHOW UNEVEN GROWTH ACROSS THE REGION (2012), http://libertystreeteconomics.newyorkfed.org/2012/09/just-released-august-indexes-of-coincident-economic-indicators-show-uneven-growth-across-the-region.html.

94. GAIL MAKINEN, CONG. RESEARCH SERV., RL31617, THE ECONOMIC EFFECTS OF 9/11: A RETROSPECTIVE ASSESSMENT 41 (2002), *available at* http://www.fas.org/irp/crs/RL31617.pdf.

95. *Id.*

96. SUBCOMM. ON MGMT., INTEGRATION & OVERSIGHT OF THE HOUSE COMM. ON HOMELAND SEC., AN EXAMINATION OF FEDERAL 9/11 ASSISTANCE TO NEW YORK: LESSONS LEARNED IN PREVENTING WASTE, FRAUD, ABUSE AND LAX MANAGEMENT 11 (2006).

97. *Id.*

98. *Id.* at 13.

99. Valli Meenakshi Ramanathan, *WTC Memorial Set to Reopen After Superstorm Sandy*, INT'L BUS. TIMES, Nov. 6, 2012, http://www.ibtimes.com/wtc-memorial-set-reopen-after-superstorm-sandy-860598.

100. David W. Dunlap, *Floodwater Pours into 9/11 Museum, Hampering Further Work on the Site*, N.Y. TIMES, Nov. 2, 2012, http://www.nytimes.com/2012/11/03/nyregion/floodwater-pours-into-9-11-museum-hampering-further-work-on-the-site.html?_r=0.

101. Christina Boyle, Phyllis Furman, Erica Pearson & Larry Mcshane, *Historic Fraunces Tavern, Other Lower Manhattan Businesses Trying to Rebound from Devastating Impact of Hurricane Sandy*, N.Y. DAILY NEWS, Nov. 22, 2012, http://www.nydailynews.com/new-york/fraunces-tavern-poured-article-1.1205443#ixzz2DARjqoai.

CHAPTER 8

Small Business Disaster Assistance

Peggy Maisel and Natalie Roman

I. Introduction

When a disaster hits, it affects the entire community. A small business, which is defined by the Small Business Administration as "one that is independently owned and operated, is organized for profit, and is not dominant in its field,"[1] is especially vulnerable because it does not necessarily have the resources to respond to a disaster or to catastrophic damage.[2] In fact, it is reported that approximately 25 percent of small businesses that close due to a disaster never reopen,[3] and 40 percent of small businesses hit directly by a serious natural disaster do not recover.[4] This is true regardless of what kind of disaster is involved, from a hurricane, a tornado, an earthquake, flooding, winter storms, or even civil unrest or terrorism.[5]

Small businesses experience a number of different problems when a disaster hits. As expected, there is the physical damage that results from a disaster, which is a more serious issue when the business is not insured or is underinsured for the damage.[6] However, the most serious and critical problem for small businesses is the loss of profits due to closure or loss of customers as a result of a disaster.[7] Sixty-two percent of businesses report the loss of sales as their main problem after a disaster.[8] Unfortunately, a large percent of businesses does not carry insurance to cover continuing operations.[9]

Fortunately, some economic assistance is available to small businesses that have suffered losses due to disasters. Immediate disaster assistance is led by state governments, which is complemented with federal assistance for disasters that qualify. Federal disaster assistance, which is generally the same regardless of the location and form of a disaster, is discussed first. This is followed by a discussion of state disaster assistance, using the state of Florida to exemplify two approaches taken by state government to provide small-business disaster relief.

II. Federal Assistance

To trigger federal disaster assistance, the Robert T. Stafford Disaster Relief and Emergency Assistance Act (Stafford Act) requires that the president declare a disaster or a catastrophe.[10] Federal disaster assistance is supplemental to state expenditures, and follows a request from the governor of the affected state indicating that "the disaster is of such severity and magnitude that effective response is beyond the capabilities of the state and the affected local governments and that the federal assistance is necessary."[11] A federal disaster declaration establishes the geographic area that is eligible for assistance, the type of assistance that is available, and those who are eligible for assistance.[12] Although a declaration opens a wide array of federal assistance for the state, federal assistance provided directly to small businesses is limited to disaster aid from the Small Business Administration (SBA) and the IRS.[13] The Federal Emergency Management Agency (FEMA) does not provide grants for businesses to recover from a disaster.[14] Indirect federal disaster assistance is also available for small businesses through the Community Development Block Grant Disaster Recovery Program (CDBG-DR) administered by the U.S. Department of Housing and Urban Development (HUD).

A. Small Business Administration

The SBA provides assistance to small businesses in the form of loans, education, advocacy, and assistance in procuring government contracts. In the wake of a disaster, the SBA also assists small businesses through its Disaster Loan Program. Between 2000 and 2009, the SBA provided 73,519 business disaster loans for a total of $7.75 billion.[15] To be eligible for these loans, the business had to be located in a federally declared disaster area and to have suffered uninsured physical harm or economic injury.

These loans are offered to help businesses repair, rebuild, and recover from economic loss after a disaster. SBA disaster loans are a form of long-term disaster assistance, with loan terms of up to 30 years.[16] They are meant to assist borrowers who, as a result of a disaster, have incurred physical losses that are not covered by insurance.[17] Unlike other loan programs administered by the SBA, which are funded by third-party lenders, the SBA's Disaster Loan Program is directly funded by the SBA[18] and is backed by the federal government.[19] The SBA's government-backed loans have lower costs than loans made by financial institutions. For example, fees paid by borrowers are capped by law.[20] Interest rates are also capped, and are usually below rates from traditional financial institutions. SBA loans are referred to as subsidized loans because fees and interest rates charged on SBA loans are insufficient to cover the cost of defaulted loans; this cost is termed the "subsidy cost."[21]

The SBA Disaster Loan Program consists of two types of loans: Business Physical Disaster Loans (BPDL) and Economic Injury Disaster Loans (EIDL).[22] As with other forms of federal disaster assistance, these two types of loans are only available in declared disaster areas.[23] A federal disaster declaration will set forth the geographic area that is eligible for assistance, as well as the type of assistance that is available, the interest rate, and those who are eligible to receive assistance.[24] For purposes of the Disaster Loan Program, disaster declarations are "official notices recognizing that specific geographic areas have been damaged by floods and other acts of nature, riot, civil disorders, or industrial accidents such as oil spills."[25] The incident is usually sudden and causes severe physical damage and/or substantial economic injury. However, small businesses that are injured by droughts and below-average water levels may also qualify if a disaster is declared.[26]

In addition to disaster declarations made by the president through the Stafford Act,[27] the SBA can also make disaster loans available to businesses through disaster declarations made directly by the SBA.[28] There are three types of SBA declarations that provide access for business to disaster loans. A physical disaster declaration made by the SBA administrator or at the request of the governor of an affected state will make disaster loans available to businesses of all sizes.[29] The SBA administrator can also issue economic injury disaster declarations when the governor of an affected state certifies that at least five small businesses have suffered substantial economic injury as a result of a disaster and there is no other viable form of financial assistance. Additionally, the SBA administrator can issue an economic injury disaster declaration when the secretary of the Department of Agriculture makes a determination of a natural disaster.[30] For example, due to the extensive drought suffered in the Midwest during the summer of 2012, more than half of the counties in the United States—1,584 in 32 states—were declared disaster areas by the secretary of agriculture.[31] As a result, small businesses located in these counties were eligible for Economic Injury Disaster Loans.[32]

1. Business Physical Disaster Loans

BPDLs are available to both large and small businesses that are located in a declared disaster area.[33] Funds derived from BPDLs can be used to repair and replace damaged real property, machinery, equipment, fixtures, inventory, and to cover uninsured or underinsured losses.[34] Additionally, the SBA has the discretion to increase a BPDL by up to 20 percent of the total amount of damage to make real property improvements that will protect the property against the same type of disasters in the future.[35] Under certain conditions, the BPDL can also be used to refinance all or part of the mortgage on the business.[36] However, loans cannot be used to expand a business unless it is required by local building codes.[37]

2. *Economic Injury Disaster Loans*

Unlike BPDLs, EIDLs are only available to small businesses.[38] EIDLs are available even if the disaster did not cause any property damage since they are designed to assist businesses with economic injury resulting from a disaster. Economic injury is defined as "economic harm to a business concern that results in its inability to meet its obligations as they mature or pay its ordinary and necessary operating expenses."[39] A "[l]oss of anticipated profits or a drop in sales is not considered substantial economic injury" for the purpose of disaster loans.[40] EIDLs are designed to provide working capital for businesses to meet the financial obligations that they could have met if not for the disaster, but not in excess of what they would have paid if the disaster had not occurred.[41] They are only available to businesses that are unable to obtain credit elsewhere. [42] Note that EIDL loans cannot refinance long-term debts or provide working capital that was needed prior to the disaster, and the EIDL cannot be used to replace sales or lost profits.[43]

Disaster loan amounts are capped at $2 million total, including physical damage and economic injury assistance.[44] The interest rate for both BPDLs and EIDLs depends on whether the borrower has credit available elsewhere: for those who do, the interest rate is capped at 8 percent; for those who do not, the interest is capped at 4 percent.[45] Although the SBA will not decline a loan if there is insufficient collateral, BPDLs over $14,000 and all EIDLs over $5,000 must be secured as much as possible, which may require a first or second mortgage on the business's damaged real property.[46] If the business does not have any real estate, the SBA will accept the best available collateral.[47] A principal of the business must personally guarantee repayment of the loan and is sometimes required to secure the loan by pledging additional collateral.[48]

Businesses can apply directly to the SBA.[49] Forms are available online[50] and the application can also be completed electronically.[51] After the application is completed and all necessary documents are provided to the SBA,[52] an investigator visits the property to estimate the cost of repair, after which the loan officer determines eligibility.[53] Once the loan is approved, the SBA disburses the first $14,000; the rest is disbursed after securing the collateral for the loan.[54] Rather than disbursing the loan in a lump sum, borrowers draw down the loan balance as repairs are made.[55]

Unfortunately, the SBA's Disaster Loan Program has not always worked efficiently and therefore has sometimes failed to timely assist those in need of its funding. One example is the experience of small-business owners after the 1992 Los Angeles riots, which was the first such disturbance to receive a presidential disaster declaration.[56] The riots, which scorched Los Angeles in April and May 1992, damaged or destroyed more than 2,500 Korean-American merchants' businesses. A survey of 150 Korean-American merchants conducted by the Mid-Wilshire Neighborhood Opportunity Center, a federal office established by the Presidential Task Force on Los Angeles Recovery, found that even though the average business loss was $180,816, the average SBA recovery loan was $136,894, supplemented only by an average of $6,636 from FEMA.[57] An estimated 20 percent of the applicants were not eligible because of insufficient collateral or other reasons.[58] According to the Mid-Wilshire Center, by December 1992, over six months after the disaster, many of the SBA applications were still pending.

By this time, emergency relief had begun to dry up while merchants continued to struggle with unpaid bills and insurance companies' unpaid claims as they entered a precarious time of transitioning from rebuilding to long-term recovery. According to another survey of 322 merchants by the Korean-American Inter-Agency Council, a community-based coalition, the greatest problem encountered by these business owners was maintaining their mortgage payments while "weav[ing] through the government maze of assistance programs, their journey hampered by shaky English."[59] More than half of business owners also did not have insurance, and those that did had difficulty collecting their insurance proceeds because their insurance companies had insufficient assets to cover claims.[60] The business owners had also found the application process for government assistance "daunting and burdensome," which was compounded by delayed check distributions due to the SBA's inefficiency, so the businesses were still unable to pay their bills.[61]

The SBA's inefficiency and delay were especially visible in the agency's response to the Gulf Coast hurricanes of 2005. Two years after Hurricanes Katrina and Rita had devastated the region, the SBA still had a backlog of unprocessed loans.[62] SBA loan approval rates, which had averaged 60 percent for previous hurricanes, dropped to 33 percent.[63] Of those that it had approved, the SBA had failed to disburse more than 90,000 loans and only 22 percent of approved loans had been fully funded.[64]

Due to these criticisms, the SBA instituted many reforms, some of which were mandated by Congress.[65] Among these were the creation of an electronic loan application and the expansion of its disaster reserve staff.[66] However, in November 2011, the SBA had not yet complied with all the congressional requirements.[67] There were still complaints that disaster loans are not available soon enough after a disaster and that it can take months for these funds to be disbursed, making it even more difficult for businesses to recover if no other funds are available.[68]

Unfortunately, this created problems when Superstorm Sandy devastated the northeastern United States in October 2012. While some improvements were seen in the SBA's response to the disaster, the SBA was slow to disburse disaster loans.[69] In early January 2013, nine weeks after the storm, even though 4,212 businesses had applied for disaster loans, only 246 applications had been approved and there were no reports of how many loans had been disbursed.[70] The SBA Disaster Loan Program was also not fully funded by Congress until January 15, 2013, when Congress finally appropriated $800 million for the program.[71]

The application continued to be cumbersome, consisting of at least 30 pages of forms and requiring supporting documentation that often had been destroyed because of the storm.[72] More concerning was the inability of many businesses to take on more debt, the only form of federal assistance available to them, especially with the uncertainty of being able to reopen.[73] Many were also overextended, running on very thin margins. With the heavy cost of rebuilding, many simply felt that they could not afford more loans since they had no prospect of customers for an extended time period.[74]

All this indicates is that the paperwork for the application process and the tax information requirement for the Disaster Loan Program continue to be burdensome.[75] As a result, the program's "laborious application process, stringent eligibility criteria, and voluminous documentation requirements often thwart attempts for businesses to access government funding."[76] This is made worse by the requirement of collateral to secure the loans. If the business does not have equipment or other assets that can serve as collateral, the principals, partners, and owners of these small businesses must secure the loan with their personal assets.[77] This is a high risk to take, and usually avoided.[78] This may make disaster loans unavailable to those businesses that are perhaps in most need of capital, and causes many of these small-business owners to deplete their personal savings and retirement accounts, take second mortgages on their homes, and max out their credit card borrowing limits in order to stay afloat.[79]

B. Internal Revenue Service

Assistance from the IRS is mainly in the form of tax deductions, waivers or extensions for making payments, and assistance in filing and obtaining copies of tax returns. Information on how to receive assistance from the IRS in the aftermath of a disaster can be found in Publication 2194, *Disaster Resource Guide for Individuals and Businesses*, available on the IRS website[80] or through the IRS Disaster Assistance Hotline.[81]

Some losses incurred by businesses as a result of a disaster can be deducted from federal income tax returns as casualty losses. Casualty losses are those that result from "the damage, destruction or loss of your property from any sudden, unexpected, or unusual event such as a flood, hurricane, tornado, fire, earthquake or even volcanic eruption."[82] These losses can be deducted if they are not covered by insurance or other form of reimbursement.[83] Although casualty losses are generally deductible in the year that they occur, if the business paid taxes the year preceding the federally declared disaster, the business can choose to receive a refund of some (or all) of the taxes paid by deducting the loss in the prior year through the filing of an amended return.[84]

During some disasters, the IRS may provide other forms of disaster relief, such as waiver of penalties, filing extensions, and other forms of disaster-specific relief.[85] However, since these classes of relief are specific for each disaster, it is not possible to know beforehand what form of relief is available. IRS assistance agents located at IRS Service Centers and FEMA Disaster Recovery Centers will be aware of the specific relief available to businesses.[86] Additionally, the IRS can make individualized decisions, and it requests those who have ongoing IRS collection matters to contact it so that appropriate consideration can be made in each case.

If a business requires assistance with filing tax returns, it can also find free assistance at IRS Service Centers and FEMA Disaster Recovery Centers.[87] This can be important, because a business needs to have filed all of its tax returns in order to qualify for federal disaster assistance. If the business needs copies of tax returns in order to apply for benefits or to file amended returns to claim casualty losses after a disaster, the IRS will also provide and expedite, free of charge, copies of tax returns or tax transcripts.[88]

It has been suggested that ad hoc IRS tax policies do not serve those affected by disasters as effectively as they could because money does not reach victims quickly enough.[89] A further criticism is that these ad hoc measures are both under- and over-inclusive and are not truly equitable to all victims of a disaster.[90] For example, tax relief after the 2005 Gulf Coast hurricanes defined six classes of victims, creating a preferential class of victims for the purpose of tax relief.[91] It is proposed that Congress enact legislation that establishes what forms of tax relief are available after a disaster and to make relief available immediately for all federally declared disasters.[92] This relief should be based on what victims will predictably need: extensions of time to file and pay taxes, removal of penalties for late payments, availability of copies of tax returns, and tax benefits for nonprofits assisting after the disaster.[93]

C. Community Development Block Grants Disaster Recovery

The CDBG program, managed by HUD, operates to "ensure decent affordable housing, to provide services to the most vulnerable in our communities, and to create jobs through the expansion and retention of businesses."[94] This section provides a general overview of the program.

The CDBG program is "the federal government's largest and most widely available source of financial assistance to support state and local government-directed neighborhood revitalization, housing rehabilitation, and economic development activities."[95] It is funded annually through congressional appropriations and grants allotted to states and local governments based on a set formula.[96]

CDBGs are extremely flexible and can be used to fund any combination of 25 eligible activities, limited only to meeting *one* of three national objectives: to "principally benefit low and moderate income persons; [to] aid in eliminating or preventing slums or blight; or [to] meet particularly urgent community development needs because existing conditions pose a serious and immediate threat to the public."[97] This flexibility exists so that community planning and urban development can remain under local discretion and control, which allow states and local governments more creativity to meet their communities' needs.[98]

Congress may also appropriate additional disaster-recovery funding for the CDBG after a presidentially declared disaster.[99] As with other forms of federal disaster relief, the largest appropriation of these CDBG-DR funds thus far took place after the Gulf Coast hurricanes of 2005, providing $19.85 billion in disaster-related relief to Alabama, Florida, Louisiana, Mississippi, and Texas.[100] For presidentially declared disaster needs occurring in 2008, Congress appropriated $6.8 billion in CDBG-DR funds.[101]

Unlike ordinary CDBG funds, disaster-related funds are only appropriated in "extraordinary circumstances that have resulted in significant unmet needs for long-term recovery."[102] Since they are meant to address only needs that are not met by other federal programs, the requirement is strict that CDBG-DR funds not duplicate or replace any other form of federal disaster-recovery assistance, such as that received from FEMA and the SBA.[103]

To determine the extent of the unmet need and to decide how to allocate CDBG-DR funds, HUD relies on damage estimates created by FEMA and the SBA.[104] It then takes into account insurance proceeds, FEMA grants, and SBA loans in estimating needs not addressed by these sources.[105] HUD will then publish a notice in the *Federal Register* regarding allocations and requirements for application submissions.[106] States and local governments must apply to HUD for CDBG-DR funding by submitting an action plan that describes the needs, strategies, and projected uses of CDBG-DR funds.[107]

As mentioned above, one of the hallmarks of the CDBG-DR program is the flexibility afforded to states and local communities in determining what activities to fund. This includes funding activities that focus on long-term recovery, as well as the restoration of infrastructure, housing, and revitalizing the economy.[108] This does not mean that there are no restrictions. First, CDBG-DR funds are restricted by the same statutory requirements that are applicable to CDBG funds.[109] This includes the requirement that CDBG allocations be used primarily to benefit low- and moderate-income residents.[110] However, while CDBG requires that at least 70 percent of the grant be used to benefit low- and moderate-income people, this requirement is often modified for CDBG-DR funding, reducing the threshold to as low as 50 percent.[111] A further restriction applicable to CDBG-DR is that funds be used solely to meet expenses related to a past disaster.[112] This means that measures purely focused on preventing or mitigating damage from future disasters cannot be funded through CDBG-DR, although they can be incorporated into rebuilding efforts that are eligible for CDBG-DR.[113]

Nonetheless, because it is not always possible at the time that funds are appropriated to determine exactly how much funding will be needed to meet recovery efforts, Congress usually grants HUD significant discretion to waive, suspend, or issue alternative requirements.[114] This includes waivers of the income threshold requirements and of statutory restrictions on the types of activities that may be funded.[115] The only requirements that can never be waived are the requirements of nondiscrimination, environmental review, labor standards, and fair housing, and that the funds be used to meet expenses related to a past disaster.[116]

However, it is argued that this broad waiver authority is subject to abuse and can end up hurting the low- and moderate-income individuals that it is supposed to assist.[117] For example, after Hurricane Katrina, the State of Mississippi received waivers from HUD that exempted over 80 percent of its CDBG-DR funds from the requirement that funds benefit low- to moderate-income individuals.[118] In fact, the State of Mississippi requested a blanket waiver of income requirements for *all* CDBG-DR funds; although HUD did not authorize the blanket waiver, it did incrementally authorize the waivers as the state submitted updates to its action plans, creating almost the same result.[119]

The diversion of funds that were initially slated for housing assistance into economic development is another example of how low- and moderate-income individuals were affected by waivers.[120] About $600 million in funds that would have been used to directly meet the dire housing needs of low- to moderate-income individuals after Hurricane Katrina were diverted to long-term recovery plans. This left the most vulnerable section of the community with few options and added to the already bleak housing crisis that existed in the state.[121] Additionally, this diversion may also have indirectly, and unintentionally, violated the CDBG-DR's unwaivable nondiscrimination requirement because it resulted in a denial of fair and affordable housing to minorities.[122]

A further criticism is the interpretation of what constitutes benefiting low- to moderate-income citizens. For example, the State of Mississippi's use of CDBG-DR funds to repair and greatly expand the Port of Gulfport as part of its economic development plan has been criticized for failing to meet this requirement.[123] Although expansion of the port is calculated to create jobs, it is estimated that only 10 percent of new jobs created will be available to low- and moderate-income individuals, which is way below the 50 percent requirement.[124]

III. State Assistance

There are two types of disaster assistance provided by states. One form of assistance is provided directly from state funds, and this assistance can be either ad hoc or can exist as established state agencies and programs set up to meet a future disaster, although these are not necessarily geared specifically for small businesses. The other form of assistance comes from state administration and distribution of federal disaster funds. This section will focus on the state of Florida as an example of one state that has an established small-business disaster-assistance program. (For an example of a state program that administers federal disaster funds, see chapter 9.)

The primary form of state disaster assistance for small businesses in Florida is the Small Business Emergency Bridge Loan Program. The program can be activated by the governor after making a declaration of a state of emergency.[125] The program was first activated after Hurricane Andrew devastated southern Florida in 1992. According to the program website, "it has been activated 13 more times following disasters and has resulted in assistance for more than 950 small businesses in 56 counties, consisting of more than $27 million in assistance."[126]

The Small Business Emergency Bridge Loan Program provides short-term, zero percent interest loans to small businesses that are damaged by a disaster.[127] These loans can serve as a cash flow between the time of the disaster and the time that the business can secure financial resources, such as insurance, SBA disaster loan proceeds, or regular profits.[128] These loans are meant to be truly at no cost to the borrower. For example, at closing, the cost of documentary stamps is paid directly from the loan fund.[129] Florida's Small Business Development Center (SBDC) Network, with offices throughout the state, can assist business owners with the application process.

Florida is one of the few states that has a bridge loan program in place to keep businesses afloat until other forms of financing become available. Other states include North Carolina, Louisiana, and New York.[130] In Florida, these loans are capped at $25,000. These loans are short term and must be repaid within 12 months.[131] They are not meant to be a primary source of funding for small businesses in the aftermath of a disaster, tying eligibility to the pursuit of other sources.[132] To be eligible for a bridge loan, a business must be located within the designated emergency disaster area and have two to 100 employees.[133] Loan proceeds can only be used to maintain or restart a business in the designated area.[134]

The state of Florida also created a special program to address the economic and environmental difficulties produced by the 2010 oil spill in the Gulf of Mexico,[135] which affected fishing, tourism, and related industries primarily in several counties of northwest Florida.[136] The Oil Spill Recovery Act,[137] enacted unanimously by the Florida Senate in 2011, consists of two separate funding sources for businesses.[138] Under either source of funding, waivers of job and wage eligibility requirements are available to businesses applying for incentives under several of Florida's economic development projects.[139]

One section of the Oil Spill Recovery Act provides that funds received by the state of Florida from private or government sources as a consequence of the 2010 Gulf oil spill in the form of fines or compensation must be preferentially distributed to eight counties deemed to be disproportionately affected by the 2010 oil spill.[140] Specifically, the act requires that 75 percent of all such funds be expended in these counties for research on the impact of the spill, environmental restoration, economic incentives, and strategies to expand and diversify the economies of the eight named counties.[141] The remaining 25 percent is to be used in any other county affected by the oil spill.

Additionally, the act appropriates $10 million a year for three years to be distributed to businesses in the form of the Industry Recruitment, Retention and Expansion Fund (IRREF) Grant Program.[142] The purpose of the program is to develop and implement "an innovative economic development program for promoting research and development, commercialization of research, economic diversification, and job creation" in the eight disproportionately affected counties.[143] Therefore, businesses applying for the grant must be able to prove that they can create "net new, sustainable, private-sector job opportunities" in the specified counties.[144] The IRREF Grant Program is meant to supplement and not substitute local and state incentives, and, therefore, an application will not be considered until all other forms of local and state economic development incentives have been proposed or denied. In other words, the program is meant to be more of a "closing fund" that is used as "a final incentive to seal the deal."[145]

The IRREF Grant Program gives preferential treatment to medium and large businesses and to those in one of Florida's targeted industry clusters[146] or strategic areas of interest.[147] To be eligible, a business must be considering locating or expanding in one of the eight disproportionately affected counties, and one for which there is significant interstate or international competition.[148] Additionally, businesses are required to commit to funding at least 75 percent of the project using sources other than Florida taxpayers.[149] Priority is given to projects located in communities with expedited permitting processes.[150] Grantees are required to locate their business within one of the disproportionately affected counties, and create 10 to 30 new, private-sector jobs, each of which must be sustained for at least three years.[151] The new jobs must pay at least 85 percent of the average wage prevailing in the location and must generate at least 51 percent of revenues outside of Florida.[152]

The IRREF Grant Program got off to a slow start. Although applications began to be accepted on October 11, 2011, the original deadline for the first disbursement had to be extended from July 1, 2012, to September 30, 2012, so that the funds would not be lost.[153] In August 2012, two businesses were finally funded through the IRREF Grant Program: Navy Federal Credit Union and iSirona, a medical software company.[154] Marjam Supply Company, a seller and distributor of building materials in 12 eastern states, was awarded a grant in December 2012.[155] Other eligible projects are currently being considered, but no other awards have been announced.[156]

IV. Conclusion

If a small business is going to recover after a disaster strikes, it must move quickly to assess and repair any damage. Failure to do so can be critical in determining whether the business can reopen and continue to operate. Nonetheless, a small business should not wait for a disaster to strike to begin preparations. Every small business should have a disaster-preparedness plan in place so that when a disaster hits it has procedures to address damage caused by the disaster. There are many resources available from the SBA, state disaster-response agencies, and nonprofit organizations to help businesses create a plan to meet future disasters.[157] Disaster preparedness also includes the appropriate level and type of insurance and, if financially feasible, business continuity insurance.

Even after taking all of these precautions, however, a small business may have insufficient resources to recover and become profitable after a disaster. Small businesses in general face unique problems, such as reduced access to loans, limited cash reserves, and more difficulty withstanding hard economic times. These same small businesses are called by President Obama "the backbone of our economy and the cornerstones of our communities."[158] When a disaster hits, it is therefore critical that these businesses bounce back quickly because their economic recovery leads to the economic recovery of the community. The programs described in this chapter are providing some assistance to businesses after a disaster. However, as discussed, there have been problems with all of these programs, which must be addressed and corrected if businesses are to recover expeditiously.

Notes

1. *What Is SBA's definition of a small business concern?* U.S. SMALL BUS. ADMIN., http://www.sba.gov/content/what-sbas-definition-small-business-concern (last visited Sept. 9, 2012). Beyond this, the SBA has size standards (defined by either the number of employees or annual sales receipts) for each industry. *See* U.S. SMALL BUS. ADMIN., TABLE OF SMALL BUSINESS SIZE STANDARDS MATCHED TO NORTH AMERICAN INDUSTRY CLASSIFICATION SYSTEM CODES (2012), *available at* http://www.sba.gov/sites/default/files/files/Size_Standards_Table.pdf.

2. IMPACT ON U.S. SMALL BUSINESS OF NATURAL & MAN-MADE DISASTERS 4 (Hewlett Packard, 2007), *available at* http://www.edwardsinformation.com/content/ImpactofDisaster.pdf.

3. *Business Needs*, FLA. SMALL BUS. DEVL. CTR., http://www.sbdctampabay.com/resources/business-needs/disaster-relief-planning/# (last visited Sept. 7, 2012); INST. FOR BUS. & HOME SAFETY, OPEN FOR BUSINESS, "*Message from Diana McClure, Vice President and Director of Business Protection, Institute for Business & Home Stafety*," *available at* http://ofb.ibhs.org/content/data/file/OpenForBusiness_new.pdf.

4. NFIB NATIONAL SMALL BUSINESS POLL: DISASTERS 2 (William J. Dennis, Jr., vol. 4, issue 5 2004), *available at* http://www.411sbfacts.com/files/disastersFINAL[1].pdf.

5. *Id.* at 3–5.

6. Seventeen percent of businesses report uninsured physical damage as their main problem after a disaster, and 12 percent report being underinsured. *Id.* at 3, 4.

7. *Id.* at 4.

8. *Id.*

9. A full 47 percent of businesses report not being insured for the loss of business. *Id.*

10. I.R.S. Pub. 2194, Disaster Resource Guide for Individuals and Businesses, at 9 (2012), *available at* http://www.irs.gov/pub/irs-pdf/p2194.pdf.

11. 42 U.S.C. § 5170 (2012).

12. Memorandum from Small Bus. Comm. Staff to Comm. on Small Bus. Members, 2 (Nov. 28, 2011) [hereinafter Memo], *available at* http://smallbusiness.house.gov/uploadedfiles/11-30_hearing_Memo.pdf.

13. Disaster assistance information can be located on the Disaster Assistance Portal at http://www.disasterassistance.gov.

14. FEMA only provides grants to individuals who qualify. If a business is not incorporated and is one that is run by a sole proprietor such that the owner files business income tax forms as Schedule C of Form 1040, it is possible that some grants from FEMA may be available to that business owner *in his/her individual capacity* and not as part of the business. Nonetheless, such assistance, by helping the owner recover personally from the disaster, can also help the business to recover.

15. BRUCE R. LINDSEY, CONG. RESEARCH SERV., R41309, THE SBA DISASTER LOAN PROGRAM: OVERVIEW AND POSSIBLE ISSUES FOR CONGRESS 16 (2010), *available at* http://assets.opencrs.com/rpts/R41309_20100629.pdf.

16. Memo, *supra* note 12, at 1.

17. *Id.*

18. This means that the SBA itself reviews, processes, closes, and services the loans. *Id.* at 3.

19. *Id.*

20. Robb Mandelbaum, *Do Romney's Budget Pledges Threaten S.B.A. Loans?*, N.Y. TIMES (Sept. 13, 2012), http://boss.blogs.nytimes.com/2012/09/13/do-romneys-budget-pledges-threaten-s-b-a-loans/.

21. *See* U.S. GOV'T ACCOUNTABILITY OFFICE, GAO-05-409, SBA DISASTER LOAN PROGRAM: ACCOUNTING ANOMALIES RESOLVED BUT ADDITIONAL STEPS WOULD IMPROVE LONG-TERM RELIABILITY OF COST ESTIMATES 5–6 (2005), *available at* http://www.gao.gov/assets/250/245994.pdf.

22. Memo, *supra* note 12, at 4.

23. LINDSEY, *supra* note 15, at 4.

24. Memo, *supra* note 12, at 2.

25. 13 C.F.R. § 123.2 (2011).

26. *Id.*

27. *See* text accompanying *supra* notes 10–11.

28. Lindsey, *supra* note 15, at 4–5.

29. *Id.* at 5.

30. *Id.*

31. Jim Suhr, *U.S. Drought 2012: Half of Nation's Counties Now Considered Disaster Areas*, Huffington Post (Aug. 1, 2012), http://www.huffingtonpost.com/2012/08/02/us-drought-2012-disaster-areas_n_1731393.html (last visited Sept. 9, 2012).

32. *Drought Disaster Assistance*, U.S. Small Bus. Admin., http://www.sba.gov/content/2012-drought-disaster-assistance (last visited Jan. 23, 2013). Farms and ranches, however, were not eligible for these loans. *Id.*

33. *Id.* at 4. Providing a definition of what is considered a small business for the purpose of qualifying for federal government programs is beyond the scope of this chapter. This is because there is not one definition for a small business, but rather a set of standards that vary by industry. *See* U.S. Small Bus. Admin., *supra* note 1.

34. Lindsey, *supra* note 15, at 3; *Business Physical Disaster Loan*, U.S. Small Bus. Admin., http://www.sba.gov/content/physical-disaster-loans (last visited Sept. 7, 2012).

35. *Id.* at 34.

36. *Id.* These conditions include not having credit available elsewhere, suffering uninsured damage affecting 40 percent or more of the value of the property, and the intent to repair the damage.

37. *Id.*

38. Lindsey, *supra* note 15, at 3. However, what is considered a small business by the SBA varies from industry to industry. *Id.* These loans are also available to small agricultural cooperatives and certain private, nonprofit organizations of all sizes provided they have suffered substantial economic injury as a result of a physical disaster or an agricultural production disaster designated by the secretary of agriculture. *Economic Injury Loans*, U.S. Small Bus. Admin., http://archive.sba.gov/services/disasterassistance/businessesofallsizes/economicinjuryloans/index.html (last visited Aug. 27, 2012).

39. 13 C.F.R. § 123.300(1) (2011).

40. 13 C.F.R. § 123.300(2) (2011).

41. *Economic Injury Loans*, *supra* note 38.

42. *Id.*

43. *Business Physical Disaster Loan*, *supra* note 34.

44. *Economic Injury Loans*, *supra* note 38.

45. Memo, *supra* note 12, at 4; *Business Physical Disaster Loan*, *supra* note 34.

46. *Business Physical Disaster Loan*, *supra* note 34.

47. *Id.*

48. *Id.*

49. *Id.*

50. *Apply for a Disaster Loan*, U.S. Small Bus. Admin., http://www.sba.gov/content/applying-disaster-loan (last visited Sept. 10, 2012).

51. *Disaster Loan Application*, U.S. Small Bus. Admin., https://disasterloan.sba.gov (last visited Sept. 10, 2012).

52. The business must submit a completed loan application and an IRS form 8821, giving permission to the IRS to provide the SBA with the business's tax return information. Additionally, the SBA will require a personal financial statement, a profit-and-loss statement, a balance sheet, and a list of debts. The SBA also requires a financial statement for each owner, partner, officer, director, and stockholder who has 20 percent or more ownership in the business. *Business Physical Disaster Loan*, *supra* note 34.

53. Memo, *supra* note 12, at 5. The SBA strongly encourages businesses to apply early and not miss the filing deadline by waiting for an insurance settlement. The final insurance information can be added when a settlement for the disaster loan has been made. The business will simply be required to apply any insurance proceeds that duplicate SBA's disaster loan to the SBA loan. *Business Physical Disaster Loan*, *supra* note 34.

54. Memo, *supra* note 12, at 5.

55. *Id.*

56. *California Fire During a Period of Civil Unrest (DR-942)*, FEMA, http://www.fema.gov/disaster/942 (last visited Mar. 10, 2013) (stating "incident period: Wednesday, April 29, 1992 to Thursday, May 28, 1992; Major Disaster Declaration declared on May 2, 1992"); *see also* Editorial, *Disaster by Any Other Name: Congress Must Probe FEMA's L.A. Failure, Too*, L.A. Times (Jan. 13, 1993), http://articles.latimes.com/1993-01-13/local/me-1098_1_natural-disasters/. As mentioned, riots and civil disorder can trigger a declaration of disaster for the purposes of making SBA disaster loans available to businesses in a designated geographic area. *See* 13 C.F.R. § 123.2, *supra* note 25, and accompanying text.

57. Jake Doherty, *Korean-Americans Lack Riot Assistance*, L.A. TIMES (Dec. 27, 1992), http://articles.latimes.com/1992-12-27/news/ci-5186_1_korean-american-merchants.

58. *Id.* For more information about the Mid-Wilshire Center's activities to support small-business development more than 20 years following the riots, visit http://www.wilshirecenter.com.

59. *After L.A. Riots, Merchant Makes Miraculous Return, Vows Another*, SEATTLE TIMES (Dec. 24, 1992), http://community.seattletimes.nwsource.com/archive/?date=19921224&slug=1531741.

60. *Id.*

61. *Id.*

62. Veronique de Rugby, *Disaster Reform Waiting to Happen*, 32 REGULATION 6, 7 (2009).

63. *Id.*

64. *Id.*

65. In 2008, Congress enacted the Small Business Disaster Response and Loan Improvements Act, requiring the SBA to effect 26 distinct changes so that it could more effectively respond to disasters in the future. U.S. GOV'T ACCOUNTABILITY OFFICE, GAO-09-755, ADDITIONAL STEPS SHOULD BE TAKEN TO ADDRESS REFORMS TO THE DISASTER LOAN PROGRAM AND IMPROVE THE APPLICATION PROCESS FOR FUTURE DISASTERS 1 (2009) [hereinafter GAO-09-755], *available at* http://www.gao.gov/assets/300/293117.pdf.

66. *Id.* at 29.

67. *See* LINDSEY, *supra* note 15, at 4; *Disaster Assistance: Is SBA Meeting the Recovery Needs of Disaster Victims?: Hearing Before the H. Comm. on Small Business*, 112th Cong. 1, 5 (2011) (statements of Roscoe G. Bartlett, Comm. Member; and William Sheer, Director, Financial Markets and Community Investment, U.S. Government Accountability Office, Washington, D.C.), *available at* http://www.gpo.gov/fdsys/pkg/CHRG-112hhrg72209/pdf/CHRG-112hhrg72209.pdf.

68. INT'L ECON. DEV. COUNCIL, AN IMPROVED FEDERAL RESPONSE TO POST-DISASTER ECONOMIC RECOVERY—FINAL REPORT 8 (2010), *available at* www.nado.org/wp-content/uploads/2011/08/pdisasterrpt.pdf.

69. Press Release, U.S. Senate Comm. on Small Bus. & Entrepreneurship, Landrieu Leads Committee Hearing to Examine Federal Response to Small Businesses Affected by Hurricane Sandy (Dec. 13, 2012), *available at* http://www.sbc.senate.gov/public/index.cfm?p=PressReleases&ContentRecord_id=501170b9-4cc2-4d1f-b24f-fcaa67e73e9b.

70. Jose Pagliery, *Inaction on Sandy by Congress Leaves Businesses in Limbo*, CNNMONEY (Jan. 4, 2013), http://money.cnn.com/2013/01/04/smallbusiness/sandy-congress/.

71. *Id.*

72. Ellen Brown, *Political Football over Disaster Relief*, HUFFINGTON POST, Jan. 5, 2013, www.huffingtonpost.com/political-football-over-d_b_2405413.html.

73. *Id.*

74. Stacy Cowley, *Sandy's Small Business Victims: We Don't Want Loans!*, CNNMONEYTECH (Nov. 2, 2012), http://money.cnn.com/2012/11/02/smallbusiness/sandy-loans/index.html. The plight of these businesses was not necessarily due to the lack of insurance, but rather due to policy provisions that exclude coverage based on whether the disaster was classified as a hurricane or a tropical storm, or whether the damage was caused by wind or by flooding. Brown, *supra* note 72. There are some businesses that did not carry flood insurance because the insurance would have provided insufficient coverage. For example, one business was offered a maximum of $500,000 insurance coverage on its $4 million equipment, and this was at exorbitant premiums. Cowley, *supra*.

75. GAO-09-755, *supra* note 65, at 31.

76. INT'L ECON. DEV. COUNCIL, *supra* note 68, at 8.

77. *Id.*

78. *Id.*

79. *Id.* at 7.

80. I.R.S. Pub. 2194, *supra* note 10.

81. The phone number for the IRS Disaster Assistance Hotline is 1-866-562-5227.

82. *Topic 515*, IRS, http://www.irs.gov/taxtopics/tc515.html (last visited Aug. 29, 2012).

83. *Id.* If a business has insurance that does not cover the entire loss, the loss not covered by insurance can be deducted as a casualty loss. *Id.* To determine the amount of the casualty loss, a business can use Publication 584-B. Business casualty losses are reported on Form 4684 Section B.

84. *Id.*; I.R.S. Pub. 2194, *supra* note 10, at 2, 9. While claiming a loss on an original or amended return for the prior year may get the taxpayer an earlier refund, it may be that claiming the loss on the current year return could result in a greater tax saving. The business should obtain tax advice on these

matters. Form 1140X is required to file an amended individual tax return (for unincorporated sole proprietors that file Schedule C with their Form 1040). To file an amended corporate return, use Form 1120X. For an S Corporation, use Form 1120-S, and check box H (4) on page 1 to indicate that the return is amended.

85. *Disaster Assistance Self-Study – Payments/Benefits and Tax Returns*, IRS, http://www.irs.gov/Businesses/Small-Businesses-&-Self-Employed/Disaster-Assistance-Self-Study---Payments-Benefits-and-Tax-Returns (last visited Dec. 5, 2012). For an example of a disaster-specific tax relief, see Patrick E. Tolan, *The Flurry of Tax Law Changes Following the 2005 Hurricanes: A Strategy for More Predictable and Equitable Tax Treatment of Victims*, 72 BROOK. L. REV. 799 (2007) (discussing tax relief after the Gulf hurricanes of 2005).

86. The relief available to taxpayers for each disaster is set forth by the National Disaster Assistance Coordinator in a Disaster Relief Guideline Memorandum.

87. I.R.S. Pub. 2194, *supra* note 10.

88. *Disaster Assistance Self-Study – Payments/Benefits and Tax Returns*, *supra* note 85. Form 4506 is required for copies of tax returns and Form 4506-T for copies of tax transcripts. The name of the disaster should be written in **red ink** at the top of the form before submitting. I.R.S. Pub. 2194, *supra* note 10, at 6.

89. Tolan, *supra* note 85, at 837.

90. *Id.* at 841–42.

91. *Id.* at 841.

92. *Id.* at 837, 843.

93. *Id.*

94. *Community Development Block Grant Program – CDBG*, HUD, http://portal.hud.gov/hudportal/HUD?src=/program_offices/comm_planning/communitydevelopment/programs (last visited Dec. 2, 2012).

95. EUGENE BOYD, CONG. RESEARCH SERV., RL33330, COMMUNITY DEVELOPMENT BLOCK GRANT FUNDS IN DISASTER RELIEF AND RECOVERY 1 (2011), *available at* http://www.fas.org/sgp/crs/misc/RL33330.pdf.

96. *Community Development Block Grant Program – CDBG*, *supra* note 94. The formula is based on community need, using measures such as the degree of poverty, size of the population, extent of housing overcrowding, age of housing, and population growth lag as compared to other metropolitan areas. *Id.*

97. BOYD, *supra* note 95, at 1. These eligible activities include economic development and job creation, which can include aid to for-profit organizations and creation of loans; public service programs, such as job counseling and training; aid to not-for-profit organizations, which include community-development corporations and faith-based organizations; purchasing, demolishing, and disposing of real property; housing assistance, including loans and grants for rehabilitation; and historic preservation. *Id.*

98. Mary Beth Johnson Pavlik, *A Look at the Recovery Act and Its Effect on the Community Development Block Grant Entitlement Program*, 62 ADMIN. L. REV. 523, 526–27 (2010).

99. Community Development Block Grant Disaster Recovery (CDBG-DR) for 2011 Disasters Frequently Asked Questions (FAQs), at 1, *available at* http://portal.hud.gov/hudportal/documents/huddoc?id=cdbg_dr_faq.pdf [hereinafter FAQs].

100. BOYD, *supra* note 95, at *Summary*.

101. *Id.*

102. FAQs, *supra* note 99, at 3.

103. *Id.* at 2.

104. *Id.*

105. *Id.*

106. *Id.* at 3.

107. *Community Development Block Grant Program – CDBG*, *supra* note 94.

108. FAQs, *supra* note 99, at 3; U.S. Dep't of Housing & Urb. Dev., CDBG Disaster Recovery Overview, at 12, *available at* http://portal.hud.gov/hudportal/documents/huddoc?id=CDBG_DR_Overview.pdf.

109. FAQs, *supra* note 99, at 3.

110. BOYD, *supra* note 95, at 4.

111. *Id.* This can be met in one of two ways: either all or a majority of people who benefit from the funded activity have low or moderate incomes *or* the funded activity takes place in an area in which at least the required percent of the population are of low or moderate income. MANAGING CDBG: A GUIDEBOOK FOR ENTITLEMENT GRANTEES ON SUBRECIPIENT OVERSIGHT, app. 1-14–1-16, http://portal.hud.gov/hudportal/documents/huddoc?id=DOC_17086.pdf (last visited Dec. 3, 2012).

112. *See* CDBG Disaster Recovery Overview, *supra* note 108, at 12, 17, 20–22.

113. *Id.*; FAQs, *supra* note 99, at 3. CDBG-DR funds also have geographic spending restrictions. *See* FAQs, *supra* note 99, at 2, 3.

114. Phyliss Craig-Taylor, *All that Glitters is Not Gold: A Critique of Waivers and Congressional Mandates on Community Block Grants*, 2 CHARLOTTE L. REV. 145, 154 (2010); BOYD, *supra* note 95, at 4; FAQs, *supra* note 99, at 3.

115. BOYD, *supra* note 95, at 4.

116. *Id.*; CDBG Disaster Recovery Overview, *supra* note 108, at 29.

117. Craig-Taylor, *supra* note 114, at 148.

118. *Id.* at 151.

119. Simon Maloy, *Media Ignored Mississippi's Use of Waivers to Redirect Funds Designated for Low-Income Katrina Victims*, MEDIA MATTERS FOR AM. (Aug. 30, 2007), http://mediamatters.org/research/2007/08/30/media-ignored-mississippis-use-of-waivers-to-re/139727.

120. Craig-Taylor, *supra* note 114, at 158.

121. *Id.* at 151–52, 156.

122. *Id.* at 180–83.

123. *Id.* at 148, 156–62.

124. *Id.* at 156–58.

125. This is indirectly authorized by Florida Statute section 252.37(2), which permits the governor to direct that funding be made available as needed in a disaster that has been declared a state of emergency.

126. *Bridge Loan Application*, FLA. SMALL BUS. EMERGENCY BRIDGE LOAN PROGRAM, http://www.floridadisasterloan.org/application.html (last visited Sept. 6, 2012).

127. The SBDC Network State Office can be contacted at (850) 473-7800 or toll-free at 1-866-737-7232. Information about the SBDC can be found at http://floridasbdc.org/main.php# (last visited Sept. 6, 2012).

128. *Frequently Asked Questions*, FLA. SMALL BUS. EMERGENCY BRIDGE LOAN PROGRAM, http://www.floridadisasterloan.org/frequently_asked_questions.html (last visited Sept. 10, 2012).

129. *Id.* Applications are available online at http://www.floridadisasterloan.org/application.html.

130. INT'L ECON. DEV. COUNCIL, *supra* note 68, at 8. North Carolina Emergency Bridge Loans of up to $10,000 are available to businesses awaiting SBA approval to be repaid from the first SBA disbursement. North Carolina's Business Disaster Assistance Program also provides loans to businesses unable to secure SBA loans or, alternatively, gives businesses rebates for three years on interest they pay on their SBA Disaster Loans. OFFICE OF THE GOV., NORTH CAROLINA DISASTER RECOVERY GUIDE 30–31, *available at* http://www.osbm.state.nc.us/disaster/DisasterRecoveryGuide.pdf. Louisiana developed an emergency bridge loan program to help businesses affected by hurricanes; New York developed a combination of business grants and short-term loans post-9/11. INT'L ECON. DEV. COUNCIL, *supra* note 68, at 8. Unlike the Florida and North Carolina programs, however, which are funded from state appropriations, the programs in Louisiana and New York were funded through CDBG grants. *See* Press Release, Disaster Recovery Unit, (La.) Office Cmty. Dev., $20 Million Awarded to Nonprofits for Small Business Loans and Technical Assistance (Dec. 6, 2010), *available at* http://www.doa.louisiana.gov/cdbg/DR/News%20Items/ILTAPrelease12-10.htm (last visited Jan. 23, 2013); TOM SEESSEL, RESPONDING TO THE 9/11 TERRORIST ATTACKS: LESSONS FROM RELIEF AND RECOVERY IN NEW YORK CITY 21, *available at* http://www.fordfoundation.org/pdfs/library/responding_to_attacks.pdf. New York also provided small businesses emergency loans of up to $25,000 after Superstorm Sandy. *See Hurricane Sandy Emergency Loan Fund FAQ*, NYC SMALL BUS. SERVS., http://www.nyc.gov/html/sbs/nycbiz/downloads/pdf/home/Emergency_Loan_FAQ.pdf (last visited Jan. 23, 2013).

131. FLA. SMALL BUS. EMERGENCY BRIDGE LOAN PROGRAM, http://www.floridadisasterloan.org/index.html (last visited Jan. 23, 2013).

132. *Eligibility & Loan Process*, FLA. SMALL BUS. EMERGENCY BRIDGE LOAN PROGRAM, http://www.floridadisasterloan.org/eligibility_and_loan_process.html (last visited Jan. 23, 2013).

133. *Id.* However, self-employed business owners with no other employees may still qualify on other guidelines on a case-by-case basis. *Frequently Asked Questions*, *supra* note 128. Loans are made to individuals that are at least 51 percent owners in the business, and only one loan is made per individual. *Id.* Therefore, a person who owns two separate businesses can only qualify for a bridge loan for one business. *Id.*

134. *Eligibility & Loan Process*, *supra* note 132. However, loans will be approved on a case-by-case basis to pay off debts already incurred to maintain or restart the business. *Id.*

135. On April 20, 2010, the Deepwater Horizon oil rig operated by BP exploded, causing a gush of oil that was not capped until July 2010. *Gulf Oil Spill Timeline and the Ensuing Legal Cases Against BP*,

Associated Press, Nov. 15, 2012, *available at* http://www.huffingtonpost.com/2012/11/15/gulf-oil-spill-timeline_n_2139515.html?utm_hp_ref=bp-oil-spill. The millions of barrels of oil that spilled into the Gulf of Mexico affected coastal communities in the states of Louisiana, Mississippi, Alabama, and Florida. Damage to Texas was mostly economic rather than environmental. Press Release, Mary Landrieu, *Shelby Lead Bipartisan Introduction of Bill to Restore Gulf Coast* (July 21, 2011), www.landrieu.senate.gov/?p=press-release&id=%201134 [hereinafter Landrieu].

136. Landrieu, *supra* note 135. State Senator Don Gaetz stated, "[S]ales and bed tax receipts were down by 40 percent or more in parts of our area and down by nearly a third overall in the seven coastal counties of Northwest Florida." Press Release, Senator Don Gaetz, Oil Spill Recovery Act on Fast Track in Senate (Jan. 11, 2011), *available at* http://www.flsenate.gov/Media/PressRelease/Show/1329.

137. 2011 Fla. Laws ch. 2011-142 §§ 497–99, *available at* laws.flrules.org/files/Ch_2011-142.pdf.

138. Lauren Sage Reinlie, *Florida Senate OKs Oil Spill Recovery Bill*, Nw. Fl. Daily News, Mar. 17, 2011, State and Regional News.

139. 2011 Fla. Laws ch. 2011-142 § 497. These waivers are available through the Department of Economic Opportunity and require notice to the governor for incentives of up to $5 million. For incentives between $5 million and $10 million, the governor, the president of the Senate, and the Speaker of the House must be notified, and the Senate president and the Speaker must concur within five days of the notice. No waivers are permitted for incentives above $10 million. *Id.*

140. The eight counties are Bay, Escambia, Franklin, Gulf, Okaloosa, Santa Rosa, Walton, and Wakulla. 2011 Fla. Laws ch. 2011-142 § 499(1).

141. *Id.* at § 499(3).

142. The IRREF Grant Program is administered by the University of West Florida's Office of Economic Development and Engagement. Information on the program can be located at http://uwf.edu/oede/initiative.cfm.

143. 2011 Fla. Laws ch. 2011-142 § 498.

144. Request for Participation, Fiscal Year 2012–2013, Northwest Florida Regional Economic Development Initiative: Industry Recruitment, Retention & Expansion Fund Grant Program 4 (2012), *available at* http://uwf.edu/oede/RFP/IRREF.pdf.

145. *Oil-Impacted Counties Looking at $10 Million in Development Funds*, Pensacola News J. (Aug. 8, 2011), http://uwf.edu/oede/news/OEDE_Aug8_2011.pdf.

146. *SEDI Frequently Asked Questions*, Univ. of West Fla., http://uwf.edu/oede/REDI_faqs.cfm (last visited Jan. 23, 2013). A targeted industry cluster is defined by Enterprise Florida Inc. as clean technology, life sciences, information technology, aviation/aerospace, logistics and distribution, defense and homeland security, and financial and professional services. *Florida Industry Clusters*, Enter. Fla., http://www.eflorida.com/contentsubpagefull.aspx?id=52 (last visited Jan. 22, 2013).

147. Florida's strategic areas of emphasis are defined by Enterprise Florida Inc. as manufacturing, corporate headquarters, and emerging technologies. *Id.*

148. Request for Participation, *supra* note 144, at 5.

149. *Id.*

150. *Id.* at 4.

151. Oil Spill Recovery Act: A Primer 6, *available at* http://www.naborhome.com/uploads/OSRA-IRREF_Overview_pptx.pdf; *SEDI Frequently Asked Questions*, *supra* note 146. A minimum of 10 jobs must be created if the project is located in a rural, brownfield, or enterprise zone, and a minimum of 30 if it is not located in these zones. *Id.*

152. Oil Spill Recovery Act: A Primer, *supra* note 151, at 6.

153. Press Release, Fla. Dep't of Econ. Opportunity, UWF Office of Economic Development and Engagement Announces Regional Economic Development Initiative (Oct. 11, 2011), *available at* http://www.floridajobs.org/news-center/news-feed/2011/10/11/uwf-office-of-economic-development-and-engagement-announces-regional-economic-development-initiative; Carlton Proctor, *State Sen. Don Gaetz Says Use BP Oil Spill Cash or Lose It*, Pensacola News J., July 15, 2012, Local News.

154. Jim Turner, *Navy Federal Gets First of Legislature's Oil Spill Recovery Funds*, Sunshine St. News (Aug. 10, 2012), http://www.sunshinestatenews.com/blog/navy-federal-gets-first-legislatures-oil-spill-recovery-funds (last visited Jan. 22, 2013); *iSirona Gets Oil Spill Grant to Add 100 Jobs in Panama City*, Econ. Dev. Blog (Aug. 30, 2012), http://www.economicdevelopmenthq.com/blog/isirona-oil-spill-grant-panama-city-fl-jobs.

155. *MarJam Supply Company Expanding to Santa Rosa Beach*, WTVY.com (Dec. 3, 2012), http://www.wtvy.com/news/headlines/MarJam-Supply-Company-Expanding-to-Santa-Rosa-Beach-181927991.html.

156. Oil Spill Recovery Act: A Primer, *supra* note 151, at 9.

157. For example, the SBA provides guidance for Small Businesses at Disaster Planning, http://www.sba.gov/content/disaster-planning (last visited Feb. 17, 2013). Businesses in Florida can go to Get a Plan! at http://www.floridadisaster.org/business for assistance in preparing a disaster plan. The Insurance Institute for Business and Home Safety also provides a disaster planning resource for businesses at Open for Business, http://www.disastersafety.org/open-for-business/ (last visited Feb. 17, 2013).

158. Katelyn Sabochik, *Small Businesses Are the Backbone of Our Economy and the Cornerstones of Our Communities*, White House Blog, http://www.whitehouse.gov/blog/2010/08/17/small-businesses-are-backbone-our-economy-and-cornerstones-our-communities (August 17, 2010, 06:02 AM EST).

CHAPTER 9

Restoring Small Business: A State Agency Response to the 2008 Iowa Disasters

Meridith Marshall

I. Introduction

In late spring of 2008, the state of Iowa experienced the most destructive series of natural disasters in the state's history. Floods, tornadoes, and severe storms affected the majority of the state, leading to 85 of Iowa's 99 counties receiving a presidential disaster declaration. Damage estimates for the state were between $8 billion and $10 billion, with business-sector damage estimates exceeding $5 billion.[1]

The majority of the disaster damage occurred in the city of Cedar Rapids, the second-largest city in Iowa. The citizens of Cedar Rapids were caught off guard when the Cedar River increased from the flood stage (12 feet) to the crest (31 feet) over a three-day period. Because the downtown area of the city is located on the Cedar River, the majority of the Cedar Rapids business sector was affected when the river crested. Over 1,100 city blocks were affected and 943 businesses experienced overland water.[2]

The rapid nature of the flood left business owners with little time to prepare; in addition, the flood-affected area extended far beyond both the 100- and 500-year floodplain.[3] Because the vast coverage of the flood affected many businesses that did not carry flood insurance, there was little help for them in terms of insurance coverage. Business owners immediately began making decisions regarding whether or not they would attempt to recover and, if they did choose to recover, how they would proceed.

Because each disaster event is unique, the recovery process will be different for all disasters. Iowa immediately recognized the devastating impact of the disaster to the state's economy and understood that a quick recovery would be the only way to minimize the negative effects. Unfortunately, the natural disasters would not be the only blow to the state's economy in 2008. Just as the recovery process began, the United States experienced the 2008 financial crisis, which compounded recovery struggles for Iowa businesses.

Assisting businesses in a post-disaster environment differs from traditional economic development and should therefore be approached differently. The state of Iowa found that in order to restore small businesses post-disaster, an immediate and targeted response was required.

II. Disaster Recovery Funding and State Assistance

On June 30, 2008, Congress appropriated $300 million under the Supplemental Appropriations Act of 2008[4], to assist with the recovery from the Midwest floods.[5] (See chapter 2.) These funds were allocated to the U.S. Department of Housing and Urban Development (HUD) and were required to be administered through entities designated by the governor of each state.[6] The Iowa Economic Development Authority (IEDA), formerly the Iowa Department of Economic Development, was the department chosen to administer these funds for the state of Iowa.

While the appropriation was made in June of 2008, the Notice of Funds Availability (NOFA), which detailed how the appropriation was divided among the disaster-affected states, was not published until September 23, 2008. IEDA used the time between the appropriation and the publication of the NOFA to construct a variety of disaster-recovery plans using varying dollar amounts. IEDA obtained damage estimates from both federal and local resources to develop disaster-recovery plans and worked with the Small Business Administration (SBA) to obtain a summary of the loss verifications completed by SBA immediately following the disaster. Many local governments and chambers of commerce completed needs assessments for their area and shared this information with IEDA. Without this information it would have been difficult to determine the disaster recovery needs for the state of Iowa. Local entities used a variety of tools in order to obtain damage estimates; for example, the Cedar Rapids Metro Economic Alliance had businesses provide individual reports via a web-based system.[7]

Because it was impossible to determine exact damage totals, estimates had to be used to prepare the State of Iowa Action Plan for Disaster Recovery.[8] HUD requires an action plan from all Community Development Block Grant Disaster Recovery (CDBG-DR) grantees prior to issuing a grant agreement. The action plan outlines the disaster-recovery needs of the grantee and includes a budget request.[9] (See chapter 1.)

Once HUD published the NOFA announcing that the state of Iowa would receive $156,690,815,[10] IEDA chose the recovery plan most aligned with the allocation and submitted the action plan to HUD for review. Because of IEDA's preparation in developing a variety of recovery plans, the state of Iowa was able to submit an action plan the day after the NOFA was published. The IEDA's action plan detailed how the state planned to use the HUD disaster-recovery funds to recover from the 2008 disasters. HUD has 45 days to review a submitted action plan and notify the recipient of the decision.[11] The state of Iowa received the approval from HUD exactly 45 days from the submission of the action plan. Frustrations mounted among flood-affected communities during this waiting period. Many businesses were attempting to recover, but they would need additional assistance to be successful in their efforts.

Total Business Assistance Program Funding
Federal Funds—$127 million HUD CDBG-DR Disaster Recovery
State Funds—$15 million state of Iowa

While the state was awaiting HUD's response to the action plan, the state legislature passed legislation for a state jump-start plan. This legislation included $15 million dedicated to business recovery needs under the Jumpstart Business Program. IEDA contracted with cities and counties for both state and federal programs. This program provided an immediate cash injection to the economies of areas affected by the disaster by providing up to $50,000 of working capital assistance and up to an additional $5,000 to purchase energy-efficient equipment. The award amount for the working capital component of the program was determined by calculating 25 percent of an approved disaster loan obtained by the business. Energy-efficiency awards were simply a reimbursement of energy-efficient equipment purchases made by the business.

Many of the businesses affected by the disaster experienced serious cash-flow issues as a result of disaster-related expenses incurred by the business. The Jumpstart Business Program was designed to address these needs by providing awards to apply toward working capital expenditures.[12] More than 900 businesses statewide were assisted with CDBG-DR funds and state funds through the Jumpstart Business Program. The Jumpstart Business Program allowed businesses that may have otherwise ended operations to continue doing business. Affected businesses were struggling post-disaster and Jumpstart was able to provide an immediate response to keep the recovery momentum moving forward. Supplementary assistance became available when Congress appropriated $6.5 billion to HUD on September 30, 2008, for expenses associated with disaster relief in areas affected by the 2008 natural disasters.[13] The state of Iowa received an additional $642 million from this appropriation to assist with recovery efforts. IEDA applied $127 million of the allocation toward disaster-related economic-development activities. Using the original damage estimates, IEDA chose to fund economic-development programs that best addressed the specific needs of disaster-affected businesses.

The first program IEDA funded through this second allocation was the Business Rental Assistance Program. This program was designed to encourage businesses to reoccupy disaster-affected property by providing up to $50,000 of rental assistance for the first six months of a market-rate lease agreement. Many of the commercial areas affected by the disaster were abandoned by the businesses occupying rental space post-disaster. This was especially true in Cedar Rapids where the core of the city is located along the Cedar River. The vacancy rate skyrocketed post-disaster due to tenants vacating the area.[14] The Business Rental Assistance Program helped to decrease the vacancy rate in disaster-affected areas by providing rental assistance to businesses that located in disaster-affected properties post-flood. This program was also an encouragement to property owners to rehabilitate their flood-affected property. More than 650 businesses used this program to obtain rental assistance to lease space within a disaster-affected property.

III. Personal Property Assistance

Additional needs were identified by the state of Iowa's CDBG-DR sub-recipients, the local entities, as the recovery efforts continued. These needs were identified through a range of methods, including online surveys, individual meetings with business owners, and ongoing discussions with local business groups. One of the largest loss categories was the loss of machinery and equipment, furniture, supplies, and inventory. IEDA expanded the Business Rental Assistance Program to include the reimbursement of business expenses associated with the purchase of these items post-disaster. Because it was difficult to gauge the potential activity level of this program, IEDA limited the award to $50,000 for the Expanded Business Rental Assistance Program (EBRAP). While this cap level allowed many businesses to participate in the program, it did not adequately assist the businesses with damages exceeding $50,000. It was impossible to know the exact damage totals at the beginning of the disaster, so IEDA had to rely on program applications to assess the damage totals. In an effort to ensure the assistance of as many businesses as possible, IEDA held the cap at $50,000 until the extent of equipment program applicants was better known. Once there was a better understanding of the amount of loss experienced by the disaster-affected businesses, IEDA began to increase the program cap incrementally. IEDA first increased the program cap to $100,000 in March of 2010 and gradually continued its increase until it reached $750,000 in March of 2012.[15] This allowed businesses with larger losses to receive an award amount more proportional to the total loss incurred.

Because EBRAP was an extension of the rental assistance program, only business owners renting their location were eligible for assistance. This created an equity issue because there were more than 100 business owners who suffered personal property loss and owned the property on which their businesses were located at the time of disaster. To address this equity issue, IEDA developed the Equipment Reimbursement Assistance Program (ERAP). This program had the same requirements and award limitations as EBRAP, but it allowed property owners to receive assistance for expenses associated with the purchase of machinery and equipment, furniture, supplies, and inventory.

IV. Commercial and Residential Rental Assistance

Commercial and residential landlords also experienced significant loss due to tenants vacating the property post-disaster. During the time spent rehabilitating their property, landlords were earning little to no rental revenue. To address the loss of rental revenue experienced by commercial and residential landlords, IEDA released the Commercial Rental Revenue Gap program[16] and the Residential Landlord Business Support Program.[17] Both programs provided lost rental revenue assistance to landlords for up to one year post-disaster. Landlords were required to provide documentation verifying that the space was occupied pre-flood as well as the rent amount for the rental space pre-flood. The award was calculated based upon the pre-flood lease amount and was limited to $15,000 for residential landlords and initially $25,000 per unit for the commercial landlords. As the commercial program continued, IEDA was informed by local entities that several disaster-affected commercial properties were large spaces with corresponding rental amounts totaling several hundred thousand dollars of lost rental revenue. As a result, IEDA increased the commercial program cap to $100,000 per unit.

V. Case Management

Another program that greatly benefited disaster-affected businesses was the case management program. The Cedar Rapids Chamber of Commerce implemented the Business Long Term Recovery Initiative in the beginning of 2010 to provide direct assistance to disaster-affected businesses. As the program expanded, the city of Cedar Rapids made a request to the state of Iowa to implement a statewide case management program funded with CDBG-DR funds. IEDA recognized the potentially positive effects of this program and amended the action plan to include the Disaster Case Management Service for Businesses Program, which was released on July 23, 2010.

Many small business owners were so busy managing the recovery efforts of their business that they did not have the time to investigate the different types of disaster assistance available. Jeff Scherrman, owner of Cedar Rapids disaster-affected business Acme Graphics, is a strong supporter of the case management program. Scherrman explained that the case management program provided great help to his business post-disaster. The case managers helped him apply for disaster-recovery business programs and create a disaster plan to aid in the event of future disasters. When asked what advice he had for a business recovering from a disaster Scherrman said, "You can't do it alone. You will be totally unsuccessful on your own."[18]

In addition to helping businesses apply for disaster assistance, the case management program helped identify issues the business community was experiencing post-disaster. While working with the business, the case manager was able to learn more about the business's needs. Case managers would compile information obtained during each one-on-one session and present this information to IEDA during weekly meetings. This helped the disaster-affected businesses to better communicate programmatic issues and, in turn, aided the state of Iowa in better assessing local business needs.

VI. Lessons Learned

Recovering from a disaster is challenging for all parties involved. The state of Iowa has learned many lessons regarding future disaster-recovery efforts. First and foremost, it is crucial to keep program design simple when developing the framework for the disaster-recovery programs. IEDA designed programs that did not require significant underwriting. When administering a recovery effort, it is important to get funds to recovering businesses as soon as possible. Keeping the program design simple allows program administrators to quickly assess applicant eligibility and reduce error in eligibility determinations.

To aid in the simplicity of the programs, IEDA worked with outside resources to establish documentation requirements to fulfill the program guidelines. IEDA consulted with the Iowa Division of Banking, the Iowa insurance commissioner, and the IRS to establish the documentation needs for each of the business programs. By working with these outside resources, IEDA was able to develop a list of required documentation that would assist with eligibility determinations.

Another opportunity to work with industry experts occurred when working to collect the required documentation. Because many businesses were unable to produce what was required due to the flood damage these records had sustained, IEDA found alternative documentation that could be provided by a third party to address the program requirements. As an example, the SBA loss-verification reports were used to support the ownership of personal property prior to the disaster for businesses applying to the disaster-recovery equipment programs. Another example included the use of canceled checks provided by the business's bank to document the rental payments made for applicants of the rental revenue programs. It is crucial to the success of any disaster-recovery business program to work with industry experts to establish program documentation that is reasonable for the business to obtain and adequately addresses the requirements of the program.

Another important lesson regarding the administration of disaster-recovery business programs is to monitor early during the program life and often throughout it.

Because the disaster-recovery programs are most likely new to both the recipient and the grantee, it is important to monitor early on in the program to ensure proper program administration. IEDA oversaw 11 cities and counties that disbursed the CDBG-DR funds across the state. Because IEDA did not have the ability to continually visit each of these entities, a process was established that required local entities to electronically submit each business applicant file deemed eligible at the local level to IEDA for review. IEDA completed an eligibility checklist for each file submitted and notified the local entity of any file deficiencies. This process significantly reduced the number of ineligible business applicant files funded at the local level. Monitoring the administration of disaster-recovery business programs early and often is beneficial in preventing potential problems later on.

IEDA maintained constant communication with the local entities through regularly scheduled conference calls and monthly email updates sent to all entities. This helped address any questions local entities had and kept IEDA informed of any issues the businesses were experiencing. IEDA hosted a training session in December 2009 and invited all local entities to attend. This session walked attendees through program guidelines, the file submission process, and documentation requirements. In addition to the initial training session, IEDA offered one-on-one webinars with all local entities to discuss administrative concerns. If there was a recurring issue the IEDA team saw while monitoring each business applicant file, an update was sent to all local entities clarifying the program requirement. Maintaining constant communication with the program administrators was critical to the success of the programs because it provided a continuous stream of information.

IEDA also discovered components that were detrimental to successful disaster recovery—for example, inadvertently writing program rules that did not reflect the intent of the program. When writing program rules, it is important to make certain the objective of the program is adequately expressed. For the state of Iowa, this came down to one word: "executed." When the Jumpstart Business Program was implemented, it was always the intent that the Jumpstart recipient would be required to provide documentation that a lender had "approved" a disaster-related loan. The approval provided due diligence regarding the business viability and the extent of the loss. However, the program rules required the recipient to provide an "executed" loan document, which would force the applicant to execute the loan agreement. IEDA administered the program with the understanding that documentation of a loan approval would be sufficient to support a Jumpstart award. However, when the CDBG-DR business programs were monitored by the Office of Inspector General (OIG), a finding was issued requiring the state to provide documentation verifying the $10.5 million was paid in accordance with Iowa law or to reimburse the funds from nonfederal sources. After communicating with the OIG and executing new administrative rules to change the requirement to a loan approval, the finding was reduced to approximately $485,645. This amount was required to be recaptured by the state of Iowa and returned to HUD. Whenever CDBG-DR programs are monitored, the auditor will monitor based upon the program guidelines; therefore, it is important to verify the guidelines accurately reflect program intent.

As previously mentioned, these disaster-recovery business programs continued to evolve throughout the disaster-recovery process. In the early stages of the disaster recovery programs there was no formalized appeals process established for businesses that did not meet the program requirements, which resulted in a continuous stream of program-modification requests submitted to IEDA. Addressing each of these requests took time away from processing applications. It was also difficult to track the number of businesses affected by this issue because requests generally represented the needs of individual businesses and not the business community as a whole. IEDA eventually established a formalized appeals process in 2010 to organize program-change requests. Not only did this provide businesses with the opportunity to appeal an award determination, it also helped IEDA to understand the magnitude of each issue presented and track the requested changes.

One of the most challenging aspects of disaster recovery is the political pressure placed on the administering agent. Disaster funds will never be able to be administered as rapidly as they are needed by the disaster-affected businesses; as a result, citizens will contact local, state, and federal officials in an effort to speed up the process. IEDA has experienced this throughout the recovery effort, and department leaders were pressured to administer funds as quickly as possible. This led to program release before administrators had a complete understanding of the program requirements, which led to funds being disbursed to ineligible businesses. In the end, this hurts the businesses that receive the funds in error, because the funds are required to be paid back. While getting funds to the businesses quickly is very important, it should never come at the expense of properly administering the program that has been developed. To a certain extent, political pressure will be present in every disaster situation. Once citizens are notified of the disaster assistance available, they will understandably request the assistance immediately in order to help with the recovery of their business. Program administrators need to consider this when beginning the disaster-recovery process to avoid potential problems.

Recipients of CDBG-DR funds can alleviate some of the pressure by preparing several disaster-recovery plans in anticipation of the NOFA. This will allow the recipient to be able to submit an action plan immediately following the NOFA publication. HUD must also work toward becoming a faster responder by publishing the NOFA earlier in the recovery process to allow recipients to respond more quickly. Program administrators must anticipate the pressure to release funds as soon as possible and must ensure program rules and regulations are not sacrificed in an attempt to distribute funds more quickly. Forgoing regulations will only hurt the businesses in the long run, because funds will be required to be recaptured.

VII. Conclusion

Although each disaster event is unique, wisdom gained from the 2008 Iowa flooding can be applied toward future disasters to effectively implement a successful disaster-recovery response. It is difficult to know the exact number of businesses that were able to come back post-disaster, but IEDA was able to assist more than 1,100 businesses through the CDBG-DR programs. Assessing the needs of the business community post-disaster and developing recovery programs addressing those specific needs are vital to the success of the recovery process. Establishing a funding plan that is efficient will significantly decrease the number of businesses that fail post-disaster. The recovery process is full of many challenges, but if the administering agent takes the time upfront to develop programs that address the needs of the disaster-affected businesses and has established programs that are easy to understand, the recovery efforts will be successful.

Notes

1. REBUILD IOWA OFFICE QUARTERLY REPORT 7–8 (2011).
2. BOB HARSCHNEK & SCOTT SWENSON, CEDAR RAPIDS AREA CHAMBER OF COMMERCE, FIRST BUSINESS CASE MANAGEMENT PROGRAM FOR A NATURAL DISASTER 3 (2012).
3. *Flood of 2008: Facts & Statistics*, CITY OF CEDAR RAPIDS, http://www.cedar-rapids.org/government/departments/public-works/engineering/Flood%20Protection%20Information/Pages/2008FloodFacts.aspx (last visited Apr. 9, 2013); *500 Year Flood Submerges Iowa*, ENV'T NEWS SERV., http://www.ens-newswire.com/ens/jun2008/2008-06-16-01.asp.
4. Pub. L. No. 110-252 (2008).
5. *Id.*
6. *Id.*
7. HARSCHNEK & SWENSON, *supra* note 2, at 13.
8. IOWA DEP'T OF ECON. DEV., STATE OF IOWA ACTION PLAN (2008).
9. CDBG Disaster Recovery Assistance website, http://portal.hud.gov/hudportal/HUD?src=/program_offices/comm_planning/communitydevelopment/programs/drsi.
10. Additional Allocations and Waivers Granted to and Alternative Requirements for 2008 Community Development Block Grant (CDBG) Disaster Recovery Grantees, 74 Fed. Reg. 41,147 (Aug. 14, 2009), http://www.gpo.gov/fdsys/pkg/FR-2009-08-14/html/E9-19488.htm.
11. HUD, BASICALLY CDBG 2–5.
12. *Iowa Jumpstart Program*, CORRIDOR RECOVERY, http://www.corridorrecovery.org/jumpstart/ (last visited Apr. 9, 2013).
13. Pub. L. No. 110-329 (2008).
14. HARSCHNEK & SWENSON, *supra* note 2, at 13.
15. IOWA ECON. DEV. AUTH., EXPANDED BUSINESS RENTAL ASSISTANCE PROGRAM GUIDELINES (2011), http://www.iowaeconomicdevelopment.com/userdocs/documents/ieda/6-20-11_Guidelines-Expanded-Business-Rental-Assistance-Program.pdf.
16. IEDA, Commercial Rental Revenue Gap Program Guidelines (2012), http://www.iowaeconomicdevelopment.com/userdocs/documents/ieda/6-20-11_Guidelines-Commercial-Rental-Revenue-Gap-Program.pdf.
17. IEDA, Residential Landlord Business Support Program Guidelines (2010), http://www.iowaeconomicdevelopment.com/userdocs/documents/ieda/6-20-11_Revised-Guidelines-Residential-Landlord-Business-Support.pdf.
18. Interview with Jeff Scherrman, President, Acme Graphics Inc. (Sept. 6, 2012).

PART 3

Housing Recovery

CHAPTER 10

The 2008 Texas Hurricanes: Working for Equitable and Transparent Redevelopment

Heather K. Way and Maddie Sloan*

I. Introduction

Following a natural disaster, after the floodwaters recede, the fires are put out, and the media vans depart, communities begin to confront the slow, hard road of long-term disaster recovery. Families leave emergency shelters to find their homes destroyed, their places of employment wiped out, and community infrastructure devastated. Historically underserved populations—the poor and people of color—face especially daunting challenges recovering from natural disasters. These populations have long lived in areas most vulnerable to flooding and other impacts of natural disasters and are less likely to have substantial assets, property insurance, or other safety nets to help them rebuild. Yet, when decisions are finally made on where to direct government rebuilding funds, the needs of these most vulnerable populations are often bypassed, their voices ignored. While the inadequate and delayed response of the Federal Emergency

*The authors wish to thank Rebecca Lightsey, executive director of Texas Appleseed; Eliza Platts-Mills, lecturer at University of Texas School of Law; and Liz Wolff for their guidance in the development of this chapter, in addition to University of Texas School of Law students Erin Gaines and Alexine Zacarias, for their assistance with the citations.

Management Agency (FEMA) to the Gulf Coast in the immediate aftermath of Hurricane Katrina was extensively dissected by policymakers and the media, there has been little national attention paid to the inequities and delays in long-term disaster recovery, particularly regarding the use of federal Community Development Block Grants Disaster Recovery funds.

The state of Texas was at the center of these issues after two hurricanes, Ike and Dolly, lashed the Texas coastline in 2008. Poor and predominantly minority neighborhoods were especially hard hit in several areas near the coast. The hurricanes destroyed thousands of homes and caused more than $29 billion in damages, including over $3 billion in housing damages.[1] In response, the U.S. Department of Housing and Urban Development (HUD) awarded Texas more than $3 billion in long-term rebuilding assistance, distributed to the state in two rounds (referred to as Round One and Round Two). The block grant award set in motion one of the largest community development and public works programs in the state's modern history.

Texas's initial program for long-term rebuilding from the 2008 hurricanes was plagued by long delays and diverted funds away from hard-hit, low-income neighborhoods. At the same time, the program skewed funds toward infrastructure projects with attenuated connections to helping the poor recover from the 2008 storms. The blue tarps over damaged roofs in low-income neighborhoods—still in place years after the storms—became an all too familiar symbol of a program that shortchanged the needs of poor families. The program's mismanagement eventually led federal officials to call Texas "the worst performing state in the country on expenditure of funds and disaster money."[2]

Affordable housing, civil rights, and low-income community advocates have worked at all levels of government to try to overcome these challenges in Texas—with the goal of ensuring that the Hurricanes Ike and Dolly disaster recovery funds are spent more equitably, effectively, and transparently to reach the needs of Texas's most vulnerable populations. Their efforts and the lessons arising out of their work are the focus of this chapter.

II. Background: The 2008 Texas Hurricanes Dolly and Ike

In July 2008, Hurricane Dolly lashed the South Texas coastal region near the U.S.-Mexico border, followed by Hurricane Ike in southeastern Texas just two months later. The damage from both hurricanes was widespread, covering more than 50 counties.

Hurricane Ike is estimated to be the fourth-costliest hurricane in U.S. history, after Hurricanes Katrina and Andrew and Superstorm Sandy, as of May 2013.[3] Ike, which first made landfall on Galveston Island, caused a storm surge from the bay side of the island that poured up to eight feet of water into buildings downtown and nearby neighborhoods, and destroyed more than 500 units of public housing. The nearby Bolivar Peninsula was devastated, with the storm surge destroying almost every structure on parts of the peninsula.[4] Ike caused extensive damages in the city of Houston as well, including flooding and widespread wind damage that ravaged roofs across the city. Nearly 2.8 million Houston-area residents were left without power, in many cases for weeks after the storm.[5]

While Hurricane Dolly was not as devastating as Hurricane Ike, Dolly's 100-mile-per-hour winds and rainfall still caused an estimated $1.05 billion in damages to homes and businesses in South Texas—one of the most impoverished areas in the United States.[6] With the region's topography and settlement patterns in low-lying areas along the Rio Grande River, flooding caused the most widespread damage.[7] Large swaths of Cameron and Hidalgo counties were flooded, up to three feet deep in some areas, destroying homes and cutting off the area's main east-west highway for several days.[8]

Both hurricanes had devastating impacts on low-income and historically disinvested minority communities. Long-standing deficiencies in infrastructure services in the impacted areas contributed to these outcomes. For example, in the Lower Rio Grande Valley, among the worst damage from Dolly was in the colonias,[9] where the area's lowest-income residents were left with standing water for weeks and even months. The colonias are so classified because of their lack of adequate infrastructure.[10] With no drainage systems for taking out rainwater, the colonias often flood after even ordinary rainstorms. With widespread reliance on inadequate septic tanks for wastewater collection, raw sewage often mixes with floodwaters following storms in the colonias, contributing to the proliferation of deadly diseases such as cholera and dysentery.[11]

In the city of Galveston, floodwaters disproportionately destroyed the housing in the island's northeast side neighborhoods.[12] These low-lying areas, which are occupied predominantly by African-Americans (including census tracts that are 80 to 100 percent African-American), were not protected by the city's seawall.[13] In contrast, the housing on the south side behind the island's seawall sustained much less damage.[14] Indeed, this outcome could have been predicted since the predominantly African-American neighborhoods on the northeast side are noted on a 2000 FEMA Vulnerability Map as being highly susceptible to flooding from tropical storms, let alone hurricanes.[15] The floodwaters also destroyed all of the island's public-housing developments for families, which were concentrated in the city's racially segregated and low-lying neighborhoods.[16]

III. The Federal Response

While the philosophy of disaster recovery places state and local governments in a leading position on recovery efforts, the reality of large-scale disasters in the United States is that federal assistance provides the bulk of disaster-recovery resources. These resources are allocated and administered in several phases.

In Texas, the first phase of federal assistance for Hurricanes Dolly and Ike began right after the hurricanes made landfall, when President George W. Bush declared a major disaster in Texas counties affected by the hurricanes, pursuant to title IV of the Robert T. Stafford Disaster Relief and Emergency Assistance Act (commonly referred to as the Stafford Act).[17] (See also chapter 1.) Under the act, a presidential declaration of a major disaster triggers a number of federal short-term assistance programs to help address the basic needs of survivors and remediate dangerous conditions created by the disaster.[18] Depending on the scope of a declaration, needs covered include emergency shelter and temporary housing assistance, debris removal, emergency repairs to essential infrastructure and public facilities damaged by the disaster, and relief services to individuals and businesses. The primary administrators of these funds are FEMA and the Small Business Administration (SBA). These agencies also participate in a Preliminary Damage Assessment: a review of damage to public and individual property that is used to allocate federal disaster-recovery resources.[19]

The second phase of federal assistance for disaster recovery begins when Congress issues one or more supplemental appropriations targeted for longer-term recovery needs. Since 1992, the bulk of these appropriations have been in the form of Community Development Block Grant Disaster Recovery (CDBG-DR) funds.[20] HUD awards these funds as block grants to states and other governmental entities[21] to address housing, infrastructure, and economic-development recovery needs unmet by the emergency assistance programs. Unless the appropriating statute otherwise restricts the funds, or HUD grants a waiver of program requirements, the same program requirements and national objectives that apply to annual CDBG grants also apply to CDBG-DR grants, with the additional requirement that the CDBG-DR grants can only fund projects related to the covered disaster. A requirement of both the annual and the CDBG-DR program is that the funds target the needs of low- and moderate-income people.[22]

Since 1993, Congress has appropriated more than $31 billion in CDBG-DR funds nationally, including $6.5 billion in 2008.[23] From the 2008 appropriations, HUD allocated $3 billion to Texas for recovery from Hurricanes Dolly and Ike. The allocation was made in two separate rounds: a Round One award of $1.3 billion in February 2009, and a Round Two award of $1.7 billion in August 2009. The $3 billion allocation to Texas in 2008 was just under half of Congress's total 2008 CDBG-DR appropriation for the entire country.[24]

Timeline: Texas Long-Term Disaster Recovery Program for the 2008 Hurricanes

July 23, 2008: Hurricane Dolly strikes Texas.

July 24, 2008: President George W. Bush issues major disaster declaration for 15 counties under Title IV of the Robert T. Stafford Disaster Relief and Emergency Assistance Act.

September 13, 2008: Hurricane Ike strikes Texas.

September 13, 2008: President George W. Bush issues major disaster declaration for 29 counties under Title IV of the Robert T. Stafford Disaster Relief and Emergency Assistance Act.

Timeline: Texas Long-Term Disaster Recovery Program for the 2008 Hurricanes

September 30, 2008: Consolidated Security, Disaster Assistance, and Continuing Appropriations Act is enacted, appropriating $6.5 billion in supplemental CDBG funds for major disasters.

February 2009: HUD allocates $1.3 billion in CDBG-DR funds to Texas (Round One).

February 20, 2009: State of Texas submits action plan for the Round One CDBG-DR funds. State designates Texas Department of Rural Affairs as lead agency for administration of the disaster recovery funds.

February 27, 2009: Texas Appleseed, Texas RioGrande Legal Aid, and Texas Low Income Housing Information Services (TxLIHIS) file administrative complaint against the State of Texas's Round One action plan for the $1.3 billion in Round One CDBG-DR funds.

March 2009: HUD issues a conditional approval of Texas's Round One action plan for $1.3 billion in CDBG-DR funds.

August 2009: HUD allocates $1.7 billion in CDBG-DR funds to Texas (Round Two).

September 2009: State of Texas submits amended action plan for the additional $1.7 billion in CDBG-DR funds.

October 2009: Texas Appleseed and TxLIHIS submit a second administrative complaint to HUD for the $1.7 billion in Round Two CDBG-DR funds.

November 2009: HUD rejects the state's amended action plan for the Round Two funds, freezing the distribution of $1.7 billion in disaster recovery funds to the State of Texas. HUD directs the state to revise and resubmit plan within 45 days.

December 2009: TxLIHIS submits a fair housing complaint to HUD against the State of Texas, joined by Texas Appleseed on February 7, 2010.

May 2010: HUD approves Conciliation Agreement between the state of Texas and advocacy groups Texas Appleseed and TxLIHIS, covering the disbursement of the Round Two funds.

June 2010: State of Texas submits amended action plan to HUD.

June 2010: HUD conditionally accepts amended action plan.

May 2011: HUD approves the Analysis of Impediments to Fair Housing required under the Conciliation Agreement.

July 1, 2011: Texas Governor Rick Perry transfers administration of the CDBG-DR funds to the General Land Office.

IV. Texas's Initial Response: Inequities and Long Delays

From the perspective of state and local governments, one of the primary benefits of the CDBG-DR program has been the flexibility it offers governments in addressing their recovery needs. Yet, the program's flexibility has also made it possible for governmental entities to stretch or even ignore compliance with federal requirements and bypass the critical needs of low-income victims. The State of Texas's

Round One program for Hurricanes Ike and Dolly epitomized these challenges. Charged with spending $1.3 billion in the Round One of CDBG-DR funds, the State of Texas proceeded to put in place a recovery program that diverted funding away from serving the state's most vulnerable populations who had been impacted by the storms.

The federal government's allocation of CDBG-DR funds to Texas was based in large part on the state's share of unaddressed housing needs compared with other states competing for the funds.[25] However, the state's initial disaster-recovery plan dedicated only the statutorily mandated minimum of $140 million in CDBG-DR funds to affordable housing. The state delegated decisions on how the rest of the funds would be spent—including the division of funds between housing and non-housing programs—to 11 different regional Councils of Governments (COGs).[26] The COGs then awarded the funds to approximately 250 local governmental entities for housing, infrastructure, and economic-development projects, leaving it largely up to the local governments to determine how to divide funds among these activities.

Texas offered no additional guidance to the regional Councils of Governments on how the funds should be further allocated and little oversight to ensure that the needs of low-income and minority victims would be addressed in accordance with federal fair housing laws and low- to moderate-income targeting requirements. Ceding the funding decisions to the COGs resulted in only 48 percent of the total Round One CDBG-DR funding going toward housing.[27] The majority of sub-recipient jurisdictions chose to prioritize infrastructure projects, which tend to serve a broader segment of the population and do not target the needs of poorer neighborhoods.[28] Excluding the City of Houston (which allocated 80 percent of its funding to housing) and the City of Galveston (which allocated 60 percent of its funding to housing), only 27 percent of the money allocated by the COGs in the other impacted areas was set aside for housing. In contrast, Louisiana and Mississippi each allocated at least 69 percent of its Hurricanes Katrina– and Rita–related CDBG-DR funding to housing.[29]

The funding allocations under the Round One program left many low-income homeowners without resources to repair their storm-damaged homes. While 12,000 applications for housing assistance were accepted by governmental entities—primarily cities, counties, and COGs—under Round One, the program was expected to assist fewer than 5,000 of the applicants.[30] Fort Bend County estimated it would be assisting only 38 out of 5,100 households whose homes were damaged by the storm.[31] The Deep East Texas Council of Governments (DETCOG) estimated that its Round One program would serve only 99 out of 809 households that had unmet housing needs from Hurricane Ike.[32] Meanwhile, DETCOG allocated funds to towns unharmed by the storm, such as a $5 million grant to the town of Lufkin to double the size of its civic center.[33]

The State of Texas's proposal for the second federal allocation of disaster-recovery funds continued to shortchange the needs of low-income communities for both housing and infrastructure improvements. Instead of allocating funds based on unmet needs and damages from the hurricanes—which formed the basis of HUD's $3 billion disaster-recovery allocation to Texas—the state's first proposed plan for the Round Two funds allocated the funds among the state's regional COGs utilizing a "weather model." Developed by the state's subcontractor, engineering firm HNTB, the weather model allocated funds to the COGs based on where the weather from the hurricanes was most intense, looking at wind speed, rainfall, and storm surge—even if the area suffered little in the way of damage to homes and businesses. For example, the weather model correctly reflected that the storm surge from Hurricane Ike was the highest in Chambers County, but the model failed to take into account that much of Chambers County is rural pastureland and that the county suffered much less housing and infrastructure damage compared with highly populated areas such as Galveston and Houston.[34]

If the state's initial Round Two plan had been accepted by HUD, the weather model would have resulted in a significant diversion of funding from areas with the highest needs. Under the model, areas far from the coast that sustained little in the way of damages from the storms were to receive millions in funds for new roads, water lines, and community centers, some with tenuous connections to disaster recovery.[35] After receiving complaints from advocates and government leaders from Galveston and Houston about the model,[36] HUD directed the state to reallocate the funds based on actual needs. The reallocation resulted in the transfer of hundreds of millions in additional funds to areas of the state with higher rebuilding needs, including $188 million to the Houston-Galveston region, an additional $20 million to southeastern Texas, and an additional $595,000 to the Lower Rio Grande Valley.[37]

The State of Texas's broad-scale delegation of spending authority and lack of oversight led to additional funding inequities at the local level. For example, in Hidalgo County, the county's disaster-recovery plans failed to address the recurrent flooding issues in the colonias, despite the fact that these were the poorest communities in the county, had the most severe drainage problems, and suffered some of the worst flooding damage following Hurricane Dolly. Instead, the county planned to invest $58 million of its $63 million Round Two infrastructure funds in a regional drainage system.[38] The proposed system, which left out the colonias, was focused on moving water out of incorporated communities during heavy rains by clearing and expanding the existing drainage system and connecting incorporated communities to the system.

Numerous other projects submitted by local jurisdictions—including construction of a conference center and a traffic-light coordination study—had questionable links to assisting low- and moderate-income residents with the hurricane recovery.[39] In Houston, while the city dedicated more funds than other areas to repairing housing for low-income victims, the city invested only $10 million of its $60 million Round One housing funds toward repairing homes of low-income homeowners. The city instead targeted the majority of its housing funds to multifamily housing developments and a down-payment assistance program for homebuyers making up to 120 percent median family income that served families outside disaster-relief areas.[40] This latter program was criticized in the media for serving unqualified buyers, and a HUD audit found that the program broke federal rules and regulations.[41]

Low-income minority disaster victims were also disadvantaged by the cursory attention state and local jurisdictions paid to fair housing issues, including the obligation to affirmatively further fair housing, in the distribution of recovery funds. (For an overview of affirmatively furthering fair housing requirements under federal fair housing laws, see chapter 15). For example, the state's Round One program and initial Round Two program required homeowners receiving disaster-recovery funds to rebuild on their pre-hurricane lot, which meant that African-American and Hispanic families living in highly segregated, flood-prone, and distressed neighborhoods were denied the opportunity to rebuild on higher ground in higher-opportunity communities.

In Galveston, despite the area's long history of racial polarization, the city's Analysis of Impediments to Fair Housing was only one sentence long and had not been updated since 2003. Public meetings turned into shouting matches between black and white residents, and public-housing opponents even resorted to circulating a rap video, alleging that it represented how public-housing residents behaved.[42] Rebuilding public housing in Galveston became the major issue in the city's May 2012 municipal elections: the mayor and members of the City Council who had supported the rebuilding of public housing lost office to candidates who opposed rebuilding the public housing.[43]

The state's decision to have local governmental entities create and run their own disaster recovery programs was problematic in other respects as well, especially given the lack of on-the-ground capacity at the local level,[44] the lack of technical assistance, and the lack of performance benchmarks. On the housing front, the delegation led to the creation of 18 new housing programs from scratch, including 18 different sets of program rules, eligibility guidelines, program activities, and application procedures—and long delays in the delivery of housing assistance. In spring 2011, almost three years after the storms, only 104 out of 3,537 contracted homes had been repaired or reconstructed, with waiting lists of more than 8,000 additional applicants.[45] Even after having funding contracts in hand for 18 months, 12 of the 18 local government entities administering housing programs had spent less than 10 percent of their awarded housing funds.[46]

The long delays in assistance from the Round One program had an especially harsh impact on low-income families whose homes were damaged or destroyed by the hurricanes. The poor often live in housing more vulnerable to natural disasters, such as older homes and mobile homes. They also lack the resources to protect their homes from disasters through disaster-mitigation improvements or property insurance.[47] In Texas, by the time the state's long-term disaster recovery program was put in place, the poor had already been disadvantaged by FEMA's aggressive denial of home-repair assistance to low-income families following Hurricanes Dolly and

Ike. For Hurricane Ike claims, FEMA denied at least 85 percent of the more than 578,000 applications for housing assistance.[48] Many of the denials by FEMA were made on the grounds that the poor conditions of the homes contributed to the storm damages.[49] Repair delays caused by FEMA's denials exacerbated direct storm damage through mold and spoilage of the damaged structures. Blue tarps, intended as an emergency measure, were still serving as roofs for many families four years after the storms.

V. Legal and Community-Based Strategies

Concerned with the plight of low-income Texans whose homes and communities were devastated by the 2008 hurricanes, low-income community and civil rights advocacy organizations have played an active role in the state's long-term rebuilding process. They have worked on both the state and local levels, integrating legal and community-based organizing strategies with the primary goals of (1) securing adequate allocations of disaster funding at the local level for the poorest and hardest-hit victims, (2) addressing the systemic disparities in infrastructure that contributed to the high levels of flooding damage in low-income minority communities after the hurricanes, and (3) institutionalizing systems and programs to facilitate long-term community engagement and structural reforms.

A. State-Level Advocacy

The state-level advocacy work was led by two nonprofit organizations working in close partnership: Texas Appleseed and Texas Low Income Housing Information Services (TxLIHIS). Texas Appleseed is a public-interest law center focused on social and economic justice on a wide array of issues. TxLIHIS is a grassroots-oriented housing and community advocacy organization with decades of experience furthering social and economic justice in state and local housing policies.

Advocates' first phase of work focused on the State of Texas's action plan process for allocating the CDBG-DR funds. The action plan process is an important vehicle through which advocacy and community-based groups can influence how long-term disaster recovery funds are allocated by a state. Before receiving a CDBG-DR grant from HUD, a state must submit and receive approval from HUD for an action plan for disaster recovery.[50] The action plan must describe the needs, strategies, and projected uses of the CDBG-DR funds, including the "method of distribution" for providing funds to sub-recipient units of general local government. Moreover, the public must have the opportunity to comment on the plan before it is approved by HUD.[51] Because Texas received two separate allocations of CDBG-DR funds from HUD, the action plan process for Hurricanes Ike and Dolly disaster-recovery funds was divided into Round One and Round Two.[52]

In the early stages of the disaster recovery, the Texas advocates worked with low-income victims and community-based groups to inform them about the public hearings for the state's action plans and the process for filing written comments to the action plans. The focus was advocating for plans that would provide an equitable allocation of funds and address the core needs of low-income communities devastated by the storms.

In advocating for an equitable distribution of the disaster-recovery funds, low-income community and civil rights advocates were challenged by the fact that the ultimate decision of how to divide funds among housing, infrastructure, and economic development was left to approximately 250 local governmental entities. At these local levels, there were limited opportunities for true community input and limited measures to ensure that the voices of historically marginalized members of the community were heard and their needs addressed.

After the Texas CDBG-DR funds had passed through three different layers of government, information on where and how the funds were ultimately being allocated became very difficult to access and thus monitor. Low-income community and civil rights advocates found that it was especially difficult to determine the extent to which the funds were benefiting low- and moderate-income households and furthering fair housing, making it next to impossible to determine the extent to which CDBG and fair housing laws were being followed.

In response to these concerns, in February 2009, Appleseed, TxLIHIS, and Texas RioGrande Legal Aid (TRLA) filed their first administrative complaint with HUD regarding Texas's Round One action plan for the first $1.3 billion in CDBG-DR funds.[53] The complaint focused on how the state's failure to identify the method for distributing the funds and the deferral of funding decisions deprived citizens of a meaningful opportunity for public comment, in violation of the federal appropriations statute and the *Federal Register* notice governing the funds. HUD notified the advocates in March 2009 that it had approved the Texas action plan, but was conditioning release of the remaining funds on receipt of information specifying how the funds would be distributed. HUD stated that it was moving forward with granting conditional approval of the Round One action plan, given the pressing need for immediate distribution of the funds.[54]

In October 2009, Appleseed and TxLIHIS filed a second administrative complaint with HUD, this time concerning the state's amended action plan governing the $1.7 billion in Round Two funds.[55] The complaint raised a series of issues with the state's failure to comply with CDBG and related federal requirements, including the following issues:

- ***Transparency and Responsiveness:*** Appleseed and TxLIHIS asserted in their complaint that the delegation of decision-making authority to the regional Councils of Governments on how the funds would be spent violated the *Federal Register* notice requirements by failing to give citizens notice and the opportunity to comment on the method for distributing the funds to local governments.[56]

- ***Equity:*** TxLIHIS and Appleseed raised several equity issues in their HUD complaint. The complaint stated that Texas's reliance on the "weather model" in the action plan, discussed in the previous section, failed to allocate the disaster-recovery funds in proportion to unmet needs from the two hurricanes, and failed to provide a method of distribution to local governments and a sufficient public participation process, in violation of the *Federal Register* notice governing the funds. The complaint also stated that the action plan failed to ensure that at least 50 percent of CDBG funds would benefit low- and moderate-income people, as required by CDBG-DR regulations.[57]

Two weeks after the complaint was filed, HUD refused to accept the State of Texas's amended action plan for the Round Two funds, freezing the distribution of $1.7 billion in disaster-recovery funds to the state.[58] This time, HUD found that there was no longer a compelling need to immediately approve the release of funds, given that Texas had not yet spent $476 million of its Round One funds.[59]

HUD's core reason for refusing to accept the state's amended action plan was that the plan did not include information on how the funds would be distributed to local units of government, and thus did not provide the public with enough information to comment on the proposed use of funds. In its letter to the state declining to accept the plan, HUD also noted several broader concerns, including:

- the state's failure to update its Analysis of Impediments to Fair Housing choice since 2003 and thus its failure to take into consideration the subsequent changes to the housing market, such as those generated by the hurricanes;
- the public opposition to the rebuilding of public housing and affordable housing in Galveston, which raised significant fair housing concerns; and
- the state's proposed use of CDBG-DR funds for mitigation of future disasters rather than addressing core recovery needs arising directly from the prior hurricanes, in contradiction of the language in the CDBG-DR appropriation that the funds be targeted to restoration of infrastructure, housing, and economic revitalization.[60]

In December 2009, TxLIHIS filed an additional complaint with HUD, later joined by Texas Appleseed, alleging a number of issues with the State of Texas's failure to comply with federal fair housing laws and allowing its sub-recipients to discriminate and perpetuate segregation on the basis of race, color, and national origin.[61] The issues raised in this complaint included the failure of the governmental entities to consider how their funding decisions would affirmatively further fair housing, the lack of awareness of fair housing obligations, the failure to have an updated Analysis of Impediments to Fair Housing, and the state's failure to give victims the ability to rebuild in higher opportunity areas.

Over the following six months, the State of Texas, Texas Appleseed, and TxLIHIS successfully negotiated a settlement of the complaints, via a Conciliation Agreement.[62] The Conciliation Agreement, which covered the disbursement of all the Round Two funds, was approved by HUD in May 2010.[63]

Increased equity. In terms of equity, the Conciliation Agreement and ongoing pressure from HUD led to a more equitable allocation of funds and advanced fair housing for minorities and people with disabilities affected by the storm. The Conciliation Agreement required that at least 55 percent of the total Round One and Round Two funds be spent on housing activities and that at least 55 percent of the funds benefit low- and moderate-income households—an increase of $150 million.

The Conciliation Agreement guaranteed the replacement of public and affordable housing destroyed by the hurricanes, and mandated specific housing programs, including a Homeowner Opportunity Program allowing affected low-income homeowners to rebuild outside of disaster-vulnerable areas with concentrations of poverty. As part of the program, the homeowners receive counseling concerning options for moving into higher-opportunity areas. Under previous disaster-recovery programs, homeowners were required to rebuild on the same site of their damaged home, locking them into low-opportunity neighborhoods vulnerable to repeat flooding.

The Conciliation Agreement also required the state to draft a new Analysis of Impediments (AI) to fair housing choice for the areas affected by the hurricanes that would address specific disaster-related, fair housing issues, listing out not only the impediments but also specific action steps Texas would take to overcome these impediments.[64] The Conciliation Agreement further required that Texas's housing and community development agency appoint an advisory committee to review and consult with the agency on the development of the AI, providing advocates with an additional opportunity to provide input on the AI.

One of the action steps that advocates pushed Texas to incorporate into the AI is the Fair Housing Activity Statement–Texas (FHAST) process. The process provides an important vehicle for assisting jurisdictions in meeting their fair housing obligations and for providing advocates with a more accessible means of tracking fair housing compliance by local governments.

Under the FHAST process, each jurisdiction is required to create a fair housing working group of at least five members to evaluate impediments to fair housing in the area. The state's guidebook lists who the jurisdiction should consider for membership in the working group.[65] Each jurisdiction receives training on how to complete the form on fair housing compliance. The FHAST process is intended to proceed as follows:

- The fair housing working group begins by reviewing demographic maps, housing discrimination complaints that have been filed in the jurisdiction, and GIS maps of where federal housing and community development benefits have been spent historically in the jurisdiction, to the extent available.

- After reviewing the data, the working group discusses each impediment to fair housing listed in the state's AI and what experiences the jurisdiction has had with that impediment. A FHAST form[66] lists all of these 16 impediments along with a detailed list of instructions and questions concerning the different impediments that the working group is supposed to respond to on the form.
- After the impediments are identified, the working group identifies specific, concrete actions that could be taken to address each impediment. The completed form is then submitted to the Texas General Land Office (GLO)—the agency administering CDBG-DR funds—for review and posted on the local jurisdiction's website in English and any other language widely spoken in the jurisdiction.
- After the state agency administering the funds approves the FHAST form, the governing body of the jurisdiction must hold a public hearing on the form. Once adopted, the form becomes part of the jurisdiction's action plan and is posted on the jurisdiction's website. The fair housing working group is responsible for ongoing monitoring of the jurisdiction's attempts to affirmatively further fair housing and is supposed to meet at least once a year to determine if any changes to the action plan are needed.

The state-level advocacy on fair housing issues has resulted in a number of additional reforms to the Texas disaster-recovery program to further fair housing compliance and advance the equitable distribution of disaster-recovery funds, including requirements in new homes to increase access by persons with disabilities and, as discussed below, tracking of demographic data for funding beneficiaries.

Increased transparency and opportunities for public input. Advocates recognized early on in the disaster-recovery process that the ability to oversee and provide input on the government's expenditure of funds is extremely limited without information about who was impacted by the storms and the governmental entities' proposed projects.

The Conciliation Agreement provides for increased transparency in a number of ways. For example, the Conciliation Agreement (together with the new state AI arising out of the agreement) requires the state to collect and report an array of data concerning the expenditure of disaster-recovery funds and guarantees advocates access to the data. The new data requirements include:

- collection of fair housing and civil rights information related to proposed projects, including funding beneficiaries' protected class status and household income;
- posting on the state website of all applications for disaster-recovery funding;
- regular reports by jurisdictions on their efforts to affirmatively further fair housing and on meeting the agreement's low- and moderate-income targeting requirements; and

- compilation and placement in a geographic information system (GIS) of current and at least 10 years of historical data on federal block grant funds awarded by the state for municipal services and housing.

As another example, all local jurisdictions setting a public hearing related to the disaster-recovery program must submit notice of the hearing to the state for posting on the state's website. The agreement also requires a methodology for determining whether an area receiving CDBG-DR funds is low- to moderate-income when this is not supported with census information. The FHAST form process required in the state's new AI, discussed on page 228, also has the potential to increase transparency into how disaster recovery funds are spent.

The advocates' goal in requiring the reporting of this information via the Conciliation Agreement was to provide the public with a clearer picture of who is receiving disaster-recovery assistance and for what types of projects. Community-based organizations and other advocacy organizations need access to easily digestible data about projects proposed for their communities so that they can provide input on the proposed use of funds and advocate more effectively for programs to benefit the needs of the most vulnerable residents.[67]

A final change to Texas's disaster-recovery program that affected the program's transparency and overall effectiveness was the governor's consolidation of disaster-recovery efforts in summer 2011 inside one state agency, the General Land Office, which is led by an elected official. These changes provided the program, in the words of Governor Rick Perry, with "more accountability."[68] The transfer over to the GLO imbued the program with stronger political leadership and put it on a path to end the long delays and mismanagement that had previously plagued the program.

B. Local Advocacy

The local advocacy work in Texas has closely coordinated legal and policy advocacy with grassroots community organizing and engagement of low-income residents and organizations impacted by the storms. The low-income residents and community organizations involved have provided intense, in-depth, firsthand knowledge of local community development and fair housing concerns, as well as political organization and advocacy. Awareness and enforcement of federal laws has also provided community-based advocates with the leverage they need to press for changes at the local level.

An important aspect of the local advocacy work in Texas has been the long-term sustained coordination between statewide policy organizations and community-based organizers. For example, local policy analysts, based in Houston and the Lower Rio Grande Valley, have worked closely on the ground with community organizations and organizers to communicate community policy priorities and needs to state-level advocates while also translating the policy expertise offered by state and national partners into usable, actionable intelligence for local organizers and housing advocates.

Given the large geographic scope of areas impacted by Hurricanes Dolly and Ike in Texas and the limited capacity of the statewide advocacy organizations, the most active coordination between state- and local-level advocacy has been focused in three areas heavily impacted by the hurricanes: the city of Houston, the Lower Rio Grande Valley (LRGV) in South Texas, and the city of Galveston. The following discussion focuses on specific issues local and state advocates faced in these areas, and some of the strategies utilized to affect the design and implementation of these local governments' disaster-recovery programs.

Houston. Houston's history of disinvestment in historically minority neighborhoods and segregated housing patterns has meant that low-income, minority homeowners have been concentrated in flood-prone areas of Houston.[69] These residents suffered from extensive flood damage from Hurricane Ike. After Houston spent the bulk of its Round One housing funds on grants to landlords to repair multifamily rental housing (only 51 percent of which had to be affordable), local advocacy efforts for Round Two focused on ensuring that an adequate level of funds were dedicated to assisting the low-income, minority communities most heavily affected by the storms, including these communities' drainage issues and single-family housing repair needs.

Advocates have also been focused on ensuring that the City of Houston develops a functional home repair program that will continue to be run effectively after the disaster recovery program ends. Prior to advocates' involvement, the city's single-family home repair program was severely troubled. For example, almost four years after Hurricane Ike, Houston had completed less than 10 percent of the homes the city had committed to repairing from the Round One funds.

The local advocacy work in Houston for Hurricane Ike disaster recovery has been led by the Texas Organizing Project (TOP). TOP is a grassroots, membership-based nonprofit organization that conducts issue advocacy, lobbying efforts, and electoral organizing to advance social and economic equity for Texas families, focusing on ensuring that the voices of low-income and minority communities are heard and that they have sufficient power to advance their issues.[70] After Hurricane Ike struck Houston, TOP organized residents to engage them in the public input process and elicit their priorities for the disaster-recovery funds. TOP also created and carried out a strategy to change Houston's disaster-recovery priorities. TOP members attended local hearings on the proposed uses of CDBG-DR funds to testify about the need for drainage and single-family home repair programs in their neighborhoods. TOP members also attended city council meetings, met with city council members and state and federal elected officials, organized information fairs about the city's housing program, and—armed with blue tarps—repeatedly confronted Houston officials about the lack of help coming to their neighborhoods.[71] As a result of TOP's organizing work, more than 300 low-income Houston residents turned out to meetings with their mayor and other city officials.[72]

The organizing work in Houston, combined with the legal mandates in Texas Conciliation Agreement, led to a historic agreement between TOP and the City of Houston in December 2011.[73] TOP's agreement with Houston moved an additional $30 million into single-family home repairs in targeted neighborhoods, and the city promised to not deny single-family homeowners assistance solely because they lived in a floodplain, a rule that had excluded many low-income, minority homeowners from the Round One home-repair program. TOP also pressured the City of Houston to request intensive technical assistance from HUD to fix its home-repair program and plan for the Round Two program. As a result, HUD is providing technical assistance to the city through Local Initiatives Support Cooperation (LISC) and Enterprise Community Partners.

In Round Two, Houston is planning to target disaster recovery funds in several narrowly defined geographic areas as opposed to spreading limited funds across the entire city. In addition to repairing homes damaged by Hurricane Ike, Houston will work to commit additional city and federal funds to institute broader-scale, community-development improvements in the target areas.[74]

Due to their organizing efforts and agreement with the city, TOP has transformed an adversarial relationship with the city into a working partnership. TOP members have been central participants and organizers in the process of selecting the potential targeted neighborhoods and continue to work with the city on both planning and administration of Houston's CDBG-DR program for Hurricane Ike. On May 9, 2012, the mayor held a press conference with HUD to announce the program and thanked TOP for its participation in the process.[75] TOP advocates also continue to work on securing funds to address the drainage infrastructure issues in minority communities affected by Hurricane Ike.

Galveston. In Galveston, advocacy efforts have focused on rebuilding the island's 569-family public-housing units that were destroyed by the storm, as well as on ensuring that low-income homeowners are able to access funds to repair their hurricane-damaged homes. Advocates have worked to ensure that the public housing units are not only rebuilt but that they are rebuilt in a manner that affirmatively furthers fair housing by desegregating public housing both economically and racially and providing housing choices in higher-opportunity areas of the city, such as near jobs at local hospitals and universities.

Before the storm, racially segregated patterns of development meant that low-income African-American residents were heavily concentrated in rental housing located on the island's northeast-side neighborhoods, including the Galveston Housing Authority's three public-housing complexes for families.[76] The housing in this area was heavily damaged by the hurricane, leaving thousands of African-Americans without a home to return to after the floodwaters receded.[77] The rebuilding of the rental housing, including the public housing, has thus been of special importance to advocates and residents wanting to ensure that low-income African-American residents displaced by the storm have the opportunity to move back to their hometown.[78]

While the Housing Authority took action to rebuild the public-housing units in compliance with a settlement agreement discussed further on page 233, fierce opposition mobilized against the rebuilding plans, generating an ugly, racially polarized discourse on the future composition of the city—a smaller-scale re-creation of the post–Hurricane Katrina struggle in New Orleans. For example, an October 4, 2009, editorial by the editor and publisher of the *Galveston Daily News* warned its readers that any new multifamily public-housing developments "will invariably become breeding grounds for crime, drug abuse and blight."[79] Meanwhile, civil rights leaders in the community charged that the drive against public housing was more about keeping low-income African-Americans from returning to Galveston than it was about public housing.[80]

In Galveston, some of the most critical advocacy happened very early in the disaster-recovery process. A few months after Hurricane Ike, the Galveston Housing Authority announced to HUD that it was going to demolish all of its 569 public-housing units for families, since they had been badly damaged by the storm.[81] The local office of Lone Star Legal Aid, representing displaced public-housing residents, promptly intervened and filed an administrative complaint with HUD opposing the demolition without a commitment to replace the units.[82] The Housing Authority quickly settled the complaint with an agreement requiring the one-for-one replacement of the demolished public-housing units.[83] A dedication of $50 million in funding for the rebuilding was also included in the HUD-approved Conciliation Agreement between the State of Texas and TxLIHIS/ Texas Appleseed.[84]

The support from HUD and the state of Texas has been essential to moving the process of rebuilding Galveston's public housing forward in the face of continued public opposition, including a 2012 municipal election that was popularly considered a referendum on public housing. In summer 2012, HUD sent a letter signed by three HUD assistant secretaries threatening to withhold $586 million in federal disaster-recovery funds and other federal funds should Galveston continue to block the rebuilding of public housing, and the HUD secretary met with representatives from Galveston to express the department's commitment to rebuilding affordable housing.[85] In August, the Texas GLO suspended all of Galveston's uncommitted nonhousing funds pending an approved plan to rebuild public housing. HUD and the GLO set a deadline of September 28, 2012, for the city to submit a rebuilding plan. The city council proceeded to approve a plan to rebuild public housing at the 11th hour—on September 28.[86]

The legal and policy advocacy in Galveston has been coordinated with the Galveston County Collaborating Organizations (GCCO), including Gulf Coast Interfaith, Galveston County Coalition for Justice, and the local NAACP chapter. In addition to several years of organizing and advocacy, GCCO was instrumental in negotiating the public-housing rebuilding plan that was ultimately approved by the Galveston City Council.

Lower Rio Grande Valley. Local advocacy in the Lower Rio Grande Valley of South Texas following Hurricane Dolly has centered on three areas: (1) addressing drainage and recurrent flooding issues in the colonias; (2) ensuring that low-income families, regardless of national origin, have access to housing rehabilitation and rebuilding funds; and (3) ensuring that low-income residents can participate in the employment opportunities generated by the investment of the Hurricane Dolly federal disaster-recovery funds through the enforcement of Section 3 of the Housing and Urban Development Act of 1968.[87]

Colonias are unincorporated communities along the Texas-Mexico border where limited infrastructure and substandard housing coincide with extremely high levels of poverty. Many colonias have inadequate drainage infrastructure and are thus extremely vulnerable to flooding.[88] Residents of colonias had long identified the recurrent flooding as one of their top concerns, and Texas's Analysis of Impediments listed the flooding as an impediment to fair housing in the area.[89]

At the local level, advocacy efforts around hurricane rebuilding activities were led by the Equal Voice Network (EVN) in South Texas, a coalition of nonprofits that advance the concerns of colonia residents. The coalition, which was started in 2008 through the Marguerite Casey Foundation's movement-building efforts, includes local community organizations, community development corporations, and other nonprofits. Staff from EVN's community groups met regularly with colonias residents, and together they decided to engage in the political process for the allocation of the funds and to press for programs and funding that would benefit their communities.

After Hidalgo County proposed using CDBG-DR funds from Hurricane Dolly on a big regional drainage project, EVN worked with statewide advocates and the local legal aid office, Texas RioGrande Legal Aid, to better understand Hidalgo County's proposal and to advocate for infrastructure improvements in the colonias.[90] Texas RioGrande Legal Aid hired an engineer to examine which areas the county's regional drainage project would serve. The engineer found that the project would not benefit the colonias but instead would benefit the higher-income incorporated areas. Working closely with the community groups, Texas Appleseed and TxLIHIS—which had legal leverage under the Conciliation Agreement—objected with the State of Texas to Hidalgo County's proposed drainage project on the ground that the project did not affirmatively further fair housing.

In January 2011, a coalition of more than 40 residents from 10 colonias spoke at a meeting of the Lower Rio Grande Development Council—the regional COG in charge of allocating a range of infrastructure funds in the region. In the public-comments session, the residents repeated over and over again their distress at the state of drainage infrastructure in their neighborhoods and frustration that little, if any, of the Round One CDBG-DR funds had been used to remedy this situation.[91] The coalition also began a coordinated, visible presence at the Hidalgo County Commissioners Court meetings, advocating for CDBG-DR funds to be spent on drainage infrastructure in colonias. Organizers also set up regular meetings for residents to discuss drainage problems with individual commissioners.

As a result of the combined state-level advocacy and local organizing efforts, the Hidalgo County Commissioners Court agreed to allocate more than $14 million in CDBG-DR funds into drainage infrastructure in the colonias damaged by

Hurricane Dolly.[92] A collateral benefit of this process is that residents are now more mobilized and engaged in regional and county-level decision making and, thus, better positioned to offer input into other funding allocations that could impact their communities. For example, as a result of the advocacy work from Hurricane Dolly, the housing committee of the Lower Rio Grande Valley Development Council now includes a representative from a colonias-based organization, and groups are now organizing around a drainage bond issue.

Community planners have been a crucial part of the local advocacy efforts in South Texas. Advocacy groups obtained grant funds from a private foundation to hire planning professionals who led workshops with residents and prepared long-term revitalization plans for seven colonias based on residents' needs and interests. The seven plans address major planning issues identified by residents, such as drainage, street lighting, trash collection, and housing repairs. These plans will serve as a blueprint for future organizing and advocacy efforts.

The second major focus of advocates in South Texas has been ensuring that new jobs arising out of the recovery efforts extend to low-income residents in the affected communities, as required by Section 3 of the Housing and Urban Development Act of 1968.[93] As discussed further in the next section, Section 3 laws and regulations require that low-income residents benefit from employment, job training, and contracting opportunities arising out of certain HUD-funded projects. These Section 3 requirements have special significance in the South Texas colonias, given the high unemployment rates and low wages in these areas.[94] Local advocates have been working with the regional COG, as well as the county and city governments in the area, to ensure that the governmental entities comply with Section 3 and that they develop Section 3 plans maximizing the ability of low-income residents to benefit from the new jobs created by the disaster-recovery efforts, in addition to annual CDBG spending and other HUD funding allocations.

Through public information requests, advocates investigated Hidalgo County's Section 3 compliance, reporting, and planning. They found that the county had no process in place for adequately tracking Section 3 compliance and had failed to identify in its annual report to HUD a single new job hire for eligible residents under Section 3. Advocates also found major discrepancies in the Section 3–related information that Hidalgo County reported to HUD and found that the county did not document any impediments it encountered in trying to provide employment or economic opportunities for low- and very-low-income residents, as required by federal law and regulations.

Supported by advocacy organizations, low-income residents met several times with political leaders and the head of Hidalgo County's Urban County Program to discuss past failures to comply with Section 3 and features they believed were essential to bringing Hidalgo County into compliance with its Section 3 obligations and maximizing hiring and contracting opportunities for low-income residents. They asked for the inclusion of the following elements in the County's Section 3 plan:

- ***Work hours:*** Low-income residents from the area must complete at least 30 percent of the work hours on projects funded by all CDBG funds (not just CDBG-DR funds) and other Section 3–covered funds. This requirement was meant to ensure that Hidalgo County met goals not only on the percentage of new hires but also took into consideration the percentage of work hours actually completed by local low-income residents. Without this provision, if contractors proceed to do the disaster-recovery work with existing staff, there are no guarantees that local low-income residents will benefit from the work opportunities.
- ***Pipeline to Jobs:*** As a condition of receiving disaster-recovery funds, contractors should be required to report their hiring needs to the local tri-county workforce development board, Workforce Solutions, and to utilize the board's referral list of eligible job seekers when hiring workers. Workforce Solutions is one of 28 government-supported nonprofits, each operating in different regions of Texas, that link employers with job seekers. Unemployed and underemployed people commonly contact the organization when looking for jobs. Providing for a common registry of available jobs creates an accessible pipeline by which unemployed and other job seekers in the community can easily locate open positions funded with the disaster-recovery funds. These job seekers can also easily register with the agency to contact them when specific types of jobs become available. In addition, Workforce Solutions can conduct outreach in the community to find people with certain qualifications for open positions and can follow up with employers about any problems they confront with workers. Finally, Workforce Solutions will track the hiring as a way to show compliance with the Section 3 program.
- ***Advisory Committee:*** A regional advisory committee should be created to monitor the county's Section 3 compliance and to provide input to the county on implementing a successful Section 3 program. The committee should consist of Section 3 residents, representatives from organizations serving Section 3 residents, and elected officials from the area. The proposed committee would meet monthly to review the county's Section 3 reports and programs and suggest program improvements.

Hidalgo County proceeded to adopt its own Section 3 plan that failed to include any of the advocates' recommendations. After failing to address advocates' concerns about ongoing Section 3 violations, TOP and TxLIHIS, represented by Texas Rio-Grande Legal Aid, filed an administrative complaint with HUD.[95]

In contrast to Hidalgo County's response, the regional COG responded favorably to the Equal Voice Network's advocacy efforts and, in 2012, adopted a regional Section 3 plan that incorporated several of the advocates' recommendations. The plan sets up clear hiring and contracting goals, develops a pipeline of Section 3 workers and businesses, and requires outreach to low-income families.[96] The COG also agreed to set up an advisory committee to guide implementation of the Section 3 plan; the committee includes representatives from community organizations, local businesses, and small contractors.

In addition to preparing the administrative complaint with HUD against Hidalgo County's Section 3 plan, lawyers with Texas RioGrande Legal Aid (TRLA) played a number of active roles to support local community groups in their job advocacy efforts.[97] Lawyers worked with policy analysts to help local community organizations understand Section 3 law and participated in negotiations on behalf of advocates with government officials concerning the adoption of the community-driven Section 3 plans.

VI. Nuts and Bolts of Section 3 Law

The following three areas of law have been critical to the Texas advocates in their work to ensure that the 2008 Texas hurricane disaster-recovery funds are spent transparently and equitably: (1) CDBG laws; (2) Affirmatively Furthering Fair Housing (AFFH) laws; and (3) Section 3 of the Housing and Community Development Act of 1968. A further discussion of CDBG and AFFH laws is available in chapters 1 and 15. The following discussion focuses on the nuts and bolts of Section 3 of the Housing and Community Development Act of 1968, which is commonly referred to in the community development field as Section 3.

Section 3 is one of the most uncharted areas of opportunity for community development lawyers to further equitable and responsive investment of federal disaster recovery funds.[98] The focus of Section 3 is to ensure that new employment and contracting opportunities created by the investment of HUD funds benefit a community's low-income residents. Local and state entities that fail to comply with Section 3 can be prohibited from receiving future HUD funding.[99]

Historically, Section 3 has been practically ignored by HUD and largely underutilized by community development advocates.[100] However, in October 2009, HUD announced its intent to provide for more robust oversight and enforcement of Section 3 compliance, opening up new opportunities for community development lawyers to advocate in this area and help bring about Section 3 reforms in local jurisdictions.[101] On the heels of a large federal disaster when millions, if not billions, of dollars in federal funding will be invested in a region, generating thousands of employment opportunities, more robust Section 3 advocacy has the potential for transformative change.[102]

Funding recipients subject to Section 3 must ensure, to the "greatest extent feasible," that new employment and contracting opportunities arising from the expenditure of HUD funds are provided to Section 3–covered residents and businesses. What this means on the hiring front, when new employees are hired in a project utilizing HUD funding covered by Section 3, is that preference should be given to filling these positions with low- and very-low-income residents—at least until the covered recipient meets HUD's safe harbor regulations, which are discussed further on the next page.

The Section 3 regulations further require that preferences be given to specific subsets of Section 3 residents, depending on the program. For CDBG-funded projects, the highest priority must be given to hiring low-income residents in the service area or neighborhood where the project is located.[103] To further facilitate the ability of Section 3 businesses to obtain contracts for HUD-funded projects, the HUD regulations also suggest, but do not require, that contract work be broken out into smaller units.[104]

The HUD-funded programs that trigger Section 3 requirements include CDBG-DR funds, as well as annual CDBG, HOME, public-housing funds and myriad other HUD programs.[105] Projects that must comply with Section 3 include housing construction, demolition, and rehabilitation, and other public construction projects such as roads, sewers, and community centers.[106] Except for projects utilizing public housing funding, two classes of funding recipients are exempted from Section 3: public and private agencies receiving $200,000 or less in funding for Section 3 projects, and contractors and subcontractors receiving $100,000 or less in funding for Section 3 projects.[107]

A Section 3–covered resident—a resident who receives hiring and contracting priorities under Section 3—is someone who is a public housing resident or a low- or very-low-income resident from the metropolitan area or nonmetropolitan county where the Section 3–covered project is located.[108] A business covered by Section 3 must meet one of the following three requirements: (1) majority ownership by Section 3 residents; (2) employment of Section 3 residents for at least 30 percent of the business's permanent, full-time staff; or (3) a commitment to subcontract to Section 3 businesses more than 25 percent of the dollar amount of an awarded contract.[109]

The Section 3 regulations set up safe harbors for establishing compliance with the "greatest extent feasible" hiring and contracting requirement. A covered recipient of CDBG funding can meet this safe harbor for the year if each of the following three benchmarks is met:

1. The recipient awards at least 10 percent of covered construction-related contracts to Section 3 businesses.
2. At least 30 percent of new hires for the year from covered projects are Section 3 residents.
3. The recipient awards at least 3 percent of covered nonconstruction contracts to Section 3 businesses.[110]

The 10 percent and 3 percent benchmarks for awarding contracts to Section 3 businesses are calculated by looking at the total dollar amount of the contracts versus the number of contracts.[111] For example, if $20 million is spent on Section 3–covered construction contracts, at least $2 million must be awarded in contracts to Section 3 businesses. If a recipient is unsuccessful in meeting the safe harbor benchmarks, the recipient must demonstrate why the benchmarks were unattainable. A jurisdiction's failure to meet the safe harbor requirements gives advocates an opportunity to force the jurisdiction to demonstrate what it has done to try to meet the benchmarks, and to push for a Section 3 plan that is more likely to result in meaningful compliance.

Funding recipients must also adopt procedures to ensure that low-income residents are aware of economic opportunities arising from Section 3 projects. Section 3 residents and businesses need to be notified about the new job training, job openings, and contract opportunities generated by the Section 3 projects.[112]

Both state and local government agencies must file an annual report with HUD that documents compliance with Section 3.[113] In 2009, HUD announced that the failure to file a Section 3 report can result in disbarment from HUD programs.[114] Each report must include the percentage of hours worked that were allocated to Section 3 residents, the total number of Section 3 businesses receiving construction and nonconstruction contracts, and the total dollar amount awarded to these businesses. The report must also include a narrative of all the measures that the agency took to comply with Section 3.[115]

State and county agencies and consortia of agencies that distribute HUD funds have additional requirements under Section 3. The agencies must file an annual report documenting all the Section 3 actions taking place in their jurisdiction, including those taken by sub-recipients. They must also assist covered sub-recipients and contractors with achieving compliance and must monitor their compliance.[116]

Governmental entities covered by Section 3 should adopt a Section 3 plan as part of their action plan for expending disaster-recovery funds, as well as HUD's five-year consolidated plan and annual action plan processes. The Section 3 plan should outline how the jurisdiction will conduct outreach, training, and education of stakeholders; what kind of job training programs for residents will be set up; and how Section 3 compliance will be documented. The plan should provide clear guidance to city staff and contractors on expectations and procedures concerning Section 3 compliance.[117]

There are a number of best practices that have arisen around the country for the development and implementation of effective Section 3 plans:[118]

1. Consolidate inside one city department all targeted hiring and contracting programs for public works projects, thus consolidating implementation of Section 3 programs with minority/woman/disadvantaged/small-business programs and other related targeted hiring programs for businesses and job seekers.
2. Designate a Section 3 coordinator to oversee the implementation of the Section 3 plan and to serve as a liaison between contractors and Section 3 residents and businesses.
3. Make the hiring of low-income residents a core operating principle in issuing and managing disaster-recovery contracts.
4. Conduct aggressive outreach to local businesses, job training programs, residents, and workers groups on Section 3 hiring and contracting opportunities.

5. Promote interagency collaboration of Section 3–related efforts.
6. Create clear hiring goals and adopt concrete action steps for reaching those goals.
7. Develop strong links with local job-training programs to prepare residents for jobs coming online as a result of the investment of federal funds.
8. Create a registry of Section 3 businesses.
9. Offer technical assistance to sub-recipients and contractors to assist them in understanding their Section 3 obligations and with ways to achieve compliance.
10. Require that targets be met on the percentage of work hours completed by Section 3 residents in addition to relying on percentage of job hires filled by the residents, given that some contracts may end up resulting in no new job hires and thus no benefits to Section 3 residents.

VII. Lessons Learned

While Texas's long-term disaster-recovery programs are ongoing, the work of advocates and government agencies in Texas over the past four-plus years of rebuilding efforts presents a number of valuable, practical lessons for how state and federal agencies, advocates, and local communities can achieve more equitable and effective outcomes in the delivery of long-term rebuilding assistance.

Integrate civil rights and community development goals. Government officials, advocates, and policymakers need to ensure that long-term disaster recovery programs incorporate both a community development and civil rights focus. This means looking beyond just the rebuilding of individual structures, to looking at the rebuilding of distressed communities in a way that supports their ability to become vibrant and safe neighborhoods offering decent infrastructure, safe and affordable homes, and access to important community services. This broader focus also means providing opportunities for victims to move and rebuild in higher-opportunity areas. Rebuilding efforts should also pay special attention to redressing the inequitable distribution of infrastructure that makes low-income communities more vulnerable to future natural disasters. As discussed earlier in this chapter, many of the issues that low-income families faced following Hurricanes Ike and Dolly were exacerbated by long-standing disparities in access to local infrastructure.

Ensure effective local community engagement. To adequately address the needs and concerns of low-income residents, a long-term rebuilding program needs to include the residents as actively engaged participants. However, the ability to effectively engage the community is limited when there is not already some sort of community organizing infrastructure in place, and building an effective public-input process takes resources and a tremendous amount of time. Foundations should consider allocating funds for building community organizing infrastructure in disaster-recovery areas where such infrastructure is not already in existence.

Adopt transparency measures. Ensuring the equitable distribution of disaster recovery funds is difficult without transparency: knowing where and how the funds have been spent in the past, and where the government is proposing the funds be spent in the current recovery program. Ideally, transparency measures are put in place before a disaster strikes.

Get involved early, but stay on for the long haul. Soon after a disaster strikes, when a community is still focused on basic needs like access to food and emergency shelter, it is easy to lose sight of the long-term recovery process. However, many essential decisions related to the long-term recovery process are made within the six months after a disaster strikes, such as how FEMA will assess long-term recovery needs in an area, what types of waivers HUD will be granting to states, and how a state plans to allocate funds to different communities and programs. To influence these decisions, advocates, government agencies, and other stakeholders need to be actively engaged within the first few months after a disaster is declared in an area, and all stakeholders need to be sure they have a seat at the table of any task force or advisory group that is created to assist with disaster-recovery efforts. Once involved, stakeholders need to be prepared to stay involved for the long haul, knowing that long-term disaster-recovery programs can take as long as five or more years to fully implement and that legal and policy advocacy will probably be needed throughout the implementation process.

Offer training and technical assistance. One of the main barriers to disaster recovery is when local governments lack the capacity to administer a recovery program. This is a common issue with housing rehabilitation programs, which require a high level of administrative sophistication. An effective training and technical assistance program can go a long way in ensuring that governmental entities have the capacity to effectively administer disaster-recovery programs. Stakeholders should try to bring in national experts early in the rebuilding process to offer their expertise.

Build from prior experiences. Rather than reinvent the wheel every time a disaster strikes, stakeholders should work together to institutionalize programs and policies that incorporate best practices and lessons learned from prior disasters. For example, instead of creating numerous new housing programs from scratch every time a disaster strikes, the federal government and states should have in place an off-the-shelf housing program that communities could quickly deploy. The same goes for advocacy in terms of building from prior experiences: Texas advocates benefited not only from their previous experiences with disaster recovery in Texas following prior hurricanes but also from the experiences of advocates in Louisiana and Mississippi who also used fair housing requirements to address problems in their state disaster recovery programs.

Build collaborative relationships. The most effective disaster programs occur when a broad range of stakeholders can build strong working relationships together, including advocates, local community groups, foundations, elected officials, and staff at all levels of government.

Recognize the benefits and challenges of local government involvement in disaster recovery. The Texas disaster recovery experience brought to bear the strengths and the weaknesses of each government sector that played a role in the disaster recovery process. At a local government level, while local officials have the most direct connections to local communities impacted by a disaster and should best grasp local redevelopment priorities, the Texas recovery efforts highlighted how the priorities of local government officials may not be aligned with the needs of low-income communities and residents. The Texas experience also highlights the inefficiencies, delays in services, and lack of accountability that came with the wholesale delegation to local governments of creating and running their own disaster-recovery programs, especially in regard to housing rebuilding programs that local government entities may not have the capacity to run. Any delegation to local governmental entities needs to address these deficiencies, including requiring more effective opportunities for input from low-income communities at both the planning and implementation stages of a disaster-recovery program. Moreover, to assist local governments in meeting the letter and spirit of the CDBG-DR program, the program needs to provide clearer rules on the types of housing programs and infrastructure projects that federal disaster recovery funds can be spent on in a disaster area. Finally, more robust federal and state technical assistance and oversight is needed to infuse more accountability into the program and ensure that local governments are using funds to assist poor and minority communities with their disaster-recovery needs.

Pursue a range of advocacy strategies. Rebuilding programs are ultimately political processes, and elected officials who are the ultimate arbiters of how disaster-recovery funds will be allocated face pressure from an array of interest groups seeking to influence the recovery program. Low-income community and civil rights advocates need to adopt a multifaceted strategy to impact long-term, disaster-recovery programs, including community engagement and media campaigns. However, advocates also need to recognize their limits and will need to prioritize the focus of their advocacy efforts, especially when working in a large geographic area.

When a governmental entity refuses requests to bring its disaster-recovery program into compliance with federal law, legal advocates will also need to consider what types of enforcement strategies will be most effective, which means deciding whether the focus should be administrative (via HUD or other federal agency), judicial (via the courts), or political (via local, state, and federal elected officials). In Texas, having the active support and involvement of HUD was critical in bringing about reforms to the state's long-term disaster-recovery program.

VIII. Conclusion

By building collaborations, engaging low-income residents, and providing vigorous oversight and enforcement, low-income community and civil rights advocacy organizations in Texas have worked for more than four years after the 2008 hurricanes to ensure that federal disaster-recovery funds are spent more equitably, effectively, and transparently, to reach the needs of Texas's most vulnerable populations. Although the final outcomes will not be known for several more years, the barriers that the advocates encountered, the strategies they have utilized, and the outcomes of their ongoing work provide a series of important lessons for all stakeholders in future disaster-recovery efforts. These lessons illuminate how recovery funds can be better utilized to improve the ability of the hardest-hit victims to rebuild their homes, obtain jobs, and improve their communities.

Notes

1. Governor Rick Perry et al., Texas Rebounds: Helping Our Communities Recover From the 2008 Hurricane Season 7–9 (2008), *available at* http://governor.state.tx.us/files/press-office/Texas-Rebounds-report.pdf.

2. Becca Aaronson, *Amid Finger-Pointing, Hurricane Relief Lags*, Tex. Tribune (Mar. 9, 2012), http://www.texastribune.org/2012/03/09/amid-finger-pointing-hurricane-relief-lags/.

3. *See* Lam Thuy Vo, *America's Most Expensive Storms*, Nat'l Public Radio (Oct. 31, 2012), http://www.npr.org/blogs/money/2012/10/31/163960418/americas-most-expensive-storms; Paul Huttner, *Sandy May Be 2nd Costliest USA Weather Disaster*, Minn. Public Radio (Nov. 27, 2012), http://minnesota.publicradio.org/collections/special/columns/updraft/archive/2012/11/sandy_may_be_2nd_costliest_usa.shtml.

4. Robbie Berg, Nat'l Hurricane Ctr., Tropical Cyclone Report: Hurricane Ike (AL092008) 10 (Jan. 23, 2009), *available at* http://www.nhc.noaa.gov/pdf/TCR-AL092008_Ike_3May10.pdf.

5. *See* Pub. Util. Comm'n of Tex., Self-Evaluation Report: A Report to the Texas Sunset Advisory Commission 31 (Sept. 4, 2009), *available at* http://www.puc.texas.gov/agency/resources/reports/sunset/2009_PUC_Texas_Self-Eval_Rpt.pdf.

6. Richard J. Pasch & Todd B. Kimberlain, Nat'l Hurricane Ctr., Tropical Cyclone Report: Hurricane Dolly (AL042008) 3 (Jan. 22, 2009), *available at* http://www.nhc.noaa.gov/pdf/TCR-AL042008_Dolly.pdf.

7. Lower Rio Grande Valley Dev. Council, Needs Assessment: Lower Rio Grande Valley Hurricane Dolly Recovery Program 2 (2011), *available at* http://www.lrgvdc.org/downloads/disaster-recovery/LRGVDC_Needs_Assessment_Combined_PDF_(Complete).pdf.

8. *See, e.g.*, Corey Ryan, *Valley Learns Lessons from Dolly Flooding,* Valley Morning Star (July 18, 2009), *available at* http://www.valleymorningstar.com/news/local_news/article_8b0793cb-29ff-5641-94fb-3135746f00e7.html; Jared Janes, *FEMA Finalizing Reimbursements for Dolly Response and Recovery*, Brownsville Herald, April 28, 2010, *available at* http://www.brownsvilleherald.com/news/valley/article_3dbad734-70b6-579b-8965-f57213c62882.html.

9. The colonias are unincorporated subdivisions in Texas near the U.S.-Mexico border that have historically lacked adequate infrastructure and are occupied primarily by poor families living in substandard housing.

10. *What Is a Colonia?*, Tex. Sec'y of State, http://www.sos.state.tx.us/border/colonias/what_colonia.shtml (last visited Jan. 16, 2013).

11. *Background on the Colonias*, Tex. Dep't of Hous. & Cmty. Affairs, http://www.tdhca.state.tx.us/oci/background.jsp (last visited Jan. 16, 2013).

12. A. Christina Wild, Hurricane Ike: Rehabilitation of Affordable Rental Units on Galveston Island 12, 18 (2009), *available at* http://soa.utexas.edu/files/csd/CSD_AH_IS_Hurricane.pdf.

13. *Id.*; *see also* Forrest Wilder, *The Castaways: Can Galveston's Black Community Survive the Community's Comeback?*, Tex. Observer (Dec. 12, 2008), http://www.texasobserver.org/archives/item/15523-2918-the-castaways-can-galvestons-black-community-survive-the-islands-comeback.

14. Wilder, *supra* note 13.

15. Wild, *supra* note 12.

16. Wild, *supra* note 12.

17. Pub. L. No. 93-288, as amended; 42 U.S.C. §§ 5121–5207 (2012).

18. 42 U.S.C. §§ 5121–5207 (2012). See also FEMA's website for a breakdown of the presidential major disaster declaration process at http://www.fema.gov/disaster-process-disaster-aid-programs.

19. *See* FED. EMERGENCY MGMT. AGENCY, 9327.1-PR, PRELIMINARY DAMAGE ASSESSMENT FOR INDIVIDUAL ASSISTANCE OPERATIONS MANUAL I-4 (Apr. 2005), *available at* http://www.ok.gov/OEM/documents/FEMA-PDA%20SOP%20SM%203-26-05.pdf.

20. EUGENE BOYD, CONG. RESEARCH SERV., RL33330, COMMUNITY DEVELOPMENT BLOCK GRANT FUNDS IN DISASTER RELIEF AND RECOVERY (2010), *available at* http://assets.opencrs.com/rpts/RL33330_20110921.pdf.

21. While most CDBG-DR funds are awarded to states, local governments and Indian tribes may also be eligible, depending on the language of the supplemental appropriation. *See CDBG Disaster Recovery Assistance*, U.S. DEP'T OF HOUS. & URBAN DEV., http://portal.hud.gov/hudportal/HUD?src=/program_offices/comm_planning/communitydevelopment/programs/drsi (last visited Apr. 9, 2013).

22. 42 U.S.C. §§ 4321, 5301(c).

23. Consolidated Security, Disaster Assistance, and Continuing Appropriations Act of 2008, Pub. L. No. 110-329.

24. *Community Planning and Development*, U.S. DEP'T OF HOUS. & URBAN DEV., http://portal.hud.gov/hudportal/HUD?src=/program_offices/comm_planning/ (last visited Jan. 18, 2013).

25. Press Release, U.S. Dep't of Hous. and Urban Dev., Preston Announces $2.1 Billion in Disaster Assistance to 13 States and Puerto Rico Impacted by 2008 Storms (Nov. 26, 2008), *available at* http://archives.hud.gov/news/2008/pr08-179.cfm.

26. TEX. DEP'T OF RURAL AFFAIRS, STATE OF TEXAS PLAN FOR DISASTER RECOVERY—AMENDMENT NO. 1 (Sept. 30, 2009) ("For all aspects of this Action Plan Amendment, local choice shall be emphasized, and the COGs shall have the right . . . to make determinations as to the allocations of funds within their regions among housing, infrastructure, and economic development programs."). The COGs are voluntary associations of local governments formed under Texas law with a focus on regional planning and fostering local government collaboration on regional problems. The COGs have limited authority and no ability to levy taxes or incur debt. The COGs are governed by a board of elected officials from each of the participating local governments.

27. *See* Method of Distribution Summaries, compiled by Tex. Dep't of Rural Affairs (Aug. 19, 2009) (on file with authors). Each sub-recipient COG prepared a Method of Distribution describing how CDBG-DR funds would be sub-allocated to its constituent local government entities.

28. A total of 18 sub-recipients ended up running housing recovery programs (although it should be noted that some of these programs were run by COGs for multiple smaller sub-recipients), and even fewer sub-recipients used the funds for economic development.

29. *See* U.S. GOV'T ACCOUNTABILITY OFFICE, GAO-07-574T, GULF COAST REBUILDING: PRELIMINARY OBSERVATIONS ON PROGRESS TO DATE AND CHALLENGES FOR THE FUTURE 6 (Apr. 12, 2007), *available at* www.gao.gov/new.items/d07574t.pdf.

30. TEX. DEP'T OF HOUS. & CMTY. AFFAIRS, NO. 11-1043, INTERNAL AUDIT REPORT 10 (2001), *available at* http://www.tdhca.state.tx.us/pdf/ia/11-AuditReport-DisasterRecoveryProgram.pdf.

31. Housing Activities Application, Fort Bend County, Texas Community Development Block Grant Program: 2008 Supplemental Disaster Recovery Fund, Hurricanes Dolly and Ike, at 24 (June 23, 2009), *available at* http://www.docstoc.com/docs/91245049/AGENDA-ITEM—Download-as-PDF.

32. General Housing Activities Application: Round 2.2, submitted by Deep East Texas Council of Governments to the Texas General Land Office, at 14 (2011) (on file with authors), *available at* http://www.detcog.org.

33. Brenda Bell, *State Outsourced Allocation of Federal Disaster Recovery to Firm with Ties to Perry*, AUSTIN AM.-STATESMAN (Oct. 4, 2011), *available at* http://www.statesman.com/news/texas-politics/state-outsourced-allocation-of-federal-disaster-recovery-funds-1893739.html.

34. *Chambers County*, TEX. STATE HISTORICAL ASS'N, http://www.tshaonline.org/handbook/online/articles/hcc09 (last visited Jan. 23, 2013); Rick Casey, Commentary, *Is God Good at Politics?*, HOUSTON CHRON. (Sept. 5, 2009), http://www.chron.com/news/casey/article/Is-God-good-at-politics-1731841.php.

35. Bell, *supra* note 33.

36. See section V for a discussion of the complaints.

37. TEX. DEP'T OF RURAL AFFAIRS, *supra* note 26, at 19.

38. Partial Method of Distribution for Round Two Disaster Recovery Supplemental Allocation, submitted by the Lower Rio Grande Valley Dev. Council to the Tex. Dep't of Rural Affairs (Aug. 26, 2010), *available at* http://www.lrgvdc.org/downloads/disaster-recovery/REVISED_Partial_MOD_LRGVDC_10-06-2010.pdf.

39. These examples were drawn from Round 2.2 Applications for Disaster Recovery Supplemental Allocation submitted by governmental jurisdictions to the Tex. Dep't of Rural Affairs and the Tex. General Land Office and reviewed by Texas Appleseed and Texas Low Income Housing Information Service (on file with authors).

40. *See CDBG Disaster Recovery Round 1 Program*, CITY OF HOUSTON HOUS. & CMTY. DEV., http://www.houstontx.gov/housing/ikerecovery2009.html (last visited Jan. 20, 2013).

41. Lise Olsen & Yang Wang, *Audit Finds City Approved Dubious Housing Grants*, HOUSTON CHRON. (Oct. 21, 2012), http://www.chron.com/news/houston-texas/houston/article/Audit-finds-city-approved-dubious-housing-grants-3969648.php.

42. Leigh Jones, *Meeting on Housing Plan Ends in Shouting Match*, GALVESTON DAILY NEWS (Oct. 20, 2009), http://www.galvestondailynews.com/news/article_e438383b-96da-57ee-a66e-1979283aa5c1.html; Rhiannon Meyers, *GHA Critics Circulate Rap Video*, GALVESTON DAILY NEWS (Feb. 25, 2010), http://www.galvestondailynews.com/news/article_a206c7e4-45cc-5b1c-8bcb-a1eae13eba29.html.

43. Robbie Whelan, *A Texas-Size Housing Fight*, WALL ST. J. (Aug. 3, 2012), http://online.wsj.com/article/SB10000872396390443545504577563271568716862.html; Harvey Rice, *Galveston OKs Housing Plan at 11th Hour*, HOUSTON CHRON. (Sept. 28, 2012), http://www.chron.com/news/houston-texas/article/Galveston-OKs-housing-plan-at-11th-hour-3903449.php.

44. A GAO report summarizing lessons learned from past disasters highlighted the need to build local capacity for recovery, stating: "State and local governments need certain capacities to effectively make use of federal assistance, including having sufficient financial resources and technical know-how." U.S. GOV'T ACCOUNTABILITY OFFICE, GAO-08-1120, DISASTER RECOVERY: PAST EXPERIENCES OFFER INSIGHTS FOR RECOVERING FROM HURRICANES IKE AND GUSTAV AND OTHER RECENT NATURAL DISASTERS (2008).

45. TEX. DEP'T OF HOUS. & CMTY. AFFAIRS, BOARD MATERIALS 540–42 (May 5, 2011), *available at* http://www.tdhca.state.tx.us/pdf/agendas/20110505-book-20110428.pdf.

46. TEX. DEP'T OF HOUS. & CMTY. AFFAIRS, NO. 11-1043, AUDIT DEPARTMENT REPORT (June 2011), *available at* http://www.tdhca.state.tx.us/pdf/ia/11-AuditReport-DisasterRecoveryProgram.pdf.

47. Debra Ballen, *Vulnerable Populations*, INST. FOR BUS. & HOME SAFETY (March 2009), http://www.oregon.gov/OSP/SFM/docs/LEPC/Vulnerable_Populations_Reducing_Disaster_Related_Losses_March_2009_IBHS.pdf; *see also* Shannon Van Zandt et. al, *Mapping Social Vulnerability to Enhance Housing and Neighborhood Resilience*, 22 HOUSING POL'Y DEBATE 29, 29–55 (2012).

48. E-mail from Ericka Lopez, FEMA External Affairs, U.S. Dep't of Homeland Sec., to Mike Snyder, Houston Chron. (June 26, 2009, 4:09 PM EST) (on file with authors).

49. Harvey Rice, *Ike Aid Rejections Have FEMA Changing Its Ways*, HOUSTON CHRON. (Feb. 10, 2011), http://www.chron.com/news/houston-texas/article/Ike-aid-rejections-have-FEMA-changing-its-ways-1682522.php.

50. *See* 74 Fed. Reg. 7244, 7246 (Feb. 13, 2009).

51. For CDBG-DR funds, HUD has authority to waive the CDBG regulatory requirements for a formal public hearing and reduce the time for public comment. Even though HUD waived the public hearing requirement for the Texas disaster recovery program, a federal register notice issued by HUD still required that Texas provide opportunities for "reasonable public notice, appraisal, examination, and comment on the activities proposed for the use of CDBG disaster recovery grant funds." 74 Fed. Reg. 7244, 7249–50 (Feb. 13, 2009).

52. Texas filed an initial Action Plan for Disaster Recovery in March 2009, covering Round One of the CDBG-DR funds allocated for the 2008 Hurricanes. The state's action plan covering the Round Two funds was technically an amendment to the Round One action plan. As of November 2012, the state had filed three additional amendments to its action plan. *See Hurricanes Ike & Dolly*, TEX. GEN. LAND OFFICE, http://www.glo.texas.gov/GLO/disaster-recovery/actionplans/ike-dolly.html (last visited Apr. 9, 2013).

53. Administrative Complaint submitted by Texas Low Income Housing Information Services and Texas Appleseed, to U.S. Dep't of Hous. & Urban Dev. (Oct. 28, 2009), *available at* http://www.texasappleseed.net/index.php?option=com_docman&task=doc_download&gid=192&Itemid=.

54. Letter from Mercedes Márquez, Asst. Sec'y for Cmty. Planning & Dev., U.S. Dep't of Hous. & Urban Dev., to Rick Perry, Governor, State of Tex. (Nov. 10, 2009), *available at* http://txlihis.files.wordpress.com/2009/11/txikeamend-11102009-1.pdf.

55. Fair Housing Complaint Against the State of Texas, submitted by Texas Low Income Housing Information Services to U.S. Dep't of Hous. & Urban Dev. (Dec. 1, 2009), *available at* http://www.texasappleseed.net/index.php?option=com_docman&task=doc_download&gid=291&Itemid=.

56. 74 Fed. Reg. 7244, 7247, 7249–50 (Feb. 13, 2009).

57. HUD gave Texas permission to lower the targeting requirement to 50 percent, a common practice allowed by federal statute. *See* Consolidated Security, Disaster Assistance, and Continuing Appropriations Act 2009, Pub. L. No. 110-329, 122 Stat. 3574 (2008); *see also* 74 Fed. Reg. 7244.

58. Márquez, *supra* note 54.

59. *Id.*

60. Márquez, *supra* note 54.

61. Fair Housing Complaint, *supra* note 55.

62. Conciliation Agreement, Tex. Low Income Hous. Info. Servs. v. State of Texas, Case No. 06-10-0410-8 and No. 06-10-0410-9 (May 25, 2010), *available at* http://portal.hud.gov/hudportal/documents/huddoc?id=DOC_4305.pdf.

63. *Id.*

64. As part of the Conciliation Agreement, the State of Texas agreed to update its statewide Analysis of Impediments (AI) and to ensure that local governments' expenditures were consistent with the state's updated AI. In order to give the state time to update its AI without halting rebuilding efforts, the agreement allowed the state to proceed with spending $458 million in funding, but provided Texas Appleseed and Texas Low Income Housing Information Services with the right to put a hold on specific expenditures from the $458 million carve out if the expenditures violated fair housing guidelines.

65. Tex. Gen. Land Office, Appendix A - FHAST Form Guide, *available at* http://www.glo.texas.gov/GLO/_documents/disaster-recovery/fair-housing-issues/fhast/appendix-a-fhast-form-guide.pdf.

66. A copy of the form in English and Spanish is available on the General Land Office's website. *See FHAST*, Tex. Gen. Land Office, http://www.glo.texas.gov/GLO/disaster-recovery/fair-housing-issues/fhast.html (last visited Apr. 9, 2013).

67. These requirements apply to the expenditure of $1.7 billion in Round Two funds. The process of distributing those funds is still under way.

68. Letter from Rick Perry, Governor, State of Texas, to Shaun Donovan, Sec'y, U.S. Dep't of Hous. and Urban Dev. (June 17, 2011) (on file with authors).

69. Mike Snyder & Matt Schwartz, *Living in Neglect: Hasty Annexation Left a Legacy of Blighted Neighborhoods*, Houston Chron., Nov. 17, 2002, at A1.

70. Tex. Org. Project, http://www.organizetexas.org (last visited Jan. 23, 2013).

71. *See* Chris Moran, *Protestors Say City Slow to Repair Ike-Damaged Houses,* Houston Chron. (Sept. 13, 2011), http://www.chron.com/news/hurricanes/article/Protesters-say-city-slow-to-repair-Ike-damaged-2169325.php; Debra Walker, Opinion, *It's Finally Time to Get Rid of Those Post-Ike Blue Tarps,* Houston Chron. (July 27, 2011), http://www.chron.com/opinion/outlook/article/It-s-finally-time-to-get-rid-of-those-post-Ike-2081377.php; John Henneberger, *On 3rd Anniversary 200 Tell Houston City Council Reforms Are Needed in Hurricane Ike Recovery Program*, Tex. Housers Blog (Sept. 14, 2011), http://texashousers.net/2011/09/14/on-3rd-anniversary-200-tell-houston-city-council-reforms-are-needed-in-hurricane-ike-recovery-program/.

72. *See* Kevin Jewell, *Houston Town Hall on Disaster Single Family Home Repair*, Tex. Housers Blog (May 21, 2011), http://texashousers.net/2011/05/26/houston-town-hall-on-disaster-single-family-home-repair/.

73. *See* Mike Morris, *Houston Mayor Agrees to Put More Ike Funds Toward Houses*, Houston Chron. (Dec. 6, 2011), http://www.chron.com/news/houston-texas/article/Parker-agrees-to-put-more-Ike-funds-toward-houses-2353072.php; Texas Organizing Project & Houston Mayor Annise Parker, Statement of Principles Regarding Single Family Home Repair (Dec. 6, 2011) (on file with authors).

74. *See* Chris Moran, *City Aiming $151M in Ike Funds at Neighborhood Revival*, Houston Chron. (May 9, 2012), http://www.chron.com/news/houston-texas/article/City-aiming-151M-in-Ike-funds-at-neighborhood-3547207.php; *$151 Million in Neighborhood Improvements*, Tex. Org. Project Blog (July 23, 2012, 12:09 PM), http://www.organizetexas.org/blog?page=2.

75. Mayor Annise Parker, *Mayor Parker and HUD Announce Target Areas to Receive $151 Million in Disaster Recovery Funds*, YouTube (May 9, 2012), http://www.youtube.com/watch?v=RNZap1vvHFE; Press Release, City of Houston, Mayor Parker, HUD, Community Leaders Announce Target Areas to Receive $151M In Disaster Recovery Funds (May 9, 2012), *available at* http://www.houstontx.gov/mayor/press/20120509.html; Moran, *supra* note 74.

76. Prior to Ike, Galveston's public housing residents were 85 percent minority and 72 percent African-American.

77. Wild, *supra* note 12.

78. The African-American community in Galveston lost population at three times the rate of the white community between 2000 and 2010: the African-American population declined by 36.7 percent, the white population by 11.4 percent. Jason Reece et al., Galveston After Ike: Moving Together Toward a Full Recovery 5 (2011), *available at* http://kirwaninstitute.osu.edu/report-galveston-after-ike/.

79. Dolph Tillotson, Editorial, *GHA's Public Housing Plan a Recipe for Disaster*, Galveston Daily News (October 4, 2009), http://www.galvestondailynews.com/opinion/columns/article_916f7710-1aab-5003-a244-6caf9e469794.html.

80. Harvey Rice, *Critics Say New Galveston Mayor Can't Block Public Housing*, Houston Chron., July 2, 2012, http://www.chron.com/news/houston-texas/article/Critics-say-new-Galveston-mayor-can-t-block-3679982.php.

81. Rhiannon Meyers, *Complaint Halts Planned Public Housing Demolition in Galveston,* KHOU .COM (Aug. 15, 2009), *available at* www.khou.com/news/local/65999727.html.

82. Administrative Complaint submitted by Lone Star Legal Aid to the U.S. Dep't of Hous. & Urban Dev., *in re* Oleander Homes (TX 017001) and Palm Terrace Apartments (TX 107006), (March 2, 2009) (on file with authors).

83. Settlement Agreement and Replacement Plan, *in re* Oleander Homes (TX 017001) and Palm Terrace Apartments (TX 107006) (Mar. 13, 2009) (on file with authors).

84. Conciliation Agreement, *supra* note 62.

85. Letter from Sandra B. Henriquez, Asst. Sec'y for Pub. & Indian Hous., Mark Johnston, Acting Asst. Sec'y for Cmty. Planning & Dev., & John Trasvina, Asst. Sec'y for Fair Hous. & Equal Opp., U.S. Dep't of Hous. & Urban Dev., to Lewis Rosen, Mayor of Galveston (July 1, 2012) (on file with authors).

86. Harvey Rice, *Galveston OKs Housing Plan at 11th Hour*, HOUSTON CHRON. (Sep. 28, 2012), http://www.chron.com/news/houston-texas/article/Galveston-OKs-housing-plan-at-11th-hour-3903449.php.

87. 12 U.S.C. § 1701u.

88. *Colonias FAQS*, TEX. SEC'Y OF STATE, http://www.sos.state.tx.us/border/colonias/faqs.shtml (last visited Jan. 23, 2013).

89. STATE OF TEXAS, ANALYSIS OF IMPEDIMENTS TO FAIR HOUSING: PHASE I, HURRICANE IMPACTED COMMUNITIES 176–77 (Mar. 2011), *available at* http://www.glo.texas.gov/GLO/_documents/disaster-recovery/fair-housing-issues/analysis-of-impediments/2011-phase-1-ai-as-approved-by-hud.pdf.

90. Hidalgo County received approximately $30 million in CDBG-DR funds for Hurricane Dolly and, in 2009, received more than $11 million in annual CDBG and HOME funding. *See Community Planning and Development Formula Allocations for FY 2009*, U.S. DEP'T OF HOUS. & URBAN DEV., *available at* http://www.hud.gov/offices/cpd/about/budget/budget09/index.cfm (last updated Feb. 18, 2010).

91. Lower Rio Grande Valley Dev. Council, Action Plan for Hurricanes Ike and Dolly Disaster Recovery, app. A (Feb. 17, 2009; Feb. 18, 2009) (Summary of Public Comments), *available at* http://www.lrgvdc.org/downloads/disaster-recovery/LRGVDC_Action_Plan_Revised_04-27-09.pdf.

92. Letter from Diana R. Serna, Exec. Dir., Hidalgo Cnty. Urban Cnty. Program, to Drew Cameron, HNTB Corp. (Oct. 19, 2011) (on file with authors); *Residents Organizing with the Equal Voice Network Win $14 Million for Drainage Improvements in Hidalgo County Colonias*, LA UNIÓN DEL PUEBLO ENTERO BLOG (Nov. 2, 2011), http://lupergv.wordpress.com/2011/11/02/residents-organizing-with-the-equal-voice-network-win-14-million-for-drainage-improvements-in-hidalgo-county-colonias/.

93. Pub. L. No. 90-448; 12 U.S.C. § 1701u. The regulations are contained at 24 C.F.R. pt. 135.

94. The unemployment rate in some colonias is more than eight times the state's rate. *Colonias FAQs*, *supra* note 88; *see also* FED. RESERVE BANK OF DALLAS, TEXAS COLONIAS: A THUMBNAIL SKETCH OF THE CONDITIONS, ISSUES, CHALLENGES, AND OPPORTUNITIES 7, *available at* http://www.dallasfed.org/assets/documents/cd/pubs/colonias.pdf.

95. Section 3 Administrative Complaint submitted by Texas Organizing Project and Texas Low Income Housing Information Services, to the Office of Fair Hous. and Equal Opp., U.S. Dep't of Hous. & Urban Dev. (April 26, 2012) (on file with authors).

96. Jared Janes, *Plan to Provide More Jobs to Local, Low-Income Workers*, MID-VALLEY TOWN CRIER, July 15, 2012, at A7.

97. For more information on roles lawyers have played in developing successful Section 3 programs and other community economic development programs, see Scott L. Cummings, *Community Economic Development as Progressive Politics: Toward a Grassroots Movement for Economic Justice*, 54 STAN. L. REV. 399, 484–87 (2001).

98. The National Housing Law Project has published *An Advocate's Guide to the HUD Section 3 Program: Creating Jobs and Economic Opportunity*, an excellent and detailed report on Section 3 that includes a write-up on Section 3's legislative and regulatory history, available at https://nhlp.org/files/03%20Sec.%203%20Guide.pdf.

99. 24 C.F.R. § 135.74(c), (d) (2012).

100. OFFICE OF INSPECTOR GEN., SURVEY OF HUD'S ADMINISTRATION OF SECTION 3 OF THE HUD ACT OF 1968 2 (Audit Case No. 2003-KC- 0001, 2003), *available at* http://nhlp.org/node/1677.

101. Press Release, U.S. Dep't of Hous. & Urban Dev., HUD Takes Action to Expand Jobs and Training Opportunities for Low-Income Residents (Oct. 14, 2009), *available at* http://portal.hud.gov/hudportal/HUD?src=/press/press_releases_media_advisories/2009/HUDNo.09-200.

102. Even before HUD's 2009 announcement, there were a number of examples of intervention by HUD and the courts in response to a Section 3 administrative complaint or lawsuit, leading to significant reforms to governmental entities' bidding, hiring, and job-training practices. *See* NAT'L HOUS. LAW PROJECT, AN ADVOCATE'S GUIDE TO THE HUD SECTION 3 PROGRAM: CREATING JOBS AND ECONOMIC OPPORTUNITY (2009), *available at* https://nhlp.org/files/03%20Sec.%203%20Guide.pdf.

103. 24 C.F.R. § 135.34(a)(2).
104. 24 C.F.R. § 135, Appendix to Part 135, II (12).
105. 24 C.F.R. § 135.5, 135.3(a).
106. *See* U.S. Dep't of Hous. & Urban Dev., Frequently Asked Questions (FAQs): Section 3 of the Housing & Urban Development Act of 1968, *available at* http://portal.hud.gov/hudportal/documents/huddoc?id=11secfaqs.pdf.
107. 24 C.F.R. § 135.3(a)(3)(ii).
108. 24 C.F.R. § 135.5.
109. 24 C.F.R. § 135.5.
110. 24 C.F.R. § 135.30(b) & (c).
111. 24 C.F.R. § 135.30(c).
112. 24 C.F.R. § 135.32.
113. 24 C.F.R. § 135.90.
114. Letter from U.S. Dep't of Hous. & Urban Dev. to Recipients of HUD Cmty. Planning and Dev. Assistance (Oct. 9, 2009), *available at* http://nhlp.org/files/13%20Section%203%20Notice.CPD%2010-08-09.pdf.
115. U.S. Dep't of Hous. & Urban Dev., Annual Section 3 Summary Reporting Requirements, *available at* http://www.hud.gov/offices/fheo/section3/Sec3-Reporting-Guidance-cpd-final.pdf
116. *Id.*; 24 C.F.R. § 135.90.
117. Nat'l Hous. Law Project, *supra* note 102.
118. HUD's website on Section 3 provides an online tool where several case studies of best practices can be accessed. *See Section 3*, HUD.GOV, http://portal.hud.gov/hudportal/HUD?src=/program_offices/fair_housing_equal_opp/section3/section3 (last visited Jan. 23, 2013). The appendix to the federal regulations for Section 3 also includes some suggested best practices at 24 C.F.R. § 135. *See also* Nat'l Hous. Law Project, *supra* note 102.

CHAPTER 11

Public Housing Post-Disaster: To Rehabilitate or Replace?

Michael H. Reardon and Nathaniel S. Cushman

I. Introduction

When a public housing project is damaged in a natural disaster, a public housing agency (PHA) must either rehabilitate the project, generally in substantially its pre-disaster form, or pursue options to replace the development in another form. This decision may be influenced by cost considerations, funding availability, current affordable housing needs in the community, and the time needed to plan a replacement scenario and to process the required approvals from the U.S. Department of Housing and Urban Development (HUD). Funding for rehabilitation often may come from existing HUD funding streams and from insurance proceeds. Disaster grant programs, described in this chapter, may be available to the PHA to secure additional rehabilitation funds, including the option in certain disasters to receive funds to implement measures to mitigate similar damage in the future.

There are also funding options to reconfigure or replace existing public housing projects. While not restricted specifically to PHAs facing the aftermath of a disaster, they nonetheless represent the replacement financing options available to a PHA in such circumstances. This chapter provides an overview of these programs, including the HUD approval process for demolition and disposition of public housing under Section 18 of the Housing Act of 1937, as amended (the Housing Act); the public housing mixed-finance process, together with the HOPE VI program and its apparent successor program, the Choice Neighborhoods Initiative (Choice Neighborhoods); and the recently authorized Rental Assistance Demonstration program (RAD). Each of these programs requires application and processing with HUD, and may also necessitate amendment to the PHA plan, notice and comment periods, and other time-consuming actions. PHAs must consider the likely time frame for any replacement scenario.

In addition to the practicalities of funding and processing, the PHA's decision involves community stakeholders, including public housing residents, HUD, local government officials, current and future development partners, and others. The decisions that must be made following a disaster may also implicate long-standing housing issues that may be controversial, including "one-for-one replacement" and principles of fair housing and site and neighborhood standards. For context, to the extent possible, this chapter includes comparisons to the events in New Orleans following Hurricane Katrina. (For further discussion on public housing post–Katrina from the tenants' perspective, see chapter 12.)

II. An Introduction to the "Big Four": The Housing Authority of New Orleans Confronts Hurricane Katrina

On August 23, 2005, Hurricane Katrina formed over the Bahamas. Over the coming days, Hurricane Katrina moved to the west, passing over southern Florida as a relatively weak storm and then rapidly building strength as it passed over the warm waters of the Gulf. Less than a week after it formed—on Monday, August 29, 2005—the hurricane made landfall in Louisiana, passing just east of the city of New Orleans. Hurricane Katrina was the deadliest U.S. hurricane since 1928 and the costliest natural disaster in American history. The hurricane and subsequent floods killed an estimated 1,200 people and caused over $108 billion in property damage.[1]

The storm's devastation affected communities along the Gulf of Mexico from Texas to central Florida; the city of New Orleans was in the center of the destruction. Nearly every one of the storm levees protecting the metropolitan area was breached. Eighty percent of the city flooded, along with substantial portions of the surrounding parishes. The storm caused major damage to infrastructure and buildings throughout the city. Recovery from Hurricane Katrina would remain a major issue of national importance for years.

Among the storm's many impacts, the Housing Authority of New Orleans (HANO) was confronted with its effect on the city's public housing. All of the city's public housing had been damaged. One estimate of the cost to renovate the damaged buildings exceeded $1 billion.[2] Much attention was focused on the "Big Four" public housing developments: B.W. Cooper (now known as Marrero Commons), C.J. Peete (now known as Harmony Oaks), Faubourg Lafitte (often referred to simply as Lafitte), and St. Bernard (now known as Columbia Parc). Of the Big Four, by early 2007, HANO considered only B.W. Cooper safe enough to allow some families to return.[3] By late 2007, HANO also determined that it would partly reopen Lafitte to returning families.[4]

HANO and other local officials needed to address complex questions. Should the Big Four be rehabilitated or replaced? If they were to be replaced, in what form, with what partners, and with what funding sources would they be replaced? How many public housing and other low-income units could or should be created on-site, and would any be made available at other sites in the same process? This last question—whether redevelopment of an existing public housing project, which requires demolition of existing public housing units, will lead to the same number of replacement public housing units being constructed—is commonly referred to as the issue of "one-for-one replacement." The issue presents a tension between two goals. On the one hand is the goal of maintaining a sufficient number of hard units (i.e., not units subsidized only with tenant-based assistance) of affordable housing to address the needs of residents and the larger community. On the other hand is the goal to avoid concentration of poverty and allow the former residents choice and mobility, for instance, as encouraged in the new RAD program.

Addressing these questions also presented a complex and tense challenge in navigating relationships with stakeholders and the public, a challenge heightened by national attention. The *Boston Globe* summarized the context this way:

> Because virtually all public housing residents in New Orleans are black, the debate about the projects' fate reflects the city's often toxic racial politics. . . . Even at best, this is yet another instance when the burden of change falls heaviest on the city's poorest residents. Yet with more than a third of New Orleans's pre-Katrina population gone and its infrastructure devastated, should the city spend scarce dollars to resurrect long-troubled housing projects that have been slated for demolition for years?[5]

In addition, nearly all of the city's public housing residents were no longer in New Orleans directly following the storm, which made finding and communicating with tenants more challenging.[6] As detailed in greater length in chapter 12 of this book, HANO and HUD's efforts on communication and transparency in decision making were frequently criticized. And HANO and HUD were not faced solely with long-term issues. Residents and activists demanded that HANO and HUD do more to provide housing, access to the decision-making process, and specific outcomes.

This chapter focuses on options and issues involved in weighing these complex considerations.

III. Rehabilitating Public Housing

When public housing is damaged in a disaster, one option for PHAs is to repair the public housing to substantially its pre-disaster state. The PHA will review the extent of the damage, determine the steps necessary to rehabilitate the project, and assess associated costs and schedules. The PHA has an obligation under the Annual Contributions Contract to operate public housing in a safe manner, which would include an obligation for the PHA to address any threats to safety caused by disaster damage.[7] Following any disaster, the Federal Emergency Management Agency (FEMA) may provide PHAs that suffer damage from the disaster with essential, emergency assistance, including debris removal, demolition of unsafe structures, and actions necessary to reduce an immediate threat to life, property, and public health and safety.[8] A portion of the demolition at the Big Four was funded by FEMA under this authority.[9] If temporary or permanent demolition of public housing is to be undertaken, generally an application under Section 18 of the Housing Act, discussed further in section IV below, is required. As a partial exception to this general rule, HUD has provided guidance for demolition in connection with exigent circumstances, including disasters. This guidance is discussed in more detail at section IV(D).

A PHA often will be able to cover most or all of the costs of permanent rehabilitation with insurance proceeds and funds otherwise available to the PHA. The PHA also may be able to access supplemental financing from FEMA or HUD. Whether the PHA looks to FEMA or HUD depends on whether a disaster is declared by the president under the Robert T. Stafford Disaster Relief and Emergency Assistance Act (the Stafford Act).[10] For presidentially declared disasters under the Stafford Act, a PHA may apply for grant assistance through FEMA's Public Assistance Program (the PA Program). For non-presidentially-declared disasters, a PHA may apply to HUD for grant assistance from emergency capital needs funds.

A. Disaster under the Stafford Act: The Public Assistance Program

Currently, PHAs may apply for grant funds under the PA Program in the case of presidentially declared disasters under the Stafford Act. This option, however, was not open to PHAs affected by Hurricane Katrina. This followed from a joint determination by HUD and FEMA made in 2001 that PHAs must look to HUD capital funds for any disaster-related assistance above the emergency assistance available from FEMA discussed above.[11] This determination was reversed by statute in 2008,[12] and PHAs are currently eligible to participate in the PA Program.[13]

The PA Program provides supplemental grant assistance to fund repair, replacement, and restoration of disaster-damaged, publicly owned facilities—such as public housing—as well as debris removal and certain emergency safety measures.[14] Grants are made to states as grantees, and further sub-grants are made to other eligible sub-grantees, which include PHAs, as well as local governments, agencies, and certain private nonprofit organizations.

The PA Program process begins with a presidential declaration of a disaster under the Stafford Act in response to a request for such a declaration by a governor.[15] Following this declaration, the state will hold a briefing for applicants, including PHAs, to review eligibility criteria for sub-grantees to receive PA Program funding, work scope, and costs. The sub-grantee begins its participation in the PA Program by filing a Request for Public Assistance,[16] a short "pre-application" form that may be completed at the initial state briefing and which must be filed with the state representative within 30 days of designation of the disaster area.[17]

In order to be eligible, costs of specific work must be (a) required as a result of the disaster, (b) located within the designated disaster area, and (c) the legal responsibility of the PHA. Costs to meet these requirements may be eligible for the repair or replacement of public housing buildings, including their contents and systems, as well as heavy equipment and vehicles. Costs must also be reasonable and necessary to accomplish the work and compliant with applicable procurement requirements.

The amount of reimbursement will also be offset by certain items, including insurance proceeds, such as from flood insurance. For general property insurance, the PHA's insurance adjustment showing actual proceeds may be used, if available. If the amount of actual proceeds is unknown, a FEMA employee will review the PHA's insurance policy against the damaged public housing and make a determination of anticipated insurance proceeds. The actual adjustment or anticipated amount will be deducted from eligible costs. For flood insurance, the reduction of eligible costs depends on whether the damaged public housing is within the Special Flood Hazard Area established under the National Flood Insurance Program (NFIP). If so, and the PHA has flood insurance but not NFIP coverage, FEMA will compare the PHA's flood insurance adjustment to what they could have received with NFIP coverage. FEMA will deduct the higher of these two adjustments from eligible costs. For eligible damage of $5,000 or more, a condition of receiving federal assistance will be that the PHA obtain and maintain insurance, protecting against future loss to the public housing from the same cause for the life of the public housing project.[18]

The initial state meeting will also cover funding options, program logistics, record keeping, and documentation requirements, as well as special requirements related to floodplain management, environmental assessments, hazard mitigation, and wetland protection.

Following the pre-application and initial meeting, FEMA officials will meet with the PHA to assess the PHA's needs, discuss disaster-related damage, and plan for the repair of the public housing. The PHA must then document the damage to the public housing and work with FEMA to identify the eligible scope of work and estimate costs associated with that scope. FEMA organizes these repair and rehabilitation efforts into "projects"; work on more than one public housing facility may be included within one FEMA project. The proposed project will be reviewed and approved by FEMA. Upon approval, FEMA will obligate the federal share of the PA Program grant, and the state is responsible for making grant funds (including the nonfederal share of grant funds) available to the PHA.[19]

FEMA considers certain projects over an annually adjusted cost threshold "large projects."[20] For these projects, funds are provided as work progresses; the PHA must apply periodically to the state for disbursements of funds for expenses already incurred or to be incurred in the near future. If during repair or rehabilitation it becomes clear that the scope of work must be adjusted or the estimated costs are too low, the PHA should request a change in scope or increase in grant funds as soon as the need is identified. Ultimately, the amount of funds will be determined under a final accounting of actual costs.

A PHA may be eligible for additional funding to implement cost-effective measures to prevent similar damage to the public housing in the future.[21] FEMA guidance states that such "[h]azard mitigation opportunities usually present themselves at sites where damages are repetitive and simple measures will solve the problem."[22] A written proposal describing the proposed measure and estimating its cost must be submitted with the PHA's application. FEMA recommends that applicants ask FEMA for help in identifying hazard mitigation opportunities and analyzing hazard mitigation proposals.[23] Undamaged public housing projects and undamaged elements of a project or project system are not eligible for hazard mitigation funding.[24]

Upon completion of the project, the state will determine the final cost of eligible work, and may perform inspections or audits in making this determination. The state then submits a final report to FEMA certifying actual cost. FEMA will review this report and may adjust the grant amount to reflect actual costs.[25]

B. Non–Stafford Act Disaster: HUD Funds for Emergency Capital Needs

When public housing is damaged by a natural disaster that is not a presidentially declared disaster under the Stafford Act, the PHA may apply for grant funds from HUD's emergency capital-needs fund. This fund has been set aside annually in recent HUD appropriations, in which Congress has indicated that a portion of the funds made available for capital needs be used for "emergency capital needs" resulting from either non-presidentially-declared disasters or crime- and drug-related activities and arising in the same fiscal year as the appropriation.[26] HUD has implemented this by allowing PHAs to apply for these funds following such disasters[27] and by making grants to PHAs for security spending on crime-prevention measures.[28]

The amount the PHA may receive in these natural-disaster grants is equal to the costs of damage caused by non-presidentially-declared disasters in the federal fiscal year, less any insurance coverage or other federal assistance, such as flood insurance.[29] The PHA may receive assistance regardless of the availability of other capital funds or reserves.[30] Grants can only be used for costs associated with repair or replacement of a public housing project damaged as a result of the disaster, not for improvements beyond the state of the project prior to the disaster or for nonroutine maintenance needs.[31]

A PHA must apply to receive a natural-disaster grant. Funds are awarded on a first-come, first-served basis, and HUD recommends that PHAs submit a preliminary grant application immediately after damage has occurred.[32] The PHA may submit a preliminary grant application even if all information relating to the damage is not yet available, and HUD may make a grant on this basis. If additional funds are required, the PHA could then later submit a final grant application.[33]

Both preliminary and final applications are made to the local HUD Field Office.[34] As part of its review, the Field Office may require a site visit to verify the work needed.[35] If the Field Office determines that the application is approvable, it forwards the application to HUD headquarters for review and approval.[36] If the Field Office determines that the application is not approvable, it will notify the PHA in writing. The PHA may appeal this decision to HUD headquarters.[37] The process from submission of the application to final headquarters should take approximately four weeks.[38]

With respect to environmental procedures, in general, the typical process under either 24 C.F.R. Part 50 or Part 58 will apply. However, the responsible entity or HUD, as applicable, may determine that disaster-related repairs are exempt from environmental review.[39]

An application for emergency capital funds involves no requirement to provide notice or a comment period either to tenants or local government officials, given the need to act quickly in the aftermath of a disaster to address immediate needs such as relocation of affected residents or repairs necessary to ensure the health and safety of the residents. However, PHAs must notify tenants and local government officials of any funding received under such an application, and HUD encourages PHAs to keep tenants and local government officials informed throughout the process.[40]

IV. Demolition and Disposition of Public Housing

As a general rule, public housing may not be disposed of or demolished, even in part, without prior HUD approval. This approval will typically be needed following a disaster if a PHA wants to replace a damaged public housing project rather than rebuild to the project's pre-disaster state. This is because replacing an existing public housing project with a new development requires demolition of the existing public housing units. Also, some redevelopment plans will also require disposition of public housing to a new owner, for instance in order to leverage federal Low Income Housing Tax Credit (LIHTC) financing. To be more specific, this requirement applies to

(a) (i) public housing developments owned by a PHA, or (ii) public housing units in a mixed finance development owned by the PHA, an affiliate of the PHA or a private owner, and
(b) which are subject to an Annual Contributions Contract under title I of the Housing Act.[41] Applications for this approval are governed by Section 18 of the Housing Act (Section 18) and federal regulations at 24 C.F.R. Part 970.[42]

In limited circumstances, HUD allows some demolition following exigent circumstances, such as disasters, without preapproval through the Section 18 process, although a Section 18 application may be required later. These special circumstances are discussed in more detail in Section IV.D.[43] Also, Section 18 requirements generally do not apply to disposal of an existing public housing project for redevelopment in accordance with the HUD public housing mixed-finance regulations—another option that a PHA may consider following a disaster in some circumstances and one which is also discussed in more detail later in this chapter.[44]

A. Section 18 General Requirements for Demolition or Disposition

Technically, under the Housing Act, HUD has relatively little legal discretion to disapprove an application for demolition and disposition of public housing that meets the statutory and regulatory guidelines. By statute, HUD "shall approve the application" if the PHA certifies to the existence of certain conditions discussed below.[45] HUD shall disapprove the application only if either those certifications are clearly inconsistent with facts known to HUD, including, for instance, the PHA's annual plan;[46] or residents, resident organizations, and local government officials were not properly consulted in developing the application. In practice, HUD's application and review process for approval of such applications is fairly detailed and can take up to six months to complete.

For all applications for demolition or disposition, the statute and regulations require the PHA to certify that it has specifically authorized the demolition or disposition and included an implementation timetable in the PHA's annual plan and that the actions contemplated by the plan comply with applicable portions of the Housing Act and regulations.[47] In order to provide this certification, the PHA would need to amend its annual plan to specifically incorporate these authorizations and timetable. The PHA should work with relevant local authorities to assure that the disposition and proposed redevelopment of the project is consistent with their comprehensive housing affordability strategy, which should be a part of the locality's consolidated plan prepared in connection with the Community Development Block Grant (CDBG) program.[48]

The PHA must also certify in any demolition or disposition application that it will comply with certain notice, comparable housing offer, and relocation requirements.[49] Notice must be provided to residents at least 90 days prior to the date they will be displaced.[50] The notice must include elements specified by statute, which include an assurance that the PHA will provide appropriate relocation benefits to those families who will be displaced.[51] The PHA must pay actual and reasonable costs of relocation of displaced residents, ensure that each placed resident is offered comparable housing, provide "any necessary counseling" for displaced residents, and relocate residents prior to demolition or disposition. The PHA must approve a relocation plan to be submitted with its application for disposition, and the relocation plan must be reviewed and approved by HUD.[52]

The PHA must also submit background facts and evidence to support an application for demolition or disposition.[53] Among the background information required, the PHA must submit the results of all consultation with residents and local officials,[54] as well as a signed resolution of the PHA's governing board.[55] The PHA must also submit the results of an environmental review. An emergency, including a disaster declared under the Stafford Act or declared by the applicable state officer or entity, or an imminent threat to health or safety may require taking action with significant environmental impact. In these cases, HUD is directed to consult with the Council on Environmental Quality about environmental arrangements. Special actions may be taken, but they are to be limited to actions necessary to control the immediate impacts of the emergency.[56] As noted in Section IV.D, however, HUD's guidance appears to allow PHA's to unilaterally take some demolition action without prior approval to protect safety, although a retroactive approval may be needed in some cases.

B. Section 18 Requirements Specific to Dispositions

In addition to these common certifications and related information, the PHA must make additional certifications depending on whether it is applying to demolish or to dispose of the public housing.[57] For a proposed disposition (e.g., a sale), the PHA must make an additional certification if the property contains dwelling units[58]—specifically, that the PHA has determined that the disposition is appropriate for the best interests of the project residents and the PHA because either

(a) conditions in the area surrounding the project (density, or industrial or commercial development) adversely affect the health or safety of project residents or operation of the project by the PHA;

(b) disposition allows the acquisition, development, or rehabilitation of other properties that will be more efficiently or effectively operated as low-income housing developments;[59]

(c) the PHA has otherwise determined the disposition to be appropriate for reasons that are consistent with the goals of the PHA and the PHA plan and that are otherwise consistent with the [Housing] Act.[60]

In providing this certification under the second or third criteria, the PHA is likely to consider the economic impact of continued ownership and operation of the project and the value of the project as part of the PHA's portfolio, compared with the alternatives afforded by disposition of the project. The PHA's board may wish to explicitly restate the consideration of these criteria in the written resolution approving the disposition.

In some dispositions, the PHA must also provide an opportunity for enumerated resident organizations to purchase in a manner detailed by statute and must certify that it has done so.[61] These requirements frequently would not apply, however, because the resident purchase process is inapplicable where "a PHA seeks to dispose of a property outside the public housing program to privately finance or otherwise develop a facility to benefit low-income families," including mixed-finance development under 24 C.F.R. Part 941 Subpart F and other low-income housing.[62] For example, all of the Big Four redevelopments were redeveloped using both public-housing funds and private financing, including LIHTCs, and consequently were mixed-finance developments that were not subject to the resident purchase requirements.

The PHA must also certify that net disposition proceeds will be used only for purposes specified in the Housing Act.[63] First, proceeds must be used to pay off any outstanding debt to HUD, although HUD has generally waived repayment if the project is being redeveloped as a mixed-finance development. Remaining proceeds may be used either for the provision of other low-income housing and for other activities that benefit public housing residents or to leverage other financing for commercial uses on public housing that are appropriate to serve the needs of the residents. Uses of disposition proceeds HUD considers acceptable include repairing or rehabilitating existing public housing units, funding certain social services, funding a HUD-approved homeownership program, or leveraging proceeds for approved mixed-finance development.[64]

The PHA must also describe the nature of the proposed disposition of the project, whether a public sale for fair market value, a negotiated sale, or a sale at less than fair market value. In cases of disposition by a previously negotiated sale or by any sale at less than fair market value, a written justification must be attached to the application.[65] This justification should refer to the appraised value of the project and explain how the negotiated price was determined, including any difference between the appraised value and the negotiated price.[66] The application also requires an explanation of how net proceeds of the sale will be used, and they must be used in accordance with the Housing Act. If the negotiated sale or other disposition of the project will be less than fair market value, then the PHA must also demonstrate that there will be commensurate public benefits to the PHA and the residents.

C. Section 18 Requirements Specific to Demolitions

For a proposed demolition, the PHA must certify that the following criteria are met:

(a) The project is obsolete as to physical condition, location, or other factors, making it unsuitable for housing purposes.

(b) No reasonable program of modifications is cost-effective to return the public housing project or portion thereof to useful life.

(c) For an application for partial demolition, the demolition will help ensure the viability of the remaining portion of the project.[67]

HUD guidance on submission of demolition and disposition applications recognizes the fact that many public housing projects are older and were not built to a standard that is acceptable to the general public today. PHAs may decide to demolish or dispose of a development for a variety of reasons, including that the costs associated with bringing the existing development into compliance with current standards are prohibitively expensive.

There may be some concern on the part of PHAs in providing a certification to HUD as to the obsolescence of a particular project. There is nothing in Part 970 of the regulations that defines the terms *obsolescence* or *obsolete*. The HOPE VI program does have a more specific definition of severely distressed or obsolete public housing contained in its statutory requirements—namely, that the housing must require "major redesign, reconstruction, or redevelopment, or partial or total demolition, to correct serious deficiencies in the original design (including inappropriately high population density), deferred maintenance, physical deterioration or obsolescence of major systems, and other deficiencies in the physical plan of the project."[68] HUD's guidance regarding demolition and disposition applications, however, even avoids using the term "obsolete" and provides for other factors that may justify the demolition/disposition of public housing.[69] Also, the regulations state that HUD generally shall not consider a program of modifications to be cost-effective if the cost of such program is greater than 62.5 percent of total development cost for elevator structures (or 57.4 percent for all other types of structures).[70]

D. Special Guidance for Exigent Cases, Including Disasters

HUD has stated that PHAs have the flexibility to take steps necessary to ensure the safety of residents, employees, and the public without waiting for HUD approval.[71] Immediately following a disaster, this flexibility may be particularly relevant. HUD specifically recognized these special circumstances and provided guidelines for PHAs facing them after the recent hurricane seasons.[72]

HUD's guidance recognizes that demolition and debris removal to maintain safe conditions or eliminate an attractive nuisance may be taken without prior HUD approval. This exception to Section 18 applies to accidental damage, including from a disaster, but not to damage from causes such as mold, mildew, or termites that takes place over time. Whether HUD approval may be required later, however, depends on if the PHA will rebuild the structure in its pre-disaster state. Where the PHA determines to rebuild in this way, no Section 18 application is needed for additional demolition necessary to accomplish the rebuilding. Where the PHA determines not to rebuild, a full Section 18 application is needed to formally remove the units from the public housing inventory.[73] In all circumstances of demolition due to accidental loss damage, HUD advises the PHA to retain records, including reports and photographs, sufficient to allow for an audit by HUD or other parties, if necessary.

V. Programmatic Options for Redevelopment of Public Housing

Redeveloping public housing typically requires new capital sources. Programs exist to provide new capital directly and to allow PHAs to leverage additional funds. PHAs have had great success integrating new sources with public housing funds through the mixed-finance program. The HOPE VI program and its apparent successor program, the Choice Neighborhoods Initiative, also provide funds for these purposes. In addition, HUD's recently developed RAD program represents a different model, one by which PHAs can convert projects out of the public housing program entirely. This may provide a PHA with additional options and a project-based subsidy stream that can enable the leveraging of redevelopment funds.

A PHA wishing to redevelop public housing following a disaster in a modified form should consider these programs—they provide options for accessing capital for any redevelopment of public housing. For example, the Big Four redevelopments following Hurricane Katrina were accomplished through the mixed-finance process. Each of these programs also requires advance planning and time for HUD review and approvals. A PHA is likely to be more successful in redeveloping a public housing project if some steps in the relevant redevelopment program have already been started prior to the urgency presented by a disaster.

In addition to the programs discussed here, a PHA should be alert to changes in the law to facilitate redevelopment following a specific natural disaster. For instance, following Hurricanes Katrina, Rita, and Wilma, federal legislation was passed into law providing additional funding and other authority for tax-exempt bonds and LIHTCs benefitting areas affected by those storms.[74] Legislation varies on a disaster-by-disaster basis, and is sometimes very significant.

A. Disposition in Support of Mixed-Finance Development

HUD has provided authorization and guidance for so-called mixed-finance development of public-housing funding through mixing HOPE VI, Choice Neighborhoods Initiative funding, and funds provided under Section 9 of the Housing Act for the operation and development of public housing (Section 9 funds) with other private and public sources of financing. Mixed-finance development has been used frequently to redevelop existing public housing sites, and the ability to leverage additional funds can greatly expand redevelopment options. A mixed-finance project is a project developed with a combination of funds from public housing or the HOPE VI or Choice Neighborhoods Initiative programs, as well as other nonpublic housing funds. The mixed-finance project may or may not include nonpublic housing units.[75] PHAs have used mixed-finance development together with HOPE VI funds[76] and are likely to do so with Choice Neighborhoods funds as well, but have also leveraged diverse sources including LIHTCs and similar state tax credits, tax-exempt bonds, HOME Investment Partnership Program (HOME) funds, project-based Housing Choice Vouchers, and other sources, including state and local grant funds. Mixed-finance redevelopments of public housing need not be mixed income, but they frequently are and may also allow for mixed use.

Mixed-finance development is governed by regulations at 24 C.F.R. Part 941, Subpart F (the Mixed Finance Regulations). After the issuance of the Mixed Finance regulations, Congress enacted the Quality Housing and Work Responsibility Act of 1998 (QHWRA), which provided statutory authorization for mixed-finance development at Section 35 of the Housing Act.[77] The process is complex and requires multiple detailed and lengthy submissions to HUD, at both the headquarters and the field office level. In our experience, development and HUD processing of a mixed-finance development requires months to accomplish.

With respect to long-term affordability, HUD requires that mixed-finance projects comply with public housing rules for at least a 40-year period. Specifically, grants to be made to PHAs to cover the development costs of public housing projects are made subject to Section 5(a)(2) of the Housing Act, which provides that the Annual Contributions Contract shall specify that the terms and conditions of such contract shall remain in effect for a 40-year period.

The Housing Act also limits the amount of public housing funds that may be used to pay the total development cost of the project.[78] Total development costs (TDC) comprise costs incurred in undertaking the planning, land acquisition, demolition, construction, or equipment; financing those undertakings; and in otherwise carrying out the development of the public housing units in the mixed finance project. However, the definition specifically excludes costs associated with the demolition of or remediation of environmental hazards associated with the public housing units that will not be replaced on the project site, or other extraordinary costs as determined by the HUD secretary.

The limitation on TDC is determined by multiplying the construction cost guideline for the project by 1.6 for elevator structures and 1.75 for non-elevator structures. The construction cost guideline is determined by HUD by averaging the current construction costs, as listed by not less than two nationally recognized residential construction cost indices, for publicly bid construction of a good and sound quality. The secretary may approve costs over 100 percent of TDC, and with a good cause determination may approve costs over 110 percent of TDC.

QHWRA amended the TDC requirements to provide that only capital assistance provided by HUD for use in the development of the public housing shall be used in the TDC calculation. It specifically excludes from the TDC calculation all other amounts used for the development of the public housing units in the mixed finance project, citing specifically HOME and CDBG funds.

In general, HUD may not make annual contributions available to a public housing project unless the project is exempt from all real and personal property taxes.[79] Mixed-finance development, however, is exempt from this requirement, as well as the requirement that the public housing units be subject to a cooperation agreement between the PHA and the local government.[80]

Legal issues not directly related to HUD approval may also arise in the context of a mixed-finance development. For example, historic preservation review requirements were raised in the context of the Big Four. As a resolution of legal claims raised on these points, original buildings from each public housing project—which became known as "legacy buildings"—were retained and renovated, most to be used for community purposes.[81]

The C.J. Peete/Harmony Oaks redevelopment provides an example of the redevelopment possibilities within this framework. Redevelopment of the project had been contemplated prior to the hurricane.[82] The project was originally constructed as 1,403 public housing units, and demolition approval for half the site was provided in 1997.[83] At the time of the storm in 2005 only about half of the original units were standing and fewer than 150 families lived on site.[84] Redevelopment was accomplished through a partnership that included HUD, HANO, the New Orleans Neighborhood Development Collaborative, McCormack Baron Salazar, and others. The redeveloped site contained 460 rental units, of which 7 were public-housing-only units, 186 were financed with both public housing and LIHTC funds, 144 were solely LIHTC units, and 123 were market-rate rental units. In addition, 50 affordable homeownership units were constructed in the local neighborhood.[85]

B. The HOPE VI Program and the Choice Neighborhoods Initiative

Historically, the first source of funding for public housing redevelopment was what became known as the HOPE VI program. Congress created the program after recognizing the need for dedicated funds to assist in planning for and accomplishing the redevelopment of obsolete public housing sites. The program has been active since initially authorized in the fiscal year 1993 appropriations act.[86] Between 1993 and 1999, the program was authorized annually in appropriations acts.[87] QHWRA then provided statutory authorization for the program at Section 24 of the Housing Act.[88]

Recently, the availability of the mixed-finance development process has provided additional options to PHAs beyond the HOPE VI program. Since 2000, the appropriations for HOPE VI have significantly diminished each year. In fiscal year 2010, just $200 million was appropriated to HOPE VI. Also, beginning with fiscal year 2011, the Obama administration has put forward the Choice Neighborhoods program to replace the HOPE VI program to some degree and to broaden the types of HUD-assisted housing that could be funded and the activities that could be undertaken with the funds. In fiscal year 2012, Congress appropriated $120 million for the Choice Neighborhoods program.

Choice Neighborhoods funding has been distributed through Notices of Funds Availability. In general, Choice Neighborhoods provides funds for the revitalization of severely distressed public housing or other HUD-assisted housing.[89] The housing project must be in an eligible neighborhood. Under the 2012 NOFA, such neighborhoods were those with at least 20 percent of residents estimated to be in poverty or to have extremely low incomes and that are also experiencing a high violent-crime rate, high vacancy or substandard housing, or inadequate schools. Each of these factors is defined in more detail in the NOFA.[90]

The Choice Neighborhoods program requires continuing affordability for the greater of 20 years or the length of the existing affordability restrictions.[91] Costs must be reasonable and realistic, and activities will be subject to cost limits to be established by HUD.[92] Certain Choice Neighborhoods activities will also require additional review and approval. For instance, it appears that public housing projects participating in Choice Neighborhoods and leveraging nonpublic housing funds will be required to undergo mixed-finance processing and approvals.[93] Also, while demolition of public housing may be approved through a Choice Neighborhoods grant without separate Section 18 processing; standard Section 18 requirements apply to disposition of public housing participating in Choice Neighborhoods.[94]

A HOPE VI grantee must comply with the grant administration requirements of 24 C.F.R. Part 85, including rules on competitive procurement,[95] conflicts of interest, OMB Cost Principles, timing of the drawdown of grant funds, and use of program income. The 2012 Choice Neighborhoods NOFA states that, generally, the 24 C.F.R. Part 85 procurement rules apply to grantees. However, applicants may, but are not required to, follow these rules in assembling the team to respond to the NOFA.[96]

Any public housing project or units that are developed with HOPE VI or Choice Neighborhoods funds are subject to Davis-Bacon wage rate requirements for laborers and mechanics, and prevailing wage-rate requirements apply to all architects, technical engineers, draftsmen, and technicians employed in the development of public housing and HUD maintenance wage rates for all maintenance laborers and mechanics employed in the operation of public housing.[97] A public housing project receiving HOPE VI funds must meet applicable site and neighborhood standards, discussed below at section VI(B). Choice Neighborhoods grantees must comply with Site and Neighborhood standards in connection with any acquisition of land for replacement units outside the target neighborhood.[98] Also, a PHA cannot carry out any activities at a HOPE VI or Choice Neighborhoods development until written approval under the applicable environmental requirements at either 24 C.F.R. Part 50 or Part 58.[99]

C. The Rental Assistance Demonstration Program

Recently, HUD announced a new demonstration program—the RAD program—which would allow, among other things, the conversion of public housing to other forms of project-based rent assistance.[100] Specifically, RAD provides a mechanism by which PHAs may apply to a competitive selection process to convert their public housing projects to Section 8 project-based rental assistance, either in the form of long-term, project-based rental assistance (PBRA) contracts (similar to project-based Section 8 contracts) or project-based housing choice voucher (PBV) contracts.[101] Applications under the initial application period were due by October 24, 2012. Following that date, additional applications will be accepted on a first-come, first-served basis until the earlier of September 30, 2015, or HUD's announcement that it has closed the application process.[102] Nonetheless, if the RAD demonstration program is successful, it may be extended in its current form or a somewhat modified form. HUD's general goals in the RAD program are also likely to remain important in any future similar program.

One reason conversion under RAD may be attractive to a PHA is an increased ability to leverage outside financing. Lenders and investors have historically been much more comfortable relying on PBV or project-based Section 8 subsidy streams in underwriting than on Section 9 public housing operating subsidy funding streams. The annual funding by Congress of operating subsidy under Section 9 has over the years been frequently less than the amount that HUD has requested in order to fully fund the operating needs of public housing projects, resulting in annual proration of operating subsidy.[103] For instance, in calendar year 2008, HUD's Financial Management Center determined that Congress appropriated sufficient operating subsidy to fund only about 89 percent of the estimated need, and a similar amount in calendar year 2009.[104] In calendar year 2011 the proration was 100 percent of need,[105] but the estimate for calendar year 2012 was approximately 95 percent of need.[106] On the other hand, HUD, to date, has fully funded Section 8 project-based assistance contracts.

The RAD program is designed to demonstrate how conversion of public housing to PBV or PBRA contracts can attract leveraged funds and facilitate long-term preservation. In designing the demonstration, HUD has taken steps intended to make RAD compatible with diverse financing sources, including FHA insurance and LIHTCs. PHAs may also find RAD attractive because requests to transfer rental assistance from a project that is uninhabitable due to unforeseen circumstances, such as a natural disaster, to a new project will be considered.[107]

In order to be eligible for RAD, a PHA must have units assisted under an Annual Contributions Contract, meet minimum requirements relating to its PHAS and SEMAP rankings, meet previous participation baselines, and have a record of fair housing compliance. RAD generally applies the rules of either the PBV or project-based Section 8 programs to converting projects, with some alterations.

Projects converting to PBVs will receive 15-year contracts, although the term may be increased to 20 years with the approval of the administering voucher agency. Contract renewal is mandatory. Long-term PBRA contracts under RAD will run for a 20-year term, with a required renewal under the Multifamily Assisted Housing Reform and Affordability Act process.[108] Under both conversion options, projects will be subject to a use agreement specific to the RAD program for a term concurrent with the new contract.[109] Rents for PBV contracts will be set no higher than "current funding" and will be adjusted annually by an operating cost adjustment factor (OCAF), subject to rent reasonableness. Rents for PBRA contracts will be set at the lesser of current funding or 120 percent of Fair Market Rent and will be adjusted annually by an OCAF. With a qualified rent comparability study, initial rents may be approved up to 150 percent of the HUD-established Fair Market Rent for the area.

HUD has included a focus on resident mobility within the RAD program. Conversion of public housing under RAD requires a choice-mobility option for residents.[110] In conversions to a PBV contract, the choice-mobility requirements of the PBV program apply.[111] For conversions to a PBRA contract, RAD outlines a similar choice-mobility requirement.[112] The RAD program also includes thorough requirements for resident notice and resident meetings prior to conversion, an allowance for a tenant comment period, and an obligation for the PHA to address comments received.

An important factor in comparing the costs and benefits of RAD participation will be the applicability of Davis-Bacon and Section 3 employment and business opportunity requirements. Presently it appears HUD will apply these requirements to most work done in public housing conversions. In the PBV program generally, a project that meets housing quality standards upon the date of execution of the PBV contract generally would be considered "existing housing," which is not subject to Davis-Bacon wage rates and Section 3 employment and business opportunity requirements. Under RAD, however, Davis-Bacon wage rate requirements and Section 3 employment and business opportunity requirements apply to public housing conversions for all initial repairs that are identified in the required financing plan, to the extent that such repairs qualify as construction or substantial rehabilitation, regardless of whether the project qualifies as "existing housing."[113] And RAD's current implementation implicates other public housing issues, as well.[114]

RAD puts forward a general blueprint for converting public housing projects to long-term, project-based subsidy, which Congress and HUD may expand upon in future years. Making this subsidy conversion may encourage leverage from private investment and allow for the repositioning of public housing projects, including those affected by disasters.

VI. Issues in Public Housing Rehabilitation and Replacement

A. One-for-One Replacement Requirement

The concept of one-for-one replacement has a long history in HUD programs and has been the cause of a fair amount of controversy. Advocates of one-for-one replacement focus on the need to preserve the availability of affordable housing. But the approach has been criticized as promoting the concentration of poverty and attendant problems for residents, as well as for limiting PHAs' flexibility in planning redevelopment.[115] The Choice Neighborhoods Initiative has required one-for-one replacement. The concept is also a continuing touchstone in public discussions in any situation in which public housing will be redeveloped, and was raised in connection with the Big Four, as discussed in greater detail below.

The legal history of the one-for-one replacement requirement sheds light on a major issue involved: What types of units are considered adequate replacement? One-for-one replacement was required by statute in 1987 for any demolition or disposition of public housing.[116] At that time, acceptable replacement units included public housing units, or units with 15-year Section 8 contracts or other federal or local assistance contracts with a 15-year term. Given funding constraints, providing replacement units was very difficult if not impossible. In 1993, HUD expanded the types of eligible replacement housing in projects funded under the Urban Revitalization Demonstration, the precursor to HOPE VI. A PHA could also use the Urban Revitalization Demonstration funding to provide other kinds of replacement housing including various homeownership opportunities.[117] Starting in 1995, one-for-one replacement was eliminated as a requirement under Section 18, initially though provisions in HUD annual appropriations acts and then permanently in the QHWRA,[118] which enabled PHAs to more easily demolish and dispose of public housing projects or portions thereof and to redevelop those projects as mixed-income communities under the HOPE VI and the mixed finance programs. Thus far, Choice Neighborhoods has included a requirement for one-for-one replacement. Under the program, grantees are required to replace demolished or disposed of units on a one-for-one basis with project-based units.[119] Grantees may, however, request an exception to allow them to replace up to 50 percent of lost units with tenant-based voucher units.[120]

Even where one-for-one replacement is not a legal requirement of a demolition or disposition plan, PHAs would do well to consider the issue and how to address likely public concerns about any loss of dedicated affordable housing units. For instance, the Big Four were not subject to a legal requirement of one-for-one replacement. Nonetheless, there was a great deal of public attention paid to the issue of demolition and replacement housing.

One topic was the appropriate baseline unit count because, at the time of the storm, only a portion of each development was occupied and there was significant variation in occupancy levels across the Big Four. In the Lafitte project, most units were occupied. While there were some differences between reported numbers, one accounting was compiled by the *Times-Picayune*; according to their numbers, 865 of 896 units were occupied. Both B.W. Cooper and St. Bernard were about two-thirds occupied; according to the *Times-Picayune*, 1,105 of 1,546 units and 963 of 1,436 units were occupied in those developments, respectively. C.J. Peete was largely unoccupied, with only 144 of 867 units occupied according to the *Times-Picayune*. In total, there were reportedly 4,601 rental units in the Big Four before Hurricane Katrina, with 3,077 of those units occupied.[121] There was thus a large distinction between replacing the total number of units and replacing the total number of occupied units, and that distinction affected the interests of various stakeholders in cross-cutting ways.

As with most mixed-income communities developed through the mixed-finance financing model, the final plans involved substantially fewer public housing units on-site than existed in the Big Four prior to demolition. By one estimate, the change represented an 80 percent drop in public housing units.[122] This statistic tells part, but not all, of the story: In addition to public housing units, the redeveloped projects also include hundreds of units that are affordable under LIHTC rules.[123]

The redevelopment of the Lafitte project reportedly included one-for-one replacement of rental units, though not all on-site, as well as development of an additional

600 for-sale units.[124] Some of the units were to be replaced through rehabilitation or new construction in the neighborhood.[125] According to the *Times-Picayune*, Jim Kelly—a member of the board of directors of Providence Community Housing, which partnered with Enterprise Community Partners in redeveloping Lafitte—said that the idea for this model was generated by former residents of Lafitte.[126]

Not everyone involved saw a need for one-for-one replacement or saw the reduction in the number of on-site public housing units as a negative. According to one report, a representative of HUD said that the agency could not, in good conscience, approve a redevelopment of the sites with an equal number of public housing units.[127] By late 2007, only about half of the residents of public housing prior to Hurricane Katrina had returned to New Orleans.

B. Fair Housing, Deconcentration, and Site and Neighborhood Standards

Another factor that may significantly impact a PHA's ability to develop replacement public housing is HUD's requirements with respect to the siting of new replacement housing and a legal requirement for the deconcentration of poverty and race. (For further discussion on fair housing compliance and public housing post-disaster, see chapter 15.) Since 1968, HUD has been required to affirmatively further fair housing in its housing assistance programs. In the public housing development context, HUD has provided guidance on how to affirmatively further site and neighborhood standards for newly constructed and rehabilitated public housing.[128] Applicable regulations provide that, for new construction, the site must not be located in an area of minority concentration or a racially mixed area if the project will cause a significant increase in the proportion of minority to nonminority residents in the area.[129] In addition, the site must promote greater choice of housing opportunities and avoid undue concentration of assisted people in areas containing a high proportion of low-income people.[130]

With respect to areas of minority concentration, the regulations provide for an exception for a new construction project if the PHA can demonstrate that sufficient comparable opportunities exist for low-income minority families outside areas of minority concentration or the project is necessary to meet overriding housing needs that cannot otherwise feasibly be met in that housing market area.[131] The overriding-need exceptions are assessed by HUD on a case-by-case basis and require HUD to determine that a project's placement in an area of minority concentration is necessary due to a lack of available sites in other areas. Another justification is that the project is an integral part of a comprehensive local strategy in a neighborhood that is undergoing concentrated revitalization as evidenced by both public and private investment in the area.

In order to facilitate demolition and mixed-finance redevelopment of public housing projects, HUD has also provided flexibility for the approval of public housing replacement sites. Following demolition of public housing units, new public housing may be constructed on the original site or in the same neighborhood if one of the following criteria is met: (i) the newly developed project contains no more that 50 percent of the public housing units that were in the original project, (ii) in cases where the project was occupied, the replacement units constructed are sufficient to house current residents who want to remain at the site, or (iii) there are no more than 25 public housing units being constructed on the site.[132] Similarly, in order to facilitate conversion of public housing to PBV or PBRA contracts, the otherwise applicable site and neighborhood standards requirements are generally waived under the RAD program, but must be met for conversion to a new site or new construction.[133]

VII. Conclusion

A PHA addressing damage to public housing following a natural disaster may wish to participate in the programs described in this chapter, whether to rehabilitate the project to its pre-disaster form or to redevelop the project in another form. The PHA's participation in many of the redevelopment options outlined in this chapter would be facilitated by planning done in advance of the disaster. Whatever the degree of advance planning, and whether the PHA determines to rehabilitate or redevelop its public housing project, the programs described in this chapter may provide resources and options to assist the PHA in accomplishing these goals.

Notes

1. *See* Richard D. Knabb, Jamie R. Rhome & Daniel P. Brown, TROPICAL CYCLONE REPORT: HURRICANE KATRINA, NAT'L OCEANIC AND ATMOSPHERIC ADMIN. (Dec. 20, 2005, updated Aug. 6, 2010 and Sept. 14, 2011), *available at* http://www.nhc.noaa.gov/pdf/TCR-AL122005_Katrina.pdf (last visited Jan. 24, 2013); NOAA Technical Memorandum from Nat'l Oceanic and Atmospheric Admin., The Deadliest, Costliest, and Most Intense United States Tropical Cyclones from 1851 to 2010 (and Other Frequently Requested Hurricane Facts), (especially tbls.2, 3a) (Aug. 2011), *available at* http://www.nhc.noaa.gov/pdf/nws-nhc-6.pdf (last visited Jan. 24, 2013).

2. *Our Story*, HOUS. AUTH. OF NEW ORLEANS, http://www.hano.org/our_story.aspx (last visited Oct. 21, 2012). As discussed elsewhere in this book, estimates of the extent of damage varied and became a point of public controversy.

3. *HANO Looks for Former Residents; More Units Are About to Open Up, It Says*, TIMES-PICAYUNE, Feb. 7, 2007, at 8 (reporting that HANO had also allowed some families to return to the Iberville, Fischer, and Guste developments at that time).

4. Gwen Filosa, *HANO to Reopen Parts of Lafitte; Agency Responding to Closure Criticism*, TIMES-PICAYUNE, Sept. 20, 2007, at 1.

5. Editorial, *Behind the Fury in New Orleans*, BOSTON GLOBE, Dec. 26, 2007, at 14A.

6. *HANO Looks for Former Residents; More Units Are About to Open Up, It Says*, *supra* note 3, at 8.

7. *See* Form Consolidated Annual Contributions Contract, HUD Form 53012-A, § 4; *cf. Demolition for an Accidental Loss*, U.S. DEP'T OF HOUS. & DEV., http://www.hud.gov/offices/pih/centers/sac/demo_dispo/accloss.cfm.

8. 42 U.S.C. § 5170b. *See also Public Assistance Guide*, FEMA, http://www.fema.gov/public-assistance-policy-and-guidance/public-assistance-guide.

9. *E.g.*, Katy Reckdahl, *HUD Expected to Break Ground on New Development to Replace "Big 4,"* TIMES-PICAYUNE, Dec. 2, 2008 (updated Oct 6. 2009), *available at* http://www.nola.com/news/index.ssf/2008/12/hud_expected_to_break_ground_o.html.

10. 42 U.S.C. §§ 5121-5207.

11. *See Public Housing Authorities (PHAs), FEMA Response and Recovery Policy 9523.7*, FED. EMERGENCY MGMT. AGENCY, http://coop.fema.gov/government/grant/pa/policy_archive/9523_7-3

_19_2001.shtm (last updated Aug. 11, 2010). For emergency assistance, *see supra* note 8, and accompanying text.

12. The Housing and Economic Recovery Act of 2008, Pub. L. No. 110-289, § 2804 (repealing then Section 9(k) of the Housing Act of 1937, under which capital funds were authorized for this purpose); *see also* S. Rep. No. 111-069, Transportation and Housing and Urban Development, and Related Agencies Appropriations Bill, at 125 (2010) (noting that this repeal "clarif[ied] that public housing capital funds cannot be used to pay for the repair of public housing damaged in Presidentially declared disasters").

13. *See* Public Assistance Funding for Public Housing Facilities, FEMA Recovery Fact Sheet 9580.205 (May 19, 2010); PIH Notice 2010-14, HUD Funding for Non-Presidentially Declared Natural Disasters, § 9 [hereinafter referred to as PIH Notice 2010-14].

14. *See generally* 44 C.F.R. pt. 206, subpart G; PUBLIC ASSISTANCE APPLICANT HANDBOOK, Handbook P-323, Fed. Emergency Mgmt. Agency (Mar. 2010) [hereinafter referred to as the PA PROGRAM HANDBOOK].

15. *See* 44 C.F.R. §§ 206.36–206.40.

16. Form FEMA 90-49, *Request for Public Assistance*.

17. PA PROGRAM HANDBOOK, *supra* note 14, page 9.

18. *See id.* at app. B.

19. In connection with disaster-related assistance provided through FEMA, for each presidentially declared disaster, the state and FEMA enter into a cost-sharing agreement, under which the federal government pays between 75 percent and 90 percent of eligible costs, and in some limited circumstances up to 100 percent of eligible costs. *See, e.g.*, 44 C.F.R. § 206.47.

20. In fiscal year 2012, the cost threshold was $66,400. *See* Notice of Adjustment of Disaster Grant Amounts, FEMA, effective Oct. 1, 2011, *available at* http://coop.fema.gov/pdf/government/grant/pa/fy12_prj.pdf.

21. *See generally* PA PROGRAM HANDBOOK, *supra* note 14, exhibit C.

22. *Id.* at C-1.

23. *Id.* at C-2. *See also id.* at C-2, C-3 (containing examples of potentially approvable mitigation measures, such as reinforcing columns damaged in an earthquake or providing shutters for windows blown out in a storm).

24. *Id.* at C-2, C-3.

25. *Id.* at 32–33.

26. *See, e.g.*, the Consolidated and Further Appropriations Act of 2012, Pub. L. No. 112-55, tit. II, Public Housing Capital Fund (indicating that HUD may use not more than $20 million of the fiscal year 2012 public housing capital fund appropriation for such purposes).

27. *See generally* PIH Notice 2010-14, *supra* note 13.

28. *See, e.g.*, Announcement of Funding Awards: Capital Fund Safety and Security Grants; Fiscal Year 2011, 77 Fed. Reg. 23,492 (Apr. 19, 2012).

29. PIH Notice 2010-14, *supra* note 13, § 4(b).

30. *Id.*

31. *Id.* § 4(c).

32. *Id.* § 4(d). HUD has also provided guidance on what materials should be included in the application. *See id.* §§ 5(f) (relating to a preliminary application) and 6(c) (relating to a final application).

33. *Id.* § 5(a).

34. *Id.* §§ 5(c), 6(a).

35. *Id.* §§ 5(h), 7.

36. *Id.* §§ 5(c), 5(h), 7(i).

37. *Id.* §§ 5(h), 7(ii).

38. *Id.* §§ 5(h), 5(i), 7, 8.

39. For part 58 reviews, *see* 24 C.F.R. § 58.34(a)(10) and for part 50 reviews, *see* 24 C.F.R. § 50.19(b)(10) (each exempting from environmental review "[a]ssistance for temporary or permanent improvements that do not alter environmental conditions and are ***limited to protection, repair, or restoration activities necessary only to control or arrest the effects from disasters*** or imminent threats to public safety . . ." (emphasis added)); *see also* PIH Notice 2010-14, *supra* note 13, §§ (5)(b), 6(c)(iv). Note that "responsible entity" here refers to the term as defined at 24 C.F.R. § 58.2(a)(7), which, where applicable, would generally refer to a state, local, or tribal government with jurisdiction over the public housing project that exercises land use responsibility.

40. PIH Notice 2010-14, *supra* note 13, § 6(c)(iv).

41. 24 C.F.R. §§ 970.3(a), 970.7(a); Section 7 of the Annual Contribution Contract (ACC); *see generally* 42 U.S.C. § 1437p; 24 C.F.R. pt. 970. Note that there is a de minimus exception under which a PHA may demolish units without approval under Section 18 of the Housing Act, if (a) the demolition within any five-year period is not more than the lesser of five units or 5 percent of the PHA's total dwelling units and (b) either (i) the space occupied by the demolished unit is used to meet resident service or other resident needs, or (ii) "the demolished unit was beyond repair." 42 U.S.C. § 1437p(f); 24 C.F.R. § 970.27. *See also* 24 C.F.R. § 970.3(b) (discussing additional exceptions to the demolition and disposition requirements discussed here).

42. The application is made on HUD Form 52860, Demolition/Disposition Application.

43. *See* notes 71 through 73 and accompanying text.

44. 24 C.F.R. § 970.3(b)(12). The mixed-finance program is governed by regulations at 24 C.F.R. Part 941, Subpart F.

45. 42 U.S.C. § 1437p(a). Similarly, the governing regulations state that HUD will approve an application for disposition upon the PHA's submission of an application for disposition with the required certifications and supporting information set forth in the regulations. 24 C.F.R. § 970.7(a).

46. PHAs' annual plans are required, generally, pursuant to 42 U.S.C. § 1437c-1 and 24 C.F.R. Part 903, Subpart B.

47. 42 U.S.C. § 1437p(a)(3); 24 C.F.R. § 970.7(a)(1).

48. *See generally* 24 C.F.R. pt. 91.

49. 42 U.S.C. § 1437p(a)(4). In addition to the certifications discussed in this section, the PHA must certify that the application does not violate any remedial civil rights order or agreement, voluntary compliance agreement, final judgment, consent decree, settlement agreement, or other court order or agreement. 24 C.F.R. § 970.7(a)(16). This is a fact-sensitive matter in which the PHA should consult its records and counsel to ensure that the certification can be provided.

50. 42 U.S.C. § 1437p(a)(4) (containing specific information to be included in the required notice). The PHA is also required to consult with the residents of the project, any resident organization affected by the disposition, and the PHA's resident advisory board. *See* 24 C.F.R. § 970.9.

51. 42 U.S.C. § 1437p(a)(4).

52. *See* 24 C.F.R. §§ 970.21, 970.23.

53. *See* 24 C.F.R. §§ 970.7, 970.15, 970.17.

54. For requirements relating to resident consultation, see 24 C.F.R. Section 970.9(a). For requirements relating to local government consultation, see 24 C.F.R. Section 970.7(a)(14).

55. 24 C.F.R. § 970.7(a)(13). Note that the resolution must be signed and dated after the completion of all resident and local government consultation.

56. 24 C.F.R. §§ 970.13(c), 50.43, 58.33; 40 C.F.R. § 1506.11.

57. 24 C.F.R. § 970.7(a).

58. If the property does not contain dwelling units, the PHA must certify in essence that the property is excess or that the disposition will not interfere with the public housing project's operation. *See* 24 U.S.C. § 1437p(a)(2)(C).

59. This justification might be appropriate when the transfer of the development to another party would be more cost-effective or efficient because that party has access to other resources that may not be available to the PHA.

60. 24 C.F.R. § 970.17.

61. 42 U.S.C. § 1437p(a)(4), (c).

62. 24 C.F.R. § 970.9(b)(3).

63. 42 U.S.C. § 1437p(a)(5).

64. *See Demolition/Disposition*, U.S. DEP'T OF HOUS. & DEV., http://portal.hud.gov/hudportal/HUD?src=/program_offices/public_indian_ housing/centers/sac/demo_dispo (last visited Dec. 2, 2012).

65. *See* Inventory Removal Application, HUD Form 52860, § 5, line 7 (Aug. 2008).

66. If the basis of the value is an appraisal, the appraisal should be included with the application. *See id.* § 5, line 8.

67. 24 C.F.R. § 970.15; 42 U.S.C. § 1437p(a)(1).

68. 42 U.S.C. § 1437v(j)(2).

69. Other factors would include changes in the surrounding community that make the site no longer optimal for residential purposes or unmarketable, such as industrialization of the area or change in demand for the type of development, or disposition that allows for acquisition of other properties better suited or more economically operated as affordable housing. *See* 24 C.F.R. §§ 970.16, 970.17

70. 24 C.F.R. § 970.15(b)(2).

71. ACC, § 4.

72. *Demolition for an Accidental Loss*, *supra* note 7.

73. This post-demolition processing is an exception to HUD's position that generally HUD will not approve Section 18 applications after the fact.

74. *See* Gulf Opportunity Zone Act of 2005, Pub. L. No. 109-135, 119 Stat. 2577 (2005). LIHTC authority under this legislation supported the redevelopment of the Big Four in New Orleans. *See, e.g.*, Bruce Alpert, *GO Zone housing tax-credit extension endorsed by U.S. Senate*, TIMES-PICAYUNE (Mar. 5, 2010), http://www.nola.com/politics/index.ssf/2010/03/go_zone_housing_tax-credit_ext.html (noting HUD Secretary Shaun Donovan statements that "the tax credits are critical, particularly in New Orleans, to help leverage private financing to rebuild the 'Big Four public housing developments: St. Bernard, C.J. Peete, Lafitte and B.W. Cooper").

75. *See generally* 24 C.F.R. pt. 941, subpart F.

76. HUD has determined that, when a PHA uses a HOPE VI grant to develop public housing, the development must be accomplished in accordance with all of the requirements of the Housing Act and the Mixed Finance Regulations.

77. 42 U.S.C. § 1437z-7.

78. *Id.* §§ 1437d(b), 1437z-7(c).

79. *Id.* § 1437d(d).

80. *Id.* § 1437z-7(e).

81. *See, e.g.*, Jeremy Alford, *Public Housing's "Legacy Buildings,"* GAMBIT WKLY. (July 24, 2012), *available at* http://www.bestofneworleans.com/gambit/legacy-buildings/Content?oid=2045710 (reporting that three original buildings were renovated at Lafitte, for a community building, a Head Start program, and administrative offices; that three original buildings were renovated at B.W. Cooper for a community building and office space; and that one 20-unit building was undergoing a gut-rehabilitation and the "projects' first administrative building [was] likewise [being] restored").

82. *See Harmony Oaks Apartments, New Orleans*, MCCORMACK BARON SALAZAR, http://www.mccormackbaron.com/component/sobi2/?sobi2Task=sobi2Details&catid=16&sobi2Id=25 (last visited Apr. 9, 2013).

83. *Id.*

84. *Id.*

85. *Id.*

86. Pub. L. No. 102-389, 106 Stat. 1571 (1992).

87. Starting in 1996, the use of funds was fairly unrestricted within the general purpose of revitalizing public housing. The funds could be used for the demolition of obsolete public housing projects, the revitalization of the remaining public housing and the sites, replacement housing that would avoid or lessen concentrations of very-low-income families, and for tenant-based assistance under Section 8 of the Housing Act. Specifically, the appropriations provided that no funds were to be used for any purpose not provided for in the appropriation act itself, in the Housing Act of 1937, or in any appropriations acts for fiscal year 1993 through fiscal year 1998.

88. 42 U.S.C. § 1437v.

89. *See* HUD's Fiscal Year 2012 NOFA for the Choice Neighborhoods Initiative—Implementation Grants, § III(A)(2) [hereinafter, the FY 2012 CNI NOFA]. *See id.* § I(C)(26) (defining "severely distressed").

90. *See id.* § III(A)(3).

91. *See id.* § III(C)(3)(j).

92. *See id.* § IV(E)(4).

93. *See id.* § III(C)(3)(m).

94. *See id.* §§ III(C)(3)(*l*), (n).

95. A private development partner of a mixed-finance project selected in accordance with procurement requirements at 24 C.F.R. § 941.602(d) is not subject to Part 85 procurement requirements. However, if the developer proposes to use an identity of interest general contractor, the award can be made only if the developer demonstrates to HUD's satisfaction that the identity of interest general contractor's bid is the lowest bid submitted in response to a public request for bids. *See* 24 C.F.R. § 941.806(n)(1)(ii)(B). HUD has provided waivers of this provision, if the developer can demonstrate through an independent third party that the construction costs are reasonable.

96. FY 2012 CNI NOFA, *supra* note 89, § III(C)(3)(bb).

97. 42 U.S.C. § 1437j; *see also* FY 2012 CNI NOFA, *supra* note 89, § III(C)(3)(r).

98. FY 2012 CNI NOFA, *supra* note 89, § III(C)(3)(p).

99. This also applies to off-site replacement public housing, with certain limited exceptions under 24 C.F.R. Part 50. With respect to Choice Neighborhoods, *see* FY 2012 CNI NOFA, *supra* note 89, § III(C)(3)(x).

100. *See generally* Notice PIH 2012-32 [hereinafter referred to as the RAD Notice].

101. RAD conversions lower the PHA's Faircloth limit. *Id.* § 1.5(D).

102. *Id.* § 1.12(C)(3).

103. *See* 24 C.F.R. § 990.210(c).

104. OFFICE OF PUB. AND INDIAN HOUS., UPDATED PRORATION ESTIMATE FOR CALENDAR YEAR (CY) 2009: PUBLIC HOUSING OPERATING FUND PROGRAM (June 8, 2009), *available at* http://www.hud.gov /offices/pih/ programs/ph/am/of/revproration.pdf.

105. OFFICE OF PUB. AND INDIAN HOUS., EXPLANATION OF FINAL OBLIGATIONS UNDER OPERATING FUND PROGRAM FOR CALENDAR YEAR (CY) 2011 (Sept. 21, 2011), *available at* http://portal.hud.gov /hudportal/documents/ huddoc?id=finalprorationexplan.pdf.

106. OFFICE OF PUB. AND INDIAN HOUS., EXPLANATION OF OBLIGATIONS COVERING APRIL THROUGH JUNE UNDER OPERATING FUND PROGRAM CALENDAR YEAR (CY) 2012 (Mar. 30, 2012), *available at* http://www.hud.gov/ offices/pih/programs/ph/am/of/revproration.pdf.

107. RAD also allows transfer of rental assistance to another project where the public housing project is economically nonviable, physically obsolete, or severely distressed.

108. *See generally* Multifamily Assisted Housing Reform and Affordability Act, Pub. L. No. 107-116 (codified at 42 U.S.C. § 1437f note).; *see, e.g.*, Michael Reardon & Tatiana Gutierrez Abendschein, *The Section 8 Housing Assistance Program*, *in* NAVIGATING HUD PROGRAMS: A PRACTITIONER'S GUIDE TO THE LABYRINTH (2012) (for additional background on project-based Section 8 contracts and renewals, and the Multifamily Assisted Housing Reform and Affordability Act process).

109. For instance, for a project converting to a PBV contract, more than 50 percent of units in a project may receive the benefit of PBVs under RAD if at least 50 percent of units qualify for the elderly, disabled, or supportive services exemptions. Supportive services may be provided to residents through a third party, and unlike the general PBV program, residents of the project at the time of the RAD conversion may opt not to receive supportive services and remain as residents of the project. Units subject to a PBV contract under RAD will continue to be subject to housing quality standards, rather than becoming subject to the Uniform Physical Condition Standards. Under RAD, the PBV deconcentration requirements are waived for all conversions and involuntary displacement of residents for income mixing purposes is not allowed.

110. "Choice-mobility" refers to certain tenant rights designed to enhance tenants' choice and mobility, primarily by conferring rights to move out of a unit assisted with a project-based assistance and receive priority for comparable tenant-based assistance. *See, e.g.*, 24 C.F.R. § 983.260.

111. RAD Notice, *supra* note 100, § 1.2.

112. *Id.* § 1.7(C)(5).

113. In addition, HUD's office of Public and Indian Housing recently issued a proposed rule that would, if adopted as proposed, make Davis-Bacon and Section 3 requirements applicable throughout the PBV program.

114. Section 18 approval will be required in many RAD conversions, although not if the conversion involves less than the greater of 5 percent of the PHA's assisted units or five units. Converted units will not count in this calculation if they have already been approved for demolition or disposition under Section 18 or have been vacant for more than 24 months. Section 18 also will not apply under RAD if the reduction in unit count would allow the owner to reconfigure apartments, such as efficiency units, or facilitate social service delivery.

115. *See, e.g.*, SUSAN J. POPKIN ET. AL., URBAN INST., A DECADE OF HOPE VI: RESEARCH FINDINGS AND POLICY CHALLENGES (May 2004), *available at* http://www.urban.org/UploadedPDF/411002 _HOPEVI.pdf (for general background on and analysis of this debate).

116. Section 121 of the Housing and Community Development Act of 1987 amended Section 18 of the Housing Act.

117. Title VI of the Housing and Community Development Act of 1987 (Pub. L. No. 100-242, 101 Stat. 1951 (1988).

118. See 1995–98 appropriations acts and QHWRA.

119. *See* FY 2012 CNI NOFA, *supra* note 89, § III(C)(3)(b).

120. Choice Neighborhoods: One-for-One Replacement Criteria and Hard-Unit Exception, *available at* http://portal.hud.gov/huddoc/2012hard-unit-exception.pdf (last updated Jan. 6, 2012). This exception is available only in soft rental markets where vouchers are currently being used primarily in lower poverty neighborhoods and a tenant issued a voucher is likely to be successful in leasing a unit. These criteria are intended to allow tenant-based vouchers as a substitute for hard units only where the vouchers would effectively promote resident mobility and "access [to] better neighborhoods." *Id.*

121. Infographic, *HUD Plans Fewer Low-Rent Units*, TIMES-PICAYUNE (Dec. 9, 2008), *available at* http://blog.nola.com/graphics/2008/12/BIG4UNITS120908.jpg.

122. Katy Reckdahl, *HUD Begins Work on St. Bernard Complex: But Critics Fault Agency for Reducing Available Units for N.O. Poor*, TIMES-PICAYUNE, Dec. 9, 2008, *available at* http://www.nola.com/frontpage/t-p/index.ssf?/base/news-12/1228804235146720.xml&coll=1.

123. Infographic, *HUD Plans Fewer Low-Rent Units*, *supra* note 121.

124. Reckdahl, *supra* note 122.

125. *Id.*

126. *Id.*

127. Reckdahl, *supra* note 122.

128. *See* 24 C.F.R. § 941.202.

129. *Id.* § 941.202(c)(1).

130. *Id.* § 941.202(d).

131. *Id.* § 941.202(c)(1)(i).

132. 24 C.F.R. § 941.202(c)

133. *See generally* RAD Notice, *supra* note 100, pt. I.

CHAPTER 12

Locked Out and Torn Down: Public Housing Post–Hurricane Katrina

Bill Quigley and Sara H. Godchaux

I. Introduction

Hurricane Katrina hit and devastated New Orleans on August 29, 2005. When the levees protecting New Orleans failed, approximately 80 percent of the city was flooded. Hurricane Katrina and the subsequent levee failures resulted in the deaths of at least 986 Louisiana residents alone, and more than 1,600 people in total. Hurricane Katrina displaced more than a million people on the Gulf Coast. As the floodwaters receded, displaced New Orleans residents began the difficult process of rebuilding their lives. Many viewed returning to their homes and communities as a critical step in that process—but that avenue was blocked off to certain individuals in the aftermath of Hurricane Katrina, as this chapter will discuss, due to an inability to access safe and affordable housing. Over seven years later, many residents are still unable to return to their homes due to government redevelopment decisions, particularly those regarding housing in post–Hurricane Katrina New Orleans.

Affordable housing was very tough to secure in New Orleans before Hurricane Katrina. Even though it was poorly managed, public housing was an extremely important part of affordable housing for the very poorest in the community before Hurricane Katrina, housing 5,146 families, with a waiting list of 17,000 people. The Housing Authority of New Orleans (HANO) was so poorly managed that it had been in receivership to the U.S. Department of Housing and Urban Development (HUD) and run by HUD appointees since 2002. Thus, the decisions made in New Orleans by the local public housing authority were actually decisions made in concert with HUD.

Despite these staggering numbers of people in need of public housing, HANO and HUD promoted the demolition of thousands of public housing apartments with unmet promises to replace the numbers of units.

Once Hurricane Katrina hit, there was an express decision by political and business leaders in the city, as well as HANO and HUD, to use this as an opportunity to demolish public housing in New Orleans. Public housing residents who wanted to return were locked out of their apartments and forced to live elsewhere. HANO swore it lost track of where former residents were displaced to after the storm, so real follow-up was impossible. Despite years of litigation, lobbying, and demonstrations, HUD demolished thousands of much-needed apartments and to date has only replaced less than 10 percent of the units. This has aggravated the affordable housing situation in New Orleans as rents are up and opportunities are down. Plus, the demolitions totally denied the idea of home and neighborhood. HANO lawyers openly said residents were better off in bigger apartments in Texas than the ones they had lived in for years in New Orleans. The idea that a home is more than the four walls was foreign to HUD and HANO and the leaders of the city. There is much literature supporting the position that displacement wrecks social networks that are important for all people, but especially families whose lives are economically precarious. Neighbors, families, schools, churches, and community groups all play a critical role. To the extent that social networks are dependent on the people who lived in the various public housing communities for years, these, too, were demolished.

This chapter examines low-income housing in New Orleans prior to the storm, in section II, with a particular emphasis on public housing before Hurricane Katrina, in section III. It then looks at the overall effect Hurricane Katrina had on low-income housing in New Orleans in section IV and the political response to the storm in section V. Section VI examines what happened to public housing tenants both during Hurricane Katrina and in its aftermath. Section VII discusses the role of HUD in response to the storm, particularly its decision to demolish, and not replace, a majority of the public housing in the city. The litigation that ensued over HUD's demolition decision, and its ultimate failure to save public housing, is summarized in section VIII. Finally, the resulting state of low-income housing in New Orleans more than seven years after Hurricane Katrina is described in section IX. This chapter shows how redevelopment after Hurricane Katrina, far from being used as an opportunity to remedy the preexisting affordable-housing crisis in the city, actually cut off opportunities for thousands of families to return to the city and added to the exclusion of African-American families from New Orleans. (For further discussion on public housing decisions post-disaster from the perspective of the public housing authority, see chapter 11).

II. Low-Income Housing in New Orleans Pre–Hurricane Katrina

Even before Hurricane Katrina hit New Orleans on August 29, 2005, the city had a substantial problem with affordable housing. According to data from the 2000 census, two-thirds of extremely-low-income households in New Orleans paid more than 30 percent of their income in rent—meaning that such households bore excessive housing costs under federal standards.[1] More than half of very-low-income households spent at least 50 percent of their income on rent.[2] Furthermore, New Orleans' affordable housing stock was already shrinking before Hurricane Katrina—making low-income housing hard to find for residents.[3]

Renting was the most important housing option for the people of New Orleans before Hurricane Katrina, partially because rental prices in New Orleans were some of the lowest in the country, and because such a large number of people lived below the poverty line.[4] In fact, 53.5 percent of all housing in pre–Hurricane Katrina New Orleans was renter occupied, while only 46.5 percent of housing was owner occupied.[5] Compare this with national numbers: In the United States as a whole, only 33.8 percent of all housing was renter occupied, while 62.8 percent was owner occupied.[6] Thus, rental property made up an important part of the New Orleans housing market before Hurricane Katrina, especially for low-income residents. A majority of the property damaged by the hurricane consisted of rental property, including more than 50,000 apartments in New Orleans alone, further exacerbating affordable housing problems in post–Hurricane Katrina New Orleans.[7]

In New Orleans, there were 5,146 occupied traditional public-housing apartments prior to Hurricane Katrina and virtually 100 percent of these households were African-American.[8] Furthermore, there were nearly 9,000 subsidized housing voucher apartments.[9] Together, these housed more than 14,000 families and a total of 49,000 people.[10] A 2000 report shows that 88 percent of those living in all types of subsidized housing in New Orleans were African-American.[11] Both the public housing and the voucher programs are managed by HANO in accordance with federal law and regulations established by the HUD.[12] However, due to gross mismanagement and the squandering of federal money, HUD placed HANO in receivership in 2002.[13] As such, HUD has managed the day-to-day operations of HANO since 2002.[14]

Before Hurricane Katrina, New Orleans had the second-highest level of poverty concentration in the United States, and families participating in government-assisted housing programs in New Orleans lived in poorer neighborhoods on average than those nationwide.[15] In 2000, about one-fourth of New Orleans' neighborhoods were considered to be ones of extreme poverty, meaning at least 40 percent of their residents lived below the poverty line.[16] Thirty-seven percent of all New Orleanians lived in neighborhoods of extreme poverty.[17] Additionally, low-income African-Americans lived in neighborhoods of extreme poverty concentration at four times the rate of low-income whites.[18] And the numbers were even worse for those participating in government-assisted housing programs. In fact, 46.9 percent of voucher users in New Orleans lived in areas of over 30 percent poverty concentration and 97.4 percent of public housing residents lived in such neighborhoods.[19] Comparatively, nationally, only 22.2 percent of voucher users in the top 50 metropolitan areas lived in areas of over 30 percent poverty concentration, as did 66.1 percent of public housing residents.[20] Thus, most New Orleans families who received government-assisted housing lived in areas of extreme concentrated poverty.[21]

Generally, these areas marked by extreme concentrated poverty and high racial segregation were the ones hit the hardest by Hurricane Katrina because the poorer neighborhoods in New Orleans are generally the lowest-lying in the city.[22] More than three-quarters of the high-concentrated poverty areas were flooded.[23] Additionally, in Orleans Parish, 272,000 residents, or 73 percent of the population affected by the hurricane, were African-American.[24] A majority of those affected were low-income renters.[25] As such, low-income, overwhelmingly African-American residents of the city of New Orleans were disproportionately affected by the hurricane, and many are still struggling to find affordable housing and rebuild their lives in the city.

III. Public Housing in New Orleans Pre–Hurricane Katrina

Public housing in New Orleans was designed as clusters of mostly two- and three-story buildings with six to eight apartments in each.[26] These complexes were not the dense high-rise towers found in other major cities.[27] On November 19, 2006, *New York Times* architecture critic Nicolai Ouroussoff criticized plans to demolish these public housing apartments, saying: "Modestly scaled, they include some of the best public housing built in the United States. Solidly built, the buildings' detailed brickwork, tile roofs and wrought-iron balustrades represent a level of craft more likely found on an Ivy League campus than in a contemporary public housing complex."[28]

Public housing apartments in New Orleans pre–Hurricane Katrina rented for very modest rents, which were tied directly to the individual residents' incomes.[29] Most tenants did not pay separate utility charges—these were included in their monthly rental payments.[30] Furthermore, most leases were essentially for life, unless someone in the household was caught breaking the law.[31] To their residents, these public housing complexes were more than just four walls and a roof to sleep under—they were close-knit communities.[32] Many residents had lived in these communities for decades—their whole families lived there, their friends, their support groups.[33] As discussed further in section IX, the storm, the displacement of residents from their homes, and the subsequent demolition of these complexes completely disrupted and destroyed these communities that were so important to the residents.[34]

Of the 5,146 public housing apartments occupied before Hurricane Katrina, 3,077 units were located in the four biggest public housing developments—C.J. Peete, Faubourg Lafitte, St. Bernard, and B.W. Cooper (collectively, the "Big

Four"). Before Hurricane Katrina, there was a waiting list of 17,000 individuals and families to get into public housing.[35] As such, even before Hurricane Katrina, HUD recognized that "[t]he need for additional public and affordable housing in the New Orleans community is at crisis proportions."[36]

However, despite this assessment, for many years prior to Hurricane Katrina, HANO and HUD had been working on forcing low-income African-American families out of public housing in New Orleans by drastically reducing the number of public housing units from more than 13,000 in 1996 to approximately 5,000 occupied units by 2005.[37] Two thousand units of public housing had been empty for years leading up to Hurricane Katrina, supposedly awaiting demolition.[38] This pattern of reducing available public housing units in New Orleans continued despite the fact that there were long waiting lists for both public housing and Section 8 rental assistance in New Orleans, and thus, the supply of public housing was being exponentially outstripped by the demand.[39]

Following national trends to eliminate public housing complexes and create "mixed income" residential communities in their place, HANO and HUD were in the process of demolishing public housing in New Orleans even before Hurricane Katrina hit, despite the overwhelming demand for it (i.e., the 17,000 families on waiting lists).[40] One notable example of this demolition was the St. Thomas housing development in the Irish Channel of New Orleans—once home to 1,510 low-income families.[41] St. Thomas was demolished in 2000 under the HUD HOPE VI program with the promise that the displaced residents would be returning to a beautiful, redeveloped mixed-income community called River Garden Apartments.[42] It is now home to a Wal-Mart and hundreds of little houses.[43] One hundred eighty-two apartments of the 660 units of new housing were reserved for public housing–eligible families.[44] A mere 100 out of the 1,510 families who used to reside at St. Thomas have been allowed to move back in.[45] Many of these families had to force their way back in with litigation by the Greater New Orleans Fair Housing Action Center.[46]

For instance, one tenant who lived in St. Thomas before it was torn down in 2000 had gotten her application approved by HUD to move back in before Hurricane Katrina hit.[47] After the storm, this tenant applied four times for an apartment, even taking a bus back from Houston where she had been evacuated, only to be told there was no room for her.[48] Another time she was denied because she was unemployed.[49] Sadly, the truth revealed HANO had leased 44 of the 63 apartments set aside for public housing residents to HANO employees after Hurricane Katrina instead of allowing the low-income public housing tenants back into their apartments after the storm.[50] Because of HANO and HUD's actions, this particular tenant was forced to live in her car, sometimes with her five-year-old child (when the child could not stay with other family or friends), or else stay with other family members living on $234 a month in food stamps and $188 in general welfare.[51]

So what happened to the other thousands of former residents of St. Thomas? Most former residents were shifted to the Section 8 voucher program, which, as discussed further in section IX, is fraught with discrimination against low-income African-American renters making vouchers an inadequate alternative to public housing and leaving such residents with few options for housing.[52] Others moved in with relatives or ended up homeless.[53] The St. Thomas/River Gardens example of what these mixed-income redevelopments really meant for public housing tenants was widely known before Hurricane Katrina and eerily foreshadowed what was in store for New Orleans public housing after Hurricane Katrina.

IV. Hurricane Katrina Damage to Public Housing

Hurricane Katrina destroyed or caused severe damage to approximately 150,000 housing units in the city of New Orleans.[54] Of these units that were damaged or lost in Hurricane Katrina, 112,000 (or 79 percent) consisted of affordable to low-income housing.[55] Furthermore, most of these units were rental properties.[56] A majority of these units have not been replaced or repaired as the post–Hurricane Katrina redevelopment plan seeks to limit the construction of affordable housing.[57]

While Hurricane Katrina destroyed much of the low-income rental property in the city of New Orleans, most of the public housing in New Orleans suffered only minimal damage. Though the extent of damage would later be contested by HANO and HUD, it was not controversial in the months before HUD announced demolition would occur. In fact, HANO initially announced that most developments could be opened with some work and they intended to clean, repair, and reopen public housing.[58] HANO first made estimates for repair and rehabilitation that were much less expensive than demolition and redevelopment.[59]

Though HANO later attempted to rationalize its decision to demolish thousands of public housing units by stating they had sustained significant damage from the hurricane, in direct contradiction to its own earlier statements that much of the public housing suffered only minimal damage and was in fact salvageable, this was soon proved to be untrue.[60] As part of federal litigation to halt the demolition of the Big Four, John Fernandez, an associate professor of architecture at MIT, inspected 140 public housing apartments in the Big Four and testified in court that he found "no structural or nonstructural damage . . . that would reasonably warrant any cost-effective building demolition."[61] Furthermore, he concluded, "[j]ustifications for demolition on the grounds that these buildings can no longer function as safe and humane housing for the people of New Orleans are not credible."[62]

This is important because the justification for demolition of public housing required by law is that it must be certified that it is unsuitable for housing purposes and no reasonable program of modification is cost-effective.[63] But since HUD had already announced demolition was coming, the rationale followed and changed.

After it was revealed to the public that the buildings were not in the state of disrepair that HANO and HUD originally represented, HANO modified its rationale for demolition. HANO then suggested that it would cost significantly more to repair the buildings than to raze them and start over.[64] However, these statements again proved to be false. Internal HANO and HUD documents revealed that the cost for repair and renovation for each of the Big Four housing developments was significantly less than for demolition and redevelopment.[65] The Housing Authority's own documents showed that Lafitte could be repaired for $20 million, even completely overhauled for $85 million, while the estimate for demolition and rebuilding many fewer units would cost over $100 million.[66] Likewise, St. Bernard could be repaired for $41 million, substantially modernized for $130 million, while demolition and rebuilding fewer units would cost $197 million.[67] B.W. Cooper could be substantially renovated for $135 million, compared with $221 million to demolish and rebuild fewer units.[68] In fact, HANO's own insurance company reported that it would take less than $5,000 each to repair the C.J. Peete apartments.[69]

The extent of damage was drastically inflated after HUD announced that the properties were to be destroyed and remained in controversy until demolition.

V. Political Response to Damaged Public Housing

"We finally cleaned up public housing in New Orleans. We couldn't do it, but God did."

—Richard Baker, U.S. Congressman (R-La.), just days after Hurricane Katrina[70]

Immediately after Hurricane Katrina, President George W. Bush and other national political leaders repeatedly expressed the same goal: to rebuild New Orleans for all interested residents and to give displaced residents an opportunity to return to their homes.[71] In furtherance of this objective, on December 30, 2005, Congress directed HUD to preserve *all* housing, which would include public housing that received project-based assistance.[72] As discussed in detail in section VII, HUD acted in direct contravention to this congressional mandate by refusing to reopen and repair public housing and subsequently approving its demolition.[73] Additionally, such actions went directly against the idea of providing displaced residents of New Orleans the opportunity to return home. As the Reverend Jesse Jackson stated in a speech given in the aftermath of Hurricane Katrina, "the right to return is hollow without a plan for transportation and a place to stay."[74]

In a similar vein, political leaders in New Orleans and across the state of Louisiana had their own agenda for public housing after Hurricane Katrina—one greatly influenced by prominent business leaders in the city.[75] Such leaders looked at the hurricane as an opportunity to redefine the contours of the demographics of the city, as well as a business opportunity to improve the city for its middle- to high-income residents and its well-connected business leaders by turning former public housing property into prime commercial developments.[76]

In fact, New Orleans' post–Hurricane Katrina redevelopment plans were merely thinly veiled attempts to rid the city of its most unpopular residents, reduce the government's role in providing housing to the poor, and create business opportunities for New Orleans' elite.[77] Sentiments expressed by some of New Orleans' political leaders confirm this. For example, U.S. Congressman Richard Baker (R-La.), just days after Hurricane Katrina, stated: "We finally cleaned up public housing in New Orleans. We couldn't do it, but God did."[78] Similarly, former City Council President Oliver Thomas admitted he was talking about African-Americans when he said, "[w]e don't need soap opera watchers all day," and if displaced residents want to come back, they better want to work.[79]

Furthermore, in 2007, the U.S. Congress considered two important pieces of legislation on low-income housing issues that proposed to save public housing in New Orleans and provide for one-for-one replacement of any public housing units destroyed.[80] Given the serious shortage of affordable housing after Hurricane Katrina along the Gulf Coast, this would have been an excellent policy from a housing point of view.[81]

The House of Representatives passed House Bill 1227, the Gulf Coast Hurricane Housing Recovery Act of 2007, on March 21, 2007, with bipartisan support—with 302 voting in favor and 125 opposed to the bill.[82] However, after this early victory, the Senate version of the bill,[83] proposed by Sen. Mary Landrieu (D-La.), was stopped short by the opposition of Louisiana senator David Vitter (R-La.).[84] While the Senate bill originally had the support of both Louisiana senators (Vitter and Landrieu), HUD and Vitter withdrew their support for the bill in September 2007.[85] Ultimately, as a result, the bill died in the Senate.[86]

While Vitter vaguely cited the reason for withdrawing his support as his belief that the proposed legislation would merely re-create the same public housing complexes as existed before Hurricane Katrina with all their problems, it is likely that Vitter's political objectives were the driving force behind his opposition to the bill.[87] At the time, Landrieu was coming up for reelection, and it served Vitter and the Republican Party's interests to ensure she would not lead a bill that would gain her the support of many Louisianans.[88] Furthermore, it served Republican political interests to stop the returning of poor, African-American residents to the city of New Orleans—a demographic that votes overwhelmingly Democratic.[89]

Thus, in the aftermath of Hurricane Katrina, both local and national political leaders ignored the needs of public housing residents displaced by the storm.

VI. What Happened to Public Housing Residents During and After Hurricane Katrina: An Unequal Opportunity to Return

What happened during the storm to the 5,146 families who occupied public housing before Hurricane Katrina? Some evacuated before the storm hit; those who were left behind were bused to shelters and then were forced to leave the city after Hurricane Katrina hit.[90] Many ended up in shelters in Houston or Atlanta; others were scattered elsewhere across the country.[91] From these shelters, some were moved into temporary housing, and others moved in with friends and family.[92] Relatively little cohesive information exists on what happened to public housing tenants during the storm. HANO has not been able to locate even 20 percent of the 3,077 former Big Four households.[93]

Public housing residents who were able to travel home to New Orleans in the months following Hurricane Katrina came home to find that HANO had locked them out of their homes.[94] Most of the housing developments were boarded up, with steel bars blocking some of the doors and 10-foot-high fences topped with barbed wire blocking off the perimeters of some housing developments.[95] Tenants at first were generally not even allowed in to retrieve their personal belongings. As such, public housing residents trying to return home were not kept out of their homes by damage from the hurricane or flooding, but instead were shut out by HANO. As discussed earlier, the storm and its aftermath did little structural damage to the developments in which most residents lived. With moderate repair and cleanup, the government could have allowed the majority of public housing residents to return to their homes. Yet by October 2006, a year after the storm, only 1,038 public housing units had been reoccupied—approximately 20 percent of the units occupied before Hurricane Katrina.[96] The rest remained closed by order of HANO, under guidance from HUD.[97]

Displaced HANO residents were absorbed into assisted housing across the country, for what most thought was a temporary stay. HANO did not try to collect rent from residents and responded to all inquiries by deflecting answers about when people could return. Residents did not have a meeting with HANO about the impending demolitions until November 29, 2006, months after HUD announced their decision to demolish.[98]

While HANO delayed reopening the public housing complexes, residents waited to return to their homes, unable to start rebuilding their lives while they waited for answers from HANO.[99] This prolonged displacement forced many residents to incur costs and hardships they did not have when they were living in public housing.[100] Families were split up and scattered across the country.[101] Furthermore, displaced residents found it hard to get jobs in their new cities because displaced persons were often discriminated against and stigmatized.[102] Unemployment rates for evacuees remaining displaced were triple those who returned to New Orleans.[103] This resulted in those displaced falling even deeper into poverty.[104] For example, one year after Hurricane Katrina in Houston alone, fewer than 20 percent of Hurricane Katrina evacuees were employed, but 60 percent were employed before Hurricane Katrina.[105]

An independent analysis of the post–Hurricane Katrina public housing crisis issued July 2006, nearly one year after the storm, confirmed: Most displaced public housing residents wanted to return; almost 80 percent of the subsidized apartments were damaged, leaving more than 16,000 families without housing; and HUD and HANO severely decreased the availability of both public housing and housing vouchers.[106]

Federal regulations do not allow demolition of public housing without a plan being submitted to HUD, notice to residents, and a number of other prerequisites.[107] However, on June 14, 2006, with no notice to the residents, nor any opportunity for residents to be heard, nor even an application for demolition filed, HUD announced in a press release that it would demolish more than 5,000 public housing apartments in the St. Bernard, C.J. Peete, B.W. Cooper, and Lafitte housing developments.[108] This promised to be the largest demolition in the city's history, destroying more than 70 percent of New Orleans public housing stock.[109]

Shocked residents fought back against HUD's planned demolition of their homes—many promised to fix up their apartments themselves if given the chance. Litigation was launched by residents. The court actions, described in section VIII, offered many opportunities for residents to turn out and show their opposition to the demolition.

One public housing resident at a public hearing ordered by a federal judge the in November of 2006 stated: "I want my house back. If I could have, I would have cleaned it. I clean for a living, and I'm proud of it."[110] And residents were not the only ones resisting the demolition—they were soon joined by preservationists, housing experts, and other community activists who expressed their support of preserving much of the Big Four, especially emphasizing renovating the complexes as the best way to address the housing crisis and recognize former residents' right to return to the city.[111] In fact, as the Advancement Project's Judith Browne Dianis explained of the movement to preserve the Lafitte housing complex, "[i]t's not about damaged units, it's about whether low-income African Americans are welcome in New Orleans."[112]

It should be noted that New Orleans public housing residents were not necessarily against the idea of mixed-income housing—many were just fearful that they would not be in the mix, that low-income public housing would not be available for everyone in need of it in the short term, and that there were no guarantees of long-term subsidized housing for former residents for the future.[113] As Tracie Washington, then director of the NAACP Gulf Coast Advocacy Center, pointed out: "It's not that people don't want mixed-income housing . . . It's that people need places to live for the short term and that evacuees have to be able to get back to New Orleans to have a place to reside in order to be a part of the long-term rebuilding process."[114] Such fears were not unfounded based on New Orleans' troubled history with razing public housing and replacing it with mixed-income communities before Hurricane Katrina. As River Gardens showed, only a small fraction of the families who had lived in these developments would be allowed to return once the mixed-income units were in place.

There were multiple protests staged at the Big Four complexes with residents and activists blocking demolition machinery and proclaiming that housing is a human right.[115]

The last step in the decision about the demolition of New Orleans public housing ultimately came down to a city council meeting at city hall on December 20, 2007, where New Orleans' leaders voted on whether to raze the Big Four.[116] Louisiana law mandated that demolition permits be approved by the city council and residents fought and won enforcement of this measure in December of 2007.[117]

Supporters of public housing, many who had traveled from all over the country back to New Orleans for the meeting, were for the most part denied a chance to speak and most were not even allowed in the building.[118] Some who insisted on speaking were arrested.[119] Much of the frustration came from the feeling that there was a lack of real consideration of public opinion and public input in the decision-making process to demolish the Big Four.[120] Ultimately, the council voted unanimously to demolish the Big Four and, within weeks, several public housing developments across the city were torn down.[121]

VII. Response of HUD

One month after Hurricane Katrina hit New Orleans, HUD got off to a bad start in New Orleans when, on September 29, 2005, HUD Secretary Alphonso Jackson, who was in charge of the development of a public housing plan for New Orleans, as well as the enforcement of fair housing opportunities and furthering fair housing in the use of federal funds, stated that post–Hurricane Katrina New Orleans "is not going to be as black as it was for a long time, if ever again."[122] On April 24, 2006, Jackson further stated that "only the best [public housing] residents should return. Those who paid rent on time, those who held a job and those who worked."[123] Perhaps that explains why 18 months after Hurricane Katrina, more than 80 percent of the 5,146 New Orleans public housing apartments remained closed by order of HUD.[124] Furthermore, although 4,300 families were given vouchers, given the difficulty of finding safe affordable housing, only 1,800 housing vouchers were in use in the city of New Orleans.[125] These actions significantly reduced the housing opportunities for the thousands of public housing families that remained displaced because they could not come home, as well as many others who were in need of housing in the city.

Then, the HUD secretary, in violation of many of HUD rules and regulations, publicly announced that thousands of public housing apartments were going to be bulldozed.[126] Without going through the required application process—which includes an application for demolition by HANO—without warning or notice or consultation with the residents, without making any arrangements with residents for them to try to arrange a purchase and renovation of their homes, HUD announced on June 14, 2006, that four major public housing developments would be demolished: Lafitte, B.W. Cooper, C.J. Peete, and St. Bernard.[127] At this time, HUD indicated it was dedicated to replacing all units occupied before Hurricane Katrina.[128]

HUD made this decision to immediately destroy more than 3,000 units of affordable public housing despite findings from the Louisiana Hurricane Housing Task Force that there was an urgent need for more than 30,000 affordable rental apartments in New Orleans in the immediate aftermath of the storm, *and* despite the congressional mandate to preserve all housing in New Orleans.[129] Perhaps in an attempt to assuage critics of its decision to act against the needs of the residents of

New Orleans, HANO also announced in June 2006 that it would reopen 1,000 public housing units in the city within 90 days.[130] However, HANO never delivered on this promise. By October 19, 2006—about 120 days later—only an additional 36 public housing units had been reopened and reoccupied.[131] One year later, on June 14, 2007, only an additional 423 units had been reopened and reoccupied.[132] In fact, the full 1,000 units promised never came into being, further hurting public housing residents who wanted to return to their homes.[133]

Until the HUD announcement that demolition had been decided, HANO, as noted in section IV, by its own assessment after the storm, found that many public housing units could have been preserved with some repairs.[134] HANO even expressed its intent to clean and repair public housing units at the Iberville, C.J. Peete, B.W. Cooper, and Lafitte public housing developments. Instead, HANO boarded up and fenced a number of these buildings, not allowing former residents back into their homes.[135] Furthermore, HANO failed to perform even basic maintenance to many units that suffered little or no damage.[136] As such, neither HUD nor HANO followed Congress's mandate[137] to preserve all housing to the extent feasible.[138]

A. Demolition or Rehabilitation?

HANO did not even submit its first application to demolish the public housing developments until October 17, 2006, 125 days after HUD had already publicly announced the demolitions. HUD reported that it reviewed HANO's demolition application under 42 U.S.C. § 1437p and its implementing regulations at 24 C.F.R. § 970. HUD decided that all the developments were obsolete and unsuitable for housing, brushing aside HANO's earlier plans to repair the apartments and the expert testimony offered by residents outlined in section IV. HUD approved the demolition on September 21, 2007, two years after the storm.[139]

HANO argued that the thousands of apartments should be demolished based on 24 C.F.R. § 970.15, which allows application for demolition when the housing is no longer suitable for housing and no reasonable program of modification is cost-effective to return the dwelling to useful life.[140] Residents argued that repair was entirely possible and cost-effective based on HANO's own survey and estimates. HUD disagreed and allowed the demolition.

B. Consultation and Offer to Residents

Federal regulations required HANO to consult with residents about its plan to demolish.[141] Further, any public housing authority that plans to dispose of property is required to offer it for sale to resident organizations, unless certain exceptions apply.[142] In violation of these rules, HUD announced the demolition 125 days before HANO even made an application.

Residents objected in court to the absolute lack of notice or consultation in the October 2006 plan for demolition filed with HUD. After a conference with the federal judge hearing the objections to the demolition, HANO was ordered to hold what they called a public hearing on November 29, 2006, to get input from residents. However, at that meeting there was no back-and-forth between residents and HANO. HANO essentially held an open microphone where residents could come up and air their questions or support or objections, but no response at all was made by HANO officials. Similar meetings were held in outlying cities, and HANO also met with the pre–Hurricane Katrina resident counsel board in December 2006. Even though residents overwhelmingly asked to return home, these meetings were enough consultation for HUD, which found this sufficient to approve demolition.[143]

Likewise, at least one of the major developments was the subject of a resident-based application for sale, triggering the requirement that the public housing agency give residents an opportunity to purchase the property proposed for demolition.[144] Residents of the St. Bernard development teamed up with the AFL-CIO to make an offer to redevelop that property after it was clear HANO and HUD were bound to demolish it. HANO and HUD found that the regulation that required offering the property to resident organizations was not applicable based on an exception in 24 CFR 970.9(3)(ii) and no negotiations were entered into with the resident organization.[145]

C. The Failures of the Federal Demolition Procedure

Another clear example of the abuse of the process engaged in by HUD and HANO is the actual application for demolition. HANO submitted its final version of its application to demolish the Big Four on September 20, 2007, and HUD approved the demolition plan on September 21, 2007—just one day after the completed plan was submitted.[146]

Throughout the application process, HANO and HUD cited a number of reasons for their decision to raze thousands of units of public housing—each of which turned out to be untrue. First, HUD attempted to rationalize its decision by claiming the buildings had sustained irreparable damage during the storm, directly contradicting its former assessments that much of the public housing stock was salvageable.[147] When this was proven to be untrue by the inspections of housing experts, HUD changed gears and cited the argument that the demolition would give New Orleans' public housing families a fresh start.[148] But a fresh start where? HUD's decision to not use a one-for-one replacement system virtually assured that many such families would not be able to make a fresh start in New Orleans because there would not be enough affordable housing available for everyone.

The HUD-approved plan provided for the replacement of the razed units with significantly fewer public housing units.[149] According to the plan, the St. Bernard development ,which had consisted of 1,400 units, would be replaced with 595 units and only 160 of those (11 percent of the original number of units) would be for public housing.[150] The C.J. Peete development, which had consisted of 723 units, would be replaced with 410 units; only 154 (21 percent of the original number of units) would be public housing units.[151] B.W. Cooper originally housed 1,546 public housing units. These would be replaced by 410 total units, of which only 154 (10 percent of the original number) would be public housing units.[152] Lafitte would be downsized in a similar way.[153] As such, HUD decided to spend hundreds of millions of Hurricane Katrina–assistance funds to end up with far fewer affordable apartments.[154]

Over the protests of many former residents, in early 2008, after getting the city council's blessing, HUD began demolitions on the Big Four.[155] All together, the agency knocked down 3,077 apartments that had been occupied before the storm.[156] As discussed further in section IX, HUD's demolition and redevelopment plans permanently displaced a significant number of low-income, African-American residents from New Orleans as they were essentially denied an equal opportunity to return to the city.

HUD's actions suggest that its goal from the start was to get out of the business of public housing, and it used the storm as an opportunity to expedite that process. By razing more than 3,000 public housing units that it had poorly managed before the storm and contracting out the management of the replacement units to third parties, HUD and the federal government have essentially removed themselves from the public housing sector. But at what human cost?

VIII. Litigation to Reopen Public Housing

Together, residents of public housing and many community leaders fought HUD's decision to demolish public housing in New Orleans.

On June 27, 2006, less than two weeks after HUD made its first public statement about Big Four's demolition, a class action lawsuit was brought in federal court against HANO and HUD on behalf of the New Orleans public housing residents who were shut out of their homes following Hurricane Katrina.[157] The suit alleged that by failing to reopen housing units that were not damaged by Hurricane Katrina, failing to repair other units, and declaring that most of the existing public housing stock in New Orleans would be demolished, HANO and HUD violated their "obligation to provide non-discriminatory access to safe, affordable housing for low-income families and breaching their contractual commitments and statutory obligations to public housing residents of New Orleans."[158] The litigation was essentially a contest between a fair housing challenge by residents versus HUD and HANO's claims that statutory rights authorized them to demolish.

The suit claimed that the actions of HUD and HANO to demolish four of New Orleans' largest public housing developments was action taken with the intent to rid New Orleans of some of its poor African-American residents. Specifically, the complaint alleged that HANO and HUD's failure to repair and reopen the developments from which the tenants were displaced violated (1) the Fair Housing Act, alleging disparate treatment, disparate impact, and a breach of the duty to affirmatively further fair housing; (2) the Housing Act of 1937; (3) the HANO lease agreements; (4) the 5th and 14th Amendments of the U.S. Constitution, alleging discriminatory intent under the Equal Protection Clause; and (5) various state laws, including constructive eviction and breach of contract.[159] The plaintiff residents asked the district court to immediately enjoin the planned demolitions, to compel HUD and HANO to repair and reopen the public housing units, and to award plaintiffs monetary damages for economic loss and emotional distress.[160]

Plaintiffs' motion for a temporary restraining order against the planned demolition was denied on November 22, 2006, because the court found that residents who received vouchers could not show irreparable harm. The court directed defendants to hold public hearings with residents as demanded by statute.[161]

In February 2007, the court denied the residents' motion for a preliminary injunction to halt the demolition of the Big Four, finding no irreparable harm, and dismissed plaintiffs' Housing Act claims. The court decided that residents could maintain private right of actions under the Fair Housing Act for claims of discrimination against HUD and HANO but did not offer sufficient evidence of discriminatory intent or effect and denied plaintiffs' motions. The court denied plaintiffs a private cause of action under section 1437 of the U.S. Housing Act and granted summary judgment for defendants for claims under it. The court also decided that since HUD had not yet approved the demolition application of HANO, the injury to residents was not imminent and denied the motions for relief.[162]

After the September 2007 HUD approval of HANO's application for the demolition, plaintiffs moved for another temporary restraining order to halt the demolition.[163] The district court again denied plaintiffs' request to enjoin the demolition.[164] Plaintiffs appealed this decision to the Fifth Circuit Court of Appeals and asked for temporary injunctive relief pending the appeal, but the Fifth Circuit denied the requests and ultimately upheld the district court's dismissal of plaintiffs' claims and its denial of an injunction to stop the demolition.[165]

A last-gasp state court injunction stopping the bulldozers was granted when it was discovered that demolition required approval of the New Orleans City Council, which had not been given. A city council meeting was rapidly convened at city hall on December 19, 2007, and New Orleans' leaders dutifully voted to raze the Big Four in a raucous meeting where people were Tasered, many residents were locked out, and others were arrested.[166]

Demolition commenced and even calls to halt public housing demolition from U.N. Special Rapporteurs on Housing and Minority Issues could not stop it. (For further discussion on the Special Rapporteurs' visits to New Orleans and an interational human rights framework to post-disaster recovery, see chapter 3.) The U.N. advisors found that the demolitions increased poverty and homelessness, did not meaningfully involve the residents in the decision making, and clearly had a racially discriminatory impact on the community.[167]

IX. Low-Income Housing in New Orleans 2012

As a result of Hurricane Katrina and the inadequate and discriminatory rebuilding process that followed, some of the most vulnerable groups have faced the steepest obstacles to returning to New Orleans. As noted by the NAACP one year following Hurricane Katrina, such "disparate opportunities for Gulf residents to return to their homes are creating rapid demographic shifts in the population of the city. Low-income communities and people of color now make up a smaller percentage of the New Orleans population than they did before the storm."[168] Data collected in the 2010 census revealed there were 118,526 *fewer* African-Americans living in New Orleans in 2010 than in 2000—making up 60 percent of the city's population in 2010, as compared with 67 percent in 2000.[169]

Such population shifts, as well as the housing decisions made in post–Hurricane Katrina New Orleans, have had a monumental impact on low-income housing in the city. For starters, the landscape of public housing in New Orleans in 2012 is essentially unrecognizable from what it was before Hurricane Katrina. The Big Four have been almost completely razed—with a few buildings here and there still being phased out.[170] The complexes have all been replaced with mixed-income housing communities and renamed: C.J. Peete is now Harmony Oaks; St. Bernard is now called Columbia Parc; Lafitte is Faubourg Lafitte; and B.W. Cooper is now Marrero Commons.[171]

HANO's own data shows that relatively few former residents have returned to the Big Four since Hurricane Katrina.[172] In fact, only roughly half (1,512) of the Big Four's 3,077 households have even returned to New Orleans.[173] Of these, only a few hundred, or roughly 7 percent of the original families, have returned to the four sites: 70 households at C.J. Peete have returned, 93 at Lafitte, 65 at St. Bernard, and a few dozen more at B.W. Cooper, which is just now filling its new apartments.[174] And of the 1,565 families who have not returned to New Orleans, there is relatively little information on where they are living and why they have not returned to the city—although it seems likely that a major reason is the destruction of their former homes.[175] Alarmingly, in the eight years since Hurricane Katrina hit, HANO has not been able to locate 20 percent of the 3,077 former Big Four households.[176]

Inherent in the actions of HANO and HUD was their belief that traditional public housing for many was inferior to newer mixed-income housing for fewer. Residents were absolutely clear that they were not opposed to mixed-income housing—they just wanted to be assured that they were going to be able to return to affordable housing in their neighborhoods. The national conversation about mixed-income housing replacing concentrated public housing appears to be heavily in favor of removing, relocating, and not concentrating poor people. However, the New Orleans experience after Hurricane Katrina was that returning home, to neighborhood, to neighbors, to church and school, and to community ties and bonds are extremely important. They may be even more important to people of little economic means who often survive only by family, church, and community relationships.

In some ways, the fate of New Orleans' public housing and its residents is not all that different from other public housing complexes that have been razed and replaced with mixed-income communities elsewhere in the United States. Generally, few public housing residents make it back to the new sites after their transformation.[177] A study by the Urban Institute of eight redevelopments nationwide found that only 19 percent of public housing households return to their rebuilt complexes.[178]

However, in other ways, the story of the Big Four is remarkably different from other redevelopments done by HUD throughout the country.[179] The Big Four were emptied of their 3,077 households in a matter of days during Hurricane Katrina, and their residents were scattered widely across the United States with no plan in place for how or where to house them in the interim.[180] This is different from other demolitions in which residents are systemically moved out and placed in alternative housing and where most residents move only a few miles away.[181]

As such, the demolition of public housing in New Orleans has had a huge impact on a number of once-vibrant New Orleans communities.[182] HUD not only razed people's homes, but also their close-knit communities, social networks, and support groups.[183] While community is important for everyone, experts say such networks are particularly important for the elderly and the poor because they rely more heavily on neighbors for everyday assistance and stability.[184] One former Lafitte resident described his community as a place where "[e]verybody knew everybody knew everybody" and where neighbors helped each other out.[185] Another Lafitte resident described how "[p]arents helped each other. You know, if it was cold outside and a kid's nose was running, the nearest parent would grab a tissue. They say it takes a village to raise a child. We had that village."[186] And even during Hurricane Katrina, neighbors in Lafitte took care of each other.[187] Just look at the numerous stories about people swimming through floodwater with elderly neighbors on their backs to get them to safety.[188] These stories and feelings are not just unique to Lafitte—former residents of all the Big Four complexes have similar stories.[189] And seven years later, these former communities are scattered throughout the country, making it hard for former residents to rebuild their lives both in New Orleans and in the cities to which many relocated.[190]

The storm and the subsequent destruction of the Big Four also had a number of consequences on low-income housing outside public housing in post–Hurricane Katrina New Orleans. The severe reduction in the number of public housing units available has resulted in an increased reliance on vouchers for affordable housing in New Orleans.[191] Many experts agree that the Housing Choice Voucher program has been an ineffective replacement for public housing in post–Hurricane Katrina New Orleans.[192] This can hardly be considered a surprise to HANO and HUD, as by their own pre–Hurricane Katrina assessments in 2003, they noted that "[r]elocation experience also demonstrates that Section 8 is not always a viable option for displaced residents transitioning from public housing."[193]

The Housing Choice Voucher program has failed to be an effective replacement for public housing in New Orleans post–Hurricane Katrina for a number of reasons. To begin with, there is currently not enough available, affordable housing in New Orleans for all former public housing tenants to rent.[194] One reason for this is the shortage of rental units in post–Hurricane Katrina New Orleans. Hurricane Katrina destroyed about half of the entire rental housing stock in New Orleans and, to date, a majority of the damaged rental property has not been replaced.[195] Thus, post–Hurricane Katrina, the demand for the remaining supply of rental housing increased and, as a result, rents skyrocketed across the metropolitan area. To illustrate, rents have increased approximately 44 percent since Hurricane Katrina, compared with 4 percent nationally during this same period.[196]

Importantly, the supply of affordable housing is even smaller for former public housing residents who now participate in the voucher program. This is because many landlords across the New Orleans metropolitan area either refuse to accept Section 8 vouchers outright, as they are not required to, or add insurmountable requirements for voucher holders in the lease terms, making it impossible for voucher holders to rent the units.[197] A 2009 report by the Greater New Orleans Fair Housing Action Center found that landlords were refusing to rent to families with vouchers about 82 percent of the time.[198] As such, in the first few years following Hurricane Katrina, thousands of housing vouchers went unused because landlords throughout the city refused to accept them.[199] A 2006 survey of all listed apartment rentals in the newspaper found that only five out of the 200 listed landlords were willing to accept Section 8 vouchers and had an available apartment.[200]

Racial discrimination affects this process as well. Of the landlords who do accept housing vouchers, many refuse outright to rent to the former public housing tenants (who are virtually all African-American) based on racial discrimination, which unfortunately still plays a significant role in the New Orleans rental market.[201] (For further discussion on the fair housing implications of the use of vouchers post-disaster, specifically post–Hurricane Katrina, see chapter 14.) The Fair Housing Action Center's 2009 report explains that a lot of the discrimination against Section 8 voucher holders is driven by racism and stereotypes about low-income African-Americans.[202] For example, the Fair Housing Action Center's report found that many landlords in the city would accept vouchers from white women, but told African-American women they did not accept vouchers.[203]

A final reason that vouchers have been an ineffective replacement for public housing is because vouchers generally do not cover costs such as security deposits or utilities, which tenants generally did not have to pay in public housing.[204] Like rents, the price of utilities increased by at least 33 percent after Hurricane Katrina, making payment of these costs an insurmountable barrier for some tenants, especially those below the poverty line, to be able to afford their Section 8 apartments.[205]

The lack of available affordable housing since Hurricane Katrina caused an explosion of New Orleans' homeless population after the storm. Despite the significant decrease in the post–Hurricane Katrina overall population of New Orleans, the city's homeless population soared to 70 percent higher than it was before the storm.[206] Currently, according to an annual homeless count by UNITY of Greater New Orleans, New Orleans has a homeless population of roughly 11,500 individuals, ranking New Orleans second in the rate of homelessness among U.S. cities.[207] In fact, New Orleans' homelessness rate is nearly three times the national average.[208] The reasons for this exponential increase in homelessness in New Orleans since the storm include the scarcity of affordable housing for New Orleans' significant low-income population. Further exacerbating the problem is the fact that many individuals' family and community safety nets were permanently displaced by Hurricane Katrina, taking away the people whom they relied on in tough times.[209]

X. Conclusion

Lessons from the tragedies in New Orleans' demolition of more than 3,000 public housing apartments and dispersal of 3,000 families can be learned.

Be transparent and democratic. The authorities must tell people what is going on, even when they are not sure of the outcome. Public housing and government officials should seek input and guidance throughout the process, listening before making final decisions. Keep people informed in all stages of the process and allow them to participate and consult in real time.

Prioritize displaced people and keep close track so people can participate in decisions about their homes and neighborhoods.

Rethink demolition of public housing and instead consider rehabilitation so people can return. Rethink mixed-income housing if the real price of that is widespread displacement of long-term residents of a neighborhood. Place and neighborhood have real values for people. Community is an important resource for all people as schools, churches, health care, jobs, friends, and family are just as important as bricks and mortar.

If authorities decide demolition is called for and mixed-income housing is going to take its place, tell the residents honestly that most residents will never return to their neighborhood. Try to relocate as many back to or as close to the neighborhood as possible. Prioritize the return of people who lived there and allow them to restart relationships and community ties.

The story of public housing in New Orleans post–Hurricane Katrina violates most ideas of transparency, accountability, and participation. Whether you agree or disagree that the former public housing developments were bad ideas and that mixed-income housing is the preferable method, there is no question that the way the old New Orleans public housing developments were replaced in the aftermath of Hurricane Katrina essentially blocked many residents from knowing what was going on and from being able to return to their homes. This was unnecessary, as the public housing units could have been used instrumentally in helping some of New Orleans' most vulnerable populations return home. Instead, the decisions about the fate of public housing were used systemically as a way to keep these people out. Currently, things are not looking a lot better for New Orleans housing eight years later, nor for the future, as the affordable housing crisis in New Orleans continues.

Notes

1. Susan J. Popkin et al., Urban Inst., Rebuilding Affordable Housing in New Orleans: The Challenge of Creating Inclusive Communities 2 (2006), *available at* http://www.urban.org/UploadedPDF/900914_affordable_housing.pdf. According to HUD:

> The generally accepted definition of affordability is for a household to pay no more than 30 percent of its annual income on housing. Families who pay more than 30 percent of their income for housing are considered cost burdened and may have difficulty affording necessities such as food, clothing, transportation and medical care. An estimated 12 million renter and homeowner households now pay more then [sic] 50 percent of their annual incomes for housing, and a family with one full-time worker earning the minimum wage cannot afford the local fair-market rent for a two-bedroom apartment anywhere in the United States. The lack of affordable housing is a significant hardship for low-income households preventing them from meeting their other basic needs, such as nutrition and healthcare, or saving for their future and that of their families.

See Affordable Housing, U.S. Dep't of Hous. & Urban Dev., http://portal.hud.gov/hudportal/HUD?src=/program_offices/comm_planning/affordablehousing (last visited Nov. 30, 2012).

2. *Id.*
3. Judith Browne Dianis & Anita Sinha, *Exiling the Poor: The Clash of Redevelopment and Fair Housing in Post-Katrina New Orleans*, 51 How. L.J. 481, 485 (2008).
4. Jeffrey Meitrodt, *Rising Rent*, Times-Picayune, Oct. 15, 2006, at A1.
5. *Orleans Parish: Housing and Housing Costs*, Greater New Orleans Cmty. Data Ctr., http://www.gnocdc.org/orleans/housing.html.
6. *Id.*
7. Fifty-one thousand rental homes in New Orleans were seriously damaged in Katrina. *See* Office of Policy Dev. & Research, *The Impact of Hurricanes Katrina, Rita, and Wilma on the Gulf Coast Housing Stock,* U.S. Housing Market Conditions, May 2006, at 9, *available at* http://www.huduser.org/intercept.asp?loc=/periodicals/ushmc/spring06/USHMC_06Q1.pdf.
8. New Orleans Housing Authority Resident Characteristics Report 2005–06, *cited in* Complaint, Anderson v. Jackson, No. 06-3298, 2007 WL 4414479 (E.D. La. 2007), 2006 WL 2263157.
9. William Quigley, *Thirteen Ways of Looking at Katrina: Human and Civil Rights Left Behind Again*, 81 Tul. L. Rev. 955, 987 (citing Hous. Auth. of New Orleans, Post-Katrina Frequently Asked Questions 1–2, October 2006).
10. *Id.*
11. Browne Dianis & Sinha, *supra* note 3, at 481–82.
12. Complaint, Anderson v. Jackson, No. 06-3298, 2007 WL 4414479 (E.D. La. 2007), 2006 WL 2032744.
13. *Id.*
14. *Id.*
15. Stacy E. Seicshnaydre, *How Government Housing Perpetuates Racial Segregation: Lessons from Post-Katrina New Orleans*, 60 Cath. U. L. Rev. 661, 674 (2011). Before Katrina, more than 125,000 people in New Orleans lived below the poverty line (27 percent of the population). *Id.*
16. *Id.*
17. *Id.*
18. *Id.*; *see also* NAACP, Housing in New Orleans: One Year After Katrina (Aug. 2006), *available at* http://www.racialequitytools.org/resourcefiles/kirwan2.pdf ("Before Katrina, New Orleans had the second-highest rate of African American concentrated poverty in the nation, with 37 percent of the city's African American population living in neighborhoods of concentrated poverty.").
19. Seicshnaydre, *supra* note 15, at 676.
20. *Id.*
21. *Id.*
22. NAACP, *supra* note 18.
23. *Id.*
24. Seicshnaydre, *supra* note 15, at 676. *See generally* Martha Mahoney, *Law and Racial Geography: Public Housing and the Economy in New Orleans*, 42 Stan. L. Rev. 1251 (1990) (for an excellent history of public housing in New Orleans).
25. *Id.*

26. Jordan Flaherty, *Floodlines: Preserving Public Housing in New Orleans*, 17(2) RACE, POVERTY AND THE ENVIRONMENT (fall 2010), *available at* http://urbanhabitat.org/17-2/flaherty.

27. *See* Nicolai Ouroussoff, *All Fall Down*, N.Y. TIMES, Nov. 19, 2006, at 1, *available at* http://www.nytimes.com/2006/11/19/weekinreview/19ouroussoff.html?pagewanted=all&_r=0.

28. *Id.* Others agreed with this assessment, including Susan Popkin, a researcher with the Urban Institute, who concluded: "These public housing buildings are some of the most sturdy housing in New Orleans, and I'm hesitant to see them torn down." Katy Reckdahl, *Like a Ton of Bricks*, GAMBIT WKLY., Oct. 24, 2006, at 9.

29. *See generally* Molly Thompson, Comment, *Relocating from the Distress of Chicago Public Housing to the Difficulties of the Private Market: How the Move Threatens to Push Families Away from Opportunity*, 1 NW. J.L. & SOC. POL'Y 267, 286–87 (2006).

30. *Id.*

31. *Id.*

32. Katy Reckdahl, *Razing a Community*, GAMBIT WKLY., Oct. 31, 2006, at 1–2, *available at* http://www.bestofneworleans.com/gambit/razing-a-community/Content?oid=1246628.

33. *Id.*

34. *Id.*

35. Advisory Group on Forced Evictions, Mission Report to New Orleans, U.S., at 13, Nov. 2010, *available at* www.unhabitat.org/downloads/docs/10009_1_593996.pdf.

36. U.S. DEP'T OF HOUS. AND URBAN DEV., PHA PLANS: ANNUAL PLAN FOR FISCAL YEAR 2003, at 6, *available at* http://www.hud.gov/offices/pih/pha/approved/pdf/02/la001v03.pdf.

37. *Id.* In 1996, there were more than 13,500 public housing units in New Orleans. However, in 2005, when Katrina hit, only 5,146 families were living in public housing.

38. *See* U.S. DEP'T OF HOUS. AND URBAN DEV., PHA PLANS, *supra* note 36, at 7 (indicating that more than 19,000 families were on the waiting list for Section 8 and 6,790 families were on the public housing waiting list in 2003).

39. *Id.*

40. The demolition of public housing in New Orleans began in the 1990s, beginning with the Imperial Drive scattered site and then moving on to some of the bigger developments such as the Desire, Florida, Fischer, and St. Thomas housing developments—all of which were replaced with smaller mixed-income developments. *See* Katy Reckdahl, *Public Housing: The Times Picayune Covers 175 Years of New Orleans History*, TIMES-PICAYUNE, Jan. 29, 2012, at 1, *available at* http://www.nola.com/175years/index.ssf/2012/01/public_housing_the_times-picay.html.

41. Sara Gran, Point of View, *Nobody Home: Agencies in Charge of Housing New Orleans Poor Prefer Not To*, TIMES-PICAYUNE, Oct. 30, 2006, at B5.

42. *Id.*

43. *Id.*

44. Richard Webster, *River Garden Residents March in Protest, Management Pushes Back*, TIMES-PICAYUNE, Jan. 24, 2013, at B1.

45. *Id.*

46. Gwen Filosa, *Tenant Admitted to River Garden After Suing*, TIMES-PICAYUNE, Dec. 7, 2006, at B1.

47. *Id.*

48. *Id.*

49. *Id.* The tenant had been employed at Loyola University before being injured in a car accident. *Id.*

50. *Id.*

51. *Id.*

52. *4 Years After Katrina: Housing Crisis Continues, Low-Income Renters Face Discrimination*, INST. FOR SOUTHERN STUDIES (Aug. 1, 2009), http://www.southernstudies.org/2009/08/4-years-after-katrina-housing-crisis-continues-low-income-renters-face-discrimination.html. *See also* section IX.

53. *Id.*

54. Press Release, La. Recovery Auth., Comprehensive New Study Reveals Updated Population No. in Storm-Affected Parishes (Oct. 5, 2006), *available at* http://lra.louisiana.gov/index.cfm?md=newsroom&tmp=detail&articleID=292&ssid=0.

55. Browne Dianis & Sinha, *supra* note 3, at 485 (citing National Low Income Housing Coalition, NLIHC Estimates 71 of Units Lost in Gulf Coast Were Low Income, Sept. 20, 2005, http://www.nlihc.org/detail/article.cfm?article_id=2670&id=48).

56. *Id.*

57. *Id.*

58. *Federal Housing Response to Hurricane Katrina, Hearing Before the Comm. on Fin. Servs. of the U.S. H.R.* (2007), Serial No. 110-1, 183–84 (citing Housing Authority of New Orleans, Post-Katrina Frequently Asked Questions (April 2006)).

59. *Federal Housing Response to Hurricane Katrina, Hearing Before the Comm. on Fin. Servs. of the U.S. H.R.* (2007), Serial No. 110-1, (testimony of Judith Browne Dianis, Esq., Co-Director, Advancement Project), *available at* http://archives.financialservices.house.gov/hearing110/htbrowne020607.pdf (citing Housing Authority of New Orleans: Preliminary Recovery Plan for the Redevelopment and Repair of Public Housing Properties: Summary).

60. Browne Dianis & Sinha, *supra* note 3, at 490.

61. Declaration of John E. Fernandez, Anderson v. Jackson, 06-3298, 2007 WL 2464530 (E.D. La. 10/23/06), *available at* http://www.justiceforneworleans.org/jfnodocs/Declaration.pdf.

62. *Id.* The testimony concludes in relevant part:

> Therefore, the general conclusions are: demolition of any of the buildings of these four projects is not supported by the evidence of the survey, replacement of these buildings with contemporary construction would yield buildings of lower quality and shorter lifetime duration, the original construction methods and materials of these projects are far superior in their resistance to hurricane conditions than typical new construction, and with renovation and regular maintenance, the lifetimes of the buildings in all four projects promise decades of continued service that may be extended indefinitely.

63. Specific Criteria for HUD Approval of Demolition Requests, 24 C.F.R. § 970.15 (2013).

64. Press Release, Advancement Project, Government Waste May Prevent New Orleans Residents From Returning (Jan. 8, 2007).

65. *Id.*

66. *Id.*

67. *Id.*

68. *Id.*

69. *Id.*

70. Charles Babington, *Some GOP Legislators Hit Jarring Notes in Addressing Katrina*, Wash. Post, Sept. 10, 2005, at A04.

71. *President Discusses Hurricane Relief in Address from the City of New Orleans Shortly After Hurricane Katrina*, George W. Bush White House, (Sept. 15, 2005), *available at* http://georgewbush-whitehouse.archives.gov/news/releases/2005/09/20050915-8.html. "Our second commitment is to help the citizens of the Gulf Coast to overcome this disaster, put their lives back together, and rebuild their communities." *Id.*

72. *See* Act of Dec. 30, 2005, Pub. L. No. 109-148, 119 Stat. 2781 (2006) ("To the extent feasible the Secretary of Housing and Urban Development shall preserve all housing within the area declared a major disaster. . . .").

73. Browne Dianis & Sinha, *supra* note 3, at 488–89.

74. Bruce Nolan, *Jackson: Housing Key to "Right to Return,"* Times-Picayune, Jan. 31, 2006, at 8.

75. Browne Dianis & Sinha, *supra* note 3, at 492.

76. *Id.*

77. *Id.*

78. Charles Babington, *Some GOP Legislators Hit Jarring Notes in Addressing Katrina*, Wash. Post, Sept. 10, 2005, at A04.

79. Eric Berger, *New Orleans Says It Won't Give Free Ride*, Houston Chron., Feb. 22, 2006, *available at* http://www.chron.com/disp/story.mpl/front/3676263.html.

80. In 1987, Congress required HUD to provide one for one replacement for demolition or sale of public housing, but that requirement was suspended in 1995 on a year-to-year basis until 1998 when it was ultimately eliminated. *See* HDR Handbook of Housing and Development Law, ch. 2, § 2:171 (2012).

81. *See* sections VI and IX, for a discussion on the lack of affordable housing post–Hurricane Katrina.

82. Gulf Coast Hurricane Housing Recovery Act of 2007, H.R. 1227, 110th Cong. (1st Sess. 2007). Specifically, Section 203 entitled One-For-One Replacement of All Public Housing Dwelling Units, provides in relevant part:

> (a) Conditions on Demolition.—After the date of the enactment of this Act, the Housing Authority of New Orleans may not demolish or dispose of any dwelling unit of public housing operated or administered by such agency (including any uninhabitable unit and any unit previously approved for demolition) except pursuant to a plan for replacement

> of such units in accordance with, and approved by the Secretary of Housing and Urban Development pursuant to, subsection (b).

Id.

83. Gulf Coast Housing Recovery Act of 2007, S. 1668, 110th Cong. (1st Sess. 2007). This proposal required that any public housing apartment torn down be replaced with another form of low-income housing—either subsidized public housing, partially subsidized "affordable" units, or vouchers that offset a portion of rents. *Id.*

84. Sue Sturgis, *Gulf Watch: New Orleans City Counsel Endorses Landrieu Housing Bill*, INST. FOR SOUTHERN STUDIES (Nov. 5, 2007), http://www.southernstudies.org/2007/11/gulf-watch-new-orleans-city-council-endorses-landrieu-housing-bill.html.

85. *Id.*

86. *Id.*

87. Sue Sturgis, *Gulf Watch: FEMA Begins Closing Katrina Trailer Parks While Affordable Housing Fight Drags On*, INST. FOR SOUTHERN STUDIES (Nov. 30, 2007), http://www.southernstudies.org/2007/11/gulf-watch-fema-begins-closing-katrina-trailer-parks-while-affordable-housing-fight-drags-on.

88. *Id.*

89. *Id.*

90. Rick Lyman, *Reports Reveal Hurricanes' Impact on Human Landscape*, N.Y. TIMES, June 7, 2006, at A16.

91. *Id.* The rule of thumb was that the poorer you were, the further you were displaced. *Id.* ("[T]he poorer and more vulnerable, who had less choice about where they landed, went to more distant cities.").

92. *Id. See also* Kris Axtman, *Katrina Evacuees Struggle to Exit Hotels*, CHRISTIAN SCI. MONITOR (Boston), Nov. 29, 2005, at 3.

93. Katy Reckdahl, *New C.J. Peete Complex Is Solid, Shiny—But Not as Social, Some Residents Say*, TIMES-PICAYUNE, Aug. 21, 2011, at 3, *available at* http://www.nola.com/politics/index.ssf/2011/08/new_cj_peete_complex_is_solid.html.

94. Browne Dianis & Sinha, *supra* note 3, at 489.

95. *Id.*

96. *Id.*

97. *Id.*

98. Memorandum of Approval from Ainars Rodins, HUD, to Cheryl Williams, HUD Dir. of New Orleans Office of Pub. Hous. (Sept. 21, 2007). This 31-page document was filed into the federal proceedings, 2:06-cv-03298 as Document 464-2 on September 24, 2007 (memo on file with authors). See subsection on Resident Consultation, page 26.

99. Browne Dianis & Sinha, *supra* note 3, at 489.

100. *Id.*

101. *Id.*

102. *Id.*

103. *Id.*

104. *Id.*

105. Rick K. Wilson & Robert M. Stein, *Katrina Evacuees in Houston: One Year Out* (White Paper), Sept. 8, 2006, *available at* http://brl.rice.edu/katrina/.

106. KALIMA ROSE & DAVID ZISSER, POLICYLINK, PRELIMINARY ANALYSIS OF NEW ORLEANS PUBLIC HOUSING CRISIS (July 19, 2006), *available at* http://www.policylink.org/atf/cf/%7B97C6D565-BB43-406D-A6D5-ECA3BBF35AF0%7D/Subsidized%20Housing%20Losses%20Policylink%208%201%2006.pdf.

107. *See* General Requirements for HUD Approval of a PHA Demolition/Disposition Application, 24 C.F.R. § 970.7 (2013).

108. Press Release, U.S. Dep't of Hous. & Urban Dev., HUD Outlines Aggressive Plan to Bring Families Back to New Orleans' Public Housing (June 14, 2006), *available at* http://archives.hud.gov/news/2006/pr06-066.cfm.

109. *Id.*

110. Gwen Filosa, *Tenants Denounce HANO Plans to Demolish Housing; Hundreds Attend Meeting at John McDonogh High*, TIMES-PICAYUNE, Nov. 30, 2006, at Metro 1. The hearing was held only after residents objected to lack of notice in the ongoing federal litigation over the proposed demolition. Consultation with residents is required by 24 C.F.R. § 970.7.

111. Katy Reckdahl, *supra* note 28.

112. *Id.*

113. Cheryl Smith, *Affordable Housing in NOLA*, AUSTIN CHRON., Sept. 1, 2006, at 1–2, *available at* http://www.austinchronicle.com/news/2006-09-01/399578/.

114. *Id.* Many public housing community leaders echoed this opinion as well. For example, B.W. Cooper resident-management vice president Donna Johnigan said: "We welcome (income) diversity in our community, but it should not come at the expense of the people who once made up our community." Katy Reckdahl, *'Big Four' Public Housing Issues Addressed by Congresswoman*, TIMES-PICAYUNE, Aug. 21, 2009, at 3, *available at* http://www.nola.com/politics/index.ssf/2009/08/big_four_public_housing_issues.html.

115. Katy Reckdahl, *B.W. Cooper Housing Site's Slow March to Rebirth Reaches Finish Line*, TIMES-PICAYUNE, May 5, 2012, *available at* http://www.nola.com/politics/index.ssf/2012/05/bw_cooper_housing_sites_slow_m.html.

116. *Id.*

117. *See* Diane Allen et al. v. HANO, CDC No. 07-15799 (Dec. 14, 2007) (on file with authors).

118. Flaherty, *supra* note 26.

119. *Id.*

120. *Id.*

121. *Id.*

122. Becky Brown et al., *Hurricane Rita: The Aftermath; Populations Shift*, HOUSTON CHRON., Sept. 29, 2005, at B1.

123. Bill Walsh, *Official Blunt on Public Housing*, TIMES-PICAYUNE, Apr. 25, 2006.

124. *See* Joe Gyan Jr., *Housing Hearing Stormy: Angry Crowd Protests Plans to Replace N.O. Projects*, ADVOCATE (Baton Rouge), Nov. 30, 2006, at A17. Only 1,000 of the 5,100 pre-Katrina public housing units were open as of June 2006. *Id.*

125. KALIMA ROSE & DAVID ZISSER, POLICYLINK, PRELIMINARY ANALYSIS OF NEW ORLEANS PUBLIC HOUSING CRISIS (July 19, 2006), *available at* http://www.policylink.org/atf/cf/%7B97C6D565-BB43-406D-A6D5-ECA3BBF35AF0%7D/Subsidized%20Housing%20Losses%20Policylink%208%201%2006.pdf.

126. *See* Press Release, U.S. Dep't of Hous. & Urban Dev., HUD Outlines Aggressive Plan to Bring Families Back to New Orleans' Public Housing (June 14, 2006), *available at* http://archives.hud.gov/news/2006/pr06-066.cfm.

127. *Id.*

128. *Id.*

129. Deon Roberts, *Urgent Need for Affordable Housing in New Orleans*, NEW ORLEANS CITYBUSINESS, Dec. 4, 2006.

130. Gwen Filosa, *Public Housing Advocates See Little Progress in N.O.*, TIMES-PICAYUNE, Sept. 13, 2006, at B1.

131. First Amended Complaint at 4, Anderson v. Jackson, No. 06-3298, 2007 WL 4414479 (E.D. La. 2007).

132. *Id.*

133. *Id.*

134. Complaint at 3, Anderson v. Jackson, No. 06-3298, 2007 WL 4414479 (E.D. La. 2007).

135. Browne Dianis & Sinha, *supra* note 3, at 488–89.

136. *Id.*

137. See section V.

138. Browne Dianis & Sinha, *supra* note 3, at 489.

139. HUD Memorandum of Approval from Ainars Rodins, HUD, to Cheryl Williams, HUD Dir. of New Orleans Office of Pub. Hous. (Sept. 21, 2007). This 31-page document was filed into the federal proceedings, 2:06-cv-03298 as Document 464-2 on September 24, 2007 (memo on file with authors) [hereinafter HUD Approval Memo, Sept. 21, 2007].

140. HUD Approval Memo, Sept. 21, 2007, *supra* note 139, at 4.

141. *See* 24 C.F.R. § 970.7(7) (2013).

142. *See* 24 C.F.R. § 970.7(8).

143. *See* HUD Approval Memo, Sept. 21, 2007, *supra* note 139, at 26-27.

144. *See* 24 C.F.R. § 970.9(b)(1).

145. *See* HUD Approval Memo, Sept. 21, 2007, *supra* note 139, at 27. The exact wording of the C.F.R. exception claimed by HANO and HUD says the requirement did not apply when "A PHA seeks disposition outside the public housing program to privately finance or otherwise develop a facility to benefit low-income families (e.g., day care center, administrative building, mixed-finance housing under 24 CFR part 941 subpart F, or other types of low-income housing)." 24 C.F.R. § 970.9(3)(ii).

146. First Amended Complaint at 4, Anderson v. Jackson, No. 06-3298, 2007 WL 4414479 (E.D. La. 2007).

147. Browne Dianis & Sinha, *supra* note 3, at 490.

148. Alphonso Jackson, *Post-Katrina Progress Housing to Help End Suffering*, WASH. TIMES, Dec. 27, 2007, at A15.

149. Press Release, Advancement Project, *Government Waste May Prevent New Orleans Residents from Returning* (Jan. 8, 2007).

150. *Id.* Another 160 units would be tax-credit mixed income and 145 would be market rate units. *Id.*

151. *Id.* Another 133 would be mixed income and 123 would be market rate. *Id.*

152. *Id.* Like C.J. Peete, another 133 units would be tax-credit mixed income and 123 would be market rate. *Id.*

153. *Id.*

154. *Id.*

155. Katy Reckdahl, *B.W. Cooper Housing Site's Slow March to Rebirth Reaches Finish Line*, TIMES-PICAYUNE, May 5, 2012, *available at* http://www.nola.com/politics/index.ssf/2012/05/bw_cooper_housing_sites_slow_m.html.

156. *Id.*

157. *See Exiling the Poor: The Clash of Redevelopment and Fair Housing in Post-Katrina New Orleans*, 51 How. L.J. 481 (2008).

158. Complaint at 2, Anderson v. Jackson, No. 06-3298, 2007 WL 4414479 (E.D. La. 2007), 2006 WL 2032744.

159. *Id.* at 25–32.

160. *Id.*

161. Order Denying TRO, Anderson v. Jackson, No. 06-3298 (E.D. La. Nov. 22, 2006) (copy on file with authors).

162. Order and Reasons, Anderson v. Jackson, No. 06-3298, 2007 WL 458232 (E.D. La. Feb. 6, 2007). *See also* Anderson v. Jackson, No. 06-3298, 2007 WL 4414479 (E.D. La. 2007).

163. *Id.*

164. *Id.*

165. Anderson v. Jackson, 556 F.3d 351, 360–61 (2009).

166. Gwen Filosa, *Live Updates on Demolition Vote from Council Chambers*, TIMES-PICAYUNE, Dec. 19, 2007, *available at* http://www.nola.com/news/index.ssf/2007/12/city_hall_girds_for_public_hou.html. *See also* Diane Allen et al v. HANO, CDC No. 07-15799 (Dec. 14, 2007) (on file with authors).

167. February 28, 2008, Statement of U.N. Advisors to the U.N. High Commission for Human Rights, *available at* http://www.prrac.org/full_text.php?text_id=1176&item_id=11258&newsletter_id=98&header=Civil+Rights+History&kc=1.

168. NAACP, *Housing in New Orleans: One Year After Katrina: Policy Recommendations for Equitable Rebuilding*, at 20, http://opportunityagenda.org/files/field_file/Housing_in_NOLA_1.pdf. The population of New Orleans fell from 484,674 before Katrina (according to the 2000 census) to an estimated 208,548 after Katrina (July 2006)—a decrease of 276,126 people and a loss of over half of the city's population. By July of 2011, the population was back up to 360,740—74 percent of what it was in 2000. The population of New Orleans was counted at 343,829 in April 2010—indicating that New Orleans lost 140,845 residents since 2000.

169. ALLISON PLYER, GREATER NEW ORLEANS CMTY. DATA CTR., WHAT CENSUS 2010 REVEALS ABOUT POPULATION AND HOUSING IN NEW ORLEANS AND THE METRO AREA (Mar. 17, 2011), *available at* https://gnocdc.s3.amazonaws.com/reports/GNOCDC_Census2010PopulationAndHousing.pdf.

170. Katy Reckdahl, *supra* note 93.

171. *Id.*

172. *Id.*

173. *Id.*

174. *Id.*

175. *Id.*

176. *Id.*

177. *Id.*

178. *Id.*

179. *Id.*

180. *Id.*

181. *Id.*

182. *Id.*
183. *Id.*
184. *Id.*
185. Katy Reckdahl, *supra* note 32.
186. *Id.*
187. *Id.*
188. *Id.*
189. *Id.*
190. *Id.*
191. *4 Years After Katrina*, *supra* note 52.
192. *Id.*
193. U.S. DEP'T OF HOUS. AND URBAN DEV., PHA PLANS: ANNUAL PLAN FOR FISCAL YEAR 2003, at 7, *available at* http://www.hud.gov/offices/pih/pha/approved/pdf/02/la001v03.pdf.
194. *4 Years After Katrina*, *supra* note 52.
195. *Id.*
196. Seicshnaydre, *supra* note 15, at 684.
197. *4 Years After Katrina*, *supra* note 52.
198. *Id.*
199. *Id.*
200. First Amended Complaint at 7, Anderson v. Jackson, No. 06-3298, 2007 WL 4414479 (E.D. La. 2007).
201. *4 Years After Katrina*, *supra* note 52.
202. *Id.*
203. *Id.*
204. First Amended Complaint at 7, Anderson v. Jackson, No. 06-3298, 2007 WL 4414479 (E.D. La. 2007).
205. *Id.*
206. Katy Reckdahl, *Report Places New Orleans' Homeless Rate at Second in the Nation*, TIMES-PICAYUNE (Feb. 5, 2012), http://www.nola.com/politics/index.ssf/2012/02/report_estimates_new_orleans_h.html.
207. 2012 REPORT OF NATIONAL ALLIANCE TO END HOMELESSNESS, *available at* http://b.3cdn.net/naeh/a18b62e5f015e9a9b8_pdm6iy33d.pdf.
208. *Id.* The national homelessness rate was 21 per 10,000 residents in 2011, while the New Orleans' rate was 56 per 10,000 residents. Katy Reckdahl, *supra* note 206.
209. Katy Reckdahl, *supra* note 206.

PART 4

Community Resilience: Challenges and Opportunities

CHAPTER 13

Wolf at the Door: Protecting Homeowners from Predatory Housing Activities in the Wake of Disaster

Kate Titford and Rutledge Simmons

I. Introduction

The past decade has been eventful for the community development field as Hurricane Katrina and other unprecedented disasters have redefined our sense of vulnerability to natural disaster, and the Great Recession has obliterated significant gains in homeownership rates and housing equity. This chapter will highlight the context and variety of predatory practices that occur in the wake of disasters, regardless of whether they are natural ones like hurricanes and superstorms or human-made ones like the housing collapse of 2008. Although natural and human-made disasters differ in how they are caused, they are remarkably similar in the ways they make homeowners vulnerable to scams. This survey of housing-related scam behavior will address: (a) contractor fraud; (b) insurance fraud; (c) government relief program fee scams; (d) mortgage fraud; and (e) government affiliation claim-based scams.[1] The chapter will go on to describe best practices of government and nonprofits responding to scammers in the aftermath of disasters, including prevention, education, and enforcement efforts. Finally, this chapter will make the case for a highly coordinated effort by government, nonprofits, and the private sector, both pre- and post-disaster, to educate consumers about scams and to provide a level of assistance that will undermine the ability of scammers to operate.

II. Challenges of the Post-Disaster Environment

The ease and success with which predatory actors target communities in crisis highlight several of the most persistent challenges in community development work. First and foremost, they remind us that achieving homeownership is just one segment of the housing wellness continuum and that ongoing education and support should figure prominently in the home-buying process. While the rise in homeownership rates in the early 2000s was applauded as a way for more Americans to build asset wealth, many homeowners entered the market with little or no equity, and saw that equity transformed into liability overnight when the housing market declined. For those families whose grasp on homeownership was tenuous from the start, the false promises of housing scammers are especially dangerous because they capitalize on the homeowner's inexperience and shamelessly oversimplify complex problems.

The prevalence of housing-related scams also reminds us that the threat to safe housing and stable communities goes beyond the physical damage of a natural disaster or the blight that may result from incomplete recovery. Protecting vulnerable homeowners from the human threat stretches the community development field beyond its usual competencies. For some community development professionals, this requires that they overcome their impulse to focus on traditional areas of expertise, such as planning and construction. Instead, housing and community development organizations must quickly design and deploy robust outreach efforts. They must also break down silos and partner with a variety of service providers, including emergency responders, legal assistance providers, lending partners, policymakers, and fellow community development professionals. Likewise, government officials face similar challenges in the post-disaster environment. While designing the recovery programs that enable their constituents to rebuild, those officials must simultaneously devise adequate protections that will ensure funds are distributed in a timely, responsible fashion and not lost to bad actors.

Whether natural or human-made, a large-scale disaster creates the perfect environment for housing fraud to occur. Homeowners are under tremendous stress following a disaster. "As a household, there is no planning for a situation where you have lost absolutely everything," said Heather Geary, who is a social worker who worked in Joplin, Missouri, following its catastrophic tornado in 2011. "People are desperate—and you are grasping at anything to get your family back into housing. If a scammer gives them an idea about how to begin, or a place to start, a lot of people will want to make that happen, because they just need something to grasp onto."[2]

In addition to experiencing the shock, anxiety, and confusion that inevitably occur, residents lack the usual resources that would help them make informed decisions about their homes and finances. Local civic leaders and insurance agents may have been displaced by the disaster, and thus find themselves ill equipped to respond to requests for information or assistance. The extremely high demand for expertise and skilled workers, coupled with a near absence of the normal municipal services and infrastructure, creates a vacuum. Unfortunately, this vacuum attracts scammers seeking to capitalize on desperate homeowners caught up in a confusing environment, short on credible service providers and reliable information, but rich in disaster recovery and other funds that homeowners may secure to rectify the damage done or pending perils. Programs that deliver recovery dollars to the disaster area are often complicated, have stringent paperwork requirements, and involve arduous time frames. In these situations, homeowner fatigue with these programs increases susceptibility to housing scams. Bound by no restrictions of fair play or conscience, scammers guarantee quick solutions and spin plausible narratives that frustrated and hopeful homeowners want to believe.

In addition to the traditional challenges of working with communities in distress, protecting homeowners from housing-related fraud has taken on a decidedly modern element in recent years, as scammers mine data to specifically target individual victims. In particular, the rise of foreclosure rescue scams in recent years has shown consumer protection advocates the stark new battle lines of carefully targeted fraudulent activity. Scam activity that might have been conducted by phishing phone calls or bulk mail a generation ago is far more difficult to combat when launched by an informed fraudster. Armed with personal data about individual consumers, obtained from their Internet use or otherwise, scammers are able to target traditionally higher-risk populations with increasing accuracy.[3] Take, for example, the increased vulnerability of a senior citizen who is contacted by a scammer who already knows most of her personal information, or the immigrant who is targeted in his native language by someone promising to act as an all-knowing intermediary who can end his housing woes.

California homeowner Jose Chirino was one such homeowner. He shared his story with the Loan Modification Scam Alert campaign, in which he described how he was contacted by phone by a company targeting his mortgage lender's customers with promises to negotiate a mortgage loan modification. Only after paying the scammer $1,500 did Chirino reach out to his lender and learn that he had been the victim of a fraud.[4]

The lucrative market that exists for consumer data was at the heart of a recent Federal Trade Commission (FTC) settlement with one of the country's largest credit reporting bureaus over allegations that the bureau had improperly sold consumer information, including credit scores and status of payment on their mortgages.[5] In its complaint, the FTC claimed that Equifax sold more than 17,000 prescreened consumer lists to companies that in turn resold those lists to third parties. These third parties then used the data to solicit consumers having debt management problems for the provision of loan modification and debt relief services. The matter with Equifax was resolved in a consent order that permanently enjoined Equifax from selling prescreened consumer lists and required Equifax to pay nearly $400,000 in fines to the FTC.[6] A related case against the alleged purchasers of the prescreened consumer lists was resolved by consent order requiring the defendants to pay $1.2 million in fines.[7]

Another modern element of housing-related fraud is that its perpetrators can operate via a sophisticated online presence that can mask their identity and thus afford consumers little contact with an identifiable person. For example, a website-based pitch might persuade a consumer to pay thousands of dollars for services one day, and then disappear offline the next. The relative ease of building a highly professional or government-affiliated looking website, and the anonymity of operating online have made it extremely difficult to protect consumers from Internet-based foreclosure rescue scams.

The facts presented in *Federal Trade Commission v. Christopher Mallett* demonstrate the egregious misrepresentations made by supposed foreclosure rescue companies.[8] In that case, a lead scam artist used more than a dozen websites—with addresses such as gov-usdebtreform.net and FHA-homeloaninfo.net—to impersonate federal government agencies and make deceptive promises about the services offered.[9] After providing their personal information via forms on these various sites, the consumers were then contacted by third-party organizations that tried to sell foreclosure rescue services. The case against Christopher Mallett was settled in June 2012, and provided for various permanent injunctions and equitable relief.[10]

Despite the old and new challenges of protecting homeowners from scams in post-disaster settings, preventing housing-related fraud is increasingly seen as an integral part of a proper disaster-recovery effort. When homeowners lose money, property, or trust after being victimized by housing scammers, the entire community suffers the consequences. A family that is displaced from its home by the scam can cost the municipality in support services and lost tax revenue. According to a 2005 report prepared for the Homeownership Preservation Foundation, a single foreclosure can impose $34,000 in direct costs on a municipality.[11] Vacant houses can accelerate blight in neighborhoods and drive down housing values. The collective loss in value surrounding a foreclosed home can total $220,000.[12] Despite renewed interest in city living and an abundant supply of affordable housing stock, vacant and abandoned buildings remain a stubborn barrier to repopulation and reinvestment.[13] Furthermore, when consumers get scammed, they develop a general sense of distrust and this can retard the pace of recovery. For example, in New Orleans, where residents were victimized by scammers throughout the post–Hurricane Katrina recovery, many homeowners developed a deep distrust of both professionals and government efforts, and this hindered the planning process around rebuilding the city.[14]

III. Predatory Housing Transactions in the Wake of Disaster

Discussed in this section are five common ways that homeowners lose their money to housing-related fraud in the wake of disasters. Although natural disasters and financial disasters differ in obvious ways, they actually create similar perils for homeowners. Each is followed by a drive to get relief money on the streets in a timely fashion. Each puts severe strain on existing systems, impeding their ability to perform their usual functions, and each generates panic by putting the typical homeowner's greatest asset at risk. This environment is fertile ground for five common scams regardless of whether they arise in the natural disaster or financial crisis context.

A. Contractor Fraud

First, as demonstrated so vividly after Hurricane Katrina struck the Gulf Coast, contractor fraud is a common occurrence after a natural disaster. The National Consumer Law Center reported that Louisiana's attorney general saw a drastic increase in housing repair–related complaints following Hurricane Katrina—from 150 per year to more than 44,000 in the two years following the storm.[15] Thousands of homeowners paid for roof repair or mold removal that never happened. The most effective scammers played to the financial limitations of the homeowner by promising to complete a project for whatever amount the insurance company had paid.[16] Contractors especially preyed on elderly homeowners, who had some money from insurance or savings but no idea how to connect the dots between their financial resources and the technical components of rebuilding, such as building plans, city building permits, and other elements of construction work.[17] Throughout the city, light poles and medians were littered with fliers for contractors promising to deliver fast affordable home repairs. After contacting a contractor and making a first payment, many homeowners never heard from the contractor again.

In the months following Hurricane Katrina, homeowners were targeted for their immediate resources: cash, insurance money, and savings. However, as federal rebuilding funds entered the Gulf Coast region through the Louisiana and Mississippi recovery programs (called the Road Home and Phase II, respectively), scams were reinvented to target homeowners who had received these funds—which, on average, totaled $72,000 per household.[18] Homeowners in Louisiana signed covenants agreeing to rebuild their houses within three years. Because those covenants run with the land, the obligation applies to the grant recipient homeowner as well as to any successors, assigns, heirs, or future owners of the subject property. This motivation to rebuild, together with an immediate infusion of recovery money and a lack of assistance with selecting reputable contractors, led homeowners to pay contractors for work that was never performed.

Donna Tally of NeighborWorks's Southern District describes the lasting visual evidence of this contractor fraud:

> When you are walking around certain neighborhoods in New Orleans, you can see it clearly—where there are just the bare beginnings of a rebuild, where work was done on the foundation and then just abandoned. The homeowners just never heard from the contractor again. Some of them had paid out $45,000 or $50,000, and now they are no closer to returning home than they were right after the storm.[19]

B. Insurance Fraud

Second, homeowners who become frustrated with the demands of their insurance companies can fall prey to scammers who charge hefty fees in exchange for the promise to win lucrative settlements with insurance companies. This practice was also common following Hurricane Katrina. Again, after receiving payment, these scammers did nothing for the homeowners, leaving them with even less money and less confidence about how to proceed in rebuilding. Perhaps the most notorious debate on the Gulf Coast was whether structural damage was covered by homeowner insurance policies that did not specifically provide for wind damage.[20] Around New Orleans, scammers took advantage of this situation by creating crude spray-painted signs on plywood and naming specific companies with messages like "We Help Win Claims Against Allstate."[21]

One New Orleans resident described the exhaustion of fighting his insurance company for 21 months before reaching a settlement:

> No wonder so many people became sick and tired of the bureaucracy of it all. Of having to call the insurance company over and over, and keep doing one more task, of having to meet insurance adjusters dozens of times. That fatigue was real. In the end, some people just walked away from their homes because it wasn't worth it. They were worn out.[22]

In many cases, housing scammers contributed to this fatigue by scamming people and creating yet another obstacle to accessing legitimate assistance from the insurance companies.[23]

C. Government Relief Scams

Third, when the federal government responds to disasters—natural and financial alike—attempts by the federal government to aid recovery through new programs are stymied by scams that charge residents for applying to receive assistance. The fraudulent scheme is aided by the fact that the programs are often complex and have burdensome paperwork requirements. Moreover, the homeowners in most dire need of help often lack the ability or technological skills to learn about and apply for the programs. Often, the existing avenues of assistance are already overwhelmed with the influx of desperate families, and the added delay and confusion leads frustrated homeowners to turn to for-profit enterprises for application assistance.

The federal housing programs of recent years have been the impetus for an increase in innovative and ingenious scams in the foreclosure rescue space. Since the collapse of the subprime mortgage market in 2008 and the subsequent years of high unemployment and declining home values, several federal programs have tried to assist homeowners facing foreclosure. The launch of an assistance program is immediately followed by an army of unsavory actors who succeed in convincing homeowners to pay them to access these free programs. For instance, the launch of the U.S. Treasury's Making Home Affordable program in early 2009 was quickly followed by a rise in loan modification scams, in which fraudsters claim to be working in some official capacity and charge homeowners to apply for their mortgage modification.[24] One such group of bad actors was sentenced to prison time and fines after its California scam operation was found to have targeted delinquent homeowners to pay for assistance using a website that falsely implied affiliation with the federal government's program.[25]

Predatory behavior also followed the launch of assistance programs like the Emergency Homeowners Loan Program and the Independent Foreclosure Review. The Emergency Homeowners Loan Program is a U.S. Housing and Urban Development (HUD) program that provides homeowners with up to $50,000 in a forgivable loan to help them recover from delinquency and make their mortgage payments if they were in default due to unemployment.[26] The application window for that program was narrow, and the application requirements were confusing to some homeowners. Scammers again targeted homeowners by charging a fee to help them apply. The Independent Foreclosure Review is an initiative of the Office of the Comptroller of the Currency to review homeowners' experiences and assess whether they were affected by servicers' practices during the foreclosure process.[27] Applying for that program is free, but the program provided an opportunity for scammers to charge homeowners to submit their packets for the review. Imitators claiming to be the official Independent Foreclosure Review sprang up and diverted homeowners from legitimate assistance. For instance, the Office of the Comptroller of the Currency was compelled to notify the public about an organization calling itself National Legal Help, which sent letters to homeowners falsely stating that the Office of the Comptroller of the Currency had directed it to reach out to homeowners. The letters also falsely stated that the consumer's mortgage lender was under investigation by the banking regulatory agencies and that the consumer could access assistance by sending $10,000 to the company.[28]

In the most despicable cases of scammers faking an affiliation to government programs, victimized homeowners have been persuaded to send their monthly mortgage payments to scammers and to avoid all contact with their servicers until the alleged loan modification negotiations have been completed. Few homeowners can recover from the severe loan delinquency resulting from nonpayment to their lender and the diversion of their funds to the scammers. The National Foreclosure Mitigation Counseling Program has interviewed a number of these homeowners and relayed their stories to policymakers in that program's *Congressional Reports*.[29] Fritz and Zoila Estrada of Lakewood, California, are homeowners who paid a loan modification scam company $4,000 to assist in negotiations with their lender. The company did nothing to help, and the bank proceeded to schedule a sale date. With the assistance of a nonprofit housing counselor, however, the Estradas were able to recover and save their home. Looking back on his very stressful experience and losing money to a scammer, Mr. Estrada recalls: "They stole my money. I don't like talking about it. They stole my money. . . . I'm just making it now, but I feel that things will soon start getting better."[30]

D. Mortgage Fraud

Fourth, natural disasters and financial crises create an environment in which blatant mortgage fraud thrives. For instance, following Hurricane Katrina, some homeowners mortgaged their homes to finance the required rehabilitation, only to realize after enduring months of construction work that they had inadvertently signed over ownership of their properties and had been reduced to mere renters in their own homes. Similarly, in the current economic downturn, homeowners facing foreclosure have entered into finance agreements intending to save their homes from foreclosure, only to learn that they have inadvertently signed away ownership.

E. Affiliation with Government Entities

Fifth and finally, as described in some of the cases above, fraudsters are consistently able to defraud consumers when they feign affiliation with a government agency. Some use the government agency seals on their websites, or design official-looking seals that closely resemble those of a government agency. Others falsely assert an affiliation with the government agency. Still other scammers capitalize on the fact that consumers have little familiarity with government agencies, and operate under company names that sound like an official governmental entity. In *Federal Trade Commission v. Christopher Mallett*, it was alleged that the defendant had engaged in all of these methods—by using websites with official-looking addresses like gov-usdebtreform.net, using the Federal Trade Commission seal on its site, and operating under the faux agency name Department of Consumer Services Protection Commission.[31] For homeowners who are already aware of government relief programs, who are eager to access government money to assist them through recovery, and are unsure about how to access government assistance, scammers posing as government representatives or affiliates are unfairly equipped to dupe such homeowners.

IV. After the Storm: Ways to Protect Homeowners from Financial Predators after Disasters

There are many stubborn challenges associated with working in a post-disaster environment and ensuring that relief funds reach their intended target. And yet, among practitioners in the community development field, there is the hopeful sense of a sea change in the way policymakers and service providers protect homeowners in crisis from financial predators. More than ever before, housing and community development organizations must expand their scope of concern beyond the traditional realm of bricks and mortar to defend against the threat to the economic well-being of their neighborhoods. Here, we outline some best practices for both preventing and responding to housing scams, and they include pursuing consumer outreach and education, creating a highly visible presence of legitimate service providers in the post-disaster environment, devising technological solutions to new scam behaviors, and encouraging law enforcement actions.

A. Consumer Education and Outreach

Several task forces have formed to fight the threat of foreclosure scams in recent years and their efforts have been directed at developing clear messaging and education for vulnerable homeowners. One such effort is the Loan Modification Scam Alert.[32] With funds appropriated by Congress, NeighborWorks America developed and launched this public education campaign with dozens of national and local partners. The resulting campaign materials for Loan Modification Scam Alert feature a bright yellow and black warning similar to police tape. Through door-to-door outreach efforts, advertising placements on buses, radio placements, and many other methods, the campaign has brought awareness of foreclosure scams to millions of consumers. The campaign is oriented toward three goals: making homeowners aware that loan modification scams exist, educating homeowners about the signs of a scam, and encouraging reporting of scams to trusted authorities.

B. Presence of High-Capacity Service Providers in the Post-Disaster Vacuum

Another important way that nonprofits and government entities can avert a scamming crisis is by cultivating a strong, legitimate presence in the post-disaster space. The role of one particular Florida nonprofit after Hurricane Andrew in 1992 is illustrative of this method. Led by Executive Director Steve Mainster, the Centro Campesino Farmworker Center helped to coordinate advocacy for affected residents and to advise homeowners on how not to be defrauded by contractors. When central Florida was pummeled by four hurricanes in a single summer in 2005, Centro Campesino again took its expertise on the road and established a satellite field office in the affected area to help coordinate relief and recovery efforts. "The goal was to gather all the resources, get the partners communicating and on the same page, and then get to work as soon as possible," said Mainster. "Back then, we had to deal with this whole range of problems—with bad repair estimates coming out of FEMA, with banks cashing the checks from the insurance company and leaving the homeowner no money to make repairs, with contractors stealing money or materials."[33] Providing a continuum of services at its Hurricane Disaster Advocacy Center, Centro Campesino helped to ensure that its clients had a local authority to help them answer the questions that come with rebuilding, and protect their limited resources from fraud.

In the months and years following Hurricane Katrina, nonprofits along the Gulf Coast also created new business lines, and this provided homeowners with additional resources as they returned home and rebuilt. This nonprofit presence helped to protect homeowners from being defrauded while they were in transition. Authors Woody Widrow, Robert O. Zdenek, and Ralph Scott highlighted some of these organizations in "Rebuilding Communities, Restoring Families: Roles for CBDOs in the Aftermath of Disasters."[34] In Austin, Texas, Foundation Communities stepped forward to respond to the immediate needs of families displaced by the storm by providing triage housing for 120 families, operating a case management program, and helping those families transition to new apartments, jobs, and even homeownership. In Mississippi, Mercy Housing and Human Development immediately reached out to homeowners to assist them with FEMA applications, and has since built case management into a permanent service. In New Orleans, Neighborhood Housing Services expanded its counseling services to include homeowner advocacy in a number of forums with applications to FEMA, insurance companies, and mortgage companies. These organizations and many others went to great lengths to contact at-risk homeowners and help them protect their homes—by public outreach on local media, staffing toll-free phone lines, and organizing mass mailings to first-time homebuyers.

This operational dexterity is not a given. Instead, it reflects a deep organizational strength. Reflecting on the unique set of skills, Marietta Rodriguez, NeighborWorks America's deputy director for homeownership programs, says, "The greatest indicator of our network's ability to assist and protect homeowners in crisis is their organizational resiliency—strength of leadership, purpose and process. An organization has to be very strong to manage the ebbs and flows in business."[35] Nonprofits that support homeowners through crisis succeed in taking their efforts to scale by getting the little things right—how they triage calls, how they manage paperwork, how they track referrals to other agencies and follow up with homeowners.

C. Design Programs That Avert Scammers' Access to Potential Victims

The ability to anticipate vulnerability of certain populations and design programs that thwart scammers is another effective way to combat predatory housing transactions in the months and years following a disaster. The Gulf Coast is still grappling with rebuilding-related scams while it undertakes initiatives to assist a newly vulnerable group of housing consumers. Such consumers are confronted by the high cost of homes and homeowners insurance, each of which has risen sharply since Hurricane Katrina, making sustainable, affordable homeownership a challenge for more residents. These homeowners are vulnerable to loss and victimization by scammers. Fortunately, by using Community Development Block Grants, the city of New Orleans has responded with a successful second-mortgage program in which homeowners receive a second mortgage to close the affordability gap, and that second mortgage is gradually forgiven as the homeowner remains in the home.[36] As of April 2012, the average second-mortgage amount through this program was $53,000, and the majority of homeowners assisted by the program earned less than 80 percent of the area median income.[37] By channeling potentially vulnerable homeowners into the program, the city has helped provide the financial resources and educational assistance these homeowners need, while ensuring program compliance using the existing network of HUD-approved housing counseling agencies.[38]

D. Develop Technology That Is Responsive to New Scams

Use of modern communication technology has made it easier for scammers to target and exploit homeowners with little personal contact. In the case of foreclosure rescue scams, it has become common for companies to target the residents of one state and—when brought to the attention of the media or law enforcement—to simply take their operations across state lines and target residents of a different state. One innovative response to this problem arose from the Loan Modification Scam Prevention Network, a national coalition of government agencies, nonprofit organizations and service providers that includes the Department of Housing and Urban Development, Fannie Mae, and Freddie Mac. Original loan modification scam complaint information is compiled and housed in the national Loan Modification Scam Prevention Network Database, which is maintained by the Lawyers' Committee for Civil Rights Under Law, located in Washington, D.C. To help combat these scams that move from state to state, and to better enable the interstate collaboration of law enforcement officials, the Lawyers' Committee for Civil Rights Under Law has built and managed a sophisticated reporting database that allows registered users to see the details of reported scams.[39]

As of October 2012, the database had grown to include 26,000 reported scams representing $63 million in losses. The database allows state and federal law enforcement officials to compare fraud complaints received by their office to the database and instantly obtain additional information about the threats they must target in their own state.[40]

E. State and Federal Enforcement Actions

Local law enforcement actions can often run a scam operation out of town, but it usually takes a more deliberate, collaborative enforcement approach to shut down scam operations altogether. This collaborative model is the hallmark of the Financial Fraud Enforcement Task Force's Mortgage Fraud Working Group, which announced in fall 2012 the results of its yearlong Distressed Homeowner Initiative. With the combined efforts of agencies, including the Federal Trade Commission, HUD, the FBI, the Consumer Financial Protection Bureau, and the Justice Department, the accomplishments were impressive. Their joint efforts resulted in 530 criminal defendants in 285 federal criminal indictments and involved more than 73,000 homeowner victims and total losses of $1 billion.[41] As these actions proceed around the country, the immediate press surrounding these cases also helps to raise awareness among the public of the prevalence and egregiousness of the scams.

State law-enforcement efforts around foreclosure scams have impaired the ability of repeat scammers to stay in business and have also raised the public awareness about the risk of scams. Perhaps most notable is California's attorney general Kamala Harris, who has been a leader in this area and has supported an active Mortgage Fraud Strike Force that investigates and prosecutes crimes related to mortgages, foreclosures, and real estate. Harris has also succeeded in charging attorneys engaged in foreclosure assistance fraud, an unfortunate consequence of the increasing involvement of lawyers in this type of activity. Her office used leads from the state bar's enforcement division to investigate and charge a law group in Northern California with grand theft by false pretense, conspiracy, and false advertising for charging homeowners up to $2,500 for loan modifications. In summer 2012, the work of Harris's office secured $4 million in restitution from a prolific, national loan modification scam company.[42]

The Federal Trade Commission has been particularly active in invoking federal enforcement powers against financial predators that target at-risk homeowners through foreclosure rescue scams. Its authority to bring these actions comes from a number of statutes related to fair practices in marketing. For instance, it has invoked section 5(a) of the Federal Trade Commission Act, which prohibits unfair or deceptive "acts or practices in or affecting commerce."[43] It has also relied on rules promulgated under Telemarketing and Consumer Fraud and Abuse Prevention Act,[44] which prohibit misrepresentations about material aspects of debt relief services and misrepresentations about the seller's affiliation with any government entity.[45] The Mortgage Assistance Relief Services Rule, promulgated in 2010, is another useful legal tool for actions brought by the Federal Trade Commission.[46] It prohibits mortgage assistance relief providers from misrepresenting any material aspect of any mortgage assistance relief service, and also requires those providers to disclose that their services are not approved by the government or the consumer's lender.

As part of the Dodd-Frank Wall Street Reform and Consumer Protection Act, a new federal agency called the Consumer Financial Protection Bureau (CFPB) was created and charged with protecting consumer interests. Since opening its doors in July 2011, the CFPB has sought to improve conditions for vulnerable consumers on a variety of fronts—including those with high-interest credit card debt, unmanageable student debt, and high risk of home foreclosure. To that end, CFPB has exercised its authority to bring enforcement actions against mortgage-relief scam artists. Two complaints filed in 2012 alleged that large-scale mortgage relief operations violated the Dodd-Frank Wall Street reform and Consumer Financial Protection Act (which prohibits unfair, deceptive, or abusive acts or practices) and Regulation O (which requires that mortgage assistance relief providers make certain disclosures, prohibits them from making certain representations, and generally prohibits them from collecting an advance fee for service).[47] In one of those cases, *CFPB v. Jalan*, CFPB alleged that the defendants—often under auspices of "National Legal Help Center"—misrepresented themselves as being affiliated with the government and as being a law firm for the purpose of collecting $1.6 million in advance payments from homeowners seeking assistance with loan modifications and other mortgage relief.[48] The CFPB alleges that the defendants owned 165 Internet domains resembling legitimate government program names, the defendant made more than 90,000 outbound calls to target new customers; the victims paid from $1,000 to over $10,000 for assistance; and the defendant sent direct mail solicitations to consumers purportedly from bank regulators threatening to proceed with a foreclosure sale. In both cases, the U.S. District Court for Central California issued temporary restraining orders, froze assets of the defendants, and appointed a temporary receiver while the cases proceeded.[49]

V. Conclusion

In the fall of 2012, an unseasonably late Superstorm Sandy plowed into New York and New Jersey, causing serious damage to densely populated coastal areas that are themselves no strangers to the dangers of storm damage. Even as the New York City subway flooded, Lower Manhattan lost power, and the storm surge took buildings and lives from coastal neighborhoods, the messages coming from government and the media included clear guidance to homeowners about how to avoid being scammed during the storm recovery period. Newspaper articles cited anecdotes from Hurricane Katrina to describe the warning signs of contractor fraud, explained how to initiate a claim with insurance companies, and what to look for in an actual contract.[50] The Consumer Financial Protection Bureau used its blog to post guidance for screening contractors and avoiding predatory reconstruction lending schemes.[51] It seems that the risk of post-disaster housing fraud has finally become part of the immediate post-disaster recovery efforts, rather than simply an afterthought. Whether these messages have actually penetrated the awareness of those affected neighborhoods will be seen in the coming months.

Over and over, housing advocates and community organizers describe the difficulty of combating fraud where desperate homeowners are eager to believe the promises of savvy scammers. In many cases, the reality is that no one can guarantee or promise that the homeowner will retain a home. The reassurance offered by predatory actors is seductive, and their message that one must pay to get quality assistance undermines in the mind of the vulnerable homeowner the value of free assistance offered by nonprofit housing counseling agencies.

When disasters strike communities, government officials and the broader community-development field see their neighborhoods placed at risk—both from the immediate ravages inflicted by the elements and the subsequent and stealthier ravages of those intent on scamming desperate homeowners. As complex federal programs are introduced in places of high need following disasters, there is increasing agreement that those programs should include a simultaneous fraud-prevention message to protect homeowners and their limited resources. Natural disasters like hurricanes in the coastal states, tornadoes in the Midwest, and unprecedented superstorms, as well as human-made disasters like oil spills and the Great Recession create environments in which homeowners, lacking sufficient access to legitimate resources for obtaining clear answers about the program processes, become susceptible to scammers promising but not delivering results and services. For players in both the natural-disaster and the economic-disaster arenas, the challenge is to further cultivate operationally strong organizations and to have ready access to the marketing methods that will deliver a clear message. While the "American Dream" has come under scrutiny in recent years, homeownership will resume its central position in asset building and intergenerational wealth stability. Protecting the integrity and resources of homeowners throughout the cycle of crisis and recovery will continue to require thoughtful collaboration and real-time responses.

Notes

1. We use the terms "fraud" and "scam" interchangeably. While fraud is a legal concept with specific elements and scam is a more casual term implying systematic targeting of consumers, both involve use of deceit to intentionally deprive consumers of their property.

2. Telephone Interview with Heather Geary, Community Initiatives Manager, Missouri Housing Development Commission (Aug. 20, 2012).

3. Lori Andrews, *I Know Who You Are and I Saw What You Did: Social Networks and the Death of Privacy*, Free Press: New York (2012) (describing the methods by which data about American consumers is collected and sold).

4. *Real Scam Stories*, LOAN MODIFICATION SCAM ALERT, http://www.loanscamalert.org/ (last visited Jan. 15, 2013).

5. Press Release, Fed. Trade Comm'n, FTC Settlements Require Equifax to Forfeit Money Made by Allegedly Improperly Selling Information about Millions of Consumers Who Were Late on Their Mortgages (Oct. 10, 2012), *available at* http://www.ftc.gov/opa/2012/10/equifaxdirect.shtm.

6. *In re* Equifax Information Services LLC, F.T.C. File No. 102 3252.

7. U.S. v. Direct Lending Source et al., S.D. Cal. No. 3:12-cv-02441.

8. Fed. Trade Comm'n v. Christopher Mallett, No. 1:11-cv-01664-ckk (D.D.C. filed Sept. 14, 2011).

9. Press Release, Fed. Trade Comm'n, FTC Asks Court to Halt Defendant from Impersonating Federal Agencies While Steering Consumers to Mortgage, Tax, and Debt Relief Services (Sept. 22, 2011), *available at* http://www.ftc.gov/opa/2011/09/usdebtcare.shtm.

10. *Fed. Trade Comm'n v. Christopher Mallett*, No. 1:11-cv-01664-CKK (D.D.C. filed Sept. 14, 2011), http://www.ftc.gov/os/caselist/1123105/120703usdebtorder.pdf.

11. William C. Apgar, Mark Duda & Rochelle Nawrocki Gorey, *The Municipal Cost of Foreclosures: A Chicago Case Study* (Homeownership Pres. Found. Hous. Fin. Policy, Research Paper No. 2005-1, 2005).

12. WILLIAM C. APGAR & MARK DUDA, HOMEOWNERSHIP PRES. FOUND., COLLATERAL DAMAGE: THE MUNICIPAL IMPACT OF TODAY'S MORTGAGE FORECLOSURE BOOM (May 11, 2005).

13. NAT'L VACANT PROPERTIES CAMPAIGN, VACANT PROPERTIES: THE TRUE COST TO COMMUNITIES (2005) *available at* http://www.smartgrowthamerica.org/documents/true-costs.pdf (summarizing the many and varied costs that vacant and abandoned buildings impose on their communities).

14. Marla Nelson, Renia Ehrenfeucht & Shirley Laska, *Planning, Plans, and People: Professional Expertise, Local Knowledge, and Governmental Action in Post-Hurricane Katrina New Orleans*, 9 CITYSCAPE 3, 38 (2007).

15. NAT'L CONSUMER LAW CTR., AVOIDING HOME REPAIR FRAUD: LESSONS FROM HURRICANE KATRINA (2008), *available at* http://www.nclc.org/images/pdf/pr-reports/report-katrina_repair_fraud_2008.pdf.

16. Telephone interview with Donna Tally, Mgmt. Consultant, NeighborWorks America (Aug. 13, 2012).

17. Telephone interview with James Ross, Mgmt. Consultant for Gulf Coast Rebuilding, NeighborWorks America (Aug. 9, 2012).

18. *Id.*

19. Telephone interview with Donna Tally, Mgmt. Consultant, NeighborWorks America (Aug. 13, 2012).

20. *Insurance Fraud*, FBI, http://www.fbi.gov/stats-services/publications/insurance-fraud (last visited Feb. 17, 2013); Austen Endersby, *Nearly Blown Away: How Policyholders Affected by Hurricane Katrina May Recover Under Their Homeowners' Insurance Policies in the Face of Anti-concurrent Causation Language*, http://digitalcommons.law.umaryland.edu/student_pubs/11/ (last visited June 30, 2012) (describing the complications after Hurricane Katrina for residents whose homeowner insurance policies contained anti-concurrent causation clauses).

21. Telephone interview with James Ross, Mgmt. Consultant for Gulf Coast Rebuilding, NeighborWorks America (Aug. 9, 2012).

22. Telephone interview with anonymous New Orleans homeowner (Apr. 9, 2012).

23. *Id.*

24. *Beware of Foreclosure Rescue Scams*, MAKING HOME AFFORDABLE PROGRAM, http://www.makinghomeaffordable.gov/learning-center/Pages/beware.aspx (last visited Jan. 15, 2013).

25. Press Release, Office of the Special Inspector Gen. for the Troubled Asset Relief Program, Operators of California-Based Mortgage Modification Scam Sentenced for Conspiracy to Commit Fraud (July 23, 2012) *available at* http://www.sigtarp.gov/press%20releases/cas_sentencing_Press_Release.pdf.

26. *Emergency Homeowner Loan Program – Summary*, U.S. DEP'T OF HOUS. AND URBAN DEV., http://www.hud.gov/offices/hsg/sfh/hcc/msgs/EHLP100810.pdf (last visited Oct. 22, 2012).

27. *Independent Foreclosure Review*, OFFICE OF THE COMPTROLLER OF THE CURRENCY, https://independentforeclosurereview.com (last visited Oct. 22, 2012).

28. *Misrepresentation of Involvement by the Office of the Comptroller of the Currency in Independent Foreclosure Grant Review Scam*, OFFICE OF THE COMPTROLLER OF THE CURRENCY (Mar. 16, 2012), http://www.occ.gov/news-issuances/alerts/2012/alert-2012-10.html.

29. NeighborWorks America, *Congressional Updates of the National Foreclosure Mitigation Counseling Program*, NEIGHBORHOOD REINVESTMENT CORP., http://nw.org/network/foreclosure/nfmcp/congressional_reports.asp (last visited Nov. 10, 2012).

30. NEIGHBORWORKS AMERICA 10 NAT'L FORECLOSURE MITIGATION COUNSELING PROGRAM CONG. UPDATE (June 11, 2012).

31. Fed. Trade Comm'n v. Christopher Mallett, Case No.1:11-cv-01664-CKK (D.D.C. filed Sept. 14, 2011).

32. *Loan Modification Scam Alert*, NeighborWorks, www.loanscamalert.org (last visited Nov. 11, 2012).

33. Telephone interview with Steve Mainster, Former Exec. Dir., Centro Campesino Farmworker Ctr. (Nov. 13, 2012).

34. Woody Widrow, Robert O. Zdenek & Ralph Scott, *Rebuilding Communities, Restoring Families: Roles for CBDOs is the Aftermath of Disasters*, NEIGHBORWORKS BRIGHT IDEAS, Spring 2006, at 6–13.

35. Interview with Marietta Rodriguez, Deputy Director, National Homeownership Programs, NeighborWorks America (July 24, 2012).

36. City of New Orleans, *Soft Second Mortgage Program*, http://new.nola.gov/softseconds/ (last visited Jan. 15, 2013).

37. Press Release, City of New Orleans, Mayor Applauds Success of "Soft Second" Mortgage Homebuyer Assistance Initiative (Apr. 26, 2012), *available at* http://www.nola.gov/sitecore/content/Root/PRESS/City-Of-New-Orleans/All-Articles/20120426-MAYOR-APPLAUDS-SUCCESS-OF-SOFT-SECOND-MORTGAGE-HOMEBUYER-ASSISTANCE-INITIATIVE.aspx.

38. Telephone interview with James Ross, Mgmt. Consultant for Gulf Coast Rebuilding, NeighborWorks America (Aug. 9, 2012).

39. Jim Puzzanghera, *Mortgage Modification Scam Watchdog Cheers Federal Crackdown*, LAWYERS COMM. FOR CIVIL RIGHTS UNDER LAW, http://www.lawyerscommittee.org/projects/fair_housing/clips?id=0628 (last visited Nov. 15, 2012).

40. *Id.*

41. Press Release, Fin. Fraud Enforcement Task Force, Financial Fraud Enforcement Task Force Members Reveal Results of Distressed Homeowners Initiative (Oct. 9, 2012), *available at* http://www.stopfraud.gov/iso/opa/stopfraud/2012/12-ag-1216.html.

42. Press Release, State of Cal. Office of the Attorney Gen., Attorney General Kamala Harris Announces Judgment in National Multi-Million Dollar Mortgage Scam (July 24, 2012), *available at* http://oag.ca.gov/news/press-releases/attorney-general-kamala-d-harris-announces-judgment-national-multi-million.

43. As in *FTC v. Mallett*, Case No.1:11-cv-01664-CKK (D.D.C.), in which the FTC alleged violations of the Federal Trade Commission Act where the defendant misrepresented his organizations' affiliation with government agencies, misrepresented that his companies were vetted and approved by the federal government, and misrepresented that consumers who used the services advertised on his websites would have their debt substantially reduced.

44. 15 U.S.C. §§ 1601–1608.

45. Similarly, in *FTC v. Mallett*, the FTC also alleged violations of the Telemarketing Sales Rule where the defendant misrepresented that his organizations were affiliated with the federal government and misrepresented material aspects of his organizations' offered debt relief services.

46. CFPB Mortgage Assistance Relief Services Rule, 12 C.F.R. § 1015 (2010).

47. Press Release, Consumer Fin. Prot. Bureau, Consumer Financial Protection Bureau Halts Alleged Nationwide Mortgage Loan Modification Scams (Dec. 11, 2012), *available at* http://www.consumerfinance.gov/pressreleases/consumer-financial-protection-bureau-halts-alleged-nationwide-mortgage-loan-modification-scams/ (last visited Feb. 10, 2013).

48. CFPB v. Jalan et al., No. SAC1V-02088 AG (C.D. Cal. ANx), *available at* http://files.consumerfinance.gov/f/201212_cfpb_nlhc-tro.pdf.

49. *Id.*; CFPB v. Gordon, No. CV 12-6147 RSWL (C.D. Cal. MRWx), *available at* http://files.consumerfinance.gov/f/201212_cfpb_preliminary-injunction-order.pdf.

50. Lewis Braham, *Tips on Hiring a Housing Contractor after the Hurricane*, BLOOMBERG BUSINESSWEEK, Nov. 14, 2012, http://www.businessweek.com/news/2012-11-13/tips-on-hiring-a-housing-contractor-after-the-hurricane (last visited Nov. 16, 2012).

51. Consumer Financial Protection Bureau, *Avoiding Loan Scams after Natural Disaster*, http://www.consumerfinance.gov/blog/avoiding-loan-scams-after-a-natural-disaster/ (last visited Nov. 13, 2012).

CHAPTER 14

Housing Choice in Crisis: Short-Term Post–Hurricane Katrina Relief

James H. Perry and Monika Gerhart-Hambrick

I. Introduction

The extent of housing challenges in the aftermath of Hurricane Katrina was greater than in any other disaster in modern-day America: the numbers of housing units decimated, the families separated, the community ties left untangled—and the short, intermediate, and long-term price tags tested the fundamentals of families, communities, private industry, and the government. None were prepared.

Just as the systems charged with meeting this historic challenge fell short, this chapter does not endeavor to provide an accounting of all housing challenges faced by Hurricane Katrina evacuees. However, it does examine a sampling of experiences and occurrences in an effort to inform and support future disaster victims seeking housing free from discrimination. Indeed, let our adversity, mishap, tragedy, and innovations outline remedies, explanations, and antidotes that might prevent the misfortune of victims of future catastrophe.

The narrative juxtaposes narrow fair housing challenges against the federal emergency management and response programs and fair housing laws intended to meet those challenges. It includes immediate relief as well as short-term to interim disaster housing, ever-changing federal disaster housing programs, and a strained private market, all while understanding that survivors experienced challenges and transitions based on their own changing personal circumstances.

Title VIII of the 1968 Civil Rights Act, as amended in 1988, otherwise known as the federal Fair Housing Act, is the legal framework guiding this discussion. The Fair Housing Act addresses systemic challenges to fair housing choice delineated by protected classes: race, color, religion, sex, disability, familial status, and national origin. The Fair Housing Act is the primary enforcement mechanism used to end discrimination in sale, rental, insurance, and most other transactions related to consumer occupied dwellings. Some cities and states have local fair housing laws that address discrimination based on source of income, gender identity, and sexual orientation. Additionally, the United States Department of Housing and Urban Development (HUD) has taken steps to prohibit gender-identity and sexual-orientation discrimination in housing provided by HUD. Further, advocates have begun working to expand the Fair Housing Act to include gender-identity and sexual-orientation protection. In response, this chapter occasionally incorporates source of income, gender identity, and sexual orientation to what may be considered prospective FHA protections.

This chapter describes the legal framework used to combat vehement levels of discrimination encountered by survivors in receiver communities, as well as other structural barriers to protected classes as institutionalized by the Federal Emergency Management Agency (FEMA) and the Robert T. Stafford Disaster Relief and Emergency Assistance Act (the Stafford Act). It concludes with policy changes that have happened since Hurricane Katrina, and still others that require change.

For the elderly, people with physical disabilities and mental illness, and others whose lives were fragile even before disaster struck, it is oftentimes nearly impossible to navigate the complex web of relief programs.

For attorneys, advocates, practitioners, government officials, and others attempting to serve disaster-affected communities in ways that are ethical, effective, and value driven, immediate and tangible gains may be made through a single civil suit or narrow focus. A lack of recognition, however, of the systemic layers of challenges facing any single individual results in Pyrrhic success that may simply shift challenges to other parts of peoples' lives. The will and intent to serve—to triage a patient bleeding out on the table—is both humble and human. But no good doctor would release a patient without working closely with a team to also treat the broken limbs and kidney disease: the trauma induced as well as chronic.

Finally, to take the triage analogy just a little further, good treatment understands that patients have arrived in current condition at least in part because of their lack of agency. Any remedy sought is only so good as it empowers the patient to future self-care and preventive health: not just lives with healed limbs, but also agency to prevent further breakage.[1]

II. Shelter as Dwelling

Under the Fair Housing act, it is unlawful to "make unavailable or deny, [sic] a dwelling to any person because of race, color, religion, sex, familial status, or national origin."[2]

The Fair Housing Act defines a "dwelling" as "any building, structure, or portion thereof which is occupied as, or designed or intended for occupancy as, a residence."[3] The most widely cited definition of "residence" is "a temporary or permanent dwelling place, abode or habitation to which one intends to return as distinguished from the place of temporary sojourn or transient visit."[4]

Courts have determined that the question of whether a structure is a "residence" under the Fair Housing Act is based on two factors: whether the occupants treat the structure as a residence and place to return, and whether the residents intend to remain for more than a brief period of time.[5] For example, homeless shelters have often been held to be a "dwelling" within the bounds of the Fair Housing Act.[6]

In defining the terms of the Fair Housing Act, HUD regulations provide that examples of "dwelling units" include, for example, "sleeping accommodations in shelters intended for occupancy as a residence for homeless persons."[7] In light of any ambiguity as to what qualifies as a dwelling under the Fair Housing Act, most courts will strongly consider HUD's regulatory stance but are not bound by it.

A strong argument can be made that, under this definition, the Fair Housing Act should apply to emergency housing solutions such as disaster shelters, FEMA trailers, hotels used for emergency shelter, and all other disaster housing assistance. However, courts have expressly excluded hotels as a covered dwelling under the FHA.[8] Further, courts have determined that some trailers are covered and some are not, depending upon the fact pattern.[9] As such, fair housing laws apply unevenly to evacuees depending on their haphazard housing placement. An evacuee who receives emergency financial rental assistance and rents an apartment would have protection under the Fair Housing Act, while a similarly situated evacuee receiving emergency housing assistance in the form of a travel trailer or hotel room may not have similar Fair Housing Act protections.

There is an argument that FEMA as a federal agency is held to a higher fair housing bar than other entities. The Fair Housing Act provides that entities that spend or receive federal funds must not only refrain from engaging in discrimination but also affirmatively further fair housing in their housing-related activities.[10] Applying this obligation, known as the Affirmatively Further Doctrine, FEMA is arguably under an obligation to extend FHA-guided protections to evacuees living in uncovered dwellings. (For further discussion on the Affirmatively Further Fair Housing Doctrine, see chapter 15.) For example, FEMA could require hotels, trailer companies, and trailer parks with whom it contracts to provide emergency shelter and to agree to be governed by the Fair Housing Act or a similar set of rules. Further, regardless of the applicability of the Affirmatively Further Doctrine, FEMA could, and likely should, codify Fair Housing Act–guided regulations that would support all evacuees who rely on FEMA emergency housing.

III. Vouchers as Disaster Housing

The use of vouchers to house people in the aftermath of disaster is authorized by section 408 of the Stafford Act, which establishes federal authority to provide, at its discretion, six types of post-disaster housing assistance: (1) temporary rental assistance, (2) repairs of owner-occupied residences, (3) replacement of owner-occupied residences, (4) direct assistance in temporary housing units, (5) permanent or interim housing construction, and (6) "other needs."[11]

FEMA had insufficient post-disaster operational housing plans in place after Hurricane Katrina, and the agency was ill equipped to cope with disaster of Hurricane Katrina's catastrophic scale.[12] This was evident from the moment the storm made landfall, and demonstrated by forensic evidence compiled through emails and lengthy investigation of Bush administration agency officials. It was not until one month after Hurricane Katrina that FEMA discussed the formation of a multiagency housing meeting to vet potential disaster-housing proposals from various agencies.[13] While HUD's initial responsibilities were limited to its own clients, not until 2007 did FEMA and HUD enter into an interagency agreement,[14] driven by persistent housing needs for non-HUD populations and coupled with increasing outrage over FEMA trailers as a long-term housing solution.

As a result, FEMA had early failures that skewed long-term resettlement patterns. For example, the very absence of an operational catastrophic disaster housing plan, the failure by the Bush administration to modify policies to address a disaster of such scale, logistical failures with temporary housing, lack of repair of rental housing, and inadequate staffing, training, and case management all exacerbated massive and urgent housing needs and limited options. These early planning and operational failures ultimately led to prolonged and sometimes permanent displacement, as further discussed in this chapter.

Most rental-housing stock in New Orleans was destroyed.[15] HUD's decision to shutter and demolish more than 5,000 units of public housing—only some of which had suffered damage—compounded the housing crisis.[16] Exacerbating these conditions were the Bush administration's constant changes, terminations, and then extensions in housing assistance or type of housing assistance, creating a constantly shifting sandbox for housing advocates and survivors that continued for years.

A. Katrina Disaster Housing Assistance Program

In September of 2005, the Bush administration created a FEMA-funded Katrina Disaster Housing Assistance Program (KDHAP), modeled after HUD's biggest rental assistance program, Section 8. Originally, HUD estimated that the program would serve close to 120,000 HUD clients. Two months later, that number was reduced by nearly half. By February 2006 the Bush administration's supplemental funding request reflected estimates of 44,000 families.[17] In September a year later, 27,000 families were served under the voucher program. Changes in estimates did not appear to be linked to data or actual need, but rather were fairly random. Without an accurate baseline for HUD families the program should have served, it is unknown how many fell through the cracks, although estimates based on calculations above indicate that tens of thousands may have been failed.[18]

The KDHAP was administered by HUD's network of more than 3,000 public housing agencies (PHAs), where voucher holders could access housing in non-disaster areas in a manner similar to a housing choice voucher, with the understanding that families could return to affected areas as housing was repaired or rebuilt, despite the fact that no solid plans were in place to do either.[19] The program is only as viable as housing stock is available, and, regrettably, many voucher holders found that receiver communities lacked sufficient units to house them. Moreover, the process of rebuilding units in storm-damaged regions was slow and arduous. So even with a voucher in hand, many storm-affected families still lacked true housing options.

In December of 2005, Congress also funded the Disaster Voucher Program (DVP), a program funded by HUD's Section 8 program, and administered similarly with wide decision-making authority by participating PHAs.[20] PHAs were then required to transition their KDHAP users into DVPs. The DVP program was then scheduled to expire but later extended on four subsequent occasions.[21] Unfortunately, in post–Hurricane Katrina communities, where stability was key, participants experienced frequent spates of unexplained terminations, transitions, and extensions of key programs.

The DVP program was, and may be still, the largest program used to provide post-disaster affordable rental housing to HUD-assisted, special-needs, and homeless survivors. While the program still makes assumptions about availability of housing stock where a participant could use a voucher, it also raises questions and distinct challenges for survivors availing to their right to fair housing choice.

For example, in tests conducted by the National Fair Housing Alliance in December of 2005 to measure race-based housing discrimination against evacuees, white callers posing as prospective renters were favored over African-American callers 66 percent of the time. The tests, conducted in 17 cities in five states, tested what white and African-American home seekers were told about rent, unit availability, and other leasing terms and conditions.[22]

Evidence of source-of-income discrimination is also well documented in the national fair housing community as well as the greater New Orleans metropolitan statistical area, providing another layer of potential discrimination beyond race-based evidence.[23] In its 2009 audit titled *Housing Choice in Crisis*, the Greater New Orleans Fair Housing Action Center found that landlords in the greater New Orleans area denied voucher holders the opportunity to rent units 82 percent of the time, either via "outright refusal to accept vouchers," or through "the addition of insurmountable requirements."[24] "Housing providers said they would accept vouchers as rental payment without any obstacles or additional terms only eighteen percent of the time."[25] Because 99 percent of voucher holders in the New Orleans area are African-American, the data demonstrates an alarming rate of discrimination impacting communities on both a race and source-of-income basis.[26]

Unfortunately, no comprehensive examination of source of income–based discrimination against DVP or KDHAP voucher holders has been conducted. This is despite the fact that some cities that received large numbers of evacuees have source-of-income nondiscrimination ordinances in place. Cities and counties that have such nondiscrimination ordinances[27] and participated in the KDHAP include Los Angeles, California; Cook County, Illinois; Iowa City, Iowa; Fredrick, Maryland; Grand Rapids, Michigan; New York, New York; Philadelphia, Pennsylvania; Memphis, Tennessee; King County, Washington; and Seattle, Washington.[28]

Another potential barrier to housing choice for disaster voucher holders was landlord preference for Section 8 versus KDHAP or DVP vouchers, given the presumed longevity of Section 8 vouchers, which are renewable. As mentioned above, KDHAP and DVP vouchers were time limited. Repeated extensions at the end of the program's term were probably ineffective in assuring potential landlords of long-term rent revenue at the program's inception. While anecdotal evidence supports this claim, no comprehensive study on the varied barriers to disaster voucher holders exists to date.

Hurricanes Gustav and Ike, which struck the Gulf Coast three years after Katrina, demonstrated that disaster vouchers have become a standing disaster-housing solution.[29]

However, fair and robust implementation of any voucher program during future disasters requires further study into multiple barriers faced by voucher holders, including the experiences of disaster voucher holders in localities with source-of-income discrimination ordinances versus those without; landlord perceptions of the program, which may vary widely by PHA; and the experiences of classes protected under the Fair Housing Act, some of which are described below.

IV. "I'm Not Racist, but Whites Only"

The federal Fair Housing Act is regarded by many as one of the strongest and most sophisticated civil rights laws on the books. Unlike equal employment law, there is no requirement that complainants exhaust administrative remedies prior to pursuing judicial claims.[30] There is no limit on punitive damages,[31] and a generally supportive line of jurisprudence has granted standing to a broad cast of claimants including both individuals and organizations.[32] Further, the codified black letter law is buttressed by the Supreme Court's definitive endorsement of mystery shopping as a means to prove that discrimination has occurred.[33] However, Hurricane Katrina helped to reveal a clear crack in the Fair Housing Act's seemingly impervious shield.

Specifically, in the wake of Hurricane Katrina, housing providers used cyberspace to reveal a challenge to the advertising component of fair housing doctrine. Survivors relied on websites designed to link them to housing resources, only to encounter the following:

> "I would love to house a single mom with one child, not racist but white only."
> "Not to sound racist but because we want to make things more understandable for our younger child we would like to house white children."
> "Provider would provide room and board for $400, prefers 2 White females."

> "Prefer white Catholic family, children welcome."
> "Room available to single white mother with child or younger to middle aged white couple."[34]

Housing providers seeking to assist Hurricane Katrina–affected home seekers posted thousands of discriminatory advertisements on websites designed to assist evacuees. In the weeks immediately following Hurricane Katrina, a concerned Gulf Coast resident alerted Fair Housing Action Center staff to websites containing the discriminatory statements quoted above. Complaints led the Fair Housing Action Center to investigate katrinahousing.org, katrinahome.com, nolahousing.org, dhronline.com and relief.welcomewagon.com. Each of the sites featured facially discriminatory ads affecting various protected class members.

While the actions of all the sites are cause for serious concern, one might argue that dhronline.com (Disaster Housing Resources online) was particularly egregious. The site was sponsored, vetted, and funded by FEMA.[35] When families whose homes had been destroyed applied for FEMA assistance online, they were referred by FEMA to dhronline.com, where many encountered government-sponsored discriminatory advertisements that clearly violated the Fair Housing Act.

The Fair Housing Action Center filed fair housing administrative complaints with HUD in an effort to enforce the Fair Housing Act against the sites. Fair Housing Action Center staff members have suggested in interviews that they initially saw the cases as open-and-shut fair housing advertising cases. And reasonably so, since the Fair Housing Act provides that it is illegal

> [t]o make, print, or publish, or cause to be made, printed, or published any notice, statement, or advertisement, with respect to the sale or rental of a dwelling that indicates any preference, limitation, or discrimination based on race, color, religion, sex, handicap, familial status, or national origin, or an intention to make any such preference, limitation, or discrimination.[36]

Some 40 years ago, the U.S. Fourth Circuit Court of Appeals set precedent when it found that a Maryland paper violated the Fair Housing Act when it published an advertisement of rental accommodations in a "white home."[37] The Second Circuit Court of Appeals expanded the fair housing advertising doctrine when it found the *New York Times* liable for discrimination for failing to include African-American models during more than 20 years of advertising.[38]

Logic provided that if it were illegal to assert rental opportunities in a "white home," then surely the expansive ban of "not racist but white only" was a per se violation of the Fair Housing Act. Indeed, few doubt the clear liability of the individual who placed the advertisement; however, questions began to arise regarding the liability of those who published the online advertisement.

While print publishers had been found liable repeatedly in prior circumstances, the Hurricane Katrina Internet cases provided a key change in the fact pattern: the publishers were Internet service providers rather than merely print publishers.

The Communications Decency Act (CDA) was passed in 1995 amending 47 U.S.C. § 223, of the Communications Act of 1934. Congress argued: "The information superhighway should not become a red light district. . . . Once [CDA] passed, our children and families will be better protected from those who would electronically cruise the digital world to engage children in inappropriate communications and introductions."[39]

Congress further offered its preference to grow the Internet and sought to fend off heavy regulation that might stunt such growth. The record provided that "[i]f we regulate the Internet at the [Federal Communications Commission (FCC)], that will freeze or at least slow down technology. It will threaten the future of the Internet."[40]

Subsequently, the courts broadly construed Congress's intention. In 1997, only two years after the passage of the CDA, the Fourth Circuit Court of Appeals upheld the district court in finding online service providers had broad immunity from liability.[41] Ironically, the court that 25 years earlier formed the judicial basis for outlawing discriminatory advertising later provided the decision that provided the most serious basis for challenges to the effectiveness of the Fair Housing Act advertising doctrine.

Citing Hurricane Katrina–affected home seekers further afflicted by discriminatory online advertising, the Fair Housing Action Center litigated the matter both in the HUD administrative complaint process and in the court of public opinion by way of two congressional testimonies.[42] Simultaneously, two court cases wound through the judicial process. *Fair Housing Council of San Fernando Valley v. Roommates.com, LLC* made its way through the Ninth Circuit, while the Seventh Circuit considered *Chicago Lawyers Committee for Civil Rights Under Law, Inc. v. Craigslist, Inc.*[43]

In the *Roommates.com* case, the Internet service provider required visitors to the site to state preferences regarding, "sex, sexual orientation and whether children will be living with them."[44] The Craigslist case was reinforced by clear and unequivocal statements in advertisements, such as "NO MINORITIES" and "Non-Women of Color NEED NOT APPLY."[45] Despite strong facts and an extensive jurisprudential record in support of the Fair Housing Act, both courts ultimately found little or no liability for Internet service providers that unknowingly and, in some cases, knowingly, allowed discriminatory content on their websites.[46]

In the face of the total physical decimation of their homes and communities, Hurricane Katrina evacuees had little choice but to rely on public and private publications for housing opportunities. When those were in print, the publishers were required to present housing opportunities free from discriminatory content. However, if those same advertisements were placed online, under the *Roommates.com* and *Craigslist* decisions, publishers were essentially allowed to publicize limitations based on race, sex, sexual orientation and other protections.[47]

In February 2006 testimony before the Housing Subcommittee of the U.S. House of Representatives Financial Services Committee, Fair Housing Action Center staff requested that Congress consider amending the CDA to provide a clear exception for Fair Housing Act claims. While subcommittee members were publicly amenable, off record they suggested that it was appropriate to allow the courts to rule before moving toward such amendments. With the 2012 Ninth Circuit *Roommates.com* decision, it has become clear that Congress must act to stem judicial harm to the Fair Housing Act advertising doctrine.

While online ads clearly tested the advertising doctrine of the Fair Housing Act for survivors seeking housing, the very concept of fair housing choice was pushed to the periphery, particularly for individuals with layered or multiple barriers, each of which alone and without disaster might pose challenges to access and opportunity.

V. Compounding Burdens: People with Disabilities

People with disabilities found themselves at the intersection of these failures. Systems designed to meet the needs of the least vulnerable people fell short, creating crisis-level circumstances for individuals with mental or physical disabilities: If disabled people with access to personal resources were nonetheless left vulnerable and powerless, circumstances for those without resources were even more life threatening.

Much has been written about mental health issues that resulted from the hurricane, but much less on the plight of those with such issues during and immediately after the storm. It is well documented that evacuation locations and emergency shelters lacked mental health supports or treatment services; they also often lacked vital medications.[48] As a result, individuals with psychiatric disabilities were often jailed, sent to psychiatric hospitals, or otherwise institutionalized when untrained shelter personnel without expertise or assistance made faulty assessments. For some sent to state psychiatric institutions or jail, all the individual may have needed was a refill on medication.[49] Once institutionalized, family reunification often became insurmountable, and the chaos that ruptured all evacuees' lives was compounded by the lack of systems and supports for people with disabilities.

Even disabled people who were informed advocates with access to personal resources suffered sometimes insurmountable obstacles in the aftermath of Hurricane Katrina, contributing to higher rates of prolonged, if not permanent, displacement among people with disabilities compared with the general population.[50] Many of these obstacles contributed to secondary medical issues that resulted in hospitalization or even death,[51] as emergency disaster shelter occupants and those evacuated out of harm's way were deprived of means to adequate self-care.[52]

While the obstacles to adequate housing choice for people with low and even moderate incomes have been well documented in previous sections of this chapter, these burdens were exponentially compounded for low-income people with mobility and other disability issues—it is dangerous to be both poor and disabled during disaster. Disability advocates such as those at the Advocacy Center of Louisiana, Mississippi Coalition for Citizens with Disabilities, and others were able to assist clients on a case-by-case basis, but no systemic means for addressing the needs of the disability population were in place.

Tragedies during evacuation were numerous, and ranged from well-publicized stories of people flooded in their beds to quiet deaths as wheelchair-bound citizens sat endless days on the interstate or roadside.[53] Individuals with physical disabilities who were successfully evacuated found themselves on airplanes with destinations unknown, placed in nursing homes, or in shelters where restrooms and showers were inaccessible. The doorways were too narrow for wheelchairs to pass, or steps made the restrooms impossible for wheelchair users to traverse. Inaccessibility of emergency shelters became special dangers for evacuees bound to wheelchairs or other mobility devices, as the inability to bathe or use the restroom for extended periods of time frequently led to infections, disease, and ultimately serious medical conditions.[54]

By far, the most common FEMA interim housing solution was the now-infamous travel trailers. Intended to bring people home to rebuild in place, the fraught-with-disaster housing solution left people with disabilities squarely out in the cold. In 2006, the Advocacy Center—along with the Mississippi Center for Justice, the Welfare Law Center of New York, and the Public Interest Law Project of California—filed a class action lawsuit[55] alleging discrimination by FEMA on behalf of plaintiffs seeking trailers with accessibility features such as ramps, wide doorways, adequate interior maneuvering space, accessible bathrooms, and accessible kitchens.[56] The suit was ultimately settled in a manner favorable to the plaintiffs.

The lawsuit successfully signaled to people with physical disabilities who are eligible for temporary housing that they can request accessible units or modifications to existing units, and that preparations to have accessible housing at the ready will be made during future disasters.

As the mandatory evacuations in New Orleans and surrounding areas were lifted and people returned, those with disabilities seeking permanent housing faced another unique set of challenges, again compounded by poverty and competition for available housing stock.

Many who returned, facing limited options, moved in with family members. These arrangements led to their own sets of challenges: besides overcrowding, many people with access and functional needs were then trapped in family homes without accessible bathrooms or wheelchair ramps, unable to leave even to get to necessary medical appointments if family members were physically unable to carry an occupied wheelchair down steps to street level. One housing advocate reported that every time he needed to use the restroom during prolonged displacement with a family member, the bathroom door had to be removed from its hinges.[57] For other returnees, the wider rental market was no kinder.

In New Orleans, the closure of approximately 5,000 public housing units[58] and the loss of 56 percent[59] of the city's rental stock meant that there was stiff competition for remaining units among disaster aid workers, returning renters, former public housing residents, and former homeowners. People with mobility or other issues that might require a reasonable accommodation or modification were often easily passed over for tenants without these requirements. Those remaining accessible units among the city's developments were immediately occupied, although not necessarily by people with disabilities. If the competition for affordable and adequate rental housing was a struggle for most, the climb was even steeper for people with physical and other disabilities.

The inadequate quantity of available rental housing increased competition and contributed to the prolonged displacement of people with disabilities, and this in turn influenced permanent resettlement patterns, where, to date, housing inventory for people with disabilities may not meet the need, despite significant federal, state, and philanthropic investment in post–Hurricane Katrina rebuilding efforts in New Orleans. For example, the Advocacy Center of New Orleans continues to serve individuals in the disability community still struggling to return. Although the Advocacy Center of New Orleans has distributed 250 vouchers, an additional 400 households remain on the Advocacy Center's voucher waiting list.[60]

In its post–Hurricane Katrina audit on housing opportunity for people with physical disabilities, *Access Denied*, the Fair Housing Action Center documents and quantifies accessibility barriers. The audit "examined twenty-two multi-family apartment complexes built after March of 1991 (such complexes are required to satisfy design and construction requirements under the 1988 Amendments to the federal Fair Housing Act)."[61] All of the complexes failed to comply with at least one of the seven design and construction requirements. Eighty-one percent of the complexes failed to comply with two or more of the requirements. On average, three of the seven design and construction requirements were lacking.[62]

While many disability advocates remain vigilant yet skeptical in the ability of future emergency response efforts to adequately meet the housing needs of people with disabilities, FEMA has come a long way. Indicators of progress include the FEMA Office of Disability Integration and Coordination, established by the Obama administration to integrate "preparedness, response and recovery for children and adults with disabilities and others with access and functional needs before, during and after a disaster,"[63] in accordance with civil rights laws and regulations. Further, the 2006 Post-Katrina Emergency Management Reform Act established the FEMA National Advisory Council, including a seat reserved for an advisory role from the disability community.[64]

Further, state-level efforts to increase the number of accessible dormitory-style units in emergency shelters, as well as recruit and train volunteers who can serve the functional needs of evacuees, are under way. For example, Louisiana's Emergency Management Disability and Aging Coalition (EMDAC), which includes organizations such as the Advocacy Center and Louisiana Assistive Technology Access Network, has successfully ensured that Medicaid-funded personal assistance services will continue in times of future disaster.[65] Advocates across the Gulf Coast also successfully ensured that portability of medical records, essential during times of disaster, was included in the Affordable Care Act of 2010.[66]

VI. Sex Discrimination

Although women shared many of the same experiences of displacement and recovery in the aftermath of Hurricane Katrina as men, special circumstances also severely limited the housing choice and safety of women in the aftermath of the storm. Besides well-documented incidences of violence, of which there are many painful and disturbing accounts, it is worth outlining systemic legal challenges for two particular populations for whom housing choice becomes equivalent to the right to life itself: survivors of domestic violence and women convicted under Louisiana's archaic "Crimes Against Nature" laws.

The summer before Hurricane Katrina, the staff of Crescent House Domestic Violence Services met with its clients and community members to discuss what would happen in the event of an emergency. Staff worked diligently to colocate multiagency services that could serve families in criminal justice, social service, and direct service needs, with a keen understanding of the layers of challenges their clients face.[67]

As Hurricane Katrina unfolded and many in-shelter residents relocated via a Catholic Charities–funded bus to partner networks in other cities, other survivors again found themselves at the margins, driven by lack of personal resources or adequate options into emergency shelters and interim housing without independent financial means, and compounded by stress and close proximity to abusers. Besides the obvious devastating stressors of the losses of Hurricane Katrina itself, short-term housing solutions put survivors and abusers together in cramped quarters, public shelters, and rented hotel rooms that in many cases narrowed options for independence from abusers to zero.

Domestic violence survivors, unlikely to leave abusers without supportive services even under ideal circumstances, followed abusers home after evacuation only to realize upon returning that they were more isolated than before they left. Reports of new abuse and escalation of existing violence were widespread. Increased severity moved verbal or emotional abuse to cutting, raping, and beatings; other physical abuse escalated to homicide.[68]

Survivors found that the single most insurmountable challenge to housing choice and access to capital were head-of-household rules, which designated one beneficiary for all relief and assistance. Whether direct FEMA or American Red Cross financial assistance, disaster housing vouchers, or FEMA trailers, head-of-household rules limited many women's ability to seek safe and secure housing separate from their abuser.[69]

While head-of-household rules may facially appear gender and race neutral, women—and particularly African-American women—again became the intersection points for severely limiting and often damaging policies. Although the Fair Housing Act does not explicitly recognize survivors of family violence as a protected class, HUD's published guidance on the issue has outlined housing discrimination claims on the basis of both sex and race. The guidance notes that women "who are denied housing, evicted, or deprived of assistance based on the violence in their homes may have a cause of action for sex discrimination under the Fair Housing Act."[70]

Family violence, and particularly in the aftermath of Hurricane Katrina, is not well researched, but many reports note that African-American women nationwide suffer domestic violence at higher rates in comparison with other racial groups.[71] Locally, these numbers are much higher; New Orleans providers estimate that African-American women make up close to 95 percent of client intake. Although African-Americans comprise only roughly 32 percent of Louisiana's population, nearly two-thirds of domestic violence deaths in Louisiana involve an African-American victim.[72] According to the National Coalition Against Domestic Violence, Louisiana ranks third in the nation for the number of women murdered by men for the last year for which statistics are available.[73]

Accordingly, HUD further determined that housing claims for domestic violence survivors on the basis of race might also be available because "[b]lack women experience intimate partner violence at a rate 35% higher than that of white females, and about 2.5 times the rate of women of other races."[74] HUD has additionally outlined foreseeable use of disparate impact analysis in demonstration of discrimination based on sex and race in domestic violence housing discrimination claims, noting that such cases often arise in the context of "zero tolerance" policies in which an entire household is evicted based on the criminal activity of one household member. "Women may be disproportionately affected by these policies because, as the overwhelming majority of domestic violence victims, women are often evicted as a result of the violence of their abusers."[75]

In the case of Hurricane Katrina, survivors with access to adequate housing choice evacuated and returned independently if they had the personal resources to do so. Direct financial assistance through FEMA and HUD disaster housing vouchers (DVP and KDHAP) were "only offered to him," as noted by Crescent House staff. Disaster assistance distributed under single head-of-household rules in most cases went to men, in this case also the abusers. These same crippling limitations again followed the BP oil spill, as the Gulf Coast Claims Facility (GCCF) awarded claims to heads of households, at the same time that workers that had lost employment were spending days inside at home, rather than at work.[76]

Legislative efforts in the aftermath of Hurricane Katrina attempted to address some of these issues. The Disaster Recovery Act of 2011, introduced to the Senate Homeland Security Committee in the 112th Congress, further addressed head of household rules for multigenerational households and survivors of domestic violence, in an attempt to prohibit denial of housing assistance to displaced individuals who are victims of domestic violence.[77] The legislation failed to clear the Senate but is clearly needed as previous efforts did not go far enough, as evidenced by subsequent disasters: in December 2012, the Fair Housing Action Center settled a DHAP claim against HUD on these same challenges, which followed Hurricane Gustav in 2008.

In that case, the client's husband served as head of household when the family received a DHAP housing voucher in the aftermath of Hurricane Gustav.[78] Violence in the client's household escalated following Hurricane Gustav and, in September of 2010, the client's husband was arrested and subsequently served time as a result of the abuse. Because quarterly case management services are required to maintain voucher compliance, and knowing that her husband would be unable to comply with case management from prison, the client went to DHAP offices to request that she be made head of household. She was denied.

One month later DHAP terminated the family's housing voucher based on failure to comply with case management services. The client and her children were evicted from their apartment and made homeless. In 2009, an investigative report issued by the U.S. Senate Ad Hoc Subcommittee on Disaster Recovery, *Far From Home*, went even further in outlining repetitive mistakes, structural mismanagement, and lessons learned from the disasters of 2005 and its predecessors.[79]

While current law is drafted to the exclusion of new or escalations in existing violence as described in the case above, providers in Orleans Parish note that the majority of services they provide are to survivors who stay in their households, receiving case management, counseling, group services, and a respite on-site when needed. According to Crescent House Program Director Deanne Bowman, "for someone who doesn't have resources before, taking her away from her supports—including his financial support—can lead to more damage."[80]

In 2008, the Housing Authority of New Orleans (HANO) set aside a limited number of vouchers to be directly administered by providers in the domestic violence service community. According to the service providers, the program was "the greatest thing ever"[81] and might easily work under DVP and DHAP in the event of future disasters, since provider networks were and are already colocated in receiver communities.

The HANO vouchers were accompanied by case management and experienced an astounding success rate. Providers such as Crescent House paid apartment rents on the private market, easing survivors into independence while helping to build self-sufficiency. Provision of voluntary services and skills training were designed to support the survivor, and coupled with incremental increases in financial responsibility. The program boasted a nearly 100 percent success rate of survivors who maintained their new homes independently once the provider transitioned out.[82] Unfortunately, funding cuts mean that new vouchers are no longer issued.

A similar provider-administered voucher program might also meet the needs of women identified by the state as "sex offenders" under Louisiana's archaic Crimes Against Nature laws, which were solidly in place at the time of Hurricane Katrina. Any woman[83] who verbally offered or agreed to engage in oral or anal sex in exchange for compensation could be charged with a Crime Against Nature by Solicitation. This was the case until legislative amendments to the Louisiana state law were implemented in June of 2011 removing the requirement to register as a sex offender for solicitation violations.[84] At the time of Hurricane Katrina, though, once convicted, these women were considered sex offenders and required to register with the state as such. In Orleans Parish in 2010, this included almost 40 percent of registered sex offenders—75 percent of whom were women,[85] and 79 percent of those of whom were African-American.[86]

There are reasonable public safety goals in regulating the activities of sex offenders. However, the effects of such laws as applied against women who are former sex workers may demonstrate that current laws are overly broad, promote or even cause recidivism, and promote harm and aggression toward former female sex workers and their families more than they protect communities from harm. Further, readers should note that men who solicit sex workers, even when arrested and convicted, face few, if any, of the long-term legal burdens and obligations detailed in this section.

These layers of discriminatory conditions that existed prior to Hurricane Katrina were made much worse during disaster. In the event of evacuation, as during Hurricane Katrina, registered sex offenders are not allowed to stay with their children or families in emergency shelters. Registered sex offenders must identify themselves as such when arriving at an emergency shelter, and must be accompanied by a police officer at all times. Shelter personnel issue a tracking number and badge for sex offenders, who are then transferred to a facility that houses the "Unique Population." The current Unique Population emergency shelter is Wade Correctional Center in Homer, Louisiana. In other words, because of a solicitation conviction, some women during Hurricane Katrina were required to give up their freedom, their children, and enter a prison to join violent offenders who are deemed potentially harmful to the general population.[87]

As the repopulation of storm-affected areas began, the impediments to housing choice described above were compounded by the net loss of the majority of the city's housing stock. The lack of community, dispersal of social and familial networks, and dismantling of place-based community infrastructure further exacerbated existing severe challenges. While no comprehensive study was undertaken to quantify discrimination specifically for this population based on sex, race, or any other factors, systemic challenges are clear: barriers to fair housing choice pre–Hurricane Katrina, coupled with post–Hurricane Katrina barriers described above, created a perfect storm for a housing crisis, with a disproportionate effect on women of color.

VII. No Se Puede

Hurricane Katrina may have affected as many as 300,000 Latinos in the Gulf Coast.[88] While this short section is not enough to do this topic justice, the housing experiences of Latinos in the aftermath of Hurricane Katrina were at least in part driven by (1) faulty assumptions on the part of federal and local relief workers about citizenship status that drove assistance and thus outcomes, (2) supportive social networks that facilitated transition in receiver communities for some groups, (3) resettlement patterns and housing opportunity based at least partially on documented versus undocumented status, and (4) prioritization by federal and local officials of immigration and customs enforcement over humanitarian assistance or personal safety.

Although undocumented people can be eligible for FEMA emergency shelter according to FEMA guidelines,[89] in many instances FEMA failed to provide temporary emergency housing or shelters to Latinos based on ignorance about its own rules and regulations, as well as faulty assumptions of citizenship status. In some instances Latinos with legal residency status were told to leave shelters or face deportation.[90] At least two American Red Cross–operated shelters were raided by local police and U.S. marshals, who racially profiled Latinos (including one shelter volunteer) and asked them to leave based on assumptions that they were undocumented.[91] As word of this and similar actions spread, many documented and undocumented people avoided shelters and emergency relief centers.

In another example, one HUD-subsidized apartment complex that was severely damaged by Hurricane Katrina housed 1,500 to 1,800 people—the majority born in Central America. Three weeks after the storm, although the complex was still without electricity and potable water, residents were still residing in their apartments because no alternate shelter was available. When area residents complained, a spokeswoman for FEMA at the time noted that "part of the problem with the Hispanic community is that if you are illegal, you cannot apply for housing," although most of the residents of the complex in question were legal U.S. residents.[92] Instead, FEMA shared limited information on eligibility or the kinds of assistance available in the Latino community, as outlined in a report by the National Council of La Raza.[93] As a result, Latinos were widely absent from shelters, and unable to access other kinds of emergency or interim housing.[94]

Besides these stereotypes and misperceptions, many of the responsible federal authorities in the disaster-affected area contributed to or exacerbated the housing challenges of the Latino community, in some instances by design. Formal FEMA communications were not bilingual or accessible for many populations. Lack of clarity in FEMA eligibility guidelines and administration of FEMA housing assistance based on false assumptions of immigration status meant that few Latinos had access to FEMA disaster-housing resources. Since many families are composed of members with different immigration statuses, including citizen children, FEMA should have made families aware of their ability to apply for FEMA-administered benefits. While undocumented adults could apply for FEMA assistance using the Social Security numbers of their citizen children, many did not because, contrary to precedents set by previous disasters, the federal government decided not to waive federal guidelines regarding immigration status.[95] Reports circulated of undocumented immigrants who applied for aid or shelter for their documented children and later faced deportation hearings.[96]

In fact, according to census data, 78.7 percent of Louisiana's foreign-born population that entered the United States before 1980 were citizens, as were 70.2 percent who entered during the 1980s, and 44.8 percent who entered during the 1990s.[97] Among these, Central Americans were predominant in the Latino population; of those most were Honduran. The Honduran population in New Orleans was 9.7 percent of Louisiana's foreign-born population in 2000.[98] In 2005 when Hurricane Katrina swept ashore, New Orleans boasted a high concentration of Hondurans,[99] many of who are Garifuna.[100]

The Garifuna population is worthy of quick mention for three reasons: (1) New Orleans is typically oversimplified in terms of race dynamics as either black or white; (2) popular perceptions of Latinos in New Orleans as "the new black" and dichotomies such as "black versus brown" pertaining especially to jobs and economic development fail to account for Latino-African descendants who have been living in the area for generations; and (3) for the Garifuna, citizenship status is but one added layer to the potential for facially disparate treatment or discriminatory impacts based on race, color, or national origin.

Writer Cynthia Garza records similar accounts of limited housing choice or other disaster assistance for Garifuna evacuees based on national origin, race, and faulty assumptions about immigration status, despite this community's multigenerational long-standing in New Orleans.[101] Because of these barriers, cultural and language identity became a basis for survival in receiver communities such as Houston,[102] where the Christian Church Garifuna Mercy of God[103] became the community focal point of the diaspora. As Garza notes in her record of the New Orleans Garifuna community in the aftermath of Hurricane Katrina, "as New Orleanians, African Americans, Latinos, Caribbeans, evacuees, residents, border-crossers, locals, foreigners, hurricane survivors (Mitch and then Katrina) . . . the men and women . . . turn[ed] a catastrophic situation into a manageable resettlement process."[104]

Thus, as with populations described in previous sections of this chapter, the ability to secure safe and habitable housing and other forms of relief seemed at least in part predicated on a provider network outside of government that was responsive to particular needs, and which ultimately drove an individual's ability to access housing and other resources.

As the repopulation of the disaster-affected region began, many Latino families found that scarcity of housing compounded discriminatory impacts of pre–Hurricane Katrina market conditions. According to HUD-sponsored pre–Hurricane Katrina research, one in four Latino renters experienced some sort of discrimination when seeking housing in the private rental market.[105] These issues of discrimination were heightened by market conditions of limited housing stock immediately after Hurricane Katrina. Unfortunately, not many investigative resources are available to quantify the level, frequency, or impact of housing discrimination during early resettlement, although poor and overcrowded conditions, lack of access to potable water or electricity, and otherwise uninhabitable living conditions were widely reported in receiver communities, at least in part due to inaccessibility of resources as noted above.

Without alternatives, many evacuees moved into shared housing with family or other community members, often in extremely overcrowded conditions. Some evacuees in Atlanta reported that they were living 14 to 15 people in a two-bedroom apartment.[106]

In another interview conducted by Drs. DeAnne Hilfinger Messias and Elaine Lacy, a survivor reported:

> My daughter . . . can't stay here because she has children . . . we don't have electricity, we only have water. This isn't the apartment we used to live in. It's one that the landlord has let us stay in. . . .But we have much to be thankful for because he [the landlord] has let us stay here even though there isn't any electricity . . . Because you can't find a place to rent anywhere. So this is a very desperate situation. . . . Everything is so expensive, so we are just taking advantage of this opportunity for a place to stay.[107]

For people who did return to find housing in the New Orleans area, nonprofit organizations serving the Latino community, such as the New Orleans Workers' Center for Racial Justice, noticed an uptick in raids in trailer parks, apartments, and single-occupancy homes by the U.S. Immigration and Customs Enforcement (ICE). Neighborhoods and apartment complexes with high percentages of Latinos seemed especially vulnerable to raids, and under the auspices of serving one person with a warrant, officials raided homes or apartment complexes with increased frequency.[108]

Despite these challenges, Hurricanes Gustav and Ike demonstrated that broad local discretion in implementation of national policy would continue to create differentiated outcomes. While federal authorities should temporarily cease immigration enforcement to prioritize humanitarian assistance during times of disaster, provide accurate information about emergency relief and assistance in languages other than English, and retain diverse staff that can provide language-accessible, culturally appropriate case management, there is little evidence that policy directives at the federal level are moving forward on these fronts, due to broad discretionary authority at the local level.

VIII. Recommendations

Perhaps Hurricane Katrina was not so mighty. By the time the hurricane neared New Orleans, its strength had waned significantly. The winds were less ferocious. It had difficulty maintaining the constant driving rain that flooded other communities along the way. In fact, some New Orleanians who had stayed to brave the storm thumped their chests as it passed with little more than a whimper. Hurricane Katrina did not actually "hit" the city of New Orleans. In fact, it was merely a passerby.

But the demise of the triple centurion city, the disaster if you will, was the failure of government to perform its duties before, during, and after the storm. The federal levees were in disrepair and ripe for failure because Congress failed to fund their maintenance for more than a decade. People were left without transportation, food, or water because local, state, and federal governments had no plan and no strategy to mobilize and provide basic necessities. And people had no shelter because FEMA had no emergency-housing plan.

This text has exposed many of the public sector's performance failures and inadequacies. Solutions are in order.

1. Federal, state, and local government officials should review all emergency programs through a fair housing lens to see if programs comply with fair housing law. The applicable standard is not merely to determine if programs refrain from discrimination; in fact, programs should affirmatively further fair housing as a minimum standard, particularly since this is the standard required of all federal agencies.
2. FEMA has repeatedly demonstrated that it lacks the sophistication to create and manage an effective housing program. The National Disaster Recovery Framework released in 2011 makes significant strides in addressing lessons learned in the aftermath of Hurricane Katrina and the attacks of 9/11. As such, HUD's leadership in the housing Recovery Support Functions (RSF) is a welcome formalization of its expected role in long-term recovery. However, because FEMA is still the lead agency under the National Response Framework's housing Emergency Support Functions (ESF), a strong interagency transitional plan should be in place. Central to any interagency agreement should be the transition in leadership from FEMA to HUD from the perspective of a consumer of disaster housing.
3. To the extent that FEMA does manage housing programs, as a federal agency it is held to a high fair housing bar. The Fair Housing Act provides that entities that spend or receive federal funds must not only refrain from engaging in discrimination but also affirmatively further fair housing in their activities related to housing. Applying the Affirmatively Further Doctrine, FEMA is under the obligation to extend Fair Housing Act guided protections to evacuees living in uncovered dwellings. FEMA should create regulations that codify Fair Housing Act guided rules to govern all of its housing related transactions.
4. FEMA and HUD should jointly commission research to determine the efficacy of the various tools in the disaster-housing toolbox through a fair housing lens. Despite the extensive use of hotels, shelters, travel trailers, vouchers, and other methods for housing evacuees, there has been no extensive study of the effectiveness of such programs in the wake of disaster. In particular, disaster voucher holders may face discrimination in both intent and impact, as demonstrated in the Fair Housing Action Center's aforementioned audit. While the audit is particular to the New Orleans area [or metropolitan statistical area], the findings demonstrate an alarming rate of discrimination against African-Americans, who were denied housing 82 percent of the time. It is plausible that voucher holders in PHAs in receiver communities may be subject to similar barriers.

5. All disaster-related housing programs should be easy to navigate, be predictable, have clear, simple rules, and have a clear and reasonable timeline. Multiple transitions, terminations, and extensions defeat the program's purpose to provide access to safe, stable, and habitable housing, at great cost to both program participants and taxpayers. Agency officials must work with Congress to establish realistic housing recovery timelines and fund disaster housing programs accordingly.
6. Federal agencies should strongly consider partial administration of disaster voucher programs for special populations through community-based service providers. As demonstrated throughout this chapter, organizations tailored to and led by the populations they serve are frequently best suited to meet the many competing and layered needs of disaster survivors. Service providers that administered vouchers did so with great success, at least in part due to the agency's awareness of and ability to provide wrap-around case management that met the layers of challenges faced by individuals.

   Practitioners and providers are uniquely situated to recognize that a single survivor might be experiencing multiple layers of circumstances that have intersected, and be well positioned to provide or connect clients to the kind of wrap-around services that will lend clients agency and ease multiple short-term needs.
7. The federal Violence Against Women Act (VAWA) should be amended to include special provisions for disasters. Such provisions would explicitly instruct federal agencies to make reasonable exceptions in program rules to ensure that federal programs do not stymie women seeking asylum and independence from abusers. States should pass similar laws that are substantially similar to the VAWA and take steps to ensure that state agencies do not stymie women seeking asylum and independence from abusers.
8. Federal, state, and local officials should prioritize humanitarian assistance and personal safety over police enforcement of immigration laws. By devoting significant resources to enforcement during times of crisis, government resources are diverted away from where they are needed most, at great harm to citizens and noncitizens alike.
9. Congress should pass the Disaster Recovery Act of 2011 to amend the Stafford Act and incorporate many of the lessons of Hurricane Katrina into emergency management law.
10. The Communications Decency Act should be amended to provide a clear exception for Fair Housing Act claims. With the advent and increased usage of smartphones to access the Internet, it is highly likely that information about housing options and availability will be increasingly found over the Internet. Lack of a legal means to monitor and enforce Internet violations harms the Fair Housing Act's ability to uphold its own tenets of nondiscrimination and fair housing choice.

Notes

1. In each and every discussion that led to chapter writing—Charles Tubre of The Advocacy Center; Jacinta Gonzalez of the Workers' Center for Racial Justice; Rosana Cruz of VOTE and Women with a Vision; Deanne Bowman of Crescent House Domestic Violence Services, as well as a long list of clients at the Greater New Orleans Fair Housing Action Center—the empowerment and agency of clients served was front, center, and woven throughout the conversation.

2. 42 U.S.C. § 3604(a) (2006).

3. 42 U.S.C. § 3602(b) (2006).

4. U.S. v. Hughes Mem'l Home, 396 F. Supp. 544, 549 (W.D. Va. 1975).

5. *See* Schwarz v. City of Treasure Island, 544 F.3d 1201, 1214 (11th Cir. 2008); Intermountain Fair Hous. Council v. Boise Rescue Mission Ministries, 655 F. Supp. 2d 1150, 1157 (D. Idaho 2009); Lakeside Resort Enters. v. Bd. of Supervisors of Palmyra Twp., 455 F.3d 154, 158 (3d Cir. 2006).

6. *See* U.S. v. Hughes Mem'l Home, 396 F. Supp. 544, 549 (W.D. Va. 1975); Villegas v. Sandy Farms, Inc., 929 F. Supp. 1324, 1328–29 (D. Or. 1996) ("Like the occupants of a homeless shelter, during the [plaintiff] farmworkers' employment by defendant, the cabins are their homes."); Woods v. Foster, 884 F. Supp. 1169 (N.D. Ill. 1995); Lakeside Resort Enters. v. Bd. of Supervisors, 455 F.3d 154, 158–59 (3d Cir. 2006); Conn. Hosp. v. City of New London, 129 F. Supp. 2d 123, 131 (D. Conn. 2001); Schwarz v. City of Treasure Island, 544 F.3d 1201, 1215 (11th Cir. 2008).

7. 24 C.F.R. § 100.201 (2011).

8. Karen Wong, *Narrowing the Definition of "Dwelling" Under the Fair Housing Act*, 56 UCLA L. Rev. 1867, 1870 (2009) (stating "[n]o court has explicitly laid out a test for distinguishing a "temporary . . . dwelling place" from a place of "temporary sojourn or transient visit," but courts have generally looked to two factors in making their decision: occupants' intended length of stay and whether occupants view the building as a place to which they will return (U.S. v. Columbus Country Club, 915 F.2d 877, 881 (3d Cir. 1990)); courts have excluded from this definition certain accommodations, including hotels, hospitals, and prisons (Patel v. Holley House Motels, 483 F.Supp. 374, 381 (S.D. Ala. 1979))).

9. *See* Hooker v. Weathers, 990 F.2d 913 (6th Cir. 1993); Walker v. Todd Vill., LLC, 419 F. Supp. 2d 743, 747 (D. Md. 2006); Implementation of the Fair Housing Amendments Act of 1988, 54 Fed. Reg. 3232, 3238 (Jan. 23, 1989). In *Hooker*, the court found that a trailer in a trailer park was covered under the Fair Housing Act, while in *Walker* the court found that trailer park "pads" are dwellings. However, when trailers are used as emergency housing, they may or may not be afforded the same protections under the Fair Housing Act. As such, if a court found that a trailer were a temporary home and the complainant had no other place of residence and intended to return to the trailer, it would likely be found to be covered under the Fair Housing Act. However, if a court treated it as a transient place of shelter, equivalent to a hotel room, it may not be covered under the Fair Housing Act.

10. Civil Rights Act of 1968 § 808(d)(5), 42 U.S.C. § 3608(d)(5) (2006). *See* Resident Advisory Bd. v. Rizzo, 425 F. Supp. 987 (E.D. Pa. 1976) *modified*, 503 F. Supp. 383 (E.D. Pa. 1980) and *modified*, 564 F.2d 126 (3d Cir. 1977).

11. 42 U.S.C. § 5174(c) (2006).

12. "FEMA's housing efforts in the aftermath of the storm . . . ma[de] it clear to the Nation that this agency had no real plan for how to house tens of thousands, hundreds of thousands of people in the aftermath of a catastrophic disaster. . . . It was evident that the agency did not have a plan in place for a housing catastrophe of this magnitude. Consistent delays, poor coordination, problems with maintenance, and a seeming lack of leadership sent a message to the Nation that it was not working," noted Sen. Mary Landrieu in hearing statements before the Ad Hoc Subcommittee on Disaster Recovery (July 30, 2008), *available at* http://www.gpo.gov/fdsys/pkg/CHRG-110shrg44585/html/CHRG-110shrg44585.htm.

13. Emails dated September 18, 2005, recovered by the U.S. Senate Committee on Homeland Security and Government Affairs, between then FEMA acting director of recovery efforts David Garrett and FEMA Deputy Chief Berl Jones, were skeptical of HUD's potential involvement based on its performance during the Northridge earthquake, which FEMA officials note "was slow because there was not a lot of Section 8 housing available" and that "HUD Housing could not meet the demand." The emails reveal both interagency conflict, lack of an operational plan that should have existed prior to the storm, and FEMA's attempts to address housing needs without fully leveraging HUD's expertise. S. Ad Hoc Subcomm. on Disaster Recovery of the Comm. on Homeland Sec. and Governmental Affairs, 111th Cong., Far From Home: Deficiencies in Federal Disaster Housing Assistance After Hurricanes Katrina and Rita and Recommendations for Improvement 162 (Comm. Print 2009) [hereinafter Far From Home], *available at* http://biotech.law.lsu.edu/blaw/FEMA/DisasterHousingInves.pdf.

14. FEMA-HUD Interagency Agreement, IAA No. HSFEHQ-07-X-0249, *available at* http://portal.hud.gov/hudportal/documents/huddoc?id=DOC_10902.pdf.

15. *Louisiana—Rebuilding New Orleans*, PolicyLink, http://policylink.info/Communities/Louisiana/NewOrleans.html (last visited Jan. 22, 2013).

16. Julia Cass & Peter Whoriskey, *New Orleans to Raze Public Housing*, Wash. Post (Dec. 8, 2006), *available at* http://www.washingtonpost.com/wp-dyn/content/article/2006/12/07/AR2006120701482.html.

17. Far From Home, *supra* note 13, at 137.

18. In December 2005, in testimony before the House Financial Services Subcommittee, when asked by Rep. Maxine Waters what HUD imagined had become of the rest of the 75,000 families, then assistant secretary Orlando Cabrera answered, "it is not an easy thing to locate people after a storm. . . ." *Id.* at 138.

19. HUD Deputy Assistant Secretary for the Office of Public Housing and Voucher Programs Milan Ozdinec noted, in interviews with Senate staff, that "what the DVP appropriators allowed us to do was to use the DVP dollars to pay the rental assistance . . . and allow those housing authorities that were affected by the storm to retain their Section 8 money. And it gave them the flexibility to use that [annual voucher] money to rebuild." *Id.* at 142.

20. PIH Notice 2006-12 (Feb. 3, 2006), U.S. Department of Housing and Urban Development, Disaster Voucher Program (DVP) Operating Requirements—Rental Assistance for HUD-Assisted Families and Special Needs Families Displaced by Hurricanes Katrina and Rita, *available at* http://portal.hud.gov/hudportal/documents/huddoc?id=DOC_9052.pdf.

21. September 30, 2007; December 31, 2007; June 30, 2008; February 28, 2009.

22. National Fair Housing Alliance, No Home for the Holidays: Report on Housing Discrimination Against Hurricane Katrina Survivors 2–3 (2006).

23. Greater New Orleans Fair Housing Action Center, Housing Choice in Crisis: Discrimination Against Housing Choice Voucher Holders 6, 11–13 (2009).

24. *Id.* at 8.

25. *Id.*

26. *Id.* at 10.

27. The Poverty and Race Research Action Council keeps an updated list of national, state, and local statutes prohibiting source of income discrimination in the housing market. Poverty and Race Research Action Council, Keeping the Promise: Preserving and Enhancing Housing Mobility in the Section 8 Housing Choice Voucher Program (2005), *available at* http://www.prrac.org/pdf/KeepingPromise.pdf.

28. "Participated" here means that there is record of disaster voucher use in these PHAs. KDHAP Participating Public Housing Authorities, Dec. 1, 2005.

29. Disaster Assistance Housing Program (DHAP)-Ike, 73 Fed. Reg. 75729 (Dec. 12, 2008), *available at* http://www.gpo.gov/fdsys/pkg/FR-2008-12-12/html/E8-29438.htm

30. 42 U.S.C. 3610 (e)–(f) (2006).

31. 42 U.S.C. 3613 (c)(1) (2006).

32. Havens Realty Corp. v. Coleman, 455 U.S. 363 (1982).

33. *Id.*

34. *Hearing before the Subcomm. on Constitution, Civil Rights, and Civil Liberties of the House Committee on the Judiciary* (July 29, 2010) (testimony of James Perry, Executive Director of the Greater New Orleans Fair Housing Action Center), *available at* http://financialservices.house.gov/media/pdf/022806jp.pdf.

35. *Hearing Before the Subcomm. on Hous. & Cmty. Opportunity*, 111th Cong. (2009) (testimony of James Perry, Executive Director of the Greater New Orleans Fair Housing Action Center), *available at* http://judiciary.house.gov/hearings/pdf/Perry100729.pdf.

36. *See* Civil Rights Act of 1968 §§ 804(d), 812(a), as amended at 42 U.S.C.A. §§ 3604(d), 3612(a); *Havens Realty*, 455 U.S. 363.

37. U.S. v. Hunter, 459 F.2d 205, 209 n.1 (4th Cir. 1972).

38. Ragin v. New York Times Co., 726 F. Supp. 953 (S.D.N.Y. 1989), *aff'd*, 923 F.2d 995 (2d Cir. 1991).

39. 141 Cong. Rec. S1953 (daily ed. Feb. 1, 1995).

40. 141 Cong. Rec. H8471 (daily ed. Aug. 4, 1995) (statement of Rep. Cox).

41. Zeran v. Am. Online, Inc., 129 F.3d 327 (4th Cir. 1997).

42. *Hearing Before the Hous. Subcomm. on Hous. & Equal Opportunity*, 109th Cong. (2006) (testimony of James Perry, Executive Director of the Greater New Orleans Fair Housing Action Center), *available at* http://financialservices.house.gov/media/pdf/022806jp.pdf.

43. Fair Hous. Council of San Fernando Valley v. Roommate.com, 666 F.3d 1216 (9th Cir. 2012); Chi. Lawyers' Comm. for Civil Rights Under the Law v. Craigslist, Inc., 519 F.3d 666 (7th Cir. 2008).

44. Fair Hous. Council of San Fernando Valley v. Roommates.com, LLC, 521 F.3d 1157 (9th Cir. 2008)

45. *Craigslist, Inc.*, 519 F.3d at 668.

46. *Fair Hous. Council*, 666 F.3d 1216; *Craigslist, Inc.*, 519 F.3d 666.

47. *Id.*

48. National Council on Disability, The Needs of People with Disabilities with Psychiatric Disabilities During and After Hurricanes Katrina and Rita: Position Paper and Recommendations 18 (2006), *available at* http://www.ncd.gov/NCD/publications/2006/07142006#5f08f6b9_f971_45e6_8c12_e398c3803e2c.

49. *Id.*

50. Vincanne Adams, Taslim Van Hattum & Diana English, *Chronic Disaster Syndrome: Displacement, Disaster Capitalism, and the Eviction of the Poor from New Orleans*, 36 Am. Ethnologist 615 (2009).

51. *Hearing Before the U.S. H.R. Ways & Means Comm.*, 109th Cong. (2005) (testimony of Marcie Roth, Executive Director, National Spinal Cord Injury Association), *available at* http://waysandmeans.house.gov/media/transcript/10183.html#Roth.

52. Interview with Charles Tubre of the Louisiana Advocacy Center, New Orleans, La. (June 14, 2012).

53. *See, e.g.*, *Nursing Home Owners Charged with Deaths*, N.Y. Times (Sept. 14, 2005), http://www.nytimes.com/2005/09/14/world/americas/14ihtweb.0914katcharges.html?_r=0; Megan Tady, *Disabled People Left Behind in Emergencies*, New Standard (Aug. 20, 2006), http://www.alternet.org/story/40443/disabled_people_left_behind_in_emergencies.

54. Interview with Charles Tubre, *supra* note 52.

55. Brou v. Fed. Emergency Mgmt. Agency, No. 06-0838 (E.D. La. 2006), *available at* http://www.fema.gov/pdf/library/brou_fema.pdf.

56. *Id.*

57. Interview with Charles Tubre, *supra* note 52.

58. Susan Saulny, *5,000 Public Housing Units in New Orleans Are to Be Razed*, N.Y. Times (June 15, 2006), *available at* http://www.nytimes.com/2006/06/15/us/15housing.html?_r=1&.

59. Margery Austin Turner et al., Affordable Rental Housing in Healthy Communities Rebuilding After Hurricanes Katrina and Rita (2007), *available at* http://www.urban.org/url.cfm?ID=411514&renderforprint=1.

60. Interview with Charles Tubre, *supra* note 52.

61. Greater New Orleans Fair Housing Action Center, Access Denied: Housing Accessibility for People with Physical Disabilities in the Greater New Orleans Rental Housing Market 7 (2009), *available at* http://www.gnofairhousing.org/2009/09/16/accessdenied/.

62. *Id.*

63. Fed. Emergency Mgmt. Agency, Planning for the Whole Community (2011), *available at* http://www.fema.gov/pdf/about/odic/all_hands_0411.pdf.

64. *National Advisory Council*, Fed. Emergency Mgmt. Agency, http://www.fema.gov/about/nac/#0 (last visited Jan. 22, 2013).

65. Pamela Fisher, *Louisiana Coalition on Disaster Preparedness Receives National Recognition*, Advocacy Ctr. (Oct. 2, 2011), http://www.advocacyla.org/index.php/news-reader/items/louisiana-coalition-on-disaster-preparedness-receives-national-recognition.html.

66. Patient Protection and Affordable Care Act of 2011, Pub. L. No. 111-148, pt. A, 124 Stat. 146 (2010), *amended by* Health Care and Education Reconciliation Act of 2010, Pub. L. No. 111-152, 124 Stat. 1029 (2010) (codified as amended primarily in scattered sections of 42 U.S.C.A.).

67. Interview with Deanne Bowman, Program Director, Crescent House, New Orleans, La. (June 23, 2012).

68. *Id.*

69. *Id.*

70. Memorandum from Sara Pratt, Deputy Assistant Sec'y for Enforcement and Programs to FHEO Office and Reg'l Dirs. (Feb. 9, 2011).

71. *Survey of Recent Statistics*, Am. Bar Ass'n (last visited Apr. 14, 2013), http://www.americanbar.org/groups/domestic_violence/resources/statistics.html.

72. Louisiana Coalition Against Domestic Violence, The Killing Must Stop: Death at the Hands of the Person You Love 24 (2010), *available at* www.lcadv.org/docs/dvfr_report.pdf.

73. *Id.*

74. Memorandum from Pratt, *supra* note 70.
75. *Id.* at 5.
76. Interview with Bowman, *supra* note 67.
77. Disaster Recovery Act, S. 1630, 112th Cong. § 206 (2011).
78. DHAP-Ike rules stated: "During the time that families are assisted under DHAP-Ike, each FEMA designated family Head of Household is required to participate in case management services. The objectives of these services are greater self-sufficiency and permanent housing for participating families." U.S. Department of Housing and Urban Development, Disaster Housing Assistance Program-Ike (DHAP-IKE) Case Management Guidelines, Notice PIH 2008-45 (HA), Dec. 10, 2008, *available at* http://www.hud.gov/offices/adm/hudclips/notices/pih/files/08-45PIHN.doc. Again, case management services "for him" may exclude essential services for survivors, although the program was designed three years after Katrina.
79. FAR FROM HOME, *supra* note 13.
80. Interview with Bowman, *supra* note 67.
81. *Id.*
82. *Id.*
83. "Woman" is used here to define individuals who identify themselves as women. Individuals who may not be identified as such by relevant authorities or other populations are included in this definition. They are also actively included in the population—and multiple layers of barriers—described in this section.
84. LA. REV. STAT. ANN. § 14:89 (2012).
85. This percentage goes up with inclusion of individuals that self-identify as women, but are not counted as such by state or parish authorities.
86. *Louisiana's Crime Against Nature Law: A Modern-Day Scarlet Letter*, CTR. FOR CONSTITUTIONAL RIGHTS (2011), http://ccrjustice.org/files/CCR-Factsheet-Crimes-Against-Nature-by-Solicitation.pdf.
87. Louisiana Department of Children & Family Services, DSS ESF-6 Protocols for Evacuating and Sheltering Registered Sex Offenders (Unique Population) (June 25, 2009), *available at* http://www.dss.state.la.us/assets/docs/searchable/OS/EmergencyPrep/PlanAppendices/O_SexOffenderShelther_UniquePopProtocols.pdf.
88. Diego Cevallos, *Thousand of Latin American Immigrants Among Katrina's Victims*, INT'L PRESS SERV. (Sept. 5, 2005), *available at* http://h-net.msu.edu/cgi-bin/logbrowse.pl?trx=vx&list=H-Afro-Am&month=0509&week=b&msg=ihDnhBHjoYaUMya8v81Eyw&user=&pw=.
89. *Questions and Answers for Undocumented Immigrants Regarding FEMA Assistance*, FED. EMERGENCY MGMT. AGENCY, http://www.fema.gov/news-release/2004/06/17/questions-and-answers-undocumented-immigrants-regarding-fema-assistance.
90. Chad Terhune & Evan Perez, *Roundup of Immigrants in Shelter Reveals Rising Tensions*, WALL ST. J., Oct. 3, 2005, at B1.
91. *Id.*
92. Ann M. Simmons, *Latinos in New Orleans Suburb Feel Slighted*, L.A. TIMES (Sept. 20, 2005), http://articles.latimes.com/2005/sep/20.
93. BRENDA MUNIZ, IN THE EYE OF THE STORM: HOW THE GOVERNMENT AND PRIVATE RESPONSE TO HURRICANE KATRINA FAILED LATINOS 4 (2006).
94. *Id.*
95. This is in contrast to, say, the attacks of 9/11. *See* Press Release, Fed. Emergency Mgmt. Agency, All Who Need Help Should Seek Help Regardless of Immigration Status (Oct. 31, 2001), *available at* http://www.fema.gov/news-release/2001/10/13/all-who-need-help-should-seek-help-regardless-immigration-status.
96. Interview with Jacinta Gonzalez, Program Director, Workers' Center for Racial Justice (July 5, 2012).
97. *2011 American Community Survey and Census Data on the Foreign Born by State*, MIGRATION POLICY INST. (last visited Apr. 14, 2013), http://www.migrationinformation.org/DataHub/acscensus.cfm#.
98. Most Hondurans came to New Orleans in the 1960s, under President John F. Kennedy's Alliance for Progress initiative. Amy Serrano, *From Punta to Chumba: Garifuna Music and Dance in New Orleans*, LA.'S LIVING TRADITIONS (2009), http://www.louisianafolklife.org/LT/Articles_Essays/garifuna.html.
99. Katharine Donato & Shirin Hakimzadeh, *The Changing Face of the Gulf Coast: Immigration to Louisiana, Mississippi and Alabama*, MIGRATION INFO. SOURCE, Jan. 1, 2006.
100. Garifuna are Caribbean descendants of West African and indigenous Arawak people that settled along the eastern coast of Central America, and made up a significant population of the New Orleans pre–Hurricane Katrina Latino community, albeit deconcentrated throughout the city. Most New Orleans

Garifuna are from Honduras or New Orleans. Since the census requires participants to either self-identify as "Hispanic" or "Black," an exact count of the New Orleans Garifuna population remains elusive. Jesse Hardman, *Garifuna Ethnic Group Seeks Voice in New York City*, NAT'L PUBLIC RADIO (Nov. 15, 2009), http://www.npr.org/templates/story/story.php?storyId=120381718. However, New York, Miami, and New Orleans are probably the largest Garifuna colonies outside of Central America. Serrano, *supra* note 98.

101. Cynthia Garza, *Twice Removed: New Orleans Garifuna in the Wake of Katrina*, *in* DISPLACED: LIFE IN THE KATRINA DIASPORA (Lynn Weber and Lori Peeks eds. 2012).

102. Garinagu communities as far as New York City held fundraisers for New Orleans survivors. GARINET, http://www.garinet.com/ (last visited Jan. 22, 2013).

103. Marla Pierson Lester, *Houston Church Assists Garifuna Storm Victims*, MENNONITE WORLD REV. (Feb. 13, 2006), http://www.mennoworld.org/2006/2/13/jouston-church-assists-garifuna-storm-victims/.

104. Garza, *supra* note 101, at 199.

105. M.A. TURNER, S.L. ROSS, G.C. GALSTER & J. YINGER, U.S. DEP'T OF HOUS. AND URBAN DEV., DISCRIMINATION IN METROPOLITAN HOUSING MARKETS: PHASE 1 (2002).

106. DeAnne Hilfinger Messias & Elaine Lacy, *Katrina Related Health Concerns of Latino Survivors and Evacuees*, 18 J. HEALTHCARE FOR THE POOR AND UNDERSERVED 443 (2007).

107. *Id.* at 459.

108. Interview with Gonzalez, *supra* note 96.

CHAPTER 15

Disasters' Long-Term Impact on Fair Housing: Rebuilding as an Engine to Perpetuate or Challenge Entrenched Segregation

Morgan Williams and Nisha Arekapudi

I. Introduction

Despite federal obligations to promote racial integration in government-funded housing programs, it has proven difficult to reverse ingrained patterns of segregation in American communities. Many cities continue to have high levels of income inequality, and "stark disparities in economic and social opportunities [are] demarcated along racial lines."[1] Unfortunately, this problem may only be exacerbated in the post-disaster context, where significant federal funds are dedicated to rebuilding.

Though housing programs often promise greater housing choice and equal opportunity, post-disaster redevelopment may be implemented in a way that significantly fortifies the patterns of racial segregation that characterized affected regions pre-disaster. Tracking federal disaster funds and recent rebuilding efforts on the Gulf Coast—following Hurricanes Katrina and Rita in 2005 and Dolly, Gustav, and Ike in 2008—depicts how government-subsidized housing programs in post-disaster regions can comport with and compound historic patterns of segregation and inequity.

This examination can also help inform communities to better plan for post-disaster redevelopment in a manner that promotes more integrated housing patterns. The obligation to affirmatively further fair housing under 42 U.S.C. § 3608 of the federal Fair Housing Act provides a framework to ensure that redevelopment funds create greater integration. Additionally, there are a number of policies that communities can rely on to ensure redevelopment furthers fair housing choice, and there are lessons learned and resources about these policies that may be helpful for those rebuilding communities post-disaster.

In order to ensure the full promise of federal disaster dollars, housing assistance must be provided in a way that functions to replace segregated communities with "truly integrated and balanced living patterns."[2] Recent federal enforcement of the section 3608 mandate to further the goals of the Fair Housing Act with the use of federal housing funds holds renewed promise, especially in the post-disaster context. However, ensuring that post-disaster housing funds are used to further fair housing requires that community stakeholders and policy makers at the local, state, and federal levels are informed and engaged in the local, state, and federal processes associated with the expenditure and obligations of federal disaster housing funds.

This chapter uses recent Gulf Coast redevelopment efforts as a lens to examine the effects of post-disaster federal housing programs on housing choice and patterns of segregation. In the wake of the 2005 and 2008 hurricanes on the Gulf Coast, several prominent programs dedicated to rebuilding the region were created and implemented. This chapter focuses on several of the most significant of these programs, including the Road Home program, the Gulf Opportunity Zone tax credit program, the redevelopment of public housing sites throughout the Gulf Coast, and the Disaster Housing Assistance Program. Each program, in its design and execution, provides insight on fair housing issues in post-disaster housing and community development. Section II examines these programs, highlighting how post-disaster redevelopment may solidify entrenched patterns of segregation along racial and economic lines. After a review of these measures, Section III aims to provide government officials and community advocates with the tools needed to address these entrenched segregation patterns and to affirmatively further fair housing in the post-disaster context. Post-disaster housing funds, and the policies that influence their expenditure, have tremendous impact on whether rebuilding efforts occur in an inclusive fashion, or whether they reconstitute patterns of segregation. The identified inclusionary policies and practices, when implemented in disaster-affected regions, can help ensure that much-needed housing assistance programs are put into practice in an inclusive and equitable fashion.

II. Recent Post-Disaster Redevelopment Programs on the Gulf Coast and the Perpetuation of Entrenched Patterns of Segregation

A. Road Home Program

In response to presidentially declared disasters, the U.S. Department of Housing and Urban Development (HUD) may provide flexible grants to help counties, cities, and states recover from emergencies.[3] These measures, which fall under the Community Development Block Grant Disaster Recovery (CDBG-DR) program, are typically noncompetitive, nonrecurring grants that "consider disaster recovery needs unmet by other federal disaster assistance programs."[4] In the aftermath of Hurricanes Katrina and Rita in 2005, Congress allocated $19.85 billion for necessary expenses related to disaster relief, long-term recovery, and rebuilding expenses in the most affected areas.[5] This plan included the federally funded Road Home program, a redevelopment program that provided housing grants to homeowners in Louisiana whose homes suffered damage during Hurricanes Katrina and Rita.

The Road Home program, created with an $11 billion budget, is estimated to be the single largest housing-recovery program in American history.[6] An estimated 330,000 homeowners "suffered from minor to complete damage of their homes across the storm affected areas of Louisiana," and it was projected that approximately 150,000 homeowners would receive grants for rebuilding or repairs.[7] The Road Home program was implemented to help get residents back into a home, whether it was a pre-hurricane home or relocated property. The stated purpose of the Road Home program was to "restore communities by helping families rebuild and return to their homes."[8]

The Road Home program and disaster-recovery programs generally are subject to both the Fair Housing Act of 1968 and the Housing and Community Development Act of 1974, which both require that housing programs not use federal redevelopment funds to perpetuate existing inequalities. The program requirements and national objectives that apply to annual Community Development Block Grants (CDBG) also apply to CDBG-DR funds, unless modified by the appropriating statute or HUD; this includes the fair housing mandate to use federal housing funds in a manner that promotes residential integration. In implementing a disaster-recovery program post–Hurricanes Katrina and Rita, the state of Louisiana was required to submit a detailed action plan associated with the use of its disaster funds to HUD.[9] In addition to detailing the intended uses of all grant funds, the action plan required a certification assuring that the state will comply with the Fair Housing Act and will affirmatively further fair housing.[10]

Despite the Road Home program's promising objective, many homeowners' efforts to return to their communities were hindered by disparities that were built into the program's very design and operation. Under the Road Home formula developed by the Louisiana Recovery Authority, residents were eligible to receive the lower of two baseline values: the pre-storm market value of the home or the cost of storm damage to the home, with the grant capped at $150,000 regardless of which baseline was used. The formula involving the use of pre-storm value meant that 81 percent of New Orleans homeowners received insufficient funds to rebuild.[11] Unfortunately, racial and economic minorities were disproportionately affected by this formula. By basing the award calculation in part on pre-storm value, the grant calculation method created "a recovery program that link[ed] housing assistance to the depressed values of black families' pre-storm segregated housing."[12]

Due to decades of racial discrimination in the Louisiana housing market, the Gulf Coast was largely segregated in residential housing before Hurricanes Katrina and Rita. New Orleans, for example, was ranked by the U.S. Census Bureau as the 11th-most-segregated city in the United States in 2000.[13] The city suffered from "acute residential segregation prior to Hurricane Katrina's landfall, which contributed to the disproportionate impact of the storm on low-income and minority communities."[14]

The Road Home program reinforced this inequality, and in November 2008, the Greater New Orleans Fair Housing Action Center, the National Fair Housing Alliance, and five African-American homeowners brought litigation against HUD and the State of Louisiana.[15] The suit represented a class of 20,000 African-American homeowners who were struggling to return to their homes because of the value of their Road Home grants. In the complaint for declaratory and injunctive relief, the plaintiffs argued that "the Road Home formula has a discriminatory disparate impact on African American homeowners because home values in predominantly African-American communities are generally lower than home values for similar homes in predominantly white communities."

Indeed, due to a legacy of racial discrimination in the housing market, homes of comparable condition, style, and quality had lower values in communities of color than did homes in predominantly white communities. This was the case for plaintiff Gloria Burns, who applied for a Road Home grant after Hurricane Katrina and subsequent flooding caused significant damage to her home. She was approved for a grant of $106,000 based on the pre-storm value of her home; however, because her grant fell short of the cost of damage by $89,000, Burns remained unable to complete the repairs.[16] Had her grant been calculated based on the damage to her home, she would have received $150,000.

Because of the Road Home grant formula, African-Americans like Burns faced larger shortfalls in rebuilding resources. Data from 2008, for example, reveals that homeowners in New Orleans' Lower Ninth Ward, a predominantly black neighborhood, lacked over $75,000 of the cost of rebuilding each home. In contrast, homeowners in Lakeview, a predominantly white neighborhood, faced shortfalls of only $44,000 per home.[17] The implementation of the Road Home program resulted in the steering of hundreds of millions of rebuilding dollars away from African-American communities, increasing the indices of blight in these neighborhoods and perpetuating the historic undervaluing of African-American neighborhoods in the region.[18]

In 2009, following the challenge raised by the fair housing suit, the Louisiana Recovery Authority amended the Road Home program in order to address the gap between home values and rebuilding costs for low-income homeowners by awarding additional funds to low-income households that had previously received a grant based on pre-storm value.[19] HUD approved the state of Louisiana to allocate $600 million to low-income grant recipients because their original grants were based on a home's pre-storm value and in many cases did not cover the costs of rebuilding. When announcing the program change, HUD Secretary Shaun Donovan stated that it was indicative of HUD's willingness to "alter barriers that hamper recovery."[20]

In spite of the state's and HUD's actions to establish the Additional Compensation Grant program to assist low-income homeowners, an estimated 10,000 homeowners remained harmed by the discriminatory Road Home formula.[21] In 2010, when it became clear that available disaster funds were being spent before the court had addressed the allegations that the Road Home program had a disparate impact on African-American homeowners and communities, plaintiffs in the fair housing suit filed for a temporary restraining order.[22] In August 2010, U.S. District Court Judge Henry Kennedy granted the plaintiffs' second motion for preliminary injunction and temporary restraining order, prohibiting the Louisiana Office of Community Development from disbursing future, initial awards under the Road Home program using the pre-storm value of the home as criterion for calculating the amount of such award. Judge Kennedy noted the following:

> The Court does not take lightly that some African-American homeowners received lower awards than they would have if their homes were in predominantly white neighborhoods. And, although the Court appreciates that all of the parties are committed to the rebuilding of a city that has suffered greatly, it is regrettable that this effort to do so appears to have proceeded in a manner that disadvantaged African-American homeowners who wish to repair their homes.[23]

In 2011, the plaintiffs reached a settlement with HUD and the State of Louisiana, under which HUD and Louisiana agreed to amend the Road Home program by creating an additional funding program that offers rebuilding grants totaling over $60 million to several thousand homeowners whose initial grants based on pre-storm value left them unable to repair their homes.[24]

When monitoring of fair housing obligations proved insufficient with regard to the design and operation of the Road Home program, civil rights advocates came forward to enforce the law. The Road Home program policy to calculate grant awards using pre-storm value illustrates how federal disaster dollars can fortify existing inequity and patterns of segregation.

B. Gulf Opportunity Zone Tax Credit Program

Following devastation from hurricanes on the Gulf Coast in 2005, the federal government attempted to "speed the restoration of affordable rental housing by channeling a vast number of tax credits" to the Gulf Coast region.[25] The Gulf Opportunity Zone (GO Zone) tax credit program provided Louisiana, Mississippi, and Alabama with $300 million in low-income tax credits that could be recouped on mixed-income, multifamily housing developments.[26] GO Zone tax credits were modeled off the Low Income Housing Tax Credit (LIHTC) program, as well as the Liberty Zone tax benefits in post-9/11 New York (for further discussion of the Liberty Zone tax benefits created after 9/11, see chapter 7), and served as the primary vehicle for redeveloping rental housing in the region. Qualifying counties and parishes received "$18 per capita in GO Zone housing credit allocations in addition to their regular state per-capita allocations." (For further discussion of the Gulf Opportunity Zone created after Hurricanes Katrina and Rita, see chapter 1.)

Despite this influx of funds to the region, however, available data suggests that GO Zone developments were more likely to be located in high-poverty and largely minority tracts. The 84 percent of the GO Zone tax-credit units scheduled for redevelopment in 2008 were projected to be developed within the city of New Orleans,[27] often in low-income communities of color. Rather than direct units where few or no affordable housing options existed, GO Zone mixed-income developments were constructed in areas of low-opportunity, thereby compounding patterns of entrenched segregation.

The consolidation of affordable housing in low-opportunity areas is a national pattern in the implementation of the LIHTC program,[28] and due to a significant influx of disaster housing investment, it is compounded in the redevelopment context. Despite established law requiring integration, it has proven extremely difficult to reverse patterns of segregation even with tax credit programs. Tulane Law School professor Stacy Seicshnaydre explains this phenomenon as a dynamic within affordable housing in which two impulses, the "anywhere-ist" and the "nowhere-ist," work together to perpetuate patterns of segregation.[29] While the anywhere-ists are primarily focused on acquiring as much government-assisted housing as possible, the nowhere-ists work to keep affordable housing out of their communities. These impulses come together to create a "path of least resistance," resulting in the construction of affordable housing in low-opportunity areas.[30]

Staunch opposition to proposed GO Zone tax credit projects persisted throughout the greater New Orleans area, and often in the context of overt racial discrimination, following Hurricane Katrina. Many jurisdictions erected policy barriers to the creation of GO Zone–funded, multifamily rental housing and launched staunch campaigns against particular proposed mixed-income housing developments.

1. St. Bernard Parish

This was the case in St. Bernard Parish, the local government just downriver from New Orleans and adjacent to the predominantly African-American Lower Ninth Ward. In the fall of 2005, St. Bernard Parish passed an ordinance restricting the redevelopment of multifamily housing in St. Bernard Parish, functionally barring the use of tax credits there.[31] Then, in the fall of 2006, St. Bernard Parish officials passed an ordinance making it illegal to rent single-family homes to people not related by blood to the owner.[32] Census data indicated that 93 precent of the homeowners in St. Bernard Parish were white.[33] As a result, few, if any, minorities were able to rent housing in St. Bernard Parish. Together, these two policies effectively restricted displaced minority and low-income residents from moving back or relocating to St. Bernard Parish. In 2007, the Greater New Orleans Fair Housing Action Center and Wallace Rodrigue, a St. Bernard Parish resident and property owner, sued the St. Bernard Parish Council, forcing them to overturn the multifamily moratorium and blood-relative ordinances.[34]

In 2008, Provident Realty Advisors, an experienced mixed-income, affordable-housing development company, received GO Zone tax credits to build four, 72-unit mixed-income developments in St. Bernard Parish. However, in August 2008, an editorial appeared on the front page of the *St. Bernard Voice* newspaper expressing strong opposition to the developments using camouflaged racial expression.[35] After public meetings where officials and the citizenry vocalized racialized fears about affordable rental housing, St. Bernard Parish officials passed an ordinance banning the construction of multifamily housing.

GNOFHAC and Provident Realty Advisors filed suit against St. Bernard Parish alleging a violation of the federal Fair Housing Act and of the terms of a prior consent decree from the 2005 moratorium and the 2006 blood-relative ordinance.[36] In her ruling that the moratorium on multifamily housing was discriminatory, U.S. District Court Judge Helen G. Berrigan wrote that "the Court concludes that the Parish and Council's intent in enacting and continuing the moratorium is and was racially discriminatory," and that "the evidence also supports a finding of discriminatory effect."[37]

St. Bernard Parish continued to fight issuing building permits for the tax credit developments and was repeatedly held in contempt of court in the summer and fall of 2009 under the fair housing consent decree until St. Bernard Parish was finally forced by court order to grant a building permit to Provident to begin construction of the affordable-housing developments in St. Bernard Parish, or face daily fines.[38]

Then, in the fall of 2009, St. Bernard Parish Council passed an ordinance to hold a public vote on a moratorium on multifamily housing in a November referendum. HUD threatened, in advance of the vote, to cut $91 million of CDBG-DR funding to Louisiana unless the state forced St. Bernard Parish to comply with the Fair Housing Act by rescinding the referendum and not proceeding with the election.[39] St. Bernard Parish had plans to build a new hospital with a significant portion of the community-development funds in question, so it moved quickly to rescind the ordinance and not have the vote.

In December 2010, following the national recession and the corresponding temporary halt in the tax credit market, Provident Realty Advisors was set to proceed with development of the GO Zone affordable-housing developments. Provident asked St. Bernard Parish to reissue the building permits because of the lapse in time since their issuance. St. Bernard Parish administrators replied by letter, noting that they would not be issued building permits because it had rezoned the zoning code to no longer allow multifamily housing in C-2 zoning districts, in which all four of the proposed developments were located. In January 2011, Provident Realty Advisors and the GNOFHAC filed a motion for contempt against St. Bernard Parish,[40] which was the fifth motion for contempt against St. Bernard Parish since 2009. Later that month, HUD Assistant Secretary John Trasvina filed a Secretary Initiated Complaint against St. Bernard Parish because it adopted a zoning ordinance that severely restricted the development of new multifamily housing.

Ultimately, on December 22, 2011, Judge Berrigan ordered St. Bernard Parish to issue occupancy certificates for the four mixed-income housing developments that have been at the center of the multiyear court battle.[41] Per the court order, St. Bernard Parish had to issue the certificates by 10 a.m. on December 23, or face penalty of $50,000 per day for noncompliance. St. Bernard Parish issued certificates of occupancy for the four developments on the very afternoon that the order was issued, and Provident immediately began the work of preparing for tenants to move in.[42]

Efforts to block the development of GO Zone tax credit mix-income projects were not unique to St. Bernard Parish in the greater New Orleans area following Hurricane Katrina. To the contrary, policies limiting or prohibiting the development of multifamily housing were consistently proposed in parishes through the disaster-affected region, with the goal of blocking the development of tax-credit-financed affordable housing.

2. *Jefferson Parish*

In 2006, the Volunteers of America received GO Zone tax credits to build an apartment complex in Jefferson Parish for low-income, elderly New Orleans–area residents, most of whom were African-American. Jefferson Parish is located directly upriver from New Orleans. As reported in congressional testimony by GNOFHAC, "After public meetings where residents and elected officials raised racialized concerns about the development's future residents, the Parish passed a resolution expressly requesting that no GO Zone tax credit developments be constructed on the west bank of Jefferson Parish, the proposed Volunteers of America site location."[43]

The resolution told the Louisiana Recovery Authority that the Jefferson Parish government objected to any applications for tax credit developments. The rationale was that Jefferson Parish did not want to invite poor New Orleans residents to move to Jefferson Parish. The Jefferson Parish councilman who sponsored the resolution remarked during a hearing to discuss the proposed policy: "You would be having folks in Orleans Parish who lived in public housing complexes into Jefferson Parish. . . . That's just not something I'm interested in."[44] The racial overtones of this statement are difficult to overlook in light of the fact that 99 percent of the residents in New Orleans public housing developments before the storm were African-American.[45] Other residents echoed this concern and, specifically, a prominent west bank landowner tellingly stated that lower-income families were "changing the whole complexion of the area."[46]

Ultimately, Volunteers of America built its proposed development in central New Orleans, in a predominately African-American neighborhood. In the face of discriminatory opposition, the development funded by the GO Zone tax credit was built in a geography that perpetuated the entrenched segregation, rather than further fair housing, in the region.

In 2008, the predominantly white city of Kenner, located in Jefferson Parish, passed a moratorium on the construction of any multifamily housing in the city, preventing any GO Zone tax credit development construction in the city. Conversation regarding the ordinance came up after residents raised concerns about a storm-damaged apartment complex that housed mostly Latino families.

As a result of these discriminatory post-disaster housing policies, the GO Zone tax credit housing that was developed in the greater New Orleans area was placed in predominantly African-American areas of the region, thus perpetuating racial segregation in the region. These "Not in my back yard" or "nowhere-ist" attitudes persisted throughout the Gulf Coast region in response to proposed developments, undercutting the hopes of the Louisiana Housing Finance Agency and other housing policy experts who view the tax-credit program as a policy initiative that may create integration through mixed-income, multifamily development.

The GO Zone tax credit program functioned as an engine in the development of much-needed affordable rental housing in the Gulf Coast region. However, the extensive opposition to the development of multifamily housing largely resulted in the site placement of new developments in predominantly low-income, African-American neighborhoods in the hurricane-affected region.[47] In this way, the utilization of GO Zone tax credits exhibits how federal disaster dollars may fortify existing inequity and patterns of segregation.

C. Redevelopment of Public Housing

Public housing provides subsidized assistance for low-income families, elderly, and people with disabilities and is administered by federal, local, and state agencies across the United States.[48] In its most common form, public housing is a housing tenure in which the property is owned and maintained by a government authority. Because "public housing is one of the only options available to very low-income people for secure, stable, and permanently affordable housing," any post-disaster redevelopment of public housing should be administered with the tenants' needs in mind.[49] Public housing authorities administer public housing developments using federal housing funds, and they are responsible for utilizing these funds in conjunction with fair housing planning to ensure meaningful resident participation and enhanced housing choice throughout the region after redevelopment.

Other chapters of this publication detail the Housing Authority of New Orleans' (HANO) post–Hurricane Katrina plans to demolish four of its largest public-housing complexes. (For further discussion of public housing post-disaster, especially following Hurricane Katrina, see chapter 11 and chapter 12.) Asserting that "HUD plans to keep low-income Black families out of New Orleans," Professor Bill Quigley, the Advancement Project, and others argued in a lawsuit that displaced families have a right to return to their homes and be consulted about the future of public housing in their city.[50] Under proposed plans, only 880 families of 5,146 displaced would be able to return to public housing complexes.[51] This displacement of thousands of African-American residents from their homes raises fundamental post-disaster fair housing questions about where and for whom public housing is redeveloped in the post-disaster context.

Following Hurricanes Dolly and Ike in 2008, the post-disaster questions of where public housing redevelopment occurred and whom it serves were raised squarely in Texas, where fair housing advocates pursued a HUD fair housing administrative complaint against the State of Texas, challenging the state's plans for using remaining disaster housing and community development funds. (For further discussion of the recovery efforts following the 2008 Texas hurricanes, see chapter 10.) A brief summary is provided below with a specific focus on the pieces related to public housing and the duty to affirmatively further fair housing.

On March 2, 2009, residents of Galveston public housing, represented by Lone Star Legal Aid, filed an administrative complaint with HUD opposing the demolition of family public-housing units on the basis that the Galveston Housing Authority had failed to comply with federal requirements for demolition of public housing, including prior approval by HUD.[52] On March 13, 2009, complainants and the Galveston Housing Authority entered into a settlement agreement with a replacement plan. Under the settlement agreement, complainant residents agreed to withdraw their opposition to the demolition of public housing based on a replacement plan that provided for the one-for-one replacement of all public housing units damaged or destroyed by Hurricane Ike in the same bedroom configuration as the pre-storm units.

The Galveston Housing Authority demolished all 569 units of public housing damaged by the hurricane but has not, at the time of the writing of this chapter, complied with the settlement agreement or replacement plan. To the contrary, a series of related complaints were filed against the state and Galveston regarding the use of disaster housing funds and the duty of both community development and public housing agencies to affirmatively further fair housing.

Congress appropriated $6.5 billion in supplemental CDBG funds for "necessary expenses related to disaster relief, long-term recovery, and restoration of infrastructure, housing, and economic revitalization in areas affected by hurricanes, floods, and other natural disasters occurring during 2008" through the Consolidated

Security, Disaster Assistance, and Continuing Appropriations Act.[53] HUD allocated $3.1 billion of this federal funding to respond to the needs of Texas residents following Hurricanes Dolly and Ike, and the governor of Texas designated Texas Department of Rural Affairs as the lead agency for administration of post-disaster programs using these funds.[54]

In 2009, HUD issued a general conditional approval of Texas's action plan for use of approximately $1.3 billion of the post-disaster housing funds, and in September 2009, the state submitted a proposal to HUD for use of an additional $1.7 billion. The Austin-based social justice advocacy groups, Texas Appleseed and Texas Low Income Housing Information Service then filed an administrative complaint with HUD, asserting that Texas's plan had not allocated enough money to low- to moderate-income families to repair their hurricane-damaged houses. The first-round funding decisions had been based on programs that required recipients to rebuild on their pre-disaster lot and denied assistance to families seeking to relocate from their pre-disaster residence. Also at issue was that the proposed rental housing rehabilitation program funded the redevelopment of multifamily rental housing in ways that reinforced patterns of segregation that existed prior to the storms.[55] Fair housing advocates called on HUD to reject Texas's amended plan for spending the federal disaster dollars until the state revised its redevelopment agenda and, upon consideration, HUD refused to accept the state's plan.[56]

Later in 2009, the Texas Low Income Housing Information Service filed a HUD fair housing complaint claiming Texas was not taking steps to further fair housing with federal CDBG funds it received after Hurricanes Dolly and Ike struck in 2008. This second complaint asserted that government funds were used to redevelop housing only in neighborhoods with high minority concentrations, as affordable housing was staunchly opposed by predominantly white communities. The complaint asserted that, in Galveston, the housing authority proposed to rebuild 569 units of public housing on sites that are "highly vulnerable to future extreme weather conditions, and in neighborhoods that are hyper-segregated, rather than develop housing in neighborhoods with greater opportunities for residents."[57] The complaint also noted that "racially charged opposition to subsidized and affordable housing, along with policy decisions that have substantially reduced the number of affordable housing units . . . are in fact impediments to fair housing."[58]

When HUD processes fair housing complaints, it is responsible for both investigating the complaint to assess whether there is reasonable cause to believe that discrimination took place and working to negotiate a conciliated resolution between the parties. In this conciliation process, Texas Appleseed and the Texas Low Income Information Service negotiated with the state about the pending claims, while HUD withheld disbursement of the $1.7 billion in CDBG-DR funds.[59]

In May 2010, the parties to the HUD complaint entered into a conciliation agreement in which Texas agreed to revise its amended action plan to require that 55 percent of the Hurricane Ike Round Two funds be spent on housing activities and that 55 percent of the recovery expenditures benefit low- to moderate-income households, and to guarantee the replacement of public housing destroyed by the hurricanes. The conciliation agreement also mandated specific housing programs, including a Homeowner Opportunity Program allowing affected homeowners to move out of disaster-vulnerable areas with concentrations of poverty, and required the state to revise its Analysis of Impediments to Fair Housing.[60]

Despite this conciliation, the Galveston mayor imposed a moratorium on plans to replace flooded public-housing units that were destroyed during Hurricane Ike.[61] HUD rejected these plans and demanded that Galveston rebuild all of the units "as part of mixed-income developments, not old-fashioned projects—or risk losing more than half a billion dollars in storm-recovery funds the city need[ed] to rebuild infrastructure."[62] On September 28, 2012, the Galveston City Council approved a plan to rebuild public housing, on the deadline established by HUD and the State of Texas, and only after the state froze nonhousing funds allocated to the city.[63] Unfortunately, "as the need for low-income rental housing rises, exacerbated by the economic downturn and the foreclosure crisis, the supply of subsidized housing has shrunk."[64]

In Texas, the persistence and ingenuity of community advocates and pressure from HUD forced the state to enter into an agreement to ensure compliance with fair housing obligations in the expenditure of remaining disaster housing and community development funds. HUD's intervention, which would have been rare prior to 2009, is an example of the federal government's greater attention to fair housing mandates in the post-disaster context.

D. Disaster Housing Assistance Program

In 1974, the Housing and Community Development Act created the Section 8 voucher program, which is operated through the Housing Choice Voucher program and authorizes the payment of rental assistance to private landlords on behalf of low-income households.[65] After securing this assistance, voucher holders contribute up to 30 percent of their income to cover rent. The program relies on the private market to meet the housing needs of low-income residents, and is designed to provide low-income residents with more housing choices that ultimately help to deconcentrate poverty and better integrate neighborhoods.[66]

In response to Hurricane Katrina, FEMA launched a voucher program to assist displaced families in need of rental housing. Taking over long-term rental assistance for approximately 45,000 displaced families, HUD then created the Disaster Housing Assistance Program in 2007.[67] Chapter 14 analyzes the FEMA and HUD post-disaster voucher programs on the Gulf Coast, but it is important to briefly assess whether these federal housing funds were employed in a way that challenged entrenched patterns of segregation.

In 2009, the GNOFHAC issued a report titled *Housing Choice in Crisis: An Audit Report on Discrimination Against Housing Choice Voucher Holders in the*

Greater New Orleans Rental Housing Market, which documented the findings of an investigation of landlords throughout the post–Hurricanes Katrina and Rita region. The report concluded from the sample of investigations performed that voucher holders were denied an opportunity to rent a unit a staggering 82 percent of the time, through outright denial or prohibitive additional terms and conditions.[68]

As a result of the discrimination against voucher holders in the post-disaster region, predominantly African-American voucher holders were more significantly able to access rental housing units in more segregated areas of concentrated poverty, thereby thwarting the purpose of the voucher program to deconcentrate poverty and promote racial integration. The report recommends that housing officials implement a study of whether the Housing Choice Voucher and Disaster Housing Assistance Program in New Orleans are meeting their goals of increasing integration and enhancing access to opportunity.

III. Fair Housing Law Mandates That Post-Disaster Redevelopment Programs Employ Federal Housing Funds to Promote Integration

With the passage of the Fair Housing Act in 1968 came the prohibition of discrimination in the sale, rental, or financing of housing. A lesser-known provision of the act, however, carried with it an obligation of the United States "to provide, within constitutional limitations, for fair housing throughout the United States."[69] Specifically, section 3608 of the Fair Housing Act requires HUD to "administer [housing] programs . . . in a manner to affirmatively further the policies" of the act.[70] This responsibility to affirmatively further fair housing extends to all executive departments and agencies that administer programs related to housing and urban development. HUD regulations require grantees of housing funding "to submit a certification that it will affirmatively further fair housing, which means that it will (1) conduct an analysis to identify impediments to fair housing choice within the jurisdiction, (2) take appropriate actions to overcome the effects of any impediments identified through that analysis, and (3) maintain records reflecting the analysis and actions in this regard."[71]

Under HUD dictates, entitlement communities[72] must engage in specific fair housing planning. This involves conducting an Analysis of Impediments (AI) to fair housing choice that should inform how a jurisdiction structures its consolidated plan and action plans, which detail a jurisdiction's plans for the use of its federal housing funds. AIs should analyze public and private practices and policies and should account for all methods of housing discrimination, including situations in which a facially neutral housing practice "actually or predictably has an effect on a group of persons (that is, a disparate impact), or on the community as a whole (perpetuation of segregation)."[73] Although not historically monitored by HUD, the AI/consolidated plan process provides a framework that enables communities, engaged with HUD and other public officials, to take deliberate actions to work toward integration in the use of federal housing funds.[74]

Courts have embraced the idea that the Fair Housing Act is a "comprehensive open housing law" that is both "broad and inclusive," especially regarding its section 3608 mandate to affirmatively further fair housing.[75] In *Otero v. New York City Housing Authority*, for example, the Second Circuit upheld a local housing authority's decision to abandon its selection preference for present and former residents of the area in order to promote racial integration in the community.[76] In that case, the court held that the section 3608 mandate "requires that consideration be given to the impact of proposed public housing programs on the racial concentration in the area in which the proposed housing is to be built."[77] Further, "action must be taken to fulfill, as much as possible, the goal of open integrated residential housing patterns and to prevent the increase of segregation."[78] This meant that simply refraining from discriminatory policies was not enough; housing officials must take affirmative steps to achieve racial integration in the housing markets funded. In *NAACP v. Secretary of Housing and Urban Development*, the court recognized this as a reflection of "the desire to have HUD use its grant programs to assist in ending discrimination and segregation, to the point where the supply of genuinely open housing increases."[79]

The fundamental obligation on HUD and local jurisdictions to ensure that federal housing and community development funds are used to promote integration was recently exemplified in Westchester County, New York. In *U.S. ex rel. Anti-Discrimination Center v. Westchester County*, a housing advocacy organization brought suit in New York when between 1996 and 2007, 75 percent of Westchester County's affordable housing was built in predominantly minority neighborhoods.[80]

From 2000 to 2006, Westchester County received over $52 million in CDBG and other housing funds. Receipt of these funds required that local housing officials repeatedly sign certifications that they are using those funds in a manner that furthers fair housing. The suit was brought under the False Claims Act, which imposes liability on individuals or government contractors for the defrauding of government programs.[81] The plaintiffs alleged that the county's fair housing certifications were false because it failed to consider race-based impediments to fair housing in the jurisdiction. The court denied Westchester's motion to dismiss, noting that "in the face of the clear legislative purpose of the Fair Housing Act . . . an interpretation of 'affirmatively furthering fair housing' that excludes consideration of race would be an absurd result."[82] With this decision, both HUD and its participating municipalities were sent a message, in the court's words, that affirmatively furthering fair housing is "not a mere boilerplate formality, but rather a substantive requirement, rooted in the history and purpose of fair housing laws and regulations."[83]

In 2009, the Department of Justice settled with Westchester County on behalf of HUD, requiring the county to pay damages and to develop and implement a housing policy that combats residential segregation.[84] The county was required to spend $51.6 million within seven years to develop at least 750 affordable housing units, primarily in municipalities with overwhelmingly white populations. Westchester agreed to submit a new AI to HUD, and pay $7.5 million to the Anti-Discrimination Center that brought the suit, along with $2.5 million in attorney fees.

Since *Westchester*, HUD has begun holding jurisdictions across the country to task with regard to their duties to affirmatively further fair housing, and in some instances threatening to withhold or rescind federal housing and community development funds if local and state jurisdictions do not take specific actions to ensure fair housing compliance with the use of the funds in question.

Recently, HUD has been particularly involved in pressuring local jurisdictions to meet their duties to affirmatively further fair housing in the post-disaster context, where significant federal funds are often involved. In Texas, as described above, HUD refused to accept the state's allocation plan, which barred the expenditure of $1.7 billion in federal funds until Texas updated its federally mandated Analysis of Impediments to fair housing choice.[85] Without intervention from HUD, fair housing advocates feared that "CDBG funds [would] not be spent on urgently needed housing recovery for vulnerable people" and that low-income, predominantly minority residents would ultimately be precluded from returning post-disaster.[86] In St. Bernard Parish, as described above, HUD threatened to rescind $91 million of CDBG funding, causing St. Bernard Parish officials to cancel their plans to hold a special election on whether to institute a moratorium on multifamily housing.

The responsibility to further fair housing with federal housing and community development funds is especially important after a disaster occurs, as the tremendous amounts of federal housing and community development funds made available for post-disaster housing represent a unique opportunity to counteract ingrained patterns of segregation and create fair housing choice. For example, in 2005, the federal government provided $11.5 billion in CDBG-DR funds to the areas affected by Hurricanes Katrina, Rita, and Wilma through the Department of Defense Appropriation Act,[87] and in 2008, Congress appropriated $6.5 billion in supplemental CDBG funds for "necessary expenses related to disaster relief, long-term recovery, and restoration of infrastructure, housing, and economic revitalization in areas affected by hurricanes, floods, and other natural disasters occurring during 2008" through the Consolidated Security, Disaster Assistance, and Continuing Appropriations Act.[88] These post-disaster federal funds dwarf the annual allocation of $3.6 billion in general CDBG funds for the entire country in fiscal year 2009.[89] The housing and community development programs that result from this influx of rebuilding funds should be subject to strict accountability.

A review of the post-disaster rebuilding programs discussed above shows that many housing-assistance programs reestablish patterns of racial segregation and inequity rather than affirmatively furthering fair housing. Indeed, the result in New Orleans and other disaster-affected communities on the Gulf Coast is a persistent affordable-housing crisis facing low-income renters, with affordable development sited and vouchers accepted in predominantly African-American neighborhoods, and with a sharp decrease in the number of public housing units.[90] Absent policies to counter neighborhood opposition to affordable housing and processes to conduct proper analysis of the impact of housing programs on housing choice, local and state community development offices may engage in future post-disaster redevelopment in a manner that repeats recent problems on the Gulf Coast.

The remainder of this chapter will briefly review specific tools—in the form of practices, policies, and enforcement techniques—that government entities and community advocates can use to ensure that federal housing and community development funds are used to ensure equity and inclusion in post-disaster redevelopment.

A. Practices Needed to Ensure Post-Disaster Redevelopment Occurs in a Manner That Furthers Fair Housing Choice

The most effective means to ensure that post-disaster federal housing dollars are utilized in a manner that bolsters fair housing choice is for local and state jurisdiction to properly engage in the required fair housing planning processes associated with the expenditure of federal housing and community development funds. Specifically, local jurisdictions must engage in a process to revise their AI to fair housing choice, and then use this analysis to inform their disaster-fund-related action plans.

Impediments to fair housing can include any private- or public-sector actions, omissions, or decisions taken to restrict housing choice or that have the effect of restricting housing choice based upon a protected class, and local jurisdictions must account for these impediments in certifying that it is working to further fair housing with the submission of action plans. This includes the protected classes of race, color, religion, national origin, sex, disability, and familial status. An AI to fair housing choice involves:

1. an extensive review of a state or entitlement jurisdiction's laws, regulations, and administrative policies, procedures, and practices;
2. an assessment of how those laws affect the location, availability, and accessibility of housing;
3. an evaluation of conditions, both public and private, affecting fair housing choice for all protected classes; and
4. an assessment of the availability of affordable, accessible housing in a range of unit sizes.[91]

HUD's guidance reminds grantees that "each jurisdiction . . .should update, where appropriate, its Analysis of Impediments to Fair Housing Choice," and "it is appropriate to update their AIs to reflect the current fair housing situation in their communities."[92] In reviewing certifications, "HUD will consider whether a program participant has made appropriate revisions to update the AI."[93]

Therefore, under existing HUD guidance, local and state jurisdictions are responsible for revising their AIs following a disaster, or any significant shifts in the housing market, and using updated AIs to inform rebuilding expenditures. Failure to do so poses the risk that HUD will revoke or rescind disaster funds, or that community advocates will pursue enforcement avenues to ensure compliance with fair housing planning requirements.

Texas had not updated its AI since 2003, long before Hurricanes Katrina, Rita, Dolly, and Ike changed the landscape for low-income families. Under the 2010 conciliation agreement with fair housing advocates, HUD released $1.7 billion in disaster funds to the state under certain conditions, including a commitment to affirmatively further fair housing,[94] and that the state would develop an updated AI for public comment and HUD approval.[95] Local and state community development offices seeking to expend disaster funds without post-disaster fair housing planning and an updated AI risk challenge to their proposed plans.

In conducting a post-disaster analysis of impediments to fair housing choice, local and state governments should comprehensively review the housing needs of disaster-affected residents and redevelopment housing programs. For example, community development departments should assess where affordable housing developments are sited in the region to ensure that, rather than reinforce patterns of segregation, the siting of affordable housing should aim to integrate communities further and provide communities of color with housing options throughout a region.[96] Similarly, jurisdictions should monitor discriminatory opposition to affordable housing.[97] The case examples detailed in section I of this chapter underscore the importance of thorough and applied fair housing planning in the context of post-disaster redevelopment.

In order to assist local and state housing officials, HUD's Fair Housing Planning Guide should be revised to account for updated planning needs that jurisdictions should endeavor to fulfill in the post-disaster context. The *Fair Housing Planning Guide* instructs communities on how and what they should consider in their fair housing planning. The guide serves to educate readers about fair housing planning and practices to allowing communities to "define the problems, develop the solutions, and be held accountable for meeting the standards they set for themselves."[98] In *Westchester*, the court relied on the HUD *Fair Housing Planning Guide* to define the obligations of entitlement jurisdictions to affirmatively further fair housing.[99]

The Guide acknowledges that "without detailed and prescriptive directives, local communities will even more aggressively ignore the need for fairness and equal opportunity." The manual fails, however, to address the intensive fair housing planning issues that arise in the aftermath of a disaster and accompany significant federal investment in rebuilding.[100] Similarly, the HUD Office of Fair Housing and Equal Opportunity (FHEO) Disaster Toolkit notes that FHEO will ensure that jurisdictions' post-disaster action plans include fair housing goals and will adjust action plans as needed to accomplish fair housing objectives. However, the Disaster Toolkit provides no guidance for jurisdictions on how to update and utilize their Analysis of Impediments in drafting their action plans.[101]

In the immediate aftermath of a disaster, there may be an uncoordinated scramble to meet urgent housing needs, and in situations where communities are displaced and communications systems are disrupted, initial planning may occur out of state and with insufficient stakeholder participation. The urgency and complicated logistics that characterize post-disaster relief efforts pose challenges for thorough and reasoned fair housing planning processes that inform the expenditure of federal housing funds, and they underscore the need for additional HUD guidance on this issue.

HUD should offer specific guidance to local and state jurisdictions, in the form of a post-disaster section added to the guide or some other supplemental guidance, in order to ensure that local and state jurisdictions are better equipped to deal with housing crises after disasters and the influx of federal disaster funds. This guidance should detail how communities engage in a fair housing planning process in a way that efficiently addresses revising and updating their AIs, while not delaying the urgent expenditure of emergency funds, and it should specify particular issues communities should evaluate and monitor in the post-disaster context.

Finally, in revising their AIs, local and state jurisdictions are required to involve members of the public and other stakeholders in developing their AIs, consolidated plans and action plans. Under these public participation mandates, housing advocates can engage in the AI, consolidated plan, and action plan processes to ensure that their public sector community development partners are adhering to fair housing obligations. The fair housing planning process is a forum for fair housing advocates to offer analysis on available data.

In 2011, the GNOFHAC and the National Lawyers' Committee for Civil Rights worked with a task force of local leaders to develop a *People's Analysis of Impediments* that consisted of proposed strategies for the city of New Orleans to affirmatively further fair housing.[102] In identifying impediments to fair housing choice, the *People's Analysis of Impediments* report served to highlight the city's need to account for the challenges faced in the post–Katrina rebuilding efforts for residents and evacuees, especially as they affect current and former residents of the Lower Ninth Ward and New Orleans East. This document served as a tool allowing the public to voice its concerns over post-disaster redevelopment and get involved in the rebuilding process, and it was used as a resource in the City of New Orleans' efforts to revise its AI and draft an updated Consolidated Plan.

Given the role of government officials and community advocates, housing and community development experts in both the public and private sectors can play an important role in ensuring that local and state jurisdictions engage in fair housing planning, in order to expend federal funds in a manner that furthers fair housing choice.

B. Policies Needed to Counteract Identified Barriers to Fair Housing Choice

In addition to identifying impediments to fair housing choice, local and state jurisdictions have a responsibility under HUD regulation to take specific actions to counteract the effects of any identified barriers. This is especially critical in the post-disaster context, when the significant influx of federal funds may be affected by identified barriers. There are many inclusionary policies that communities across the country have adopted to counteract barriers to fair housing choice. These include rent control, counseling services, regional coordination, housing trust funds, higher density zoning, housing mobility programs, reasonable accommodation request procedures, and more.[103] This section will focus on the following four inclusionary policies because they specifically address the types of barriers to fair housing choice identified in Section II.

Inclusionary Zoning. Post-disaster communities may want to consider inclusionary zoning as a possible solution to the problem of concentrating affordable housing in low-income areas. Inclusionary zoning refers to local planning ordinances that require a given share of new construction to be affordable by people with low- to moderate-income.[104] Incentives may include density bonuses, expedited permitting, and reduced fees. Where incentives are insufficient, developers may have alternative means of meeting the inclusionary zoning requirement, such as in-lieu fees or dedication of land for affordable housing. This policy serves to ensure that post-disaster, private-market residential developments include a certain percentage of housing units affordable to low- and moderate-income households.

Fair Share Programs. The Fair Share Program apportions affordable housing funds geographically by need to ensure that jurisdictions without affordable housing gain access to it. Generally applied on a regional or statewide basis, a formula is used to calculate the number of affordable housing units a given municipality will need to create to meet their "fair share" of regional housing needs. Basic variables to assess housing need generally include employment growth, available land, and population growth, and the allocation processes differ by state. This policy functions to ensure that publicly subsidized affordable housing units are distributed throughout post-disaster regions rather than concentrated in low-income neighborhoods.

Source-of-Income Protections. The Housing Choice Voucher program serves as a primary vehicle in post-disaster emergency housing relief; however, as noted above and detailed further in chapter 14, significant discrimination against voucher holders often relegates the use of vouchers in low-income areas, perpetuating patterns of segregation. In light of this barrier to fair housing choice, many local and state jurisdictions have passed laws prohibiting discrimination on the basis of source-of-income discrimination in the sale, rental, or financing of housing.[105] Source-of-income protections ensure that voucher holders and other recipients of federal assistance in housing do not face discrimination from landlords unwilling to rent to them, making it easier for low-income residents, including people with disabilities, to find housing in low-poverty neighborhoods.

Tenant Participation. Indeed, "residents are an under-utilized resource for the management and improvement of public housing."[106] Public housing tenants should be consulted in order to ensure that their interests are fully accounted for in decisions about whether, how, when, and where to redevelop public housing. Any displaced tenants should be tracked to ensure that displaced residents have housing during redevelopment and upon their return to the region, and to allow displaced tenants a voice in the process of rebuilding.

With the influx of federal funds that shape post-disaster redevelopment, it is important that local and state governments, and specifically their community development agencies, institute policies that function to overcome any barriers to fair housing choice they may identify through their fair housing planning. Implementing these and other inclusionary policies may require specific skills that may exceed the capacity of the agencies responsible for implementation, such that government entities and community advocates should ensure that responsible administrators have the appropriate training and skill development needed to carry out any associated programs. Fair housing training in particular can be provided by HUD or local fair housing offices.

C. Enforcement Techniques Available to Challenge Post-Disaster Redevelopment Plans That Do Not Further Fair Housing Choice

Local and state governments are responsible both for employing federal housing and community development funds in a way that furthers fair housing choice and for implementing policies that counteract identified barriers. When these jurisdictions fall short of their duties, it is HUD's and housing advocates' role to challenge these jurisdictions to ensure compliance with the expressed duties associated with affirmatively furthering fair housing. Enforcement mechanisms available to housing advocates in challenging local and state jurisdictions to meet their fair housing responsibilities include HUD fair housing complaints, compliance review requests, and section 3608 enforcement.

While fair housing planning and inclusive policy implementation serve as a proactive avenue for a community to meet its duties to affirmatively further fair housing, the enforcement options outlined below detail a reactive path to address fair housing violations after they have occurred. If jurisdictions fail in their duties under the Fair Housing Act, housing advocates can take several actions to exercise leverage in negotiations with their public-sector partners over decisions about the use of the federal housing and community development funds in question.

HUD Fair Housing Complaint. Any aggrieved person may file a complaint with HUD within one year after the alleged discrimination occurs or ceases, and then HUD must conduct an investigation to determine whether there is reasonable cause to believe that discrimination has taken place.[107] These complaints alert HUD that discriminatory housing actions are taking place in the specified jurisdiction, and, in the case of federal funds being expended in a manner that discriminates or simply does not further fair housing choice, a complaint may serve as a vehicle to trigger some HUD action in policing the behavior of one of its grantees. In addition to investigating complaints, HUD is responsible for working to facilitate a negotiated resolution, and this conciliation process may provide a forum to negotiate with local or state housing officials regarding the proposed or ongoing use of federal funds. Advocates in Texas used the HUD complaint process, as described above, to halt expenditure of $1.7 billion in disaster funding and to negotiate an agreement regarding how these funds should be spent.

HUD Compliance Review Request. Any person may file a compliance review request to initiate a HUD review of grantee activities to determine whether the grantee is complying with fair housing duties. All agencies that receive financial assistance from HUD, including local and state governments and public housing authorities that administer federal housing and community development funds, are subject to these reviews and must allow HUD officials access to their facilities, books, records, accounts, and other sources of information.[108] If after conducting a review HUD finds the presence of discriminatory practices or a failure to affirmatively further fair housing, local jurisdictions can be subject to termination, suspension, or the refusal to grant or continue financial assistance. This is similar to a fair housing complaint, except rather than engaging in the process as a complainant and party to any negotiated resolution, HUD institutes the review independent of the party that forwards the request.

Section 3608 Enforcement. Community advocates may wish to take legal action to enforce section 3608 of the federal Fair Housing Act, which requires HUD grant recipients to act affirmatively to further fair housing choice. There is no private right of action under section 3608[109]; however, housing advocates have employed other methods to litigate enforcement of this section and its associated HUD regulations. One avenue for legal action may be the False Claims Act, as used in the *Westchester* case. This act establishes liability when any person or entity defrauds the government in the course of receiving or avoids payment. Because local and state governments must certify that they are furthering fair housing with the receipt of federal housing and community development funds, jurisdictions that are not using those funds to promote integrated living patterns may be defrauding the federal government with their certifications.

The False Claims Act requires a complaint must be filed under seal with the Department of Justice, with a comprehensive memorandum detailing the factual underpinnings of the complaint, allowing the government the opportunity to decide whether to intervene and take over the case as lead plaintiff. If the government does intervene in the suit, the private party may proceed with the action. Jurisdictions may be liable for "deliberate ignorance" and "reckless disregard" of the truth,[110] and may be subject to treble damages under the False Claims Act.

Fair housing advocates have also challenged failures to further fair housing under section 3608 and other civil rights violations using the Administrative Procedures Act, which allows federal courts to directly review the decisions of federal agencies. Under the Administrative Procedures Act, courts can only set aside HUD actions that are determined to be an arbitrary or capricious violation of section 3608, and these suits can result only in injunctive relief. In 2008, the Administrative

Procedures Act was used to assert a violation of 42 U.S.C. § 5301, requiring that 50 percent of CDBG-DR funds benefit low- and moderate-income people, in a case involving the Port of Gulfport Expansion Project after HUD approved Mississippi's plan to divert $570 million in CDBG funds from "programs addressing the housing needs of low- and moderate-income survivors of Hurricane Katrina to the financing of a major expansion of the commercial Port of Gulfport."[111] The suit resulted in a settlement to reallocate over $132 million in CDBG-DR funds and other funds to programs designed to address the unmet housing needs of low-income homeowners and renters.

These and other enforcement tools present housing advocates with options to challenge local and state governments regarding the use of federal housing and community development funds, to ensure they are expended in a manner that promotes greater housing choice and integrated living patterns, especially in the post-disaster context. To local and state housing officials across the country, the examples and prospect of enforcement action—the *Westchester* litigation, HUD's post-disaster threats to withhold or rescind federal funds in Texas and St. Bernard Parish, and the risk that local fair housing offices may pursue any of the described enforcement tools—serve to send a strong message that a failure to affirmatively further fair housing has real consequences.

IV. Conclusion

In spite of the influx of federal disaster housing funds on the Gulf Coast and obligations to promote fair housing choice, many resulting rebuilding programs developed housing and allocated federal funds in a manner that corresponded with entrenched patterns of segregation. In order to prevent this from happening again, local and state governments should use the framework of affirmatively furthering fair housing to take proactive steps toward reversing segregated housing patterns in post-disaster rebuilding efforts. Disaster funds can serve to challenge entrenched patterns of segregation, as long as HUD and local jurisdictions commit to fair housing planning practices and implementing inclusionary policies. Of course, this cannot be done without the aid of community advocates, who can provide the much-needed pressure to ensure adherence to these mandates. These practices and policies help ensure not only that housing assistance is provided to low-income and other affected residents but that disaster funds are expended in a way that helps create more integrated and equitable housing patterns.

Notes

1. Judith Browne Dianis & Anita Sinha, *Exiling the Poor: The Clash of Redevelopment and Fair Housing in Post-Katrina New Orleans*, 51 How. L.J. 481, 481 (2008).
2. 114 Cong. Rec. 3422 (1968) (statement of Sen. Mondale).
3. *CDBG Disaster Recovery Assistance*, U.S. Dep't of Hous. & Urban Dev., *available at* http://portal.hud.gov/hudportal/HUD?src=/program_offices/comm_planning/communitydevelopment/programs/drsi (last visited Oct. 29, 2012).

4. *Id.*

5. Eugene Boyd, Cong. Research Serv., Community Development Block Grant Funds in Disaster Relief and Recovery, RL3330 (Sept. 21, 2011), *available at* http://congressionalresearch.com/RL33330/document.php?study=Community+Development+Block+Grant+Funds+in+Disaster+Relief+and+Recovery (last visited Oct. 31, 2012).

6. *Implementation of the Road Home Program Four Years After Hurricane Katrina: Hearing Before the Subcomm. on Hous. and Cmty. Opportunity of the H. Comm. on Fin. Servs.* (2009) (statement of Matthew Colangelo, Serial No. 111-70) [hereinafter Colangelo], *available at* http://financialservices.house.gov/calendar/eventsingle.aspx?EventID=231865 (last visited October 31, 2012).

7. Kalima Rose, Annie Clark & Dominique Duval-Diop, *A Long Way Home: The State of Housing Recovery in Louisiana 2008*, PolicyLink, www.policylink.org/threeyearslater/ (last visited Apr. 17, 2013).

8. Complaint at 2, Greater New Orleans Fair Hous. Action Ctr. v. U.S. Dep't of Hous. & Urban Dev. (D.D.C. 2008).

9. See the State of Louisiana action plan and amendments for Hurricanes Katrina and Rita at http://www.doa.louisiana.gov/cdbg/DR/DR_firstapprovedplan.htm.

10. *See* 71 Fed. Reg. 7671; 71 Fed. Reg. 63,339; 72 Fed. Reg. 70,472.

11. Rose et al., *supra* note 7.

12. Colangelo, *supra* note 6.

13. Opportunity Agenda, Housing: Welcoming Katrina's Victims Back Home, *available at* http://opportunityagenda.org/files/field_file/Katrina%20Housing.pdf (2005).

14. *Id.*

15. Complaint at 1, Greater New Orleans Fair Hous. Action Ctr. v. U.S. Dep't of Hous. & Urban Dev. (D.D.C. 2008).

16. *Id.* at 12.

17. Colangelo, *supra* note 6.

18. *Id.*

19. David Hammer, *Road Home Changes Address Gap*, Times-Picayune, Nov. 3, 2008, http://www.nola.com/hurricane/index.ssf/2009/11/road_home_changes_target_gap_b.html.

20. Katie Reckdahl, *Road Home Program Amended to Assist Owners of Homes of Modest Value*, Times-Picayune, Oct. 16, 2009, http://www.nola.com/hurricane/index.ssf/2009/10/road_home_program_amended_to_a.html.

21. *Protecting the American Dream: Advancing and Improving the Fair Housing Act on the 5-year Anniversary of Hurricane Katrina: Statement to the Subcomm. on Constitution, Civil Rights, and Civil Liberties of the House, Comm. on the Judiciary* (July 29, 2010) (testimony of James Perry).

22. Brief for Plaintiff at 1, Greater New Orleans Fair Hous. Action Ctr. v. U.S. Dep't of Hous. & Urban Dev. (D.D.C. 2008).

23. Greater New Orleans Fair Hous. Action Ctr. v. U.S. Dep't of Hous. & Urban Dev., at 8 (D.D.C. 2008), http://www.naacpldf.org/files/case_issue/Opinion.pdf.

24. Michael A. Fletcher, *HUD to Pay $62 Million to La. Homeowners to Settle Road Home Lawsuit*, Wash. Post, July 6, 2011, http://www.washingtonpost.com/business/economy/hud–to–pay–62–million–to–la–homeowners–to–settle–road–home–lawsuit/2011/07/06/gIQAtsFN1H_story.html.

25. Kate Moran, *GO Zone Tax Credit Program Critiqued*, Times-Picayune, July 13, 2008, http://www.nola.com/business/index.ssf/2008/07/go_zone_tax_credit_program_cri.html.

26. Peter Lawrence, *GO Zone Placed in Service Deadline*, Enter. Cmty. Partners, http://www.enterprisecommunity.com/policy-and-advocacy/issues/tax-incentives/go-zone-in-service-deadline (last updated Apr. 28, 2012).

27. Stacy E. Seischnaydre, *How Government Housing Perpetuates Racial Segregation: Lessons from Post-Katrina New Orleans*, 60 Cath. U. L. Rev. 661, 687 (2011).

28. Kirk McClure, *Are Low-Income Housing Tax Credit Developments Locating Where There Is a Shortage of Affordable Units?*, 20 Housing Pol'y Debate 153, 169 (2010).

29. Seischnaydre, *supra* note 27.

30. *Id.*

31. St. Bernard Bureau, *Judge OKs Accord in Housing Bias Suit*, Times-Picayune, Feb. 29, 2008, http://www.gnofairhousing.org/wp-content/uploads/2012/02/2-29-08-St.-Bernard-Settlement.pdf.

32. *Id.*

33. *Id.*

34. Greater New Orleans Fair Hous. Action Ctr. v. St. Bernard Parish, 648 F. Supp. 2d 805 (E.D. La. 2009).

35. *Id.* at 805.

36. *Id.* at 806.

37. *Id.* at 819. Brentin Mock, *Keeping St. Bernard Parish White*, ROOT, Aug. 25, 2009, http://www.theroot.com/views/keeping-st-bernard-parish-white.

38. Campbell Robertson, *Housing Battle Reveals Post-Katrina Tensions*, N.Y. TIMES, Oct. 4, 2009, http://www.gnofairhousing.org/wp-content/uploads/2012/02/10-4-09_NYTimes_Battle_over_low-income_housing.pdf.

39. Benjamin Alexander-Bloch, *HUD Chief: St. Bernard Resists Fair Housing*, TIMES-PICAYUNE, May 8, 2011, http://www.nola.com/politics/index.ssf/2011/05/hud_chief_st_bernard_resists_f.html.

40. Brief for Plaintiff at 1, Greater New Orleans Fair Housing Action Ctr. et al. v. St. Bernard Parish et al., 648 F. Supp. 2d 805 (E.D. La. 2009).

41. Order and Reasons at 1, Greater New Orleans Fair Housing Action Ctr. v. St. Bernard Parish, 648 F. Supp. 2d 805 (E.D. La. 2009) (No. 06-7185).

42. *St. Bernard Parish Issues Permits, Avoids Massive Fines*, WDSU NEWS (Dec. 23, 2011), http://www.wdsu.com/St-Bernard-Parish-Issues-Permits-Avoids-Massive-Fines/-/9854144/10975310/-/qmbrldz/-/index.html#ixzz2PzmRt16Q.

43. *Protecting the American Dream: Advancing and Improving the Fair Housing Act on the 5-year Anniversary of Hurricane Katrina: Statement to the Subcommittee on Constitution, Civil Rights, and Civil Liberties of the House, Committee on the Judiciary* (July 29, 2010) (testimony of James Perry).

44. Meghan Gordon, *Jefferson Council Opposes Housing Tax Credits*, TIMES-PICAYUNE, Oct. 18, 2006, at A1.

45. New Orleans Housing Authority Resident Characteristics Report 2005-06, *cited in* Complaint, Anderson v. Jackson, 2007 WL 4414479 (E.D. La. 2007) (No. 06-3298), 2006 WL 2263157.

46. Deon Roberts, *Land Shortage Stifles for Large Apartment Development in New Orleans*, NEW ORLEANS CITYBUSINESS, May 15, 2006, *cited in American Dream Part III: Advancing and Improving the Fair Housing Act on the 5-year Anniversary of Hurricane Katrina: Statement to the Subcomm. on the Constitution, Civil Rights and Civil Liberties Cong. of the United States, H.R. Comm. on the Judiciary* (2010) (testimony of Stacy E. Seischnaydre), *available at* http://judiciary.house.gov/hearings/pdf/Seicshnaydre100729.pdf.

47. Rose et al., *supra* note 7.

48. *Public Housing*, U.S. DEP'T OF HOUS. & URBAN DEV., http://portal.hud.gov/hudportal/HUD?src=/program_offices/public_indian_housing/programs/ph (last visited Oct. 29, 2012.

49. ANITA SINHA, ET AL., RIGHT TO THE CITY ALLIANCE, WE CALL THESE PROJECTS HOME: SOLVING THE HOUSING CRISIS FROM THE GROUND UP (2010), *available at* www.wehavenoart.net/public/righttocitycolor4-10-10.pdf.

50. Press Release, Advancement Project, Federal Agencies Sued for Violations of the Fair Housing Act Against New Orleans Public Housing Residents (2006), *available at* http://www.wafb.com/story/5085595/federal-agencies-sued-for-violations-of-the-fair-housing-act-against-new-orleans-public-housing-residents.

51. Kalima Rose & David Zisser, *Preliminary Analysis of New Orleans Public Housing Crises*, POLICYLINK (July 19, 2006), http://www.policylink.org/atf/cf/%7B97C6D565-BB43-406D-A6D5-ECA3BBF35AF0%7D/Subsidized%20Housing%20Losses%20Policylink%208%201%2006.pdf.

52. Robert Stanton, *Galveston Agency Backs Off on Tearing Down Housing*, HOUSTON CHRON., Mar. 3, 2009, http://www.chron.com/news/houston-texas/article/Galveston-agency-backs-off-on-tearing-down-housing-1729790.php.

53. S. REP. NO. 112-157 (2012).

54. *Id.*

55. Fair Housing Complaint, Tex. Appleseed v. Texas (Oct. 28, 2009), *available at* http://www.texasappleseed.net/index.php?option=com_docman&task=doc_download&gid=192&Itemid=.

56. *Id.*

57. Fair Housing Complaint, Tex. Low Income Hous. Info. Service v. Texas (Dec. 1, 2009), *available at* http://www.texasappleseed.net/index.php?option=com_docman&task=doc_download&gid=291&Itemid=.

58. *Id.*

59. Michael Allen, *The Revival of Civil Rights Obligations in HUD Funding Programs*, EMORY LAW SCH. (Sept. 6, 2010, 1:04 AM), *available at* http://sciencestage.com/v/33689/michael-allen-speaking-on-the-westchester-county-case.html.

60. Conciliation Agreement, Texas Low Income Hous. Info. Serv. v. Texas, No. 06-10-0410-8, (HUD May 25, 2010) (private agreement filed with HUD) (on file with author).

61. Michael A. Smith, *Feds: Remove Public Housing Moratorium*, GALVESTON DAILY NEWS, July 25, 2012, http://df3.galvnews.com/story/329998.

62. Robbie Whelan, *A Texas-Size Housing Fight*, WALL ST. J., Aug. 3, 2012, http://online.wsj.com/article/SB10000872396390443545504577563271568716862.html.

63. Harvey Rice, *Galveston OKs Housing Plan at 11th Hour*, HOUSTON CHRON., Sept. 28, 2012, http://www.chron.com/news/houston-texas/article/Galveston-OKs-housing-plan-at-11th-hour-3903449.php.

64. *Id.*

65. GREATER NEW ORLEANS FAIR HOUS. ACTION CTR., HOUSING CHOICE IN CRISIS: AN AUDIT REPORT ON DISCRIMINATION AGAINST HOUSING CHOICE VOUCHER HOLDERS IN THE GREATER NEW ORLEANS RENTAL HOUSING MARKET (2009), *available at* http://www.gnofairhousing.org/wp-content/uploads/2011/09/HousingChoiceInCrisis2009.pdf.

66. *Id.*

67. 42 U.S.C. § 5301 (1988); *see also Disaster Housing Assistance Program (DHAP)*, U.S. DEP'T OF HOUS. & URBAN DEV., http://www.hud.gov/news/dhap.cfm.

68. GREATER NEW ORLEANS FAIR HOUS. ACTION CTR., *supra* note 65.

69. 42 U.S.C. § 3601 (2006).

70. 42 U.S.C. § 3608 (2006).

71. 24 C.F.R. § 570.601(a)(2) (Mar. 20, 1996); 24 C.F.R. § 91.225(a) (April 11, 2011).

72. Entitlement communities can be principal cities of Metropolitan Statistical Areas, cities with populations of at least 50,000, or qualified urban counties with populations of at least 200,000. *See CDBG Entitlement Communities Grants*, U.S. DEP'T OF HOUS. & URBAN DEV., http://portal.hud.gov/hudportal/HUD?src=/program_offices/comm_planning/communitydevelopment/programs/entitlement (last visited Apr. 17, 2013).

73. 76 Fed. Reg. 70,921, 70,924 (Nov. 16, 2011), *available at* http://www.gpo.gov/fdsys/pkg/FR-2011-11-16/html/2011-29515.htm.

74. Robert G. Schwemm, *Overcoming Structural Barriers to Integrated Housing: A Back-to-the-Future Reflection on the Fair Housing Act "Affirmatively Further" Mandate*, 100 KY. L.J. 125 (2011).

75. *Id.*

76. Otero v. NYC Hous. Auth., 484 F.2d 1122, 1124 (2d Cir. 1973).

77. *Id.* at 1134.

78. *Id.*

79. NAACP v. Sec'y of Hous. & Urban Dev., 817 F.2d 149, 155 (1st Cir. 1987).

80. United States *ex rel.* Anti-Discrimination Ctr. v. Westchester Cnty., 668 F. Supp. 2d 548, 550 (S.D.N.Y. 2009).

81. False Claims Act, 31 U.S.C. §§ 3729–3733 (2006).

82. *Id.*

83. *Id.*

84. *See* Stipulation & Order of Settlement & Dismissal, United States *ex rel.* Anti–Discrimination Ctr. v. Westchester Cnty., 668 F. Supp. 2d 548 (S.D.N.Y. 2009) (No. 06-2860).

85. Rhiannon Meyers, *State Plan for Ike Money Draws 2nd Complaint*, GALVESTON DAILY NEWS, Dec. 9, 2012, http://galvestondailynews.com/story.lasso?ewcd=1de84bde0dcc7bf2.

86. *Id.*

87. Press Release, U.S. Dep't of Hous. & Urban Dev., HUD Katrina Accomplishments—One Year Later (June 29, 2012), *available at* http://www.hud.gov/news/katrina05response.cfm/.

88. EUGENE BOYD, CONG. RESEARCH SERV., RL33330, COMMUNITY DEVELOPMENT BLOCK GRANT FUNDS IN DISASTER RELIEF AND RECOVERY, *available at* http://congressionalresearch.com/RL33330/document.php?study=Community+Development+Block+Grant+Funds+in+Disaster+Relief+and+Recovery.

89. U.S. GOV'T ACCOUNTABILITY OFFICE, GAO-10-905, HOUSING AND COMMUNITY GRANTS: HUD NEEDS TO ENHANCE ITS REQUIREMENTS AND OVERSIGHT OF JURISDICTIONS' FAIR HOUSING PLANS 4–5 (2010) [hereinafter GAO REPORT], *available at* http://www.gao.gov/new.

90. Browne Dianis, *supra* note 1.

91. U.S. DEP'T OF HOUS. & URBAN DEV., FHEO, PROMOTING FAIR HOUSING (Jan. 28, 2008).

92. U.S. Department of Housing and Urban Development, *Guidance Memorandum; Analysis of Impediments to Fair Housing Choice Reissuance* (Sept. 2, 2004).

93. *Id.*

94. Michael Allen, Presentation at Emory Law School, Affirmatively Furthering Fair Housing: Using the Westchester Case to Address Racial Segregation and Other Impediments to Fair Housing Choice, Apr. 15, 2010, www.prrac.org/pdf/Emory_Law_AFFH.pdf.

95. Harvey Rice, *HUD Gives Galveston 30-day Ultimatum on Public Housing Plan*, Houston Chron., http://www.chron.com/news/houston-texas/article/HUD-gives-Galveston-30-day-ultimatum-on-public-3732081.php.

96. Sarah Pratt & Michael Allen, Hous. Alliance of Pa., Addressing Community Opposition to Affordable Housing Development: A Fair Housing Toolkit (2004), *available at* http://content.knowledgeplex.org/kp2/cache/documents/68549.pdf.

97. *Homelessness Res. Ctr.*, Substance Abuse & Mental Health Servs. Admin., http://homeless.samhsa.gov/%28S%2851ozyg45vntwdf55qp0msrb2%29%29/Search.aspx?search=NIMBY+%28Not+in+My+Backyard%29&tagString=NIMBY+%28Not+in+My+Backyard%29&AspxAutoDetectCookieSupport=1 (last visited Apr. 17, 2013) (accessed by searching for "NIMBY").

98. U.S. Dep't of Hous. & Urban Dev., Fair Housing Planning Guide (vol. 1 1996) [hereinafter Fair Housing Planning Guide], *available at* http://www.hud.gov/offices/fheo/images/fhpg.pdf.

99. *Promoting Fair Housing*, U.S. Dep't of Hous. & Urban Dev., http://portal.hud.gov/hudportal/HUD?src=/program_offices/fair_housing_equal_opp/promotingfh (last visited Apr. 17, 2013).

100. Fair Housing Planning Guide, *supra* note 98.

101. Office of Fair Hous. & Equal Opportunity, Disaster Toolkit (2007), *available at* http://portal.hud.gov/hudportal/documents/huddoc?id=DOC_7744.pdf.

102. Greater New Orleans Fair Hous. Action Ctr. & Lawyers' Comm. for Civil Rights Under Law, People's Analysis of Impediments (AI) for New Orleans (2011), *available at* http://www.lawyerscommittee.org/admin/community_development/documents/files/12-20-11-Peoples-AI-FINAL.pdf.

103. *Strategies to Affirmatively Further Fair Housing: Proposals for the City of New Orleans Comprehensive Zoning Ordinance (CZO) and Beyond*, Greater New Orleans Fair Housing Action Center and Lawyers' Committee for Civil Rights under Law, Apr. 28, 2011, *available at* http://www.lawyerscommittee.org/admin/community_development/documents/files/4-28-11_Strategies_to_Affirmatively_Further_Fair_Housing.pdf.

104. *Inclusionary Zoning*, PolicyLink, *available at* http://www.policylink.org/site/c.lkIXLbMNJrE/b.5137027/k.FF49/Inclusionary_Zoning.htm (last updated 2003).

105. *Source of Income Discrimination*, Nat'l Hous. Law Project, http://nhlp.org/node/805 (last visited Apr. 17, 2013).

106. Right to the City Alliance, *supra* note 49.

107. A detailed overview of the HUD fair housing complaint process is available at http://portal.hud.gov/hudportal/HUD?src=/program_offices/fair_housing_equal_opp/complaint-process.

108. Compliance and Enforcement Procedures for Title VI of the Civil Rights Act of 1964, *Compliance Review* (May 30, 2007), http://www.hud.gov/offices/adm/hudclips/handbooks/fheh/80401/80401c2FHEH.pdf.

109. MHANY Mgmt., Inc. v. Cnty. of Nassau, 843 F. Supp. 2d 287 (D.N.Y. 2012).

110. *See* 31 U.S.C. § 3729.

111. *Port of Gulfport Expansion*, Lawyers' Comm. for Civil Rights Under Law, http://www.lawyerscommittee.org/projects/fair_housing/page?id=0082 (last visited Apr. 17, 2013).

CHAPTER 16

Innovative Post-Disaster Community-Based Housing Strategies

Diane Glauber and David Zisser*

I. Introduction

From the perspective of lawyers who provide pro bono assistance to nonprofit organizations involved in affordable housing and community development, there is no shortage of challenges in post–Hurricane Katrina New Orleans and Mississippi. Prior to Hurricane Katrina, Louisiana and Mississippi were two of the poorest states in the nation.[1] The devastation of the storm, the failure of the levees, the ruined homes and lives, and the bungled government responses exacerbated the already fragile communities and challenged residents in extraordinary ways.

Many confronted these challenges head-on. Natives and transplants, as well as temporary volunteers, worked tirelessly with nonprofit organizations to rebuild homes and communities. With the support of the philanthropic sector and private individuals, these dedicated advocates continue to develop new initiatives to address ongoing challenges of displacement, poverty, disinvestment, and a dearth of affordable housing. The

*The authors would like to acknowledge law school interns Vaneeta Chintamaneni, Jennifer Henry, and Eva Seidelman; college intern Sidney Beaty; and Law Fellow and Associate Counsel Melissa Gallo, all of whom provided significant contributions to this chapter, including research, writing, and thoughtful insights and ideas.

community-based efforts described in this chapter are just a few examples of the ingenuity of countless individuals. Some are the stories of the authors' clients and partners; others are stories the authors learned about from allies and friends on the ground. The authors hope these stories will serve as replicable models in other communities.

While this chapter takes a brief look at the problems, barriers, and frustrations, it is ultimately about community-based solutions that rely on creativity and tenacity rather than on government funds and programs, to get people into affordable, quality homes, and to rebuild communities ravaged by disaster.

II. Barriers to Rebuilding

For both low-income and minority renters and affordable housing developers, Hurricane Katrina exacerbated housing problems that had already existed. In particular, the difficulty of finding quality private rental housing in low-poverty, racially integrated neighborhoods with or without a voucher, as described elsewhere in this book, illustrates the importance of building and preserving physical units of affordable housing. But NIMBY (not in my backyard) efforts and associated exclusionary zoning decisions and policies passed by local officials often stop the development of affordable housing in its tracks. In addition, unwieldy government-funding programs, failures in the banking sector, contractor fraud, and duplicative planning processes were just some of the formidable barriers facing low-income residents of New Orleans looking for homes.

A. Exclusionary Zoning

Exclusionary zoning policies and ordinances often result from concerns expressed by some community members and exclude certain groups of residents, socioeconomic classes, or racial groups from an area; they may include large lot zoning, placement of restrictions on exclusion of multifamily housing, onerous permitting restrictions, and restrictions on mobile and non-permanent homes.[2] Claims that such restrictions will protect property values often mask discriminatory intentions. The cumulative effect of such exclusionary zoning policies is racial and economic segregation.[3]

Louisiana and Mississippi serve as important examples of ways in which exclusionary zoning has been and continues to be utilized to exclude individuals in a post-disaster context. While exclusionary zoning was used in ways that impeded affordable housing prior to Hurricane Katrina, it has had a significant effect on post-disaster rebuilding.[4]

The Katrina Cottages are a prime example of how the intent to provide disaster relief can be undone by local community efforts to exclude. Following Hurricane Katrina, the Federal Emergency Management Agency (FEMA) housed people in temporary trailers. As that program expired, Congress gave FEMA several hundred million dollars to make prefabricated housing units in Louisiana and Mississippi, part of the Alternative Housing Pilot Program.[5] Mississippi built approximately 3,500 of these units with over $280 million of federal money. Despite designs that met manufactured housing standards and building codes for permanent housing, energy efficiency, and sturdy construction featuring porches and brightly colored exteriors, many cities refused to grant permits to those receiving the units, citing potential decreases in property values.[6] As a result of these fears, many of the cottages in Mississippi that were initially marketed as temporary-to-permanent housing were unused for years and eventually changed to temporary housing. In Louisiana, a multitude of problems, including budget issues and inexperienced developers, and local resistance to temporary housing resulted in delays. Currently, only 461 Katrina Cottages have been completed, at a cost of $130,000 per unit.[7]

Although Mississippi's program was much more cost-efficient than Louisiana's, in order to avoid claims that installing them would reduce property values, the Mississippi Emergency Management Agency distributed cottages as temporary shelters. After 18 months of habitation, the cottages were offered for sale at prices as low as $450.[8] If residents did not buy the cottages, they were forced to vacate and the cottages were removed.[9] Meanwhile, thousands of these cottages sat unused in warehouses,[10] while others sat unused even after they had been installed on lots.[11] For example, in 2007, 74-year-old James Johnson, a longtime Mississippi native whose home was destroyed by Katrina, was living in a 300-square-foot government trailer while approximately 700 new Katrina Cottages remained uninhabited across a fence near his property.[12]

The reasons behind such exclusionary practices are based largely on stereotypes and misinformation. Exclusionary zoning practices are often enacted at the behest of local constituents, based on fear over the types of residents that will move in if such policies are not implemented. These fears stem from racial stereotypes and from associating affordable housing with high poverty and crime, as well as the failure to distinguish between mixed-income housing, single-family cottages, and the old image of large public-housing developments. While these fears are not new to Louisiana and Mississippi, it is more important than ever to dispel the myths and misunderstandings through education and political initiative. Political will, however, has mirrored the will of local constituents, and there has therefore been little motivation to eliminate exclusionary zoning policies and practices.

The result of practices like exclusionary zoning is racial and economic segregation. In New Orleans, for instance, affordable housing is disproportionately located in high-poverty, high-minority areas of the city.[13] Though this pattern existed prior to Hurricane Katrina, current discriminatory practices, in conjunction with the increased need for housing post–Hurricane Katrina, will continue to worsen patterns of segregation.

B. Government Programs

Community opposition was not the only barrier residents faced in their attempts to return to their communities. Government programs that were intended to help often hindered residents' ability to obtain the funds they needed to rebuild and return to their storm-damaged homes. Government programs were poorly run and failed to get money to the people who desperately needed it. In 2006, a Government Accountability Office report found that most of the Hurricane Katrina money had been wasted, "with evidence of double payments, aid given to foreign exchange students, and a major failure to recover money paid out for illegitimate claims."[14]

The Road Home program, a more than $9 billion federally funded initiative[15] with a goal of helping homeowners repair and return to their homes within three years, has been plagued with problems, resulting in severe delays and waste. The program offers grants to help homeowners repair their homes or buyouts for those who sell their homes and move. Problems included fraudulent contractors, property owner debt, and a $150,000 grant cap, too small for some homes to be repaired. Many displaced property owners who wanted to rebuild and return to their homes were unable to do so even years after the hurricane, and eventually were forced to sell their property to the program. Road Home properties sometimes became blighted or a nuisance for their neighbors because the program prevented the Louisiana Land Trust, which was formed to manage the properties that the state purchased under the Road Home program, from utilizing program funds to rehabilitate the properties it purchased. Problems with the Road Home program also included facially neutral policies that disproportionately affected African-American homeowners, and such policies were eventually changed due to civil rights litigation. (For further discussion on the Road Home program and civil rights litigation, see chapter 15.)

As a result of these deficiencies, hundreds of millions of federal dollars designated for housing rehabilitation had remained unspent years into the program. In April 2010, for example, $188 million was still available through the Road Home program.[16] However, fewer than half of program participants had been able to return to their homes seven years after the storm, and data suggest that somewhere between 700 and 1,000 homes out of 1,435 participating remain unoccupied as of 2012.[17]

C. Private-Sector Barriers

Problems in the private sector also contributed to homeowners failing to receive money to rebuild their homes. Thousands of homeowners were unable to finish rebuilding their homes because of forced mortgage payoffs, whereby homeowners voluntarily or involuntarily used their Road Home grants or insurance proceeds to pay off a pre-storm mortgage, leaving insufficient funds to rebuild.[18] Other factors included contractor fraud or the unexpected expenses that arose during the long rebuilding process.[19] Banks administering government programs sometimes did not have strong enough requirements to ensure that recovery money would benefit homeowners. For example, in initiating a multimillion-dollar loan program, the city of New Orleans failed to require the program's banks to create a new loan product that catered to the specific circumstances of the rebuilding program, and instead allowed them to use existing products that disqualified many would-be applicants because they had poor credit, despite the fact that the loans were secured by Road Home money.[20]

D. Planning Problems

Local planning after Hurricane Katrina, which included three citywide plans, provided another layer of confusion and distrust. The first was Mayor Ray Nagin's Bring New Orleans Back (BNOB) Commission, which was heavily criticized for its infamous "green dots" indicating future green space located on residential areas deemed inappropriate for redevelopment because of insufficient population.[21] The second planning initiative was the Lambert Plan developed by consultant Paul Lambert, which was criticized for failing to adequately incorporate public input, using the BNOB boundaries that did not align with informal community boundaries, covering only a portion of the city, not incorporating the neighborhood plans into one comprehensive document, and not including the city planning commission.[22] Finally, the Unified New Orleans Plan (UNOP), which did include all of the city's neighborhoods in one final document, split the city into 14 districts, each with its own plan.[23] In contrast to BNOB, where districts largely ignored informal community boundaries and planning teams were assigned without consulting community members, the assignment of planning teams for UNOP included some community input.[24] The UNOP document was officially approved by the mayor, city council, and city planning commission on August 28, 2006.[25]

Although the post-disaster landscape can be a disheartening picture, the response from community development corporations, neighborhood associations, grassroots coalitions, and innovative individuals offers some hope for rebuilding homes and communities.

III. Community-Based Strategies

The most successful affordable housing programs are community driven, usually led by local nonprofit organizations. Mission-driven nonprofit developers and intermediaries, such as Providence Community Housing, Harmony Neighborhood Development, and Enterprise Community Partners, are utilizing the federal Choice Neighborhoods Initiative program, and groups continue to rely on traditional programs, such as project-based vouchers in Section 8 and low-income housing tax credits. Several organizations, some with the support of the Lawyers' Committee for Civil Rights Under Law (Lawyers' Committee), have developed or adopted new approaches that are not driven by government programs, though some utilize government financing and government-acquired land. These strategies do not provide a panacea, but they do offer potentially replicable models that are community driven and thereby less prone to the problems created by bureaucratic government programs. Four of these innovative solutions are described below: community land trusts, utilizing vacant land, volunteer construction, and title clearing.

A. Community Land Trusts

A community land trust (CLT) is a nonprofit organization that owns land and leases it for a nominal fee to individuals who own the buildings, usually a home, on the land.[26] Because the homeowner does not have to pay for the land, the home is more affordable. The homeowner's resale amount and equity is restricted, and the home must be sold to another income-eligible family, making it a "limited equity" or "shared equity" model. CLTs generally include homeowners and other community members on their boards. They provide their homeowners with financial counseling and other support to ensure that families are able to stay in their homes.

CLTs exist throughout the country and have proven to be a good model for affordable housing. Currently, more than 250 CLTs support more than 10,000 homes,[27] and in 2008, CLT homes had a foreclosure rate of just 0.52 percent, compared with a national average of 3.3 percent.[28] Many CLT homeowners go on to buy traditional homes. The CLT model cropped up in the 1970s, but its roots go back much further, drawing from Native American traditions, *kibbutzim* in Israel, the civil rights movement, and the Bhoodan-Gramdan Movement in India.[29] Its application to post-disaster settings, however, is relatively new.

CLTs are often used as a tool to address the pressures of gentrification—to keep land affordable and in community control as development threatens to displace low- and moderate-income families. It may be difficult, then, for some to reconcile using the CLT model in communities such as the Lower Ninth Ward in New Orleans or North Gulfport in Mississippi, which have large amounts of vacant and inexpensive land and none of the upscale retail stores and amenity-laden apartment complexes that signal gentrification and displacement of residents and small businesses. There is also a perception that CLTs do not amount to "real" homeownership because the land is not owned outright. In places with deep roots to land rights and to passing land from generation to generation, where African-American homeownership has been a point of pride, the notion of owning just the home and not the land may not resonate.

Grassroots efforts have resulted in the creation of CLTs that attempt to address the unique circumstances of these post–Hurricane Katrina communities. In some cases, it is about protecting land from speculation and for uses appropriate and beneficial to the existing community (i.e., holding off the pressures of gentrification). In others, however, it is about ensuring permanent affordability and a chance for some form of homeownership, as well as a holistic approach to creating community.

1. New Orleans: Crescent City CLT

Crescent City CLT officially formed in 2011 after the National Community Land Trust Network and the Ford Foundation conducted a two-year feasibility study. The study found that in addition to preventing future development from fueling displacement as the economy improves and gentrification occurs, a CLT in New Orleans could also prevent displacement and foreclosures in a stagnant economy.[30] Crescent

City CLT acknowledges that the role of a CLT is different in a place like New Orleans, which continues to deal with high vacancy rates, "blight," disinvestment, and diminished property values. Many current housing programs—both homeownership and rental—have affordability periods of just a few years, despite significant subsidies. These subsidies, however, benefit only the first homeowner, who can then sell the property to the highest bidder. But with the additional resources and attention that Hurricane Katrina brought, some believe there is a unique responsibility—and opportunity—to ensure that significant public investments in housing result in long-term or permanent affordability. Crescent City CLT aims to create the opportunity to pass on affordability for generations and to help significantly more families own their homes and build wealth.

A Holistic Approach

The original vision included two entities: a commercial CLT that would develop land itself and a citywide residential "central server" that would support neighborhood-based CLTs with technical assistance. Eventually, the CLT Advisory Committee, which included people working at the local and state foundations and various housing and community development organizations, as well as the prospective boards of the two organizations, agreed that the initiatives were intimately connected and could and should operate from the same organization. In order to attract people to homes, the homes needed to be a part of a more comprehensive approach that included blight remediation and the development of commercial assets. Crescent City CLT takes this holistic approach to rebuilding in New Orleans, envisioning development in three arenas: residential, commercial, and vacant land.[31]

Crescent City CLT's residential program utilizes a "central server" approach modeled in part after the Atlanta Land Trust Collaborative, which supports three neighborhood-based CLTs near the developing Atlanta Beltline project.[32] As a central server, Crescent City CLT provides technical assistance and support to neighborhood-based CLTs engaged in developing affordable housing throughout New Orleans, recognizing that these local leaders best understand the needs of the residents and the challenges and pressures in their communities. The residential program has three main goals: (1) to create permanently affordable housing for low- and moderate-income residents by increasing affordable homeownership, rental units, limited-equity cooperatives and lease-to-purchase arrangements; (2) to retain public and private funds invested in affordable housing in a cost-efficient manner, enabling one-time subsidies to serve generation after generation, not only the initial occupants; and (3) to provide opportunity for CLT-assisted residents to build wealth and ensure long-term family success.[33]

Crescent City CLT's commercial development plans will complement residential development by creating jobs, fresh-food stores, space for small businesses and nonprofits, and other community assets beneficial to low-income residents. The CLT will also bring in revenue for other projects through commercial lease arrangements.

Most importantly, sustainable commercial development will make the city "a place where people actually want to live," according to Executive Director Van Temple.[34]

Crescent City CLT's vacant lot initiative is also centered on sustainable and livable communities. It is initiating a pilot project in New Orleans with the Tulane City Center in which the CLT would own parcels and build fences and trees in order to create "pocket parks." If, after three to seven years, demand for housing has returned, homes could be placed on those lots.

Although Crescent City CLT has yet to develop any housing, it is making strides. For example, it is partnering with other local organizations on an exciting mixed-use project and collaborating closely with Jane Place Neighborhood Sustainability Initiative (Jane Place) in the Mid-City neighborhood, which has experienced significant disinvestment and vacancy.[35] Jane Place views the CLT as a critical tool in addressing the nearby BioDistrict development, which "is focused on the development of a biosciences industry in New Orleans" and will encompass 1,500 acres and attract new market-rate residential development.[36] Prior to Hurricane Katrina, nearly three-quarters of occupied units in the neighborhood were rental households[37] and a third of the residents were living in poverty.[38] Most of the homes in the community were damaged by floodwaters,[39] and Jane Place acquired multiple buildings in the neighborhood in an effort to convert these parcels to affordable rental units and shared equity cooperatives.

2. *Community Land Trust Challenges*

Challenges remain in educating longstanding residents about this shared-equity approach and prioritizing long-term neighborhood preservation and stability over short-term individual gains. Many potential homeowners may be uncomfortable or unfamiliar with this "in between" status—not renters but not homeowners with full equity rights and land ownership. Others worry that because they do not own the land, they do not have a key asset to pass on to their children. The CLT movement, including individual CLTs such as Crescent City CLT, continues to educate community members about the benefits to individuals, subsequent generations, and the community as a whole.

Additionally, it is often difficult to garner support from traditional lenders and government entities, including property assessors, that ascribe to a narrow definition of homeownership and property value that does not include the land and caps the resale amount. Crescent City CLT continues its outreach for CLT properties to receive a fair assessment of their value and that homeowners have the ability to acquire a mortgage, noting that the CLT itself plays a "stewardship" role that helps ensure that a homeowner does not end up in foreclosure.

CLTs have gained steam in the post–Hurricane Katrina Gulf Coast context as a viable revitalization tool that can benefit traditionally marginalized communities over the long term. Local stakeholders have largely driven the CLT initiatives in the region, along with support from foundations, technical assistance providers, and community development corporations, helping to create an environment that encourages alternative models that focus on long-term housing affordability and community control of land, key aspects of community development.

B. Developing Vacant and Blighted Properties

In the wake of a disaster—or disinvestment in general—cities must grapple with an influx of vacant and blighted properties. New Orleans was already facing a significant inventory of vacant properties prior to Hurricane Katrina. The hurricane and its aftermath resulted in an almost twofold increase of vacant housing units, from 26,000 to more than 47,000 in 2010.[40] The city of New Orleans has responded with a number of strategies to address the high vacancy rates. One example is the Lot Next Door Program, which provides residents living adjacent to properties controlled by the New Orleans Redevelopment Authority (NORA) the first opportunity to purchase and redevelop these properties.[41] This program has had modest success.

Another moderately successful program was launched by Project Home Again, a nonprofit created by Barnes & Noble founder and New York philanthropist Leonard Riggio. This program gives a family a new house in exchange for the home or lot they own.[42] The houses come fully constructed, landscaped, and furnished,[43] and with fully forgivable five-year mortgages equal to the difference between the appraised values of the old and new house,[44] held by the program to encourage residents to live in their homes for at least five years.[45] The $20 million donation from Riggio's family foundation is believed to be the largest from any private donor following the storm[46] and resulted in 101 homes.

Like Crescent City CLT, Project Home Again realized the importance of rebuilding communities, not simply rebuilding single homes. A rehabbed house that sits between and across the street from vacant lots may be a home, but a rehabbed house with neighbors is a home *and* part of a community with the potential to grow. Project Home Again clustered the homes primarily in three sections of the Gentilly neighborhood of New Orleans, making a real difference in those areas. In order to accomplish this, Project Home Again built homes on well-located lots they received from participating homeowners; if the lots were not located well, the organization swapped them for other properties owned by NORA for lots that were closer to others that Project Home Again already owned.[47]

The program does not serve everyone, however. Designed to serve a specific income range (e.g., a family of four must earn between $29,712 and $74,280 annually), it has strict eligibility requirements: the resident must have lived in New Orleans during Hurricane Katrina (some program literature states that two years of residency in the Gentilly neighborhood prior to the hurricane is required),[48] must agree to live in the home for five years, and must agree to purchase flood and liability insurance for the duration of residency.[49] Moreover, the property must be ready to swap, and program participants must have paid off their old property's mortgage and have clear title to participate in the program.[50] Renters may also participate but are required to take financial literacy classes, clear up any outstanding debt, and agree not to purchase any other homes until the new mortgage is paid off.[51]

Although the program provides a potentially scalable model, its impact should not be overstated given that the program built only 101 houses, costing approximately $190,000 each despite program efficiencies like reusing architectural designs.[52] Moreover, as the program states, it does not have the capacity to deal with repairing individually owned homes, only to construct new homes.[53]

Even with $20 million in hand, the program struggled from 2005 until 2008, when the project gained two important resources that allowed it to be more successful. The first was land. Because the program needed a large tract of land to accomplish the clustering effect, Riggio struggled to get the nonprofit off the ground until 2008, when it purchased a large plot of land for the project's first 20 homes (through a generous donation of land from the Winingder family).[54] The second important resource was program staff. In 2008, Carey Shea (formerly a Rockefeller Foundation program officer) came on board as executive director.[55] She made the program more efficient and lean, cutting program consultants and bringing the staff down to just three employees.[56]

The city of New Orleans has long engaged in similar land swapping arrangements. In 1974, for example, under Mayor Moon Landrieu, the city traded 3.7 acres of city land for 1.5 more-valuable acres of developer land, which allowed the developer to proceed with the Canal Place high-rise development project on the edge of the French Quarter.[57] The West End neutral ground became New Basin Canal Park thanks to a successfully negotiated land swap.[58] In the years immediately following the storm, the Office of Recovery Management under Edward Blakely (an aide to then–Mayor Nagin) announced a $1.1 billion recovery plan including a land swap element.[59] Janet Howard, leader of the nonprofit group Bureau of Governmental Research, often criticized Nagin's BNOB Commission but supported land swaps as a way to shrink the city's footprint without destroying neighborhood integrity.[60]

Despite Project Home Again's modest successes and limitations, it has demonstrated the benefits of clustering homes in areas with high vacancy rates. Moreover, with so many vacant lots available, the program illustrated the need and capacity for flexibility, working with NORA to swap scattered lots for lots in clustered areas. It is important to continue to engage in thoughtful planning and development that prioritizes location of affordable homes at least as much as sheer production to ensure that residents have access to the safety and other benefits of community, including proximity to transit, good jobs, schools, open space, and healthy food. Building homes is not enough without also building community.

C. Volunteer Construction Model

Since Hurricane Katrina, more than a million volunteers have traveled to New Orleans to help rebuild homes and provide services for disadvantaged groups.[61] Dozens of new nonprofit organizations emerged after the disaster to coordinate volunteers to rebuild, and other existing organizations diverted resources to the region. While some claim that this volunteer construction model is not the most efficient way to build homes, it has some significant upsides.

First, using volunteers decreases labor costs, especially over time, as nonprofits develop systems to coordinate volunteers and construction efforts. The savings allow organizations to build more homes for more families. Some organizations require the future homeowners to pay for the costs of supplies while some residents qualify to have their homes constructed for free. Many of the coordinating organizations hire volunteer coordinators, construction coordinators, and skilled workers to do some of the work. The remainder of the work is carried out by the unskilled volunteers.[62]

Additionally, the volunteer model brings overall resources for affordable housing reconstruction to regions in need. Many organizations require volunteers to pay an administration fee, which helps pay for coordination, certain paid positions, and volunteer housing and other costs, ultimately increasing affordability for homeowners and capacity for the organizations.[63] Others require volunteers to raise money to support affordable housing advocacy groups and campaigns before they build.[64]

Finally, the model can promote civic engagement, leadership development, and job training among outside volunteers and local residents and provide free additional support to the prospective homeowners.[65] The exchange builds empathy among people of different backgrounds as volunteers often work alongside local residents. Some organizations use the model as a job-training program as well.

1. National Efforts

The volunteer model has been employed by many large-scale national organizations in the Gulf Coast, which can create efficient economies of scale for home-building. National organizations that existed before Hurricane Katrina already had systems in place to disperse volunteers to various sights and coordinate massive service weeks. For example, Rebuilding Together, which has 30 years of experience, administered the Fifty for Five program to employ its 46 regional chapters and other groups to mobilize more than 1,000 volunteers from all over the country for one week in August 2010. The effort generated 50 homes for low-income families within the short period.[66] Rebuilding Together New Orleans, its local affiliate, claims to have generated $40 million in total construction investment for the city of New Orleans.[67] National organizations also recruit volunteers nationwide and year-round for longer periods.

Habitat for Humanity, a worldwide organization that has built more than 500,000 homes globally, is an example of a large-scale organization that successfully employs the volunteer model.[68] Habitat for Humanity has been actively involved in the Hurricane Katrina disaster relief efforts. Immediately after the hurricane, Habitat for Humanity was able to organize 50,000 volunteers and raise $127 million for the relief effort.[69] The organization worked with its 21 Gulf Coast affiliates to mobilize volunteers to build, rehabilitate, and repair houses.[70]

Habitat for Humanity launched several initiatives in response to the destruction left behind by Hurricane Katrina. Operation Home Delivery was implemented with the goal of providing long-term housing solutions for the hurricane-affected families in the Gulf Coast area. In 2008, the program was phased out with the ongoing Gulf recovery effort, with local affiliates taking over the program.[71] Habitat for Humanity also started its Habitat "house-in-a-box" program, which builds house frames remotely, and then ships them out for use in the Gulf Coast.[72] Finally, Habitat for Humanity established the Musicians' Village, an 8.2-acre tract of land in the Upper Ninth Ward of New Orleans that consists of 72 single-family homes, five elder-friendly duplexes, a park, and a music center.[73] The village's goal is to provide housing for the city's displaced traditional jazz and blues musicians, although the village is open to nonmusicians as well.[74] While these are just some examples of Habitat for Humanity's involvement in the Gulf Coast region, these projects showcase the organization's ability to tailor its services to fit the needs of the population at hand.

Because of its effort post–Hurricane Katrina, the New Orleans chapter of Habitat for Humanity became the largest affiliate in the country.[75] As of early 2012, Habitat for Humanity had built or rehabilitated 557 homes in the Gulf Coast since Hurricane Katrina.[76] Volunteers have gutted more than 2,400 homes.[77] Additionally, the organization has coordinated more than 285,000 volunteer opportunities.[78] Through its work, Habitat for Humanity has contributed greatly to the Gulf Coast's recovery after Hurricane Katrina as it continues to respond to the needs of the community.

2. *Grassroots Efforts*

It is the smaller, neighborhood-based organizations, however, that have sprung up since Hurricane Katrina to mobilize countless volunteers to build relatively inexpensive homes. Developing these programs has its challenges, including the logistics and liability of managing hundreds of volunteers, the seasonal nature of volunteer assistance (spring break is an especially popular time), the need for oversight and labor by professional contractors on some phases of the work, and affording the cost of construction materials. Nevertheless, both Lowernine.org and Common Ground Relief, operating on tight budgets, continue to work in the most devastated area of New Orleans: the Lower Ninth Ward. Both organizations take a holistic approach to rebuilding, by working with community leaders and other organizations to train residents and outside volunteers to build and repair homes while also helping residents in other ways.[79] Common Ground Relief focuses specifically on working with communities to "rebuild their lives in sustainable ways," while also engaging in environmental advocacy, job training, and providing legal and social services. Common Ground gutted more than 3,000 homes immediately after Hurricane Katrina and mobilized more than 35,000 volunteers.[80]

St. Bernard Project's Rebuilding Program (SBP) rebuilds homes within a few neighborhoods "for senior citizens, people with disabilities and families with children who cannot afford to have their homes rebuilt by contractors. A typical SBP project takes approximately eight to 12 weeks of volunteer labor."[81] During the rehabilitation process for each client, the SBP goes through a multistep process. First, a case manager is assigned to support the homeowner through the process. Then, a skilled construction manager oversees all phases of the rebuilding process, including purchasing and delivering all necessary building materials. Finally, the SBP "places a skilled site supervisor onsite to supervise the volunteers and to serve as the direct point of contact for each client."[82]

SBP has grown, partly because it has developed partnerships with government institutions, large foundations, and corporate sponsors. Through several state- and city-administered grant programs, SBP has received $4.1 million in Community Development Block Grants from the U.S. Department of Housing and Urban Development to rebuild clients' homes. Additionally, the U.S. Department of Energy has partnered with SBP to focus on energy efficiency in new affordable homes.[83]

Human capacity in reinvigorating a disaster-ravaged city has proved to be an enormous resource in post–Katrina New Orleans. Volunteers have not only built thousands of affordable homes for disadvantaged families, but have also developed relationships with the region and its people. Ultimately, the volunteer model has been successful at connecting a sustainable stream of labor, financial resources, and attention to the region for years after the disaster.

D. Title Clearing

Attorneys at Southeast Louisiana Legal Services (SLLS) and The Pro Bono Project, along with the slew of housing counseling organizations in New Orleans, have known for years about the challenge of clouded title. Many families—in New Orleans and around the country—have no reason to even think about title to homes that have been in their families for generations until a tragedy like Hurricane Katrina occurs. In order to acquire Road Home and other grants to rebuild and return to their homes, thousands of families who were forced from their homes were suddenly required to prove they owned their homes, a fact many of them took for granted.

Without traditional access to legal assistance, African-American families, in particular, confront the related issue of "heir property." Since emancipation, property has passed intestate—without the use of a will—from generation to generation, meaning that few, if any, legal records exist to show who owns the land. And in many cases, multiple family members, sometimes more than a hundred, share legal ownership because of inheritance rights. Such fractured ownership makes it difficult for family members actually living in the home to refinance, obtain home equity loans, sell the property, or obtain rebuilding grants.[84] For instance, as of May 2012, nearly 2,700 Road Home applicants were deemed "ineligible" because of "title/heirship issues."[85] As of July 2012, just 80 families received grants through the pilot Non-Profit Rebuilding Pilot Program (NRPP), a state program that contracted with nonprofit housing counseling organizations to administer rebuilding funds rather than distributing funds directly to homeowners.[86] Case managers at several of the participating nonprofits had cited lack of clear title as a barrier to receiving grants.

In April 2010, the Lawyers' Committee met with representatives of dozens of housing organizations in New Orleans, including nonprofit developers and housing counseling organizations, to hear about the issues facing the housing community and develop strategies to help. Lack of clear title was a recurring theme. Counseling and rebuilding groups like Rebuilding Together, the United Way, and SBP reported being unable to obtain grants through NRPP because their clients could not show clear title. Affordable-housing developers reported being unable to acquire property from homeowners or from NORA for the same reason. The state of Louisiana had set up a Limited Legal Assistance program, but it was underutilized and under-advertised, and it lived up to its name—it was "limited" in the services it could provide. Moreover, it was difficult even for attorneys and nonprofits to get information about these services, and even harder for individual residents to do so. It is unclear how many residents were served by these services.

But some local legal aid lawyers already knew the variety of title issues involved—co-ownership, successions, blight judgments, tax sales, property liens, etc.—and, more importantly, the legal solutions. Legal aid attorneys at SLLS and The Pro Bono Project had been helping clients clear title, but they were not funded to specifically and strategically address this uniquely complex and aggravating problem. At the same time, Louisiana Appleseed, as part of a national effort to address heir property, had been steadily chipping away at state law to make it easier to consolidate and prove ownership.

In the context of Road Home and NRPP, these groups all wanted to bring title clearing to scale—to help more people. The expertise and the will were there, but with stretched budgets and staff resources, the missing ingredient was funding. The Greater New Orleans Foundation had helped facilitate the Lawyers' Committee's meetings and was administering the Ford Foundation–supplied Community Revitalization Fund (CRF). Together, SLLS, PBP, Louisiana Appleseed, and the Lawyers' Committee obtained a two-year grant from the CRF for a coordinated effort to clear title for 400 owners and to continue changing the laws to conform to the realities of heir property and title. SLLS and The Pro Bono Project were able to hire dedicated staff to provide direct legal services to Orleans Parish homeowners, Louisiana Appleseed would direct outreach and public policy efforts, and the Lawyers' Committee would coordinate the initiative.

As of January 2013, the collaborative, known as Save New Orleans Homes, had met with nearly 2,500 people at more than 60 community events and helped more than 400 homeowners and co-owners successfully resolve their cases. The collaborative has also trained dozens of volunteer attorneys and completed training manuals on several related issues, including successions, liens and judgments, and property tax sales.

The results of this collaborative are real for people like a 91-year-old disabled African-American woman, "Bessie," living in a home in the Upper Ninth Ward neighborhood in New Orleans. Bessie and her two brothers had inherited the home from a family member. Bessie's two brothers were now deceased, and she was attempting to get a Road Home rebuilding grant to repair damage from Hurricane Katrina, but could not because of title issues. SLLS located the heirs of the two brothers and filed small succession affidavits for both of them, clearing the way for Bessie to receive a Road Home grant. Without the help of SLLS attorneys, Bessie may not have been able to navigate the process of locating family members and completing the necessary documentation and filings to clear title to her home.[87]

Moreover, Louisiana Appleseed had successfully advocated for the unanimous passage of a bill, which became Act 323, to refine Louisiana's small successions law to allow any co-owner of real property damaged by natural disaster to work directly with the state or federal agencies to recover repair money and compensation in order to rebuild the damaged property without the need to do any probate work.[88] The rights granted by this act were extended to non-Louisiana residents who own real property within the state.[89]

This type of strategic collaboration among direct legal service providers, state and national advocacy organizations, case management organizations, and funders is crucial to providing dedicated resources and coordination that allow for a more efficient implementation of multiple strategies at various levels, including direct legal assistance, community education and outreach, and policy reform. Training volunteer attorneys, creating manuals, building the capacity of the legal aid organizations, strengthening relationships among community organizations, and changing the laws create a sustainable impact that will last beyond the term of the grant.

IV. Lessons Learned

In the aftermath of Hurricane Katrina, it is clear that the absence of effective and coordinated housing policies and strategies by local, state, and federal governments severely impeded rebuilding efforts. Programs such as Road Home and even low-income housing tax credits were stymied by bureaucracy and a poor economic climate. Meanwhile, the government did little to address long-standing residential segregation that resulted in NIMBYism, exclusionary zoning, and discrimination based on source of income, disability, and race, all of which were exacerbated by the displacement of thousands of mostly African-American residents.

Community-based efforts, however, have offered some hope for alleviating and mitigating Hurricane Katrina's damage. Strategies such as community land trusts, the utilization of vacant land, volunteer models of rebuilding and construction, and title clearing have provided alternatives to government programs, allowing communities to rebuild with fewer bureaucratic barriers and more community involvement. These innovative strategies, which have had varying levels of success in places like New Orleans, can be used by other communities working to give people the chance to return home.

Any approach must be thoughtful and holistic. Identifying existing assets and considering what resources are missing are essential components of planning and creating opportunity. Although the devastation of disasters like Hurricane Katrina cannot truly be undone, it can provide opportunities for ingenuity and, more importantly, for rebuilding communities stronger and more equitably than before.

Notes

1. *See* Joseph Dalaker, U.S. Census Bureau, *Poverty in the United States: 2000*, CURRENT POPULATION REP., Sept. 2001, at 1, 11, *available at* http://www.census.gov/prod/2001pubs/p60-214.pdf (showing the 1998–2000 average poverty rates were 18.6 percent for Louisiana and 15.5 percent for Mississippi, whereas the national average was 11.9 percent).

2. *See* 83 AM. JUR. 2D *Zoning and Planning* § 74 (2012); "Zoning," BLACK'S LAW DICTIONARY (9th ed. 2009).

3. *See* RADHIKA K. FOX ET AL., POLICYLINK & CMTY. DEV. P'SHIPS NETWORK, SHARED PROSPERITY, STRONGER REGIONS: AN AGENDA FOR REBUILDING AMERICA'S OLDER CORE CITIES 121 (2d ed. 2006), http://www.policylink.org/atf/cf/%7B97c6d565-bb43-406d-a6d5-eca3bbf35af0%7D/SHAREDPROSPERITY-CORECITES-FINAL.PDF.

4. *See* GREATER NEW ORLEANS FAIR HOUS. ACTION CTR. & LAWYERS' COMM. FOR CIVIL RIGHTS UNDER LAW, STRATEGIES TO AFFIRMATIVELY FURTHER FAIR HOUSING 3–4 (April 28, 2011), *available at* http://www.lawyerscommittee.org/admin/community_development/documents/files/4-28-11_Strategies_to_Affirmatively_Further_Fair_Housing.pdf.

5. *See Mississippi Alternative Housing Pilot Program*, FED. EMERGENCY MGMT. AGENCY, http://www.fema.gov/mississippi-alternative-housing-pilot-program#0 (last visited Jan. 14, 2013).

6. *See id.*

7. *See* Tom Gogola, *Katrina Cottages: Years Late and $1 Million over Budget in the 9th Ward*, THE LENS (May 3, 2012), *available at* http://thelensnola.org/2012/05/03/katrina-cottages-for-sale/.

8. *See* Bruce D. Snider, *Spotlight: Mississippi Alternative Housing Program*, AM. INST. OF ARCHITECTS (Feb. 28, 2011), *available at* http://www.residentialarchitect.com/affordable-housing/spotlight2.aspx.

9. *See id.*

10. *See* Spencer S. Hsu, *FEMA Taking Hit on Sale of Surplus Trailers*, WASH. POST (Mar. 8, 2007), http://www.washingtonpost.com/wp-dyn/content/article/2007/03/07/AR2007030702628.html.

11. *See* Spencer S. Hsu, *For Some Displaced by Hurricane Katrina, Permanent Housing Is Still Out of Reach*, WASH. POST (June 13, 2009), http://www.washingtonpost.com/wp-dyn/content/article/2009/06/12/AR2009061203958.html.

12. *See id.*

13. *See* GREATER NEW ORLEANS FAIR HOUS. ACTION CTR. & LAWYERS' COMM. FOR CIVIL RIGHTS UNDER LAW, *supra* note 4.

14. Carol Anne Clark Kelly, *Much Katrina Aid Wasted, GAO Report Says*, NAT'L PUB. RADIO (Dec. 6, 2006), http://www.npr.org/templates/story/story.php?storyId=6587188; *see* U.S. GOV'T ACCOUNTABILITY OFFICE, GAO-07-252T, HURRICANES KATRINA AND RITA DISASTER RELIEF: CONTINUED FINDINGS OF FRAUD, WASTE, AND ABUSE BEFORE THE S. COMM. ON HOMELAND SEC. AND GOV'T AFFAIRS, 109th Cong. (2006) (statement of Greg Kutz, Managing Dir., Forensic Audits and Special Investigations), *available at* http://www.gao.gov/products/GAO-07-252T.

15. *See The Road Home Program*, ROAD HOME, http://www.road2la.org (last visited Jan. 16, 2013) (discussing funding made possible for the program by the U.S. Congress and Louisiana).

16. *See* Robin Keegan, La. Disaster Recovery Unit, Disaster Recovery Budget and Program Updates, Presentation to the Louisiana Recovery Authority (Apr. 16, 2010), http://lra.louisiana.gov/assets/docs/searchable/meetings/2010/Board%20Meeting%204-16-10/BudgetUpdate4-16-10.pdf.

17. *See* David Hammer, *New Orleans Redevelopment Authority Continues to Deal with Road Home Problems*, TIMES-PICAYUNE (Apr. 30, 2012), http://www.nola.com/politics/index.ssf/2012/04/new_orleans

_redevelopment_auth_5.html (citing M.A. Sheehan) ("State and Census Data suggest that 700 to 1,000 homes out of 1,435 to get Road Home rebuilding grants are not reoccupied.").

18. *See* Memorandum from Greater New Orleans Hous. Alliance et. al, to the Select Comm. on Hurricane Recovery, Still Not Home: A Summary of Unmet Needs and Recommended Solutions (Aug. 17, 2010), http://gnoha.files.wordpress.com/2012/05/unmet-needs-memo-for-select-committee.pdf.

19. *See* TRANSITION NEW ORLEANS TASK FORCE, HOUSING 18 (Apr. 2010), *available at* http://www.policylink.org/atf/cf/%7B97c6d565-bb43-406d-a6d5-eca3bbf35af0%7D/MAYOR%27S%20HOUSING%20TASKFORCE.PDF.

20. Phone interview with Andreanecia Morris, Vice President, Providence Community Housing (July 10, 2012).

21. *See* Jedidiah Horne & Brendan Nee, An Overview of Post-Katrina Planning in New Orleans (Oct. 18, 2006) (unpublished graduate school project, UC Berkeley), *available at* http://blog.bn.ee/wp-content/uploads/2006/10/An_Overview_of_the_Unified_New_Orleans_Planning_Process.pdf; *see also* Bring New Orleans Back Comm'n et al., *Action Plan for New Orleans: The New American City*, NAT'L PUB. RADIO (Jan. 11, 2006), *available at* http://www.npr.org/documents/2006/jan/CityPlanningFinalReport.pdf?.

22. *See* Gwen Filosa, *N.O. Neighborhoods Plans Unveiled*, TIMES-PICAYUNE (Sept. 24, 2006), *available at* http://www.nola.com/katrina/articles/planningreports.html; *see also* Abigail Williamson, Citizen Participation in the United New Orleans Plan (Mar. 21, 2007) (unpublished Ph.D. research project, Harvard Univ.), *available at* http://americaspeaks.org/wp-content/_data/n_0001/resources/live/citizenpartstudy1.pdf.

23. *See* Horne, *supra* note 21.

24. *See id.*

25. Memorandum of Understanding Between the City of New Orleans, New Orleans City Council, City Planning Commission, Greater New Orleans Foundation, and New Orleans Community Support Foundation, Aug. 28, 2006, http://www.nolaplans.com/plans/UNOP/MOU-66608.pdf.

26. *What Are Community Land Trusts*, NAT'L CMTY. LAND TRUST NETWORK, http://www.cltnetwork.org/index.php?fuseaction=Blog.dspBlogPost&postID=1396 (last visited Jan. 16, 2013).

27. *U.S. Directory of CLTs*, NAT'L CMTY. LAND TRUST NETWORK, http://www.cltnetwork.org/index.php?fuseaction=Main.MemberList (last visited Jan. 16, 2013); *see also* EMILY THADEN, VANDERBILT UNIV., COMM. RESEARCH & ACTION PROGRAM, SHARED EQUITY HOMEOWNERSHIP: SHARING THE COSTS AND BENEFITS (2008), http://peabody.vanderbilt.edu/docs/pdf/ccs/Shared%20equity%20primer.pdf.

28. *Foreclosure*, NAT'L CMTY. LAND TRUST NETWORK, http://www.cltnetwork.org/index.php?fuseaction=Blog.dspBlogPost&postID=36 (last visited Jan. 17, 2013).

29. *History*, NAT'L CMTY. LAND TRUST NETWORK, http://www.cltnetwork.org/history (last visited Jan. 16, 2013).

30. *See* Nat'l Cmty. Land Trust Network, *Assessing the Potential for a Community Land Trust in New Orleans*, 3–5, *available at* http://www.cltnetwork.org/doc_library/Summary%20Report%20-%20New%20Orleans%20CLT%20Assessment%20060809.pdf (last visited Jan. 17, 2013).

31. *See* Phone interview with Van Temple, Executive Director, Crescent City CLT (July 12, 2012).

32. *See* ATLANTA LAND TRUST COLLABORATIVE, www.atlantaltc.org (last visited Jan. 28, 2013).

33. *See* Interview with Van Temple, *supra* note 31.

34. *Id.*

35. *See id.*

36. BIODISTRICT NEW ORLEANS, http://www.biodistrictneworleans.org (last visited Jan. 17, 2013).

37. *See History and Neighborhood Snapshot*, JANE PLACE NEIGHBORHOOD SUSTAINABILITY INITIATIVE, http://www.jpnsi.org/ (last visited Jan. 17, 2013).

38. *Id.*

39. *Id.*

40. *See* Allison Plyer, *Population Loss and Vacant Housing in New Orleans Neighborhoods*, GREATER NEW ORLEANS CMTY. DATA CTR., http://www.gnocdc.org/PopulationLossAndVacantHousing/index.html (last updated Apr. 15, 2011).

41. *See The Lot Next Door*, NEW ORLEANS REDEV. AUTH., http://www.noraworks.org/residents/lot-next-door (last visited Jan. 28, 2013).

42. *See* Roger Hahn, *Moving Back Home to New Orleans*, HOME ENERGY, Sept./Oct. 2010, at 32–38, *available at* http://www.projecthomeagain.net/home_energy_septoct2010_article.pdf.

43. *See id.*

44. *See id.*

45. *See Project Home Again Frequently Asked Questions*, New Orleans Neighborhoods P'ship Network, http://npnnola.com/CMSuploads/PHA-FAQs.pdf (last visited Jan. 17, 2013).

46. *See* Kate Moran, *Barnes & Noble Exec Aids Katrina Victims*, Times-Picayune (Sept. 7, 2008, 8:00 AM), http://blog.nola.com/tpmoney/2008/09/barnes_noble_exec_aids_katrina.html.

47. *See* Rebecca Mowbray, *Project Home Again Finishes 100 Homes in Gentilly—Plus 1 for Lagniappe*, Times-Picayune (Nov. 10, 2011), http://www.nola.com/katrina/index.ssf/2011/11/project_home_again_finishes_10.html.

48. *See Project Home Again Frequently Asked Questions*, *supra* note 45.

49. *See* Project Home Again Eligibility, New Orleans Neighborhoods P'ship Network, http://npnnola.com/CMSuploads/PHA-GuideEligibility.pdf (last visited Jan. 17, 2013); *see also Person of the Week—Helping Hands—Noble Cause*, New Orleans Living, http://www.livingneworleans.com/?p=3575 (last visited Jan. 17, 2013).

50. *See Project Home Again Frequently Asked Questions*, *supra* note 45.

51. *See* Hahn, *supra* note 42.

52. *See id.*

53. *See Project Home Again Frequently Asked Questions*, *supra* note 45.

54. *See* Mowbray, *supra* note 47; *see also* Moran, *supra* note 46; *see also Person of the Week—Helping Hands—Noble Cause*, *supra* note 49.

55. *See* Hahn, *supra* note 42.

56. *See id.*

57. Memorandum from Mike Lockerby to John Heinz, Moon Landrieu Confirmation Hearings (Sept. 4, 1979) (on file with the Carnegie Mellon Library Special Collections), *available at* http://shelf1.library.cmu.edu/cgi-bin/tiff2pdf/heinz/box00295/fld00017/bdl0008/doc0001/heinz.pdf.

58. Bari Landry, *An Updated Look at a Charming Neighborhood*, Preservation Res. Ctr. of New Orleans: Preservation in Print, May 2008, at 19, *available at* http://www.prcno.org/programs/preservationinprint/piparchives/2008%20PIP/May%202008/18.html.

59. *See* Audrey McFarlane, *Fighting for the High Ground: Race, Class, Markets, and Development Done Right in Post-Katrina Recovery*, 14 Wash. & Lee J. Civil Rts. & Soc. Just. 77, 90 (2007), *available at* http://scholarlycommons.law.wlu.edu/cgi/viewcontent.cgi?article=1235&context=crsj; *see also* Sean Almonte, *Helping to Rebuild New Orleans*, American Planning Ass'n (Oct. 2, 2007), http://www.planning.org/katrina/almonte.htm.

60. *See* Dan Baum, *Letter from New Orleans—The Lost Year: Behind the Failure to Rebuild*, New Yorker (Aug. 21, 2006), *available at* http://www.newyorker.com/archive/2006/08/21/060821fa_fact2.

61. *See* Rebecca Solnit, *In New Orleans, Kindness Trumped Chaos*, Yes! (Aug. 27, 2010), *available at* http://www.yesmagazine.org/issues/a-resilient-community/in-new-orleans-kindness-trumped-chaos.

62. Interview with Laura Paul, Executive Director, Lowernine.org (May 8, 2012); *see also St. Bernard Project Rebuilding Program,* St. Bernard Project, http://www.stbernardproject.org/our-programs/rebulding-program/ (last visited Jan. 18, 2013).

63. *See id.*

64. *See* Bike & Build, http://bikeandbuild.org/cms/ (last visited Jan. 18, 2013) (showing that Bike & Build, not focused on the Gulf Coast, has raised millions of dollars to benefit affordable housing groups).

65. *See Vision and Mission*, Hands On New Orleans, http://www.handsonneworleans.org/About_Us (last visited Jan. 18, 2013).

66. *See* Brian Clark Howard, *5 Years After Katrina, 1,000 Volunteers Help New Orleans Rebuild Green*, Daily Green (Aug. 30, 2010), http://www.thedailygreen.com/environmental-news/latest/rebuilding-together-new-orleans-460810#ixzz20og37D6X.

67. *See Volunteer*, Rebuilding Together New Orleans, http://www.rtno.org/give-time/volunteer (last visited Jan. 18, 2013).

68. *See Fact Sheet*, Habitat for Humanity, http://www.habitat.org/how/factsheet.aspx (last visited Jan. 18, 2013).

69. *See* Leslie Eaton & Stephanie Strom, *Volunteer Group Lags in Replacing Gulf Houses*, N.Y. Times (Feb. 22, 2001), http://www.nytimes.com/2007/02/22/us/22habitat.html?pagewanted=all&_r=0.

70. *See Five Years After Hurricanes Katrina and Rita*, Habitat for Humanity, http://www.habitat.org/newsroom/2010archive/08_09_2010_HFHI_5_Year_Katrina_Anniversary.aspx (last visited Jan. 18, 2013).

71. *See Hurricanes Katrina and Rita Recovery Effort*, Habitat for Humanity, http://www.habitat.org/disaster/programs/details/Gulf_Recovery_Default.aspx (last visited Jan. 18, 2013).

72. *Id.*
73. *See Musicians' Village*, HABITAT FOR HUMANITY, http://www.habitat-nola.org/about/musicians_village (last visited Jan. 18, 2013).
74. *See id.*
75. *See* Natasha Robin, *Habitat for Humanity Contributing to City's Recovery*, FOX NEWS (June 22, 2012), http://www.fox8live.com/story/18743466/habitat-for-humanity-contributing-to-citys-recovery.
76. *See Fact Sheet*, NEW ORLEANS AREA HABITAT FOR HUMANITY, http://www.habitat-nola.org/filestorage/NOAHH%20Fact%20sheet%2006-26-12.pdf (last visited Jan. 18, 2013).
77. *See id.*
78. *See id.*
79. *See About*, LOWERNINE, http://lowernine.org/wordpress/about-2/ (last visited Jan. 18, 2013).
80. *See About Us*, COMMON GROUND RELIEF, *available at* http://www.commongroundrelief.org/about (last visited Jan. 18, 2013).
81. *See St. Bernard Project Rebuilding Program*, ST. BERNARD PROJECT, http://www.stbernardproject.org/our-programs/rebulding-program/ (last visited Jan. 18, 2013).
82. *Id.*
83. *See id.*
84. *See* LOUISIANA APPLESEED, PROTECT YOUR PROPERTIES: HEIR PROPERTY IN LOUISIANA (rev. 2011), *available at* http://www.appleseednetwork.org/wp-content/uploads/2012/05/Protect-Your-Property.pdf.
85. *See* THE ROAD HOME, HOMEOWNERSHIP ASSISTANCE PROGRAM, WEEK 309 SITUATION & PIPELINE REPORT 1 (May 25, 2012), *available at* http://road2la.org/Docs/HAP/Situation%20and%20Pipeline%20Reports/week309%2006-05-2012.pdf.
86. *See* Graph on Investments in Residential Construction, REBUILD LA., www.rebuild.la.gov/Residential.aspx (last visited Jan. 18, 2013).
87. *See Title Clearing Collaborative Has Reached over 300 Clients and Counting*, LAWYERS' COMM. FOR CIVIL RIGHTS UNDER LAW (Oct. 12, 2013), http://www.lawyerscommittee.org/projects/community_development/clips?id=0340.
88. *See* Small Successions Act, LA. CODE CIV. PROC. ANN. art. 3431 (1960), *amended by* 2011 La. Act 323.
89. *See id.*

CHAPTER 17

Disaster as a Catalyst for Collaboration and Innovation: Workforce Development in Mississippi Following Hurricane Katrina

Ed Sivak

I. Introduction

Over the last 30 years, incomes among the bottom quintile of households grew, on average, by only $1,330 after adjusting for inflation. During the same period, households in the top fifth of income experienced increases of $2,550 per year.[1] Explanations for the nearly stagnant wage growth among low-income households include globalization and the ensuing loss of low-skilled manufacturing jobs, the evolution of technology, the decline of union participation, and the erosion of the purchasing power of the minimum wage. Regardless, the vastly different wage trajectory for low-income households underscores the importance of acquiring skills and education in today's economy. For those who obtain relevant training—especially for jobs that are in demand—a clear path to family economic security exists. In contrast, individuals with low levels of educational attainment often experience limited opportunities beyond low-wage work.

Amid the backdrop of increased skill requirements for the attainment of gainful employment lies at least one conundrum in the labor market. On one hand, the Bureau of Labor Statistics reports that as of November 2012, the country had 4 million fewer jobs than at the start of the

Great Recession. On the other hand, job vacancies exist—especially in middle- and high-skill occupations—and employers report ongoing challenges in filling the positions.[2] Rectifying the skills mismatch between the existing workforce and the needs of employers remains a priority of any comprehensive community and economic development strategy.

When disasters occur, the mismatch in skills among workers and employer needs is often exacerbated. In the immediate aftermath, individuals with expertise, particularly in the construction and building trades, may be displaced at a time when demand for their skills is heightened. Individuals who work in other sectors and who have not been displaced may find that their previous employment arrangement is not readily available. Finally, overlaying the post-disaster labor market dynamic includes the very real human challenges of rebuilding a home, reuniting with loved ones and navigating financial hardships.

During the recovery and rebuilding period following the landfall of Hurricane Katrina on the Mississippi Gulf Coast, the challenges faced from both the labor demand (employers) and labor supply (workers) converged. Workforce developers with the Mississippi Department of Employment Security, the community colleges, and employers were faced with the question: How does a state implement a plan that will attract, support, and train workers that have encountered significant stress for in-demand jobs that meet the needs of short-term recovery and long-term growth? Using a case study approach, this chapter lifts the response to the question from the perspective of 10 workforce development stakeholders in Mississippi in the employment security, community college, and nonprofit sectors following Hurricane Katrina. It concludes with lessons learned.

II. Case Examples

A. Hurricane Katrina Damage Estimates

On August 29, 2005, Hurricane Katrina made landfall on the Gulf Coast and continued its path of destruction through the state of Mississippi. Once on land, the storm maintained hurricane status until it was 150 miles beyond the Gulf of Mexico. In the days, weeks, and months following the storm, the sheer vastness of its path came into clear view. More than 230 Mississippians lost their lives and 80 percent of the state's nearly 3 million residents had lost power.[3] Forty-nine of 82 counties received the highest level of disaster declaration by the Federal Emergency Management Agency (FEMA).[4]

The effects of the storm on employment were largely associated with the level of damage encountered by Mississippi businesses during the storm. Of 2,678 establishments affected, 47 percent were classified as receiving catastrophic damage. Catastrophic damage is the FEMA classification for the destruction of all solid and light structures.[5] Solid structures are buildings and homes made from concrete, whereas light structures are made from wood and steel. Within the Mississippi establishments that received catastrophic damage, 16,294 jobs were lost—79 percent of the total job loss attributed to Hurricane Katrina[6] (see Table 1).

Table 1
Mississippi Businesses Affected by Hurricane Katrina

	Establishments December 2004	Employment Change December 2004–2005
Total	2,678	−20,551
Flooded Area	57	−174
Non-flooded Area		
Limited Damage	794	−1,028
Moderate Damage	468	−1,731
Extensive Damage	95	−1,324
Catastrophic Damage	1,264	−16,294

Source: Bureau of Labor Statistics Quarterly Census of Employment and Wages. Monthly Labor Review August 2006
Note: Data is restricted to businesses located in Hurricane Katrina–damaged areas during the third quarter of 2005.

The impacts extended well beyond the businesses encountering catastrophic damage along the Mississippi coastline. Reviews of administrative records at the Mississippi Department of Employment Security revealed that 6,774 businesses had employees that successfully filed a claim for Disaster Unemployment Assistance (DUA). In total, 69,413 employees received DUA. It should be noted that the employees included in the DUA counts only included employees who were covered by the unemployment insurance program. Hence, government employees and self-employed individuals not covered by the program were not included.[7]

Following the storm, surveys of Mississippi business owners stated that identifying workers with the requisite skills to fill vacant positions remained a challenge. In fact, 86 percent reported that it was more difficult to find skilled workers than before the storm. Businesses responded by reducing hiring requirements, increasing hours of existing employees, increasing wages, limiting the hours of operation, and engaging in intense recruitment and retention strategies. Within the spectrum of services available through the Workforce Investment Network (WIN) job centers, employers cited skills training, along with recruitment, as the most important services available for their operations following the storm.[8]

From the employee perspective, a number of recovery obstacles emerged in the post–Hurricane Katrina environment. For those who were not displaced by the storm, housing was the primary challenge, followed by employment and transportation.[9] More than 30,000 FEMA trailers were placed into service to meet short-term housing needs, while significantly increased property insurance rates post-storm hindered rebuilding efforts. Low-income residents encountered shortages in the affordable rental market as well.[10] Mental health needs, inadequate access to health care, and a lack of financial resources and services—such as bank accounts and credit cards particularly among low-income residents of the Mississippi Gulf Coast—compromised efforts to return to work.[11]

Coastal Counties - Mississippi

Rates of unemployment increased significantly in the three southernmost coastal counties immediately following the storm—particularly for minorities. Whereas the unemployment rate for whites rose from 4.2 percent to 9.0 percent from 2004 to 2006 in Harrison County, the unemployment rate for African-Americans increased from 8.7 percent to 17.8 percent over the same period of time.[12] Six years after the storm, Hancock, Harrison, and Jackson counties all experienced growth in the civilian labor force composed of minorities. In contrast, Hancock and Harrison counties saw the white labor force decline and remain relatively stable in Jackson county.

B. Workforce Development before Hurricane Katrina

Along the Mississippi Gulf Coast, the workforce development programs primarily consisted of the services funded by the U.S. Department of Labor and managed by the Mississippi Department of Employment Security through its WIN job centers and through Mississippi Gulf Coast and Pearl River Community Colleges. Through the presence of a large shipbuilding cluster, apprenticeship programs also served as an important training resource in that industry. Very little training occurred via the nonprofit sector.

At the time, while the coastal counties of Hancock, Harrison, and Jackson were home to 12.8 percent of the state's population, the three counties provided 14 percent of the state sales tax revenue and 18.6 percent of the state's corporate income and franchise tax revenue.[13] Anchored by hospitality (gaming) and manufacturing (shipbuilding), the Gulf Coast offered employment opportunities at levels not experienced in other parts of the state. Training and education opportunities supported both industries, as well as other sectors such as health care and construction. The community colleges also provided pathways to additional higher education at four-year institutions.

In practice, the availability of training and education resources alongside job opportunities may have slowed efforts to collaborate across traditional agency boundaries before the storm. Since jobs were available, clients from the WIN job centers and students coming out of the colleges were finding employment. Innovation and collaboration were not a prerequisite for successful placement of trainees in jobs. As a result, curriculum development within the colleges that incorporated employer feedback may not have occurred as efficiently as employers would have preferred. Additionally, training opportunities were not always offered during times such as on weekends or at night, and in blocks most conducive for the retraining of low-skill workers. The conditions created a workforce delivery system that could collaborate but did not always maximize opportunities for employers and residents seeking to acquire skills to come together.[14]

C. After Katrina: The First Weeks of Recovery

Going into the storm, the Mississippi Department of Employment Security (MDES) started planning for the storm several days before it reached Mississippi. In an interview with Les Range, the former executive director of the MDES, Range stated that the agency followed precedent set during previous hurricanes: equipment and offices were secured and staff from field offices in other parts of the state was on call to assist with DUA claims.[15] DUA is a federal program managed by MDES that provides financial assistance to individual workers or the self-employed who could not return to work because a job no longer existed or was not reachable. DUA also exists for individuals who could not return to work due to a disaster-related injury. Preparations were also made to request funding through the U.S. Department of Labor National Emergency Grant (NEG) program—if necessary.

The NEG provides funding to state and local governments for the training and employment of large numbers of people who have lost their jobs due to unforeseen events such as mass layoffs, disasters, and the closure of military bases. NEG disaster grants typically focus on temporary jobs related to the cleanup needed following the disaster for six months. States may submit modification requests to expand the scope of the NEG when additional training is required for temporary job workers to acquire skills that are in demand in the post-disaster labor market. Only states, Native American tribal government, and local workforce investment boards are eligible to apply for NEG funds.[16]

Hurricane Katrina's size and strength, however, created conditions that exceeded the limits of the MDES plan. The state office for MDES had to be closed because hurricane-force winds were still present when the storm reached Jackson—185 miles inland. Both power and communications were lost for nearly two days. On the Gulf Coast, offices that would have been used for staging in Jackson and Harrison counties were completely destroyed and many of the employees from MDES lost their own homes.

As soon as the power returned, the NEG application was faxed to the U.S. Department of Labor and efforts to restore all agency services—particularly the ability to take DUA claims and connecting people to work—became the priority. Forty staff members from other parts of the state were mobilized to work with people who had been displaced and lost their jobs. Additionally, 19 other states sent people to the Gulf Coast to assist MDES. Mobile offices were in place where WIN job centers had been demolished, and all other offices were back on line by September 12, 2005. Two additional offices were also opened during this time period.[17]

Within the community college system, Mississippi Gulf Coast Community College lost 25 percent of its students and encountered $21 million in property damage.[18] Pearl River Community College experienced upward of $30 million in damage, losing classrooms, residence halls, and a sports coliseum largely from wind as the hurricane passed directly over its campus. While Pearl River addressed classroom constraints through portable units, residence-hall space was scarce. Not only were students returning to a campus with fewer rooms, demand for the space increased as commuters relocated onto campus because the storm destroyed their homes. Immediate space constraints were addressed by assigning three residents to one room.[19]

D. National Emergency Grant Program

Within four days of Hurricane Katrina's landfall, the U.S. Department of Labor awarded the state of Mississippi $50 million through the NEG program. A verbal commitment of another $45 million was made in December of 2005 to address workforce training needs.[20] Over the last 12 years, no other state has received a NEG for a single disaster as large as the NEG for Hurricane Katrina recovery in Mississippi.[21]

From the onset, administration of the NEG rested within the centralized location of the Mississippi Department of Employment Securities—an executive agency in the Office of the Governor. Rebekah Staples, a former policy advisor for Governor Haley Barbour, articulated the rationale of the approach. By centralizing decision making surrounding the implementation of the grant-funded programs with significant input from those on the ground, the state of Mississippi could use the unprecedented level of NEG resources to address priorities in both the short term and to plan for the future. Alternatively, MDES could have devolved the strategic decision making to local and regional governments on the execution of the NEG. Such action, however, may have resulted in the over-prioritization of short-term needs and the resetting of ineffective structures that would ultimately reduce the amount of resources available to position the Gulf Coast to compete in the future.[22] Taking the centralized approach, initial plans requested temporary jobs funding, workforce training—both in the classroom and on the job—and business recapitalization.

E. Temporary Jobs

One of the primary activities funded by the NEG program included the support of temporary jobs for the cleanup of debris, recovery assistance to individuals, and restoration of communities. In 2005, federal regulations limited participation in the temporary-jobs program to six months or 1,040 hours of work with an earnings cap of $12,000 not including benefits.[23] Mississippi's first temporary jobs—debris removers, disaster recovery workers, teaching assistants, clerical workers, and a harbormaster—were filled in October 2005.[24]

Accounts from the time indicate that existing regulations on the temporary-jobs component of the grant were insufficient to address the gravity of the post-disaster needs. For many individuals, there was simply not a job to which they could return. In Hancock County alone, many businesses were completely washed away, along with much of the local government infrastructure. Gary Lukens highlighted the challenges in Hancock County: "Temp jobs were an absolute necessity. There was no infrastructure, no tax base, no businesses and the state could not afford to put it back together. Temp jobs put people back to work when there was no other place to turn."[25]

The volume of cleanup activities coupled with the uncertainty faced by businesses on the Gulf Coast prompted multiple modification requests, ultimately accepted by the U.S. Department of Labor, of the temporary jobs program. In the end, it extended eligibility to 24 months with total wages not to exceed $48,000.[26] Despite having all costs covered, many factors limited enrollment in and the successful completion of NEG-funded training during the first two years of recovery. First, for individuals who lost their home and their job, it was simply not comprehensible that one's employer would not return. Yolanda Boone, the manager of the Grants Management Office with the MDES raised the challenge, "It takes individuals six months to one year to accept that a job isn't coming back and that skills need to be upgraded for existing opportunities."[27] The temporary jobs provided a stream of income where an individual could delay a decision to retrain—especially if the individuals possessed skills from previous employment that were no longer in demand. "Every time the temporary jobs program was extended, we experienced delays in the take-up of training" said Boone.[28] Second, the realities of rebuilding simply compromised an individual's ability to complete training. Families were trying to locate housing, rebuild homes, navigate recovery payments, get kids to school, and generate an income. These activities crowded out the time required to go to class and learn a new skill without earning any money. Third, if small children were present in a family, child-care options were limited because many of the centers experienced catastrophic damage.[29] Finally, for individuals that wanted to start a new career, particularly those previously employed in low-wage hospitality jobs, the differences between hospitality and the in-demand occupations in the construction trades proved challenging for retention in training programs. For example, upon training, individuals who had previously worked indoors in positions that required less activity decided that the physical demands of the trades in an outdoor environment were not a good fit.

F. Workforce Training: Mississippi Gulf Coast

By the end of 2007, training participation began to increase across the Gulf Coast and in adjacent rural areas. With the temporary-jobs program winding down, the pace of participation in training programs increased. The recruitment challenges faced earlier significantly decreased with the end of the temporary-jobs program, according to Yolanda Boone.[30] Additionally, the urgency of the moment catalyzed collaboration between MDES and the community colleges in new ways that made training more accessible to those recovering from the disaster.

Mississippi Gulf Coast Community College implemented a number of programs to address labor force shortages in the state's southernmost counties. Carpentry, drywall, electrical, and roofing were among the short-term training programs put in place to meet the immediate demand for workers with construction skills. Participants received 160 hours of basic training. Additionally, more advanced courses in HVAC and network cabling were offered. Courses were also rapidly scaled up in the health-care professions for nursing assistants and phlebotomists, including a licensed practical nursing program. Finally, other retraining programs were offered for individuals in the gaming and hospitality sector.

In many ways, the requirement for a rapid response accelerated the evolution of the college's approach to training. Demand for skilled workers was incredibly high post-storm, and families could realize opportunities if training aligned with the needs of the employers. To respond to the conditions, Mississippi Gulf Coast Community College worked hand in hand with Gulf Coast employers to design the training curricula for the skills most needed.

According to Anna Faye Kelley-Winders with Mississippi Gulf Coast Community College, the partnership with employers exceeded levels that existed before the storm and resulted in new efficiencies. The traditional pace of curriculum development within the community college shortened drastically. The long-standing recruitment relationship with the WIN job centers reached new levels of synergy. Recognizing that people needed the daytime hours to work and rebuild, night and weekend classes began to be offered for select programs much more frequently than before the storm. Finally, the college took a more deliberate approach to marketing programs than before Hurricane Katrina to raise awareness among prospective employers and employees of the trainings offered.[31]

By embracing an ethos of partnership, historical barriers broke down to garner the necessary resources for recovery. For example, Northrop Grumman Corporation reached out to MDES for funding to support a crane simulator. Due to the high cost of materials being moved and the risk associated with using equipment improperly by on-the-job trainees, incoming crane operators required preparation on a simulator.

To make such a purchase using NEG funds, a waiver was needed from the U.S. Department of Labor Employment and Training Administration. Such action required support from organized labor in Mississippi. While organized labor typically opposed the governor on policy matters, it supported the administration's request to use NEG funds to purchase a simulator in partnership with the Mississippi Gulf Coast Community College, and the Department of Labor granted the waiver.

At the same time, program implementation was not without hurdles. First, finding qualified instructors emerged as an ongoing challenge. In the construction trades, given the extremely high demand for skilled workers, individuals versed in the trades and with the proper certifications were working—often for wages at much higher levels than could be earned as an instructor. Likewise, shortages of clinical instructors in the health professions increased following the storm. Second, for many individuals—especially low-income individuals—the opportunity cost of participating in training proved to be too high. Going 30 days without an income was not an option. Low-income individuals without services such as child care and transportation also experienced a much longer road to completion and employment in the post-disaster environment.

G. Workforce Training in Rural Areas

At Pearl River Community College (PRCC), two successful workforce training programs post-disaster coalesced around heavy-equipment operation and the training of electrical linemen. The two programs addressed both a short-term need—to rebuild the infrastructure—and a long-term need, as the average age of a lineman was 52 years old. To make the programs more accessible to students, PRCC developed curricula that took advantage of block scheduling. By breaking the training modules down into segments of two weeks on and two weeks off, individuals took jobs that allowed for the application of new skills on the job while in school. Many of the students who enrolled in the heavy equipment training programs were previously employed in other sectors in which their jobs simply did not return. Heavy equipment instructor Brad Ladner cited various reasons for success in the program, including previous experience and supportive services such as money for gas to drive to school.[32] The lineman training program got off the ground in 2008 and maintains a 100 percent hire rate for those who complete the course. Randy Henry, lineman instructor with PRCC, underscored the importance of having a seasoned instructor with strong ties to the industry to build successful programs.[33]

Another need met by PRCC included the development of building code classes. Scott Alsobrooks, director of workforce education at Pearl River Community College, emphasized the importance of the classes. In many of the rural counties hit hard by the storm, building codes either did not exist or existed at levels below current standards. Following the storm, many of the counties adopted the International Building Codes to regulate rebuilding efforts. Many of the local contractors were not familiar with the newly adopted building codes. PRCC's code classes—which included a test for certification—became classes in high demand in the months immediately following the storm.[34]

According to Alsobrooks, another phenomenon encountered at PRCC included the arrival of evacuees from the town of Chalmette, Louisiana. Largely from a community of shrimpers and oystermen, the Chalmette evacuees required training for employment in a completely new field. The NEG provided significant resources by way of financial aid and career counseling for people looking to retrain for jobs in the post-disaster environment. The evacuees from Chalmette took advantage of the resources, which proved to be a critical success factor in the retention of the evacuees and the successful attainment of employment post-training.

H. Women in Construction Program

Prior to the storm, opportunities for women to train for and participate in the construction fields were limited. When asked about opportunities for women to train for nontraditional employment, Julie Kuklinski, the director of the Women in Construction Program, stated that, before the storm, women in search of employment and training "were connected to low skilled positions, like a secretarial position or a nurse's aide position."[35] Her comments reflected a general view of gender bias by occupation.

Following the storm, hundreds of volunteers from all over the country flocked to the Gulf Coast to assist with the rebuilding of homes—many of whom were women. In Kuklinski's view, the visibility of women using tools and equipment to rebuild homes coupled with the immense need for workers changed perceptions about women in the trades on the Gulf Coast. "Seeing women on the job site, created a space for people to see women out there," said Kuklinski.[36]

From that phenomenon, the Women in Construction Program emerged following Hurricane Katrina. In partnership with a number of organizations, Moore Community House (located in East Biloxi), a mission agency of the United Methodist Church, conducted an assessment of whether or not a training program geared toward the needs of low-income women for employment in nontraditional occupations was viable. The interest of Moore Community House (Moore) revolved around the theory that it could connect low-income women being served by the agency to training that could prepare them for placement in well-paying jobs in the construction fields. Following the promising assessment, the program received foundation funding to launch the program. Over time, the program expanded to include both welding and construction training where women acquired nationally recognized certifications. Since the program's inception, more than 100 women have been trained and funding is in place to offer classes for the next two years.

As enthusiasm for the program grew, Moore made the intentional decision to target its program toward low-income women—many of whom were single parents and minority women. Often, the traditional training providers were not resourced to manage the barriers experienced by at-risk populations. Many of the women were homeless, without an income, and victims of domestic violence. The challenges faced by the women led the Women in Construction Program to offer a comprehensive set of support services. Support services, which include child care, transportation, mental health counseling, and financial education, were identified by Kuklinski as the single most important aspect of the success of most women in the program.[37]

The program leadership also credits the simulation of on-the-job participation requirements for program completion as critical for success. Participants are provided a stipend to assist with living costs during the training. Receipt of the stipends is tied to a rigorous attendance policy. Jonathan Gonzalez, instructor for the Women in Construction Program cited the policy as an important factor of success: "[I]f you don't show up, you don't get paid. We try to make our class as close to real world situations that we can." By creating real-world opportunities and consequences, attendance and completion rates remain high.[38]

III. Lessons Learned

Almost eight years since Hurricane Katrina made landfall in Mississippi, several clear lessons have emerged. Four lessons bear relevance for workforce developers in a post-disaster environment.

A. Do Not Waste a Crisis

Immediately following the disaster, there was a period where collaboration occurred that would not have otherwise taken place. In particular, individuals in different state agencies that shared similar goals deepened relationships. As people got to know each other across agency boundaries, trust developed and people worked together. On one level, the collegiality increased because people deeply wanted to help their fellow Mississippians who had experienced tremendous loss. On the other hand, procuring and mobilizing federal recovery resources demanded authentic partnership. In Mississippi, post–Hurricane Katrina, the colleges moved rapidly to ensure that curricula for post-storm employment were aligned tightly with employer needs. Additionally, the colleges adjusted course offerings to meet the scheduling demands of a population in recovery. As these changes were made, the whole workforce development system—from referrals at the WIN job centers to enrollment in training to placement in a job worked more efficiently than before the storm. The successes fostered a culture of collaboration and the adoption of meaningful change across the workforce system. For example, flexible schedules and employer engagement, while in place before the storm, are much more prevalent on the Gulf Coast today than they were in the summer of 2005.

B. Hierarchy of Needs Matters

In general, people will not participate in workforce training—even if it is free and for a high-quality job—if they do not have shelter, transportation, mental health access, or unmet children's needs. Such a finding underscores the need for comprehensive recovery and rebuilding programs that include resources and strategies for stabilizing families to position individuals to take advantage of the available workforce training.

C. Supportive Services Matter—Particularly for Low-Income Families

Repeatedly, workforce developers in the colleges, the employment security system and nonprofit sector highlighted the importance of support services. Within the public sector, child care and transportation were cited as critical for the recruitment and retention of individuals in training programs. In the Women in Construction Program, a more in-depth set of services—including resources to address domestic violence when necessary—was essential to the success of its training participants.

Investments in support services also remain critical within the context of moving people into training programs for in-demand careers as a means of closing employment gaps by race. In each of the three southernmost counties, the unemployment rate for African Americans is several percentage points higher than the unemployment rate for whites. The gap is particularly acute in Jackson County where the African-American unemployment rate is 18.8 percent compared with the unemployment rate for whites, which is 8.9 percent, and exceeds the state level gaps.[39] Support services provide the means for low-income families—which are more likely to be minority families—to enroll, persist in, and complete the necessary training for jobs that pay self-sufficiency wages.

D. Nonprofits Have a Role to Play—Yet Scale Remains a Challenge

As seen from this case study, nonprofit organizations—especially those with a long and continuous track record of service—can fill a niche not filled by traditional public-sector approaches. At the same time, nonprofit strategies can experience challenges in going to scale and are susceptible to the boom-and-bust cycle of philanthropy following a disaster. After five years, the Women in Construction Program served 100 people. In contrast, tens of thousands of individuals have been served by the public sector. At the same time, the Women in Construction Program figured out how to serve a population facing significant barriers to employment that the public sector is not resourced to assist. Such findings underscore the importance of including nonprofit organizations in the disaster response to ensure that the needs of populations most at risk are met.

IV. Conclusion

Following a large-scale disaster, the communities most significantly affected encounter a skills mismatch between the existing workforce and the needs of employers engaged in rebuilding. In some instances, the jobs for which residents were previously employed vanish; in others, long delays occur before businesses come back on line. It is the job of workforce developers to prepare the labor supply to adequately meet the labor demand.

In developing the response, workforce developers have the opportunity to make lasting changes. To the extent that long-standing divisions exist among agencies, disasters open a window of collaboration that public administrators can use to implement innovation and to catalyze the evolution of systems to serve the public more effectively than before a disaster. To the extent that decision making can be centralized at the state level with substantial input from the affected communities, there is an increased likelihood of investment in long-term change. Finally, in a post-disaster environment, implementing workforce development programs that serve at-risk populations requires deep investment in support services and a prolonged partnership with entities that are in communities and that have a track record of moving people from distress to stability.

Notes

1. Elizabeth McNichol, Douglas Hall, David Cooper & Vincent Palacios, Ctr. on Budget & Policy Priorities, Econ. Policy Inst., Pulling Apart: A State-by-State Analysis of Income Trends (2012), *available at* http://www.cbpp.org/cms/index.cfm?fa=view&id=3860.

2. Harry J. Holzer, *Better Skills for Better Jobs*, Issues in Sci. & Tech., Winter 2012, at 31–40, *available at* http://www.issues.org/28.2/holzer.html.

3. Office of Gov. Haley Barbour, One Year After Katrina (2006).

4. *Designated Areas: Mississippi Hurricane Katrina*, Fed. Emergency Mgmt. Agency (Aug. 29, 2005), http://www.fema.gov/disaster/1604/designated-areas.

5. ESRI, ESRI Gulf Coast Updates Methodology (2006).

6. Bureau of Labor Statistics, *The Labor Market Impact of Hurricane Katrina: An Overview*, 129 Monthly Labor Rev. August 2006, at 3–10, *available at* http://www.bls.gov/opub/mlr/2006/08/contents.htm (last visited Aug. 21, 2012).

7. Domenico Parisi, Steven Michael Grice & Jed Pressgrove, *Mississippi Business Environment Before and After Katrina: Challenges and Opportunities*, 22(2) S. Rural Soc., 64–82 (2007).

8. *Id.*

9. Holly Bell, Elissa Madden, Elisa Vinson Borah, Laura Lein & Julie Beausoleil, *Case Management with Hurricane Katrina Survivors: Perspectives of Case Managers and Supervisors*, J. Soc. Sci. Res., 2010, at 216–29.

10. Brian Sanderson, Gulf Coast Bus. Council Research Found., Mississippi Gulf Coast 3.0 (2008).

11. David Abramson, Richard Garfield & Irwin Redlener, Nat'l Ctr. for Disaster Preparedness, The Recovery Divide: Poverty and the Widening Gap Among Mississippi Children and Families Affected by Hurricane Katrina (Mailman School of Public Health Columbia Univ. 2007).

12. Miss. Dep't of Emp't Sec., Labor Market Information for Affirmative Action Programs, Jackson: MDES, 2005 and 2007.

13. Miss. State Tax Comm'n, Annual Report: Fiscal Year Ending June 30, 2005 (2005), *available at* www.dor.ms.gov/docs/stats_fy05annualreport.pdf.

14. Interview with Anna Faye Kelley-Winders, Vice President, Mississippi Gulf Coast Community College (July 2, 2012).

15. Interview with Les Range, Former Exec. Dir., Miss. Dep't of Emp't Sec. (July 7, 2012).

16. *National Emergency Grants*, U.S. Dep't of Labor Employment & Training Administration, May 3, 2012, http://www.doleta.gov/neg/admin_req.cfm (last visited May 16, 2013).

17. Interview with Les Range, *supra* note 15.

18. *Mississippi Gulf Coast Community College Rapid Response Skills Training*, Southern Growth Policies Bd., http://www.southernideabank.org/items.php?id=2640 (last visited May 16, 2012).

19. Pearl River Cmty. Coll., *Hurricane Katrina Strikes PRCC*, Dixie Drawl, Sept. 2005, at 1, 3.

20. Les Range, HURRICANE KATRINA NATIONAL EMERGENCY GRANT OVERVIEW Jackson, n.d. (unpublished report, on file with the author).

21. Bureau of Labor Statistics, *The Labor Market Impact of Hurricane Katrina: An Overview*, 129 MONTHLY LABOR REV. August 2006, at 3–10, *available at* http://www.bls.gov/opub/mlr/2006/08/contents.htm (last visited Aug. 21, 2012).

22. Interview with Rebekah Staples, Former Policy Advisor, Office of Gov. Haley Barbour (June 19, 2012).

23. Department of Labor Employment and Training Administration Workforce Investment Act: National Emergency Grants—Application Procedures; Notice, 69 Fed. Reg. no. 81, at 23062 (2004).

24. Yolanda Boone, Jackson, Mississippi Dep't of Employment Security, Two Years after Katrina Progress Report (2007) (unpublished).

25. Interview with Gary Lukens, Workforce Area Dir., Twin Districts (May 17, 2012).

26. Interview with Yolanda Boone, Manager, Grants Mgmt. Office Miss. Dep't of Emp't Sec. (May 7, 2012).

27. *Id.*

28. *Id.*

29. Interview with Kelley-Winders, *supra* note 14.

30. Boone, *supra* note 24.

31. Interview with Kelley-Winders, *supra* note 14.

32. Interview with Brad Ladner, Instructor of Constr. Equip., Pearl River Cmty. Coll. (June 14, 2012).

33. Interview with Randy Henry, Lineman Instructor, Pearl River Community College (June 14, 2012).

34. Interview with Scott Alsobrooks, Dir. of Workforce Educ., Pearl River Cmty. Coll. (June 14, 2012).

35. Interview with Julie Kuklinski, Dir., Moore Community House (Nov. 14, 2012).

36. *Id.*

37. *Id.*

38. Interview with Jonathan Gonzalez, Instructor, Moore Community House (Nov. 14, 2012).

39. MISS. DEP'T OF EMP'T SEC., LABOR MARKET INFORMATION FOR AFFIRMATIVE ACTION PROGRAMS (2012), *available at* http://mdes.ms.gov/media/8285/affact2012_WEB.pdf (last visited May 16, 2013).

Resources

The following section is designed to provide practitioners with both useful tools and information for further reading. The resources were suggested primarily by the chapter authors. They are organized similar to the structure of the table of contents, with a focus first on the framework for recovery and then topical attention to affordable housing and community economic development considerations that arise in a post-disaster setting. Much like the book as whole, it provides information about lessons learned from previous disasters and guidance in implementing those lessons in preparation for and response to the next one. The end of this section presents resources specific to six select disasters representing the range and variety of natural and human-made disasters covered in this book.

FEDERAL GOVERNMENT RESOURCES

Tools You Can Use

- Ready.gov, http://www.ready.gov —National public service advertising campaign managed by FEMA; designed to educate and empower Americans to prepare for and respond to emergencies including natural and human-made disasters.

- DisasterAssistance.gov, http://www.disasterassistance.gov—Federal government portal providing centralized information on how individuals might be able to get help from the U.S. government before, during, and after a disaster.
- FEMA Housing Portal, http://1.usa.gov/YkKDPb—Helps individuals and families who have been displaced by a disaster find a place to live.
- RestoreYourEconomy.org, http://www.restoreyoureconomy.org—Federal government portal providing "resources and best practice information for public and private stakeholders seeking to rebuild their local economies after a major disaster as well as assisting the business community to prepare for a disaster."
- Financial Fraud Enforcement Task Force, http://www.stopfraud.gov/.

Consumer Financial Protection Bureau

- Statement on Supervisory Practices Regarding Financial Institutions and Borrowers Affected by Hurricane Sandy, http://1.usa.gov/ZpKqdB.
- *Protecting and Rebuilding Your Finances after a Disaster*, http://1.usa.gov/WBkVL2.
- *Avoiding Loan Scams after a Natural Disaster*, http://1.usa.gov/15EUZyN.
- *How Do I Recognize and Prevent against Fraud after a Natural Disaster?*, http://1.usa.gov/W8qPCg.

Federal Emergency Management Agency (FEMA)

- National Disaster Recovery Framework, http://1.usa.gov/13MBiGJ.
- Presidential Disaster Declarations:
  - By State/Tribal Government and Year, http://www.fema.gov/disasters.
  - Disaster Declaration Process, http://www.fema.gov/declaration-process.
  - Disaster Aid Programs, http://1.usa.gov/145niZc.
  - Policies and Guidance, http://1.usa.gov/Z7WZtd.
- Public Assistance Grants:
  - Overview, http://1.usa.gov/13MzGwF.
- Public Assistance Applicant Handbook, FEMA P-323, http://1.usa.gov/10o28jX.
- Guidance to State Administrative Agencies to Expedite the Expenditure of Certain DHS/FEMA Grant Funding, http://1.usa.gov/16HlbKt.
- *Long Term Recovery*, http://1.usa.gov/11bl1ak.
- *Office of Disability Integration and Coordination*, http://1.usa.gov/ZpGhWW.

- Midwest Floods of 2008 in Iowa and Wisconsin, http://1.usa.gov/YSym7j.
- Hurricane Sandy Recovery Resources, http://www.fema.gov/hurricane-sandy.
- Photo Library (searchable by date, disaster, geography), http://www.fema.gov/photolibrary.

Internal Revenue Service

- *Around the Nation* (provides IRS news specific to local areas, primarily disaster relief, or tax provisions that affect certain states), http://1.usa.gov/15UQyQz.
- Individuals:
  - *Tax Relief in Disaster Situations*, http://1.usa.gov/WQsJsD.
- Small Businesses:
  - Disaster Assistance Hotline, 1-866-562-5227.
  - *Disaster Assistance and Emergency Relief for Individuals and Businesses*, http://1.usa.gov/ZLE8VO.
  - *Topic 515—Casualty, Disaster, and Theft Losses (Including Federally Declared Disaster Areas)*, http://1.usa.gov/13MD0YJ.
  - *Disaster Assistance Self-Study: Payments/Benefits and Tax Returns*, http://1.usa.gov/13OaiqT.
  - *Gulf Oil Spill: Questions and Answers*, http://1.usa.gov/XTdOfN.
- Nonprofit Organizations:
  - IRS Webinar: Starting and Operating Charities for Disaster Relief, http://1.usa.gov/YiFs5z.
  - Postponement of Deadline for Transitional Relief Under Notice 2011-43 for Certain Small Organizations Affected by Hurricane Sandy, Notice 2012-71, http://1.usa.gov/WQm15W.
  - Published Guidance for Charities about Disaster Relief, http://1.usa.gov/YiO4sW.
- Low-Income Housing Tax Credit:
  - Low-Income Housing Credit Disaster Relief for Hurricane Sandy, Notice 2012-68, http://1.usa.gov/ZLx6Am.
  - For compilation of IRS LIHTC disaster-related rules, guidance, and relief: National Council of State Housing Agencies Disaster Relief Center, http://bit.ly/XTefqD.
- Tax-Exempt Bonds:
  - Current Refundings of Tax-Exempt Bonds in Certain Disaster Relief Bond Programs, Notice 2012-3, http://1.usa.gov/112iQWx.
  - Tax-Exempt Bonds in Certain Disaster Areas, Notice 2010-10, http://1.usa.gov/YIZhSL.

- Time for performing certain acts postponed by reason of service in a combat zone or a presidentially declared disaster, Rev. Proc. 2002–71, page 890, http://1.usa.gov/15fmDAj.

Small Business Administration (SBA)

- List of SBA Disaster Recovery resources: http://1.usa.gov/XHLO0T.
- Fact Sheet for SBA post-disaster aid: http://1.usa.gov/WdEN4N.
- Business Physical Disaster Loans: http://1.usa.gov/13YwLkG.
- Economic Injury Loans: http://1.usa.gov/12DX9kt.
- Military Reservist Economic Injury Loan: http://1.usa.gov/WMZ7MT.
- Disaster Loan:
  - Overview: http://1.usa.gov/10o8uji.
  - Application: disasterloan.sba.gov.
- Disaster Preparedness and Recovery Plan: http://1.usa.gov/Yf4oLf.
- BP Oil Spill, http://1.usa.gov/WDzvRl.
- SBA Searchable list of small business resource centers by state, http://1.usa.gov/YSH4Cp.

U.S. Department of Agriculture

- USDA Disaster Declarations in response to drought, http://1.usa.gov/Z7XcN3.
- Disaster and Drought response and tracking: http://1.usa.gov/XT2Yqd.
- Disaster Assistance Programs, http://1.usa.gov/XSVGmk.
  - Emergency Farm Loans, http://1.usa.gov/104HLd2.
  - Disaster Debt Set-Aside Program, http://1.usa.gov/111vZiF.
  - Emergency Conservation Program for damaged farmland, http://1.usa.gov/WxjVFC.
  - Many others available at Disaster Assistance Program link above.
- Funding Distribution Maps by State for Select Programs, http://1.usa.gov/Wuz2kw.
  - Spreadsheets of distribution data by State and County, http://1.usa.gov/XSVGmk (scroll to bottom).
- Disaster Assistance Eligibility Tool, http://1.usa.gov/132ygza.
- Rural Development Handbook 2-3560, Section 6: Special Procedures for Declared Disasters, http://1.usa.gov/142i3sY.
- Multi-Family Housing Rentals search for USDA rental housing, http://1.usa.gov/ZTvOEW.
- BP Gulf Oil Spill—USDA Response, http://1.usa.gov/ZYbtON.

U.S. Department of Commerce Economic Development Administration

- RestoreYourEconomy.org (provides resources and best practice information for public and private stakeholders seeking to rebuild their local economies after a major disaster as well as assisting the business community to prepare for a disaster).
- Disaster Recovery Overview, http://1.usa.gov/WQA2AC.
- FY 2012 Disaster Relief Opportunity Funds, http://1.usa.gov/105MEmh.
- EDA Disaster Recovery Webinar (Aug. 2, 2012), http://bit.ly/15UXnBs.

U.S. Department of Housing and Urban Development (HUD)

- Disaster Recovery Tool Kit, http://bit.ly/ZLol9n.
- HUD Funding for Non-Presidentially Declared Natural Disasters, PIH Notice 2010-14, http://1.usa.gov/WTS27N.
- HUD Announces Foreclosure Protection for Displaced Storm Victims (this is Maryland example, but similar announcements made for other disaster-declared states) (Nov. 26, 2012), http://1.usa.gov/ZBWJVX.
- HUD Interests Affected by Hurricane Sandy, Interactive Map, http://bit.ly/WQkQn7.
- Hurricane Sandy Recovery Resources, http://1.usa.gov/WxvxIP.
- National Housing Locator System (NHLS) (built as lessons learned from Hurricane Katrina and other disasters, NHLS is a searchable database of available rental housing and available government-owned single-family homes nationwide), https://hudapps.hud.gov/nhls/.

Community Development Block Grants-Disaster Recovery (CDBG-DR)

- Overview, http://1.usa.gov/142aDpI.
- HUD Releases Model Programs for Use by Communities Seeking CDBG-DR Funding (2013), http://1.usa.gov/16y5RzL.
- Allocations, Common Application, Waivers, and Alternative Requirements for Grantees Receiving CDBG-Disaster Recovery Funds in Response to Hurricane Sandy, 78 Fed. Reg. 14329–49, No. 43 (Mar. 5, 2013) http://1.usa.gov/YB5Qnl.
- CDBG Training (a series of eight webinars), http://1.usa.gov/10wwHaW.
- CDBG Recipients by state, http://1.usa.gov/16hO4gh.

Federal Housing Administration (FHA)

- Single Family:
  - Guidance for FHA-Approved Mortgagees Originating and Servicing Mortgages in Presidentially-Declared Major Disaster Areas, Mortgagee Letter 2012-23 (Nov. 16, 2012), http://1.usa.gov/104Z0ea.
  - Disaster Relief Options for FHA Homeowners, http://1.usa.gov/1425Zru.
  - HUD Homes and Other Options Available in Presidentially-Declared Disaster Areas, http://1.usa.gov/WQhC2L.
  - Mortgage Insurance for Disaster Victims Section 203(h), http://1.usa.gov/14260vQ.
  - 203k Rehabilitation Mortgage Insurance, http://1.usa.gov/XT42KL.
  - Title 1 Home Improvement Loans, http://1.usa.gov/YB1H2P.
- Multifamily:
  - Hurricane Sandy/Superstorm Response—Expedited Processing for FHA Multifamily Mortgage Insurance Applications, Notice H 13-05 (Feb. 12, 2013), http://1.usa.gov/YB1I6E.
  - HUD Handbook 4350.1, Chapter 38, Multifamily Asset Management and Project Servicing, Multifamily Emergency/Disaster Guidance, http://1.usa.gov/YIzp9C.
  - Special procedures memorandum regarding FHA Multifamily Mortgage Insurance Processing for the New Orleans Program Center Office (2007), http://1.usa.gov/XT4Or6.
- Multifamily Servicing Policies to Assist Victims of Presidentially-Declared Disasters, Mortgagee Letter 2004-38 (Sept. 22, 2004), http://1.usa.gov/116X4Vn.

HOME

- HOME Program Waivers Related to Hurricane Sandy, http://1.usa.gov/1173i7u.

Office of Public and Indian Housing

- Public and Indian Housing Hurricane Recovery Resources, http://1.usa.gov/111O1B6.
- Vouchers:
  - Disaster Voucher Program (Hurricanes Katrina and Rita), http://1.usa.gov/Yizdig.
  - 2007 HUD and FEMA Interagency Agreement, http://1.usa.gov/WVygsJ.

- Disaster Housing Recovery Assistance Program, http://1.usa.gov/1425JZR.
- Disaster Housing Assistance Program—Ike (DHAP-Ike), http://1.usa.gov/Z83BrJ.
- Buildings:
  - Demolition/Disposition Technical Assistance Package, http://1.usa.gov/Zai0pg.
  - Demolition for an Accidental Loss, http://1.usa.gov/15mCm2e.
- Rental Assistance Demonstration, http://1.usa.gov/13MAz8F.
- Choice Neighborhoods, http://1.usa.gov/Y1agYm.

Office of Fair Housing and Equal Opportunity

- DISASTER TOOLKIT (2007), http://1.usa.gov/ZkncrL.
- Guidance to Allow Housing for Older Persons to Admit Evacuees (Nov. 6, 2012), http://1.usa.gov/WxviNX.
  - Final Rule, Equal Access to Housing in HUD Programs—Regardless of Sexual Orientation or Gender Identity, No. FR 5359-F-02 (2012), http://1.usa.gov/YIGuap.
- Fair Housing Information for Disaster Survivors, http://1.usa.gov/WQkLzJ.
  - File a Housing Discrimination Complaint, 1-800-669-9777, http://1.usa.gov/142ae6A.

Section 3 of the HUD Act of 1968

- Notice to Submit Form HUD-60002 on Section 3 Hiring and Contracting (2009), http://bit.ly/VV8BUL.
- Annual Section 3 Summary Reporting Requirements: Technical Assistance on Form HUD-60002, http://1.usa.gov/YN53mb.
- Understanding the Basics of Section 3 and Vicinity Hiring Preferences for the NSP Program (2011), http://bit.ly/Ykfbjl.
- The National Housing Law Project, *An Advocate's Guide to the HUD Section 3 Program* (2009), http://bit.ly/Y1dJ9u.

U.S. Department of Justice

- National Center for Disaster Fraud, http://1.usa.gov/YkUlU2.
- Antitrust Division—Disaster Recovery (reporting anticompetitive behavior following disaster in violation of the Antitrust Act, e.g., bid rigging, price fixing, customer or market allocation), http://1.usa.gov/WMYaUC.

- Joint guidance on antitrust activity post–Hurricanes Katrina and Rita, http://1.usa.gov/ZGRrXz.
- Emergency Authorization for Disaster Relief (portal for requesting authorization to quickly move controlled substances in response to domestic or international disaster relief efforts), http://1.usa.gov/Xei6dZ.
- An Americans with Disabilities Act Guide for Local Governments: Making Community Emergency Preparedness and Response Programs Accessible to People with Disabilities, http://www.ada.gov/emergencyprepguide.htm.

U.S. Department of Labor

- List of Department of Labor's Disaster Recovery Resources, http://1.usa.gov/Z4MvuN.
- National Emergency Grants, http://www.doleta.gov/neg.
- Disaster Unemployment Assistance, http://1.usa.gov/Yhov8r.
- Severe Storm and Flood Recovery Assistance, http://1.usa.gov/XefAVh.
- Fact Sheet: Worker Adjustment and Retraining Notification Act—Katrina Natural Disaster (2005), http://1.usa.gov/YhnKME.
- OSHA, Hurricane Preparedness, http://1.usa.gov/ZdiyM7.
- OSHA, Keeping Workers Safe During Hurricane Sandy Cleanup and Recovery, http://1.usa.gov/16yDt0q.
- DOL Responds in the Gulf, http://1.usa.gov/ZbCEDx.

TRIBAL GOVERNMENTS

- Statements in support of Sandy Recovery Improvement Act of 2013, which included an amendment to the Stafford Act to clearly reflect federally recognized tribal governments' status as sovereign nations and to directly request federal disaster assistance for the impacts within their own borders, http://www.fema.gov/tribal.
- National Congress of American Indians, http://www.ncai.org.
    - Tribe Directory (searchable by geography), http://www.ncai.org/tribal-directory.
- FEMA Tribal Affairs: http://www.fema.gov/tribal.
    - Tribal Homeland Security Grant Program, http://1.usa.gov/13OcbDX.
    - Executive Order 13175, Consultation and Coordination with Indian Tribal Governments (2000), http://1.usa.gov/WS6ClI.
- Tribal Emergency Management Association, http://itema.org.
- Northwest Tribal Emergency Management Council, http://www.nwtemc.org.
- National Tribal Emergency Management Council, http://ntemc.org.

- Inter Tribal Long Term Recovery Foundation, http://itltrf.org.
- Heritage Preservation, Getting Ready in Indian Country: Emergency Preparedness and Response for Native American Cultural Resources, http://bit.ly/15WFSRe.
- United South and Eastern Tribes, Inc., http://www.usetinc.org.
  - Tribal Emergency Relief Fund (Hurricane Sandy), http://bit.ly/135MTSj.

EVALUATIONS OF FEDERAL SUPPORT POST-DISASTER

- U.S. GOV'T ACCOUNTABILITY OFFICE, GAO/RCED-98-1, GUIDANCE NEEDED FOR FEMA'S "FAST TRACK" HOUSING ASSISTANCE PROCESS (1997), http://1.usa.gov/148wPPe.
- U.S. GOV'T ACCOUNTABILITY OFFICE, GAO-03-385, SMALL BUSINESS ADMINISTRATION: RESPONSE TO SEPTEMBER 11 VICTIMS & PERFORMANCE MEASURES FOR DISASTER LENDING (2003), http://1.usa.gov/XabPFY.
- U.S. GOV'T ACCOUNTABILITY OFFICE, GAO-03-926, DISASTER ASSISTANCE: INFORMATION ON FEMA'S POST 9/11 PUBLIC ASSISTANCE TO NEW YORK CITY (2003), http://1.usa.gov/VUT5sb.
- U.S. GOV'T ACCOUNTABILITY OFFICE, GAO-04-72, SEPTEMBER 11: OVERVIEW OF FEDERAL DISASTER ASSISTANCE TO THE NEW YORK CITY AREA (2003), http://1.usa.gov/ZsGwE5.
- U.S. DEP'T OF HOUS. & URBAN DEV., OFFICE OF INSPECTOR GENERAL, SURVEY OF HUD'S ADMINISTRATION OF SECTION 3 OF THE HUD ACT OF 1968 (Audit Case No. 2003-KC-0001) (2003), http://bit.ly/Yk7B8p.
- NYC OFFICE OF THE COMPTROLLER, 9/11 THREE YEARS LATER: SECURING THE FEDERAL PLEDGE (2004), http://bit.ly/16hEQAp.
- U.S. DEP'T OF HOUS. & URBAN DEV., CURRENT HOUSING UNIT DAMAGE ESTIMATES: HURRICANES KATRINA, RITA, AND WILMA (2005), http://bit.ly/Yk602l.
- U.S. DEP'T OF HOUS. & URBAN DEV., OFFICE OF POLICY DEVELOPMENT AND RESEARCH, THE IMPACT OF HURRICANES KATRINA, RITA, AND WILMA ON THE GULF COAST HOUSING STOCK (2006), http://bit.ly/VUWiYH.
- MATT FELLOWES & AMY LIU, BROOKINGS INSTITUTION, FEDERAL ALLOCATIONS IN RESPONSE TO KATRINA, RITA AND WILMA: AN UPDATE (2006), http://bit.ly/WdtQQD.
- BRENDA MUÑIZ, NATIONAL COUNCIL OF LA RAZA, IN THE EYE OF THE STORM: HOW THE GOVERNMENT AND PRIVATE RESPONSE TO HURRICANE KATRINA FAILED LATINOS (2006), http://bit.ly/10wlkzR.
- U.S. DEP'T OF LABOR, *The Labor Market Impact of Hurricane Katrina: An Overview*, MONTHLY LABOR REV. (2006), http://1.usa.gov/XahOdS.
- U.S. GOV'T ACCOUNTABILITY OFFICE, GAO-06-870, NATIONAL EMERGENCY GRANTS: LABOR HAS IMPROVED ITS GRANT AWARD TIMELINESS AND

DATA COLLECTION, BUT FURTHER STEPS CAN IMPROVE PROCESS (2006), http://1.usa.gov/10Madx9.

- U.S. GOV'T ACCOUNTABILITY OFFICE, GAO-07-574T, GULF COAST REBUILDING: PRELIMINARY OBSERVATIONS ON PROGRESS TO DATE AND CHALLENGES FOR THE FUTURE (2007), http://1.usa.gov/13MxKo4.
- U.S. GOV'T ACCOUNTABILITY OFFICE, GAO-08-88, DISASTER ASSISTANCE: BETTER PLANNING NEEDED FOR HOUSING VICTIMS OF CATASTROPHIC DISASTERS (2007), http://1.usa.gov/YATyeJ.
- *Federal Housing Response to Hurricane Katrina, Hearing Before the Comm. on Fin. Servs. of the H.R.* (Serial No. 110-1, 2007), http://1.usa.gov/10wnwrf.
- *Financial Services Committee Hearing to Examine Federal Housing Response to Hurricane Katrina Before the H.R.* (2007) (testimony of Judith Browne Dianis, Advancement Project), http://1.usa.gov/WTKvWt.
- U.S. GOV'T ACCOUNTABILITY OFFICE, GAO-07-88, DISASTER ASSISTANCE: BETTER PLANNING NEEDED FOR HOUSING VICTIMS OF CATASTROPHIC DISASTERS (2007), http://1.usa.gov/YATyeJ.
- ANNIE CLARK & KALIMA ROSE, POLICYLINK, BRINGING LOUISIANA RENTERS HOME: AN EVALUATION OF THE 2006–2007 GULF OPPORTUNITY ZONE RENTAL HOUSING RESTORATION PROGRAM (2007), http://bit.ly/18IakA1.
- KALIMA ROSE ET AL., POLICYLINK, LONG WAY HOME: THE STATE OF HOUSING RECOVERY IN LOUISIANA 2008 (2008), http://bit.ly/X1sFky.
- U.S. GOV'T ACCOUNTABILITY OFFICE, GAO-08-1120, DISASTER RECOVERY: PAST EXPERIENCES OFFER INSIGHTS FOR RECOVERING FROM HURRICANES IKE AND GUSTAV AND OTHER RECENT NATURAL DISASTERS (2008), http://1.usa.gov/14HBgfz.
- U.S. SENATE COMM. ON HOMELAND SEC. AND GOVERNMENTAL AFFAIRS, FAR FROM HOME: DEFICIENCIES IN FEDERAL DISASTER HOUSING ASSISTANCE AFTER HURRICANES KATRINA AND RITA AND RECOMMENDATIONS FOR IMPROVEMENT (2009), http://bit.ly/15EOeNq.
- *The Role of the Community Development Block Grant Program in Disaster Recovery Before the U.S. S. Ad Hoc Comm. on Disaster Recovery* (2009) (testimony of Dominique Duval-Diop, PolicyLink), http://bit.ly/12KeNTD.
- *U.S. H.R. Comm. on Fin. Servs. Subcomm. Housing & Cmty. Opportunity Field Hearing on the Implementation of the Road Home Program Four Years After Hurricane Katrina* (2009) (testimony of Dominique Duval-Diop, PolicyLink), http://bit.ly/WjbP3w.
- U.S. DEP'T OF AGRIC., FOOD AND NUTRITION SERV., FNS 2008 AND 2009 DISASTER LESSONS LEARNED AND BEST PRACTICES REPORT (2009), http://1.usa.gov/ZYdMBo.
- EUGENE BOYD, CONG. RESEARCH SERV., RL-33330, COMMUNITY DEVELOPMENT BLOCK GRANT FUNDS IN DISASTER RELIEF AND RECOVERY (2010), http://bit.ly/Y6fHEC.

- CONG. RESEARCH SERV., R40810, FEMA DISASTER HOUSING: FROM SHELTERING TO PERMANENT HOUSING (2010), http://bit.ly/YCV7bT.
- U.S. SMALL BUS. ADMIN., OFFICE OF THE INSPECTOR GENERAL, NO. 10-13, SBA'S ROLE IN ADDRESSING DUPLICATION OF BENEFITS BETWEEN SBA DISASTER LOANS AND COMMUNITY DEVELOPMENT BLOCK GRANTS (2010), http://1.usa.gov/146405K.
- NYC INDEP. BUDGET OFFICE, FEDERAL AID 10 YEARS AFTER WORLD TRADE CENTER ATTACK (2011), http://bit.ly/pOoIjb.
- ENTERPRISE CORP., MEASURING THE RESPONSE TO HURRICANE SANDY: FEMA ASSISTANCE ANALYSIS (2013), http://bit.ly/ZiB4Uf.

INTERNATIONAL HUMAN RIGHTS LAW

Tools You Can Use

- Walter Kälin, *Guiding Principles on Internal Displacement Annotations*, 38 STUD. IN TRANSNAT'L LEGAL POL'Y (2000), http://bit.ly/YbWHCq.
- The Pinheiro Principles: United Nations Principles on Housing and Property Restitution for Refugees and Displaced Persons (2005), http://bit.ly/11rHs8S.
- U.S. HUMAN RIGHTS NETWORK, HURRICANE KATRINA AND VIOLATIONS OF ICCPR ARTICLES 6 AND 26: A RESPONSE TO THE THIRD PERIODIC REPORT OF THE UNITED STATES OF AMERICA (2006), http://bit.ly/XvYWGl.
- ADVOCATES FOR ENVTL. HUMAN RIGHTS, *U.S. Disaster Response Law vs. Human Rights Standards on Internal Displacement*, http://bit.ly/YsFhAP.
- Eric Tars, Who Knows What Lurks in the Hearts of Human Rights Violators? The Shadow (Reporter) Knows, *Human Rights Shadow Reporting: A Strategic Tool for Domestic Justice*, 42 CLEARINGHOUSE REV. 475, Jan.-Feb. 2009, http://bit.ly/WcPzJB.
- NAT'L LAW CTR. ON HOMELESSNESS & POVERTY, HOUSING RIGHTS FOR ALL: PROMOTING AND DEFENDING HOUSING RIGHTS IN THE UNITED STATES (2011), http://bit.ly/X8nZJJ.

For Further Reading

- American Society of International Law, www.asil.org.
- Brookings-LSE Project on Internal Displacement, http://bit.ly/XTiu5q.
- United Nations, Economic Commission for Latin America and the Caribbean, *The Impact of Disaster on Women*, *in* HANDBOOK FOR ESTIMATING THE SOCIO-ECONOMIC AND ENVIRONMENTAL EFFECTS OF DISASTERS (2003), http://bit.ly/WeRJav.

- Advocates for Envtl. Human Rights, *U.S. Disaster Response Law vs. Human Rights Standards on Internal Displacement*, http://bit.ly/YsFhAP.
- Representative of the Secretary-General, *Report on the Guiding Principles on Internal Displacement, delivered to the Commission on Human Rights*, U.N. Doc. E/CN.4/1998/53/Add.2 (1998), http://bit.ly/10P9Jfs.
- U.S. Agency for Int'l Dev., PD-ACA-558, USAID Assistance to Internally Displaced Persons Policy (2004), http://1.usa.gov/ZJkCdN.
- Miloon Kothari, the United Nations Special Rapporteur on Adequate Housing, and Gay McDougall, the U.N. Independent Expert on Minority Issues, Statement on the Demolition of Public Housing in New Orleans (2008), http://bit.ly/WofnkX.
- *Special Issue on 10 Years of the Guiding Principles on Internal Displacement*, Forced Migration Rev. (2008), http://bit.ly/Z3IeL5.
- Advisory Grp. on Forced Evictions, Mission Report to New Orleans, U.S. (2009), http://bit.ly/YbNWYW.
- Ctr. for Constitutional Rights and Loyola Univ. of New Orleans Coll. of Law, International Human Rights Obligations and Post-Katrina Housing Policies (2009), http://bit.ly/YalWrW.
- Elizabeth Ferris et al., From Responsibility to Response: Assessing National Approaches to Internal Displacement (2011), http://bit.ly/X8bIox.

EQUITABLE RECOVERY

Tools You Can Use

- PolicyLink, www.policylink.org.
  - Equitable Development Toolkit, http://bit.ly/ZhcUYl.
  - Safety, Growth, and Equity: Infrastructure Policies that Promote Opportunity and Inclusion (2006), http://bit.ly/10ylBi3.
  - Victor Rubin, Economic Development for the State and Its Regions in the Wake of the Storms (2006), http://bit.ly/ZvNpRV.
  - Investing in Equitable Recovery: Philanthropy Confronts the Historic Neglect of the Gulf Coast (2007), http://bit.ly/13Qq1Fq.
  - Kalima Rose et al., Nonprofits Filling the Gaps in Recovery: New Orleans Nonprofits Address Voids Left by Housing Recovery Programs (2008), http://bit.ly/YWZWgd.
  - New Orleans at Five: Reviewing Key Reforms After Hurricane Katrina (2010), http://bit.ly/10ylBi3.
  - One Gulf, Resilient Gulf: A Plan for Coastal Community Recovery (2010), http://bit.ly/Xlmc9R.

- Sarah Treuhaft et al., Fostering Equitable Foreclosure Recovery (2012), http://bit.ly/Yg1qW0.

For Further Reading

Assessment of Vulnerability

- Ctr. for Health Equality, Publications Addressing Emergency Preparedness for Racially and Ethnically Diverse Communities (Drexel Univ. 2007), http://bit.ly/ZbOteQ.
- Sharona Hoffman, *Preparing for Disaster: Protecting the Most Vulnerable in Emergencies*, 42 U.C. Davis L. Rev. 1491 (2009), http://bit.ly/Ylhpir.
- Nat'l Org. on Disability, Report on Special Needs Assessment for Katrina Evacuees (SNAKE) Project, http://bit.ly/dX5EGG.

Impact of Inequalities

- There Is No Such Thing as a Natural Disaster: Race, Class, and Hurricane Katrina (Charles Hartman & Gregory D. Squires eds., 2006).
- Manuel Pastor, Robert D. Bullard, James K. Boyce, Alice Fothergill, Rachel Morello-Frosch & Beverly Wright, In the Wake of the Storm: Environment, Disaster, and Race after Katrina (2006).
- NAACP, Housing in New Orleans: One Year After Katrina: Policy Recommendations for Equitable Rebuilding (2006), http://bit.ly/ZvQP6U.
- Lex Friedan, Nat'l Council on Disability, The Needs of People with Psychiatric Disabilities During and After Hurricanes Katrina and Rita: Position Paper and Recommendations (2006), http://1.usa.gov/XALE9i.
- Rebecca A. Clark, Lynn Besch, Mary Murphy, Jan Vick, Colin Gurd, Stephanie Broyles & Kathleen Lincoln, *Six Months Later: The Effect of Hurricane Katrina on Health Care for Persons Living with HIV/AIDS in New Orleans*, AIDS Care, Vol. 18 S59–S61 (2006).
- David Abramson, Richard Garfield & Irwin Redlener, The Recovery Divide: Poverty and the Widening Gap Among Mississippi Children and Families Affected by Hurricane Katrina (2007), http://bit.ly/13WFxjs.
- Enterprise Corp., Measuring the Response to Hurricane Sandy: FEMA Assistance Analysis (2013), http://bit.ly/ZiB4Uf.

Community Resilience Measurements

- Natural Hazards Research and Application Information Center:
  - Holistic Disaster Recovery: Ideas for Building Sustainability After a Natural Disaster (2005), http://bit.ly/10qhh4l.

    - Chapter 6: *Promoting Social and Intergenerational Equity during Disaster Recovery*, http://bit.ly/ZBpXnx.
    - Chapter 8: *Incorporating Disaster Resilience into Disaster Recovery*, http://bit.ly/YOMldT.
- Fran H. Norris et al., *Community Resilience as a Metaphor, Theory, Set of Capacities, and Strategy for Disaster Readiness*, 41 AM. J. COMMUNITY PSYCHOL. (2008), http://bit.ly/WAqys1.
- DeAnne Hilfinger Messias & Elaine Lacy, *Katrina Related Health Concerns of Latino Survivors and Evacuees*, 18.2 J. of Health Care for Poor & Underserved 443 (2007).
- JOHN TWIGG, U.K. DEP'T FOR INT'L DEV., CHARACTERISTICS OF A DISASTER-RESILIENT COMMUNITY: A GUIDANCE NOTE (2007), http://bit.ly/14K8hYl.
- Lung Vu, Carl L. Bankston III, Mai Do & Mark J. VanLandingham, *Evacuation and Return of Vietnamese New Orleanians Affected by Hurricane Katrina*, 22 ORG. & ENV'T, 422–36 (2009).
- RESILIENCE AND OPPORTUNITY: LESSONS FROM THE U.S. GULF COAST AFTER KATRINA AND RITA (Roland Anglin, Amy Liu, Richard Mizelle & Allison Plyer eds., 2011).
- Robert B. Olshansky, Laurie A. Johnson & Kenneth C. Topping, *Rebuilding Communities Following Disasters: Lessons from Kobe and Los Angeles*, 32 BUILT ENV'T 354, http://bit.ly/10yvX5o.
- DISPLACED: LIFE IN THE KATRINA DIASPORA (Lori Peck & Lynn Weber eds., 2012).
- Shannon Van Zandt et al., *Mapping Social Vulnerability to Enhance Housing and Neighborhood Resilience*, 22 HOUSING POL'Y DEBATE (2012).

STATE GOVERNMENT RESOURCES

- National Council of State Housing Agencies, Disaster Relief Resource Center, http://bit.ly/XTefqD.
- State Agencies and Offices of Emergency Management Offices, http://1.usa.gov/132Ycuy.
- Emergency Management Assistance Compact, www.emac.org.
- Model Intrastate Mutual Aid Legislation, http://bit.ly/117BDDu.
- For guidance on the Presidential Disaster Declaration process, see above section "Federal Government Resources—FEMA."

LOCAL GOVERNMENT RESOURCES

- FEMA National Disaster Recovery Framework, Local Disaster Recovery Managers Responsibilities (2011), http://1.usa.gov/XlGv1j.

- Lessons Learned Information Sharing (LLIS.gov), "State and Local Government Continuity of Operations Planning: Elements of a Continuity of Operations Plan," http://bit.ly/XRJjZY.
- National Association of Regional Councils, www.narc.org.
- National Association of Counties, Lessons Learned: Everything You'll Want to Know about Disaster Recovery, http://bit.ly/1448M3w.
- Association of Bay Area Governments, Recovery Toolkit for Local Governments, http://bit.ly/14473v3.
- Am. Planners Ass'n, A Planner's Toolkit: Planning for Post-Disaster Recovery and Reconstruction, http://bit.ly/XVdxcu.
- DANA DOUGHTY, PREPARING NEIGHBORHOODS FOR DISASTER: AN ANALYSIS OF SMART PRACTICES IN THE BAY AREA AND RECOMMENDATIONS FOR THE CITY OF HAYWARD (2012), http://bit.ly/YUczsf.
- U.S. DEP'T OF JUSTICE, AN AMERICANS WITH DISABILITIES ACT GUIDE FOR LOCAL GOVERNMENTS: MAKING COMMUNITY EMERGENCY PREPAREDNESS AND RESPONSE PROGRAMS ACCESSIBLE TO PEOPLE WITH DISABILITIES (2008), http://www.ada.gov/emergencyprepguide.htm.
- RICHARD C. WILSON, CITY MANAGER OF SANTA CRUZ, THE LOMA PRIETA QUAKE: WHAT ONE CITY LEARNED (1991).
- George C Mader, *Recovery, Mitigation, and Planning*, *in* PRACTICAL LESSONS FROM THE LOMA PRIETA EARTHQUAKE (1994), http://bit.ly/ZafRbc.
- For more information on funding assistance available to local governments, see above resources on FEMA Public Assistance Grants and HUD CDBG-DR Grants.
- For information on fair housing obligations, see below resource sections "Fair Housing" and "2008 Texas Hurricanes."

NONPROFIT AND RELIGIOUS ORGANIZATIONS

(See additional resources in section "Federal Government Resources—Internal Revenue Service.")

- American Bar Association Young Lawyers Division Disaster Legal Hotlines, http://bit.ly/ZbDJLy.
- American Red Cross, www.redcross.org.
- Citizen Corp, www.citizencorps.gov.
- Federal Alliance for Safe Homes, www.flash.org.
- Guidestar, www.guidestar.org.
- Habitat for Humanity, www.habitat.org.
- National Disaster Legal Aid, http://www.disasterlegalaid.org.
- National Voluntary Organizations Active in Disaster, www.nvoad.org.
- NeighborWorks, http://www.nw.org/network.
- Nonprofit Risk Management Center, www.nonprofitrisk.org.

- Public Entity Risk Institute, www.riskinstitute.org/peri.
- PolicyLink:
  - INVESTING IN EQUITABLE RECOVERY: PHILANTHROPY CONFRONTS THE HISTORIC NEGLECT OF THE GULF COAST (2007), http://bit.ly/13Qq1Fq.
  - KALIMA ROSE ET AL., FILLING THE GAPS IN RECOVERY: NEW ORLEANS NONPROFITS ADDRESS VOIDS LEFT BY HOUSING RECOVERY PROGRAMS (2008), http://bit.ly/YWZWgd.
- Woody Widrow, Robert O. Zdenek & Ralph Scott, Rebuilding Communities, RESTORING FAMILIES: ROLES FOR CBDOS IS THE AFTERMATH OF DISASTERS (2006).
- NEIGHBORWORKS, DISASTER PREPAREDNESS AND RECOVERY FOR COMMUNITY DEVELOPMENT ORGANIZATIONS MANUAL (2009), http://bit.ly/Ylanv5.

EMERGENCY HOUSING

- Mary C. Comerio, *Housing Issues After Disasters*, 5(3) J. CONTINGENCIES & CRISIS MGMT. (1997).
- CONG. RESEARCH SERV., R40810, FEMA DISASTER HOUSING: FROM SHELTERING TO PERMANENT HOUSING (2010), http://bit.ly/YCV7bT.
- EXPERIENCES OF HURRICANE KATRINA EVACUEES IN HOUSTON SHELTERS: IMPLICATIONS FOR FUTURE PLANNING (2006), http://1.usa.gov/XX2UIl.
- SARAH B. LADITKA ET AL., *Providing Shelter to Nursing Home Evacuees in Disasters: Lessons From Hurricane Katrina*, 98(7) AM. J. PUB. HEALTH (2008), http://1.usa.gov/Yl3nkV.
- City of New York Urban Post-Disaster Housing Design Program, http://on.nyc.gov/117P4Qj.
- U.S. GOV'T ACCOUNTABILITY OFFICE, GAO/RCED-98-1, GUIDANCE NEEDED FOR FEMA'S "FAST TRACK" HOUSING ASSISTANCE PROCESS (1997), http://1.usa.gov/148wPPe.
- U.S. GOV'T ACCOUNTABILITY OFFICE, GAO-07-88, BETTER PLANNING NEEDED FOR HOUSING VICTIMS OF CATASTROPHIC DISASTERS (2007), http://1.usa.gov/YATyeJ.

FAIR HOUSING

(See additional resources in the sections "Evaluations of Federal Support Post-Disaster," "Federal Government: Tools You Can Use," and "2008 Texas Hurricanes.")

- POVERTY & RACE RESEARCH ACTION COUNCIL, STATE, LOCAL, AND FEDERAL LAWS BARRING SOURCE-OF-INCOME DISCRIMINATION, http://bit.ly/Ylc4aJ.

- Greater New Orleans Fair Housing Action Center, www.gnofhac.org.
    - ACCESS DENIED: HOUSING ACCESSIBILITY FOR PEOPLE WITH PHYSICAL DISABILITIES IN THE GREATER NEW ORLEANS RENTAL HOUSING MARKET (2009), http://bit.ly/Y3DPW4.
    - FOR RENT, UNLESS YOU'RE BLACK: AN AUDIT REPORT AND STUDY ON RACE DISCRIMINATION IN THE GREATER NEW ORLEANS METROPOLITAN RENTAL HOUSING MARKET, http://bit.ly/14bO0dN.
    - HOUSING CHOICE IN CRISIS: AN AUDIT REPORT ON DISCRIMINATION AGAINST HOUSING CHOICE VOUCHER HOLDERS IN THE GREATER NEW ORLEANS RENTAL HOUSING MARKET (2007), http://bit.ly/WC6ypT.
- LAWYERS COMM. FOR CIVIL RIGHTS UNDER LAW & GREATER NEW ORLEANS FAIR HOUS. ACTION CTR., STRATEGIES TO AFFIRMATIVELY FURTHER FAIR HOUSING, http://bit.ly/15XaFO1.
- INST. FOR SOUTHERN STUDIES, 4 YEARS AFTER KATRINA: HOUSING CRISIS CONTINUES, LOW-INCOME RENTERS FACE DISCRIMINATION (2009), http://bit.ly/10yrdg5.
- Jeannie Haubert Weil, *Finding Housing: Discrimination and Exploitation of Latinos in the Post-Katrina Rental Market*, ORG. & ENV'T 22(4): 491–502 (2009).
- FURMAN CTR. FOR REAL ESTATE & URBAN POLICY, SANDY'S EFFECTS ON HOUSING IN NEW YORK CITY (2013), http://bit.ly/YUIjh3.
- Litigation Resources:
    - Timeline and resources for lawsuit against St. Bernard's Parish for discriminatory land use ordinances following Hurricane Katrina, http://bit.ly/XVG0yB.
    - Timeline and resources for lawsuit against HUD and state of Louisiana for disparate impact of the federal Road Home Program, http://bit.ly/XVG1Tf.

PUBLIC HOUSING

(See additional resources in the sections "Evaluations of Federal Support Post-Disaster" and "Federal Government: Tools You Can Use.")

- Kalima Rose & David Zisser, PolicyLink, Preliminary Analysis of New Orleans Public Housing Crisis, http://bit.ly/10KABx4.
- U.S. DEP'T OF HOUS. & URBAN DEV., OFFICE OF POLICY DEVELOPMENT AND RESEARCH, THE IMPACT OF HURRICANES KATRINA, RITA, AND WILMA ON THE GULF COAST HOUSING STOCK (2006), http://bit.ly/VUWiYH.
- *Financial Services Committee Hearing to Examine Federal Housing Response to Hurricane Katrina Before the H.R.* (2007) (testimony of Judith Browne Dianis, Advancement Project), http://1.usa.gov/WTKvWt.

- Miloon Kothari, the United Nations Special Rapporteur on Adequate Housing, and Gay McDougall, the U.N. Independent Expert on Minority Issues, Statement on the Demolition of Public Housing in New Orleans (2008), http://bit.ly/WofnkX.
- THE INST. FOR SOUTHERN STUDIES, 4 YEARS AFTER KATRINA: HOUSING CRISIS CONTINUES, LOW-INCOME RENTERS FACE DISCRIMINATION (2009), http://bit.ly/10yrdg5.
- JORDAN FLAHERTY, FLOODLINES: PRESERVING PUBLIC HOUSING IN NEW ORLEANS, RACE, POVERTY AND THE ENVIRONMENT (2010), http://urbanhabitat.org/17-2/flaherty.
- Litigation Resources:
    - Anderson v. Jackson: class action to enjoin demolition of 5,000 public housing units in New Orleans post–Hurricane Katrina.
        - Class Action Complaint for Declaratory Relief, Injunctive Relief, and Damages, 2006 WL 2263157 (Jun. 27, 2006).
        - First Amended Complaint (No. 06-3298), 2007 WL 4414479 (E.D. La. 2007).
        - Declaration of John E. Fernandez (No. 06-3298) (E.D. La. Oct. 23, 2006).
        - Summary of pleadings and resources available via National Housing Law Project, http://nhlp.org/node/906#attachments.
        - Opinion of the U.S. Fifth Circuit Court of Appeals, 556 F.3d 351, C.A.5 (La. January 26, 2009).
        - *Financial Services Committee Hearing to Examine Federal Housing Response to Hurricane Katrina Before the H.R.* (2007) (testimony of Judith Browne Dianis, Advancement Project), http://1.usa.gov/WTKvWt.
- Administrative Complaint Resources:
    - Lone State Legal Aid of Texas filed an Administrative Complaint with HUD to halt the destruction of and rebuild over 500 public housing units in Galveston, Texas.
        - *In re* Oleander Homes (TX 017001) and Palm Terrace Apartments (TX 107006), Administrative Complaint submitted by Lone Star Legal Aid to the U.S. Dep't of Hous. & Urban Dev. (March 2, 2009), http://bit.ly/138KmXk.
        - *In re* Oleander Homes (TX 017001) and Palm Terrace Apartments (TX 107006), Settlement Agreement and Replacement Plan (Mar. 13, 2009).
        - Conciliation Agreement, Tex. Low Income Housing Information Servs. & Tex. Appleseed v. Texas, No. 06-10-0410-8 and No. 06-10-0410-9 (May 25, 2010), http://1.usa.gov/158bzF3.

PREDATORY FINANCIAL TRANSACTIONS

(See additional resources in the section "Federal Government: Tools You Can Use.")

- NAT'L CONSUMER LAW CTR., AVOIDING HOME REPAIR FRAUD: LESSONS FROM HURRICANE KATRINA (2008), http://bit.ly/WGGhqE.
- Loan Modification Scam Alert Campaign, www.loanscamalert.org.
- Prevent Loan Scams (a project of the Lawyers' Committee for Civil Rights Under Law), http://www.preventloanscams.org.

SMALL BUSINESSES

(For more information, see above section "Federal Government Resources—SBA" and the section below on "2008 Iowa Storms.")

- U.S. GOV'T ACCOUNTABILITY OFFICE, GAO-03-385, SMALL BUSINESS ADMINISTRATION: RESPONSE TO SEPTEMBER 11 VICTIMS & PERFORMANCE MEASURES FOR DISASTER LENDING (2003), http://1.usa.gov/XabPFY.
- U.S. SMALL BUS. ADMIN., OFFICE OF THE INSPECTOR GENERAL, SBA'S ROLE IN ADDRESSING DUPLICATION OF BENEFITS BETWEEN SBA DISASTER LOANS AND COMMUNITY DEVELOPMENT BLOCK GRANTS (2010), http://1.usa.gov/146405K.
- Insurance Institute for Business and Home Safety, www.disastersafety.org.
- Florida Resources:
  - Bridge Loan Application, http://bit.ly/WTTRHd.
  - Florida's Small Business Development Center, http://bit.ly/11fEHxE.
  - Enterprise Florida, Florida's Disaster Assistance for Businesses, http://bit.ly/Y104C9.
  - Industry Recruitment, Retention and Expansion Fund, http://bit.ly/WBQP8j.
- Pennsylvania Small Business Development Center, Disaster Recovery, http://bit.ly/WBOOss.
- Mid-Wilshire Neighborhood Opportunity Center (Los Angeles), http://www.wilshirecenter.com.
- Red Cross Business Readiness Evaluation Tool, http://www.readyrating.org.

WORKFORCE DEVELOPMENT

- U.S. Dep't of Labor, National Emergency Grants, http://www.doleta.gov/neg/.
- U.S. Dep't of Labor, MONTHLY LABOR REVIEW, Special Edition: Hurricane Katrina (August 2006), http://1.usa.gov/XahOdS.

    - *The Labor Market Impact of Hurricane Katrina: An Overview.*
    - Richard L. Clayton and James R. Spletzer, *Worker Mobility Before and After Hurricane Katrina.*
    - Molly Garber et al., *Hurricane Katrina's Effects on Industry Employment and Wages.*
    - Sharon P. Brown et al., *The Effect of Hurricane Katrina on Employment and Unemployment.*
- Charles S. Colgan & Jefferey Adkins, Hurricane Damage to the Ocean Economy in the U.S. Gulf Region in 2005, http://www.bls.gov/opub/mlr/2006/08/art7full.pdf.
- David Abramson, Richard Garfield & Irwin Redlener, The Recovery Divide: Poverty and the Widening Gap Among Mississippi Children and Families Affected by Hurricane Katrina (2007), http://bit.ly/13WFxjs.
- Domenico Parisi, Steven Michael Grice & Jed Pressgrove, *Mississippi Business Environment Before and After Katrina: Challenges and Opportunities*, 22 S. Rural Soc. 64 (2007), http://bit.ly/Z3nzH4.
- Southern Growth Policies Bd., 2007 Report on the Future of the South (2007) (highlighting Mississippi Gulf Coast Community College Rapid Response Skills Training following Hurricane Katrina as an Innovator award winner), http://bit.ly/15Nl2Up.
- Brian Sanderson, Gulf Coast Bus. Council Research Found., Mississippi Gulf Coast 3.0 (2008), http://bit.ly/ZMfrvY.

CENTERS AND THINK TANKS

- National Hazards Research and Application Information Center, www.colorado.edu/hazards.
- National Resource Center on Advancing Emergency Preparedness for Culturally Diverse Communities, www.diversitypreparedness.org.
- American Planning Association National Center/Hazards, http://bit.ly/15ner0T.
- Emergency Management Magazine-on-line periodical, www.emergencymgmt.com.
- American Bar Association Committee on Disaster Response and Preparedness, http://bit.ly/Y0JK44.
- National Law Center on Homelessness & Poverty, www.nlchp.org.

SELECT DISASTER-SPECIFIC RECOVERY RESOURCES

New York City Post–9/11

- Lower Manhattan Development Corporation, http://www.renewnyc.com.
- CONG. RESEARCH SERV., RL31617, THE ECONOMIC EFFECTS OF 9/11: A RETROSPECTIVE ASSESSMENT 5 (2002), http://bit.ly/Xjmqsk.
- U.S. GOV'T ACCOUNTABILITY OFFICE, GAO-03-926, DISASTER ASSISTANCE: INFORMATION ON FEMA'S POST 9/11 PUBLIC ASSISTANCE TO NEW YORK CITY (2003), http://1.usa.gov/VUT5sb.
- U.S. GOV'T ACCOUNTABILITY OFFICE, GAO-03-385, SMALL BUSINESS ADMINISTRATION: RESPONSE TO SEPTEMBER 11 VICTIMS & PERFORMANCE MEASURES FOR DISASTER LENDING (2003), http://1.usa.gov/XabPFY.
- U.S. GOV'T ACCOUNTING OFFICE, GAO-04-72, SEPTEMBER 11: OVERVIEW OF FEDERAL DISASTER ASSISTANCE TO THE NEW YORK CITY AREA (2003), http://1.usa.gov/ZsGwE5.
- NYC OFFICE OF THE COMPTROLLER, 9/11 THREE YEARS LATER: SECURING THE FEDERAL PLEDGE (2004), http://bit.ly/16hEQAp.
- SUBCOMM. ON MGMT., INTEGRATION AND OVERSIGHT OF THE HOUSE COMMITTEE ON HOMELAND SECURITY, AN EXAMINATION OF FEDERAL 9/11 ASSISTANCE TO NEW YORK: LESSONS LEARNED IN PREVENTING WASTE, FRAUD, ABUSE AND LAX MANAGEMENT (2006), http://1.usa.gov/15Nxcgc.
- Joseph J. Salvo, Arun Peter Lobo & Joel Alvarez, A Pre- and Post 9/11 (2000–05) Look at Lower Manhattan, NYC Dep't of City Planning, delivered at March 2007 Population Association Meeting in New York City, http://on.nyc.gov/Yaxifo.
- NYC INDEP. BUDGET OFFICE, FEDERAL AID 10 YEARS AFTER WORLD TRADE CENTER ATTACK (2011), http://bit.ly/pOoIjb.

2005 Hurricane Katrina

- Judith Browne Dianis & Anita Sinha, *Exiling the Poor: The Clash of Redevelopment and Fair Housing in Post-Katrina New Orleans*, 51 HOW. L. J. 481 (2008).
- *Financial Services Committee Hearing to Examine Federal Housing Response to Hurricane Katrina Before the H.R.* (2007) (testimony of Judith Browne Dianis, Advancement Project), http://1.usa.gov/WTKvWt.
- The Inst. for Southern Studies, 4 Years after Katrina: Housing Crisis Continues, Low-Income Renters Face Discrimination (2009), http://bit.ly/10yrdg5.

- Jordan Flaherty, *Floodlines: Preserving Public Housing in New Orleans,* Race, Poverty and the Environment (2010), http://urbanhabitat.org/17-2/flaherty.
- Nicolai Ouroussoff, *All Fall Down*, N.Y. Times, Nov. 19, 2006, § 4, at 1, 14.
- Kalima Rose & David Zisser, PolicyLink, Preliminary Analysis of New Orleans Public Housing Crisis, http://bit.ly/10KABx4.
- William P. Quigley, *What Katrina Revealed*, 2 Harv. L. & Pol'y Rev. 361 (2008).
- William P. Quigley, *A Place to Call Home? Affordable Housing That Working and Poor People Can Afford in New Orleans Since Katrina*, 42 Wake Forest L. Rev. 393 (2007).
- William P. Quigley, *Thirteen Ways of Looking at Katrina, Human and Civil Rights Left Behind Again*, 81 Tul. L. Rev. 955 (2007).
- Stacy E. Seicshnaydre, *How Government Housing Perpetuates Racial Segregation: Lessons from Post-Katrina New Orleans*, 60 Cath. U. L. Rev. 661 (2011).
- FEMA, Hurricane Katrina Flood Recovery Maps, http://www.fema.gov/response-recovery/hurricane-katrina-flood-recovery-maps-louisiana.
- Greater New Orleans Community Data Center, http://www.gnocdc.org/.
- HUD, Housing Recovery in the Gulf Coast Phase 1: Results of Windshield Observations in Louisiana, Mississippi and Texas (December 2010), http://www.huduser.org/portal/publications/commdevl/hsgrec_gulfcoast1.html.
- HUD, Housing Recovery in the Gulf Coast Phase 2: Results of Property Owner Survey in Louisiana, Mississippi and Texas (November 2011), http://www.huduser.org/portal/publications/commdevl/hsgrec_gulfcoast_phase2.html.
- *The New Orleans Index at Six: Measuring Greater New Orleans' Progress Toward Prosperity*, Greater New Orleans Community Data Center (August 2011), https://gnocdc.s3.amazonaws.com/reports/GNOCDC_NewOrleansIndexAtSix.pdf.
- Resilience and Opportunity: Lessons from the U.S. Gulf Coast After Katrina and Rita (Amy Liu et al. eds., 2011).

2008 Texas Hurricanes

- CDBG Disaster Recovery (CDBG-DR) Round One Program, http://bit.ly/Yf0lyo.
- Texas filed an initial action plan for disaster recovery in March 2009, covering Round One of the CDBG-DR funds allocated for the 2008 hurricanes. The state's action plan covering the Round Two funds was technically an

amendment to the Round One action plan. The state has filed 3 additional amendments to its Action Plan, all of which are at http://bit.ly/13U48oD.

- Administrative Complaint:
  - Resources related to the above CDBG-DR allocations:
    - Administrative Complaint, submitted to U.S. Dep't of Hous. & Urban Dev. by Tex. Low Income Hous. Info. Servs. & Tex. Appleseed, Oct. 28, 2009, http://bit.ly/WMVgza.
    - Fair Housing Complaint, submitted by Tex. Low Income Hous. Info. Servs. to U.S. Dep't of Hous. & Urban Dev., Dec. 1, 2009, http://bit.ly/158bq4q.
    - Conciliation Agreement, Tex. Low Income Hous. Info. Servs., Tex. Appleseed & the State of Texas, Approved by the Asst. Sec'y for Fair Hous. and Equal Opportunity on behalf of the U.S. Dep't of Hous. & Urban Dev., No. 06-10-0410-8 (Title VIII) and No. 06-10-0410-9 (Section 109), http://1.usa.gov/158bzF3.
    - Fair Housing Activity Statement—Texas, Form Guide, http://bit.ly/10ZxxND. A copy of the form in English and Spanish is available on the General Land Office's website at http://bit.ly/YxpzUP.
  - Resources related to Lone State Legal Aid of Texas filed an Administrative Complaint with HUD to halt the destruction of and rebuild more than 500 public housing units in Galveston, Texas.
    - *In re* Oleander Homes (TX 017001) and Palm Terrace Apartments (TX 107006), Administrative Complaint submitted by Lone Star Legal Aid to the U.S. Dep't of Hous. & Urban Dev. (March 2, 2009), http://bit.ly/138KmXk.
    - *In re* Oleander Homes (TX 017001) and Palm Terrace Apartments (TX 107006), Settlement Agreement and Replacement Plan (Mar. 13, 2009).
    - Conciliation Agreement, Tex. Low Income Housing Information Services & Tex. Appleseed v. Texas, No. 06-10-0410-8 and No. 06-10-0410-9 (May 25, 2010), http://1.usa.gov/158bzF3.
- U.S. GOV'T ACCOUNTABILITY OFFICE, GAO-08-1120, DISASTER RECOVERY: PAST EXPERIENCES OFFER INSIGHTS FOR RECOVERING FROM HURRICANES IKE AND GUSTAV AND OTHER RECENT NATURAL DISASTERS (2008), http://1.usa.gov/14HBgfz.
- A. Christina Wild, Hurricane Ike: Rehabilitation of Affordable Rental Units on Galveston Island (Summer 2009) (unpublished Final Report) 12, 18, http://bit.ly/15UQSyG.
- Fed. Reserve Bank of Dallas, Texas Colonias: A Thumbnail Sketch of the Conditions, Issues, Challenges, and Opportunities, http://bit.ly/WozKyu.

2008 Iowa Storms

- Iowa Finance Authority, *Midwestern Disaster Area Bonds*, http://bit.ly/WBLs8V.
- Iowa Commission on Volunteer Service, *Requesting Funds from Embrace Iowa: 2008 Iowa Disaster Fund*, http://bit.ly/YSw9Zs.
- Iowa Legislature, 2008 Disaster Recovery Efforts, http://bit.ly/ZHIG15.
- Iowa State University Extension, Economic Impacts of the 2008 Floods in Iowa, http://bit.ly/Y0Njr1.
- Rebuild Iowa Office, *Disaster Recovery Lessons Learned*, http://bit.ly/Y7wPI2.
- FEMA, MITIGATION ASSESSMENT TEAM REPORT: MIDWEST FLOODS OF 2008 IN IOWA AND WISCONSIN, http://1.usa.gov/YSym7j.
- Internal Revenue Service, Iowa Storm, Tornado Victims May Qualify for IRS Disaster Relief, http://1.usa.gov/1464qJo.
- U.S. DEP'T OF AGRICULTURE, FOOD AND NUTRITION SERVICE, FNS 2008 AND 2009 DISASTER LESSONS LEARNED AND BEST PRACTICES REPORT (2009), http://1.usa.gov/ZYdMBo.
- U.S. SMALL BUS. ADMIN., OFFICE OF THE INSPECTOR GENERAL, SBA'S ROLE IN ADDRESSING DUPLICATION OF BENEFITS BETWEEN SBA DISASTER LOANS AND COMMUNITY DEVELOPMENT BLOCK GRANTS (2010), http://1.usa.gov/146405K.
- *Corridor Recovery Jumpstart*, CORRIDOR RECOVERY, http://www.corridorrecovery.org/jumpstart/ (last visited Apr. 9, 2013).
- BOB HARSCHNEK & SCOTT SWENSON, CEDAR RAPIDS AREA CHAMBER OF COMMERCE, FIRST BUSINESS CASE MANAGEMENT PROGRAM FOR A NATURAL DISASTER (2012), *available at* http://www.cedarrapids.org/cwt/external/wcpages/recovery/business_case_management_final_report.aspx.
- IOWA DEP'T OF ECON. DEV., BUSINESS DISASTER RECOVERY PROGRAMS: COMMERCIAL REVENUE GAP PROGRAM, PROGRAM GUIDELINES, *available at* http://www.iowaeconomicdevelopment.com/userdocs/documents/ieda/6-20-11_Guidelines-Commercial-Rental-Revenue-Gap-Program.pdf.
- IOWA DEP'T OF ECON. DEV., BUSINESS DISASTER RECOVERY PROGRAMS: EXPANDED BUSINESS RENTAL ASSISTANCE PROGRAM, PROGRAM GUIDELINES, *available at* http://www.iowaeconomicdevelopment.com/userdocs/documents/ieda/6-20-11_Guidelines-Expanded-Business-Rental-Assistance-Program.pdf.
- IOWA DEP'T OF ECON. DEV., BUSINESS DISASTER RECOVERY PROGRAMS: RESIDENTIAL LANDLORD BUSINESS SUPPORT PROGRAM, PROGRAM GUIDELINES, *available at* http://www.iowaeconomicdevelopment.com/userdocs/documents/ieda/6-20-11_Revised-Guidelines-Residential-Landlord-Business-Support.pdf.
- IOWA DEP'T OF ECON. DEV., STATE OF IOWA ACTION PLAN, (2008), *available at* http://www.niacog.org/_notes/disasterrecoveryactionplan.pdf.

- Pub. L. No. 110-252 (2008), *available at* http://www.gpo.gov/fdsys/pkg/PLAW-110publ252/pdf/PLAW-110publ252.pdf.
- Consolidated Security, Disaster Assistance, and Continuing Appropriations Act of 2009, Pub. L. No. 110-329 (2008), *available at* http://www.gpo.gov/fdsys/pkg/PLAW-110publ329/pdf/PLAW-110publ329.pdf.
- Press Release, Rebuild Iowa Office, Governor Culver Announces Funding Distribution for Jumpstart Iowa Programs (Sept. 22, 2008), *available at* http://www.inrcog.org/pdf/JUMPSTART%20IOWA%20FUNDING.pdf.
- Interview with Jeff Sherman, President, Acme Graphics Inc. (Sept. 6, 2012).
- STATE OF IOWA ACTION PLAN FOR DISASTER RECOVERY #2, *available at* http://www.iowaeconomicdevelopment.com/userdocs/documents/ieda/actionplan2.pdf.
- Supplemental Appropriations Act of 2008, Pub. L. No. 110-252, 122 Stat. 2323.
- *Quarterly Report & Economic Recovery Strategy*, REBUILD IOWA OFFICE (Univ. of Iowa School of Urban and Regional Planning 2012), *available at* http://rio.urban.uiowa.edu/resources/reports/2011.04_RIO_Quarterly_Report.pdf.
- U.S. Department of Housing and Urban Development, Additional Allocations and Waivers Granted to and Alternative Requirements for 2008 Community Development Block Grant (CDBG) Disaster Recovery Grantees, *available at* http://portal.hud.gov/hudportal/documents/huddoc?id=DOC_11978.pdf.
- Office of Block Grant Assistance, *Activity Selection and Implementation*, BASICALLY CDBG, http://portal.hud.gov/hudportal/documents/huddoc?id=DOC_16471.pdf.
- *CDBG Disaster Recovery Assistance*, U.S. DEP'T OF HOUS. AND URBAN DEV., http://portal.hud.gov/hudportal/HUD?src=/program_offices/comm_planning/communitydevelopment/programs/drsi.

2010 BP Oil Spill

- RestoretheGulf.gov—The official federal website for the BP oil drilling disaster response and recovery, http://www.restorethegulf.gov.
- DEEPWATER HORIZON CLAIMS CTR., *Economic and Property Damage Claims*, http://bit.ly/XXbBjz.
- Advocates for Envtl. Human Rights, Know Your Rights: Damage Recovery After the BP Oil Drilling Disaster, http://bit.ly/15YxfFR.
- NAACP SPECIAL INVESTIGATION, "MY NAME IS 6508799": STATE OF THE GULF, ONE YEAR AFTER THE OIL DRILLING DISASTER (2011), http://bit.ly/ZQKMdm.
- NATURAL RES. DEF. COUNCIL, THE BP OIL DISASTER AT ONE YEAR: A STRAIGHTFORWARD ASSESSMENT OF WHAT WE KNOW, WHAT WE DON'T, AND WHAT QUESTIONS NEED TO BE ANSWERED (2011), http://bit.ly/YEpSxo.

- NAT'L COMM'N ON THE BP DEEPWATER HORIZON OIL SPILL AND OFFSHORE DRILLING, FINAL REPORT, DEEP WATER: THE GULF OIL DISASTER AND THE FUTURE OF OFFSHORE DRILLING (2011), http://1.usa.gov/ZskArL.
- STATE OF FLORIDA, OIL SPILL ACADEMIC TASK FORCE, *Legal Issues*, http://bit.ly/ZQKTFP.
- U.S. ENVTL. PROTECTION AGENCY, *Cooperative Agreements to Support Communities Affected by the BP Oil Spill*, http://1.usa.gov/WTMWxO.
- U.S. DEP'T OF AGRIC., *BP Gulf Oil Spill—USDA Response*, http://1.usa.gov/ZYbtON.
- U.S. SMALL BUS. ADMIN., *BP Oil Spill*, http://1.usa.gov/WDzvRl.
- U.S. DEP'T OF LABOR, *DOL Responds in the Gulf*, http://1.usa.gov/ZbCEDx.

2012 Hurricane Sandy

- CFPB, Statement on Supervision of Institutions and Borrowers Affected by Hurricane Sandy, http://1.usa.gov/ZpKqdB.
- ENTERPRISE CORP., MEASURING THE RESPONSE TO HURRICANE SANDY: FEMA ASSISTANCE ANALYSIS (2013), http://bit.ly/ZiB4Uf.
- FEMA Hurricane Sandy Recovery Resources, http://www.fema.gov/hurricane-sandy.
- IRS Notice 2012-71, Postponement of Deadline for Transitional Relief under Notice 2011-43 for Certain Small Organizations Affected by Hurricane Sandy, http://1.usa.gov/WQm15W.
- IRS Notice 2012-68, Low-Income Housing Credit Disaster Relief for Hurricane Sandy, http://1.usa.gov/ZLx6Am.
- FHA Notice H 13-05, Hurricane Sandy/Superstorm Response—Expedited Processing for FHA Multifamily Mortgage Insurance Applications (Feb. 12, 2013), http://1.usa.gov/YB1I6E.
- FURMAN CTR. FOR REAL ESTATE & URBAN POLICY, SANDY'S EFFECTS ON HOUSING IN NEW YORK CITY (2013), http://bit.ly/YUIjh3.
- HUD, Allocations, Common Application, Waivers, and Alternative Requirements for Grantees Receiving CDBG-Disaster Recovery Funds in Response to Hurricane Sandy, 78 Fed. Reg. 14329–49, No. 43 (Mar. 5, 2013), http://1.usa.gov/YB5Qnl.
- HUD, HOME Program Waivers Related to Hurricane Sandy, http://1.usa.gov/1173i7u.
- HUD, Interactive Map, *HUD Interests Effected by Hurricane Sandy*, http://bit.ly/WQkQn7.
- HUD, Hurricane Sandy Recovery Resources, http://1.usa.gov/WxvxIP.

- HUD Announces Foreclosure Protection for Displaced Storm Victims (Nov. 26, 2012) http://1.usa.gov/ZBWJVX (this is Maryland example, but similar announcements made for other disaster-declared states).
- New Jersey Statewide Hurricane Sandy Business Recovery Assistance, http://bit.ly/14acHfu.
- New York Business Solutions, Hurricane Sandy Business Recovery Information, http://on.nyc.gov/ZbGuMN.
- New York Hurricane Sandy Emergency Loan, http://on.nyc.gov/ZHLhYP.
- New York State, Hurricane Sandy: Disaster Relief, http://bit.ly/ZQR1Ov.
- Occupy Sandy Recovery, http://interoccupy.net/occupysandy.
- OSHA, *Keeping Workers Safe during Hurricane Sandy Clean Up and Recovery*, http://1.usa.gov/16yDt0q.
- USDA, Housing Assistance to Rural East Coast Residents, http://1.usa.gov/1466Qrp.
- United South and Eastern Tribes, Inc., Tribal Emergency Relief Fund (Hurricane Sandy), http://bit.ly/135MTSj.

Index

A

Abkhazia, 69
Access Denied, 329
Acme Graphics, 209–210
Additional Compensation Grant program, 349
Addressing Internal Displacement: A Framework for National Responsibility, 59
Administrative Procedures Act, 366
Advertising, 324–327
Advisory Group on Forced Evictions (AGFE), 71, 79, 80, 81, 83
Advocacy
- with Human Rights Committee, 76–77
- local, 230–237
- for people with disabilities, 327
- policy, 57
- state-level, 225–230
- strategies, 242

Advocacy Center, 328
Advocacy Center of Louisiana, 327
Advocacy Center of New Orleans, 329
Advocates for Environmental Human Rights (AEHR), 76–77
AEHR. *See* Advocates for Environmental Human Rights (AEHR)
AFFH. *See* Affirmatively Furthering Fair Housing (AFFH)
Affirmatively Furthering Fair Housing (AFFH), 237, 321
Affordable Care Act of 2010, 329
AFI IDA. *See* Assets for Independence Individual Development Account (AFI IDA)
African-Americans
- displacement of, 354
- domestic violence and, 330–332
- employment, 98
- households in New Orleans, Louisiana, 277–278
- issue of heir property, 383
- Jefferson Parish, Louisiana, 352–353
- neighborhoods in Galveston, Texas, 219, 232–233
- public housing redevelopment for, 282
- racial discrimination of, 292
- reliance on public transportation, 100
- Road Home grant formula and, 348–349
- as sex offenders, 333
- St. Bernard Parish, Louisiana, 351–352

AGFE. *See* Advisory Group on Forced Evictions (AGFE)
Agricultural Disaster Assistance Act, 15
AI. *See* Analysis of Impediments (AI)
Alabama, 95
Alabama A&M University, 99
Alternative Housing Pilot Program, 372
American Red Cross, 4, 20–21, 30, 139–140, 142
American Society of Civil Engineers (ASCE), 112
Analysis of Impediments (AI), 228, 230, 356, 357
Andrews, Al, xxxiv
Arad, Michael, 179
ASCE. *See* American Society of Civil Engineers (ASCE)
Assets for Independence Individual Development Account (AFI IDA), 152–154
Association of Records Managers and Administrators, 101
At-risk populations, 113
Austin Chronicle, 148

B

Babister, Elizabeth, 137
Baker, Richard, 282
Bank of America, 177
Bank of New York, 177
Barriers
- exclusionary zoning, 372–373
- to fair housing choice, 362–364
- government programs, 373–374
- planning problems, 375
- private-sector, 374
- to rebuilding, 372–375

Barton, Clara, 139
Basic Principles and Guidelines on Development-Based Evictions and Displacement, 74
Battery Park City, 169–170
Beaumont, Texas, 118
Bergmark, Martha, 145
Berrigan, Helen G., 351, 352
Big Four public housing developments
- demolition of, 252, 280–281, 283–285, 287–290
- historic preservation review requirements, 261, 284
- Housing Authority of New Orleans and, 250–251
- Hurricane Katrina damage to, 280–281
- one-for-one replacement requirement, 266–267
- redevelopment funding sources, 258, 260
- residents of, 283, 290–291

Blakely, Edward, 380
Blatchford, Laurel, 46
Bloomberg, Michael R., xxxvii, 136
BNOB. *See* Bring New Orleans Back (BNOB)
Bonus depreciation deduction, 20
Boone, Yolanda, 398
Boston Globe, 251
BP Oil Drilling Disaster, 92, 94, 96, 101, 429–430
BRG. *See* Business Recovery Grant Program (BRG)
Bridge loan programs, 195–196
Bring New Orleans Back (BNOB), 375, 380
Brookings Institution, 59
Burns, Gloria, 348
Bush administration, 322
Bush, George W., 7, 168, 172, 219, 281
Business Recovery Grant Program (BRG), 175
Business Rental Assistance Program, 208
B.W. Cooper public housing development, 250, 278, 290

C

Calatrava, Santiago, 174
California, 313–314
Carter, Jimmy, 5, 30
Case management, 209–210
Case studies
federal recovery funds, 172–174
housing rights of internally displaced people in post–Katrina New Orleans, 75–83
HUD toolbox for recovery, 32–33
immediate housing needs, 38–40
intermediate housing needs, 40–42
Iowa buyouts, 36–37
meeting housing needs, 33–42
multifamily needs, 33–35
role of HUD in the overall federal response, 43–45
single-family rehabilitation, replacement, foreclosure prevention, 35–36
use of CDBG-DR grants, 42–43
workforce development in Mississippi following Hurricane Katrina, 392–401
Castillo, Joey, xxxiv
CAT. *See* Convention against Torture and Other Forms of Cruel, Inhuman, or Degrading Treatment or Punishment (CAT)
Catastrophic damage, 392
Catholic Charities, 330
CBOs. *See* Community Based Organizations (CBOs)
CDA. *See* Communications Decency Act (CDA)
CDBG. *See* Community Development Block Grant (CDBG)
CDBG-DR funds. *See* Community Development Block Grants Disaster Recovery (CDBG-DR) funds
CDOs. *See* Community Development Organizations (CDOs)
Cedar Rapids, Iowa, 205–210
Cedar Rapids Metro Economic Alliance, 206
CEDAW. *See* Convention on the Elimination of All Forms of Discrimination against Women (CEDAW)
Center for Constitutional Rights, 80
Center for Research on the Epidemiology of Disasters (CRED), 134
Centers and Think Tanks, 424
Centro Campesino Farmworker Center, 311
CERD. *See* Convention on the Elimination of All Forms of Racial Discrimination (CERD)
CFPB v. Jalan et al., 314
Chain of Eco-Homes, 127
Chamlee-Wright, Emily, 148
Charitable organizations, 21, 175
Cheyenne River Indian Reservation, 17
Chicago Lawyers Committee for Civil Rights Under Law, Inc. v. Craigslist, Inc., 326
Chirino, Jose, 305
Choice Neighborhoods. *See* Choice Neighborhoods Initiative (Choice Neighborhoods)
Choice Neighborhoods Initiative (Choice Neighborhoods), 250, 260, 262–263, 265, 375
Chrysler Building, 169
Church Mutual Insurance Company, 159
Civil Rights Act of 1968, Title VIII, 320
C.J. Peete public housing development, 250, 262, 278, 290
Clinton, William J., 7
COG. *See* Council of Governments (COG)
COGP. *See* Continuity of Government Plan (COGP)

Collaboration for Disaster Mitigation, 111
Collaborative relationships, 241
Columbia Parc, 250, 290
Commercial assistance, 209
Committee on the Elimination of Racial Discrimination, 77–79
Common Ground Relief, 382
Commonwealth of Pennsylvania, 113
Communication, 158–159
Communications Decency Act (CDA), 326, 338
Community, 135–136
Community-based housing strategies
- barriers to rebuilding, 372–375
- community land trust, 376–379
- developing vacant and blighted properties, 379–380
- innovative post-disaster, 371–389
- lessons learned, 385–386
- solutions, 375–385
- title clearing, 383–385
- volunteer construction model, 380–383

Community Based Organizations (CBOs), 144, 159
Community Development Block Grant (CDBG)
- for FEMA Hazard Mitigation Grant Program, 37
- overview of, 193–195, 220
- role of Mississippi Center for Justice and, 145
- second-mortgage program and, 312
- St. Bernard Parish and, 359
- use by HUD, 31
- Westchester County and, 358
- World Trade Center redevelopment and, 174

Community Development Block Grants Disaster Recovery (CDBG-DR) funds
- allocation to Texas, 222
- fair housing choice and, 359
- flood buyout practice and, 31–32
- overview of, 10–11, 121–122
- process of, 220
- resources, 409–410
- role of disaster-recovery plans and, 212
- Section 3 requirements, 238
- for small business disaster assistance, 193–195
- use in Midwest floods of 2008, 206–207
- using for long-term activities, 42–43

Community Development Organizations (CDOs), 142–143, 144
Community land trust (CLT), 376–378
Community resilience measurements, 417–418
Community Revitalization Fund (CRF), 384
Compliance review requests, 365
Conciliation Agreement, 228, 229–230, 231, 233, 234
Congressional Act of 1803, 4
Congressional Reports, 309
Consolidated Security, Disaster Assistance, and Continuing Appropriations Act of 2009, 36, 354–355, 359
Consumer education and outreach, 311
Consumer Financial Protection Bureau (CFPB), 313, 314, 315, 406
Contextual equity, 93
Continuity of Government Plan (COGP), 116
Continuity of Operations Plan (COOP), 116

Contractor fraud, 307
Convention against Torture and Other Forms of Cruel, Inhuman, or Degrading Treatment or Punishment (CAT), 55, 84
Convention on the Elimination of All Forms of Discrimination against Women (CEDAW), 65, 66
Convention on the Elimination of All Forms of Racial Discrimination (CERD), 55, 78
Convention on the Rights of the Child (CRC), 65
COOP. *See* Continuity of Operations Plan (COOP)
Coordination, 157–158
Council of Governments (COG), 117–118, 222–223, 234–237
Covenant Community Capital, 152
CPD. *See* Office of Community Planning and Development (CPD)
Craigslist, 326
Cranston-Gonzalez National Affordable Housing Act, 33
CRC. *See* Convention on the Rights of the Child (CRC)
CRED. *See* Center for Research on the Epidemiology of Disasters (CRED)
Crescent City CLT, 376–378
Crescent House, 332
Crescent House Domestic Violence Services, 330
CRF. *See* Community Revitalization Fund (CRF)
Crimes Against Nature laws, 332
Crystal Building, 170

D

(Daily) *The Daily Texan*, xxxiv
Declarations, 6, 252
Deconcentration standards, 267–268
Deep East Texas Council of Governments (DETCOG), 222
Deepwater Horizon, 94
Defining Equity: A Framework for Evaluating Equity in the Context of Ecosystem Services (McDermott et al.,), 92
Delaunay, Sophie, xxxvii
Demolition
  Big Four public housing developments, 252, 280–281, 283–285, 286–290
  failures of federal procedure, 287–288
  lessons from tragedies in New Orleans, 293
  litigation to halt, 288–289
  Section 18 general requirements for, 256–257
  Section 18 requirements specific to, 258–259
Deng, Francis, 59
Department of Consumer Services Protection Commission, 310
Department of Defense Appropriations Act of 2006, 40
Department of Housing and Urban Development Reform Act of 1989 (HUD Reform Act), 32
DETCOG. *See* Deep East Texas Council of Governments (DETCOG)
Deutsche Bank Tower, 170
DHAP. *See* Disaster Housing Assistance Program (DHAP)
DHS. *See* U.S. Department of Homeland Security (DHS)
Disability discrimination, 66
Disaster Case Management Service for Businesses Program, 209

Disaster Housing Assistance Program (DHAP), 12–13, 41–42, 331–332, 346, 356–357
Disaster Loan Program, 174, 192
Disaster Preparedness and Recovery for Community Development Organizations (Ude), 142
Disaster Recovery Act of 2011, 331, 338
Disaster Recovery Enhancement Fund (DREF), 36
Disaster Recovery Guidance by Multifamily Housing After a Presidentially-Declared Disaster, 34
Disaster recovery resources
- Hurricane Katrina, 425
- New York City post–9/11, 425

Disaster Recovery Tool Kit, 45, 361
Disaster relief
- chart of eligible activities and funding source, 24
- creation of funding sources, 4–7
- disaster recovery funding and state assistance, 206–208
- elements for successful, 21–23
- funding incentives and public support, 19–21
- lessons for, 240–242
- resources, 7–18
- for tribal governments, 16–18

Disaster Relief Act of 1950, 4
Disaster Relief Act of 1970, 30
Disaster Relief Appropriations Act of 2011, 9
Disaster Relief Appropriations Act of 2013, 47
Disaster Relief Fund (DRF), 9
Disaster Relief Opportunity Funds, 13–14
Disaster Resource Guide for Individuals and Businesses, 192
Disasters
- evaluations of federal support post-disaster, 413–415
- frequency of, 134
- impact on business, 101
- impact on community infrastructure, 99–100
- impact on employment, 98
- impact on housing, 96–97
- impact on transportation, 100
- national response to, 4–5
- presidential declarations, 6
- process for presidential declaration of, 6–7
- recommendations, 102–103
- redevelopment following, 101–102
- socio-cultural impacts of, 94–95
- state and local responses to, 5–6

Disaster Voucher Program (DVP), 40, 323–324
Discrimination
- Fair Housing Act and, 320–321, 357
- fair housing advertising and, 324–327
- gender, 66
- income-based, 323–324, 385
- internally displaced persons and, 65–67
- against Latinos, 330–333
- people with disabilities, 327–330, 385
- racial, 65–66, 292, 348, 385
- sex, 330–333
- working with Committee on Elimination of Racial Discrimination, 77–79

Disposition
- Section 18 general requirements for, 256–257

Section 18 requirements specific to, 257–258
Distressed Homeowner Initiative, 313
Distributive equity, 92
Doctors Without Borders, xxxvii
DOD. *See* U.S. Department of Defense (DoD)
Dodd-Frank Wall Street Reform and Consumer Protection Act, 314
Domestic violence, 96, 330–332
Donovan, Shaun, 46, 349
DOT. *See* U.S. Department of Transportation (DOT)
DPs. *See* Internally displaced persons (IDPs)
DREF. *See* Disaster Recovery Enhancement Fund (DREF)
DRF. *See* Disaster Relief Fund (DRF)
Duany, Andres, 150
DVP. *See* Disaster Voucher Program (DVP)

E

East Central Iowa Council of Governments (ECICOG), 118
East Grand Forks, Minnesota, 121–122, 125
EBRAP. *See* Expanded Business Rental Assistance Program (EBRAP)
ECICOG. *See* East Central Iowa Council of Governments (ECICOG)
Economic Development Administration (EDA), 13–14
EDA. *See* Economic Development Administration (EDA)
EDPs. *See* Externally displaced persons (EDPs)
Edwards, Frances L., 111
EMAC. *See* Emergency Management Assistance Compact (EMAC)
EMDAC. *See* Emergency Management Disability and Aging Coalition (EMDAC)
Emergency declarations, 6
Emergency Homeowners Loan Program, 309
Emergency housing, 137–139, 420
Emergency Management Assistance Compact (EMAC), 116–117, 119
Emergency Management Disability and Aging Coalition (EMDAC), 329
Emergency Relief Act of 1932, 4
Emergency Supplemental Appropriations Act of 1993, 33
Emergency Support Functions (ESFs), 43
Empire State Development Corporation (ESDC), 43, 175
Employment, 98. *See also* Workforce development
Enterprise Community Partners, 143, 375
Equal Voice Network (EVN), 234, 236
Equifax, 305
Equitable Life Assurance Building, 168
Equity
    in allocation of Texas CDBG-DR funds, 227–229
    assessment of vulnerability, 417
    community resilience measurements, 417–418
    definition of, 92
    in disasters, 92
    framework, 92–93
    impact of inequalities, 417
    preexisting vulnerabilities, 93–94
    recovery resources, 416–418
ESDC. *See* Empire State Development Corporation (ESDC)
ESFs. *See* Emergency Support Functions (ESFs)

Estrada, Fritz, 309
EVN. *See* Equal Voice Network (EVN)
Exclusionary zoning, 372–373, 385
Executive Order 12127, 5
Executive Order 13632, 46
Expanded Business Rental Assistance Program (EBRAP), 208
Externally displaced persons (EDPs), 137

F

Facebook, 144
Fair housing. *See also* Fair housing choice
    advertising, 324–327
    complaints, 364–365
    resources, 420–421
    standards, 267–268
Fair Housing Act, 44, 289, 320–321, 329, 330, 346, 351, 357
Fair Housing Action Center, 325, 329, 331
Fair Housing Activity Statement–Texas (FHAST), 228–230
Fair housing choice. *See also* Fair housing
    Analysis of Impediments to, 360
    barriers to, 362–364
    enforcement techniques to further, 364–366
    practices needed to ensure, 360–362
    redevelopment and, 360–362
Fair Housing Council of San Fernando Valley v. Roommates.com, LLC, 326
Fair Housing Planning Guide, 361
Fair share programs, 363
False Claims Act, 358, 365
Fannie Mae, 313
Farber, Daniel A., 92
Far From Home, 332
Faubourg Lafitte, 250, 266–267, 278, 284, 290, 291
FBI. *See* Federal Bureau of Investigation (FBI)
FDAA. *See* Federal Disaster Assistance Administration (FDAA)
Federal Bureau of Investigation (FBI), 313
Federal Disaster Act of 1950, 30
Federal Disaster Assistance Administration (FDAA), 4, 30
Federal Emergency Management Agency (FEMA)
    Affirmatively Further Doctrine and, 321
    Alternative Housing Pilot Program, 372
    American Red Cross and, 139, 140
    creation of, 5
    criticism of, 5
    Disaster Recovery Centers, 192–193
    eligibility determinations for temporary rental housing, 34
    federal disaster response and, 30–31
    Hazard Mitigation Grant Program, 37
    home-repair assistance following Hurricanes Ike and Dolly, 224–225
    Hurricane Katrina damage estimates, 392–394
    Iowa buyouts and, 37
    Katrina Disaster Housing Assistance Program, 40
    Latino community and, 334
    National Advisory Council, 329
    National Disaster Housing Strategy, 44

National Response Framework, 43–44
Office of Disability Integration and Coordination, 329
Preliminary Damage Assessment, 6–7
Public Assistance Program, 8, 120–121, 252–254
public housing agencies and, 252
Ready website, 140
recommendations for emergency-housing plan, 337–338
reorganization of, 5
resources, 406–407
response to Hurricane Katrina, 38–42, 218, 322
responsibility for care of displaced people and, 61
Road Home, xxxiv
trailers, 62, 78, 328, 372, 393
voucher program, 356
Vulnerability Map, 219

Federal government resources, 405–412
Federal Housing Administration (FHA), 35, 41, 264, 306, 320, 321, 410
Federal Insurance Administration, 30
Federal Register, 194, 226, 227
Federal Strategic Plan to Prevent and End Homelessness, 82
Federal support post-disaster, evaluations of, 413–415
Federal Trade Commission Act, 314
Federal Trade Commission (FTC), 305, 310, 313, 314
Fed. Trade Comm'n v. Christopher Mallett, 306, 310
FEMA. *See* Federal Emergency Management Agency (FEMA)
Fernandez, John, 280
FHA. See Federal Housing Administration (FHA)
FHEO. *See* Office of Fair Housing and Equal Opportunity (FHEO)
FHFC. *See* Florida Housing Finance Corporation (FHFC)
Financial Fraud Enforcement, 313
Fink, Sheri, xxxvii
Fire Management Assistance Declarations, 6
Fiterman Hall, 170
Flood Control Act, 4
Florida, 195–196, 311
Florida Housing Finance Corporation (FHFC), 34
Folkes, Abigail, 96
Ford Foundation, 384
Foundation Communities, 311–312
Franklin, Peter, xxxiv
Fraud
contractor, 303, 307
insurance, 303, 308
mortgage, 303, 305, 308–309
Freddie Mac, 313
Fritz, Zoila, 309
FTC. *See* Federal Trade Commission (FTC)
Fuller, Linda, 141
Fuller, Millard, 141

G

Galveston County Collaborating Organizations (GCCO), 233
Galveston Daily News, 233
Galveston Housing Authority, 354
Galveston, Texas, 123, 219, 222, 224, 232–233, 354
GAO. *See* Government Accountability Office (GAO)
Garifuna, 335
Garza, Cynthia, 335

Gateway Plaza, 170
GCCF. *See* Gulf Coast Claims Facility (GCCF)
GCCO. *See* Galveston County Collaborating Organizations (GCCO)
Geary, Heather, 304
Gehry, Frank, 179
Gender discrimination, 66
General federal assistance, 8
General Services Administration, 30
Georgia, 69
Ginnie Mae, 41
GLO. *See* Texas General Land Office (GLO)
GNO, Inc., xxxvi
Goldman Sachs Group, Inc., 178
Government Accountability Office (GAO), 31, 374
Government relief scams, 308–309
GO Zone. *See* Gulf Opportunity Zone (GO Zone)
Greater New Orleans Fair Housing Action Center, 292, 348, 351–352, 356, 362
Greater New Orleans Foundation, 384
Greensburg, Kansas, 126–127
GRID-Arendal Center, 134
The Guardian, xxxvi
Guidance for Public Housing Agencies in Assisting Families Displaced by Hurricane Katrina, 39
Guiding Principles on Internal Displacement
    family, 71–72
    life and health, 71
    national government responsibilities, 61
    prohibition on discrimination, 66–67
    rights articulated in, 59
    rights in planning for displacement, 67–68
    right to housing, 69–71
    right to participate in government, 72–73
    Robert T. Stafford Disaster Relief and Emergency Assistance Act vs., 62–64
    as standard-setting document, 53
    steps for implementing, 84–85
    United States government and, 54, 60
Gulf Coast Claims Facility (GCCF), 331
Gulf Coast Hurricane Housing Recovery Act of 2007, 282
Gulf Opportunity Zone Act of 2005, 19
Gulf Opportunity Zone (GO Zone), 180, 346
    bonds, 19–20
    bonus depreciation deduction, 20
    New Market Tax Credits, 20
    overview of, 19
    tax credit program, 350–353

H

Habitat for Humanity, 381–382
Habitat for Humanity International, 141–142
HANO. *See* Housing Authority of New Orleans (HANO)
Hanukkah Eve Wind Storm of 2006, 109, 112
Harmony Neighborhood Development, 375
Harmony Oaks, 250, 262, 290
Harris, Kamala, 313–314
Hastings, Alcee, 78
Hazard mitigation, 8
Hazard Mitigation Grant Program (HMGP), 37

HCD Act. *See* Housing and Community Development Act of 1974 (HCD Act)
HCV. *See* Housing Choice Voucher (HCV)
HDC. *See* New York City Housing Development Corporation (HDC)
Hecht, Michael, xxxvi
Heir property, 383
Henderson, Tom, 150
HFA. *See* New York State Housing Finance Agency (HFA)
Hidalgo County, 223, 234–237
Hierarchy of needs, 401–402
HMGP. *See* Hazard Mitigation Grant Program (HMGP)
Holistic Disaster Recovery, 122
HOME Investment Partnerships Act, 11
HOME Investment Partnerships Program, 11, 33, 260, 410
Homelessness, 96, 292–293
Homeowner Opportunity Program, 228, 356
Homeownership Preservation Foundation, 306
Hope Community Development Agency, 145–146
HOPE VI program, 250, 260, 262–263, 266
Housing. *See also* Community-based housing strategies; Fair housing; Fair housing choice; Public housing
  challenges in the aftermath of Hurricane Katrina, 319–343
  disasters and, 96–97
  emergency, 137–139, 420
  income-based discrimination and, 323–324
  internally displaced persons and, 69–71
  for Latinos, 333–336
  for people with disabilities, 327–330
  racial discrimination and, 324–327
  recommendations for
    emergency-housing plan, 337–338
  sex discrimination, 330–333
  shelter as dwelling, 320–321
  use of vouchers, 321–322
Housing Act of 1937, 249, 252, 257, 261
Housing and Community Development Act of 1968, 237
Housing and Community Development Act of 1974 (HCD Act), 32, 356
Housing and Home Finance Agency, 4
Housing and Urban Development Act of 1968, 234, 236, 237–240, 411
Housing Authority of New Orleans (HANO), 250–251, 276, 280–281, 283, 286–290, 332
Housing Choice in Crisis, 356–357
Housing Choice Voucher (HCV), 39, 40, 291, 363
Houston, Texas, 222, 231–232
Howard, Janet, 380
HRC. *See* Human Rights Committee (HRC)
HUD. *See* U.S. Department of Housing and Urban Development (HUD)
HUD Reform Act. *See* Department of Housing and Urban Development Reform Act of 1989 (HUD Reform Act)
Human Rights Committee (HRC), 76
Human Rights Council, 82
Human rights, indivisibility of, 66–67
Human rights law
  domestic legal effect of, 55–57
  resources, 415–416
  in United States, 55

Human rights law ***(continued)***
using in domestic courts, 57
using in policy advocacy, 57
using to defend housing rights of internally displaced persons, 58
Human rights monitors, 79–81
Human rights treaties, 55–56
Hurricane Agnes, 30, 31
Hurricane Andrew, 5, 33, 195
Hurricane Camille, 30
Hurricane Charley, 33–34
Hurricane Disaster Advocacy Center, 311
Hurricane Dolly
Analysis of Impediments to, 361
federal response, 219–220
home-repair assistance following, 224–225
local advocacy following, 233–237
overview of, 218–219
public housing redevelopment following, 354–355
role of Council of Governments after, 119
Hurricane Floyd, 141
Hurricane Frances, 34
Hurricane Gustav, 324, 331–332
Hurricane Hugo, 5
Hurricane Ike
Analysis of Impediments to, 361
federal response, 219–220
home-repair assistance following, 224–225
overview of, 218–219
public housing redevelopment following, 354–355
role of Council of Governments, 118
use of disaster vouchers following, 324
Hurricane Isaac, xxxvi, 94
Hurricane Katrina, 159
Analysis of Impediments to, 361
BP Oil Drilling Disaster and, 94
CDBG-DR funding and, 194–195
cost of homes and homeowners insurance since, 312
damage estimates, 392–394
damage to Big Four public housing developments, 280–281
domestic violence following, 330–333
effects of, 275
FEMA response to, 5
homeless population created by, 292–293
Hope Community Development Agency and, 146
Housing Authority of New Orleans and, 250–251
HUD response to, 285–288
immediate housing needs, 38–40
impact on Big Four public housing developments, 250–251
impact on community infrastructure, 99–100
impact on employment, 98
impact on housing, 96
impact on transportation, 100
information packet for, 142
insurance fraud following, 308
intermediate housing needs, 40–42
international human rights law and victims of, 54
Katrina Cottages, 150
Mary Queen of Vietnam Catholic Church and, 148–149
Mississippi businesses affected by, 393

NEG fund use after, 15
predatory housing activities following, 306
preexisting vulnerabilities, 93–94
recovery resources, 425–426
role of American Red Cross after, 140
role of nonprofit and religious organizations after, 143
seventh anniversary, xxxiv–xxxvi
Hurricane Rita, 159
Analysis of Impediments to, 361
BP Oil Drilling Disaster and, 94
Hope Community Development Agency and, 146
information packet for, 142
intermediate housing needs, 41–42
NEG fund use after, 15
role of American Red Cross after, 140
temporary rental voucher assistance for families displaced by, 40
Hurricane Sandy, 159
disaster relief funding and, 104
Facebook postings, 144
FEMA response to, 5
HUD response to, 46–47
impact on World Trade Center site, 181–182
implementation of EMAC, 119
problems created by, xxxvii–xxxviii, 92
rebuilding costs, 112, 124
recovery resources, 430–431
redevelopment following, 101–102
replacement housing, 113
risk of post-disaster housing fraud and, 315
Hurricane Sandy Rebuilding Task Force, 46
Hyogo Framework for Action, 141

I

IAA. *See* Interagency Agreement (IAA)
ICCPR. *See* International Covenant on Civil and Political Rights (ICCPR)
ICE. *See* U.S. Immigration and Customs Enforcement (ICE)
ICERD. *See* International Covenant on the Elimination of All Forms of Racial Discrimination (ICERD)
IDA. *See* Individual Development Accounts (IDA)
IEDA. *See* Iowa Economic Development Authority (IEDA)
Inclusionary zoning, 363
Income-based discrimination, 323–324
Independent Foreclosure Review, 309
Individual Development Accounts (IDA), 150–155
Industry Recruitment, Retention and Expansion Fund (IRREF), 196–197
Infrastructure, 99–100, 112
Institute for Building Technology and Safety, 111
Insurance fraud, 308
Interactive Corporation, 177
Interagency Agreement (IAA), 41
Inter-Agency Standing Committee, 73
Internally displaced persons (IDPs)
definition of, 59–60
general principles regarding, 60–67
human rights of, 58–60
indivisibility of human rights, 66–67
international lessons, 137–138
national responsibility of, 60–65
nondiscrimination, 65–66

Internally displaced persons (IDPs) ***(continued)***
- post–Katrina case study of housing rights for, 75–83
- rights during displacement, 68–69
- rights in planning for displacement, 67–68
- right to housing, 69–71
- right to participate in government, 72–73
- status in United States, 60
- using human rights law to defend housing rights of, 58–75
- victims of Hurricane Katrina as, 54

Internal Revenue Service (IRS), 192–193, 407–408
International Association of Emergency Managers, 110
International Covenant on Civil and Political Rights (ICCPR), 55, 57, 65, 67, 70–71, 75
International Covenant on Economic, Social and Cultural Rights (ICESCR), 56, 57, 65, 70, 80
International Covenant on the Elimination of All Forms of Racial Discrimination (ICERD), 65
International Labor Organization Convention No. 169, 68
International Red Cross, 139
Internet, 144, 338
Intrastate Mutual Aid Compact, 117
Iowa buyouts, 36–37
Iowa disasters of 2008
- case management, 209–210
- commercial and residential rental assistance, 209
- disaster recovery funding and state assistance, 206–208
- overview of, 205–206
- personal property assistance, 208–209
- recovery resources, 428–429

Iowa Economic Development Authority (IEDA), 206–212
Iowa State Homeland Security and Emergency Management, 37
IRREF. *See* Industry Recruitment, Retention and Expansion Fund (IRREF)
iSirona, 197

J

Jackson, Alphonso, 285
Jackson, Jesse, 281
JCWAA. *See* Job Creation and Worker Assistance Act of 2002 (JCWAA)
Jefferson Parish, Louisiana, 352–353
JFO. *See* Joint Field Office (JFO)
Jindal, Bobby, xxxvii
Job Creation and Worker Assistance Act of 2002 (JCWAA), 176
Johnson, James, 373
Joint Field Office (JFO), 43
Joplin, Missouri, 21, 44–45, 304
Joyce Theater Foundation, 179
Jumpstart Business Program, 207
Jurisdiction, 112–113

K

Katrina Cottages, 150, 372–373
Katrina Disaster Housing Assistance Program (KDHAP), 40, 322–324
KDHAP. *See* Katrina Disaster Housing Assistance Program (KDHAP)
Kelley-Winders, Anna Faye, 398
Kelly, Jim, 267
Kelman, Ilan, 137
Kennedy, Henry, 349
King County Department of Natural Resources and Parks, 112
King County, Washington, 109

Kothari, Miloon, 78
Kriger, Brett, 111
Kuklinski, Julie, 400, 401

L
Lacy, Elaine, 336
Ladner, Brad, 399
Lafitte public housing development, 250, 266–267, 278, 290
Landrieu, Mary, 282
Landrieu, Mitch, xxxiv, xxxvii
Landrieu, Moon, 380
Latinos, 330–333
Law Center. *See* National Law Center on Homelessness and Poverty (Law Center)
Lawyers, 157
Lawyers' Committee for Civil Rights Under Law, 313, 375, 384
LEED certification, 127
Legal and community-based strategies, 225–237
Liberty Zone, 176–177, 180, 350
Liberty Zone Bonds, 170, 176–177
LIHTC. *See* Low-income housing tax credits (LIHTC)
Limited Legal Assistance program, 384
LMDC. *See* Lower Manhattan Development Corporation (LMDC)
LMSB&WRP. *See* Lower Manhattan Small Business & Workforce Retention Project (LMSB&WRP)
Loan Modification Scam Alert campaign, 305
Loan Modification Scam Prevention Network, 313
Loan Modification Scam Prevention Network Database, 313
Local community engagement, 240–241
Local government
- benefits and challenges in disaster recovery, 242
- challenges for, 123
- disaster planning, response, and recovery, 111–116
- federal support for disaster response, 120–122
- framework for long-term recovery, 122–123
- planning and cooperation, 116–117
- post-disaster role, 110–111
- redevelopment opportunities, 124–127
- resources, 418–419
- state government interaction, 118–120

Local Initiatives Support Corporation, 143
Lone Star Legal Aid, 354
Long Term Community Recovery Planning Process, 123
Long-term recovery, 241
Lot Next Door Program, 379
Louis Berger Group, 43
Louisiana, 331, 332–333, 348–349, 351–353, 372–373, 384
Louisiana Appleseed, 384, 385
Louisiana Assistive Technology Access Network, 329
Louisiana Economic Development, xxxvi
Louisiana Recovery Authority, 349, 352
Lower Manhattan Development Corporation (LMDC), 43, 171–172, 174–175, 179
Lower Manhattan Small Business & Workforce Retention Project (LMSB&WRP), 175
Lowernine.org, 382
Lower Rio Grande Valley (LRGV), 231, 233–237
Low-income housing, New Orleans, 289–293

Low-income housing tax credits (LIHTC), 34, 255, 260, 266, 350
Loyola University New Orleans College of Law, 80
LRGV. *See* Lower Rio Grande Valley (LRGV)

M

Mainster, Steve, 311
Making Home Affordable program, 308
Mallett, Christopher, 306
March 23, 2012, flood, 138
Mardi Gras, xxxiv, xxxv
Marjam Supply Company, 197
Marrero Commons, 250, 290
Mary Queen of Vietnam (MQVN) Catholic Church, 148–149
May Day New Orleans, 80
MDES. *See* Mississippi Department of Employment Security (MDES)
Mennonite Disaster Service, 30
Mental health issues, 327
Mercy Housing and Human Development, 312
Messias, DeAnne Hilfinger, 336
Millennium Hilton, 170
Mississippi, 194–195, 312, 372–373
Mississippi Center for Justice (MCJ), 144–145, 158, 328
Mississippi Coalition for Citizens with Disabilities, 327
Mississippi Department of Employment Security (MDES), 393, 395–396
Mississippi Emergency Management Agency, 373
Mississippi Gulf Coast, xxxviii
Mississippi Gulf Coast Community College, 396, 398
Mixed-finance development, 260–262
Monnet, Claudette, 147
Monnet, Willie, Sr., 147
Moore Community House, 400
Mortgage Assistance Relief Services Rule, 314
Mortgage fraud, 303, 305, 308–309
Mortgage Fraud Strike Force, 313
Mortgage Fraud Working Group, 313
Mouzon, Steve, 150
MQVN Catholic Church. *See* Mary Queen of Vietnam (MQVN) Catholic Church
Multifamily Disaster Clarification of Notice H 04-22 and Additional Guidance, 35
Multifamily needs, 33–35
Mutual aid compacts, 116–117

N

NAACP. *See* National Association for the Advancement of Colored People (NAACP)
NADO. *See* National Association of Development Organizations (NADO)
Nagin, Ray, xxxiv, 375, 380
Nation, xxxvii
National Advisory Council, 329
National Association for the Advancement of Colored People (NAACP), 140, 233, 284, 290
National Association of Development Organizations (NADO), 118
National Coalition Against Domestic Violence, 331
National Congress of American Indians, 18
National Council of La Raza, 334
National Disaster Housing Strategy (NDHS), 44
National Disaster Recovery Framework (NDRF), 43–44
National Economic & Social Rights Initiative, 80
National Emergency Grant (NEG), 14–15, 395, 396

National Environmental Policy Act, 45
National Fair Housing Alliance, 348
National Flood Insurance Program (NFIP), 30, 253
National Foreclosure Mitigation Counseling Program, 309
National Guard, 140
National Housing Act (NHA), 35
National Housing Locator System (NHLS), 44
National Law Center on Homelessness and Poverty (Law Center), 78–79, 80, 82, 142
National Lawyers' Committee for Civil Rights, 362
National Legal Help, 309
National Oceanic and Atmospheric Administration (NOAA), 9
National Response Framework (NRF), 43–44
National Voluntary Organizations Active in Disaster (VOAD), 140
National Weather Service, 9
Native American tribes, 15–18, 45, 92, 120, 412–413
Natural-disaster grants, 254–255
Navy Federal Credit Union, 197
NDHS. *See* National Disaster Housing Strategy (NDHS)
NDRF. *See* National Disaster Recovery Framework (NDRF)
NEG. *See* National Emergency Grant (NEG)
Neighborhood Housing Services, 312
Neighborhood Investment Corporation (NeighborWorks), 142
Neighborhood standards, 267–268
NeighborWorks. *See* Neighborhood Investment Corporation (NeighborWorks)
Network for Good, 142
New Basin Canal Park, 380
New Market Tax Credits, 20
New Orleans, Louisiana. *See also* Big Four public housing developments; Housing Authority of New Orleans (HANO); Hurricane Katrina
  demolition of public housing in, 285–289
  Hurricane Katrina damage to public housing, 280–281
  low-income housing in, 277
  political response to damaged public housing, 281–282
  public housing in, 278–280
  residents of, 282–285
New Orleans Redevelopment Authority (NORA), 379
New York City
  aid for transit, small businesses, and economic development, 174–175
  building World Trade Center Tower and Battery Park City, 169–170
  charitable giving for, 175–176
  creation of Lower Manhattan Development Corporation, 171–172
  Downtown, 168–169
  federal recovery funds for, 172–174
  impact of 9/11 on housing and community economic development, 170–171
  Liberty Bonds, 176–177
  Liberty Zone tax benefits, 176–177, 180
  post–9/11 disaster recovery resources, 425
  rebuilding, 177–179, 180–181
New York City Economic Development Corporation, 43
New York City Housing Development Corporation (HDC), 177

New York State Housing Finance Agency (HFA), 177
New York Stock Exchange, 176
New York Times, xxxvii, 112, 278
New York Times Magazine, xxxvii
NFIP. *See* National Flood Insurance Program (NFIP)
NGOs. *See* Nongovernmental organizations (NGOs)
NHA. *See* National Housing Act (NHA)
NHLS. *See* National Housing Locator System (NHLS)
NIMBYism, 385
9/11. *See* September 11, 2001, terrorist attacks
9/11 Memorial, 179, 182
1950 Act. *See* Federal Disaster Act of 1950
1970 Act. *See* Disaster Relief Act of 1970
90 West Street, 170
Nixon, Richard M., 30
NOAA. *See* National Oceanic and Atmospheric Administration (NOAA)
NOFA. *See* Notice of Funds Availability (NOFA)
Nongovernmental organizations (NGOs), 56, 67
Nonprofit organizations
  coordination between religious organizations and, 157–158
  local initiatives, 143–146
  resources, 419–420
  role of, 139–143, 402
Non-Profit Rebuilding Pilot Program (NRPP), 383, 384
NORA. *See* New Orleans Redevelopment Authority (NORA)
Northrop Grumman Corporation, 398
Nothstine, Ray, 147
Notice of Funds Availability (NOFA), 206–207, 212, 262
NRF. *See* National Response Framework (NRF)
NRPP. *See* Non-Profit Rebuilding Pilot Program (NRPP)

O

Obama, Barack, xxxvii, 7, 43, 46, 197
ODMNS. *See* Office of Disaster Management and National Security (ODMNS)
Office of Community Planning and Development (CPD), 39
Office of Disability Integration and Coordination, 329
Office of Disaster Management and National Security (ODMNS), 31
Office of Fair Housing and Equal Opportunity (FHEO), 44, 361, 411
Office of Policy Development and Research (PD&R), 42
Office of Public and Indian Housing (PIH), 38–39, 410–411
Office of Recovery Management, 380
Office of the Comptroller of the Currency, 309
Oil Spill Recovery Act, 196
One-for-one replacement requirement, 265–267
Ouroussoff, Nicolai, 278
Outside Online, xxxvii
Oxfam GB, 68

P

Pakes, Francis J., 135
PBRA. *See* Project-based rental assistance (PBRA)
PBV. *See* Project-based housing choice voucher (PBV)
PD&R. *See* Office of Policy Development and Research (PD&R)
PDA. *See* Preliminary Damage Assessment (PDA)

Pearl River Community College (PRCC), 399–400
People's Analysis of Impediments, 362
People with disabilities, 327–330
Permanent statutory authorities, 32
Perry, Rick, 230
Personal property assistance, 208–209
Perth-Andover, New Brunswick, Canada, 138
PHAs. *See* Public housing agencies (PHAs)
PIH. *See* Office of Public and Indian Housing (PIH)
Pinheiro, Paulo Sergio, 73
Pinheiro Principles, 73–74, 80
Place-based IDA. *See* Assets for Independence Individual Development Account (AFI IDA)
Policy advocacy, 57
Pontiac, Michigan, 113
Portable Individual Development Accounts, 152–155
Port Authority of New York and New Jersey, 169
Port of Gulfport Expansion Project, 366
Posner, Michael, 82
Post-Katrina Emergency Management Reform Act, 5, 329
Power, Matthew, xxxvii
Pratt City, Alabama, 95
PRCC. *See* Pearl River Community College (PRCC)
Predatory housing activities
- affiliation with government entities, 310
- challenges of post-disaster environment, 304–306
- consumer education and outreach, 311
- contractor fraud, 307
- government relief scams, 308–309
- high-capacity service providers in post-disaster vacuum, 311–312
- insurance fraud, 308
- programs that avert scammers' access to victims of, 312
- protecting homeowners from, 303–318
- resources, 423
- scams, 303
- state and federal enforcement actions, 313–315
- technology that is responsive to, 313
- types of transactions, 306–310
- ways to protect homeowners from, 310–315

Preliminary Damage Assessment (PDA), 6–7
Preparedness, 156–157, 197
Presidential declarations, 6, 252
Prison population, 96
Private-sector barriers, 374
Pro Bono Project, 383, 384
Procedural equity, 92
Project-based housing choice voucher (PBV), 263–265, 268
Project-based rental assistance (PBRA), 263–265, 268
Project Home Again, 379–380
Providence Community Housing, 375
Provident Realty Advisors, 351–352
Public Assistance Program, 8, 120–121, 252–254
Public housing, xxxvii
- demolition and disposition of, 255–259
- fair housing, deconcentration, and site and neighborhood standards, 267–268
- Galveston, Texas, 232–233

Public housing (*continued*)
- Hurricane Katrina damage to, 280–281
- impact of Hurricane Katrina on, 38–39
- issues in rehabilitation and replacement, 265–268
- litigation to reopen, 288–289
- in New Orleans pre–Hurricane Katrina, 278–280
- one-for-one replacement requirement, 265–267
- political response to damaged, 281–282
- post–Hurricane Katrina, 275–300
- programmatic options for redevelopment of, 259–265
- rebuilding, 224
- redevelopment of, 353–356
- rehabilitating, 251–255
- resources, 421–422
- special guidance for, 259
- status of residents during and after Hurricane Katrina, 282–285

Public housing agencies (PHAs)
- Katrina Disaster Housing Assistance Program and, 40
- Public Assistance Program, 252–254
- response to Hurricane Katrina, 38–39
- role in obtaining rehabilitation funds, 249–250, 254–255

Public Interest Law Project of California, 328

Public Management Magazine, 111

Public support, 20–21

Q

QHWRA. *See* Quality Housing and Work Responsibility Act of 1998 (QHWRA)

Quality Housing and Work Responsibility Act of 1998 (QHWRA), 260, 261, 262, 266

Quigley, Bill, 354

Quinault Nation, 17

R

Racial discrimination, 65–66, 292, 348, 385

RAD. *See* Rental Assistance Demonstration program (RAD)

REAC. *See* Real Estate Assessment Center (REAC)

Real Estate Assessment Center (REAC), 34

Rebuilding Communities, Restoring Families (Widrow, Zdenek & Scott), 311

Rebuilding Together, 381, 384

Rebuilding Together New Orleans, 381

Reconstruction Finance Corporation, 4

Recovery Support Functions (RSFs), 43–44

Redevelopment
- barriers to rebuilding, 372–375
- exclusionary zoning, 372–373
- fair housing choice and, 360–362
- Fair Housing law and, 357–366
- following disasters, 101–102
- mixed-finance development, 260–262
- programs on the Gulf Coast, 347–357
- of public housing, 353–356
- recommendations, 102–103
- role of local government in, 124–127
- use of federal housing funds to promote integration, 357–366
- World Trade Center, 177–179

Reflecting Absence, 179

Refugees, 137–138

Religious organizations
- coordination between nonprofit and, 157–158
- local responses, 147–149
- resources, 419–420
- role of, 146–147

Rental Assistance Demonstration program (RAD), 250, 260, 263–265
Reservations, understandings, or declarations (RUDs), 56
Residential rental assistance, 209
Resilience, 136
Resilience Alliance, 136
Resources
- Centers, 424
- emergency housing, 420
- equitable recovery, 416–418
- evaluations of federal support post-disaster, 413–415
- fair housing, 420–421
- federal government, 405–412
- international human rights law, 415–416
- local government, 418–419
- nonprofit organizations, 419–420
- predatory financial transactions, 423
- public housing, 421–422
- religious organizations, 419–420
- select disaster-specific recovery, 425–431
- small businesses, 423
- state government, 418
- Think tanks, 424
- tribal governments, 412–413
- workforce development, 423–424

Riggio, Leonard, 379–380
River Gardens, 280, 284
Riverwalk Center, 122
Road Home program, xxxiv, 346, 347–350, 374, 383, 384, 385
Robert T. Stafford Disaster Relief and Emergency Assistance Act (Stafford Act), 320
- as basis for disaster relief, 58
- federal disaster response and, 31
- Guiding Principles on Internal Displacement vs., 62–64
- overview of, 7–9
- as primary federal law addressing disasters, 54
- responsibility for care of displaced people and, 61
- role of president and, 119, 188, 220, 252
- section 310, 32
- section 312, 37, 46
- section 408, 39
- use by Federal Emergency Management Agency, 44
- use of vouchers as authorized by, 321–322

Rodrigue, Wallace, 351
Rodriguez, Marietta, 312
Rolnik, Raquel, 80
Roommates.com, 326–327
Roper v. Simmons, 57
RSFs. *See* Recovery Support Functions (RSFs)
RUDs. *See* Reservations, understandings, or declarations (RUDs)
Ruffino, Mark, xxxv

S

San Bernardino, California, 113
Sandy Recovery Improvement Act of 2013, 16
Sarasota Gold, LLC, xxxviii
Save New Orleans Homes, 384
SBA. *See* U.S. Small Business Administration (SBA)
SBDC. *See* Small Business Development Center (SBDC)

SBP. *See* St. Bernard Project's Rebuilding Program (SBP)
Scams, 303
Scherrman, Jeff, 209–210
Scott, Ralph, 311
Second-mortgage programs, 312
Section 3 law, 234, 236, 237–240, 411
Section 8 programs, 38
Section 108 Loan Guarantee Program, 12
Section 3608 enforcement, 365–366
Seedco, 175
September 11, 2001, terrorist attacks
 aid for transit, small businesses, and economic development, 174–175
 charitable giving for families of victims, 175
 charitable organizations and, 21
 creation of the Liberty Zone in, xxviii
 federal recovery funds, 172–174
 FEMA response to, 5
 impact on housing and community economic development, 170–171
 New York's disaster response resources and, xxxvii
 recovery resources, 425
 role of American Red Cross after, 139
 role of private investment after, 22
 use of CDBG-DR in recovery from, 42–43
September 11th Fund, 175
Serino, Richard, 110
SETRPC. *See* South East Texas Regional Planning Commission (SETRPC)
Sex discrimination, 330–333
Sex offenders, 332–333
SFARG. *See* Small Firm Attraction and Retention Grant Program (SFARG)
Shea, Carey, 380
Shelby, Richard, 94
ShelterBox, 150
Single-family rehabilitation, replacement, foreclosure prevention, 35–36
SLLS. *See* Southeast Louisiana Legal Services (SLLS)
Small Business Development Center (SBDC), 196
Small business disaster assistance
 federal assistance, 188
 from Internal Revenue Service, 192–193
 low-interest loans, 13
 resources, 423
 role of Small Business Administration, 188–192
 for September 11, 2001, terrorist attacks, 174–175
 state assistance, 195–197
Small Business Emergency Bridge Loan Program, 195–196
Small Firm Attraction and Retention Grant Program (SFARG), 175
Smartphones, 338
Smoking for Jesus Ministry, 147–148
Source-of-income protections, 363
Southeast Louisiana Legal Services (SLLS), 383, 385
South East Texas Regional Planning Commission (SETRPC), 118
South Ossetia, 69
Special Rapporteur on Adequate Housing, 58, 68, 78–79, 289
Special Rapporteur on Racism, 78–79
Spirit Lake Long-Term Flood Recovery Plan, 45
Spirit Lake Tribe, 45

Stafford Act. *See* Robert T. Stafford Disaster Relief and Emergency Assistance Act (Stafford Act)
Stallworth, Bill, 146
State government
enforcement actions on predatory housing activities, 313–315
local government interaction, 118–120
recommendations for emergency-housing plan, 337–338
resources, 418
response to Hurricanes Ike and Dolly, 221–225
role in Midwest floods of 2008, 206–208
small business disaster assistance, 195–197
St. Bernard Parish, Louisiana, 123, 351–352
St. Bernard Project's Rebuilding Program (SBP), 382–383, 384
St. Bernard public housing development, 250, 278, 287, 290
St. Bernard Voice, 351
St. Nicholas Church, 170
Storr, Virgil Henry, 148
St. Thomas public housing development, 279–280
Superstorm Sandy. *See* Hurricane Sandy
Supplemental Appropriation Act of 2008, 36
Supplemental appropriations, 32
Support Hurricane Sandy Relief, 142
Support services, 402

T

Targeted Lending Initiative (TLI), 41
Tax incentives, 19, 180, 260
TDC. *See* Total development costs (TDC)
Teachers, 100
Technical assistance, 241
Tenant participation, 363–364
Texas
allocation of CDBG-DR funds, 225–230
allocation of Texas CDBG-DR funds, 355–356
Analysis of Impediments to, 361
Conciliation Agreement, 228, 229–230, 231, 233, 234
Foundation Communities, 311–312
Hurricanes of 2008, 217–248
local advocacy, 230
long-term disaster recovery program for 2008 hurricanes of 2008, 220–221
recovery resources, 426–428
role of Council of Governments after, 118, 119
Smoking for Jesus Ministry, 147–148
state government response to Hurricanes Ike and Dolly, 221–225, 354–355
state-level advocacy, 225–230
use of Section 3 law in, 237–240
Texas Appleseed, 225–228, 234
Texas Asset Building Coalition, 152
Texas General Land Office (GLO), 229, 230
Texas Low Income Housing Information Service (TxLIHIS), 225–228, 234, 355
Texas Organizing Project (TOP), 231–232
Texas RioGrande Legal Aid (TRLA), 226, 234, 236, 237

Think tanks and Centers, 424
Thomas, Faynell, xxxvi
Thomas, Oliver, 282
Three Mile Island nuclear power plant accident, 4
Tidwell, Mike, xxxvii
The Times-Picayune, xxxv, 266, 267
Title clearing, 383–385
TLI. *See* Targeted Lending Initiative (TLI)
TOP. *See* Texas Organizing Project (TOP)
Tornadoes
  Alabama, 95, 97
  Joplin, Missouri, 44–45, 304
Torrens Resilience Institute, 136
Total development costs (TDC), 261
Tourism, 180–181
Training, 241
Transparency, 226–227, 229–230, 241
Transportation, 100
Trasvina, John, 352
Treaties. *See* Human rights treaties
Tribal governments, 15–18, 120, 412–413
TRLA. *See* Texas RioGrande Legal Aid (TRLA)
20 Exchange Place, 176
TxLIHIS. *See* Texas Low Income Housing Information Service (TxLIHIS)
Typhoon Durian, 68

U
Ude, Susan, 142
UDHR. *See* Universal Declaration of Human Rights (UDHR)
Unemployment, 394
UNEP. *See* United Nations Environment Programme (UNEP)
UN-HABITAT. *See* United Nations Human Settlements Programme (UN-HABITAT)
UNHRC. *See* United Nations Human Rights Council (UNHRC)
Unified New Orleans Plan (UNOP), 375
United Houma Nation, 95
United Nations
  Declaration on the Rights of Indigenous Peoples, 68
  General Assembly, 68, 70
  Guiding Principles on Internal Displacement, 54
  human rights monitors, 79–81
  Independent Expert, 78–79
  Special Rapporteur on Adequate Housing, 58, 68, 78–79, 289
  Special Rapporteur on Minority Issues, 289
  Special Rapporteur on Racism, 78–79
  Special Rapporteur on the Rights of Internally Displaced Persons, 58, 59
  Universal Declaration of Human Rights (UDHR), 57, 65, 70
United Nations Environment Programme (UNEP), 134
United Nations Human Rights Council (UNHRC), 56
United Nations Human Settlements Programme (UN-HABITAT), 71, 79, 80
United States
  case study of housing rights for internally displaced persons post–Katrina, 75–83
  human rights treaties and, 56–57, 70
  international human rights law in, 55
  status of internally displaced persons in, 60
United Way, 384
UNITY of Greater New Orleans, 292
Universal client tracking system, 158

Universal Declaration of Human Rights (UDHR), 57, 65, 70
Universal Periodic Review (UPR), 56, 81–83
UNOP. *See* Unified New Orleans Plan (UNOP)
UPR. *See* Universal Periodic Review (UPR)
Urban Revitalization Demonstration, 266
U.S. Agency for International Development (USAID), 60
USAID. *See* U.S. Agency for International Development (USAID)
U.S. Army Corps of Engineers, 10, 37, 77, 94
U.S. Bureau of Labor Statistics, 391
U.S. Congress, 10, 32, 84, 142, 176, 181, 206, 281, 282, 326, 354
USDA. *See* U.S. Department of Agriculture (USDA)
U.S. Department of Agriculture (USDA), 13, 408
U.S. Department of Commerce, 13, 30
U.S. Department of Commerce Economic Development Administration, 409
U.S. Department of Defense (DoD), 11, 30
U.S. Department of Homeland Security (DHS), 5, 43, 82
U.S. Department of Housing and Urban Development (HUD)
    Additional Compensation Grant program, 349
    allocation of Texas CDBG-DR funds, 226
    Analysis of Impediments to, 360–361
    avenues for providing assistance, 32–33
    best practices and lessons learned, 45–46
    case studies, 32–45
    CDBG-DR funding and, 11, 194
    compliance review requests, 365
    demolition of Big Four public housing developments, 280, 283–284, 286–290
    emergency capital-needs fund, 254–255
    Emergency Homeowners Loan Program, 309
    enforcement actions on predatory housing activities, 313
    evolution of disaster recovery role, 31–32
    failures of federal demolition procedure, 287–288
    Fair Housing Act and, 320–321, 357
    fair housing choice and, 359
    fair housing complaints, 364–365
    Fair Housing Planning Guide, 361
    Federal Disaster Assistance Administration, 4
    historical involvement in federal disaster response, 30–31
    Housing Authority of New Orleans and, 276, 283–284, 286
    housing claims for domestic violence survivors, 331
    Office of Community Planning and Development, 39
    Office of Fair Housing and Equal Opportunity, 44, 361
    Office of Policy Development and Research, 42
    public housing agencies and, 249
    recommendations for emergency-housing plan, 337–338
    resources, 409

U.S. Department of Housing and Urban Development (HUD) ***(continued)***
  response to Hurricane Dolly, 218, 220
  response to Hurricane Ike, 218, 220
  response to Hurricane Katrina, 38–42, 285–286
  role in Midwest floods of 2008, 206–207
  role in overall federal response, 43–45
  role in post-disaster community recovery, 29–52
  Section 3 law, 234, 236, 237–240, 411
  Section 8, rental assistance program, 322
  Section 3608 enforcement, 365–366
  St. Bernard Project's Rebuilding Program and, 383
  Universal Periodic Review process and, 82
U.S. Department of Justice, 81–82, 84, 313, 358–359, 411–412
U.S. Department of Labor, 14–15, 101, 395, 396, 412
U.S. Department of Health and Human Services, 82
U.S. Department of State, 81–82
U.S. Department of Transportation (DOT), 174
U.S. Department of Treasury, 308
U.S. ex rel. Anti-Discrimination Center v. Westchester County, 358, 366
U.S. Human Rights Network, 76
U.S. Immigration and Customs Enforcement (ICE), 336
U.S. Interagency Council on Homelessness (USICH), 82, 84
U.S. Senate, 56, 57
U.S. Small Business Administration (SBA), 10, 13, 174, 187, 188–192, 206, 408
U.S. Supreme Court, 57, 324

V

Vacant and blighted properties, developing, 379–380
VAWA. *See* Violence Against Women Act (VAWA)
Violence Against Women Act (VAWA), 338
Vitter, David, 282
VOAD. *See* National Voluntary Organizations Active in Disaster (VOAD)
Volunteer construction model, 380–383
Volunteer fire departments, 113
Volunteers of America, 352
Vouchers, 321–322
Vulnerability, assessment of, 417

W

Wade Correctional Center, 333
Waiver authorities, 32
Walke, James A., 120
Walker, Peter, 179
Wall Street, 176
Washington, 109, 117
Welfare Law Center of New York, 328
Westchester County, 358–359
WHO. *See* World Health Organization (WHO)
Widrow, Woody, 311
Williams, Darren, xxxvi
Winstone, Jane, 135
Women, 96, 400–401
Women in Construction Program, 400–401
Woolworth Building, 168
Workforce development
  before Hurricane Katrina, 394–395

incomes, 391
in Mississippi following Hurricane Katrina, 391–404
resources, 423–424
temporary jobs, 397–398
Women in Construction Program, 400–401
workforce training along Mississippi Gulf coast, 398–399
workforce training in rural areas, 399–400
World Conference on Disaster Reduction, 141
World Financial Center, 170, 178
World Health Organization (WHO), 134
World Trade Center. *See also* September 11, 2001, terrorist attacks
arts center, 179
building of, 169–170
commercial space, 177–179
impact of Hurricane Sandy, 181–182
memorial, 179
1993 bombing of, xxxvii
rebuilding, 177–179
as target, 169
World Vision, 142
World War II, 55
Wright, Stan, 96
WTC. *See* World Trade Center

Z

Zdenek, Robert O., 311